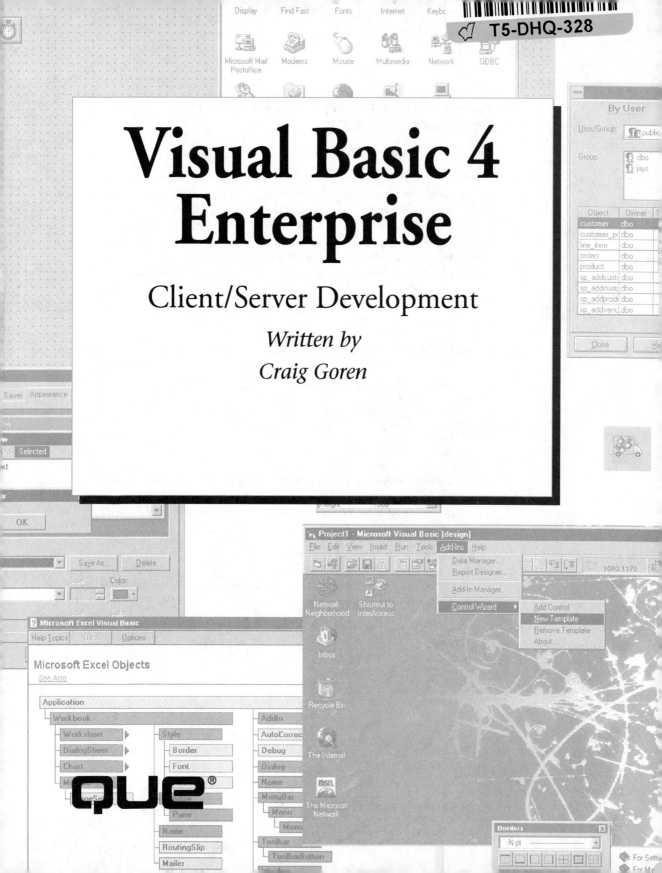

Visual Basic 4 Enterprise

Client/Server Development

Written by

Craig Goren

que®

Visual Basic 4 Enterprise Client/Server Development

Library of Congress Catalog No.: 95-71429

ISBN: 0-7897-0099-9

98 97 96   6 5 4 3 2 1

Interpretation of the printing code: the rightmost double-digit number is the year of the book's printing; the rightmost single-digit number, the number of the book's printing. For example, a printing code of 96-1 shows that the first printing of the book occurred in 1996.

Screen reproductions in this book were created by using Collage Plus from Inner Media, Inc., Hollis, NH.

Composed in *Stone Serif* and *MCPdigital* by Que Corporation.

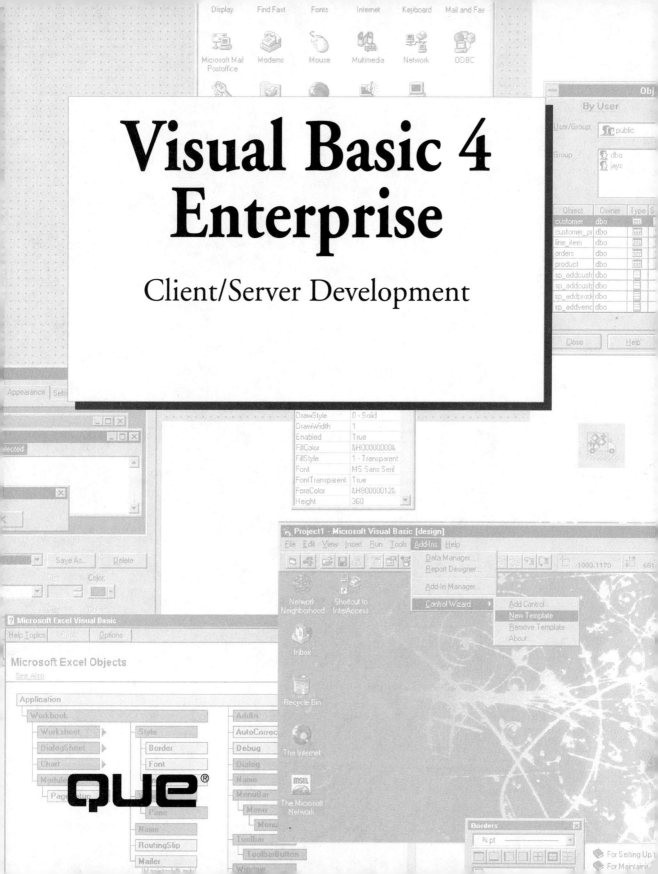

Credits

President and Publisher
Roland Elgey

Associate Publisher
Joseph B. Wikert

Editorial Services Director
Elizabeth Keaffaber

Managing Editor
Sandy Doell

Director of Marketing
Lynn E. Zingraf

Senior Series Editor
Chris Nelson

Title Manager
Bryan Gambrel

Acquisition Editor
Fred Slone

Product Director
Stephen L. Miller

Production Editor
Don Eamon

Editors
Anna Huff
Patrick Kanouse
Jeff Riley
Caroline D. Roop

**Assistant Product
Marketing Manager**
Kim Margolius

Technical Editor
Mark Streger

Technical Specialist
Nadeem Muhammed

Acquisitions Coordinator
Angela C. Kozlowski

Operations Coordinator
Patricia J. Brooks

Editorial Assistant
Michelle R. Newcomb

Book Designer
Ruth Harvey

Cover Designer
Dan Armstrong

Copywriter
Jennifer Reese

Production Team
Brian Buschkill
Jason Carr
Chad Dressler
Joan Evan
DiMonique Ford
Trey Frank
Amy Gornik
John Hulse
Damon Jordan
Daryl Kessler
Bob LaRoche
Michelle Lee
Scott Tullis

Indexers
Ginny Bess
Jeanne Clark

About Clarity Consulting, Inc.

Clarity Consulting, Inc., is a Chicago-based consulting firm that specializes in the design and implementation of client/server information systems. The corporation's primary business objective is helping organizations achieve clear, logical, and well-planned solutions to modern business and information system problems.

Clarity has extensive experience in custom application development, strategic planning, technical design, and project management within the Fortune 500 community. The corporation uses leading edge client/server technologies, including Visual Basic, Powerbuilder, Visual C++, SQL Server, Oracle, Sybase, DB2, Access, OLE 2.0, Windows NT, and UNIX, as well as enabling technologies involving the Internet, voice processing, imaging, and hand-held devices.

Clarity is a Microsoft Solution Provider. Applications developed by Clarity consultants have won industry awards and been featured in national publications. Dedicated to continued education and maintain high profiles within the developer community, Clarity's consultants are full-time, salaried employees committed to the success of the company and client engagements.

If you have project work that might benefit from Clarity's services, or if you are interested in joining Clarity, Clarity can be reached via the Internet at **info@claritycnslt.com** or via fax at **(312) 266-1006**.

About the Authors

Craig Goren is president of Clarity Consulting, Inc. Craig holds a degree in computer science from Northwestern University. He is recognized in the industry as an expert in client/server technology. Craig has written several articles on client/server topics, and is often quoted in the national trade press. He has spoken at Microsoft Tech*Ed and the Visual Basic Insider's Technical Summit (VBITS) on Visual Basic topics. Craig has architected many large client/server systems with Visual Basic, supporting hundreds of users and hundreds of gigabytes of data. Certified in several Microsoft products, including Visual Basic, Craig is a section leader in the client/server section of VBPJFORUM on CompuServe. He also volunteers as Director of Computer Education for the Cabrini Green Youth Program in Chicago. You can reach Craig via the Internet at **cgoren@claritycnslt.com**, via CompuServe at **72773,1062**, and via fax at **(312) 266-1006**.

James Schmelzer, a consultant with Clarity Consulting, Inc., holds a degree in management information systems from Indiana University. Jay has architected a number of enterprise client/server solutions with tools such as Visual Basic, PowerBuilder, SQL Server, and Oracle. He has written articles for several technical journals, including *Visual Basic Programmer's Journal*. You can reach Jay via the Internet at **jschmelz@claritycnslt.com** and via fax at **(312) 266-1006**.

Jeffrey Smith is a consultant with Clarity Consulting, Inc. Jeff holds a degree in biomedical engineering from Northwestern University and has designed, developed, and deployed several three-tier client/server solutions for Fortune 500 companies, utilizing Visual Basic 4. He has contributed to other books on Visual Basic, and he has written articles for several technical journals, including *Visual Basic Programmer's Journal*. You can reach Jeff via the Internet at **jdsmith@claritycnslt.com** and via fax at **(312) 266-1006**.

Acknowledgments

We would like to thank several people for helping out with this book.

For support and patience, we would like to thank **Emily Baran** and **Gina Smith**.

For technical and product assistance, we would like to thank **Cornelius Willis**, **Jon Roskill**, **Kirby Lulle**, **Scott Swanson**, **Tim McBride**, **Chris Dias**, **Greg Hinkel**, **John Eikanger**, **Ron Martinsen**, **Christopher Flores**, and the VB4 product team.

For QA work, we would like to thank **Chuck Follen**, **Loren Kaneshige**, **Jon Rauschenberger**, **Dave Greene**, and **J. Jason Lyons**.

And finally, we would like to thank **Jim Johnson** for keeping us focused on the book's objective.

We'd Like to Hear from You!

As part of our continuing effort to produce books of the highest possible quality, Que would like to hear your comments. To stay competitive, we *really* want you, as a computer book reader and user, to let us know what you like or dislike most about this book or other Que products.

You can mail comments, ideas, or suggestions for improving future editions to the address below, or send us a fax at (317) 581-4663. For the on-line inclined, Macmillan Computer Publishing now has a forum on CompuServe (type **GO QUEBOOKS** at any prompt) through which our staff and authors are available for questions and comments. The address of our Internet site is **http://www.mcp.com** (World Wide Web).

In addition to exploring our forum, please feel free to contact me personally to discuss your opinions of this book. You can reach me on CompuServe at 76103,1334, or through the Internet at slmiller@que.mcp.com.

Thanks in advance—your comments will help us to continue publishing the best books available on computer topics in today's market.

Stephen L. Miller
Product Development Specialist
Que Corporation
201 W. 103rd Street
Indianapolis, Indiana 46290
USA

Contents at a Glance

Client/Server Concepts

OLE

The Service Layers

Application Enhancements

Sample Applications

Contents

4 Visual Basic Application Architecture   77

6 Creating OLE Objects   163

13 Architecting Security 465

14 Architecting Error Processing 489

16 Distributing Applications 549

17 Extending Visual Basic 587

18 Developing International Applications

19 Version Control and Team Development   643

20 Creating Development Guidelines   727

21 Organizing the Development Approach   765

V Sample Applications   787

24 Sample Application #3: A Three-Tier Order Processing System 891

Forward

From its inception, Microsoft designed Visual Basic as a general purpose Windows development tool. With each release we've tried to expose the latest software technology in a way that makes it easily accessible to the broadest audience of developers. For VB 1.0, this meant developers could suddenly create Windows applications without learning the hundreds of calls in the Windows API. Version 2.0 gave Visual Basic developers easy access to important and topical technologies, such as multimedia, pen computing, and communications. Version 3.0 was the first version of Visual Basic to have built-in database support and the first development tool to support integrating other applications through OLE. Today, Visual Basic 4.0 is again moving the development community forward, by providing an intuitive, high productivity tool for developing high performance, distributed enterprise applications.

Visual Basic 4.0 represents much more than just an upgrade to Visual Basic 3.0. It is the culmination of more than five years of development work that completely rearchitected the product. Ever since Visual Basic 1.0 was released, Microsoft has been researching and refining open, component based software development. Well, Visual Basic 4.0 is now built entirely from OLE components. We have replaced the VB 3 language engine with Visual Basic for Applications (VBA), which is optimized for the manipulation of OLE objects. And all components, including controls and database components, have been redesigned as OLE objects.

Rearchitecting Visual Basic into a collection of OLE components gave us complete flexibility to enhance and replace components without sacrificing backward compatibility. It allowed us the flexibility to introduce new pieces of functionality that address specific developer needs. A good example of this is the Remote Data Object (RDO) and the Remote Data Control (RDC) found in VB 4 Enterprise. These OLE objects were designed to give developers high performance data access to remote servers such as Microsoft SQL Server, Oracle, or any other ODBC data source. In VB 4 we were able to implement these features as an OLE Server and an OLE Control (OCX). Now that Visual Basic can host OLE components, both Microsoft and ISVs can extend the

Visual Basic environment by simply inserting OLE server objects that perform any task required by a developer.

By now, it should be apparent that all of Microsoft's operating systems, development tools and applications will continue to incorporate OLE at the core of their architecture. The best way to describe OLE is as a standard way of exposing interfaces in objects that allow other applications to manipulate these objects. OLE is the infrastructure that every major product from Microsoft will use for many years to come. OLE objects will also come from third parties. There are OLE interfaces defined for specific vertical markets such as banking, health care, and insurance. There are also OLE interfaces for telephony, messaging, and database access. The OLE architecture allows us to add support for these new types of OLE interfaces into Visual Basic as they become available.

Today, with Visual Basic 4.0, anyone who can program Visual Basic can create reusable EXEs and DLLs that expose OLE interfaces. This capability gives the VB developer the feature they have been asking for since VB 1.0 introduced the VBX—the ability to create, compile, and distribute reusable components written in Visual Basic. Unlike the VBX, the OLE Automation Servers created by Visual Basic 4.0 can be used by any application that supports OLE Automation. Visual Basic developers now can create reusable OLE components in the form of in-process DLLs or cross-process EXEs. This book takes you on a guided tour of the ins and outs of designing, coding, and deploying OLE Automation servers.

These days, you can hardly pick up a computer industry trade publication without finding at least one article that mentions "three-tier computing." The Enterprise Edition of VB 4.0 takes OLE server creation one step further by allowing you to remote these objects and place them on application servers located throughout your LAN or WAN. The beauty of Remote Automation is that your objects do not need to be recompiled or altered in any way to take advantage of this functionality. Your applications continue to call the same methods on the same objects. I will never forget remoting a Visual Basic application via Remote Automation for the first time. I moved one of my Visual Basic created OLE servers to my Windows NT machine and proceeded to call it from my Windows 95 client. I had not rewritten any of the code in either portion of the application. Yet, it ran across the two machines without modification. It might appear that I am over-simlifying a very complex process, but I'm not. The beauty of Remote Automation lies in how the complexity of creating distributed computing objects is masked and presented to the Visual Basic developer in a paradigm they already know and understand—OLE Automation.

Visual Basic 4.0 does for OLE and distributed computing what VB 1.0 did for Windows application development. You might think that this is an exaggeration. However, think back to the days before Visual Basic 1.0 was available. All Windows applications had to be written in C. The Windows developer had to be intimately familiar with the Windows API. Writing "Hello World" took 100 lines of C code. Then, along came Visual Basic and a developer could write "Hello World" in a single line of code. The number of available Windows applications exploded. With Visual Basic 4.0, it is now possible to write distributed "Hello, World" application in two lines of code (after all, you do need one line of code for the client application and another for the server application).

I had first heard of Clarity Consulting during the Visual Basic 4.0 beta. Craig Goren had come to Redmond from Chicago to demo some of the applications Clarity was developing with VB 4.0 for the Enterprise Technical Summit that Microsoft hosted for industry analysts and press. After watching his demo, it was immediately apparent to me that he was not only writing powerful applications, but he possessed a strong grasp of the significance of easily creating reusable OLE components with Visual Basic 4.0..

Throughout the beta process, Craig constantly stressed Remote Automation to its limits. He was always posting messages on CompuServe, asking us about issues such as capacity tuning, object pool management, security, and any other feature he happened to be pounding on a particular day. Now that Visual Basic 4.0 is shipping, I still receive e-mail from Craig every few weeks telling me about some new way he has found to implement a feature in a business object he is writing for a customer. I have encountered few people outside of the Visual Basic group that have spent more time understanding, designing, and implementing distributed applications using Visual Basic 4.0 Enterprise.

Visual Basic's investment in both creating OLE Automation objects and using OLE to create Visual Basic itself, let Microsoft quickly incorporate the latest and most important technologies as they emerge. Future versions of Visual Basic will expand on key areas such as object creation, enhanced remote data access, and distributed applications. Of course, the a critical new type of distributed application are applications running across the Internet. Visual Basic will be a compelling tool for the Internet because of the extensibility provided via OLE.

VB developer surveys have shown that 80 percent of all VB applications deal with databases in some form. Regardless of whether your application involves a corporate LAN or the Internet, Visual Basic will continue to be enhanced to help developers build high-performance distributed database applications that take advantage of the latest Database technologies. While Visual Basic 4.0 makes it easy to create and deploy a distributed application, the road to distributed computing is full of twists, turns and some potholes.

In this book, Craig Goren, Jay Schemelzer, and Jeff Smith provide you with a comprehensive guide to designing, creating, deploying, and supporting distributed OLE applications. As you begin to develop reusable components, it will quickly become apparent that although Visual Basic 4.0 looks very similar to past versions of Visual Basic, there is much more here than meets the eye. New concepts such as Class Modules, early binding versus late binding of OLE objects, and object model design introduce a new set of issues to be understood and dealt with. The information in this book is based on the first hand experience of Clarity Consulting and the authors who have created such applicationsations with Visual Basic 4.0 Enterprise Edition. There is no doubt in my mind that this book will become one of that small number that earns a spot next to your monitor, and will quickly become dog eared and highlighted as you begin to build and deploy distributed applications using Visual Basic 4.0.

Scott Swanson

Visual Basic Product Planning Manager, Microsoft Corporation

October, 1995

Introduction

Microsoft Visual Basic is enormously popular with corporate client/server database developers. Its popularity can be attributed to its ease of use, extensibility with custom controls, and flexibility.

Visual Basic is a general programming language. In fact, Visual Basic 1.0 did not contain any built-in data access methods. Visual Basic differentiates itself from its 4GL counterparts—like PowerBuilder and SQL Windows—by being a general programming language, suitable for developing applications that don't require any database access.

But this distinctive advantage was also Visual Basic's biggest weakness—it simply was not as powerful or as easy to use as its counterparts for large scale, client/server team development. Tools like PowerBuilder grew up around client/server databases.

Visual Basic 4.0 finally closes the gap by providing advanced features so crucial to corporate client/server development—features like source code control, team development, and high-performance data access. In addition, VB4 raises the stakes in the client/server tools war by being the first mainstream development tool capable of building three-tiered, distributed applications. It does all these while still maintaining its traditional advantage of being an open, easy-to-use general Windows programming language.

Visual Basic: The Enterprise Edition

Visual Basic 4.0 Enterprise Edition builds on the features of Visual Basic 3.0 to facilitate large-scale team development of three-tiered, distributed enterprise applications.

With over two million units sold, Visual Basic is the most popular Windows-based development tool. Also, VB has the largest third-party following of any development tool. Its popularity is due to both its rapid application development capabilities and its flexibility, allowing development of a wide range of projects.

Visual Basic 3.0 was widely adopted by professional developers, who account for more than 85 percent of VB's user base. Most of these developers—who generate approximately 50 percent of all Visual Basic sales—are in corporations. The remaining 35 percent of professional developers who use Visual Basic are consultants, VARs, or ISVs.

Microsoft has recognized the success of Visual Basic and is proliferating it into all of its business applications. For example, at the time of this writing, Visual Basic for Applications (VBA) appears in most Office applications. Microsoft has committed to adding VBA scripting applications into the remainder of its Office line as well as into its BackOffice line, such as SQL Server and Exchange.

Visual Basic is the only development language a corporate developer needs to know to create components and services in all three tiers of an enterprise client/server system. This book shows you how to create such services, and thus, how to build "The Visual Basic Enterprise."

Purpose of This Book

This purpose of this book is to provide both theoretical and how-to information on how to construct distributed, three-tier corporate client/server applications with Visual 4.0 Enterprise Edition.

There are many VB language and "how-to" references. There are many books on client/server theory. This book merges the two concepts and provides real-world, three-tier client/server how-to information, based on solid theory and business practices.

Enterprise Client/Server Development for Visual Basic 4 focuses on building "mission-critical" applications—line-of-business transaction processing applications capable of scaling to large databases and many users. In doing this, this book discusses issues often overlooked by developers and other books—issues like error-processing architecture, security architecture, team development, version control and release management, and development strategies.

This book does not focus on "local" database development. For example, it does not address database access with the Microsoft Jet Engine or Data Access Objects. Instead, this book focuses on a new client/server data access method known as Remote Data Objects (RDO).

Architecting distributed client/server applications involves many choices. This book makes specific recommendations and shows you how to construct components with code examples. But it also provides you with an in-depth discussion of the theory behind three-tier client/server applications, so that you are armed with the theoretical background required to make good design decisions in your own systems environment. After reading this book, you should feel comfortable that you are capable of creating a three-tiered, enterprise-wide application.

Therefore, three types of readers will benefit from reading this book:

- The corporate database developer familiar with VB3, looking to understand VB4 database development

- The corporate database developer already familiar with VB4, but looking to understand three-tier client/server with VB

- The corporate database architect or manager, looking to understand three-tiered client/server architecture

Because this book is targeted at the corporate developer, all examples and code are in the context of fictitious businesses.

What You Need to Use This Book

This book covers features found only in the Enterprise Edition of Visual Basic 4.0. Therefore, you should have and use a copy of VB4EE while reading this book.

This book is not a language reference. It assumes that you have a basic understanding of the Visual Basic programming language. Before reading this book, you should have some experience in developing Visual Basic applications. Because, however, most of the features introduced in VB4 from Visual Basic 3 are applicable to the content of this book, you need only have experience with VB3—all of the new VB4 features applicable to enterprise client/server development (such as RDO and creating OLE automation servers) are covered in detail.

There are many Visual Basic 4 language-oriented books available. If you are not very familiar with VB4 or VB3, it is recommended that you read one of these books, such as Que's *Using Visual Basic 4*, before reading this one. This book, instead, is application oriented. It focuses on specific techniques and design issues for creating three-tier client/server applications. This book is focused on database and OLE development because these are the primary technologies used by VB to construct a services application.

We strongly recommend that you have an environment that is capable of running the sample applications. We recommend the following:

- A client workstation, running Windows 95 (or greater)

- A server workstation running Windows NT Server 3.51 (or greater) and SQL Sever 6.0 (or greater)

- A network connection between the client and the server

This minimum configuration will enable you to test all the sample applications and VB4EE functionality. Because the three-tier architecture is a logical and not a physical design, you can run all tiers on a single machine, but this will prevent you from experimenting with one of the significant new features in VB4—remote automation—which requires a network.

Because many of the VB4EE features (such as RDO) run only in a 32-bit environment, this book will focus on 32-bit application development. A case will be made later in the book that you consider developing all "mission-critical" applications in a 32-bit environment anyway. All of the sample applications were created with the 32-bit version of VB4.

You should have a basic understanding of databases, relational database theory, and Structured Query Language (SQL). Much of the discussion of three-tier architecture is written in the context that the reader already has a basic understanding of traditional two-tiered or file-server database application development.

How This Book Is Organized

This book is organized into five parts, with 24 total chapters that cover all aspects of three-tier client/server development with VB4. This books assumes that you are reading in order from Chapter 1 to Chapter 24. The following sections provide an overview for each of the five parts of the book.

Part I: Introduction to Client/Server Concepts, Architecture, and Methodology

This part of the book provides the reader with an overview of the book, as well as covers the theoretical background behind the three-tiered services model.

Chapter 1, "The Visual Basic Enterprise," discusses the purpose of this book and new features in Visual Basic 4 Enterprise Edition.

Chapter 2, "Application Architecture," surveys traditional application architectures, such as centralized and file-server architectures. It then presents a theoretical overview of the three-tiered architecture and its advantages.

Chapter 3, "Understanding OLE," provides an overview of OLE in general and within the context of Visual Basic. It shows you exactly how OLE is the glue that binds distributed components together.

Chapter 4, "Visual Basic Application Architecture," is a brief summary of the three-tiered architecture. It maps out all of the pieces of The Visual Basic Enterprise from a technical standpoint. This chapter will help you understand the "big picture" and how everything relates before diving into architectural specifics.

Part II: OLE

Chapter 2 described OLE in general. This part of the book shows you specifically how OLE is leveraged within Visual Basic.

Chapter 5, "Controlling OLE Objects," shows you how to control OLE objects with VB. Objects include OLE documents, OLE automation severs, and OLE controls.

Chapter 6, "Creating OLE Objects," shows you how to create OLE objects with VB. VB can create OLE automation servers, which can then be controlled by other applications, such as those creating in Excel, VB, or PowerBuilder.

Chapter 7, "Managing OLE Objects," shows you how to manage OLE objects. It discusses remote automation—a method of controlling OLE automation objects across a network. It also discusses the Component Manager, a tool included in VB4 that enables you to store and categorize OLE objects.

Part III: The Service Layers

Chapter 8, "Architecting Tier 1: Client Applications," shows you how to create components in the user services layer. It covers things like GUI design and controlling business servers.

Chapter 9, "Architecting Tier 2: Business Servers," shows you how to create components in the business services layer. This is one of the more significant chapters in the book—it shows you how to create the new, line-of-business objects. It also shows you how to performance tune such objects for remote automation.

Chapter 10, "Architecting Tier 3: Data Servers," shows you how to create components in the data services layer. Most of these components will be bought, not built, such as DBMS data services like SQL Server. But it also presents ideas on how to leverage other data services, such as the Internet and mainframe applications.

Part IV: Application Enhancements

Chapter 11, "Remote Data Objects," shows you how to use RDO, the best way for a VB business server to access a client/server RDBMS.

Chapter 12, "Advanced Coding Techniques," shows you how to make the most of VB by incorporating such advanced coding techniques as collections, callbacks, and reusable code modules.

Chapter 13, "Architecting Security," discusses suggested corporate security goals within the three-tier services model. It then makes suggestions on how to meet those goals with VB4.

Chapter 14, "Architecting Error Processing," discusses error-processing techniques in all tiers of the services model. It also makes suggestions for corporate error-processing standards.

Chapter 15, "Adding Help to an Application," shows you how to link user and business services to help files. It also shows you how to create help files.

Chapter 16, "Distributing Applications," shows you how to use the Setup Kit to distribute applications. It discusses issues regarding distribution of OLE objects.

Chapter 17, "Extending Visual Basic," shows you how to extend your VB applications with custom controls, add-ins, and API calls.

Chapter 18, "Developing International Applications," discusses issues involved in creating applications that will be distributed to different locales. It shows you how to use resource files to manage text strings.

Chapter 19, "Version Control and Team Development," shows you how to use SourceSafe to manage application versions as well as manage large project teams.

Chapter 20, "Creating Development Guidelines," discusses the importance of development standards and provides some suggested approaches.

Chapter 21, "Organizing the Development Approach," discusses the issues and opportunities for approaching development of distributed, component-based services that differ from traditional development approaches.

Part V: Sample Applications

Throughout this book, sample code will be presented. Most of this code is excerpted from three sample applications included on the companion disk. These sample applications are outlined in detail in the last three chapters of the book.

Chapter 22, "Sample Application #1: An OLE Document Manager," is three-tiered application that allows you to check-in and check-out OLE documents from a centralized DBMS.

Chapter 23, "Sample Application #2: An Instance Manager," is a pool manager application that manages OLE automation business servers across a network.

Chapter 24, "Sample Application #3: A Three-Tier Order Processing System," is a sample three-tiered application, the GOLF System, that incorporates most of the architectural aspects presented in this book.

About the Companion Disk

The disk included with the book includes all sample source code found in the book's chapters. It is organized by chapter, and each chapter has its own subdirectory off of the root directory. For example, you can find the Chapter 18 sample code in the companion disk directory, \CHAP18.

Chapters 22, 23, and 24 include one sample application per chapter. These sample applications are fully documented in their respective chapters.

Conventions Used in This Book

To make this book easier to use, the following typographical conventions are used:

- A word or phrase used for the first time appears in *italic* and is usually accompanied by a definition.

- Screen displays, code examples, and on-screen messages appear in a special monospace type. Any code used in Visual Basic—function names, methods, and so on—also is in monospace format.

- A value or phrase that you are asked to type is shown in **bold monospace**.

- *Italic monospace* is used to indicate placeholders and variables—words that you are supposed to replace with a setting.

This book also includes these other features to enhance its usability:

> **Note**
>
> This is an example of a Note. Notes provide additional information that may help you avoid problems or that you should consider in using the described features.

Occasionally, the lines of code that you see in this book may be too long to fit onto one printed page. When this condition occurs, you will see the code continuation character shown in the following line:

```
'This is an example of a line of code that should be typed as a
 ➥single line but is too long to fit onto one line of the printed
 ➥page.'
```

This character indicates that the line was broken to fit on the printed page. If you decide to type a line of code that contains this character, you should *not* use the Enter key. Just ignore the character and type both lines, as a single entry, before pressing Enter.

Additionally, descriptive code listing heads were added to help you more easily find and use the code-sample and application files throughout this book. The only exceptions to this new feature are Chapters 22, 23, and 34. In these chapters, you will find complete sample-code and application file locations in tables, near the beginning of each chapter. All of the listing heads contain the file name of the sample code or application that you can find on the companion disk.

Part I

Introduction to Client/Server Concepts, Architecture, and Methodology

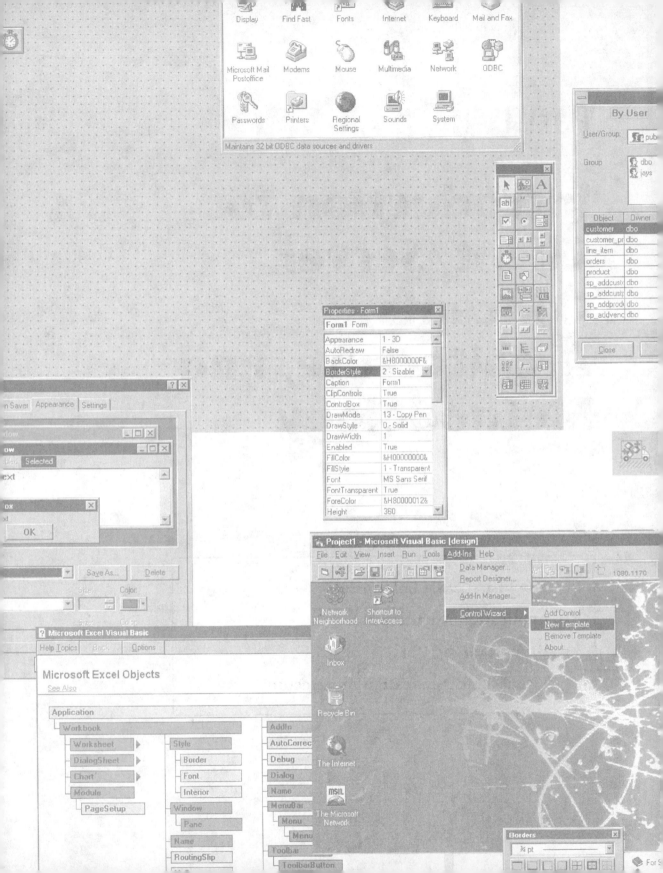

Chapter 1

The Visual Basic Enterprise

Visual Basic 4 Enterprise Edition makes three-tier client/server a reality. A number of new features introduced in VB4EE enable this. This chapter will cover:

- Key three-tier VB4 Enterprise Edition features
- The three-tier services model
- Why you will want to use the services model

Key Three-Tier VB4 Enterprise Edition Features

As more business-critical corporate applications are built with first generation two-tier client/server tools, it is becoming more clear that they have requirements that are not met by current products. Visual Basic 4.0 addresses the following key issues regarding business application creation:

- 32-Bit development environment
- Team development
- Business rule encapsulation
- Distribution of components
- High-performance DBMS data access
- Extensible integrated development environment

32-Bit Development Environment

VB4 is a 32-bit application, allowing developers to create 32-bit applications that run on Windows NT 3.51 and Windows 95. Developers can develop applications for these environments using a single set of source code. VB4 also includes a source code compatible 16-bit version for managing the transition to a 32 bit environment. Corporate developers can now deploy their custom, line-of-business applications on robust 32-bit operating systems.

Team Development

The Enterprise Edition environment includes tightly integrated Visual SourceSafe, Microsoft's version-control software. SourceSafe's project-oriented approach to source-code control promotes code reuse and management of multiple releases while helping prevent accidental code loss or alteration. Development teams can work effortlessly in concert without ever having to leave the environment of Visual Basic 4.0

Business Rule Encapsulation

Business rules and other services can be encapsulated in reusable OLE automation severs. VB4 allows developers to create both in-process and out-of process servers OLE Automation servers.

Distribution of Components

VB4 includes Remote Automation technology, which allows developers to create distributed multi-tier client-server applications. Distributed applications can conveniently be created and debugged on a single machine and then deployed across the network. Using the Component Manager, developers can deploy OLE objects anywhere throughout the network to create high-performance, network leveraged applications.

High Performance DBMS Data Access

VB4 has addressed the corporate need for high performance DBMS data access with a new object library, Remote Data Objects (RDO). Like Jet's Data Access Objects (DAO), RDO is an easy-to-use object-based database interface. Unlike DAO, however, RDO is ideal for high-performance server-based ODBC data access with support for such advanced options as stored procedures, bound parameters, error processing, and cursor support.

Extensible Integrated Development Environment

Part of the success of Visual Basic can be attributed to its extensibility. In version 3.0, extensibility typically came in the form of a custom control.

Additional extensibility came from a few innovative vendors that managed to restructure the Visual Basic IDE, integrating their tools with the Visual Basic design environment, thus extending the capabilities of Visual Basic in a whole new direction.

In addition to exposing Data Source Control interfaces, VB4's development environment has been exposed as an OLE object that can be manipulated programmatically with OLE Automation. By doing this, Microsoft encourages development of extensibility enhancements in a new direction. Many third-party tools can now be created and integrated with the VB4 development environment. The new Add-In menu item and Add-In Manager have been added specifically to support this functionality. Using the new exposed interfaces, third parties can do the following:

- Add menu items to the Visual Basic menu structure

- Modify Visual Basic projects such as adding forms, controls, and code

- Support two-way communication between third-party tools and Visual Basic

The open IDE enables high-end corporate design and CASE tool vendors to seamlessly integrate their products with Visual Basic.

Like custom controls, these capabilities promise to be utilized for functionality not yet imagined. However, the following areas provide some of the first examples of tools utilizing these capabilities.

Source-code control

The ability to add menu items to the Visual Basic IDE provides integration with the most popular source-code control tools. Microsoft SourceSafe has been integrated in this manner in VB4. In addition to providing the capability to add menu items, VB4 also provides a new set of events caused by file-related activities—such as File Open and File Close—that are included to allow source-code control vendors to achieve an extremely high level of integration.

CASE and Data Modeling

CASE and Data Modeling tools can integrate with the VB4 application development environment. For example, tools can be created such that once the designer is finished specifying a high-level object or database-structure design, the modeling tool can "drive" Visual Basic, creating the first pass of the Visual Basic project.

Form and Code Design Aids

Design aids can be integrated with the VB4 development environment. Design aids include things like form templates for often-used forms and wizards for interactive-form generation and code library management. Because VB IDE add-ins can be created with VB itself, VB provides the corporate developer with customization capabilities by allowing individuals to create their own wizards.

Open, Component-Based, Distributed Solutions

In other engineering disciplines, designers start a project with a catalog and price list and then decide which components must be purchased and which must be custom made to complete the project. However, for most client-server software projects, most developers must start a project from scratch, with nearly every part of most software projects built new and by hand.

The Industrial Revolution came about at the end of the last century because manufacturers developed universal standards that resulted in consistent products for consumers and interchangeable parts. For example, an engineer knows now that the thread count of a quarter-inch bolt and a quarter-inch nut work together. Achieving a level of interoperability similar to that achieved as a result of universal standards is Microsoft's primary goal in establishing the component object model (COM) in OLE. COM provides a set of interfaces that allows components from various vendors to work together in custom software applications.

Microsoft's pragmatic approach to the design of OLE—a standard set of component interfaces supported at the system level—allows a component created in one vendor's environment to interoperate with components created in other computing environments. This provides developers with best-of-breed products and third-parties opportunities to provide add-on products for OLE.

Microsoft will support OLE components as it carries these components forward to future releases of its operating system products. Microsoft will continue to expose its operating system and application technology via OLE to ensure interoperability between Microsoft products and those of other vendors. Microsoft will continue to provide tools for creating and integrating components—such as Microsoft Visual Basic. Microsoft also will continue to work closely with third parties to encourage them to promote interoperability between their products and other OLE components. In addition, Microsoft will encourage the creation of OLE components that can be used in other environments.

With Visual Basic 4.0, Microsoft has advanced this strategy significantly. For the first time, reusable OLE components can be created easily in a high-level rapid applications development (RAD) tool. With Visual Basic 4.0 Enterprise Edition, these components now can be accessed over networks in a multi-tier distributed solution.

Three-Tiered Model for Enterprise Solutions

Client-server computing continues to represent an increasingly popular alternative to legacy host-based solutions. It can offer faster and more cost-effective performance and enables the development of entirely new solutions based on the broad-based availability of information and analysis at all levels of the organization. Client-server solutions are becoming larger and increasingly support the corporation's "mission-critical" line-of-business functions.

But the classic two-tiered client-server model fails to provide adequate scalability, performance, and ease of management—a necessity for any business-critical solution. For this reason, many vendors are adopting a three-tiered, distributed-computing model. This model, known as a *services model*, modifies the role of traditional "server" and "client" and adds a new architectural component, "business services." To date however, no vendor has offered the combination of a three-tiered application architecture with mainstream, rapid application development tools.

In first-generation client-server architectures, business logic is captured in one of two ways: it's either coded into the client graphical user interface, necessitating that any maintenance change be reinstalled to perhaps hundreds or thousands of desktops, or it's coded into stored procedures on the server machine. While SQL is a widely accepted standard, it is primitive in its control flow, data structures, maintenance capability, and debugging capability in comparison to full-blown programming languages such as BASIC and C. In the three-tier model, volatile business-service logic is logically isolated from client and data services, maintained in a secure, centralized business object.

As business conditions become more competitive, custom business solutions must be adapted much more quickly to meet competitive threats and sales opportunities. The typical client/server application now has a maintenance cycle of less than six months.

This services model is a way of viewing applications as a set of features or services that are used to fulfill end-user requests. By encouraging the developer to model an application as a collection of discrete services, features and functionality can be packaged for reuse, sharing and distribution across functional and computational (such as hardware) boundaries. For example, an airline reservation system can maintain the business rules, describing pricing and availability in a separate pricing and availability service that is shared by thousands of users. When prices change these services are easily updated. Through this networked service architecture many services are available to an application builder in "ready-to-use" form. The components that provide these services can be developed in-house or purchased from a number of outside vendors.

There are three categories of services:

- User services (roughly analogous to the traditional client)
- Business services (a new model component)
- Data services (roughly analogous to the traditional server)

User Services

User services provide the visual interface for presenting information and gathering data. They also secure the business services needed to deliver the required business capabilities and integrate the user with the application to perform a business process. User services are generally identified with the user interface and normally reside in an executable program located on the client workstation. Even here, however, there are opportunities for identifying services to reside in separate components for shared application usage and easy updating.

Business Services

Business services are the bridge between user and data services. They respond to requests from the user (or other business services) to execute a business task. Business services accomplish this by applying formal procedures and business rules to the relevant data. When the needed data resides on a database server, business services secure the data services needed to accomplish the business task or apply the business rule. This insulates the user from direct interaction with the database. Because business rules change more frequently than the specific business tasks they support, they are ideal candidates for encapsulating components that are physically separate from the application logic itself. This makes it easier to update enterprise-level solutions without having to update a large number of individual clients or servers.

Data Services

Data services define, maintain, access, and update data. They manage and satisfy business services requests for data. They may be physically implemented in a particular database management system (DBMS) or by a heterogeneous collection of databases that reside on multiple platforms and combinations of servers, mainframes, and other data sources.

Why Use the Services Model?

The three-tier VB architecture is capable of scaling to meet the needs of the enterprise and prepares you for future architectural evolution. This architecture is not appropriate in every situation, however—it might be overkill for a department, workgroup, or small company.

Likewise, it might not be appropriate for decision-support applications characterized by data retrieval and browsing, not transactions. Some companies have begun releasing three-tier decision support and on-line analytical processing (OLAP) engines, but most have not. Most DSS front-end tools require direct access to the DBMS database, bypassing the middle tier in the services model. This lack of front-end tool support may mean that the difficulty in building a three-tier DSS application may not be cost effective, even though it's a better long-term architecture.

In addition, design trade-offs will probably require you to occasionally bypass these lofty architectural goals. Three-tier client/server is still evolving. There is no "right" way—or a commonly accepted way—to design a business object. Physical constraints such as network performance, for example, may dictate the logical design of your business objects. As always, you should consider your organization's specific needs and apply these techniques to meet them where appropriate—and abandon techniques that are less useful.

A migration of new and existing application development to the services model should, however, begin in organizations where this architecture is appropriate. This core set of business components is what enables a company to easily assemble new solutions that use existing business processes. Visual Basic 4 Enterprise Edition is the best tool for creating such rich enterprise components.

From Here...

This chapter provided a high-level overview of all the pieces of a three-tier Visual Basic application architecture. You now should have a good introductory understanding of what The Visual Basic Enterprise looks like.

The remainder of the book covers these topics in detail. For further information related to topics covered in this chapter, see the following:

- If you feel you need more experience with the VB language, the VB documentation is an excellent reference. There are a number of books on the market that cover VB4 programming as well.

- For more information on three-tier client/server development with VB4, read *Building Client/Server Applications*, which is included with VB4EE.

- For an excellent general overview of distributed applications see *Client/Server Strategies: A Survival Guide for Corporate Reengineers*, by David Vaskevitch (IDG Press).

Chapter 2

Application Architecture

Before you can sit down and design a client/server application, you must understand the various client/server architectures. This chapter presents a survey of the various architectural scenarios, details the emerging three-tier architecture, and then discusses features of *Visual Basic Enterprise Edition* that enables three-tier application development.

Creating three-tiered applications in Visual Basic is the focus of the remainder of this book.

This chapter covers the following application architecture features:

- Centralized, file-server, and two-tier application architectures

- Typical two-tier client/server application features and limitations

- A three-tier and n-tier architecture approach

- Three-tier VB features

Application Architecture

Architecture is a term often used when designing software applications, particularly client/server applications. The *architecture* of an application refers to the way in which it is both logically and physically designed.

The physical design specifies exactly where the individual physical pieces of the application will reside—pieces like disks, software executables, network cable, and personal computers.

The logical or conceptual design, on the other hand, specifies the structure of the application and its components without regard to where the physical software, hardware, and infrastructure is located. Concepts such as order processing, customer maintenance, and commission tracking are the logical components of an organization's systems.

Too much emphasis usually is placed on the physical design of an application. Additionally, application developers often incorrectly assume that a logical design has a one-to-one correspondence to a physical design. A properly constructed logical design should be able to map to many physical scenarios. As you will see, this mapping capability is a desirable trait that leads to application flexibility and scalability.

What Is Client/Server?

The term *client/server*, in its broadest definition, can be accurately used to describe an application in which two or more separate logical processes work together to complete a task.

The *client* process requests the *server* process to perform some work on its behalf. This operation is known as *cooperative processing* because two separate processes are cooperating to complete a task.

The processes may or may not be located on the same physical machine. The processes of a client/server application can be located on a single PC or separated by thousands of miles of telephone wire. The logical design, not the physical design, determines to what degree an application is client/server.

A simple network print server, therefore, is a client/server system. The end-user PC tells a word-processing application to print. The word-processing application in turn hands over the job to the network print-server PC, which in turn queues up the request and handles all the dialog with the printer. While the print server PC spools the print job to the printer, the client PC is freed up to allow the user to perform other tasks. After the print job is complete, the server notifies the client that the job is done, and the user sees a message, indicating that printing is complete (see fig. 2.1).

Server Type	Description
File server	Redirects the server's hard drive across a network
Database server	Processes SQL commands against a database and sends results back to the client
Mail server	Processes electronic mail commands for the client (get mail, send mail, and so on)

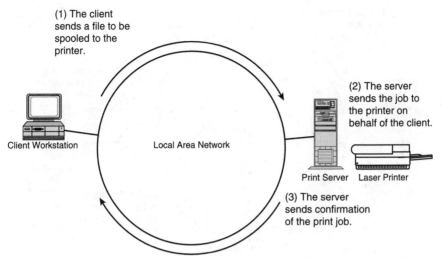

Fig. 2.1
A print server is
a client/server
application: the
client requests the
server to spool
output to a printer;
notifies client.

(1) The client
sends a file to be
spooled to the
printer.

(2) The server
sends the job to
the printer on
behalf of the client.

Client Workstation   Local Area Network

Print Server   Laser Printer

(3) The server
sends confirmation
of the print job.

You explore application partitioning at a high level for the remainder of this chapter. It's important to understand these concepts before diving into either design or development of your application. A fundamental change is occurring in client/server application design, and before you can understand the future of application design (which is the road you now are taking), you must understand both where it was in the past and where it is today.

After the concepts are laid down, the remainder of this book shows you exactly how to construct such applications with Visual Basic 4 Enterprise Edition (VB4EE).

A Centralized Architecture

In a mainframe terminal emulation environment, the computer terminal with which the user interacts doesn't exhibit much intelligence. It simply marshals keystrokes to the mainframe, which in turn marshals back character-based "green screens" to the terminal.

This architecture is known as *centralized* because the bulk of the processing occurs on the central mainframe computer (see fig. 2.2).

This architecture still may employ a client/server database such as Oracle or DB2, but the application and database reside within the same mainframe process. The application cannot be partitioned any further.

Fig. 2.2
A centralized architecture. Only terminal characters and screens pass from client to server. All the processing is done on the mainframe.

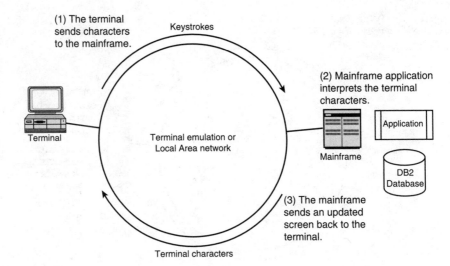

This architecture is not limited to mainframes. For example, a common method of accessing Oracle running under UNIX is to establish a simple *telnet* session on the same host that is running Oracle. This setup is a centralized architecture because the client PC is acting only as a terminal emulator.

A File-Server Architecture

Databases like Microsoft Access and Paradox are based on a file-server architecture. The database consists of just a database file—no database engine runs on the server side of the network. The only server required is a simple file-server because the only services required are file services. Therefore, these databases run as easily over a file-server network as they run on a local PC hard drive.

In a file-server architecture, the database engine actually runs on the client machine, closely tied to the client application. When the user asks the engine to execute a SQL statement, the engine searches the database file located across the network by using standard file reads and writes (see fig. 2.3). For Microsoft Access, the database engine is known as the *Jet* engine, and it is composed of several DLLs that reside on the client machine.

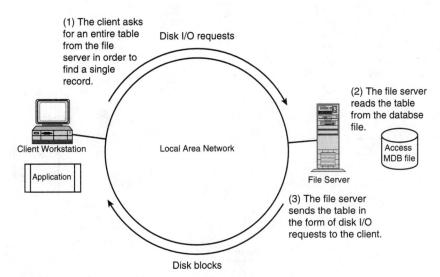

(1) The client asks for an entire table from the file server in order to find a single record.

Disk I/O requests

Client Workstation

Application

Local Area Network

(2) The file server reads the table from the databse file.

Access MDB file

File Server

(3) The file server sends the table in the form of disk I/O requests to the client.

Disk blocks

Fig. 2.3
A file-server architecture. The entire table passes over the network and the searching is done on the client.

Client/Server Concepts

What Most People Call Client/Server

Although the previous architectures could be referred to as client/server applications, when most people think of "client/server," none of those examples come to mind because the server part of client/server is often, and incorrectly, used synonymously with a database server. Unfortunately, this incorrect designation has led to a lot of confusion in the industry and innumerable heated debates.

When most people think of a client/server architecture, they think of an active database server process. This database server process could be SQL Server, Oracle, DB2, Informix, Watcom, or Sybase. In the client/server architecture, the client passes requests for data to the server. The server then actively processes the requests for data and returns only the results back to the client (see fig. 2.4).

Client requests are made in the form of SQL (Structured Query Language, pronounced "Sequel") statements. A request statement might look like the following example:

```
SELECT
      customer_id,
      customer_desc
FROM
      customers
WHERE
      customer_id = 3001234
```

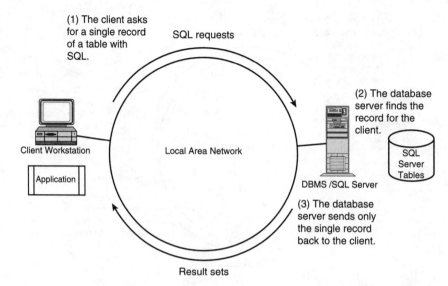

Fig. 2.4

A two-tier client/ server architecture. Only the result set passes over the network, and the searching is done by the server.

The server decides where to find the raw data on its hard disk(s), and passes only the particular customer information back over the network. Contrast this process with the file server architecture, where, in order to find a single customer, the file server passes back the *entire* customer table over the network.

Advantages of Client/Server

If both file-server databases, such as Microsoft Access and client/server databases, (for example SQL Server process SQL statements), and the file-server database is simpler and easier to use, why would an organization ever use a client/server database? For several reasons:

- When the database server actively processes the query, response time (the time it takes the system to complete a user's query) depends upon the server machine, not the client machine. Organizations can invest in a high-end server that benefits all users.

- The active server process returns only result sets over the network (as opposed to large file i/o blocks), so network traffic is reduced. This process also enables an organization to build applications that access large amounts of data over a modem, which has a narrow bandwidth.

- An active server process can better ensure the integrity of its data. Active servers manage data integrity features, such as transactions, rollbacks, logs, and so on. File-server databases also can do this on a limited basis, but the client application database engine still has access to the underlying raw data. In a client/server database, only the robust server engine has access to the data.

In this section, database servers were called "client/server." Remember, however, to be properly called a server, a process can provide any service, not necessarily just a database service. So, although centralized and file-based architectures are not commonly thought of as client/server, they do exhibit client/server characteristics.

File-Based Versus Server-Based

Why this ambiguity exists is understandable. Mainstream development tools such as Visual Basic, PowerBuilder, and SQL Windows that operate against database management systems like SQL Server and Oracle all rightfully claim to produce client/server applications. These tools are client/server development tools, and it's easy to understand why applications that don't look like the kind of applications these tools produce are incorrectly assumed to not be client/server.

Another common source of confusion is equating a file-server and database server database. A typical developer, for example, might not understand the architectural differences between a Visual Basic application that uses a Microsoft Access database and an application that uses a SQL Server database.

In this case, the developer is overlooking an important point: in file-based and database server scenarios, the server is performing very different tasks. When a query request for data is executed by VB in the Access scenario, the VB client process actually searches the physical Access .MDB file for the appropriate records. The complexity might be hidden from the programmer, but the client's CPU is chugging through the file. Microsoft Access is not a database server because its engine is not a separate partition (even if the database is placed on a shared file server).

In the SQL Server scenario, the client passes a SQL request to the SQL Server process. The server process, in turn, searches through the physical data. After the results are obtained by the server, only the results are sent back to the client. If you've ever used Oracle or SQL Server, for example, you know that you don't need any kind of file/drive mapping in order to query the server.

It is important to understand the strict definition of client/server so that you can understand the rest of this book. The database server example—the one most people call client/server—is known as a two-tiered client/server architecture. After fully examining the traditional two-tier architecture, you will explore more complicated three-tier and n-tier architectures, as well as examine services other than SQL database management systems.

Typical Two-Tier Client/Server Application Partitioning

Most client/server applications built with fourth-generation language (4GL) tools in production today were designed with a two-tiered architecture. They are partitioned into two logical layers: the front-end and the back-end, which is explained in Table 2.1.

Table 2.1 The Logical Layers of a Two-Tiered Client/Server Architecture	
Tier	**Characteristics**
1. Front-End	GUI Interface; SQL calls; desktop application; 4GLs
2. Back-End	SQL database server; multitasking operating system

The front-end process is developed in a 4GL, such as Visual Basic or PowerBuilder. It is known as the *front-end* because it is the layer with which the user interacts on their PC.

The front-end executable code is composed of GUI elements: buttons and menus, GUI form flow, SQL statements, data validations, and so on.

The back-end process is a database server such as SQL Server or Oracle. It is known as the *back-end* because it typically resides on a centralized server machine in a controlled environment.

The back-end database is composed of elements such as data tables, triggers, referential integrity definitions, security policies, and so on.

You can easily see why separating this logical architecture from the physical is confusing: ordinarily, the logical front-end is deployed on a Windows-based client workstation and the logical back-end is deployed on a large server machine. The logical architecture is almost always a one-to-one mapping of the physical architecture in a two-tiered client/server environment (see fig. 2.4).

Now that we defined a two-tier architecture, let's discuss the limitations of this architecture.

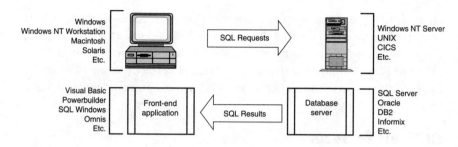

Fig. 2.5
A typical two-tier client/server architecture.

Client/Server Concepts

Limitations of Two-Tier Applications

Thousands of two-tier Windows-based applications in production run many large businesses throughout the world.

If, however, you've ever been in an organization that developed this kind of application, you know that the architecture is not perfect.

Difficult to Manage Front-End Enhancements

In a two-tier environment, what happens when the SQL needs to be changed because a new column has been added to a database table? What happens if old customers should now be marked as inactive rather than deleted from the database?

Hundreds, sometimes thousands, of client workstations need to be upgraded with a new version of the front-end simultaneously with the database change. This is not an easy change, especially if the client applications are geographically dispersed.

If *multiple* front-end applications are affected, just analyzing the dependencies of a change is difficult.

Difficult to Share Common Processes

After the business process is painstakingly designed and coded into an application, it is difficult to then reuse this process in another application.

An integrated order processing application, for example, has been written for several hundred customer service reps. Senior management is going through a typical Total Quality Management and Business Process Re-engineering phase and decides it's beneficial to empower sales reps to query order status, query shipment information, and enter orders. The sales reps neither need nor want the same full-blown application that customer service reps use. Instead, they want this functionality integrated into their existing sales force work-flow application.

To do this, MIS must develop a completely new set of code—even though it is composed of functionality that was already developed in another application. If the original order-processing application was well-designed, however, it might be possible to rip out the code that relates to the processes of interest. But even then, two identical (and complex) business processes must be maintained in two different applications.

Difficult to Secure

In a two-tier environment, security is either:

1. Enforced by the database server back-end (database security)

2. Enforced in the client application front-end (application security)

Each option has limitations. The following two sections describe each approach in detail.

Database Security

Database server security consists of assigning privileges to database objects and users. For example, a user may be allowed only SELECT privileges on a table, or the user may be allowed SELECT, UPDATE, and INSERT privileges. The problem with giving the user this ability is that there usually are so many different entities in a large organization's database that, even when you group users together to assign rights, it's nearly impossible to determine who should have exactly what privileges.

Additionally, the DBMS doesn't provide the level of granularity an organization typically requires. Sometimes, organizations need to ensure the security and data integrity beyond what can be expressed in simple table-based row and column privileges.

Organizations don't need to just secure *what* data can be changed and accessed, they need to secure *how* the data can be changed and accessed. A human resources employee, for example, may have access to update a salary table, but only if the change was approved by a manager. These types of security policies are nearly impossible to define with simple database views and grants.

Application Security

The second scenario, enforcing security at the front-end, is probably the more popular scenario. Although the user still logs on to the database with the DBMS user ID and password, the front-end application uses a series of custom user/group tables to determine what things the user is allowed to do within the front-end application.

This scenario has two problems:

- Because none of the database objects are secure, users have wide-open access to the database with tools other than the front-end application (such as Microsoft Excel or a query tool).

- The application security implementation must be developed, deployed, and maintained across all of the organization's custom applications.

Both problems are serious, but the former problem is probably more serious because just about every desktop application now ships with ODBC database links. MIS can expect that, if given authority, users will be browsing around the database.

Users Must Use MIS's Applications

Because so many important business rules are incorporated into the front-end, it would be unacceptable to allow the users to develop their own front-end that operated against the database and to bypass these rules.

If a sales rep, for example, had a large recurring order for a major customer, he/she could not be trusted to build an Excel VBA macro that entered the order into the SQL Server database. Too many complicated steps must occur in the creation of an order, and the production order-processing system is too important to allow users such free reign.

But MIS should *want* the users to be able to adapt the system to their particular, individual needs. Users don't want to go through MIS for minor application presentation changes, and MIS wants to empower users to perform their own presentation maintenance.

The Business Model: Buried in Front-End Code and Back-End Design

The business is modeled around high-level entities (such as a customer or order) and processes that manipulate these entities (such as print order or update customer). These entities and processes define the organization's business rules. Unfortunately, our logical *business* model doesn't have a one-to-one mapping to our logical *application* design. Rather, the business entities (things) and processes (actions) that make up the business model are scattered throughout front-end presentation code and back-end database code.

There isn't an explicitly identified layer in the two-tiered architecture where the business rules and objects are kept. Instead, the attributes of a high-level business entity, such as a customer, are modeled in a cryptic set of database tables and relations. Likewise, the valid processes associated with these entities, such as deleting a customer, are maintained as 4GL code on the client workstation.

Maintaining, understanding, and changing the systems that support the business model in this architecture is difficult.

No Business Process Engine

Mainframe COBOL code tends to keep the business moving in legacy environments. Although two-tier client/server tools have been around for a while, the front-end and back-end tools don't enable an application developer to easily develop the background processes that keep the business humming— for example, the two-tier environment is missing the following tools:

- A batch-processing language to chug through large amounts of data during month-end processing or move data from an operational database to a decision support database

- A server-based process that coordinates orders from electronic data interchange (EDI) data sources

- Transaction monitors that can manage transactions across multiple databases or even other data sources

So, although the two-tier environment provides great tools for the front-end and back-end, the corporate developer must resort to 3GLs such as C and COBOL to create the batch processes.

A Three-Tier and N-Tier Architecture: The Services Model

Databases, development tools, and corporations are moving toward a three-tiered application architecture to overcome the limitations or the two-tiered architecture.

The additional tier provides an explicit layer for the business rules that sits between what once was called the front-end and back-end. This middle tier encapsulates the business model (or "business rules") associated with the system and separates it from the presentation and database code.

Table 2.2 shows a summary of the tiers of services in a three-tiered architectural approach.

Table 2.2	**A Summary of the Three Tiers**			
Tier	**Service Type**	**Characteristics**	**Responsible For**	**Tools**
(1) User services	Client applications	GUI interface	Presentation & navigation	4GLs; desktop applications
(2) Business services	Business servers	Business object properties & methods	Business policies, rules, & security	Some 4GLs, COBOL, C
(3) Data services	Data servers	Raw data-based managers	Integrity of decision independent data	Databases, messaging systems

In the Visual Basic documentation, Microsoft correctly calls client applications *user services* because they directly interact with end-users. This book, however, uses the term *client application* because it is easier to understand a reference to a "client application" than to a "user service."

The Services Model

A tier communicates within its parent, child, or sibling, which means that it can make requests and return answers to a process within its own tier, immediately above its tier, or immediately below its tier (see fig. 2.6). Usually, the only communication that doesn't occur is a client application communicating directly with a data service.

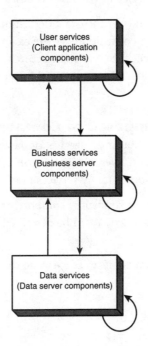

Fig. 2.6
The layers in a three-tier client server application architecture or "services model."

In a traditional layered architecture, a layer can communicate only with another layer directly above or below it. Notice, however, that the user services, business services, and data services can communicate with themselves. This model is known as the *services* model because, unlike a layered model, any service may invoke another service within its tier.

An example of this model would be an order business server that uses a customer and product business server to help fulfill an order, without the client application having visibility to the business servers' interaction.

So, a single client application request can involve many business servers. Because such a request involves more than a single data and business server interaction, this request is often referred to as an *n-tier* architecture.

This book uses the terms three-tier, n-tier, and services model as equivalent terms.

A client application request to update an order, for example, may be asked directly of an order processing business server, which in turn requests a shipment business server to schedule shipments, which both use an underlying database service. In this example, a single client application request involved two business servers and one data server.

Remember, these tiers do not necessarily correspond to physical locations on a network. Rather, they are logical layers that give the developer flexibility to deploy the particular service to wherever is best.

Just as there is confusion over the exact definition of two-tier client/server computing, there also is confusion over the exact definition of three-tier. In this book, a three-tier client/server architecture (or services model) is simply an architecture that is logically partitioned into user service, business service, and data service layers.

Services Are Composed of Components

A particular user service, business service, or data service is composed of *components*. Every component lives within the context of a single tier and single service, and each tier houses many services made up of components.

While a service is a logical concept, a component describes a physical packaging of functionality. So, a *service* can be described as a logical grouping of physical components.

Components are the actual pieces of software that are deployed on computers.

Therefore, the following rules hold:

- The client application tier is composed of client applications—such as order entry and customer maintenance—which are made up of client application components.

- The business server tier is composed of business servers—such as order processing and warehouse management—which are made up of business server components.

- The data server tier is composed of data servers—such as orders and customers—which are made up of data server components.

It's a simple hierarchical construct. Many times, a single server is made up of only one component. Some servers, however, provide very complex services, so rather than creating giant monolithic servers, they're broken down into components.

A client application, for example, is a user service. An order processing client application may be made up of several components: multiple Visual Basic EXEs, OCXes, and VBXs. The same concept applies to business and data servers.

Components are the lowest common denominator; they cannot be broken down any further. Components are black boxes: what goes in and what comes out is well defined, but it is unknown and irrelevant what happens inside the component.

The Client Application

Throughout this book, a particular service in the first tier will be referred to as a client application. As is typical, services within this tier may be named many different things in the real world, including the following:

- A user service

- The client

- The application

- The front-end

- The presentation layer

- The GUI

As you have seen, however, this tier isn't the only tier that acts as a "client"—it's not the only tier that requests services of other processes.

The function of the client application is to provide the user a graphical interface to the business services. A well-designed client application enables a user to do the following:

- Understand the business services as a whole

- Navigate through the business services efficiently

Client applications usually are created with 4th-generation languages, like Visual Basic, and desktop applications such as Microsoft Excel. Physically, client applications usually reside as executables (EXEs) on the end user's workstation.

Business Services

The new tier is the *business services* tier. Business services provide the link between the client applications and data services.

As the following list shows, the function of this logical layer is two-fold:

1. To enforce business policies

2. To encapsulate a model of the business and expose that model to client applications

Business services enforces the business policies of the organization and maintains the consistency of the data services in the third tier. The client application is insulated from the complexities of the raw data services.

Business policies are rules that restrict and control the flow of business tasks. They encapsulate policies, such as those shown in the following examples:

- Orders that have been shipped cannot be canceled.

- Delivery trucks should be routed from customer to customer with a least-cost algorithm.

- An e-mail message should be sent to an account executive who's national account customer hasn't placed an order in over four weeks.

Business rules tend to change more frequently than the user presentation. For example, an additional "credit check" business rule might be put in place, but the basic times that credit is checked in the business process probably will not change.

So, the internal workings of the "black box" business server has changed, but the type of data that goes in and out has not. Because these changes are frequent in the corporate environment, business rules are excellent candidates for encapsulation.

Note that, by enforcing business policy in the business server tier, we are moving away from enforcing business policy in the data-server tier. In a two-tier environment, the business policy was enforced both at the front-end with 4GL code and at the back-end with database objects, such as triggers.

Moving the business rules out of the front-end probably is an easy sell—most people are familiar with the kinds of limitations that exist when doing this.

Moving the business rule out of the database and into middle tier probably is a more difficult sell. DBMS constructs such as triggers, rules, stored procedures, and defaults work—so why would you not want to take advantage of them? Because these constructs can't enforce *all* the business rules, and you don't want the organization's raw data tied to such rules, nor do you want logical rules distributed among multiple tiers.

Security and auditing are just additional business policies. Business services enforce the following kinds of security-related policies:

- Salesmen cannot be reimbursed for more than their expense account

- Customer EDI transmissions must be specially encrypted

- Human-resource coordinators can view salaries only in their assigned department

- All retail sales over $50,000 generate a page to the store manager

Business services are built with programming languages such as Visual Basic, COBOL, C, and CASE tools.

Data Services

The third tier is composed of data servers. The most common data service is the SQL-based database management system. SQL Server and Oracle are data servers.

Data servers manage the raw business information and handle transactions for business servers. The primary responsibility of data services is to provide business services with low-level transactional work and to ensure the integrity of their data. They ensure the meaningfulness of the data they store.

These types of generic data servers are mature technologies. They have been successfully deployed and understood in many organizations.

The existence of the new business server that uses the data server, however, in no way lessens the importance of good database design. Just because the business server gives us a lot of flexibility in constructing transactions, it doesn't mean that underlying database entities can be poorly designed.

Don't be too quick to narrowly equate data servers with only relational database servers, however. Data servers, for example, can be:

- File servers
- Imaging servers
- Messaging/mail servers
- Reporting servers
- Workflow servers
- Legacy mainframe applications
- Object Oriented DBMS (ODBMS)

Process Communication

As you saw in figure 2.6, the three-tier architecture depends upon the capability of interprocess communication—the capability of one service to communicate with another.

For two services to communicate, they both must speak the same language, or *protocol*. Some examples of interprocess communication you may have heard of include the following examples:

- Microsoft's Object Linking and Embedding (OLE)
- Windows's Dynamic Data Exchange (DDE)
- The Object Management Group's Common Object Request Broker Architecture (CORBA)
- Database-oriented middleware, such as Oracle's SQL*Net or Sybase's DB-LIB
- The Windows Sockets specification (WinSock)

All these protocols are not equal, but they all share one common characteristic: they enable two or more services to communicate.

You will see later that services developed in Visual Basic use OLE to communicate.

A Conceptual Example

What is an example of a process flow through the three tiers? The following example shows an order processing system (see fig. 2.7):

1. A clerk enters an order for a customer into a customer service client application. The client application displays to the user a series of forms, asking for a customer name, line items, shipping information, and so on.

2. After the user enters the order, the client application sends the order information to the order-processing business server. The server checks to make sure all the information is valid by communicating with the customer and product business servers. If valid, the order server initiates a series of transactions with the database server that actually reflect the new order in the database.

3. The data server manages the transaction for the order manager business server.

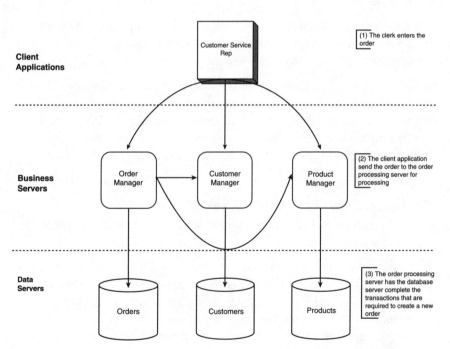

Fig. 2.7

A three-tier conceptual example.

Benefits of a Three-Tier Architecture

The benefits of a three-tier client/server application architecture mirror the limitations of the two-tier architecture described previously.

System Enhancements Are Manageable

Because you have layered the architecture, changes in one service—if properly designed—should not affect the other services.

If changes occur to the internal workings of a service and not to its interface, no other services need to be modified. For example, if the order processing business server needs to change the way inventory is adjusted, the change can be made to the server without changing the client application.

If a service's interface needs to be changed, it can be redesigned so that the changes are *downward-compatible* with the existing interface. Downward-compatible means that, although the interface has been modified, existing services still should run even if they weren't modified to take advantage of the change.

Releasing changes of the client application usually is logistically difficult. Unlike the business and data servers, which tend to be centralized, the client application tends to be physically located on many machines.

In the two-tier environment, where the front-end and back-end are closely related, changes need to occur simultaneously for all end-users. When the client application needs to change in a three-tier environment, the changes can be distributed at your leisure, without regard to the other layers. An unchanged client application still runs because the business services it uses aren't changed.

Business Servers Can Be Shared

In the three-tier architecture, the business logic is not bound and intertwined with the desktop application.

If three separate client applications need order entry functionality, the complicated business processes do not need to be redundantly coded and maintained in three separate places. Rather, a single order-processing business server services all three client applications. Likewise, the developer of the client application doesn't have to deal with the underlying business or data service code.

This technique is known as *code reuse*. You're not reusing small objects, like an "OK" button or listbox, but instead you are reusing objects that have a business value: a billing server, a shipping server, warehouse management server, and so on.

Surprisingly, most organizations look at object orientation and think of objects at the micro level. It's no wonder "object orientation" hasn't taken the corporate world by storm: there really isn't much business value to be gained by developing an enterprise-wide "OK" button.

The real value of objects is standardizing on and sharing organizational objects at the macro level—objects that are expensive to build and manage redundantly, which is what three-tier and the services model is all about. You're building large business server objects that can be shared, and as you shall see, you don't need a 100 percent object-oriented programming language like C++ or SmallTalk to create these objects or realize their enormous benefits.

The Business Objects and Processes Can Be Secured

Security can be moved out of the data services and client application into the business services tier, where it belongs. The client application does not have direct access to the data services, so there are no "back-doors" available that would allow an end user to corrupt the data. The business servers, therefore, can implement security in the manner most appropriate to the organizations.

The business server environment can control not only *what* data is changed and accessed, but *how* that data is changed and accessed.

Most important, however, the business server can implement security into its own rich business processes, as in the following examples:

- Security can be enforced in ways too complex to express in the RDBMS security schema

- Specific alerts can be written to an event log

- E-mail messages can be sent

Users Can Create their Own Client Applications

Because all the business rules were stripped out of the front-end and placed in the business servers, you no longer have "fat" clients. The term *fat client* refers to a two-tier front-end application that is interwoven with complex business rules. Instead, the client applications consist only of lightweight forms, controls, and navigational code.

This paradigm shift is going to be the most difficult for MIS professionals. MIS developers spend their lives trying to understand database theory and developing applications—and they still make serious mistakes (occasionally). Yet now we're saying users can create their *own* applications?

MIS probably has already tried this approach and learned the hard way that no matter how many ads they see for easy-to-use query tools, a single user can bring down the entire database with an errant query.

The thought of allowing a user to write their own order-processing client application isn't even taken seriously. In the two-tier world, MIS would be correct in this attitude. In a two-tier architecture, it would mean the user creating database transactions and directly modifying database tables—not something to take lightly.

But in a three-tier architecture, does it really matter if the user develops a personal application in Excel VBA that enters orders? Simply, no.

Because the user doesn't have access to the data services, they *can't* corrupt an organization's data. If the business server is developed properly, it won't allow the user to do anything that may jeopardize the organization's data. In fact, a good litmus test of whether of not a business server was designed properly is to ask the question, "Would I let an end user create a client application that uses this business server?"

This question may sound like an oversimplification. It's true—the business server should provide a simple interface, but this doesn't mean it was simple to design or develop. "But how will I know who is doing what?" Put auditing into the business server. "But how will I prevent the sales rep from ordering more than their allotted hot product?" Put a product allocation limit into the server. These are business rules.

You can see why allowing a user to create his or her own client application is such a good test—if you want to control something, it's a business rule and belongs in the business server.

This capability doesn't imply that MIS is no longer developing client applications—this will continue to happen. It means that users now can augment the MIS applications with their own personal applications. It also implies, as you shall see later, that the MIS client application developer doesn't need to have the same skills as the business services developer and the data services developer.

The Business Model Has its Own Tier

A *business object* is composed of properties and methods.

An object, such as an order, has attributes—an order number, customer number, an order date, and so on. An order also has a number of valid business processes associated with it, such as creating the order, shipping part of the order, canceling the order, or printing an invoice of the order.

The three-tier architecture has a specific layer in which to model these business entities and processes. In the two-tier world, the entities are modeled in a cryptic set of relational tables, and the processes are encapsulated in a combination of the front-end code (such as Visual Basic) and back-end code (such as SQL Server Transact-SQL).

In the three-tier world, properties and methods are attributes of objects. Application developers and end-users alike can browse these documented objects.

The Business Process Engine Has a Tier

Batch processing and unattended business queues occur in the business server. So, there are two types of processes in a logical business server:

- A set of processes that model the business and communicate directly with the client application

- A set of processes that run unattended and automatically

An order-processing object, for example, may interact with the client applications to allow the user to browse customers, enter orders, and delete orders. This order-processing object is an example of the first type of processing.

After an order is entered, the order-processing object may communicate with other business processes to complete the life of the order. It may, for example, reduce on-hand inventory, schedule multiple shipments over an extended period, issue an invoice during month end, or purge and archive older orders. This processing may occur during the day, or it may occur in batch at night.

So, the middle tier not only provides a model of the business to the client applications, it also handles what traditionally is considered the batch processing of the organization.

You might argue that a properly designed system may no longer require batch processing. Perhaps, but probably not.

Certainly, the design goal should be to eliminate batch queues that slow the business process by running only once a night. But there probably always will be a need for organizations to operate on large quantities of data that their hardware and software *must* perform in batch. Sometimes, an organization has limited processing power, and big processes must run at night when users aren't interacting with the system.

If you're beginning to think that business servers look like transaction processing monitors, you are right. A transaction processing or teleprocessing monitor (TP Monitor) is a process that manages and coordinates data server processes. These products have been around in commercial form for some time, and include products such as CICS from IBM, Tuxedo from Novell, and Encina from Transarc Corp. This book shows how to implement TP monitor functionality into the Visual Basic business server tier.

Distributed Systems Are Possible

The authors have drawn a distinct line of separation between the three tiers and also said that within each tier, there exists distinct services. Examples of these services are shown in Table 2.3.

Table 2.3 Examples of Services within Tiers	
Tier	**Service**
Client application	Order processing Customer maintenance Product maintenance
Business servers	Order processing Accounts receivable Warehouse management
Data servers	DBMS: product DBMS: customer DBMS: orders Messaging: Lotus Notes Communications: EDI server

As you can see, the system as a whole is partitioned into many distinct pieces.

In a two-tier architecture, an application usually is partitioned into only two distinct pieces: the front-end and back-end.

A *distributed system* is physically located on many machines in many locations. The degree to which an application can be distributed is directly proportional to the degree in which it is logically partitioned because it is difficult to break up a single partition to run on multiple machines. In fact, the act of breaking up an application to run on multiple machines may be considered partitioning.

In a two-tier environment, the front-end and back-end usually are tightly bound. Therefore, distributing the application involves either breaking the bond and partitioning the application, or distributing the back-end.

The first scenario is painful and, at times, impossible without a code rewrite. The second scenario can be accomplished if the database supports it, but it also is difficult and has a performance ceiling that correlates directly to specific back-end hardware and software.

In the three-tier environment, where the individual services can communicate over a network, any service can be distributed to any machine (see fig. 2.8). Different services can run under different operating systems. It also is possible to have all three tiers run on the same physical machine and operating system—this might be appropriate for a sales rep with a laptop.

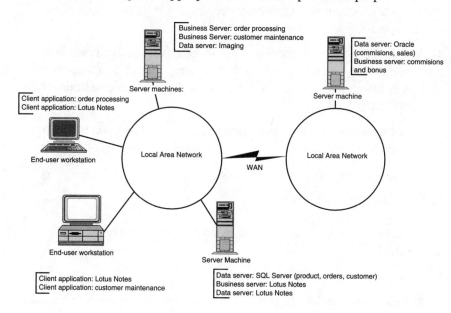

Fig. 2.8

Examples of physically distributing the logical services of a three-tier architecture.

Why would you want to create a distributed system? For flexibility and scalability.

An application that can be distributed is flexible. A business server, for example, can be placed out in a local field office to eliminate the need for a high-speed wide-area network.

An application that can be distributed is scaleable. When a data server exceeds capacity or is performing poorly, one of the logical partitions can be placed on a new, inexpensive server.

OLE: The Great Communicator

The three-tier architecture is dependent on an agreed upon way for processes to communicate. A common denominator must exist that enables any process, no matter what it was developed in, to communicate with any other.

The communication should occur *locally* (on the same machines) or *remotely* (on separate machines). It should be transparent to the process whether or not the communication occurs locally or remotely.

In this book and in the Windows environment, the communication mechanism is Object Linking and Embedding (OLE, pronounced "Oh-Lay"). OLE is a part of the Windows Open Systems Architecture (WOSA), which is Microsoft's all-encompassing specification on how Windows applications should operate.

OLE is based upon the Component Object Model (COM). COM defines the core functionality of OLE in which other services are built. In a following section of this chapter you take a closer look at COM and the additional OLE services built upon it.

In order for two services to communicate, they must agree upon the following two protocol issues:

- A well-defined, published interface

- A way to transport their dialog

The interface is the OLE object interface, and the transport is OLE automation.

An OLE automation server object exposes:

- **Properties**, which are attributes of business entities. An order exposes "customer" and "shipment date" properties.

- **Methods**, which are processes of business entities. An order exposes "update" and "print invoice" methods.

- **Member Objects**, which are dependent objects, each with their own properties and methods. An order may have a dependent line item object.

- **Collections**, which are bundles of objects, each with their own properties and methods.

The combination of an object's properties, methods, member objects, and collections is known as its *interface*. An object's interface can remain the same, even though the business logic it encapsulates changes.

A service's behavior and functionality, therefore, is encapsulated and made available through a well-defined published interface.

The method by which two services access each other's interface is OLE automation. OLE automation is handled by the service's development environment. In Visual Basic, for example, OLE automation is handled like any other "dot" operation.

When OLE communication is handled all within the context of the same machine, it is referred to as either *local automation* or just *automation*. When handled over a network, it is known as *remote automation*.

Many tools—including Microsoft Excel, Word, Access, PowerBuilder, and Visual Basic—can access OLE automation servers (see fig. 2.9).

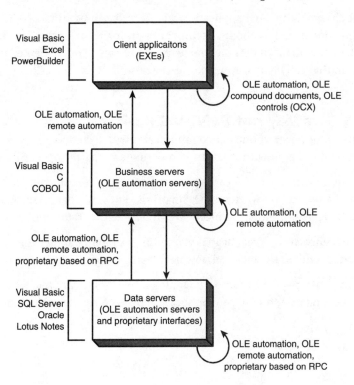

Fig. 2.9
Common tier tools and communication mechanisms.

Three-Tier and Visual Basic Enterprise

The authors have spent so much time discussing three-tier architecture with little mention of Visual Basic for the following two reasons:

- Well-designed systems are a competitive advantage.

- Although you can create all your organization's applications with Visual Basic, you don't have to.

Well-Designed Systems Are a Competitive Advantage

Client/server technology is changing rapidly. Unfortunately, large organizations cannot afford to rewrite applications immediately after significant technology changes occur, which is why you still see (and will continue to see) 132-character-column mainframe reports.

Conversely, organizations cannot afford to *not* change applications after significant technology breakthroughs. The business marketplace is growing more competitive, and when your competitor's systems enable them to provide better customer service than ours, you *must* respond.

A well-designed three-tier application architecture can be enhanced in specific functional areas without affecting or requiring changes in other functional areas. Enhancements are inexpensive and can be implemented quickly. A system that can change as quickly as the business is a competitive advantage.

Every Tier May not Be Visual Basic

When a component of one tier communicates with a component of another tier, should it matter with what the components were developed? Simply, no.

Each service within a tier encapsulates its underlying complexities. It doesn't matter if a service was written in C, SmallTalk, PowerBuilder, COBOL, or Visual Basic. It still should fit nicely into the three-tier framework.

This "fit" allows for a great deal of vendor independence and enables the designer to choose the most suitable development tool for a particular task.

Therefore, before you dive into developing a specific Visual Basic application, you must understand how your application fits into the three-tier framework.

Why Visual Basic?

The business server tier is the missing piece of the two-tier client/server architecture. It is the tier that enables you to create truly scaleable and reusable Windows-based client/server applications.

Visual Basic 4 is the first mainstream development tool that lets you easily create applications that operate in the business server tier and create applications that can use OLE to communicate in all three tiers.

There are a number of new features in *Visual Basic 4 Enterprise Client/Server Development* that enable the typical corporate MIS department to begin three-tier development.

Visual Basic Can Create OLE Automation Servers

OLE automation is a standard that defines how communication occurs between applications.

An OLE automation server can be accessed by other applications. The business servers will be OLE automation servers, and some data services will be encapsulated by OLE automation servers that are created in Visual Basic.

These components can be developed in-house or purchased from third-party vendors.

Visual Basic Includes Remote Automation Capability

Remote automation is a standard that defines how OLE automation can operate transparently over a network. Visual Basic either can transparently automate an object or can be automated over a network.

OLE and remote automation makes possible encapsulating and deploying services across a network. Neither the client nor the server knows nor cares where the other object is physically located.

Visual Basic Can Create 32-Bit Applications

Business servers are an important part of the three-tiered architecture. Like the data services, they must reside on a fault-tolerant machine, running a fault-tolerant operating system.

Visual Basic can create business servers that run in native mode under Windows NT.

Visual Basic Has High-Performance Data Server Support

Besides the traditional VB data access methods such as Jet, the ODBC API, and VBSQL.VBX, VB4EE includes two new database server interfaces—*remote data objects* (RDO) and the *remote data control* (RDC).

The remote data objects are a light object-based ODBC interface analogous to the Access/Jet database engine. The remote data control is analogous to the Access/Jet data control.

Both interfaces provide server-specific functionality such as engine side cursors, multiple result sets, error processing, and excellent performance. Both also provide an object-based interface and operate against multiple DBMSs.

Who Else Is Doing Three-Tier?

Before Visual Basic, products that implemented a three-tier architecture tended to be expensive, proprietary, or difficult to use.

Products such as Forte and R/3 by SAP are based on a three-tier architecture. TP monitors like CICS and Tuxedo are based upon a three-tier architecture. These expensive products have separate proprietary scripting languages and separate proprietary interfaces. At the time of this writing, TP monitors such as Top End from AT&T/GIS have an entry price of around $50,000.

A three-tier application also can be built in 3GLs like C. C, however, is inappropriate for most corporate developers: it has a steep learning curve, is difficult to use, and yields long development times.

PowerSoft and other vendors eventually will release 4GL products that can create three-tier applications. It will be interesting to see if they rely on proprietary interfaces. Remember, if a tool supports only a proprietary interface (instead of OLE), then the code reuse benefit can be realized only if you stick with the proprietary tool that can access this interface.

Three-Tier Is a Guideline, not a Requirement

The services model is a logical model, not a physical one. It describes how the application is designed, not deployed. The designer should strive to create logical services with physical components that do not cross service boundaries.

Unfortunately, the real world is not this neat. Design tradeoffs probably demand that you occasionally bypass these lofty architectural goals.

For example, DBMS triggers and stored procedures are reliable, fast, and mature. To conform to the services model, you would not encapsulate business rules in these data server constructs. If, however, they operate significantly faster than an equivalent Visual Basic business server, you may have to do so.

Also, although we said that all our services communicate with each other through OLE, some services may not support OLE. For example, you probably should not scrap your DB2 database and mainframe just because you can't find an OLE-based interface into the DBMS.

This situation isn't all that bad, as long as you understand—and reflect in your design documentation—that a portion of your business services reside in the DBMS data server.

These are design goals. Understand them, but apply them when they best suit your particular organization's requirements.

VB Is not Just Three-Tier

Visual Basic is a flexible fourth-generation programming language. Applications built with Visual Basic are not inherently three-tier, just as applications built with C, SmallTalk, or PowerBuilder are not inherently three-tier. Visual Basic doesn't force the developer to adhere to any methodology or architecture. It's up to the system architect to design the services so that they fit into a logical three-tier model.

The rest of this book shows how to create services within the three tiers by using Visual Basic—services such as VB client applications, VB business servers, and VB-based interfaces to third party data services such as SQL Server, Oracle, and mainframe sessions.

This book shows that although you can create services with other tools, Visual Basic is the only programming language a corporate developer *needs* to know to create complete three-tier client/server application services.

From Here...

This chapter covered various architectures of modern client/server information systems and explored, in depth, the advantages of a three-tier architecture over a two-tier architecture. This chapter also reviewed the new features in VB4EE that enable you to create such three-tier applications.

For further information related to topic covered in this chapter, see the following:

- Chapter 3, "Understanding OLE," provides more information about OLE.

- Chapter 8, "Architecting Tier 1: Client Applications," provides more information on creating user services.

- Chapter 9, "Architecting Tier 2: Business Servers," provides more information on creating business services.

- Chapter 10, "Architecting Tier 3: Data Servers," provides more information about creating data services.

Chapter 3

Understanding OLE

In Chapter 2, "Application Architecture," we discussed how OLE is the foundation used to build interoperable components in a multi-tier client/server architecture.

Before moving on to Chapter 4, "Visual Basic Application Architecture," which discusses exactly how to put together all the pieces with Visual Basic, you need to look more closely at OLE.

This chapter discusses OLE concepts and terms in detail, and then shows how these general OLE concepts apply in the Visual Basic environment.

What Is OLE?

OLE (pronounced "Oh-Lay") is Microsoft's view of shared objects and components. OLE is a language independent, binary standard.

Microsoft currently supports OLE on the Windows platforms (Windows 3.*x*, Windows 95, and Windows NT) and on the Macintosh platform. Microsoft has agreements with other vendors to port OLE to additional platforms. Bristol Technology, for example, currently is working on porting OLE to the UNIX environment.

Although OLE is an acronym for Object Linking and Embedding, it has progressed well beyond these two functions. In fact, because the acronym does so little justice in describing what OLE is about, Microsoft no longer uses the term's verbose description.

OLE is a part of the Windows Open Systems Architecture (WOSA), which is Microsoft's all-encompassing specification on how Windows applications should operate. OLE is based on the Component Object Model (COM). COM defines the core functionality of OLE in which other services are built. Later in this chapter, you take a closer look at COM and the additional OLE services built upon it.

Why Learn OLE?

OLE is not only the foundation for today's three-tier Visual Basic applications, it is the foundation for Microsoft's long-term operating system infrastructure strategy. Because OLE defines the standard on how application components communicate, every Windows developer—now matter what programming language is used—needs to understand OLE. When applications developed with different programming languages need to work together, the applications need to communicate with a common language interface—this language is OLE.

OLE is a natural progression from a call-level interface (CLI) to an object-based interface. A *call-level interface* is an application programming interface (API) based on function calls. These acronyms may sound confusing but as an experienced programmer, you probably are familiar with APIs and CLIs.

Most Visual basic programmers, for example, are familiar with the Windows API. The Windows API is a set of C-based function prototypes that are stored in operating system DLLs. These prototypes allow a developer to access operating system services. Visual Basic can access these functions by declaring them with the VB *Declare* statement. For example, Visual Basic 3 didn't include any native functions to manipulate INI files. VB3 programmers often used the Windows API *GetPrivateProfileString()* to access Windows INI files.

Open Database Connectivity (ODBC) is an example of a CLI. ODBC, through the ODBC.DLL, abstracts a specific database's functionality into a universal set of function calls. ODBC, therefore, is said to *encapsulate* the native database function calls with its own set. The Oracle ODBC driver, for example, encapsulates Oracle's native API, the Oracle Call Interface (OCI).

OLE Versus Traditional APIs

An OLE object based interface can provide a much richer interface than a traditional C-based interface. For example, an OLE interface can:

- Expose a hierarchy of functionality—a workbook object can contain worksheet objects that can contain cell objects

- Communicate across a network or different operating systems

- Handle complex data structures, such as compound documents and applications

OLE eventually will replace traditional function-based APIs in the Windows environment, just as 4GLs have begun to replace 3GLs for application development.

Future versions of Windows, such as the next version of Windows NT (code named Cairo), will be based exclusively on OLE. In this environment, the operating system API and file system will *be* OLE—they use OLE as a native process, not as an extension.

Acronyms

As you have seen, we're barely through the introduction to OLE and already you encountered a slew of acronyms. Table 3.1 summarizes the acronyms of which you'll need a firm grasp after reading this chapter.

Table 3.1 Acronyms Associated with OLE	
Acronym	**Definition**
CLI	Call-level interface
CLSID	Class identifier
COM	Component Object Model
DCOM	Distributed Component Object Model
GUID	Globally unique identifier
IDL	Interface definition language
IID	Interface identifier
OA	OLE automation
OCX	OLE custom control
ODL	Object description language
OLE	Object Linking and Embedding
RPC	Remote procedure call
SCM	Service Control Manager
TLB	OLE type library

The History of OLE

This section summarizes how OLE and interprocess communication has evolved in Windows.

Before OLE and Windows, when you wanted to move data from one application to another, you had to export the data to a file from the source application, run the destination application, and import the file into the destination application. To further complicate matters, this worked only if both applications understood a common file format.

When Windows was introduced, the Clipboard allowed you to transfer data from source application to destination application with simple menu commands, avoiding the intermediate export file.

OLE 1, introduced shortly after Windows 3.1, allowed document linking and embedding. The data no longer had to be physically stored in two spots—the source and destination. Linking allows the user to get to the data by creating an icon in the destination document that points to the source document. Embedding physically stores the source document data in the destination document.

Dynamic Data Exchange (DDE), also introduced shortly after OLE 1, allowed one application to perform simple tasks in another application.

OLE 2 introduced additional enhancements, including in-place activation of embedded documents. *In-place activation* allows the user to edit the embedded document from within the container document, even if the documents were created with different applications. For example, an Excel spreadsheet might contain an embedded Word document. With in-place activation, when the user edits the embedded Word document, the Excel container's menus and toolbars merge with Word's.

The Component Object Model

The Component Object Model (COM) is the heart of OLE. COM is the foundation in which all other, more complex, OLE services are built.

OLE is a client/server model. Chapter 2 discussed the meaning of client/server—that the term doesn't apply only to DBMS systems like SQL Server.

OLE objects can communicate and ask each other to perform tasks. This communication is client/server. In OLE terminology, an *object user* is a client and an *object implementer* is a server.

In a traditional client/server model an entity is either a client or a server. OLE breaks this barrier. OLE objects can be clients and servers at the same time. In fact, if two way communication is needed between objects, two OLE objects can simultaneously be both clients and servers to *each other*. In this scenario, the client first passes an object reference to the server. The server then performs some work and invokes the client's object reference—the relationship is reversed.

For example, Chapter 2 introduced the concept of a business server. Figure 2.7 showed a business server object known as the *Order Manager*. This OLE object takes requests from a *Customer Service Rep* client application, makes requests to the *Customer Manager* and *Product Manager* business servers, and makes requests to the *Orders* data server. Therefore, the *Order Manager* OLE object is a server to one client application, a client to two business servers, and a client to one data server respectively.

COM provides the standard by which objects communicate. It is built upon several Windows DLLs, the heart of which is COMPOBJ.DLL.

COM enables objects created in different languages or residing on different machines to communicate. COM defines the object interface, how to create objects, and how to destroy objects. It provides memory management, error handling, interface negotiation, and interprocess communication.

This abstraction and standardization of these low level aspects makes OLE powerful and flexible.

Other Object Models

As of this writing, there are several emerging standards similar to OLE. Table 3.2 summarizes these standards.

Table 3.2 Other Object Models		
Acronym	**Definition**	**Primary Sponsor**
CORBA	Common Object Request Broker	Object Management Group
OpenDoc	OpenDoc	Component Integration Lab
SOM	System Object Model	IBM
DOE	Distributed Objects Everywhere	SunSoft

Most of the other object models provide services similar to those in OLE. Some models provide additional functionality, some provide less. This book doesn't go into detail of these other object models.

OLE will become a de facto object model standard, at least in the Windows environment. Microsoft is committed to basing its operating systems and applications on OLE. Given the current and anticipated Windows and Microsoft application installation base, OLE has a bright future. Other object models may claim technological advantages over OLE, but the biggest reason to invest in OLE is that it is here today, and Microsoft is strategically committed to OLE across all its product lines.

It's a safe assumption, however, that if another object model gains widespread industry popularity, technologies will emerge that allow OLE to interoperate with it. For example, Microsoft and DEC already have agreed to add OLE to DEC's ObjectBroker technology.

OLE Objects

Everything in the OLE environment—a disk file, piece of data, application, operating system, or hardware platform—is an *object*. Anything that can have a computer representation is an OLE object. This definition of an object is different from the definition you might find in object-oriented programming languages.

Although this definition is rather ambiguous, it is accurate. OLE objects can be word-processing documents, cells in a spreadsheet, order processing servers, database engines, animation clips, and applications.

OLE is a specification that sits on top of the underlying operating system, hardware, and programming language. OLE requires the developer to follow a strict set of rules independent of the environment.

Object interfaces are described with an OLE object definition language (ODL) and type libraries (TLB). When ODLs are compiled, they produce TLBs.

In-Process Versus Out-Of-Process

As mentioned previously in this chapter, OLE is a client/server model. When two OLE objects interact, the client is the object that makes the request and the server is the object that satisfies the request.

An OLE server can be either an *in-process* or *out-of-process* server. An in-process server is implemented as a DLL, and an out-of-process server is implemented as an executable. Table 3.3 summarizes these architectures.

Table 3.3 In-Process and Out-Of-Process Servers		
Server Type	**OLE Client**	**OLE Server**
In-Process	EXE or DLL	DLL
Out-of-process	EXE or DLL	EXE

What does this all mean? An in-process server runs in the same address space as the client, while an out-of-process server runs in its own address space. An in-process request, therefore, is similar to a traditional DLL function call; an out-of-process request is similar to a DDE function call.

Visual Basic can create both in-process and out-of-process servers. Pros and cons exist with each scenario, which are discussed in Chapter 6, "Creating OLE Objects." In general, you can't use in-process servers in as many scenarios as out-of-process servers (such as across a network), but in-process servers operate significantly (20 times or more) faster. A single instance of an out-of-process server, however, can serve multiple clients simultaneously.

Object Management

Objects and pieces of objects are identified by *globally unique identifiers*, or GUIDs (pronounced "Goo I.D."). A GUID is a 128-bit number unique for each interface and object class. When represented visually, a GUID is enclosed in braces and consists of 32 hexadecimal digits in the form, {*xxxxxxxx-xxxx-xxxx-xxxx-xxxxxxxxxxxx*}.

The following line shows an example of a GUID:

    {8F0E48D4-8A1A-11CE-B781-00AA006EC3D4}

The OLE SDK provides special facilities to randomly generate GUIDs. Because GUIDs are so large, they are statistically guaranteed to be unique if generated randomly. The same principle applies with credit cards: if you pick a random credit card number, most likely it will not be used by anyone.

Every standard object is defined by a GUID known as a class ID (CLSID). Every standard interface is defined by a GUID known as an interface ID (IID).

CLSIDs and IIDs are stored in the registry database that contains the inventory of available objects. Because all objects are defined in the registry, objects can be available across a network, even if they don't exist on the same physical machine. Figure 3.1 shows how a CLSID for an Excel worksheet is stored in the registry.

Fig. 3.1
A CLSID for a
Microsoft Excel
worksheet.

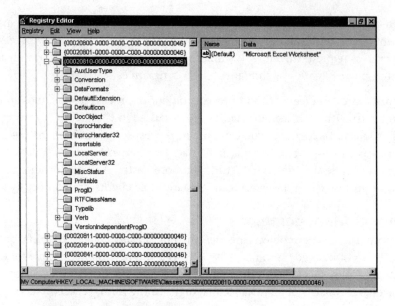

Object Error Handling

Because OLE operates across languages and machines, OLE error handling must be language and machine independent. So, rather than raising exceptions, COM must use return codes to indicate errors.

OLE error handling in Visual Basic is described in greater detail in Chapter 14, "Architecting Error Processing." In OLE, an error consists of 13 bits of facility information and 16 bits for an error code. Examples of facility information include: dispatch, Win32, RPC, persistent storage, and so on. The error code is specific to the facility.

OLE also supports external debugging libraries. These libraries allow the developer to invoke external hooks to other debuggers. This capability is significant—without it, debugging across multiple programming languages (which OLE allows) would be difficult.

In Visual Basic, for example, although OLE applications are in different projects, you can step through code across these projects.

OLE Services

This section describes COM and the services layered on top of COM. The aggregation of these services is OLE. Some of these services are not yet available, and you can expect that additional OLE services will be introduced in the future.

Table 3.4 shows the list of services that this chapter discusses. This list is not exhaustive.

Table 3.4 Key OLE Services	
Service	**Description**
Marshaling	Basic mechanism for OLE communication
Structured storage	Compound document data and directory
Monikers	Linked data pointer
Uniform data transfer	Data distribution method
Drag and drop	Interactive cut and paste
Compound document processing	Files that contain multiple class objects
Linking	Storing a pointer to a document in a document
Embedding	Storing a document within a document
In-place activation	Interactively editing one document within the container of another
OLE automation	Remotely controlling an object
OCX	An OLE custom control
Distributed OLE	OLE automation across a network
Nile	OLE for databases

Figure 3.2 shows these services and gives you an idea about how the services interoperate and depend on each other. The figure is not complete and doesn't show all the complex interactions that really take place. For example, although drag and drop applies to compound document processing, compound document processing doesn't have to support drag and drop.

Although this figure looks complex, it is not something you have to memorize in order to use OLE. This capability is one of the advantages of OLE—it handles the OLE service management behind the scenes. For example, although you might be using an OCX in your Visual Basic application, you don't need to know that, behind the scenes, OLE automation and inside-out in-place activation is occurring. You just need to know what an OLE control does and how to use it.

Fig. 3.2
An overview of
OLE services.

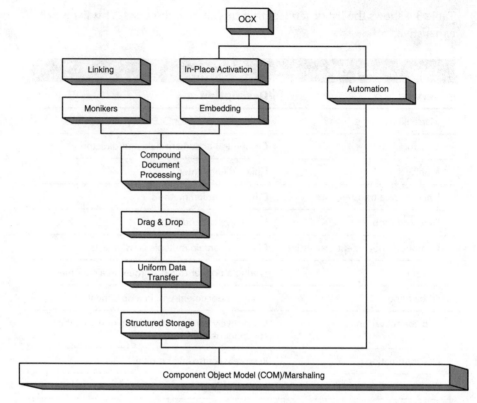

Still, a sophisticated VB developer should understand how all the various OLE services interoperate. This knowledge makes it easier to understand new OLE services and to debug and manage complex enterprise applications.

Although each of the services listed is described in Table 3.4, most of the lower-level services are not directly exposed to the Visual Basic developer. For example, developers don't really need to know how marshaling and OLE automation works behind the scenes to use them.

Marshaling

Marshaling is the process of passing function calls and parameters across process boundaries. For example, when one OLE client application controls an OLE server application, the client needs to be able to make function calls to the server. This server may be written in a different programming language and may reside on another computer. Marshaling packages the client function call and parameters up and invokes it on the server.

The marshaling process is actually more complicated than it sounds, but this is its beauty—a very complex operation occurs in a simple and transparent interface.

Marshaling involves a *proxy* on the OLE client and a *stub* on the OLE server. The proxy packages up the function call and parameters in a standard OLE format and sends them to the server. The stub receives the function call and parameters, converts them to a form the server can understand, and executes them. This proxy/stub relationship is transparent to both the client and server.

Under the covers, marshaling is done with light-weight procedure calls (LRPC) under local Win16, and DCE Compliant remote procedure calls (RPC) under Win32 and remote Win16. You don't need to know this information for Visual Basic, but it may be useful to know in the context of other programming languages.

COM handles 16-to-32-bit marshaling seamlessly. Marshaling is not required when operating with an in-process server, which contributes to in-process server's better performance.

Marshaling is completely transparent to the VB developer. But because it introduces a performance impact, as a VB developer, you should understand when it is and is not occurring.

Structured Storage

Structured storage is the mechanism OLE uses to store documents that contain other documents. Structured storage uses compound files instead of a traditional file system interface.

A compound file is a file-system file that stores multiple documents. An Excel file—for example, MYSHEET.XLS—may contain an embedded Word and Visio document. These two documents are stored within the compound file, MYSHEET.XLS.

Today, OLE structured storage sits on top of the native file systems (such as DOS FAT, Windows NT NTFS, or Macintosh). In future versions of Windows, such as Cairo, structured storage will be the primary storage mechanism.

A compound document is composed of *streams* and *storages*. Streams are the unstructured data that is a document. Storages are similar to directories; they organize and contain hierarchical streams and storages.

Both streams and storages support transactions, similar to database transactions. This support is helpful for "undo" operations, and helps ensure the integrity of the documents, similar to the way a DBMS ensures the integrity of its data.

When an OLE object or compound document is stored on a permanent medium such as a disk drive, it is known as a *persistent object*. The native file-system file, such as MYSHEET.XLS above, is known as *root storage*.

Structured storage also includes support for *property sets*, which are placeholders for information about the data. Word documents, for example, contain "Subject" and "Author" property sets.

Monikers

OLE uses *Monikers* to point a reference to a linked object within a compound document to its source document. For example, an Excel document that contains a link to a Word document uses a moniker to maintain the reference to the Word document.

Uniform Data Transfer

Uniform data transfer (UDT) is the mechanism by which OLE transfers data from client to server. It is OLE's equivalent to DDE and the clipboard cut-and-paste capability rolled into one. UDT supports notification as to when the data has changed as well as negotiation of the format of the data which will be transferred. UDT also supports transfer of just a handle to the data rather than the data itself.

Drag and Drop

Drag and drop is similar to cutting and pasting OLE objects but it is handled in one step. Drag and drop is the process of selecting one object in one application and—with the left mouse button held down—dragging it into another application or to a different area of the same application.

The source application is known as the *drop source*, and the destination application is known as the *drop target*.

You can drag, for example, the file MYSHEET.XLS from the Windows 95 Explorer (the drop source) into a Word document (the drop target).

OLE Documents

OLE documents, sometimes referred to as compound documents, can contain data from several different application sources. As mentioned previously, they are represented internally with OLE structured storage.

Because compound documents are a structured storage, they can be represented in a single file, memory location, or database record.

The *container application* is the application that contains the compound document with linked or embedded documents (described in the following sections). When compound documents are loaded into a container application, they exhibit the characteristics of the application that created the component.

Because compound documents are examples of OLE structured storage, they store information in property sets. For example, from the Windows 95 Explorer you can select *File..Properties* from the menu while a Word document is selected and see the author and title of the document. Property sets also store operating system and hardware information, so that documents can be truly cross-platform.

All major Microsoft desktop applications—including Word, Excel, PowerPoint, and Project—now use OLE compound files as their native format.

As you will see, Visual Basic can manipulate compound documents in a number of ways: through linking, embedding, in-place activation, and automation.

Linking

Linking enables a client object to reference a server document object. When an object is linked, only a reference to the server document object is stored. The actual data, therefore, is stored outside of the compound document. This road map to get at the data outside of the compound document is known as a *moniker*, as you learned previously in this chapter.

The linked data may be stored in a non-OLE file or in OLE structured storage. A rendered image of the linked object, however, is stored in the client compound document.

For example, the MYSHEET.XLS spreadsheet may have a linked Word document, MYDOC.DOC. When the user double-clicks on the rendered image of the Word document in the Excel compound file to edit the document, Excel uses a moniker to find MYDOC.DOC, and then start Word.

Embedding

An embedded object in a compound document is much like a linked object, but the actual object is stored in the compound file.

Client/Server Concepts

For example, the spreadsheet, MYSHEET.XLS, may have an embedded Word document. In this case, the Word document doesn't have a file name because it is stored within the Excel file. When the user double-clicks the rendered image of the Word document in the Excel compound file to edit it, Word launches, and the user can edit the Word document from within Word. Rather than saving the document within Word to a file, however, the user updates the file only in the Excel compound document.

In-Place Activation

In-place activation takes embedding a step further by allowing the user to edit the embedded document without leaving the container application. Rather than launching the embedded document's application, the relevant parts of the server application are merged with the container application while the user is working on the embedded document.

In-place activation enables the two applications to appear to the user as one application.

In the example, when the user double-clicks on the rendered image of the Word document within the Excel compound file to edit it, the Excel menus and toolbars are merged with the Word menus and toolbars.

Figure 3.3 shows an Excel worksheet with an embedded Word document. Figure 3.4 shows the same worksheet with the Word document activated in place. Notice how the menu items and toolbars are now Word's.

Fig. 3.3
An Excel worksheet, with an embedded Word document.

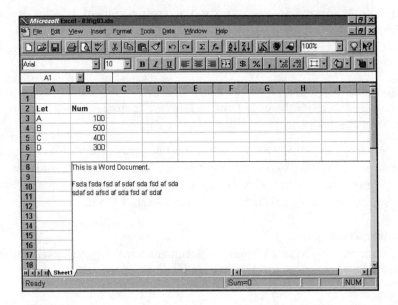

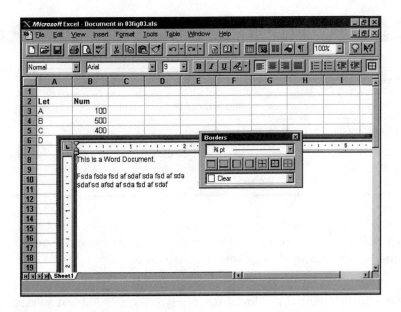

Fig. 3.4
An Excel
worksheet, with an
embedded Word
document that is
activated in-place.

Client/Server Concepts

OLE Automation Servers

OLE automation (OA) is the mechanism by which one application controls or
automates another application. The client and server pieces of OLE automation can be named several things synonymously. Table 3.5 summarizes these
other commonly used names.

Table 3.5	Names for OLE Automation Clients and Servers
Piece	**Synonymous Names**
Client	OLE automation client
	Controlling application
	OLE automation controller
	OLE client component
Server	OLE automation server
	OLE object application

OLE automation server objects are neither linked nor embedded. An OLE
automation server exposes properties, methods, member objects, and collections of member objects. The sum of the parts of an object is known as the
object's OLE *automation interface*. Automation allows programmers to manipulate this interface from within other applications. Table 3.6 summarizes
the attributes of an OLE automation interface.

Table 3.6 Attributes of an OLE Automation Interface	
Object Attribute	**Description**
Property	A characteristic of the object, such as Font
Method	An operation the object can perform, such as Print
Member object	A dependent object within the object, such as an ActiveWorkbook within an Application object
Collection	An array of member objects, such as Cells within a Workbook object

Microsoft makes a recommendation on how to construct the object interface of an OLE automation server. All OLE applications, for example, should have a top-level object named "Application." Chapters 6, "Creating OLE Objects," and 9, "Architecting Tier 2: Business Servers," describe this in detail.

Objects are hierarchical within the OA interface. Figure 3.5 shows an example of Excel's object model from the Excel VBA Help File. Within each of these objects and collections are hundreds of properties, methods, member objects, and collections.

Fig. 3.5
Excel's object model.

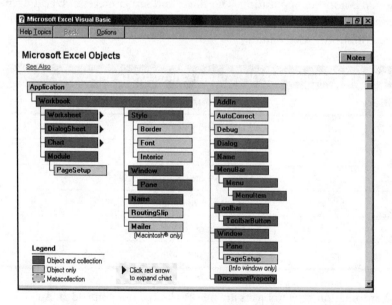

When the OA application is created, the OLE automation interface is stored either in a library (TLBs and OLBs) or as a resource within the DLL. The registry then stores this information for OLE controllers, which enables the automation controllers to view property prototypes, method prototypes, and interface help. The registry also enables early binding so the automation controller can check for syntax errors during development.

Figure 3.6 shows an example of Visual Basic 4's Object Browser, browsing Excel's Worksheet object and `Range` method.

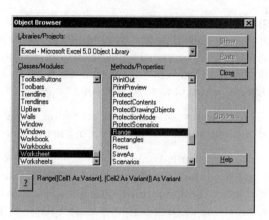

Fig. 3.6
Browsing Excel's
Worksheet object
and Range method
with Visual Basic's
Object Browser.

An OLE automation server is said to be running *local* when running on the same machine as the client, and *remote* when running on a different machine. With remote automation, a single OLE automation object can run either local or remote.

The capability of creating OLE automation servers probably is the most important feature added to Visual Basic 4, which makes three-tier client/server possible. Although Excel was used as an example of an OLE automation server in this chapter, OLE automation servers you build for your applications will be business server objects, such as the *OrderManager* and *ProductManager* examples in Chapter 2, "Application Architecture."

OLE Controls

An OLE custom control (OCX) is a special form of OLE automation object. OLE controls can be 32-bit or 16-bit. Like an OLE automation object, these controls have properties, methods, member objects, and collections.

Unlike an OLE automation object, however, OLE controls can perform the following tasks:

- Draw (place visual attributes) directly on their client (container) application, like in-place activation

- Support property sheets, which enables them to provide the user a quick method of setting multiple properties

- Detect licensing in a design versus runtime environment

- Support an extended interface that allows it to fire events

- Support data "binding," like VBXs

OLE controls are always activated within the client application. In contrast, an OLE document supports *outside-in* activation—only the image of the embedded object is seen in the container application until the user explicitly activates it by double-clicking. When the user moves focus to another part of the container, the embedded object is deactivated.

An OLE control, however, supports *inside-out* activation. OLE controls are *always* activated and appear like any other part of the container application.

OLE controls can be implemented only as DLLs—they can be only in-process servers because, unlike automation objects that use LRPC or RPC, OLE controls use a more efficient communication system analogous to function calls. This system is required for speed because it is unacceptable for a user of the container to see a performance hit when using an OLE control.

In Visual Basic, an OLE control is an extension to the Visual Basic Toolbox and is used like any other built-in control, such as a text box.

OLE controls are intended to replace VBXs in the Visual Basic environment and also be accessible to other environments. In the future, versions of Windows (such as Cairo) will support OCXes within the operating system itself.

Distributed Component Object Model

The Distributed Component Object Model (DCOM) is the process by which OLE communicates across a network. It sometimes is referred to as Distributed OLE.

Before going too far into a discussion of DCOM, note that as of this writing, it hasn't yet been fully implemented.

The specification is being reviewed but is not expected to be fully adopted until Cairo. Visual Basic 4 Enterprise Edition, however, introduces a subset of DCOM named remote automation (RA).

DCOM

DCOM is a fairly open specification. Although driven by Microsoft, it—like other WOSA services—is subject to industry review.

The revised version of COM, which includes DCOM, was introduced in March of 1995. DCOM is based on the Open Software Foundation's (OSF) Distributed Computing Environment (DCE) remote procedure calls (RPC). This wordy basis is often referred to, as you may have guessed, as OSF/DCE RPC. The actual network protocol is based on the 1994 X/Open DCE RPC Common Applications Environment (CAE) specification. The VB developer only needs to know that OLE is based upon industry standards.

DCOM is required for true application partitioning; it enables the developer to place an OLE object anywhere on the network. DCOM allows location transparency and object scalability. It handles marshaling across CPUs.

DCOM will use the DCE security specification, naming conventions, and directory services. The OLE interface definition language (IDL) is based on DCE IDL.

DCOM works by creating an in-process proxy on the client that handles communication with a stub on the server. The Service Control Manager (SCM) manages the connections to the server. Figure 3.7 shows this architecture.

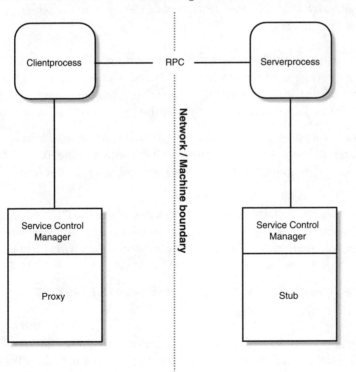

Fig. 3.7
DCOM RPC.

Remote Automation

Remote Automation is a compatible subset of DCOM. Some of the differences between DCOM and RA include the following:

- Remote Automation comes only with Visual Basic Enterprise Edition. As of this writing, you must incorporate Visual Basic on either the client or server end in order to use RA without violating Microsoft licensing.

- Rather than having integrated operating system support like DCOM, RA requires special utilities, such as the Remote Automation Manager.

- Although RA provides secure connections, it doesn't have the full-blown integrated security that DCOM will have, such as client impersonation across multiple objects.

- RA doesn't provide integrated operating system load balancing and resource management on the server. Instead, you must manually create "pool managers" in VB that manage server resources.

- RA doesn't support any type of visual interface on the client machine, although the server can display visual elements on the server, such as a status message.

Remote automation still accomplishes the most important task of DCOM: it provides transparent access to OLE objects across a network. It was the lack of a simple way of accomplishing this access that inhibited widespread adoption of three-tier client/server architectures in the past.

Remote automation is accomplished by replacing the original OLE proxy/stub with a remote automation RPC proxy/stub contained in the *AUTPRX*.DLLs* and a special program, the Remote Automation Manager, that runs on the server.

The registry on the local computer determines where the OLE server component is located. This registry is managed by the Component Manager and the Remote Automation Connection Manager, both of which are included with Visual Basic 4 Enterprise Edition.

RA is discussed in detail in Chapter 7, "Managing OLE Objects."

Nile

Nile is a Microsoft code name for a COM-based data integration specification. Like DCOM, it is not yet fully implemented in any product, nor is it expected to be until Cairo. As this book goes to press, little is known about the Nile specification.

The traditional procedure of programmatically accessing a database server has been through a call-level interface (CLI), which can be either an open, driver-based interface (such as ODBC) or by way of the database vendor's proprietary interface (such as DBLIB for SQL Server or OCI for Oracle).

Recently, proprietary object-based DBMS data access methods have emerged, such as Oracle Objects for Oracle or Sylvain Faust's SQL Sombrero for SQL Server.

Given Microsoft's stated direction, you probably can expect that Nile will be an OLE-based data access method that accesses both multiple, nontraditional data sources and standard DBMS data sources. Presumably, it also provides location independence and manages transactions across multiple data sources. For DBMS data sources, it probably will resemble an object-based version of ODBC and/or Jet.

Visual Basic 4 Enterprise Edition introduces a new high-performance data access method, Remote Data Objects (RDO). Although little is known about Nile now, we probably can expect that the migration from RDO to Nile will be smooth.

RDO is a thin COM layer on top of ODBC. It is the first DBMS-independent, high-performance, object-based DBMS interface for Visual Basic. RDO is discussed in detail in Chapter 10, "Architecting Tier 3: Data Servers."

COM Service Support

You now should have a solid understanding of the OLE services built upon COM. As time passes, more and more applications will support these services.

Table 3.7 summarizes known application support for various OLE services at the time of this writing. Notice that this table doesn't have a one-to-one correspondence to the services listed in Table 3.4 because this table is intended to list services that are of interest to the application programmer, not general OLE services.

For programming languages such as Visual Basic, Visual C++, and PowerBuilder, a "C" or an "S" indicates that the programming language is capable of *creating* such an object, *not* that the programming environment is capable of performing such service. For example, an "S" under Visual C++ for OLE automation means that Visual C++ is capable of creating applications that can operate as OLE automation *servers*, not that the Visual C++ *IDE* (integrated development environment) can operate as an OLE automation server (although VB4's IDE can!).

Table 3.7   Application Support for OLE Services

OLE Service	VB4	VB3	Visual C++	Power-Builder 4	Excel 5	Access 2	Word 6
Drag and drop	C S		C S	C	C S	C	C S
Linking	C	C	C S	C	C S	C	C S
Embedding	C	C	C S	C	C S	C	C S
In-place activation, standard	C	C	C S	C	C S	C	C S
In-place activation, menu and toolbar replacement	C		C S	C	C S	C	C S
OLE automation	C S	C	C S	C	C S	C	S
OLE controls	C		S			C	

A C means the application is capable of operating as a client and an S means the application is capable of operating as a server.

Visual Basic 4 and OLE

Applications that were created with Visual Basic can operate as clients and servers for many OLE services. This section walks you through these services in the context of VB4. Chapter 4 then shows you how the pieces fit together, Chapter 5 shows how VB acts as an OLE client, and Chapter 6 shows how VB acts as an OLE server.

In Visual Basic you can use objects supplied with VB, such as command buttons and forms, or you can use OLE objects from other applications, such as OCXes and Excel. You also can create your own objects within Visual Basic.

Each object within VB is defined as a class. A class is a blueprint for an object. Sometimes, class and object are used interchangeably. Formally, however, an object is an instance of a class. So when we use the term, "Worksheet object," we are referring to the more precise nomenclature, "an object instance of the Worksheet class."

For example, a *TextBox* in the VB toolbox is a representation of the *TextBox* class. After a *TextBox* is drawn on a form in the design environment, this textbox becomes an object instance of the *TextBox* class.

Objects and classes, then, are analogous to variables and datatypes respectively.

Figure 3.8 shows the relationship between objects and classes in VB. The properties window, under the caption, shows that we have an object of the class *TextBox* named *txtMyTextBox*.

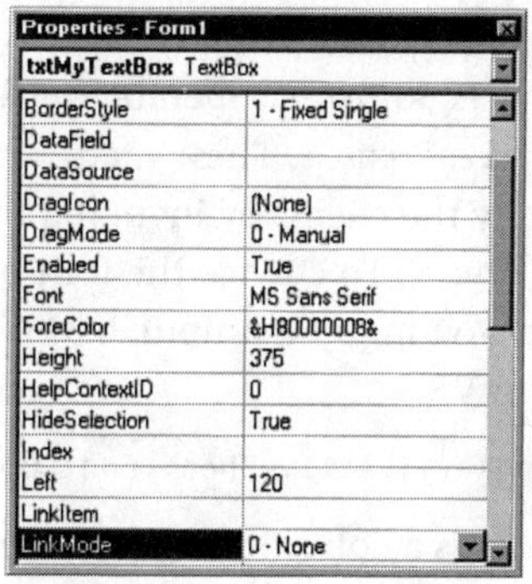

Properties - Form1	
txtMyTextBox TextBox	
BorderStyle	1 - Fixed Single
DataField	
DataSource	
DragIcon	(None)
DragMode	0 - Manual
Enabled	True
Font	MS Sans Serif
ForeColor	&H80000008&
Height	375
HelpContextID	0
HideSelection	True
Index	
Left	120
LinkItem	
LinkMode	0 - None

Fig. 3.8
Objects and classes as represented in the VB properties window.

When objects are first created, they have default values as defined by the class. This process is known as *instantiating* an object. After it is instantiated, however, the programmer can use the object's interface to change its values. So, each *TextBox* class drawn on a form is in an individual object with its own name, text, and size property values.

Microsoft has said that VB is "the glue that binds objects together." This much is true, but it doesn't do full justice to VB's capabilities. A more accurate description might be, "Visual Basic is the most powerful environment for assembling distributed applications from disparate components and partitioning them across the enterprise."

Controlling OLE Controls

Visual Basic 4 can act as a client to OLE custom controls with support for events and bound data access. VB4 cannot, however, create custom controls.

OLE controls can be added directly to a form during design time from VB's ToolBox.

Controlling OLE Automation Objects

Visual Basic 4 can act as a remote and local OLE automation controller like any VBA (Visual Basic for Applications) application. OLE automation client support is built into the VBA language. The `CreateObject()` and `GetObject()` functions allow the programmer to create new instances of an automation server class.

After an object is instantiated, its attributes can be accessed with VB "dot" operations. A *WorkSheet* object, for example, has a `Print` method that can be invoked by executing *WorkSheet.Print* in VB.

Table 3.6 listed the attributes of an OLE automation object. An automation object contains other objects, known as member or dependent objects, and arrays of objects, known as *collections*. These members and collections can be referenced only one way by the client: by invoking their dot operation to return a reference to the object. To change the font of a single cell in a spreadsheet, for example, you might manipulate the object hierarchy by executing the following in VB:

```
Application.WorkBooks(1).ActiveSheet.Font.Bold = True
```

In this example, *WorkBooks* is a collection; *Application*, *ActiveWorksheet*, and *Font* are objects; and *Bold* is a property.

Controlling OLE Documents

Visual Basic 4 can act as a client to OLE documents. OLE documents can be drawn on forms during design, like OLE controls, or they can be placed inside an OLE container control. VB can support both linked and embedded documents, with full menu negotiation and toolbar replacement.

If the server application supports OLE automation, you also can automate the object programmatically through the OLE control's *Object* property. Some objects, such as Microsoft Excel, can be both automation and in-place activation servers. So, when do you use OLE automation versus in-place activation? If you want the object to have a visible interface within your VB application, such as displaying an Excel graph, you need to use the OLE control and create an in-place object. If you only want to control the object, such as using Excel's pivot table engine, then use the `CreateObject` or `GetObject` functions to create the object.

Chapter 5, "Controlling OLE Objects," describes in detail how to control OLE documents.

Creating OLE Automation Objects

Visual Basic 4 can create both remote and local OLE automation server objects. The same is not true for OLE documents and controls, however. You can't create anything analogous to an Excel workbook in VB and paste it into the OLE control or a Word document.

You can use class modules and forms to define your custom-built OLE classes. Class modules and forms can expose properties, methods, and objects to OLE automation controllers.

A project can be compiled as an OLE application, both as an EXE and DLL. The compiled application exposes *classes* which, when instantiated by a client, form objects.

Visual Basic can create both 16-bit and 32-bit applications. Win16 didn't support OLE natively, so OLE DLLs must be distributed with 16-bit Visual Basic applications. Windows 95, Windows NT, and other 32-bit Windows operating systems include native support for OLE, so OLE DLLs do not need to be distributed for 32-bit applications.

Because 32-bit operating systems support OLE natively, they allow 16- and 32-bit OLE objects to interoperate. The process of going between 16- and 32-bit function calls is known as *thunking*. Client applications use the same process to instantiate an object, whether the object is in-process, out-of-process, local, or remote.

Visual Basic, however, has several limitations for 16-bit applications and OLE. For example, 16- and 32-bit applications cannot interoperate in-process, only out-of-process. Nor can in-process or 16-bit OLE server applications operate over remote automation.

Chapter 6, "Creating OLE Objects," discusses the creation of OLE automation objects in VB in detail.

The Future of OLE

OLE becomes a de facto standard for Windows object-based development and communication. And Windows is the de facto standard for business applications.

OLE has been criticized for being slow. OLE is not slow, but recent implementations of OLE are slow. For example, before Windows 95 and VB4, most people's experience with OLE automation was in automating Office applications like Excel under Windows 3.1. This probably is the worst-performing

OLE scenario: 16-bit OLE automation to a huge out-of-process server application (such as Excel). A Visual Basic OLE server, operating in-process, is significantly faster than the Excel scenario.

In the future, operating systems like Cairo will be built predominantly upon OLE. Microsoft continues to invest in OLE for linking and building objects across the enterprise and even between organizations (over the Internet, for example).

From Here...

This chapter covered the OLE from a high level. You were introduced to VB4's OLE capabilities as well as Microsoft's vision for OLE.

For further information related to topics covered in this chapter, see the following:

- Chapter 5, "Controlling OLE Objects," provides more information on controlling OLE controls, automation servers, and documents.

- Chapter 6, "Creating OLE Objects," provides more information on creating OLE automation servers.

- Chapter 7, "Managing OLE Objects," provides more information on managing OLE objects and remote automation.

Chapter 4

Visual Basic Application Architecture

The first three chapters covered the purpose of this book, three-tier client/server architecture and the foundation of this architecture—OLE.

The remainder of the book shows you exactly how to build all of these pieces of a three-tier system with Visual Basic. But before the discussion of individual components within the three-tier services model can begin, you should have a general understanding of just how all of these objects are going to look in Visual Basic.

This chapter presents a high level summary of all of the various Visual basic components. It shows how they interact and gives you a feel for the overall design.

We've written a great deal about theory and abstract descriptions of the three-tier services model in previous chapters. But sometimes, it's difficult to understand the theory without examples of how real-world products fit into the abstract architecture. Likewise, it's sometimes difficult to understand individual pieces of the architecture without having seen the "big picture." This chapter shows you the big picture, so that you can understand how the details of the remaining chapters relate to one another.

The topics of the remainder of the book are only introduced in this chapter, they all will be discussed in detail in the remainder of the book. Likewise, this chapter may seem redundant because it provides a basic introduction to all topics. This chapter will cover the following topics:

- Controlling OLE objects
- Creating OLE objects

- Managing OLE objects
- User services
- Business services
- Data Services
- Physical deployment

Visual Basic Object Applications

The programs in the user, business, and data service layers that communicate with one another are known as *object applications*. The design of object applications differs from other types of applications with which you may be more familiar.

Programming Paradigm Shift

For example, you probably moved from a procedural language, such as Microsoft C or QuickBasic, to an event-driven languages, such as Visual C++ or Visual Basic. Although the syntax of the core language remained relatively unchanged, the fundamental way in which you designed applications changed. Procedural languages require that your program has a specific start and a specific end. Therefore, a significant programming effort was required to implement user input—usually the program implemented tight loops that waited for user input.

Event-driven languages such as Visual Basic manage user input for you. Rather than a specific beginning and end to a program, you simply place code in pre-defined events. When the development environment or operating system detects that a user generates such input, it invokes the appropriate event in which you placed code. The actual syntax of the code, however, was not very different from the syntax of its procedural equivalent. The syntax of Visual Basic, for example, isn't too different from the syntax of QuickBasic.

With Visual Basic 4 you enter into another fundamental programming design evolution: components. Just like procedural QuickBasic applications evolved into event-driven Visual Basic 3 GUI applications, monolithic event-driven VB3 applications will evolve into partitioned and distributed Visual Basic 4 component applications.

When designing Visual Basic 4 programs, think about concepts such as code-reuse, object interfaces, and OLE automation. Visual Basic 4 can create and control OLE automation servers: applications which can be used by other applications at run time, much like DLLs but more powerful.

Object-Oriented Programming Techniques

Object-oriented programming techniques employed in Visual Basic differ from traditional techniques that view the world as a single program that works on isolated data. The concept of a "program" changes in this environment. A business solution is no longer composed of a single monolithic VB application, but rather, a collection of shared services. In VB, each of these services is an individual VB project executable.

The purists wouldn't say that Visual Basic is not truly object-oriented because it doesn't support all of the functionality of OOP, such as inheritance and polymorphism, within the programming language. But it does provide what is really needed in the services model—the capability to create reusable components with well-defined, easy-to-use OLE interfaces that can work together across a network. So, a more strict definition is that Visual Basic is capable of creating component objects, but it is not fully object-oriented.

The capability to create and manipulate OLE objects is particularly suited for the three-tier services model. For example, Visual Basic can create OLE data services by wrapping up legacy data services in OLE automation servers, such as 3270 mainframe applications. It can create custom OLE automation business servers that encapsulate order entry functionality. It can create reusable user services, such as a database logon dialogs. The sum of these parts—Visual Basic applications interoperating in all tiers across the network—is what this book refers to as "The Visual Basic Enterprise."

Controlling OLE Objects

OLE involves client/server communication between objects. In OLE, the controlling application is referred to as the "controller" or "OLE client," while the controlled application is referred to as the "OLE server." Visual Basic can control or act as a client to all types of OLE objects: OLE controls, OLE automation servers, and OLE documents.

OLE Controls

OLE controls generally have GUI elements and generate events in response to user input. They typically, therefore, are used in the user-services tier. A client application will use an OLE spreadsheet control, for example, to present users with lists of data and use a tab control to create advanced dialogs. Business servers and data servers still may use OCXes, however. A business server might maintain a status box on the server, indicating which client applications are currently using it. A data server might use a communications OLE control to provide business servers access to a dial-up Internet connection.

OLE controls exist as files with an .OCX extension. Before you can use them in your application, you need to add them to your project by choosing Tools and Custom Controls from the Visual Basic menu. After a control is added, it appears in the Visual Basic toolbar. Instances of the control's class then can be added to your VB form by dragging and dropping. After the instance is added, its name appears in the properties windows in the object combo box on the form.

OLE Automation Servers

OLE automation servers usually do not have GUI elements. Because OLE automation servers are generally used to encapsulate business processes, client applications and business servers control other business servers through OLE automation.

A client application. for example, might control an order entry business server to enter orders. This order entry business server may control a product business server to verify that valid products were included in the order.

Business servers also use OLE automation to control data services. Visual Basic's Remote Data Objects (RDO), for example, provide an OLE interface into ODBC SQL servers, such as Oracle and Microsoft SQL Server.

User services access other user services with OLE automation. All client applications, for example, might share a common OLE automation logon dialog box, or a user service might invoke Microsoft Excel's pivot table engine to perform crosstabs on result-set data.

Unlike OLE controls, which are added to the project during design time in the IDE, OLE automation servers are accessed by way of code during runtime. An OLE object is instantiated with the `CreateObject()` or `GetObject()` functions or with the *New* keyword in conjunction with a *Set*, *Dim*, *Public*, *Private*, *Set*, or *Static* statement.

OLE Documents

OLE documents are useful for editing and storing free-form data. A client application, for example, might allow a user to create and store an invoice in a Microsoft Excel spreadsheet or a proposal in Microsoft Word.

OLE documents also are useful for data presentation. For example, Microsoft Excel's chart and print engines provide a powerful means of creating and printing graphs.

OLE documents with OLE visual editing also can be used for structured data entry, but this is *not* recommended. You might allow a user, for example, to enter orders into an order-entry business server with an imbedded Excel worksheet in a client application, but the OLE document server application (Excel in this example) usually is large and is designed for free-form data entry. OLE controls (such as a spreadsheet control) usually are smaller, faster, and better suited for such structured data entry than their full-blown application counterparts.

Client applications usually control OLE documents while data services usually store them, but business servers may also have a use for controlling OLE documents, particularly for printed batch output. An invoicing business server, for example, might use Excel or Word to create invoices that can be stored in the database.

Visual Basic applications can instantiate OLE documents two ways. Like an OLE control, an OLE document class can be added to the toolbar by choosing Tools, Custom Controls from the VB menu, and then subsequently drawn on a VB form. An OLE document also can be contained within an instance of the OLE container control that comes with Visual Basic.

When using controlling OLE document from within Visual Basic, you almost always will want to use the OLE container control rather than adding the document class to the toolbar. The container control provides a number of methods and properties that are helpful in programmatically controlling the imbedded document object.

Chapter 5, "Controlling OLE Objects," details how to control OLE objects through Visual Basic.

Creating OLE Objects

Although Visual Basic 4 can control all types of OLE objects, it can only create OLE automation servers. It cannot create OLE controls or OLE documents.

In the services model, most OLE automation servers you create will live in the business services tier. Servers such as *OrderMgr*, *ProductMgr*, and *CustomerMgr*, for example, will encapsulate the properties and methods of your business objects.

Unlike OLE controls and OLE documents, OLE automation servers cannot merge their GUI with their controller. An OLE automation server, for example, cannot place a control such as a text box directly on the controlling application's form. An OLE automation server, however, can display its own forms, which makes OLE automation servers useful for creating common dialogs, such as a logon dialog, in the user services tier.

OLE automation servers can be used to create data services. More likely, however, you will buy—not build—your data services. For example, you will not build your own DBMS, you will go to Microsoft and pick up a copy of SQL Server. Some data services, however, do not provide OLE automation interfaces. You may, therefore, wrap the data service's non-OLE interface with an OLE interface created in VB. You might wrap, for example, a legacy 3270 mainframe order-entry program in an OLE automation server that provides east-to-use properties and methods, or you might wrap an Internet WWW server in an OLE interface so that business servers and client applications have access to its Internet functionality.

OLE automation servers are created by using new constructs introduced in Visual Basic 4—class modules. Class modules are like standard .BAS modules—they are code modules with no GUI that contain functions, procedures, and variables.

But a class module defines an object class, and as such, it can be instantiated as an object within the Visual Basic application, much like a control, form, or OLE automation server can be instantiated. Every variable and function within the class module can be defined as either *public* or *private*. Private functions and variables are used internally by the class module and cannot be accessed externally, while public functions and variables are accessible outside of the class module by the controller.

An application can be compiled as an OLE automation server by choosing Options from the Tools menu and selecting OLE Server in the Project tab. When an application is compiled as an OLE server, it can be instantiated by other applications through OLE automation.

When an application is compiled as an OLE server, every class module who's Public property was set to True can be instantiated by other applications through OLE automation. In addition, every function declared as Public is available as a method, and every variable declared as Public and every Property procedure are available as properties.

In 32-bit Visual Basic, an OLE automation server can be created either as an out-of-process EXE or as an in-process DLL server by choosing Make EXE File or Make OLE DLL File from the File menu, respectively.

Remote automation doesn't work with in-process servers, so, in general, OLE automation business servers that need to be accessed by user services are created as out-of-process because you may want to place the user servers on different physical machines than the business servers. Typically, for example, you will want to place the user service on the user's workstation and the business servers on a secure server machine.

Accessing in-process methods and properties is significantly faster than accessing out-of-process methods and properties. So, generally, users services (such as a common logon dialog) that you will always want to place on the same machine as the client application will be created as in-process servers.

Chapter 6, "Creating OLE Objects," details how to create OLE automation servers in Visual Basic.

Managing OLE Objects

The are advantages and disadvantages to managing a three-tier services model versus the more traditional two-tier architecture. In the services model, it's easier to build new solutions and change existing functionality. In the services model, however, there are more pieces to manage and these pieces may change physical locations frequently.

Visual Basic 4 provides a number of mechanisms for connecting, registering, and managing distributed OLE objects.

When Visual Basic compiles an OLE server project, it generates a unique class ID (CLSID) for each public class module. This CLSID also is represented as a combination of the project name plus the name of the class module. A project, for example, who's name is *OrderMgr* and that has a public class module named *Application* will expose a class name, *OrderMgr.Application*, as shown in figure 4.1.

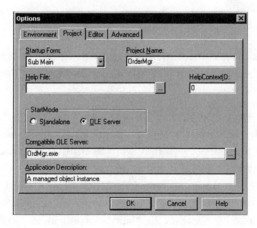

Fig. 4.1
The project name shown in the dialog plus the class module name equal the fully qualified class name.

The Windows registry database on every machine tells that machine where to find a particular object class. So, when you execute either of the following, Visual Basic looks to the Windows registry to figure out where to find the *Application* class of the *OrderMgr* project:

```
Set MyOrderMgr = CreateObject("OrderMgr.Application")

Dim MyOrderMge as New OrderMgr.Application
```

Object classes get registered when they are executed, with one of the utilities mentioned in the following text, or with a setup application. Chapter 16, "Distributing Applications," discusses application and component distribution.

Visual Basic 4 introduces remote automation functionality. Remote automation enables a controlling application to access the properties and methods of an OLE automation server across the network. VB includes a number of tools that facilitate remote automation.

The Remote Automation Manager runs on the server machine and handles remote requests for its objects. The Remote Automation Connection Manager enables the server to set security on clients requesting objects, and also allows you to easily point to local or remote servers. The Component Manager enables a developer or end user to easily browse, search, and register individual components.

Here are other chapters that cover features related to the Remote Automation Manager:

- Managing OLE objects and remote automation is discussed in Chapter 7, "Managing OLE Objects."

- Visual Basic can control such things as the Class ID of an object and its version. Version control is discussed in Chapter 19, "Version Control and Team Development."

- Business servers typically reside on a server machine across a network. To provide client applications with quick response time and to maximize server resources, you may want to control areas such as the maximum number of business server instances that can be created at once. The Visual Basic manuals refer to an application that manages class instances on the server as a "Pool Manager." A sample instance managers is discussed in Chapter 23, "Sample Application #2: An Instance Manager."

Putting All the Services Together

A *system* is a collection of services that work together. Systems are composed of services. Services, in turn, are composed of components.

You should understand at this point that a system is partitioned into many services, many of which are Visual Basic object applications. This section shows how a system is partitioned into logical service layers and shows you a sample system.

The GOLF system is a three-tier order processing and maintenance system. The GOLF system is included on the companion disk that accompanies this book. It consists of various service components located in all three tiers. This and previous chapters already presented some of the GOLF system services as examples. We will continue to use this sample system for examples. Chapter 24 discusses the GOLF system in detail. This chapter provides a broad overview of its components. The GOLF system file are included on the companion disk that accompanies this book, in the directory tree located at \CHAP24\APP.

Figure 4.2 shows the services that comprise the GOLF system. The GOLF system is composed of two user services, *GolfClient* and *LogonMgr*, three business services, and five data service entities.

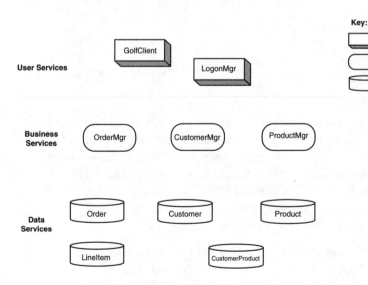

Fig. 4.2
The service architecture of the GOLF system.

User Services

Within a three-tier system, a single user service usually can be identified as the *controlling client application*. This controlling client application coordinates the rest of the user services within the system, provides the primary interface to the user, and manages the communication between the user and business services.

For example, the controlling client application in the GOLF system is the *GolfClient* Visual Basic application. This VB application coordinates the remainder of the user services—in this case, the *LogonMgr* OLE automation object. The *GolfClient* is responsible for the bulk of the interaction between the user and the system—the only other interface the user has with the system is the LogonMgr dialog box. Figure 4.3 shows the user service layer interaction.

Fig. 4.3
The user services layer of the GOLF system. Arrow tails indicate OLE controllers, and arrow heads indicate OLE servers.

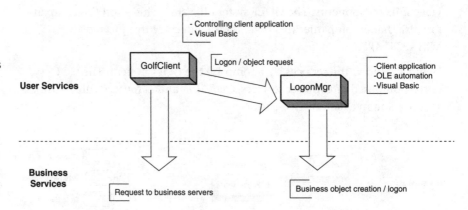

The controlling client application usually is a standard Visual Basic application. It doesn't have to be an OLE automation server because it usually doesn't need to be controlled by any other service. Because this controlling client application contains most of the presentation Visual Basic code, it looks most like the traditional two-tier VB client application. The difference, of course, is that it isn't "fat"—it doesn't contain SQL, database access, or business logic, it contains only presentation code.

The controlling client application could have been written in any number of languages that support forms-based development and OLE automation, including PowerBuilder, Delphi, and Microsoft Excel. Visual Basic usually is the best choice, however. Visual Basic provides better support for OLE automation and OLE controls than most mainstream development tools.

Most organizations will want to build at least one general controlling client application for each of the business servers. For example, the *GolfClient* is primarily an order-processing application that makes use of the *OrderMgr*, *ProductMgr*, and *CustomerMgr* business servers, but the *OrderMgr* business server also might be used by a specialized Excel client application that allows a single sales rep to enter standing orders for a large customer.

Desktop tools such as Excel can make suitable controlling client applications in some scenarios, such as client applications created by end users, proto- types, and applications with short life spans. But for applications that require multiple developers, complex GUI interaction, and life spans measured in years, Visual Basic is the better choice. Visual Basic, for example, has better version control, supports team development tools, doesn't make source code available to users, is faster than VBA macros, and so on.

As mentioned in the previous section, when user services that are built with Visual Basic will be placed on the same physical machine as the controlling client application, they should be built as in-process servers for performance.

The arrows between the user services and business services represent OLE automation calls that will generally pass across the network via remote automation.

Notice that the user service doesn't talk directly to the data services. This has a big implication for Visual basic developers: VB bound controls don't fit into the three-tier architecture today. Bound controls automatically link a GUI OLE control with a database. But GUI controls in the user service layer inter- act directly with the business services, not the data services layer. Because OLE controls cannot be bound to OLE automation servers created in Visual Basic 4, we cannot yet bind OLE controls to our business services. Instead, the GUI elements must be populated via code from business server objects, col- lections, properties, and methods. Microsoft publicly announced, however, that in future versions of Visual Basic, you can expect to see the capability to bind client application controls to any OLE automation server.

Although not using bound controls requires more code, the three-tier archi- tecture still has a distinct advantage over traditional two-tier architectures from a presentation standpoint: the client application is not just a mirror image of the logical database design. There is no reason the user should be presented with nothing more than a one-to-one mapping of the logical data- base design. Instead, a client application should be fine-tuned to flow the way the user works. Different users may require very different interfaces to the same business server.

Chapter 8, "Architecting Tier 1: Client Applications," details the creation of user services.

Business Services

Business servers contain all the business logic of the system. It is the business servers that control how the underlying enterprise data is managed via the data services.

Generally, business servers are large objects that manage a specific business entity. In the context of application partitioning, business servers are often referred to as "service objects" or "line-of-business objects" (LOBjects).

Business Server Design

Business objects model business entities. A business object encapsulate the attributes and functions of a business entity. Because business objects are OLE automation servers, the business attributes become properties and the business functions become methods in the context of OLE automation.

Although business objects can be "small," encapsulating just a small piece of business functionality, you should probably strive to create larger, more universal business objects.

For example, an organization might have a complicated credit-check algorithm to determine a customer's credit rate. This algorithm could be implemented as a either an individual object or as a method to a larger *customer* object. The latter is generally more preferred for a number of reasons:

- Instantiating (creating) and releasing objects across the network is generally a slow operation. A model that has a few large objects requires less "creates" than a model that has many smaller objects.

- Object management tools are still immature; managing, finding, and understanding few larger objects is an easier task than performing the same actions with many smaller objects.

- Modeling larger business entities as objects composed of smaller entities is more intuitive then modeling just the smaller entities. For example, a *line item* is always associated with an order, so it doesn't require its own business service—its functionality is provided for in the *order* business service.

These business objects should be universal. Their design should accommodate the entire enterprise. For example, building a universal *customer* business object might be a daunting task for a large multinational corporation. Even if the business object isn't going to serve all of the organization's subsidiaries, for example, it should be designed so that eventually it can accommodate the entire organization without breaking existing systems.

The easiest way to envision business object partitioning is to think about your organization's main logical business entities. These entities often are often apparent when you start to group your database tables by subject matter. For example, most organizations use the same common entity dimensions: orders, products, customers, employees, vendors, and so on.

Because the business object shields the user services from the data services, a business object such as a *customer* object can provide a universal customer interface, even if customer information is spread across multiple heterogeneous legacy data services.

Just as it is standard practice to normalize databases, business servers also should be "normalized" to eliminate redundancy. A business function or property should be built only once. If two services perform the same functionality, that functionality should be encapsulated in its own service and invoked from the other two.

The GOLF system's business servers encapsulate three main business entities: orders, products, and customers. Each business object manages the specific entity, therefore they are named *OrderMgr*, *ProductMgr*, and *CustomerMgr*, respectively. Each business object exposes a single class, the *Application* class. When a client application needs to use a specific entity, for example, it creates an instance of the *Application* class. For example, either of the following two examples would set the variable, *MyOrderMgr*, to an instance of the class running on the server:

```
Set MyOrderMgr = CreateObject("OrderMgr.Application")
Dim MyOrderMge as New OrderMgr.Application
```

Exposing just a single *Application* class simplifies access to the object. A client application need only create a single *OrderMgr* object for "one stop shopping" on the order entity.

From this point, the client application could create new orders, edit existing orders, and print invoices by invoking properties and methods of *MyOrderMgr*. For example, `MsgBox MyOrderMgr.Order.CustomerName` will display the customer name of the existing order, and `MyOrderMgr.Order.PrintInvoice` has the server print an invoice to the invoice printer. Figure 4.4 shows the object interface of the OrderMgr object.

Fig. 4.4

The object interface of the OrderMgr object.

Objects

Order Mgr Object Interface

	Application	Orders	Order	LineItems	LineItem
Collections:	Orders		LineItems		
Member objects:		Item		Item	Parent
Properties:	Id	Count	OrderID	Count	LineID
	UserId		CustomerID		ProductID
	Password		OrderDate		OrderQty
			ShippedFlag		ShipQty
			RemovedFlag		
Methods:	Initialize	LoadOrders		Add	
		UpdateOrders		Remove	
		Add			
		Remove			
(Performance tuning):		CollectionGet	PropertyGet	CollectionGet	PropertyGet
		CollectionSet	PropertySet	CollectionSet	PropertySet

An object interface is composed of properties, methods, member objects, and member object collections. An example of a property in the *OrderMgr* business server's *Application* object is *UserID*, which specifies the UserId of the client application that instantiated the object. AddInit, which initializes the object, is an example of a method. The *Order* member object contains all the properties and methods used to modify orders. And the *Orders* collection is used to view and browse multiple orders.

There aren't a lot of tools currently available for business server design. There are, however, many tools that facilitate data service design, such as LogicWorks ErWin and Asymetrix InfoModeler. These tools, particularly the ones that have already begun modeling business entities as objects, will begin to also model the business services tier. Eventually these tools will generate VB object class code, just as their data service counterparts generate SQL stored procedure and SQL data definition code.

Chapter 9, "Architecting Tier 2: Business Servers," covers the design and creation of business servers.

Business Server Deployment

Visual Basic can create an OLE automation servers who's instance is referenced either by multiple controllers or just a single controller. The setting of the class module's *Instancing* property determines whether the class is not creatable, creatable for a single user, or creatable for multiple users.

Because an OLE automation servers created in Visual basic are single threaded, they can only service one controller at a time. So, although a class instance who's *Instancing* property is set to *Creatable Multi-Use* can be referenced by many controllers, it can respond to them only one at a time because it is a single process (and, therefore, a single thread).

This situation is not suitable for a services architecture, where multiple client applications need to be served simultaneously by a business server. If a Visual Basic OLE application class's *Instancing* property is set to *Creatable Single-Use*, when a controller asks to create an instance of the object class a new instance is created and a new process is started. That is, when a client application asks to create an instance of the business server, a new instance of the executable process is loaded because any previously instantiated instances are only allowed to service a single process.

If the business server is running under a preemptive multitasking operating system such as Windows NT, each instance of the business server gets its own process, which the operating system multitasks—exactly what you want.

In general, then, business servers usually will be *Creatable Single-Use*, and user servers usually will be *Creatable Multi-Use*.

This Creatable Single-Use/Creatable Multi-Use nomenclature is confusing but correct. It sounds backwards: Creatable Multi-Use is better for a single-user environment, and Creatable Single-Use is better for multi-user environment! This is because the property value describes the object process's instantiation, not the number of users simultaneously served.

As you may expect, this means client applications are capable of launching programs on your server machines—the business servers. Servers, however, have finite resources available to them. You may need to place a ceiling on the number business servers that can be created simultaneously, or you may want to load-balance instances between multiple server machines without having the user aware of the load balancing.

This process is accomplished by placing an intermediate server "on top" of the standard business server. The Visual Basic documentation calls this intermediate server a "Pool Manager." The pool manager manages instances of business servers. This book refers to the intermediate application as an *instance manager*, so that you don't confuse this book's sample application with the sample that comes with VB.

An instance manager can accomplish several objectives, such as the following:

- Put a ceiling on the maximum number of instances that can be running simultaneously on the server machine.

- Pre-create instances, so when a client application asks for a new instance, the instance manager just passes the client application a reference to the pre-created instance. The client application doesn't need to wait while the instance is being instantiated.

- Load balance instances across multiple server machines transparently to the client application.

- Monitor instances and destroy those that are allocated to a client application but haven't been used for a while (a time-out).

- Provide additional levels of security and auditing.

The GOLF system uses an Instance Manager for each of its business objects. Figure 4.5 shows how the *OrderMgrs* instance manager might be used by the client application. In this figure, each box represents an instance of the class, not the class itself.

Fig. 4.5
The OrderMgrs instance manager. When the GolfClient needs to use an OrderMgr object, it tells the LogonMgr to ask the OrderMgr's object for an instance from its created pool.

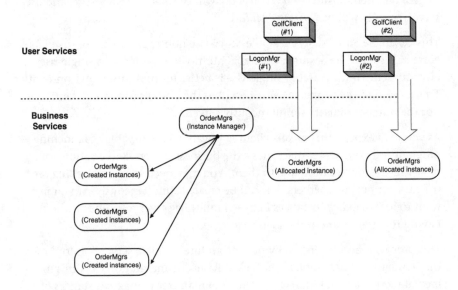

The instance manager for the *OrderMgr* business object is named *OrderMgrs*, the plural of the object, because it manages and maintains a reference to many *OrderMgr* objects. This is analogous to the way a collection of objects usually is named—the plural of its member objects.

So, the figure shows that the *OrderMgrs* instance manager has three unused instances available in its pool and has already allocated two instances to two client applications.

The *GolfClient* asks the *LogonMgr* for an *OrderMgr* object. The *LogonMgr* then asks the *OrderMgrs* instance manager for an *OrderMgr* object. If *OrderMgrs* has an available object, it returns the handle of the instance back to the *LogonMgr*, which in turn passes the handle back to the *GolfClient*. *OrderMgrs* then releases its handle on the freshly allocated instance.

When the *GolfClient* ends or releases its handle to its *OrderMgr* instance, the *OrderMgr* instance terminates and it notifies *OrderMgrs*. Periodically, *OrderMgrs* wakes up and adjusts its created instances' pool size.

When using the instance manager from the companion disk provided with this book, a client application must perform different steps when getting an object. When creating an object through an instance manager, for example, the code will look like the following example:

```
Set MyOrderMgrs = CreateObject("OrderMgrs.Application")
Set MyOrderMgr = MyOrderMgrs.GetInstance("MyUserId", "MyPassword")
```

Code that doesn't involve an *Instance Manager* looks like the following example:

```
Set MyOrderMgr = CreateObject("OrderMgr.Application")
MyOrderMgr.AddInit "MyUserId", "MyPassword"
```

Notice that in the second case, *OrderMgrs* is not involved. However, you still need to initialize the *OrderMgr* object (which was accomplished during *OrderMgrs.GetInstance* in the first example).

OrderMgrs.Application has its *Instancing* property value set to *Creatable Multi-Use* so a single instance will serve multiple requests, but one at a time. This is acceptable in the GOLF system because client applications talk to the instance manager only when they need an object (relatively infrequently), not when they actually use the *OrderMgr* object.

Chapter 23, "Sample Application #2: An Instance Manager," details an a simple instance manager and discuses additional things that can be accomplished with it.

Batch Processing

In an ideal world, your Visual Basic business servers and data services should react to all requests, in real-time. Unfortunately, because technology resources are finite, certain processes may have to be performed off-hours, when the system usage is low.

Management, for example, may need to look at monthly sales history for the past three years. Ideally, this is done "on-the-fly," off the orders data service. But realistically, most large organizations lack the computing resources to keep three years of order history available for querying and summarization. So instead, organizations sum up this detail to a monthly level and allow applications to go after this sum. Because this summarization is a resource-intensive process—possibly requiring locks on entire database tables—it must be performed off-hours.

Organizations will continue to need to develop this kind of processing for at least the next five years, and possibly forever. Batch systems should be used sparingly—the system design should strive to eliminate them—but more than likely, a need for them will continue.

The services model, therefore, needs to address batch processing. The solution is fairly straightforward—build a Visual Basic business service that performs the batch processing. Design a specialized client application that operates the batch business service. This client application may be no more than a GUI scheduling package. You probably should separate the batch business server from the on-line business server because end users usually have no need to initiate these kinds of batch processes.

Figure 4.6 shows an example of the only batch-based business servers in the GOLF system. For clarity, the *OrderBatch* business server and the *BatchClient* client application were omitted from previous GOLF system diagrams.

Batch processing business servers look a little different than their interactive counterparts. These business servers probably need to be instantiated only once because they only need a single process, so their Instancing property should generally be Creatable Multi-Use. Likewise, they are invoked from only a single specialized client application. This client application may be run on the server itself (in an operations room, for example).

In the GOLF system, the OrderBatch business server is always instantiated. The specialized BatchClient application can schedule *OrderBatch* to perform batch processing at regular or specific intervals.

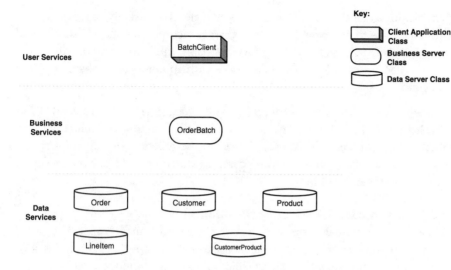

Fig. 4.6
OrderBatch encapsulates all the batch processing that relates to orders and is controlled by a simple, specialized client application, BatchClient.

You may be tempted not to partition your batch process into user and business services, but instead, you may decide to throw the GUI interface right into the same Visual Basic program as the batch logic itself. This may be acceptable, but it means that you will not be able to remotely monitor the batch processes or invoke them from other client applications. You may someday, for example, want to create a single client application that monitors all batch processing.

Accessing Data Services

Data services can be any source of data. Most likely, the bulk of an organization's data services will be contained in client/server database management systems, such as SQL Server and Oracle.

Data Access Methods

There are many ways to access SQL-based databases though Visual Basic, such as bound controls, data access objects (DAO), and the SQL Server Programmer's Toolkit (VBSQL).

This book recommends using a data access method that was introduced in VB4—remote data objects (RDO). RDO provides a fast, consistent interface for getting at SQL server data from multiple sources. It's based on Open Database Connectivity (ODBC), so theoretically, it should work against any database that provides an ODBC driver.

Using RDO, your business servers can access data services in either of two ways—via dynamic SQL statements or via stored procedures.

The advantage of dynamic SQL is that SQL dialects are usually compatible from database to database. If a business server incorporates SELECT statements from Oracle, that business server probably will work unmodified against a Microsoft SQL Server data service with an identical database schema.

The advantage of stored procedures is that they are faster and are a good mechanism of insuring that the data service's database integrity remains intact. Unfortunately, stored procedure syntax is generally incompatible from database to database, so when using complex stored procedures, you give up seamless database portability.

Business and Data Service Entity Relationships

Usually, an individual business server's purpose is to manage a specific business entity, such as an order. The database usually encapsulates this entity in one or more database tables. These tables loosely correspond to a business server's object collections, and the columns on these tables loosely correspond to object properties.

For example, in the GOLF system the OrderMgr business server—for the most part—accesses the *Order* and *LineItem* tables exclusively. Figure 4.7 shows which business servers manage which data service entities.

Fig. 4.7
The GOLF system's data entities and the business servers that manipulate them.

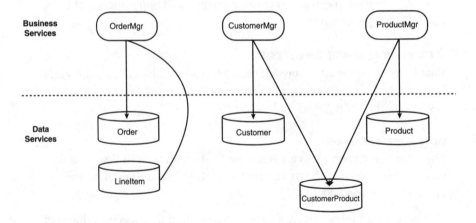

Some tables, however, are referenced by multiple business servers. The CustomerProduct table, for example, which contains attributes like a customer's price for a specific product, is accessed by both the CustomerMgr and ProductMgr business servers.

Tables loosely correspond to a single business server because all business rules associated with this data service entity probably were encapsulated in a single business server during its partitioning design. This doesn't mean a business server doesn't use data that is associated with a different business entity, however. When creating an order, for example, you may need to look up products or adjust a customer's credit rating. In this case, the OrderMgr probably will ask the ProductMgr to do the lookup and the CustomerMgr to adjust the credit rating. In this way, it doesn't need to understand the logical database design or business rules of other entities.

When a business server is associated with many tables, the ancillary tables are often represented as collections within the business server object, especially when they have a one-to-many relationship. When the OrderMgr represents a specific order, for example, it does so by setting the Order object's properties to the columns of the corresponding row in the Order table, but it also creates a LineItems collection of the associated line items from the LineItems table.

A method of a business server loosely corresponds to one or more SQL statements or stored procedures in the data service. Although the business rules are contained in the second tier, such as credit limit computations, the fundamental data service integrity still is contained with database objects using database objects like triggers, referential integrity, and stored procedures.

The GOLF system uses stored procedure exclusively to access SQL Server data services. Figure 4.8 shows some of these stored procedures. The Update method of the *OrderMgr.Application.Order* object, for example, will invoke one sp_addorder stored procedure and many sp_addlineitem stored procedures.

The association between business objects and data service tables is rarely an exact one-to-one correspondence. Some tables, for example, cross business object boundaries and are used by multiple servers. In the GOLF system, for example, *Product* and *Customer* has a many-to-many relationship, as represented by the *CustomerProduct* table. You can choose to have either the *CustomerMgr*, *ProductMgr*, or both manage this *CustomerProduct* entity. Or, if the *CustomerProduct* has many attributes, you may choose to create its own business server, named *CustomerProductMgr*. This business server may manage customer pricing, for example.

So, usually, a single business object manages a set of data service tables. The columns on these tables are represented as properties in the business object. Ancillary tables are represented as collections within the business object. A method within the business object is represented by one or more stored procedures or SQL statements.

Fig. 4.8

Sample stored procedures, used by the business servers to manipulate the data service.

Objects

Order Mgr Object Interface

	Application	Orders	Order	LineItems	LineItem
Collections:	Orders		LineItems		
Member objects:		Item		Item	Parent
Properties:	Id	Count	OrderID	Count	LineID
	UserId		CustomerID		ProductID
	Password		OrderDate		OrderQty
			ShippedFlag		ShipQty
			RemovedFlag		
Methods:	Initialize	LoadOrders		Add	
		UpdateOrders		Remove	
		Add			
		Remove			
(Performance tuning):		CollectionGet	PropertyGet	CollectionGet	PropertyGet
		CollectionSet	PropertySet	CollectionSet	PropertySet

Data Tier:		sp_Get_Orders	sp_Add_Order		sp_Add_LineItem
			sp_Delete_Order		

Chapter 10, "Architecting Tier 3: Data Servers," further discusses accessing SQL databases in detail.

Other data services, such as mail or mainframes applications, may have their own API for accessing their data. Chapter 10 discusses accessing these other data services in detail.

Data Services

While business rules are stored in the business service tier, the fundamental data to which these rules apply lives in the data services tier.

The majority of data services that the Visual Basic developer will use are SQL-based client/server DBMSs. Client/server DBMSs such as Oracle, SQL Server, Sybase, Informix, and DB2 are mature technologies. The way in which data is modeled in these systems is fairly well understood. The way in which these data services store data in the three-tier services model doesn't differ much from the way in which they store data in the two-tiered model—relational database theory and good design still apply in the three-tier architecture.

The preceding section highlighted one of the significant changes, however—business rule placement. Because no good, centralized place existed to put business rules in the two-tier world, database vendors began to expand the functionality of their stored procedure syntax. As the syntax started to look more like a traditional programming language, developers were able to add more complex business logic into stored procedures. The three-tier world halts this trend.

Business rules manifest themselves in code as complex *Case* or *If* statements. These rules must deal with security and multiple heterogeneous data services. They must be developed in a team environment. Visual Basic is a more suitable tool than stored procedures to develop and debug complex business logic.

Stored procedures, however, will not go away. They are still exceptionally useful for encapsulating elementary data functions, such as "add order header," "add line item," and "adjust inventory." One or more of these elementary data functions usually will compose a business service method, such as "create order."

Any *elementary data function* is a function that leaves the enterprise's data in a valid state. An "add order header" function, for example, will insure that the order belongs to an existing customer, but will not necessarily adjust the customer's credit rating (a business rule).

Sometimes, the distinction between what is a business rule and what is an elementary data function is not clear. A good litmus test to determine if a rule is a business or data rule is to ask, "Do I anticipate that management might ever make a decision that changes the validity of this rule?" If the answer is yes, it probably is a business rule. If the answer is no, then it's probably a data rule.

This book recommends using stored procedures for all your database access if you don't anticipate switching back-end databases. Although you need to rewrite the stored procedures if you decide to move to a different DBMS, stored procedures offer a number of advantages, including the following:

- The DBA has visibility to all SQL that are being run on the server.

- Because stored procedures are pre-compiled, they execute more quickly.

- It's easier to administer security against only stored procedures versus all database objects (tables, views, and so on).

- Your elementary data functions are defined *on the data server*, rather than being defined in the business server Visual Basic code.

- Changing your database schema involves recompiling only the elementary data functions, not the business servers.

- People who specialize in database design and performance tuning can write the elementary data function SQL used by the business servers, which usually is not possible if the SQL is imbedded into the Visual Basic business server.

These advantages were more important in the two-tier world, when client machines were directly accessing the database. It's less important in the three-tier environment, where centralized business servers are accessing the database, but it's still recommended.

So, where does Visual Basic fit into a DBMS data services? Today it really doesn't—there are no places in a DBMS data service where VB is applicable. With the promulgation of VBA into Microsoft products, however, expect Microsoft SQL Server's Transact-SQL syntax to eventually be augmented with VBA.

Chapter 10, "Architecting Tier 3: Data Servers," discusses DBMS and other types of data services.

Visual Basic Libraries

You now have a feel for how Visual Basic is used to create client applications and business servers, and how it is used sparingly in the data services tier.

There are other places where you will find Visual Basic code. Regardless of tier, it often helps to create Visual Basic code libraries that developers can incorporate into their applications, whether user, business, or data service.

In other programming languages these are often referred to as *libraries* or *statically linked libraries*. In Visual Basic, they generally manifest themselves as class modules with a .CLS extension that developers add to their project. This book refers to this code as *reusable code libraries*.

Routines that manipulate the registry, for example, call Windows APIs, or implement sort algorithms often are good candidates for reusable code libraries—basically, anything that multiple developers will find of value, but is not appropriate or overkill to implement as an in-process OLE automation server.

Chapter 12, "Advanced Coding Techniques," discusses Visual Basic code libraries and coding techniques.

Physical Design

One powerful aspect of the services model is that, to the model, where you place the physical code on the network doesn't matter. Unfortunately, the real world isn't nearly this flexible. Operating systems, networks, and Visual Basic limit, for all practical purposes, where you can deploy service components.

Operating Systems

At the time of the writing of this book, Windows 95 was just recently released, Windows NT Workstation and Windows NT Server were at version 3.51, and most of the world was still running Windows 3.1 or its companion, Windows for Workgroups 3.11.

Windows 3.1 (Win31) is a 16-bit operating system that isn't capable of preemptively multitasking applications.

Windows 95 (Win95) is a 32-bit operating system that can preemptively multitask 32-bit applications. It also can run 16-bit applications. It's a more stable environment than Win31, makes better use of system resources, and provides good management facilities.

Windows NT (WinNT), both Server and Workstation, are 32-bit operating systems that can preemptively multitask 32-bit and 16-bit applications. WinNT provides a more stable environment than Win95, strong (C2) security, better resource management, and operates on non-Intel machines.

Visual Basic 4 can create both 16 bit (Win31) and 32-bit (WinNT and Win95) applications. It imposes several limitations on 16-bit applications, however—particularly with Enterprise-specific features. VB cannot use remote data objects (RDO), create 16-bit in-process OLE servers, use the 32-bit Win95 custom controls, or create secured business servers.

Most organizations now face the challenging question of how to migrate users from Win31 to Win95 or WinNT. Win95 and WinNT provide many long-term advantages to an organization, especially in management costs, but they impose many short-terms costs, such as hardware upgrades, support, and training.

The system architect, however, needs to decide how to accommodate the different operating systems from a custom application standpoint.

Custom application development is time-consuming and expensive—it usually exceeds the cost of the hardware on which it is deployed. Most organizations will acknowledge that they are moving to 32-bit platforms. Given these two facts, the advantages of 32-bit Visual Basic over 16-bit, and the advantages of Win95 and WinNT over Win16, a compelling argument can be made to develop all new applications in 32-bit.

A good strategy, therefore, may be to identify the current 16-bit users of the new three-tier system and incorporate an operating system upgrade for them into the system development workplan.

Because Visual Basic imposes several limitations applicable to three-tier development, the focus of this book is on 32-bit application development.

Deployment of Services

At the time of this writing, Visual Basic can create applications that run only on Intel processors under Win31, WinNT, or Win95. The services described in this book are created in Visual Basic, and therefore can be deployed only on Intel machines running a variation of Windows. This section talks about each service layer.

User Services

Client applications usually will execute entirely on the client machine.

The disadvantage of deploying client applications on the users' workstations is that, when the application needs updating, the update must propagate to many physical machines. Because client applications incorporate presentation logic and don't contain critical business logic, updating these user services isn't a time-sensitive task. The business doesn't stop running if version 2.1 of the presentation application doesn't make it to all 1,000 end-user workstations simultaneously.

Additionally, although the process runs on the users' workstations, the executables and DLLs can sit in a single spot on a shared file server. Also, management tools such as Microsoft System Management Server will continue to mature and make such propagation and desktop software management easier.

For the reasons mentioned in the previous chapter, either Win95 or WinNT Workstation are suitable operating systems to run client applications.

Business Services

Business services usually should reside on a centralized server machine. Because they perform the bulk of the business process logic, locating them on a central server provides a number of advantages, including the following:

- Performance can be scaled centrally

- Capacity can be increased centrally

- System usage is easily monitored

- Business functionality is "locked-up" in a secure environment

- Changes in the business logic, which are often time sensitive, need only occur on the central server

The architecture described in this book assumes that business servers are located on a server machine.

Another alternative is executing the business servers on the end-user's workstation. This alternative has a number of disadvantages, including the following:

- Performance cannot be scaled without upgrading all user workstations

- Capacity cannot increase without upgrading all users workstations

- Business server usage is difficult to monitor

- Confidential business functionality is distributed across many machines

- Changes in the business logic may need to occur simultaneously over many workstations.

The disadvantages of placing the business services on the end-users' workstations in some respects mirror the disadvantages of a two-tier client/server architecture.

Business servers are critical to the day-to-day operations of the system. They are accessed by many client applications via remote automation. For these reasons, business servers should be run under WinNT on high-performance, fault-tolerant machines. Because business servers are created in Visual Basic, they cannot reside on machines running other fault-tolerant or multitasking operating systems, such as UNIX.

Data Services

Because the bulk of the data services are DBMS servers that you buy (not that you build in Visual Basic), you have some flexibility in the kind of operating system and hardware in which they are deployed.

Microsoft SQL Server runs only under WinNT, but other DBMSs such as Oracle, Sybase, and DB2 run on a number of operating systems, such as UNIX and OS/2, and on a number of different hardware platforms, such as IBM, Hewlett-Packard, and Digital.

Data services are used by a number of business server clients. Data services support the organization's line-of-business applications. As such, they should reside on centralized, fault-tolerant machines.

Non-RDBMS data services, such as OLE automation "wrappers" () around legacy mainframe applications or messaging systems, also should reside on centralized servers. (A "wrapper" is a custom OLE automation interface that encapsulates some other type of application.) The type of data service dictates where it can be deployed.

Physical Deployment Example

This section makes some recommendations as to where the services should physically reside. Figures 4.9 and 4.10 show two scenarios of how the GOLF system may be deployed.

Figure 4.9 shows the GOLF system business and data services, deployed on a single physical server on a LAN. The single WinNT machine runs SQL Server, the interactive business servers, and the *OrderBatch* batch business server.

Fig. 4.9

A simple deployment of the GOLF system. All the business and data services reside on the same physical server.

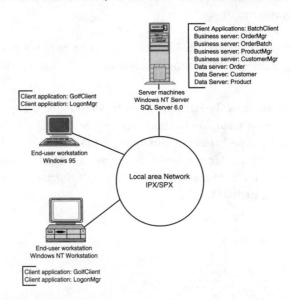

Figure 4.10 shows a more complex partitioning scheme. Although, as a whole, the system looks the same to the client applications as it looked in figure 4.9, the server distribution is different. The business servers are partitioned into two main areas, orders and customer/product. The *OrderMgrs* instance manager maintains a pool of *OrderMgr* instances across three Windows NT server machines. The business servers are accessing the data services across the WAN, and the data is partitioned across two machines, running two different operating systems and two different DBMSs.

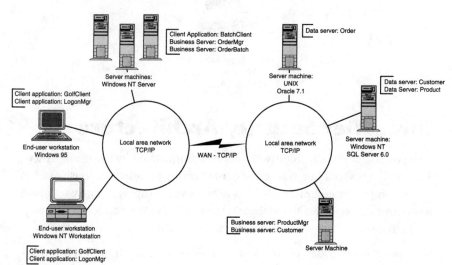

Fig. 4.10
A complex deployment of the GOLF system. The business and data services are deployed across a WAN and on several physical machines.

Sometimes, deploying all three tiers on a single machine is desirable. The system, for example, may be required to support remote sales reps in the field with laptops that cannot always dial into the corporate network. Figure 4.11 shows an example of this kind of deployment. In this scenario, the data services tier uses a local Microsoft Access database. The batch processes are no longer applicable, so they are omitted. Of course, the GOLF system has to be modified to replicate transactions if a "master" data server were established to store all users' transactions.

Fig. 4.11
Deploying all
services on a
stand-alone
laptop.

Client application: GolfClient
Client application: LogonMgr
Business server: OrderMgr
Business server: ProductMgr
Business server: CustomerMgr
Data server: Order
Data server: Customer
Data server: Product

End-user workstation
Windows 95
Microsoft Access

Three-Tier Security Architecture

In the three-tier model, security should be administered by the business service tier. Users should be granted or denied access to individual business objects' properties and methods. This enables you to apply security to business entities (as opposed to database tables) and also lets you secure the way in which data is changed, not merely the data itself.

Because the business servers reside on Windows NT machines, you can make use of Windows NT security. With remote automation, you can grant or deny users access to individual object classes running on the server. Each object class has an access control list (ACL) associated with it. The ACL is set with the Remote Automation Connection Manager utility.

In a properly designed three-tier architecture, users are not allowed to directly log into and manipulate the database with end-user tools such as Microsoft Excel.

Chapter 13, "Architecting Security," details security.

Organizing System Development

Because this architecture is logically partitioned into three distinct tiers, we also can logically partition our application developers.

Client/server systems involve many rapidly changing technologies. And, although it's good to have the entire system development team understand each others' work, you cannot expect everyone to maintain expertise in all the areas of client/server technology.

Building a large three-tier system, for example, requires knowledge of database design, database performance tuning, GUI design, business-requirements gathering, batch-processing, security, business-entity modeling, stored procedure development, and so on. It is reasonable to expect a three-tier system to require development in four or more programming languages.

The type of work involved in creating the client applications differs from the type of work involved in creating the business services, although both are written in Visual Basic. The business service requires modeling skills, operations knowledge, and so on. The user service requires intuitive presentation, good artistic skills, and so on. Likewise, stored procedure development and database design are different from both the user and business services.

The three-tier services model enables developers to specialize in technologies. Because each layer and service has a clearly defined interface, developers need only agree upon the interface. From there on, they can work independently.

Client/server development and modeling tools differ radically from traditional mainframe tools. The development approach should reflect these differences. Chapter 21, "Organizing the Development Approach," outlines a three-tier Visual Basic development approach.

From Here...

The three-tier Visual Basic architecture is capable of scaling to meet the needs of the enterprise, and prepares you for future architectural industry direction. The GOLF system demonstrates all the aspects of such an architecture.

Occasionally, this architecture is inappropriate, however. It may be overkill, for example, for a departmental, work group, or small company. Likewise, it may not be as appropriate for decision support applications that are characterized by data retrieval and browsing, not transactions.

Throughout this book, you will be provided recommendations in order to "jump start" your development efforts. You should recognize them as such and evaluate their applicability to your own environment and system needs.

A migration of new and existing application development to the services model should, however, begin in organizations where this architecture is appropriate. This core set of business components created in Visual Basic is what enables a company to easily assemble new solutions that use existing business processes.

This chapter provided a high-level overview of all the pieces of a three-tier application architecture. You now should have a good introductory understanding of what The Visual Basic Enterprise looks like. The remainder of the book covers these topics in detail.

For further information related to topics covered in this chapter, see the following chapters:

- Chapter 8, "Architecting Tier 1: Client Applications," provides more information on creating user services.

- Chapter 9, "Architecting Tier 2: Business Servers," provides more information on creating business services.

- Chapter 10, "Architecting Tier 3: Data Servers," provides more information on creating data services.

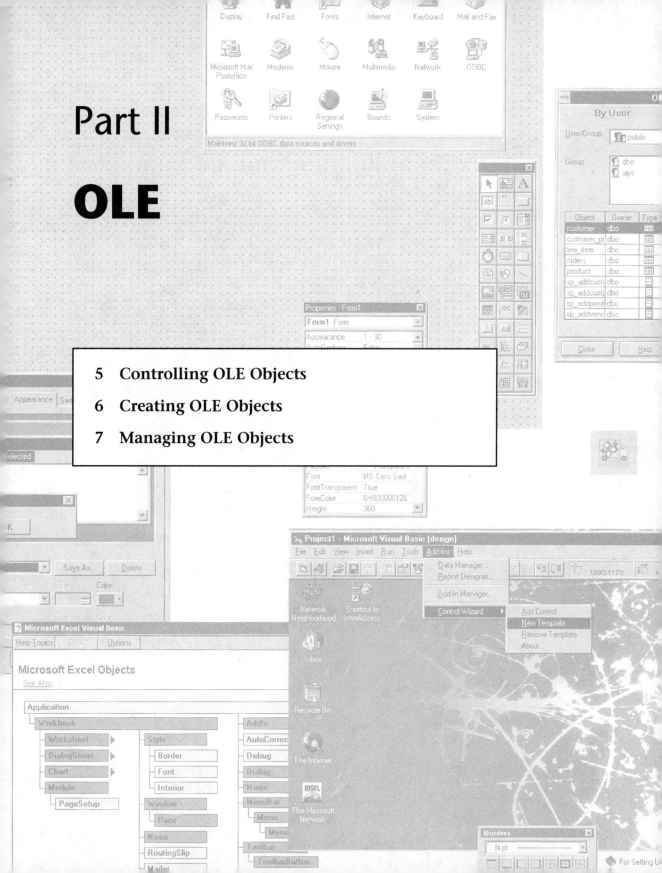

Part II

OLE

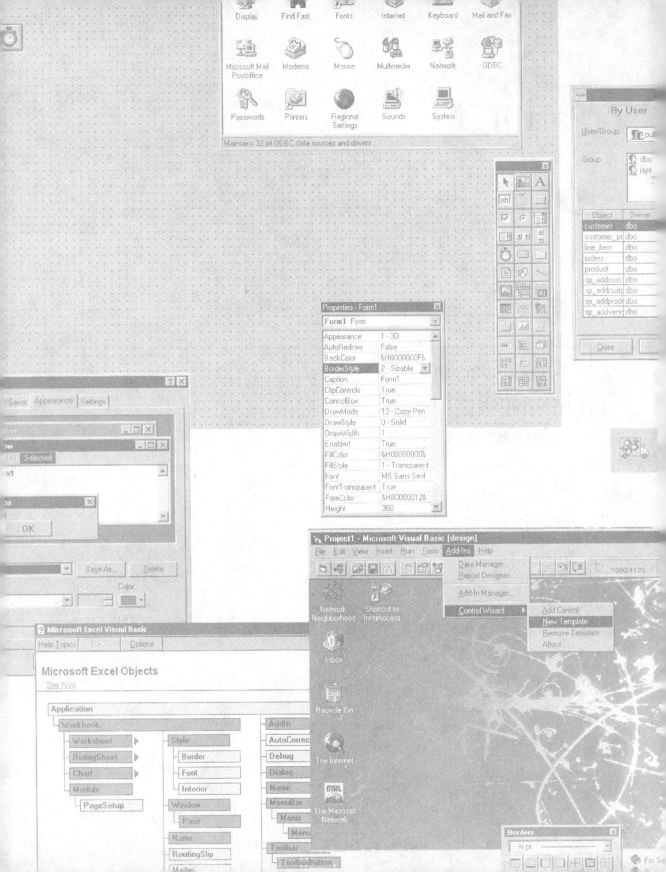

Chapter 5

Controlling OLE Objects

In Chapter 4, "Visual Basic Application Architecture," you learned about OLE and its role in a three-tier client/server architecture. This chapter discusses how you can control OLE objects with Visual Basic.

In this chapter, you learn about:

- Objects that Visual Basic can control
- Understanding the OLE object interface
- Manipulating different types of OLE objects from Visual Basic
- Using the Object Browser

This chapter explains how to use VB to create, manipulate, and destroy each object type. You learn that the OLE interface to all object types is similar, and that learning how to manipulate one object type enables you to easily learn how to manipulate others.

An Overview of OLE Objects

An OLE *object* (or just "object") is a combination of code and data that can be treated as a unit. These objects can be a part of an application, such as a *Chart* or *Worksheet* in Excel, or an entire application, like Excel.

Each object in a Visual Basic project is defined as a *class*. An instantiated object is created as an identical copy of its class. To help understand this example, consider an automobile assembly line that uses machines to assemble the cars.

The machines are programmed with a blueprint to follow when creating the automobile. This blueprint tells the machine how to stamp out the body of the car—where all of the bolts go, where the steering wheel goes, and so on.

When each auto rolls off of the assembly line, each unit is a replica of the blueprint programmed into the assembling machines. Each car is identical in weight, shape, and size.

When *you* purchase the car, you can change the basic attributes of the auto. You can change the color of the car by painting it. You can put a sunroof in the top of the car. You may accidentally bang into the garage when backing the car out of it, altering the shape of the car's body. Another owner might reupholster the interior of a car, install a new stereo system, or put new whitewall tires on the car.

Although these actions make each copy of the car look different, no change affects the original blueprint of the car. When the next batch of cars rolls off of the assembly line, they are identical in weight, shape, and size.

How does this relate to classes and objects? In our example, the original blueprint is the class, but each auto that comes off the assembly line is an object, or an instance of the class. Each copy shares a common set of characteristics—size and shape—defined by the class. Once created, each copy is a separate entity that can be altered. In our example, the cars were painted, reupholstered, or crashed. Likewise, objects are created as identical copies of their class. After an object is created as a unique entity, its properties can be changed. If you created a *Chart* object, for example, you can change the Chart's axis, color, and title.

Objects are beneficial to developers because they allow you to reuse pieces of functionality that are already developed. The physical implementation of one or more objects in an object application is often referred to as a "component." Because Excel exposes its Chart object, you don't need to create the code necessary to generate a chart. You can reuse the engine provided by Excel.

Because each object is an exact copy of its class, developers must make modifications in only one place. After the changes are made, every object created (or "instantiated") from the class includes the updates.

Objects that Visual Basic Can Control

The OLE objects that Visual Basic is capable of controlling fall into three main categories:

- OLE controls
- OLE automation servers
- OLE documents

OLE controls are the most common type of object used in Visual Basic, including controls such as text boxes, command buttons, and list boxes. OLE controls are generally used to make up the graphical interface of a client application, but can also implement non-visual functionality, such as modem communications.

OLE automation servers are applications that can be controlled through OLE automation. See Chapter 6, "Creating OLE Objects," for details on creating OLE automation servers in VB.

Because you can create OLE automation servers with Visual Basic, they often are used in the three-tier client server architecture to create business servers, encapsulating the business logic of an application. The capability to package automation servers in standalone executables makes them easy to distribute and allows developers to maintain business rules in one location.

OLE documents are objects contained in other applications that can be inserted into Visual Basic applications by using the OLE Container control. Examples of OLE documents include Word documents, Excel worksheets, and Visio diagrams.

OLE documents differ from OLE automation servers: a document always has a visible interface. Many kinds of OLE documents permit visual editing. Visual editing allows you to edit an OLE document, such as a Word document or an Excel spreadsheet, from within another application, such as a Visual Basic order processing application.

Each of these objects has a programmatic interface that may include properties, methods (or events), members, and collections of the object. Each of the interface elements can be manipulated by Visual Basic. The object interface is discussed in detail in following sections of this chapter.

Choosing Communication Methods

As you saw in the preceding section, applications can control many types of OLE objects. Visual Basic's development environment coordinates and consolidates these objects. VB allows you to combine objects from different sources—text boxes, Excel worksheets, Word documents, and so on—into a single application and to communicate between all these sources.

Visual Basic can control objects through OLE. But why use OLE? Certainly Windows provides many methods for exchanging data and communicating between applications.

II

OLE

As you learned in Chapter 4, in early versions of Windows, users used the Clipboard to exchange data. In later versions, they used DDE to transfer data and send commands to other applications. Although you still can copy data to the clipboard and still can use DDE to transfer data and send commands, OLE provides the capability to embed other applications or pieces of an application directly into applications you develop.

Visual Basic can perform functions that use both DDE and OLE. DDE is similar to OLE automation, but doesn't address the features of OLE controls or OLE documents. OLE automation, however, usually is a better choice for the following reasons:

- With DDE, only data appears in the source application. Visual elements, such as the source application's toolbars and menus, don't appear in your application.

- DDE can exchange only text between applications. DDE is incapable of sharing graphics, charts, and other visual elements.

- The performance of OLE usually is better than DDE.

- Future versions of operating systems, such as Windows 95 and Windows NT, will continue to build upon OLE.

In some situations you may need to use DDE. Many applications still exist that don't expose an OLE automation interface. In these situations, DDE is the only option.

Understanding the OLE Object Interface

Visual Basic allows you to control an object's properties, methods, events, member objects, and collections. Collectively, these components make up an object's *interface*. Through OLE, VB can alter the characteristics of an object by manipulating the object's interface. Table 5.1 describes each attribute of the object interface.

Table 5.1 The Elements of an Object Interface

Attribute	Description
Properties	An object's data settings
Methods	Procedures used to operate on an object

Attribute	Description
Event	An action recognized by an object
Member/Dependent Object	A constituent element of a collection or object
Collections	A type of object that contains a set of related objects

Object Properties

Properties refer to an object's data settings. *Color*, *FontSize*, *Visible*, and *Locked* all are examples of properties.

You can change an object's characteristics by setting its properties. Excel's *Application* object, for example, has a *Visible* property. When you set the Visible property of the application object to False, the application no longer is visible on a user's desktop.

Object Methods

Methods are procedures that are used to perform operations on an object. You can use methods to affect properties. The `Move` method of a an object, for example, might reposition an object on the screen by changing the object's the Top and Left properties.

Methods don't need to affect properties. They may cause some action to occur in an application. Invoking the `ChartWizard` method of Excel's Application object, for example, instantiates a new Chart object. Calling the `DatabaseLogon` method of a user created object can result in the user logging onto a database.

Object Events

An *event* is an action recognized by an object, such as clicking the mouse, typing a key, or destroying the object. Events occur when an aspect of the object changes. You can write code that responds to an object's events.

Not all objects can respond to events. The OLE container control, for example, responds to events in Visual Basic, but Visual Basic cannot respond to events within the OLE document contained by the container control. If a user clicks on a cell within an embedded Excel worksheet, Visual Basic cannot respond to the event. Currently, the only type of OLE object that supports events is the OLE control object.

II

OLE

Member and Dependent Objects

A *member* is a constituent element of an object or collection. In Microsoft Excel, for example, the Application object is at the highest level of the object hierarchy (the hierarchy is shown in figure 5.5), which means that the Application object is the *parent* to all other objects.

If you follow the hierarchy down to the next level, you see the Workbook object. Because the Workbook object lies below the Application object in Excel's object hierarchy, the Workbook object is a *member* object of the Application object. Likewise, if you follow the hierarchy down another level, you see that the Worksheet object lies below the Workbook object; the Worksheet object is a member object of the Workbook object.

As you will see in a following section of this chapter, member objects make up collection objects. Additionally, member objects can be used to create references to object without using the `CreateObject()` statement.

Dependent objects are a special type of member object. Dependent objects cannot be created externally by the controlling application, such as Visual Basic. They *depend* on a parent object. The *ListItem* object, for example, which is a member object, cannot exist without the *ListView* control. In other words, you cannot begin to add items to a list without first having a list.

To use a real-world example: a bank account can be seen as a dependent object. The account requires that a bank object is in place before it can be created. After the bank object is in place, you can begin to create its member objects—bank accounts.

Object Collections

A *collection* is an object that contains a group of objects. All Visual Basic applications, for example, have a *Controls* collection. The *Controls* collection is a group of all controls contained on a form within a VB project.

You use a collection much like you would an array. You can obtain information about the entire collection, such as the number of elements within it. You can also obtain information about individual elements within a collection, such as the *Text* property of the collection's fourth element.

Besides properties, collection objects can have methods. The *Nodes* collection of a *TreeView* control, for example, has an `Add` method that you use to add additional nodes to the *TreeView* control.

Using an Object Interface

To control objects in Visual Basic, you interact with an object's interface. Interacting with the interface changes the characteristics of an object, which allows you to change an object's appearance or invoke a procedure within the object.

With OLE, you can create powerful applications by using properties, methods, events, members objects, and collections exposed through an object's interface without writing all the code needed to carry out the functions, which helps you develop professional-looking applications in a shorter amount of time.

Controlling OLE Controls

OLE controls, or OCXes, generally make up the largest portion of objects used in the client application. They provide the visual elements of a VB program, such as toolbars, text boxes, and command buttons.

Like all objects, you must instantiate an OLE control. After an OLE control is instantiated, you can use code to change the control properties or to invoke the control's methods. OLE controls differ from other OLE objects in their capability to respond to events, such mouse clicks or key presses. You can create code that responds to these events.

Although Visual Basic custom controls (VBXs) resemble OLE controls from an object interface standpoint, OLE controls have a more open architecture and richer interface characteristics. For example, OLE controls can be controlled from applications other than VB, such as Visual C++.

The following section may seem basic if you already are familiar with programming VBXs in versions of Visual Basic prior to version 4. Because the concept of objects and OLE may be new, this book first presents the techniques associated with OLE in its simplest form—controlling OLE controls. Later, when you learn about other types of objects, such as OLE documents and OLE automation Servers, you will see that many techniques used to control OLE controls are the same techniques used to control OLE automation servers and OLE documents.

Instantiating OLE Controls

In a Visual Basic project, OLE controls are displayed in the toolbox. Figure 5.1 shows the Visual Basic toolbox.

II

OLE

Fig. 5.1

The Visual Basic toolbox.

Previous versions of Visual Basic used VBXs instead of OCXes. For compatibility reason, Visual Basic 4.0 still supports VBXs, but because they are 16-bit DLLs, they can only be used in 16-bit applications.

Most third-party vendors have developed or are developing 32-bit OCX versions of their VBXs. Microsoft added OCX versions of all the VBXs included with prior versions of Visual Basic. Because of their inability to operate in a 32-bit environment and their closed architecture, VBXs have a limited future. So, this book focuses on controlling only OCXes.

Before you can use an OCX in a project, it must be added to the toolbar. To add an OLE control to the toolbox, follow these steps:

1. Select the Custom Controls command from Visual Basic's Tools menu.

2. The Custom Controls dialog box is displayed. In the Available Controls list, all custom controls and externally creatable classes contained in the object libraries referenced by your project are displayed. Select the custom control you want to add to the toolbar.

   To display only custom controls in the Available Controls list, select only the Controls check box in the Show group box. To see only controls that are currently displayed in the toolbar, select the Selected Items only check box.

3. After you finish, click the OK button. The OLE control is displayed in the toolbox.

After an OCX class is added to the toolbar, it can be instantiated form by double-clicking on it or dragging it from the toolbar onto a form. Figure 5.2 shows a Visual Basic form, with an added command button.

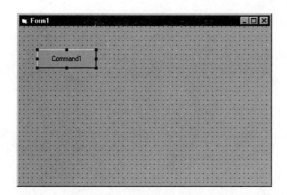

Fig. 5.2
A form, with a command button OCX added.

You also can add an OLE control to a form at run time by using Visual Basic's *Load* statement. The Load statement allows you to create a new instance of a control that is part of a control array. For more information on creating controls at run time, refer to the Visual Basic documentation.

Manipulating an OLE Control's Properties

An OLE control's properties, like VB variables, can be both set and retrieved. Property values, however, can be set and retrieved at run time or design time. During design time, property values can be set with the VB property window, or by bringing up the control's property sheet.

Setting Property Values

When you want to change the value of an OLE control's property, such as the *Text* property of a text box, you set it. To set the value of a property, use the following syntax:

```
object.property = value
```

The following example demonstrates setting a property in an OLE control:

```
txtUserName.Text = "Jane User"
txtUserNumber.Text = "100"
```

This kind of syntax often is known as *dot notation* because when the statement is read aloud, the periods are pronounced "dot." The following line of code would be read as "object-dot-text," for example:

```
object.Text
```

Retrieving a property also uses dot notation. Each dot operation (or occurrence of a dot in a statement), evaluates to some value. To determine the value of the entire operation, you follow the dot tree down, from left to right, to final value. Each dot operation, therefore, is an internal evaluation that requires processing.

Retrieving Property Values

You retrieve an OLE control's property when you want to know the current value of the property, which usually is done before your application performs another action. You may retrieve the Checked property of a check box control, for example, to determine if a user answered "Yes" to a question before carrying out a save operation.

Usually, you retrieve the value of a property by using the following syntax:

```
variable = object.property
```

The *object.property* expression evaluates to a value, just like a variable. It can, therefore, be used in any valid VB construct where a variable, constant, or literal may be used. You also can set and retrieve property value as part of complex expressions. In the following example, the current Text property of a text box is used to reset the property to a new value:

```
txtSearchResults.Text = txtSearchResults.Text + " found."
```

If you plan to use the value of a control's property more than once, your code will run faster if you assign the value to a variable and use it in place of the property expression, because VB can evaluate a variable much faster than it can evaluate an object's property. The following code fragment, for example

```
Sub FillListBox ()

    ''

    ' Assign value of Text property to a variable
    lsTextItem = txtListItem.Text

    ' Add items to list
    For liCounter = 1 to 1000
        lstListBox.AddItem lsTextItem & liCounter
    Next liCounter

End Sub
```

runs faster than this code fragment:

```
Sub FillListBox ()

    ''

    ' Add items to list using the Text property
    For liCounter = 1 to 1000
        lstListBox.AddItem txtListItem.Text & liCounter
    Next liCounter

End Sub
```

Performing Actions with an OLE Control's Methods

As you learned previously in this chapter, methods are used to invoke an action from the object. You can affect a list box's *ListCount* property, for example, by clearing all the items in the list box with the `Clear` method. Methods also can carry out an operation within an application—for example, the `Circle` method can be used to draw a circle on a form.

Calling an OLE control's methods in code is similar to retrieving or setting an object's properties. The general syntax for invoking a method is shown in the following line:

```
object.method
```

Remember that unlike a property that can be assigned a value, a method isn't an attribute and cannot be assigned a value. Therefore, the equal-sign character (=) never should appear to the right of the *object.method* statement.

Methods can accept arguments. For example, the `AddItem` method of the *ListBox* OCX has two arguments—*Item* and *Index*. The Item argument is a string that specifies the item to add to the object. The Index argument specifies the position within the object where the new item is placed. When passing arguments to an OLE control's method, the following syntax is used:

```
object.method argument1, argument2, ...
```

Some methods have optional arguments, that is, not all arguments are needed to invoke the method. If we did not pass the index argument in the `AddItem` method, for example, the new item is added to the end of the list or, if the list is sorted, in its appropriate alphabetical order.

Many methods expect arguments in a predefined order. These arguments are known as positional arguments. When an argument isn't passed to a method, you use a comma to indicate the argument's place. The *ListView* control, for example, has a `FindItem` method that accepts four arguments: *string*, *value*, *index*, and *match*. Only the first argument, string, is needed to call the method. If you call the method, passing only the first and fourth arguments, the syntax will resemble the following example:

```
ixListItem = ListView.FindItem ("Item", , ,lvwPartial)
```

In this case, the method causes the application to search the ListView control's *ListItems* collection, looking for the string, "Item," and accepting a partial match on the string. Note how the commas are used to hold the position of the unpassed arguments.

Some methods also support *named arguments*. Named arguments allow you to pass arguments in any order, not just the order expected by the syntax. When calling a method that supports named arguments, you don't need to use commas to hold a place for unpassed arguments. You also can pass named arguments in any order.

II

OLE

The OpenConnection method of the rdoEnvironment object, for example, has four named arguments: dsName, Prompt, ReadOnly, and Connect. Therefore, the following syntax is a valid call to the method:

```
rdoConnection = rdoEnvironment.OpenConnection
➥(dsName :="Database1", ReadOnly:=True)
```

You also can use the following syntax to make the call:

```
rdoConnection = rdoEnvironment.OpenConnection
➥(ReadOnly := True, Name := "Database1")
```

Notice that in the OpenDatabase and FindItem method, you surrounded the arguments with parentheses. When a method returns a value, you must enclose the arguments in parentheses. The syntax for a method of an OLE control that returns a value is shown in the following example:

```
variable = object.method (argument1, argument2, ..)
```

Using an OLE Control's Events

One aspect of OLE controls that differentiates them from other types of OLE objects is the capability to respond to events. Visual Basic is an event-driven language. You write code in response to user events, such as clicking a mouse or typing keys. OLE controls respond to these same types of events.

To add code to an OLE control's event, double-click the OLE control and select an event from the Procedure drop-down list box. Figure 5.3 shows the code window for the Click event of a CommandButton.

Fig. 5.3
A CommandButton's Click event code window.

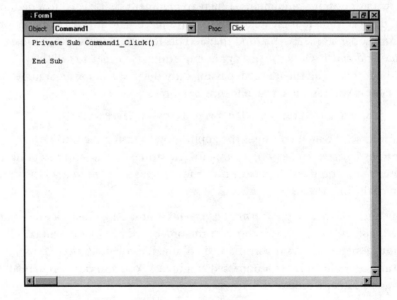

Currently, Visual Basic doesn't allow you to create OLE controls that respond to events. Using C++, however, you can create OLE controls that can respond to user events.

Using Member Objects

A *member object* is an object that is a constituent element of a parent object. For example, the ListView control allows you to add items to a list. When you add a new item, you actually create a new object. In the ListView control, this object is a *ListItem*. A ListItem object, therefore, is a member object of the ListView control.

Like their parent, a member object has its own object interface that can be controlled through Visual Basic. The ListItem member object, for example, has a *Selected* property that, when the item is selected in a list, evaluates to True. The ListItem member object also has a EnsureVisible method that guarantees that a specific ListItem object is visible on the screen.

An OLE control's member object's interfaces are manipulated the same way an OLE control's object interface is manipulated—by affecting the properties, methods, events, and collections of the member object. The code used to manipulate the member object's interface is also identical.

You also can create object variables that reference member objects, which can be used to minimize OLE "dot" operations in your code and increase performance. It also helps save time during development because you won't continually have to type long object references. This will help make your code more legible.

To create a reference to a member object, first declare an object variable, and then assign the variable to the member object by using the *Set* keyword. Declaring object variables is explained in detail in the following section, "Controlling OLE Automation Objects." To create a variable, for example, that references a ListItem member object, use the following code:

```
Dim loMemberObject as Object
Set loMomberObject = lvwListViewControl.ListItems(1)
```

The *loMemberObject* variable now references the first ListItem object in the ListItems collection object. More information on collection objects is provided in the following section. Notice, however, that unlike other variable types such as integer, object variables like loMemberObject don't hold a copy of the assignment, but rather a pointer reference to the member object.

Using a generic *object* datatype is known as *late binding* because syntax is not checked until run-time. You also can declare a variable of type *member object*. This is known as *early binding* because VB can check syntax during compile-time. In the previous example, rather than declaring an object variable as type Object, we can use the following statement:

```
Dim loMomberObject as ListItem
```

This object can be used only to reference a ListItem object. Late binding versus early binding is discussed in a following section of this chapter.

Using an OLE Control's Collection Objects

Collection objects, or collections, are containers for groups of other objects. A ListView control, for example, has a ListItems collection that makes up all the Items that were added to the ListView control.

Because they also are objects, collections can have their own methods and properties. The ListItems collection, for example, has properties such as *Count*, which returns the total number of objects in the ListItems collection. The ListItems collection also has an Add method that adds a new ListItem object to the collection.

Collections provide a convenient way to track a set of objects that are of the same type. In an order processing business service, for example, you may have a collection of *Order* objects contained in an *Orders* collection, or a collection of LineItem objects in a LineItems collection. The LineItems collection has a Count property that returns the total number of line items in the LineItems collection, and an Add method that adds additional LineItem objects to the collection.

Notice that the LineItems collection object and the Orders collection object are named in the plural form of the objects that they contain. This naming convention is standard for a collection.

Not only do other applications expose collections, Visual Basic also has its own collection data type that allows you to maintain collections of objects. A collection is essentially a linked list that can be accessed by an index or a key.

Using VB's Collections

You instantiate a collection object in Visual Basic the same way you instantiate any other object type.

You declare a collection object as you declare any type of object in Visual Basic, but you use the Collection data type. The following code, for example, creates a new collection object named, lcCollectionObject:

```
Dim lcCollectionObject as New Collection
```

After a collection is instantiated, you can add items to it, using the collection object's Add method, which has the following syntax:

> *object*.Add(*item, key, before, after*)

The Add method syntax has the following object qualifier and named-arguments, shown in Table 5.2.

Table 5.2 The Add Method's Object Qualifiers and Arguments	
Part	**Description**
object	**Required**. The collection object to which a new item will be added.
item	**Required**. An expression of any type that specifies the member to add to the collection.
key	**Optional**. A unique string expression that specifies a key string that can be used, rather than a positional index, to access a member of the collection.
before	**Optional**. An expression that specifies a relative position in the collection. The member to add is placed in the collection before the member identified by the before argument. If a numeric expression, before must be a number from 1 to the value of the collection's Count property. If a string expression, before must correspond to the key specified when the member referred to was added to the collection. You can specify before or after positions but not both.
after	**Optional**. An expression that specifies a relative position in the collection. The member to add is placed in the collection after the member identified by the after argument. If numeric, after must be a number from 1 to the value of the collection's Count property. If a string, after must correspond to the key specified when the member being referred to is added to the collection. You can specify before or after positions but not both.

To add a *TextBox* named *txtNewTextBox* to the lcCollectionObject collection, we just created the following syntax:

```
lcCollectionObject.Add(txtNewTextBox, "txtNewTexBox", 1,)
```

This statement adds the TextBox item to the first position in the collection.

In addition to collections exposed by external objects and collections you create, a Visual Basic application has three commonly used collections. These collections are listed in Table 5.3.

Table 5.3 Commonly Used Collection Objects Provided by Visual Basic	
Collection	**Description**
Forms	Contains loaded forms
Controls	Contains controls on a form
Printers	Contains all available printer objects

Each collection has methods and procedures that can be accessed through Visual Basic code.

Referring to Objects within a Collection

To refer to an item within a collection, you use the Item method of the collection. The Item method requires that you specify the item's *key* or *index* within the collection. A key is a unique string that identifies an object within a collection. With Visual Basic's Controls collection object, a control's key is its *Name* property. An object's index is a number that specifies the objects position in the collection.

The general syntax for referring to an object in a collection is

    object.Item(*index*)

or

    object.Item(*key*)

The following code, for example, adds text to the text box (the fourth element) in the Controls collection of the Visual Basic form, *frmSampleForm*:

```
frmSampleForm.Controls.Item(4).Text = "Some Text"
```

Because the Item method is the default method for a collection object, you don't need to specify it when calling the method. The following line of code is equivalent to the previous method:

```
frmSampleForm.Controls(4).Text = "Some Text"
```

Both of these examples reference an object's index, which can become confusing as more controls are added and removed from a form. Because each TextBox object on an form also has a key, which is its *Name* property, we can also refer to the fourth LineItem in the LineItems collection by name. This is shown in the following line:

```
frmSampleForm.Controls("txtTextBox").Text = "Some Text"
```

Using a Collection's Properties and Methods

A collection's methods are accessed the same way any OLE object's properties and methods are accessed, by using the *object.property* and *object.method* syntax. The previous two sections showed how to use a collection object's Add and Item methods.

An important point to remember is that a collection object has its own methods and procedures that are independent of the objects contained in the collection. A ListItem object of the ListView control, for example, has an InsureVisible method. The ListItems collection object cannot execute this method. Conversely, the ListItems collection object has an Add method, used to add more ListItem objects to the collection. This method is unavailable to the ListItem object.

Removing Objects from a Collection

To remove an object from a collection, you use the collection object's Remove method. The Remove method uses either of the following two syntax examples:

> *collection*.Remove(*index*)

> *collection*.Remove(*key*)

As with the other collection methods, the Remove method requires that you supply the index or key of the object that you are removing from the collection.

Using an OLE Control's Container Property

Many Visual Basic OLE objects can act as containers to OLE controls. Several of these objects are shown in the following list:

- Form

- Frame control

- Picture box control

- Sheridan 3D frame control

- Sheridan 3D panel control

- Sheridan 3D tab control

An OLE control typically contains a *Container* member object. The Container member object points to the object in which the member object resides. The Container object in an OLE control is analogous to the parent member object in an OLE automation server.

II

OLE

Using the Container member object, an OLE control can be moved between container objects at run time. The following steps show how to move a command button placed within a frame control to a picture box control:

1. Create a form in a Visual Basic project.

2. Place a picture box control and a frame control on the form.

3. Place a command button control within the Picture box control.

4. In the forms click event, add the following code:

```
Private Sub Form_Click()
    Set Command1.Container = Frame1

End Sub
```

5. Run the project and click the form.

When the form is clicked, the CommandButton control moves from the picture box to the frame control.

Freeing Resources Used by OLE Controls

Every object in an application uses system resources. OLE controls, OLE documents, and OLE automation servers each require some amount of memory when they are instantiated in a project.

After you have finished using an object, good programming practice dictates that you free the resources used by the object. Freeing the resources helps insure that your application performs optimally.

Resources are freed when an object is uninstantiated. An object becomes uninstantiated when all references to the object are removed. A reference exists when a variable points to the object or when the object exists in a container control (because the object is referenced behind the scenes). The number of references made to an object is referred to as the object's reference count. Therefore, the object's resources are freed, and the object is destroyed when its reference count is equal to zero.

OLE controls created at design-time automatically free resources when the form that contains them is unloaded or when execution of the application is halted. OLE controls created at run time using the Load command also free resources when the form that contains them is unloaded or when the application is stopped.

If you are finished with an OLE control that you created at run time and are not unloading the form that contains it or halting the execution of the application, use the Unload command to free the system resources that the control is using.

Controlling OLE Automation Objects

In addition to controlling OLE controls, VB can also control OLE automation objects. An OLE automation object is exposed to other applications or programming tools through an OLE interface. An OLE automation object differs from an OLE control object in that it may lack a visible interface. OLE automation objects may expose analysis and calculation capabilities as objects. Both Excel and Word, for example, expose their spell-checking engines through OLE automation objects, and Project allows you to access its Calendar functions.

An Excel Worksheet class is an example of an OLE document class. Its server—Excel—exposes a visual interface and can be visually edited within the OLE container control. However, an Excel Worksheet's server—Excel—also is an OLE automation server. Excel can be automated outside of the OLE container control by using OLE automation constructs and can be manipulated with code, while never exposing a visual interface to the user.

As with OLE documents and OLE controls, OLE automation objects expose a standard OLE interface of properties, methods member objects, and collection. They do not support events.

OLE automation objects are typically used in both the user and business services tiers of the three-tier client/server architecture. A client application may use OLE automation objects to generate printed Excel charts or Word documents.

Client applications also use OLE automation to access business services. These OLE automation business servers control access to the data service tier, enforce business rules, and insure that data doesn't become corrupted. Business servers also use OLE Automation to access other business and data services. An *Order Manager* business service, for example, may create a reference to a *Customer Manager* OLE automation object that also resides in the second tier. The Customer Manager object may verify the name and address of a customer who places an order for the *Order Manager*. A business sever also might use Remote Data Access objects to access a data service and retrieve database information.

Instantiating OLE Automation Objects

The first step in using an OLE automation object is declaring an object variable and referencing an OLE automation object. The techniques that you use to instantiate an OLE automation object differs from the techniques used to instantiate both OLE documents and OLE controls.

II

OLE

Declaring Object Variables

When you declare an object variable you use the Dim statement. The syntax for declaring an object variable is either

> Dim *variable* As Object

or

> Dim *variable* As *class*

The first syntax declares a *generic* object variable. This is known as late binding. A generic object variable can refer to any externally creatable OLE object, such as an Excel worksheet or a Word document.

The second syntax creates a *specific* object variable. used to create an object of the class specified by the *class* argument. This is known as early binding. Remember that the class argument is composed of two parts: *application* and *objecttype*. Application refers to the OLE server that contains the OLE automation object, such as Word or Excel, and objecttype refers to the object's class, such as *Sheet*, *Range*, or *Document*.

Late Binding

Use generic object variables when you don't know what type of object will be created at design time or if you plan to use a single object variable and assign many different types of objects to it.

Usually, when you create reference to OLE automation objects, you use the Object generic variable type. The Object generic variable type can refer to any parent, member, or dependent object exposed by an OLE automation server.

Early Binding

Although less flexible that generic object variables, calls made to objects that are declared as specific object types execute faster than calls made to objects declared an generic types.

For example, both of the following statements *Dim* an object variable and create a reference to an Excel.Application object:

```
Dim loExcelObject as Object
Set loExcelObject = CreateObject ("Excel.Application")

Dim loExcelObject as Excel.Application
SetloExcelObject = CreateObject ("Excel.Application")
```

Subsequent calls to the *loExcelObject* created with the second method execute faster than calls made to the loExcelObject created with the first method because Visual Basic resolves the second method's type information at compile time, instead of run-time. Early binding also enables VB to check for things like type mismatches at compile-time instead of run-time, making your code more bug-free.

Because of their enhanced performance and better debugging information, it's a good idea to use specific object types rather than generic types wherever possible. To determine what object types an OLE server exposes, use the Object Browser. For more information on the Object Browser, see the "Using the Object Browser" section that follows in this chapter.

Using the New Keyword

The *New* keyword applies to several VB constructs: *Dim*, Set *Public*, Set *Private*, and Set *Static*. In all cases, *New* tells the construct to instantiate a new instance of the class (rather than making an assignment to another object reference, for example).

The `CreateObject`, `GetObject`, and `New` functions all perform the same operation—they instantiate a class. For example, the code

```
Dim MyObj as New Excel.Application
```

is the same as

```
Dim MyObj as Excel.Application
Set MyObj = New Excel.Application
```

Each of the preceding operations produce the same end result—they instantiate a new instance of a class. The *Dim New* construct can be used only to create a new instances of externally creatable OLE objects that were referenced by the Visual Basic application. You also can use the *Dim New* construct to create an instance of any class modules that are part of the current project. The Dim New construct cannot be used to declare variables of any intrinsic data types, such as integers or strings, nor can it be used to create instances of dependent objects, which generally have their own special methods, such as Add, to create new instances (see "Member and Dependent Objects," a previous section in this chapter, for more information on dependent objects).

When you use the Dim New construct to declare an object variable, the object is not created until it is referenced in code for the first time. For example, if you were to Dim a new instance of a form in your project, *Form1,* for example, the new instance will not be created until you made a reference to Form1, such as Form1.Show. The new instance doesn't not begin to consume resources until after the first reference is made.

II

OLE

If you set the instance of Form1 created with the Dim New construct to *Nothing*, and no other objects have made reference to it, it is removed from memory. If you then re-reference the Form1 object, a compltetely new instance of the form is created. The new instance of Form1 regains all its default properties.

You may not have realized it, but when you display multiple instances of a form in an MDI application, you actually are instantiating multiple instances of your child form class. If you have an application with a form named "Form1," for example, you can add the following code to the Click event of a command button to display multiple copies of the form.

```
Dim frmNewForm as New Form1
frmNewForm.Show
```

When you run this code and click the command button several times, you see multiple instances of the Form1 object being created.

Using the CreateObject Function

The CreateObject function has the following syntax:

Set *objectvariable* = CreateObject (*"class"*)

Here, *objectvariable* is an object variable that previously was declared and "class" is an argument composed of two parts—the name of the application that supplies the OLE automation object (Excel or Word, for example) and the type of object being created (such as a worksheet or document). The class argument has the format, *application.objecttype*.

If, for example, you want to use the CreateObject function to create a reference to an Excel worksheet object, you can use the following code:

```
Dim loExcelSheetObject as Object
Set loExcelSheetObject = CreateObject("Excel.Sheet")
```

When you create a reference to the object, the OLE server that contains the object is started automatically if it isn't already running.

Creating a reference to an OLE automation server created with Visual Basic is no different than creating a reference to an OLE automation object exposed by Excel or Word. After declaring the object variable, you can use the CreatObject function to create a reference to your OLE automation objects. The following code, for example, creates a reference to an OLE automation object known as Orders that is part of the OLE automation server OrderMgrs. The OrderMgr server was created with Visual Basic:

```
Dim loExcelSheetObject as Object
Set loExcelSheetObject = CreateObject("OrderMgr.Orders")
```

Using the GetObject Function

You can use the GetObject function to create a reference to an existing object in another application. The GetObject function uses the following syntax, similar to the CreateObject function:

Set *objectvariable* = GetObject ([*pathname*] [,*class*])

The *objectvariable* argument is a valid object variable that was previously declared. The *pathname* argument can have one of three values: the fully qualified path to an existing file, an empty string, or it can be entirely omitted.

If pathname is a file path, the GetObject creates a reference by using the existing instance of the OLE server. The server must be provided in the second argument or, if the server is registered, the class argument can be omitted.

To use the GetObject function, for example, to create a reference to an Excel worksheet object and use an existing Excel file, you can use the following code:

```
Dim loExcleSheet as Object
Set loExcelSheet = GetObject ("NEWSHEET.XLS")
```

Because Excel is registered when it is installed, you don't need to include the Excel.Sheet class argument. This code creates a new instance of Excel and loads the file, NEWSHEET.XLS.

If you pass an empty string as the pathname argument, the GetObject function behaves like the CreateObject function. For example, the following code creates a new instance of an application object:

```
Dim loExcleApplication as Object
Set loExcelSheet = GetObject ("", "Excel.Application")
```

If the pathname argument is omitted, the OLE server that contains the object being referenced must be running. If it is not, the GetObject function causes an error. Additionally, the class argument must be passed. If the application is running, the GetObject function references an existing object.

You also can use the GetObject function to activate only a portion of a document file. For example, you may want to create a reference to a specific range of cells within an existing worksheet.

To specify the portion of the file that you want to access, you add an exclamation point to the end of the file name, followed by a string that identifies the part of the file you want to access. Excel, for example, uses R1C1 syntax to specify a range of cells. You can use the following code to create a reference to a cell range in the NEWSHEET.XLS file:

II

OLE

```
Dim loExcelSheet as Object
Set loExcelSheet = GetObject ("NEWSHEET.XLS!R1C1:R10C20")
```

In the preceding example, an instance of Excel is started, the file NEWSHEET.XLS is loaded, and the range of cells specified is activated. Notice that the name of the OLE server application—Excel—was never used in the function call. OLE can determine which application and object to activate based on the file name.

When to Use GetObject and CreateObject

The main difference between the GetObject function and the CreateObject function is that GetObject usually cannot be used to create a new instance of an OLE object. That is, if you haven't previously started an OLE server using the CreateObject command, the GetObject command returns an error. For example, if you use the GetObject function to create a reference to a Word document and Word isn't yet running, the function call returns an error message.

Several applications provide an exception to this rule. Using the GetObject function to create a new instance of an object contained within Microsoft Excel is the functional equivalent of using the CreateObject function. It does not retrun an error. As a general rule, use the CreateObject function to create references when no current instance of an object exists or if you want to create a new instance of an OLE server that may already be running. If a current instance exists, or if you want to load an object that is stored in a file, use the GetObject function.

Note that the GetObject function isn't supported by any class in an application created with Visual Basic. Rather, you always must use the CreateObject function.

Accessing an Automation Object's Interface

After you reference an OLE object with an object variable, the object can be manipulated in Visual Basic by accessing the object's interface. The way in which you manipulate an OLE automation object's interface is identical to the way you manipulate an OLE control's interface.

Just like the OLE controls section, this section examines how an OLE automation object's properties, methods, member objects, and collections are exposed and modified with Visual Basic.

Using an Automation Object's Properties and Methods

The following syntax is used to set and retrieve an automation object's property values:

```
object.property = value
```

To invoke an OLE automation object's methods, use the following syntax:

```
variable = object.method (argument1, argument2...)
```

This syntax should look familiar because it's the same syntax used to access the interface of OLE controls. As you will see in the following chapter, it's also the syntax used to access the interface of OLE documents. This feature is one of the most powerful tools of OLE: the capability to program objects from many different applications with the same code constructs.

In the "Controlling OLE Controls" section, for example, you saw how to change the value of a TextBox object's Text property. To do so, you use the following code:

```
txtUserName.Text = "Jane User"
```

If you want to perform a similar operation by using an OLE automation object instead of an OLE control, you can do so with the code in Listing 5.1, which you can find in the \CHAP05 directory, on the companion disk.

Listing 5.1 CODE01.TXT—Sample procedure to change content of an Excel worksheet's cells

```
Private Sub ChangeCellText ()
    ' Procedure changes the value of text in an Excel worksheet
    ' Declare the object variable
    Dim loExcelSheet as Object
    ' Create a reference to an Excel worksheet
    Set loExcelSheet = CreateObject ("Excel.Sheet")
    ' Change the value of a cell
    loExcelSheet.Cells(1,1).Value = "Some New Text"
End Sub
```

Notice the similarity of the two statements used to actually change the Value property:

```
txtUserName.Text = "Jane User
loExcelSheet.Cells(1,1).Value = "Some New Text"
```

The following code uses the SaveAs method of an Excel worksheet object to save the worksheet to a file:

```
loExcelSheet.SaveAs (filename := "NEWSHEET.XLS")
```

The preceding example used the SaveAs method of the Excel sheet. Notice that this method was called just like the methods of the OLE controls were called, by using the *object.method* construct. We also passed a named argument, *filename*, to the method.

You can now see how easily methods and properties of any type of object from any application can be manipulated.

Using OLE Automation Object's Member Objects

Just as OLE controls have member objects, OLE automation objects also have member objects. Because of the number of automation objects that many server applications expose, a single OLE automation object may have many levels of member objects.

To understand these multiple levels of member objects in OLE server applications, it helps to understand the object hierarchy of an OLE automation server.

Every object exists somewhere in an application's object hierarchy. When you create a reference to the object, you can do so directly if the object is externally creatable, such as an Excel worksheet, using the object hierarchy. You saw this in the "Controlling OLE Controls" section, when we created a new object variable by using a *ListView* controls member object. Figure 5.4 shows the ListView controls object hierarchy.

Fig. 5.4
The ListView control's object hierarchy.

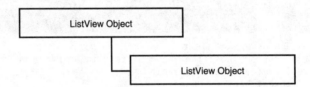

In this hierarchy, the *ListView* control is a parent of the *ListItem* object. At the same time, the *ListItem* object is a member object of the ListView control.

Figure 5.5 shows Excel's object hierarchy.

You can see from this model that all objects within Excel stem from the *Application* object. Most large applications have an Application object at the top of their hierarchy.

In Excel's object hierarchy, the Application object is a parent of the *Workbook* object, which also means that the Workbook object is a member object of the Application object. Just as you saw with OLE control's, you can create a reference to a member object by using its parent object.

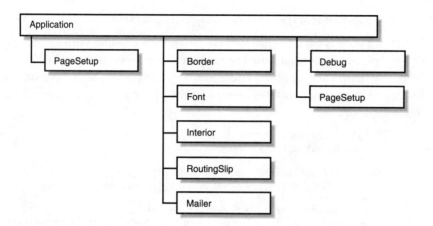

Fig. 5.5
Excel's object
hierarchy.

For example, if you already created a reference to Excel's *Application* object in
your application by using the `CreateObject` statement, you can use the Workbook object's relationship to the Application object to create a reference, as
shown in the following example:

```
Dim loApplicationObject as Object
Dim loNewWorkbookObject as Object
' '
' '
Set loApplicationObject = CreateObject("Excel.Application")
Set loNewWorkbookObject = loApplicationObject.Workbook
```

The *loNewWorkbookObject* variable now contains a reference to an Excel workbook object. You can call any workbook property or method by using the
object variable.

Of course, you also can use `CreateObject` to reference a workbook object because it's externally exposed. You aren't limited to creating objects that have
a simple parent-member relationship. The object model of Excel, for example,
shows you that a *Worksheet* object is a member object of the Workbook object. Using the following code, you can create a reference to a Worksheet
object:

```
Dim loApplicationObject as Object
Dim loWorkbookObject as Object
Dim loWorksheetObject as Object

' Create the application object
Set loApplicationObject = CreateObject ("Excel.Application")

' Create a reference to a WorkBook object
Set loWorkbookObject = loApplicationObject.Workbooks(1)

' Create a reference to a Worksheet object
```

```
Set loWorksheetObject = loWorkbookObject.Worksheets(1)
```

This much code is a lot of work to create an reference to one Worksheet object. Fortunately, Visual Basic enables you to transverse down the object hierarchy when creating object references. You can create a reference, for example, to the same Worksheet object on the previous example by using the following code:

```
Dim loApplicationObject as Object
Dim loWorksheetObject as Object

' Create the application object
Set loApplicationObject = CreateObject ("Excel.Application")

' Create a reference to a Worksheet object
Set loWorksheetObject = loWorkbookObject.Workbooks(1).Worksheets(1)
```

Certain objects in a hierarchy, such as Excel's EditBox object, are *dependent* objects. Dependent objects cannot be created or referenced by using the CreateObject statement—the only way a reference can be created to a dependent object is by referencing member objects in the hierarchy.

Because the EditBox object is a member object of the Worksheet object, you can use the Worksheet object to create a reference. For example, the following code creates a reference to an existing Excel Worksheet object, and then creates a reference to an existing EditBox object and fills in some text:

```
Dim loExcelSheet as Object
Dim loExcelEditBoxObject as Object

' Create reference to existing worksheet
Set loExcelSheet = GetObject("SAMPLE.XLS")

'Create reference to an existing EditBox object
Set loExcelEditBoxObject = loExcelSheet.EditBoxes(1)
' Set the text property of the EditBox object
loExcelEditBoxObject.Text = "Some New Text"
```

In a business application, dependent objects generally are implemented to enforce business rules by insuring that a certain type of object cannot be created without first creating an instance of its parent object. In an order processing application, for example, business rules may say that a LineItem object cannot be created without first creating an Order object. Therefore, the LineItem object is implemented both as a member object and as a dependent object of the Order object, which ensures that the only way to create a LineItem object is to first create an *Order* object.

Using an OLE Automation Object's Collections

Just as OLE container object's have collection objects, OLE automation objects have collection objects. Generally, these collection objects are composed of objects of a similar type.

Individual objects within a collection can be accessed by using an index. This index may be either a number or a string. If you had an Order object containing ten line items, for example, you can refer to the fourth LineItem in the LineItems collection by using the following code:

```
loOrderObject.LineItems(4).Text = "Fourth Line Item"
```

Responding to Busy OLE Servers

If you try to create a reference to an OLE automation server that is currently busy with another task, you receive a message, indicating that the OLE automation server is busy. While you cannot prevent OLE automation servers from being busy, Make sure your controlling application is capable of handling the error.

Chapter 14, "Architecting Error Processing," provides information on how "server busy" errors should be handled from a controlling application.

If you will access an OLE automation server frequently, and you find that the server often responds with a "server busy" message, there are several settings in Visual Basic that you can tune. These settings may help lessen or eliminate the server busy problem.

Visual Basic's *App* object has several properties associated with an OLE server busy message. They are listed in Table 5.4.

Table 5.4   The App Object's "Server Busy" Related Properties

Property	Description
OLEServerBusyMsgText	Allows you to set or determine the Text displayed when an OLE Server Busy message occurs.
OLEServerBusyMsgTitle	Allows you to set or determine the Title of the message box that displays an OLE Server busy message.
OLEServerBusyRaiseError	Allows you to set whether Visual Basic displays a message box when an OLE server busy situation occurs, or if Visual Basic will raise a trappable error. If the property is set to True, Visual Basic raises error number &h80010001.
OLEServerBusyTimeout	Allows you to set or determine the number of milliseconds that Visual Basic will retry OLE automation requests before an OLE server busy message is displayed. The default value is 10000 milliseconds.

II

OLE

You may experience OLE server busy problems when using an OLE automation server as a pool manager. Suppose that you had an OLE server that ran lengthy queries in the background, then returned the results to a client application. The client application would first call a method of the OLE automation server to register itself and indicate which query it wanted to run. The OLE automation server would periodically "wake-up" and determine which queries should be run.

When the OLE automation server is running a query, it cannot receive new registrations from OLE clients. If the query is long, the time span during which clients cannot be registered also will be long. Any client attempting to register during this time may receive an OLE automation server busy message.

By manipulating the App object's OLE automation server properties, you can control how the client application responds to this kind of situation. For example, you could set the *OLEServerBusyTimeout* value to a very high number. This will cause the client application to attempt to register itself with the OLE automation server for a longer period. If, however, the query execution takes minutes, your user will be forced to wait until a registration or a time-out occurs.

You may not want to display the OLE automation server busy message box to the end-user. If this is the case, set the App object's *OLEServerBusyRaiseError* property to *True* and raise a trappable error when a time-out occurs rather than displaying the message box. You then can use the error-processing mechanisms that Visual Basic provides to handle the exception.

If you choose to display the "server busy" message box, you can set the text displayed in the message box and the message box's title by manipulating the App object's *OLEServerBusyMsgText* and *OLEServerBusyMsgTitle* properties, respectively. You may want to create a message more understandable to an inexperienced user, such as `Could not complete your query. Try again later`.

The App object provides additional means to handle OLE automation server busy errors. This aids you in developing an application that responds gracefully to OLE automation server busy exceptions.

Freeing Resources

After you finish using an object variable, it's good programming practice to release all references associated with the variable. This release uninstantiates the object and frees all resources associated with the object.

To release references held by an object variable that references an OLE automation server, you set the variable to *Nothing*. The Nothing keyword sets the value of an object variable to nothing and frees all resource associated with the object, as long as the object is not being referenced by any other sources.

For example, the following code sets and creates an object variable (loExcelObject), assigns it to an Excel application object, and then sets the object to *Nothing*:

```
Private Sub ProcessApplicationObject()
    Dim loExcelObject as Object

    ' Create the application object
    Set loExcelObject = CreateObject("Excel.Application")

    ' Perform necessary processing
    ..
    ..

    ' Remove references from variable
    Set loExcelObject = Nothing
End Sub
```

If no other references are made to the Excel.Application object by any other controlling applications, the Excel.Application and the resources consumed by it will be released from memory. If, however, another application has created a reference to the Excel.Application object, the object will continue to reside in memory and use system resources.

Controlling OLE Documents

When developing a client application, you may want to include some kind of functionality for which a highly specialized application already exists. For example. you may want to allow an end user to create a thank-you letter and provide full formatting capabilities.

You can write the code to provide this functionality, but word processing applications already exist which provide this kind of functionality. OLE provides you the capability to insert a part of the word processing application into your application.

Inserting other application's objects is accomplished through *OLE documents*. OLE documents are a third type of object that Visual Basic can control. OLE documents are objects contained by an application, such as Word documents or Excel worksheets. These objects can be linked or embedded into Visual Basic by using the OLE container control.

II

OLE

Because of their graphical interface, OLE documents are a good choice for displaying documents that require formatting, such as sales reports or confirmation letters.

The primary difference between linked and embedded OLE documents is where their data is stored. Linked objects allow you to reference data associated with a document object, such as the data in the cells of an Excel worksheet. In a linked object, the data is stored by the application that supplied the object. Visual Basic only stores link references that display an image of the source data. The data itself is stored in a separate file.

Linked Objects

When an object is linked, any application that contains a link to this object can access and change the object's data. If Visual Basic application has a link to a Word document, for example, the document can be modified by any application linked to it: Word, another Visual Basic application, or another word processing application that can read Word documents. Whenever you open the linked object in Visual Basic, the object is updated to include all modifications made to the file that contains the data.

If a user double-clicks on the linked object, the application containing the linked data, such as Word or Excel, starts automatically. The user can edit the data using Word or Excel. Editing is handled in a separate window, outside the OLE container control.

Embedded Objects

When you embed an object in a Visual Basic container application, all the data associated with the object is contained in the container application. Therefore, if a Word document is embedded in a Visual Basic application, all the data associated with the document is contained in the OLE container control.

Unlike linked objects, only the application that contains the embedded object has access to its data. This limitation makes embedded objects useful in applications where only one user at a time is permitted to edit an object.

If the user selects an embedded object while working with the Visual Basic application, the object's *server application*—Word in this example—is started and the document is edited without leaving the Visual Basic application. This is known as *visual editing* or as *in-place activation*.

If both the server application and the container application support menu and toolbar negotiation, the toolbars and menus of your Visual Basic application merge with the toolbars and menus of the server application. This merging allows a user to use many of the server application's features without exiting the Visual Basic application.

You may use an embedded Excel worksheet, for example, to display the results of a query in a formatted chart. An embedded Word document also might create a thank-you letter in an order-entry application. An order processing business service might generate an invoice by using Excel.

Creating OLE Documents

In VB, OLE documents are instantiated with the *OLE container control*. The OLE container control allows you to instantiate linked or embedded objects at design time or run time, from either an existing file or as a new document object.

You can use several methods to create a linked or embedded object in the container control. The method that you use depends on whether you need to create the object at design time or at run time, and whether or not you decide to create a linked or embedded object. The three methods used to create a linked or embedded objects are shown in the following list:

- Using the Insert Object or Paste Special dialog box

- Setting the Class, SourceDoc, and SourceItem properties of the OLE container control

- Using the CreateEmbed or CreateLink method of the OLE container control

Preparing the OLE Container Control

Before you create any type of object in the OLE container control, there are several properties of the container control that should be set. These properties relate specifically to the types of objects that can be created in the container control, how the contained object is displayed, and the behavior of the container control when an object is inserted. Table 5.5 lists these properties, which can be set at both run time and design time, but it's often a good idea to set them at design time. This helps ensure that the OLE container control behaves in the manner you expect at run time. It also helps you develop code that handles events, such as resizing the form.

II

OLE

Table 5.5 Important OLE Container Control Properties	
Property	**Description**
DisplayType	Specifies whether the object is displayed with content or as an icon
OLETypeAllowed	Determines the type of object you can create (Linked, Embedded, or Either)
OLEDropAllowed	If True, the OLE container control is a drop target for OLE drag-and-drop operations
SizeMode	Determines how an object's icon or data image is displayed in the OLE container control

The following is a more in-depth discussion of the elements listed in the above table:

- The **DisplayType** property determines whether the OLE container control displays the linked or embedded object's content or an icon that represents the object. Setting the property to *Icon* displays an icon that symbolizes the type of document being inserted. Setting the property to Content displays an image of the documents data when the object is inserted. The *DisplayType* property cannot be changed while an object is instantiated inside the container control but you can delete the object, change the DisplayType setting, and then insert a new object.

- The **OLETypeAllowed** property insures that only objects of a specified type can be instantiated. If you allow users to insert documents by selecting them from the Insert Object dialog box (described in a following part of this section), and you want only embedded documents inserted into the control, for example, this property aids you in enforcing this rule.

- The **OLEDropAllowed property** determines whether the object can be a drop target (and source) for an OLE document drag-and-drop operation. Because of the emphasis that Microsoft has placed on creating applications that support drag-and-drop functions, you will see more and more applications using drag-and-drop functionality. You may want to include property in your client applications. For more information on drag and drop, see Chapter 8, "Architecting Tier 1: Client Applications."

- The **SizeMode property** determines how the OLE container control is sized with respect to its contained document object. The SizeMode property has four settings: Clip, Stretch, AutoSize, and Zoom, which are described in the following paragraphs.

Setting the property to *Clip* causes the OLE document to display at its actual size. If the object is larger than the OLE container control, its image is clipped by the control's borders. With an Excel worksheet, for example, the clip setting may cause the scroll bars on the right and bottom edges of the inserted document to be hidden.

Choosing the *Stretch* setting causes the object's image to resize to fill the OLE container control. The image may not maintain the original proportions of the object. If a user resizes the control, the OLE document is resized to fit within the control's new dimensions. This resizing can cause problems if the user shrinks the form to a small size.

Selecting the *AutoSize* setting causes the OLE container control to be resized to display the entire object when it is inserted. This setting may pose a problem if a user is permitted to resize the OLE control. The setting allows a user to resize the OLE container, but after the resizing occurs, the OLE document readjusts the size of the container to preserve its proportions. The second resize event may cause the edges of the OLE document to exceed the bounds of the form on which it sits.

Finally, if the property is set to *Zoom*, the OLE document is resized to fill the OLE container control as much as possible while attempting to maintain the original proportions of the object. Because the OLE document tries to maintain its original dimensions, enlarging the document causes the image of the document to grow smaller and smaller—enlarging the control has the effect of zooming out. Conversely, making the document smaller has the effect of zooming in on the document's image.

Creating Objects at Design Time

When you place an OLE container control on a form, the Insert Object dialog box is displayed. You use this dialog box to create a linked or embedded object at design time.

Alternatively, you also can use Visual Basic's Paste Special dialog box to create a linked or embedded object at design time. This section outlines the steps needed to create objects, using both methods.

Using the Insert Object Dialog Box

Figure 5.6 shows the Insert Object dialog box, displayed when you place an OLE container control on a form.

Fig. 5.6
The Insert Object
dialog box.

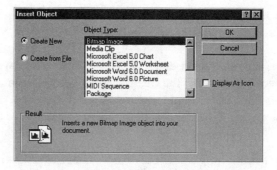

The Insert Object dialog box presents a list of document object classes that you can link or embed into an application. Besides selecting which type of object you insert, you need to determine whether the object will be a new object or if it is created from an existing file.

Only objects created from existing files can be linked to a Visual Basic application. When you select the Create from File option on the Insert Object dialog box, the Insert Object dialog box changes. The Create from File version of the Insert Object dialog box is shown in figure 5.7.

Fig. 5.7
The Insert Object
dialog box, with
the Create from
File option
selected.

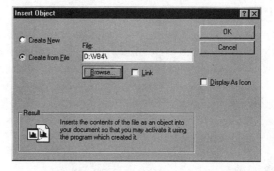

You create a linked object at design time by selecting the Link check box on the Insert Object dialog box. When you click OK, the object you selected is linked or embedded into your application.

When an object is selected, the *Class*, *SourceDoc*, and *SourceItem* properties of the OLE container control are set for you. The *Class* property corresponds to the class of the object that you are inserting.

If you choose to create an object from a file, the *SourceDoc* property indicates the name of the file from which the object is created. The *SourceItem* property refers to the data within the file, such as a range of cells in an Excel spreadsheet. If you create a new object, the SourceDoc and SourceItem properties are set to an empty string.

After you create a linked or embedded object in the OLE container control, you can change it by selecting the *Class* property in the property window and clicking on the ellipses. This action displays a list of insertable classes.

Using the Paste Special Dialog Box

Another way to create a linked or embedded object at design time is through the Paste Special dialog box, shown in figure 5.8.

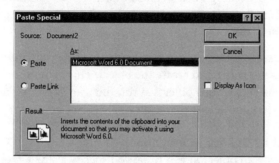

Fig. 5.8
The Paste Special dialog box.

The Paste Special dialog box is useful if you want to use only a portion of a file, such as a range of cells in an Excel worksheet.

To create an object by using the Paste Special dialog box, follow these steps:

1. Run the application that contains the data you want to link or embed.

   To illustrate the example, we will follow the steps necessary to insert a Word document into the container control.

2. Select the data you want to link or embed. In the Word 6.0 scenario, you would select the text you want to embed.

3. From the OLE server's Edit menu, choose Copy. In this example, you would select the Copy command from Word's Edit menu.

4. In Visual Basic, click the OLE container control with the right mouse button and choose the Paste Special command.

5. Select the Paste option if you want to create an embedded object. Select the Paste Link option if you want to create a linked object.

6. If an object already exists in the OLE control, you are asked if you want to delete the existing object.

7. Choose OK to create the object.

After you create the embedded object, you can edit it by double-clicking on the container control. This allows you to, among other things, add new information to the document, edit data present in the document, or change formatting properties within the document.

Creating an Object at Run Time

You may not always know what type of object needs to be created in an OLE container control at design time. For example, you may be developing an application that allows users to insert many different kinds of objects into one container control.

When you create an object at run time, you use properties and methods of the OLE container control to create the object. This section shows how to create linked and embedded objects at run time, and also demonstrates the methods used to allow a user to decide what type of object to insert.

Creating Linked Objects at Run Time

When you create an object at run time, you specify a single piece of information—the name of the document to which you want to link. In previous versions of Visual Basic, you accomplished this in two steps. You accomplished the first step—defining the type of object to be created—by setting the OLE container control's SourceDoc property. The SourceDoc property indicated the name of the document to which you wanted to link. After setting the SourceDoc property, you used the Action statement to create the link.

In Visual Basic 4.0, you can use the CreateLink method of the OLE container control to create a link to a file at run-time. The CreateLink method takes two arguments—*sourcedoc* and *sourceitem*. These two arguments are the same as the arguments that you use when inserting an object at design time. The *sourcedoc* argument is the name of the file to which you want to create a link. The *sourceitem* argument is an optional argument that specifies the data you want to link from within the sourcedoc.

For example, the following code creates a linked object to an Excel worksheet at run time:

```
oleContainer.CreateLink "C:\MSOFFICE\EXCEL\SAMPLE.XLS"
```

If you want to create a link to specific cells within the Excel file, you use the following code:

```
oleContainer.CreateLink "C:\MSOFFICE\EXCEL\SAMPLE.XLS", "R1C1:R4C4"
```

Creating Embedded Objects at Run Time

As with creating a linked object, creating an embedded object from an existing file at run time in previous versions of Visual Basic required two steps.

The first step was accomplished by setting the OLE container control's SourceDoc property to the name of the file. The second step was carried out by executing the *Action* statement which created the embedded object. Additionally, if you wanted to create a new embedded object—one that wasn't based on a file—you set the OLE container's Class property to the class of the object that you wanted to create. You then used the Action property to create the object.

In Visual Basic 4.0, the CreateEmbed method is used to accomplish these tasks. The CreateEmbed method has two arguments—*sourcedoc* and *class*. *Sourcedoc* determines the template file for the new embedded object, and *class* determines the object type.

For example, the following code creates an embedded object from an Excel worksheet:

```
oleContainer.CreateEmbed "C:\MSOFFICE\EXCEL\SAMPLE.XLS"
```

If you specify a *sourcedoc* argument, the class argument is ignored. For example, in the following code fragment, the class argument of "Excel.Sheet" is ignored and a sheet object is created from the specified sourcedoc:

```
oleContainer.CreateEmbed "C:\MSOFFICE\EXCEL\SAMPLE.XLS",
    "Excel.Sheet"
```

Conversely, to create an empty Excel worksheet, you specify the class argument and pass an empty string as the *sourcedoc* argument. For example, the following code can be used to create an empty Excel worksheet in an OLE container control:

```
oleContainer.CreateEmbed "", "Excel.Sheet"
```

Allowing Users to Select Objects at Run Time

If you are developing a document-management application, you may want to allow an end user to create an insertable object at run time. For example, if you are developing an application that allows users to create marketing reports, the users may need to insert Word documents, Excel charts, and Visio drawings into a single document.

You can do this by using the InsertObjDlg and PasteSpecialDlg method of the OLE container control. The InsertObjDialog method displays the Insert Object dialog box, while the PasteSpecialDlg method displays the Paste Special dialog box.

As you learned previously in this chapter, the Insert Object dialog box presents a list of available object types. When the user selects an object from the list, the object is created in the OLE container control. The Paste Special dialog box allows the user to paste an object from the system clipboard, such as an Excel chart or a paragraph from a Word document, into an OLE container control.

The code in Listing 5.2 shows how you can use the InsertObjDlg method to create a new compound document in the OLE container control at run time. The following code (which you can find on the companion disk, in the \CHAP05 directory) also uses a property of the OLE container, the OLEType property, to determine if an object was created.

Listing 5.2   CODE02.TXT—Sample procedure for creating a compound document

```
Private Sub prcCreateAnObject ()
      'Display the Insert Object Dialog
      oleContainer.InsertObjDlg
      'Determine if an object was created
      If oleContainer.OLEType = vbOLENone Then
            ..
            'Object not created code goes here
            ..
      End If
End Sub
```

When the dialog box is displayed, if a user chooses an object type and presses OK, the new object is created by Visual Basic. You don't need to write additional code. If the user clicks Cancel on the Insert Object dialog box, the OLEType property of the OLE container is set to *vbOLENone*.

The PasteSpecialDlg method works like the InsertObjDlg method of the OLE container control. When using the PasteSpecialDlg method, however, an additional property of the OLE container should be checked before displaying the Paste Special dialog box. Remember that the Paste Special dialog box allows you to paste objects that were copied to the system clipboard into an OLE container control. The *PasteOK* property of the OLE container control allows you to determine if the information in the system clipboard can be pasted in the container control.

Listing 5.3 (which you can find on the companion disk, in the \CHAP05 directory) shows how to check the clipboard for a valid OLE object, display the Paste Special dialog box, and check whether or not the user clicked Cancel.

Listing 5.3   CODE03.TXT—Sample procedure to check the clipboard for a valid OLE object before trying to paste the object in an OLE container control

```
Private Sub prcCreateAnObject ()
    ' Determine if information on clipboard can be pasted
    ' into the OLE container
    If oleContainer.PasteOK = True Then
        'Display the Insert Object Dialog
        oleContainer.PasteSpecialDlg
        'Determine if user clicked the Cancel button
        If oleContainer.OLEType = vbOLENone Then
            ..
            'Object not created code goes here
            ..
        End If
    End If
End Sub
```

As with the InsertObjDlg method, after the Paste Special dialog box is displayed on-screen and the user selects either the Paste or Paste Link option, the compound document is created by Visual Basic.

Placing Frequently Used OLE Documents in the Toolbox

If you regularly create the same type of OLE documents, you can place them in the toolbox. The object appears as an icon that you can drag onto a form to create an embedded instance of the object in your application.

To create an insertable instance of an object class in the toolbox, take the following steps:

1. Select the Custom Controls command from Visual Basic's Tools menu.

2. The Custom Controls dialog box is displayed. In the available controls list, all externally creatable classes contained in the object libraries referenced by your project are displayed. Select the class for which you want to create an insertable instance.

3. After you finish, click the OK button. The insertable object is displayed in the toolbox.

Because insertable objects are more difficult to control than document objtecs contained in the OLE container control, it's usually best to use the OLE container control when inserting OLE documents.

II

OLE

Manipulating a Compound Document's Methods and Properties

The *Object* property of the OLE container control is a read-only property that returns a reference to the object in the instantiated in the OLE container control. If, for example, you instantiated an Excel worksheet in the OLE container control, the container control's Object property will be set to the *worksheet* object.

The Object property allows you to access the OLE interface of the inserted object. The following line shows the general syntax for calling a method:

oleContainer.Object.*method (argument1, argument2...)*

How do you call a method or property by using the Object property? If you inserted an Excel worksheet object into the OLE container control, and then wanted to change the value of one of the worksheet cells, you can use the following code:

```
oleContainer.Object.Cells(1,1).Value = "Some New Text"
```

If you then wanted to use the SaveAs method of the worksheet to save the worksheet to a file, use the following code:

```
oleCOntainer.Object.SaveAs "NEWTEST.XLS"
```

You can see that manipulating the instantiate object inside of the container control is just like manipulating any other object's interface.

This ease of manipulation is important to the corporate developer because they don't have to learn completely different coding techniques to access objects of different types. The coding constructs used to access an OLE container control's object are identical to the constructs used to manipulate OLE controls and OLE automation servers.

Using an OLE Document's Member Objects

The OLE container control itself has no member objects. However, the OLE document contained in the control may have member objects. As with methods and properties, you use the OLE container control's Object property to access the OLE document's member objects.

The general syntax you use to manipulate an OLE document's member objects is the same that you use with OLE controls' member objects and OLE automation servers' member objects. If, for example, you previously inserted an Excel worksheet object into an OLE container control and wanted to invoke the Count method of the *EditBoxes* collection, you use the following code:

```
liCounterVariable = oleOLEContainer.Object.EditBoxes
➡("ebxExcelEditBox").Text
```

This statement returns the value of the *text* property of the EditBox object named ebxExcelEitBox.

You also can create references to dependent objects of the document that is contained in the OLE container control by using the Object property. To create a reference to the CommandButton dependent object by using an Excel worksheet that was inserted into a container control, for example, you use the following code:

```
Dim loCommandButtonObject as Object
Set loCommandButtonObject = oleOLEContainer.Object.CommandButtons(1)
```

Using an OLE Document's Collection Objects

Just as the OLE document in an OLE container control may have member objects, it also may have collection objects. The collection objects are identical to the collection objects exposed by OLE automation objects, and you can use the same syntax to access them.

You must use the OLE container's Object property to access any collection objects exposed by the inserted document. For example, the previous section used the Object property to retrieve the *text* property of an EditBox object on an Excel worksheet.

The example actually used the Item method of the EditBoxes collection to retrieve the property. Remember that because the Item method is the default method for a collection object, it doesn't need to be specified. So, the following code actually uses the EditBoxes collection of the inserted OLE document to obtain the text value of the EditBox:

```
liCounterVariable = oleOLEContainer.Object.EditBoxes
➡("ebxExcelEditBox").Text
```

Like any collection object, you can use the Add, Item and Count, and Remove methods of any collection object that the OLE document exposes. You can invoke the methods by using the same syntax that was used to invoke methods of OLE automation collection object methods.

Saving an Object's Data

Because all data that is associated with an embedded object is stored within your Visual Basic application, this data is not persistent. In other words, when you close the application that contains the object or insert a new object into the container control, all unsaved data that is associated with the object is lost.

The data of an embedded object uses a structured storage format to store the data internally. To save data from an object in the OLE container control to a file, you use the container control's SaveToFile method. You can use the SaveToFile method to save objects in the OLE container control to an open, binary file.

If, for example, you decided to embed a Word document into the OLE container control, made changes to it, and then decided to save this data—with changes—to a file, you could use the code in Listing 5.4 (which you can find on the companion disk, in the \CHAP05 directory).

Listing 5.4   CODE04.TXT—Sample procedure to save an OLE document embedded in the OLE container control to a file

```
Private Sub SaveOLEObject ()
    ' Create a File Number
    llFileNumber = 1
    ' Open a file
    Open "SAVEOBJ.OLE" For Binary As #llFileNumber
    ' Save the file
    oleCOntainer.SaveToFile llFileNumber
    ' Close the file
 'Close #llFileNumber
End Sub
```

After you save the object's data to a file, you probably will want to read it later. To read data from a file into the OLE container control, you use the container control's ReadFromFile method.

The code in Listing 5.5, which you can find in the \CHAP05 directory on the companion disk, shows how to read the data (saved in the previous example) back into the OLE container control.

Listing 5.5   CODE05.TXT—Sample procedure to read an OLE document that was previously saved to a file into the OLE container control

```
Private Sub ReadOLEFile ()
    ' Get the file number
    llFileNumber = 1
    'Open the OLE file
    Open "SAVEOBJ.OLE" For Binary AS #llFileNumber
    ' Read the file
    oleContainer.ReadFromFile llFileNumber
    'Close the file
    Close #llFileNumber
End Sub
```

When you read data stored in an OLE file back into the OLE container control, you don't need to specify the class of the object that is being inserted or create an empty embedded object by using the `CreateEmbed` method. When the file is loaded, the correct type of object is by default embedded into the container control.

The OLE container control's `Update` event is triggered each time a change is made to the data of an embedded object. You can create a form level variable and set the variable in the container control's `Update` to indicate that the object needs to be saved. When you save the object, reset the variable.

The `SaveToFile` and `ReadFromFile` methods apply only to embedded objects. Linked objects contain link information and an image of an object's data. The application used to create the object actually maintains the object's data. To save the changes to a linked file, a user must select the Save command from the OLE server application's File menu.

Uninstantiating an OLE Document Object

Because objects inserted into the OLE container control consume memory resources, it's good programming practice to uninstantiate the object when you are finished with it to free its resources. The OLE container control's `Delete` method is used to remove an object from the container control and free the memory resources associated with it.

The following line shows the syntax for the `Delete` method:

```
object.Delete
```

Here, *object* is the name of the OLE container control that contains the linked or embedded object.

The `Delete` method allows you to explicitly delete a reference to an object. Linked and embedded documents are implicitly deleted when the form that contains the OLE container control is unloaded, because removing the form removes all references to the object.

Considerations When Creating Linked Objects

Linked objects pose several problems that should be accounted for when developing an application. Two important considerations to take into account are:

- Because linked files can be updated from any source, data in a linked object can change while your Visual Basic application is running.

- All users must have access to the file path named in the link.

II

OLE

If the linked file is opened by another application and changes are made and saved, the linked file in the OLE container control changes to reflect the modifications. If two users are modifying the same file, they may overwrite each other's changes.

Because the path of a linked object is needed to create the linked object, applications distributed to remote users may cause difficulty. If users plan to link to objects, the path needed to access the files stored on a remote network may be different than the path used to access a file stored on a local drive. You must account for these types of differences in your code.

Performing Multiple Actions on Objects

In the previous sections of this chapter, you learned how to control OLE controls, OLE documents, and OLE automation servers from Visual Basic. In each case, you saw how to use an object's properties and methods to control the object and change its characteristics. In each case, only one method or property was affected at a time.

Two statements are available in the Visual Basic programming language that either allow you to either perform multiple actions on a single object or allow you to perform actions on all objects within a collection. These two statements are shown in the following list:

- With...End With
- For Each...Next

Using the With...End Statement

The *With...End* statement allows you to reference a single OLE object multiple times, without explicitly referring to the object's fully qualified name each time or using a temporary variable. Suppose that you wanted to change the *Text*, *Height*, and *Width* properties of a TextBox control. You can use three separate statements as follows:

```
txtSample.Text = "New Text"
txtSample.Height = 220
txtSample.Width = 1000
```

Alternatively, you could use the With...End statement. Performing the same operation as the preceding example with the With...End statement looks like the following example:

```
With txtSample
    .Text = "NewText"
    .Height = 220
    .Width = 1000
End With
```

In the latter example, the With...End statement doesn't appear to provide much benefit over the first example beyond readability. In fact, you actually had to write two more lines of code when you used the With...End statement. When you begin to use OLE automation objects that have long object names, however, the benefits become more apparent. For example, suppose that you had an object named:

```
loOleObject.Application.Worksheet.Range.Cells(1,1)
```

You can set the *Value*, *Bold*, and *Italic* properties by using the following code:

```
loOleObject.ActiveSheet.Range.Cells(1,1).Value = 500
loOleObject.ActiveSheet.Range.Cells(1,1).Bold = True
loOleObject.ActiveSheet.Range.Cells(1,1).Italic = False
```

If you perform the same operation by using the With...End statement, your code looks like the following example:

```
With loOleObject.ActiveSheet.Range.Cells(1,1)
    .Value = 500
    .Bold = True
    .Italic = False
End With
```

Because each dot (.) operator in the code requires that Visual Basic makes another call to the OLE automation server, the second statement will execute faster than the first because fewer dot operations need to be completed. This is especially true for out-of-process OLE automation servers.

Using the For Each...Next Statement

The *For Each...Next* statement allows you to perform actions on each object in a collection. Suppose that you were using OLE automation to control an Excel workbook that contained ten worksheets. You decided that you want to print each one of these worksheets. You can make a separate call to each worksheet in the workbook as follows:

```
loExcelObject.Worksheets(1).PrintOut
loExcelObject.Worksheets(2).PrintOut
loExcelObject.Worksheets(3).PrintOut
..
..
loExcelObject.Worksheets(10).PrintOut
```

This approach is not only time consuming to you as a developer, it also is inefficient because Visual Basic must execute many dot operations. You can set up a temporary object variable and reference the worksheets collection, which in code looks like the following example:

```
Dim loWksheetCollection as Object
Dim liCounter as Integer
Dim liSheetCount as Integer

liSheetCount = loWorksheetCollection.Count

For liCounter = 1 to liSheetCount
    Worksheets(liCounter).PrintOut
Next liCounter
```

This construct is just as fast as the previous example, but requires three temporary variables. You can use the For Each...Next statement to perform the same function. Using the *Worksheets* collection and the *For Each..Next* statement, your code looks like the following example:

```
For Each Sheet in loExcelObject.Worksheets
    Sheet.PrintOut
Next
```

The general syntax of the *For Each..Next* statement is:

```
For Each element In group
    [statements]
    [Exit For]
    [statements]
Next [element]
```

Group is the name of the object collection or array, and *element* is a placeholder variable dimensioned as either *Object* or the collection's member object class. The collection can be any object collection, including collections exposed by OLE automation servers and OLE controls. OLE collections created in VB (as you will see in Chapter 6, "Creating OLE Objects"), however, cannot be used in this construct.

For more information on the For Each...Next and With...End statements, refer to the documentation included with Visual Basic.

Using the Object Browser

In this chapter you saw that applications can expose classes of many different kinds. Excel exposes an *application* class, a *worksheet* class, a *chart* class, and so on. Word exposes the *Word Basic* class and a *Document* class. How does a developer know what types of object classes an application exposes and what OLE interface attributes apply to the class?

In addition to the documentation provided with most OLE automation servers, Visual Basic provides the *Object Browser*. You can use the Object Browser to browse the interface of external OLE automation classes, such as Excel, as well as the internal object interface of your VB project (its form and class modules).

You access the Object Browser by selecting the Object Browser item from Visual Basic's View menu. Figure 5.9 shows the Object Browser.

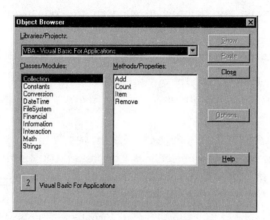

Fig. 5.9
Visual Basic's
Object Browser.

Understanding the Object Browser Interface

The Object Browser displays information about objects in a three-level hierarchy. First, the Libraries/Projects drop-down list box contains a list of all projects and libraries referenced by Visual Basic. Referencing projects and libraries is explained in a following part of this section.

After a project or library is selected from Libraries/Projects list box, the classes and modules contained within the library or project are displayed in the Classes/Modules list box.

When you select a class or module from the Classes/Modules list box, the methods and properties associated with it are displayed in the Methods/Properties list box.

Many methods and properties have an associated help topic. If a method or property has a help topic, the command button at the lower left corner of the object browser labeled with a question mark (?) is enabled. Clicking on the button displays the help topic associated with the method or property.

Pasting Properties and Methods into Your Code

Besides displaying help topics for methods and procedures, the Object Browser enables you to paste code templates for certain methods and procedures. If a method or procedure has an associated code template, the Paste button at the right side of the Object Browser is enabled.

To paste a template of Visual Basic code for a method or property into a procedure, follow these steps:

1. Place the insertion point where you want the code fragment to appear in the Code window.

2. Select the method or property in the Object Browser.

3. Click the Paste button to copy the procedure template for the selected item into the Code window.

Referencing Other Object Libraries

Before you can browse any object library or project, you must reference it. After a library or project is referenced, Visual Basic automatically displays it in the Libraries/Projects list box on the Object Browser.

A reference is a type of link between your Visual Basic application on an object library. It allows Visual Basic to look inside of the library and determine its contents. Not only can you browse a referenced OLE automation appllication, but referencing enables VB to early-bind to the object which, as mentioned earlier, enables VB to do type checking during compile-time.

To reference a object library or project, follow these steps:

1. Open the References dialog box by selecting the References item from Visual Basic's Tools menu.

2. The Reference dialog box displays a list of registered object libraries. If the object library you want to reference appears in the Available References list box, select the check box next to its name.

   If the library or project doesn't appear in the list, click the Browse button. After you locate the item, it appears in the Available References list box. You then can reference it by selecting the check box that is beside its name.

3. After the item is selected, it appears in the Libraries/Project list box of the Object Browser.

After you have created the reference, you can use the Object Browser to examine the object's interface.

From Here...

This chapter provided information on controlling OLE objects from a Visual Basic application. You now should understand what types of OLE objects VB is capable of controlling, and realize that the techniques used to control the different OLE objects are very similar.

For more information related to topics covered in this chapter, see the following:

- Chapter 3, "Understanding OLE," provides on overview of OLE.

- Chapter 8, "Architecting Tier 1: Client Applications," provides information on user services which can be used to control OLE objects.

- Chapter 12, "Advanced Coding Techniques," for more information on creating an OLE Server capable of running queries in the background.

- Chapter 14, "Architecting Error Processing," provides information on developing an error handling architecture for all aspects of your system.

- Chapter 24, "Sample Application #3: A Three-Tier Order Processing System," walks you through a sample three-tier application that controls OLE objects.

Chapter 6

Creating OLE Objects

This chapter discusses methods for designing and developing OLE automation servers, using Visual Basic. Before you begin the design and development of an OLE automation server, you first must understand what exactly is meant by the term *OLE automation server*.

After you gain an understanding of what an OLE automation server is, you will look at the types of OLE objects that exist, and we will discuss methods that you can use to design these OLE objects. After the objects are designed, this chapter will go into detail on the methods by which OLE objects and servers can be created.

In this chapter we will cover the following areas of OLE automation server design and development:

- Techniques for designing OLE automation servers

- Techniques for developing OLE automation servers

- OLE automation server design standards

- Visual Basic features for creating OLE automation servers

What Is an OLE Automation Server?

Before discussing the design and development of OLE automation server applications, you first must understand exactly what an OLE automation server is, and what benefits they can provide to application developers and users.

Definition

A Visual Basic application, or any application, is an OLE automation server when it exposes at least one object class using OLE automation. An OLE automation server is an application that provides objects to other applications.

For a Visual Basic application, at least one of its class modules is defined as either *Creatable—Single-Use* or *Creatable—Multi-Use*. The specifics of these two settings are described in following sections of this chapter.

Benefits of OLE Automation Servers

The use of OLE automation servers provides many benefits to application developers. Some of these benefits include the following:

- Capability to encapsulate common application functionality in a central location

- Capability to use common functionality without having to embed it within the application

- Capability to partition an application across multiple machines

OLE Automation servers provide the capability for common application features to be encapsulated and, therefore, more easily shared by multiple applications. These shared features or services can be located within the user or business services tiers of the three-tier application architecture, depending on the functionality they provide.

The GOLF System, for example, uses an OLE automation server to encapsulate the user login. By developing this functionality in the form of an OLE automation server, multiple-client applications can provide the consistent look and feel of the LogonMgr without reinventing the wheel. The LogonMgr is an example of an OLE automation server that must reside within the user-services tier of the three-tier architecture because, if the user hasn't yet logged in, it displays a logon form to prompt the user for a name and password. The considerations to think about when developing an OLE automation server that will graphically interact with the user are discussed in detail in following sections of this chapter.

The GOLF System's OrderMgr, on the other hand, is an example of an OLE automation server that would reside within the business-services tier of the three-tier application architecture. The OrderMgr encapsulates all of the functionality that is needed to create and maintain orders. This functionality can be made available to distributed client applications from central locations— the business servers. When updates are made to the OrderMgr, they need to be distributed only to the business servers that exist within the enterprise, not to all of the client applications. The individual client applications will have access to the update, without distributing a new version of the client software.

As you will see in later chapters of this book, OLE automation servers are key components within the services layers of a three-tier client/server architecture.

Designing OLE Automation Servers

Now that you understand what is meant by OLE automation server and OLE object, you can begin to design some OLE automation servers.

The process of designing an OLE automation server involves the following two main steps:

- Identifying objects and their hierarchical relationships
- Defining object interfaces

Taking time to perform a complete design when working with OLE automation servers pays off during development. Without a well laid out object design, the developer easily can get lost in the objects that are being created.

Defining Objects and Hierarchies

The object hierarchy is the most important design aspect of an OLE automation server. The OLE automation server's object hierarchy serves not only as a skeleton for the development of the OLE automation server, but also as documentation for other developers that may incorporate this server in their applications.

C++ developers are familiar with class hierarchies that describe *inheritance*. Inheritance is the manner in which objects are derived from similar objects, inheriting their behavior.

Visual Basic OLE automation server object hierarchies, on the other hand, describe *containment*. Containment describes how one object can contain other objects. The *GOLF System's OrderMgr*, for example, contains an *Order* object that contains a collection of *LineItem* objects.

The OLE automation server object hierarchy provides a physical representation of the objects that exist within an OLE automation server. Besides simply presenting the objects that are exposed, the hierarchy also illustrates the relationships that exist between the objects.

Figure 6.1 shows the object hierarchy for the Customer Manager OLE automation server, developed as part of the GOLF System sample application provided with this book.

Fig. 6.1
The Customer Manager's object hierarchy.

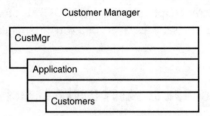

Besides defining objects and their hierarchical relationships, you also must determine which types of objects exist within the OLE automation server. Two types of objects may exist within an OLE automation server's object hierarchy—*Creatable* objects and *Dependent* objects. The difference between these object types is discussed in detail in following sections of this chapter.

Identifying Object Interfaces

An object's *interface* consists of the properties, methods, objects, and collections that are exposed to external applications. This interface provides the mechanism by which external applications interact with the OLE automation server.

Properties

Properties define the attributes of an OLE object. These attributes can be defined so that the controlling application has read-only, write-only, or read and write access to the property.

In the GOLF System, the Customer Manager's Customer object exposes all of the attributes of a customer. These attributes include the Customer Number, Name, Address, and Contact.

Methods

Methods define the actions that apply to the OLE object. These actions can be any function that applies to the object, such as changing object properties, accessing a database, or performing a calculation.

In the GOLF System, the Customer Manager's Customers object exposes both an Add method that allows the client application to add customers and an Update method that allows the client application to update customer information.

Collections

Collections are groups of OLE objects. Collections enable the client application to work with multiple OLE objects at the same time. Although a collection can be used to implement groups of different objects or data types, an OLE automation server collection typically exposes collections of identical objects.

The GOLF System's Customer Manager exposes a *Customers* collection that consists of multiple Customer objects. This object allows the controller to perform actions that are applied to a group of Customer objects. These actions include adding a customer to the collection, updating all of the objects in the collection, and retrieving a specific customer object from within the collection.

Object Instantiation

As you learned previously in the chapter, two types of objects can be exposed by an OLE automation server—Creatable objects and Dependent objects. This section goes into detail about the differences between the two objects.

Externally Creatable Objects. Within the OLE automation server application, objects can be created from any class that exists within the application. OLE client applications, however, can create objects only from the classes that the OLE automation server exposes. These exposed classes provide the blueprints for what are known as *externally creatable objects.*

An externally creatable object is an object that the OLE client application can create, using the New operator with the Set statement, calling the `CreateObject` or `GetObject` functions, or by declaring a variable, *As New.*

An example of a creatable object is the *Customer Managers Application* object. An OLE client application can create this object by using one of the following syntax examples:

```
Set CustomerMgr = CreateObject("CustMgr.Application")

Set CustomerMgr = New CustMgr.Application

Dim CustomerMgr As New CustMgr.Application
```

When one of the preceding statements is used by an OLE client to request an object, OLE automation instantiates a new object, and then provides the client with a reference to the created object. When the client is done with the reference, it sets the object variable equal to *Nothing* or allows the variable to go out of scope. OLE then tells the OLE automation server to destroy this instance of the object.

II

OLE

Making an OLE object externally creatable is discussed in detail in "Developing OLE Objects," a following section of this chapter.

Dependent Objects. Often, objects exist as an attribute of another object—for example, the collection of LineItem objects that apply to a single Order object in the OrderMgr sample application. In this example, it makes no sense for an OLE client application to be able to create an instance of the LineItems class without creating the Order object that the LineItems relate to—LineItems cannot exist separately from an Order object. These kinds of objects are known as *dependent objects*.

Although an OLE client application can access the interface of a dependent object, it cannot directly create an instance of the dependent object. Often, the OLE automation server will provide an Add method that allows the client to create a new instance of the dependent object.

As previously mentioned, the difference between creatable and dependent objects are apparent only to the controlling client application. The OLE automation server can create all internally defined classes.

Object Design Tools

Currently, few tools are available that assist in the processes of defining an object hierarchy and interface. You will begin, however, to see vendors offer object modeling tools similar to traditional database modeling tools.

You should choose a consistent mechanism to portray the OLE automation server's object model. You can create the object hierarchy diagram, as shown in figure 6.1, in a graphics drawing package, such as Shapeware's Visio or Microsoft PowerPoint. Any tool can be used, provided the end result represents the objects and their relationships to each other in an understandable manner.

One method of documenting the object hierarchy is to create a help file that shows the object hierarchy. This help file also should detail the properties and methods of each object within the hierarchy. This layout provides an easy way for the developers of OLE client applications to use the OLE automation servers that you created. The creation of an OLE help file is discussed in Chapter 15, "Adding Help to an Application." The Visual Basic Architecture section that follows in this chapter discusses the methods by which the help file can be linked to the Object Browser.

Developing OLE Objects

This section discusses the specific methods available within Visual Basic to create OLE automation servers. Throughout this section, we will use the GOLF System's Customer Manager as an example.

First, this section talks about the Visual Basic project settings that you need to set in order to develop an OLE automation server. After you have your project set up correctly, the roles that class modules, standard modules, and forms play in creating an OLE automation server are discussed. After you have the modules needed for your OLE automation server, the techniques available for creating the properties and methods that OLE clients will use to interact with the OLE automation server are discussed.

Project Settings

To use Visual Basic to create an OLE automation server, some settings must be changed in the Options dialog. These settings determine part of the OLE class name, OLE automation server's descriptive name, and the run mode that Visual Basic uses when starting the application from within the Visual Basic development environment.

From the Visual Basic Tools menu, choose Options to display the Options dialog box. In the Options dialog box, click the Project tab to display the options that need updating when creating an OLE automation server. Figure 6.2 shows the Project tab of the Visual Basic Options dialog box.

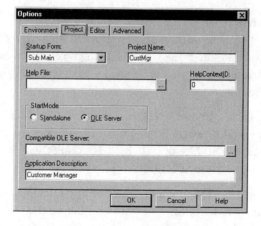

Fig. 6.2
The Visual Basic Project options used when defining OLE Automation server settings.

II

OLE

StartMode Option

The StartMode option needs to be set to OLE server. This setting only affects the way the application acts within the Visual Basic development environment. This setting has no effect on the executable file that is created for the OLE server.

Under normal circumstances, an OLE automation server is destroyed when no active references to its objects remain. In the Visual Basic development environment, the application would close immediately when it is started, not giving the developer time to switch to the test application.

When the StartMode is set to OLE Server, Visual Basic keeps the OLE server application running until the first request by a client for an instance of one of its objects.

Project Name Option

The Project Name option is used to specify the first part of any fully qualified class name when creating objects from the OLE server. This project name also is used to identify the OLE server within the Windows registry.

When the Project Name option is combined with the name of a class within the OLE automation server, a unique class name is produced. In the Customer Manager, for example, the Project Name, *CustMgr*, combined with the *Application* class produces the unique class name, *CustMgr.Application*. This unique class name can be used by the CreateObject function to obtain a reference to the Customer Manager application object.

Compile Options

Another option that is recommended, but not required, to set is the Compile option. The Advanced tab of the Options dialog box, displayed in figure 6.3, contains the option that allows the developer to determine when application compilation takes place.

As shown in figure 6.3, do not select the *Compile On Demand* option. When Compile On Demand is used, Visual Basic only compiles the application during the creation of an EXE of DLL. By deselecting this option, the application is compiled every time it's run.

Using this option, errors that would cause the application to restart, like renaming parameters to methods, can be caught before the OLE server and client are started. These kinds of development standards are discussed in greater detail in Chapter 20, "Creating Development Guidelines."

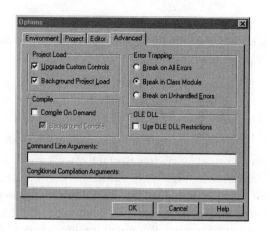

Fig. 6.3
The Advanced tab
enables you to set
additional project
options.

Class Modules

Class modules within Visual Basic have a one-to-one correspondence to the object classes that are available within the OLE automation servers that you create. As was previously mentioned in this chapter, OLE automation servers expose two basic types of objects—externally creatable and dependent objects.

When working with class modules, anything defined as Public—variables, functions, sub procedures, and property procedures—are visible to the controlling application. These Public aspects of the class module make up the class's interface, which is discussed later in the chapter.

Instancing

For OLE automation servers developed with Visual Basic, the *Instancing* property of the class module determines whether the object is an externally creatable or a dependent object. Setting the Instancing property to **Creatable Single-Use** or **Creatable Multi-Use** creates an externally creatable class. The specifics of these two settings are discussed in a following section of this chapter. Setting the Instancing property to **Not Creatable** makes this class dependent and doesn't allow controlling applications to create an instance of the class.

For all types of classes or objects exposed by an OLE automation server, the Public property of the class module must be set to True. Setting the Public property to True allows controlling applications to manipulate the object within the OLE-server object hierarchy. When the Public property is set to False, only the OLE automation server application can create an instance of the object class.

Class Events

Class modules have two events that are associated with the creation and destruction of an instance of the class.

Initialize. The Initialize event of a class module is executed when an OLE client application requests a reference to an instance of the class. This event is fired before any objects' properties are set or before the client application can execute any of its methods.

Because this event is fired every time the OLE class is instantiated, give careful thought to the code that is placed within this event. Because the forms and dialogs, for example, presented by an OLE automation server application will display on the machine where the OLE service is running, it is recommended that the Initialize event not require interaction with the end user. Although this does not present a problem for OLE automation servers located in the user-services tier, it does present a problem if it is moved to the business-services tier. Moving an OLE automation server that interacts with the user during the Initialize event from the user-services tier to the business-or data-services tier may cause the OLE automation server to appear to be hung when the client application attempts to create an instance of the server. In actuality, the OLE automation server is waiting for the user to respond to the form displayed on the server.

Terminate. The Terminate event of a class module executes after all references to its objects are released and the OLE automation server object is about to be destroyed. No additional OLE automation server code is executed after this event fires.

Again, because this event is fired every time an instance of the OLE class is destroyed, you should give careful thought to the code placed within this event. For example, it's also recommended that the Terminate event require no interaction with the end user.

With the introduction of remote automation, the client isn't required to have knowledge of the location of any OLE automation server objects that it references. Therefore, even if the OLE automation server will reside on the client machine, interactive code shouldn't be placed in the Initialize or Terminate events of the OLE automation server in case they are moved to another machine in the future.

Forms

Sometimes it's necessary for OLE automation servers to display forms to obtain information from the OLE client application's end user. Other times, an OLE automation server may be run in either of two modes:

- Interactive mode, when the user is sitting at the machine

- Hidden mode, when it is accessed by an OLE client application

This section discusses some issues the application developer needs to be aware of when creating these types of OLE automation servers.

Obtaining Information from the User

Like any other Visual Basic application, when an OLE automation server needs to obtain information from the end user, it must display forms or modal dialog boxes to obtain this information. The forms and dialogs displayed by OLE automation servers will behave differently when implemented by in-process and out-of-process servers. Because no relationship exists to handle the focus and modality between the forms exposed by different applications, a modal form displayed by an out-of-process server does not necessarily appear on top of the client application. Therefore, OLE automation servers that need to interact with the end user should be implemented as in-process OLE automation servers.

An example of this kind of OLE automation server is the Logon Manager, included with this book. The Logon Manager prompts the user for a user name and password to determine if they have access to the functionality of the application. The Logon Manager displays a modal dialog box to obtain the user name and password from the current user.

As previously mentioned in this chapter, remote automation servers provide another twist to this scenario. When an OLE automation server displays a form, the form is owned by the process in which the OLE automation server is executing. For remote automation servers, the process is executing on the remote machine, which means that the form is displayed on that remote machine, not at the client workstation.

Interactive Mode

Some OLE automation server applications can operate both as interactive client applications and OLE automation servers controlled by other client applications. Microsoft Excel is an example of this kind of application. The user can run Excel by double-clicking the Excel icon in the Windows Program Manager. In this case, Excel displays a user interface to allow the user to interact with the application. Excel also can be controlled by other OLE client applications, without displaying a visible user interface.

Visual Basic allows you to create OLE automation servers that provide the same functionality. In this case, the Visual Basic App object's read-only

StartMode property can be used to determine how the application was started. The value of StartMode identifies whether the application was started by the user double-clicking the application or by an OLE client application that requests a reference to one of its objects. The read-only value of StartMode is unaffected by the design time setting of StartMode made within the Visual Basic design environment.

Forms also affect the destruction of the OLE automation server. Visual Basic will tell OLE to destroy an instance of an OLE automation server when no controlling applications remain that hold a reference to an object of the OLE automation server and when the OLE automation server has no loaded forms.

This rule requires only that the form is loaded—not visible—to prevent OLE from destroying the instance of the object. A loaded but hidden form, for example, prevents Visual Basic from destroying the OLE automation server application.

Creating Properties

Now that the object classes that will exist within this OLE automation server have been defined and the interface requirements—if any—have been determined, we can start developing the object interface that will be exposed to client applications.

OLE automation server properties can be implemented in the following two ways:

- Public variables
- Property Procedures

Property procedures allow the developer more control over the manner in which the OLE automation server's properties are changed, and a *public variable* implementation gives the client application complete control of the property value. These two methods of implementing properties are discussed in the next section.

Public Variables

One way the properties of OLE objects are implemented is by defining Public variables within the class module that are associated with the properties to be exposed—any variable defined as Public within a class module is a property of that class. Client applications can read and write its value just as they can read and write any other value. The client application has complete control of how these properties are used.

This technique is the most basic way of creating a property, but it doesn't give the server much capability to control what is happening to the OLE object. With this implementation, for example, the server cannot prevent the client application from updating the properties with illegal values.

The Customer Manager's Customer class could have implemented its properties in this manner. The Customer class would expose properties that relate to the attributes of a customer within the GOLF System, which is implemented by declaring Public variables that represent each Customer property. In this case, the values that the client application manipulates do not require validation. If the client application updates the Name property, for example, with a series of numbers, like 123456, rather than the expected character value, Joe's Golf Shop, the system will not break:

```
'declare the object properties
Public CustomerId As Integer
Public Name As String
Public Street As String
Public City As String
Public State As String
Public Zip As String
Public Attn As String
```

All of these properties can be accessed and updated by an OLE client application.

Property Procedures

The second method of implementing a property in a class module is with property procedures. Property procedures allow the OLE automation server to have more robust control over the way in which the controlling application can manipulate the property values.

Property procedures, for example, can be used to implement properties that do the following:

- Execute code when the property is accessed

- Are read-only

- Are visible within the Object Browser

The following table lists the three types of property procedures available within Visual Basic:

Procedure	Description
Property Let	Executed when property is written with a value
Property Set	Executed when property is written with an object reference
Property Get	Executed when property is read

When properties are created by using property procedures, a private variable is created within the class module and is made accessible to the client applications through Property Let, Property Set, and Property Get methods. The following example demonstrates the implementation of the OrderDate property of the OrderMgr's Order object. In this example, the property value is kept in the private variable, prvOrderDate, which is defined in the declarations section of the Order class module:

```
'These values are read-only
Private prvOrderDate As Date
```

This property value is exposed to the client applications through the Property Get and Property Let OrderDate procedures. The Property Get procedure is defined like a public function that returns a date value that is set to the contents of prvOrderDate.

```
Public Property Get OrderDate() As Date

    OrderDate = prvOrderDate

End Property
```

The Property Let procedure is defined in a way similar to a public sub procedure that contains a single parameter, the new value of the OrderDate property.

```
Public Property Let OrderDate(OrderDate As Date)

    prvOrderDate = OrderDate

End Property
```

Property procedures allow the OLE automation server developer to create procedures that can read and write property values that use the same name. The capability to retrieve and update the property values, for example, could have been implemented by using standard Public functions and procedures. They would, however, require different names for example GetOrderDate() and SetOrderDate().

Implementing Read-Only Properties

OLE objects may need to expose properties that can be read but not modified by the controlling application.

The Customer Manager's Customer object, for example, could expose a read-only property that indicates whether or not any changes were made to the other properties of the OLE object. The property would be declared as a private variable within the class module. Declaring the variable as private prevents the OLE client application from having any visibility to the property.

```
'declare a read-only modified property
Private prvModified As Boolean
```

A property procedure must be created that allows the OLE client application to obtain the value of the property.

Dependent Objects

The OLE automation server's interface exposes dependent objects in a way similar to the way it exposes properties—through public variables or property procedures. The difference between the two ways is that the public variable or property procedure returns a value, not a reference to an object.

When the client application reads a property, the OLE automation server returns a copy of the property value. When the client application accesses a dependent object, the OLE automation server returns a reference to the object. The client application then can interact with the dependent object's interface, accessing its exposed properties and methods, which introduces the main difference between dependent objects and properties; properties cannot have additional "dot" operations to the right of the property but dependent objects can.

The GOLF System's Customer Manager provides one Externally creatable object, the Application object, and a dependent object, the Customer object. For this dependent object to be accessible to OLE client applications, the Application object must expose the Customer object.

Like property values, dependent objects can be implemented as either public variables or property procedures defined within the parent class module. In the Customer Manager example, the Customer dependent object is exposed by the Application class by using the following public variable declaration:

```
'declare the links to the Customer object
Public Customer As New Customer
```

II

OLE

The following code demonstrates how the Customer object could be implemented using a property procedure:

```
'declare the links to the Customer object
Private prvCustomer As New Customer

Public Property Get Customer() As Customer

    Set Customer = prvCustomer

End Property
```

The Customer Manager example demonstrates the common use of a dependent object. Usually, the dependent object is a reference to an instance of another class module that is defined within the OLE automation server application. This situation, however, is not a requirement; an OLE automation server can expose a dependent object that is a reference to any object, including objects exposed by other OLE automation server applications.

Creating Methods

An object's methods are implemented as procedures and functions created within the object's class module. Much like properties, only the functions and procedures that are declared as Public are available to the OLE client applications.

When a function or procedure is declared as Public in the class module, it becomes a method of the OLE object. Procedures that are used internally to the object and that are not intended to be invoked by a controlling application should be declared as Private.

Because Visual Basic supports optional parameters, methods can be created that perform differently, depending upon the parameters that are passed.

Using the Customer Manager's Customers object as an example, you can look at the LoadCustomers method, which uses an optional parameter. If the OLE client application supplies a value for the Active parameter, the selection of customers will be limited based on its value. If no value is supplied by the controlling application, all of the customers are returned.

Listing 6.1 shows the implementation of the LoadCustomers method. This code can be found on this book's companion disk, in the \CHAP24\GOLF\TIER2\CUSTMGR directory.

Listing 6.1   CUSTS.CLS—The Customers LoadCustomers method

```
Public Sub LoadCustomers(Optional Active As Variant)

Dim qryGetCustomers As rdoPreparedStatement
Dim rstGetCustomers As rdoResultset
Dim NextCustomer As Customer

Set prvCustomers = Nothing

If IsMissing(Active) Then
    Active = "%"
End If

Set qryGetCustomers = db.CreatePreparedStatement( _
                    "sp_get_customers", _
                    "{call sp_get_customers (?)}")
qryGetCustomers.rdoParameters(0).Value = Active
Set rstGetCustomers = qryGetCustomers.OpenResultset(_
                    rdOpenForwardOnly, _
                    rdConcurReadOnly)

Do Until rstGetCustomers.EOF

    Set NextCustomer = New Customer

    'add these to the collection
    With NextCustomer
        .CustomerID = rstGetCustomers.rdoColumns("CustomerID")
        .Name = rstGetCustomers.rdoColumns("Name")
        .Street = rstGetCustomers.rdoColumns("Street")
        .City = rstGetCustomers.rdoColumns("City")
        .State = rstGetCustomers.rdoColumns("State")
        .Zip = rstGetCustomers.rdoColumns("Zip")
        .Attention = rstGetCustomers.rdoColumns("AttentionName")
        .RemovedFlag = rstGetCustomers.rdoColumns("ActiveFlag")
    End With

    prvCustomers.Add Item:=NextCustomer

    'get the next customer
    rstGetCustomers.MoveNext
Loop


'close up
rstGetCustomers.Close
qryGetCustomers.Close

End Sub
```

II

OLE

When developing the methods of an OLE automation server application, the developer must decide whether to use procedures (Subs) or functions. Procedures and functions that you use to create these methods act just like other procedures or functions that exist within a Visual Basic application—functions can return a value, procedures cannot. Therefore, the decision of which to use when creating an OLE object method depends on whether or not the method needs to return a value.

Methods that return a value must be implemented as Public functions within the class module; methods that do not return a value should be implemented as Public Sub procedures.

Public Functions Versus Property Procedures

In many cases, you can use Public functions to accomplish the same functionality provided by implementing Property Get procedures. For example, the Count property of the Customer Manager's Customers object can be implemented by using the following Property Get procedure:

```
Property Get Count() As Integer

    'return the count of customer object
    'currently in the collection.
    Count = prvCustomers.Count

End Property
```

The Count property of the Customer Manager's Customers object also can be implemented by using the following Public function:

```
Function Count() As Variant

    'return the count of customer object
    'currently in the collection.
    Count = prvCustomers.Count

End Function
```

Both of these implementations return the number of objects that are in the Customer collection. So, the difference between the two implementations is that Property procedures allow the client application to retrieve and set property values using procedures with the same name. For example, the Customer object exposes a Name property that contains the name of the customer. Using property procedures, the OLE client can set the property value by using the following syntax:

```
CustObj.Name = lsNewName
```

and could retrieve the property value by using a procedure with the same name:

```
lsCurName = CustObj.Name
```

If the same functionality was implemented though Public functions and procedures, the OLE client might have to use the following syntax to set the property values:

```
CustObj.SetName = lsNewName
```

The OLE client also needs to use the following syntax to obtain the current value of the name property:

```
lsCurName = CustObj.GetName
```

> **Note**
>
> Property procedures also allow help topics to be linked to the properties when they are viewed within the Object Browser.

Linking help files to OLE objects created within Visual Basic is discussed in detail in following sections of this chapter.

Creating Collections

A *collection* is an OLE interface attribute that exposes a special array of objects. The collection object allows operations to be performed on a group of objects rather than on an object-by-object basis. Like the other OLE objects that were discussed, a class module is associated with each collection object within the OLE automation server application.

Again, like the other interface attributes that were discussed, collections can be implemented in two ways—as a public collection variable, or as a private variable that points to a special collection class. Like properties, when a collection is implemented as a public variable, the controlling application has complete control over how the collection is used, including the addition and removal of collection members. The private variable implementation, however, gives the OLE automation server developer the control over the way in which the controlling application interacts with the collection.

The collection object includes a number of default properties and methods often that are not desirable to be fully exposed to the controlling application. For this reason, collections often are implemented as private collection variables within a class module of the OLE automation server.

Implementing the collection object as a private variable within the class module allows the OLE automation server to expose to the controller only the methods and properties it wants. The controlling application cannot directly manipulate the collection object without going through the OLE automation server's methods and procedures because it cannot see the actual collection object.

The standard collection Item method, for example, is implemented as a function within the Customer Manager's Customers collection. This function simply invokes the standard collection Item method to retrieve the specified member of the collection.

```
Function Item(Key As Variant) As Customer

    'return the requested collection member
    Set Item = prvCustomers.Item(Key)

End Function
```

The Item method is a fundamental collection interface component because it provides the only mechanism by which a client application can obtain a reference to a specific member within the collection. The Item method allows the client application to request a collection member based on the "key" value used when the collection was created. The Customer Manager's Customers collection, for example, uses the customer number as the collection key.

As mentioned previously, by implementing the collection object as a private variable within the class module, the client applications are prevented from being able to make use of the powerful default Add method of the collection object. This method accepts an object of any type, and therefore can place objects into the collection that were not intended to be there, causing problems for the OLE automation server. The Add method also accepts an option key value that is used when searching the collection. By allowing the client application to access the default Add method, the OLE automation server loses control over the values placed in the key.

The collection object also can be used to implement advanced coding features, such as linked lists. By implementing a linked list as a collection, the addition, removal, and location of an element within the list is automatically done by calling a method of the collection. No additional code or development time is needed.

Although collections are slower than arrays of user-defined structures, their added power and functionality usually is well worth the decrease in performance.

Error Handling

Although error handling is discussed in more detail in Chapter 14, "Architecting Error Processing," the OLE automation server developer should be aware of the following aspects of error handling that are encountered when developing OLE automation servers:

- OLE automation servers can run on a machine other than the machine in which the OLE client application is running.

- OLE automation servers provide references to their objects to OLE clients, sudden closure of the OLE automation server leaves the client with an invalid reference.

To prevent the OLE automation server from locking up the client or leaving the client with an invalid reference to its objects when an error occurs, the OLE automation server must be developed to recover from errors when possible and notify the client of errors that it cannot handle.

An OLE automation server notifies the controlling application that an error occurred in one of two ways—it may raise an error, or it may return an error value.

Raising Errors

The preferred method of notifying the client of an error is to raise an error from within the OLE automation server application. This method uses the `RaiseError` method to generate an error exception within the client application. To the controlling application, this exception looks like any other runtime error encountered by the application. Notifying the controller in this fashion has several advantages.

First, the controlling application has the option as to how it implements its own error handling. The OLE controller can implement in-line error handling by using *On Error Goto 0* and checking the `Err` object after every method is executed. Because the `RaiseError` method of the OLE automation server generates an error in the client application, the client can use Visual Basic's *On Error Goto* construct to handle the error like any other, by placing an error handler in the procedure.

The second benefit is that, no matter how the controlling application handles the error—even if they do not—the error is returned to the client, and it presents the error to the user. If no active error handlers are present in the client application, the active calls list is traced until either an error handler is found or the application is ended.

The RaiseError method of an OLE automation server works no matter how or in what language the client application was developed because it uses OLE's error mechanisms.

Returning Errors

You can develop an OLE automation server to return a value that indicates the successful completion of a method, or the value of the error that was encountered. When this is done, an exception isn't raised within the client application. In this case, the OLE client must implement an in-line method of error processing, whereby it checks the return value of every method it executes.

If errors are going to be returned to the controlling applications, then only the error value should be returned. The method shouldn't attempt to return a result if successful and an error value if it failed; this adds unneeded complexity and confusion for both the OLE-server and client-application developers. If a method needs to return both a value or object to the client *and* a completion status, the method should require that a parameter is passed by reference that can be updated by the OLE automation server with the return value.

The controlling application shouldn't be required to determine if the return value of the method represents the result or an error code.

Chapter 14, "Architecting Error Processing," goes into detail about designing an error-processing architecture and the methods available to trap and handle errors that are encountered within an application. See Chapter 14 for specific techniques for implementing error handling in both OLE-server and OLE-client applications.

OLE-Server Design Standards

When designing OLE automation servers, it is important to keep a set of standards in mind. For application developers to easily incorporate the functionality of your OLE automation server into their applications, your server should adhere to the common standards accepted by other OLE automation servers. A consistent OLE automation look-and-feel is as important as a consistent GUI look-and-feel.

Naming Conventions

Chapter 20, "Creating Development Guidelines," discusses application development standards that you should incorporate in all applications. This section, however, briefly discusses some guidelines to follow when creating OLE automation server interfaces.

The following list describes some basic rules that you should follow when naming elements of an OLE automation server's interface.

- When possible, use entire words or syllables. It's much easier to remember entire words than abbreviations.

- Don't separate words with underscores; use mixed case.

- Use consistent names. OLE automation servers will be used by other developers and users—make the object, property, and methods names something that is meaningful to them.

- When naming collection classes, use the plural of the object name contained within the collection.

- Provide property and method names similar to those used by other OLE automation server applications.

If you follow these naming conventions, you will make it easier for other application developers to reference your OLE automation server.

Object Standards

OLE automation servers should provide a set of standard objects and name them in a manner meaningful to the user of the server. This section describes two kinds of objects found in almost all OLE automation servers—the Application object and a Collection object.

The Application Object

An *Application object* usually is defined at the highest level of an OLE automation server's object hierarchy. Application objects defined in this manner represent the executing instance of the OLE automation server.

The Application object is useful if the automation server has only one creatable object because it provides a place to identify the properties and methods of the server. The Customer Manager's Application object, for example, contains a Customers collection that provides access to the properties and methods of the Customer objects.

When the OLE automation server exposes multiple creatable objects, the Application object provides a place for the properties and methods that apply to the server as a whole to be identified. In this case, the Application object may contain a read-only Version property, denoting the compile version of the OLE automation server.

II

OLE

Because OLE automation servers can be shared by multiple controlling applications, the properties and methods must relate to the instance of the OLE automation server and not to the specific controlling application. The instancing options available when creating OLE automation servers are discussed in a following section of this chapter.

Collection Objects

Collection objects should be named as the plural of its member objects. Collections should be implemented as private collection objects, within a separate class module, which prevents the controlling applications from accessing the default properties and methods of the collection object.

Exposing the private collection object by using a class module allows the OLE automation server to perform additional checks when the standard properties and methods of the collection object are invoked by the client application. The default Add method of the collection object, for example, accepts an object and an optional key value. If the OLE automation server exposes this method through a class module, the Add method's parameters can require a specific type of object.

In the GOLF System's Customer Manager, for example, if the Customers collection exposed the default collection methods, nothing stops a client application from adding an Order object as a new member of the Customers collection. Because the Customer Manager expects the collection to contain only Customer objects, the Order object causes an error to be generated within the Customer Manager or possibly corrupt its data.

Collection objects should contain the properties and methods described in Table 6.1. The specifics of implementing these methods are discussed in a following section of this chapter.

Table 6.1 Standard Properties/Methods of a Collection

Property/Method	Description
Add	Method that adds an item to the collection
Count	Property that returns the number of items in the collection
Item	Method that returns a specific item from the collection, based on either the collection index or key value
Remove	Method that removes an item from the collection, based on the collection index or key value

Properties

No standard set of property values that all OLE objects should expose exists, except for collection and application objects. Property names, however, should subscribe to the naming conventions mentioned previously in this section.

Methods

As discussed previously, collection objects should expose a set of standard properties and methods.

For performance reasons, OLE automation objects intended for remote deployment should expose standard methods that allow the OLE client application to retrieve and set multiple properties by using a single call. Implementing methods of this nature reduce network traffic by setting or retrieving all desired property values at the same time.

The GOLF System's Customer Manager exposes the following `PropertyGet` method that has optional parameters that correspond to each of its properties. This method, shown in Listing 6.2, uses the Visual Basic `IsMissing()` function to determine which parameters were passed to the method and modifies them appropriately. The code for this procedure can be found in the \CHAP24\GOLF\TIER2\CUSTMGR directory of this book's companion disk.

Lisitng 6.2   CUST.CLS—Customer objects PropertyGet method

```
Public Sub PropertyGet(Optional CustomerID As Variant, _
                       Optional Name As Variant, _
                       Optional Street As Variant, _
                       Optional City As Variant, _
                       Optional State As Variant, _
                       Optional Zip As Variant, _
                       Optional Attention As Variant, _
                       Optional RemovedFlag As Variant)

    'Return the property values that the caller asked for
    If IsMissing(CustomerID) = False Then
        CustomerID = prvCustomerId
    End If
    If IsMissing(Name) = False Then
        Name = prvName
    End If
    If IsMissing(Street) = False Then
        Street = prvStreet
    End If
    If IsMissing(City) = False Then
        City = prvCity
    End If
```

(continues)

Lisitng 6.2   Continued

```
    If IsMissing(Zip) = False Then
        Zip = prvZip
    End If
    If IsMissing(Attention) = False Then
        Attention = prvAttention
    End If
    If IsMissing(State) = False Then
        State = prvState
    End If
    If IsMissing(RemovedFlag) = False Then
        RemovedFlag = prvRemovedFlag
    End If
```

The Customer Manager's Customer object also exposes a PropertySet method
that allows the client application to update the value of multiple properties
with only one procedure call. This method, shown in Listing 6.3, is implemented in the same manner as the PropertyGet method. This code can also
be found in the \CHAP24\GOLF\TIER2\CUSTMGR directory of this book's
companion disk.

Listing 6.3   CUST.CLS—Customer objects PropertySet procedure

```
Public Sub PropertySet(Optional Name As Variant, _
                       Optional Street As Variant, _
                       Optional City As Variant, _
                       Optional State As Variant, _
                       Optional Zip As Variant, _
                       Optional Attention As Variant, _
                       Optional RemovedFlag As Variant)

    'update the specified property values
    If IsMissing(Name) = False Then
        prvName = Name
    End If
    If IsMissing(Street) = False Then
        prvStreet = Street
    End If
    If IsMissing(City) = False Then
        prvCity = City
    End If
    If IsMissing(Zip) = False Then
        prvZip = Zip
    End If
    If IsMissing(Attention) = False Then
        prvAttention = Attention
    End If
    If IsMissing(State) = False Then
        prvState = State
    End If
```

```
    If IsMissing(RemovedFlag) = False Then
        prvRemovedFlag = RemovedFlag
    Else
        prvRemovedFlag = custUpdate
    End If

End Sub
```

Avoiding Circular References

When you develop OLE automation server applications, you should be careful not to create circular object references. Circular object references occur when one object further down in the hierarchy contains a reference to an object that exists further up the object hierarchy. Because of the way Visual Basic handles the destruction of an object, a circular reference prevents the OLE automation server from terminating. Remember that one of the criteria that Visual Basic uses to determine when to tell OLE to destroy an object is when applications no longer hold references to the OLE automation server's objects.

Using the GOLF System as an example, you can see where using a circular object reference makes sense, and how to avoid improper use. The GOLF Systems OrderMgr exposes an Order object that contains all the information about an order, including the line item information, customer information, and other order-specific information such as order date and order number. The order information can be exposed by using a reference to a LineItems collection that contains all the line items for the order; a reference to a Customer object, exposed by the CustomerMgr, and various properties that contain information such as the order number and order date.

On the surface, there appears to be no problem at this point. Suppose that the Customer object exposes a LastOrder property, which returns a reference to an Order object. Now, you have a circular reference, the CustomerMgr cannot be destroyed because the OrderMgr's Order object contains a reference to a Customer object. At the same time, the OrderMgr cannot be destroyed because the CustomerMgr's Customer object contains a reference to an Order object.

To avoid this, the Customer property of the Order object can be exposed as a standard text property that acts as a pointer to the customer information, using the Customer number for example. You can do the same for the Customer object's LastOrder property, which prevents the circular reference from occurring and allows both OLE automation servers to be destroyed when no more references to them remain.

For more information on circular references and working with them when they are needed, refer to the book, *Creating OLE Automation Servers*, supplied with Visual Basic.

Creating a Test Application

When developing an OLE automation server, you need to spend the time to create a test application. A thorough test application ensures that your OLE automation server works properly, as well as enables you to run your server interactively because an OLE automation server doesn't always have its own interface.

This section first discusses the process of designing an OLE client test application. After you have an understanding of what the test application should accomplish, you will look at the development of the test application by using the Customer Manager test client as an example. This section is intended to provide guidelines for your own testing applications—it isn't written as a comprehensive authority on what is or is not a solid system-testing approach.

Designing the Test Client

The goal of the test client is to ensure that the OLE automation server's interface—its properties, methods, dependent objects, and collections—work correctly. The test client can be as simple or complex as needed to accomplish this goal.

At the simplest, you can develop the test client as a series of procedures that interact with the OLE automation server and its exposed objects. These procedures can pass hard-coded test values to the parameters of the methods. You don't always need to get fancy with the test application.

In some cases, you may want to test the OLE automation server interface more completely, using dynamically changing values. In this case, you should develop a test client that provides GUI elements such as test boxes that are associated with each parameter that is passed to the automation server.

Now that you have an understanding of the goal of our test client application and the different complexity levels that can be provided, now take a look at the test client application that was used to develop the GOLF system's Customer Manager.

A Sample Test Client

The Customer Manager Test Client application was developed by using the simple technique described in the preceding section. The client interface isn't fancy, and the values being passed to the OLE automation server are hard coded. Figure 6.4 shows the test client application.

Fig. 6.4
The Customer Manager Test Client application.

To test the OLE automation server application, first run the OLE automation server within Visual Basic. This temporarily registers the OLE automation server with Windows and provides the Typelib and other runtime files that are needed for a controlling application. Next, start another instance of Visual Basic and open your test client project.

For the test client to reference the OLE automation server using early binding, Visual Basic must be told where to find the information about the interface to the OLE automation server. You tell Visual Basic where to find this information by adding a reference to the OLE automation server in the test instance of Visual Basic. To do so, select the References option from the Visual Basic Tools menu, which displays the References dialog box shown in figure 6.5. Scroll through the list of Available References until you find the OLE automation server application—in this case, the Customer Manager. Add a reference to this object by selecting the object and checking the checkbox.

Adding a reference to the object allows Visual Basic to check the interfaces available when compiling an OLE client application that references an object. The reference added here was to the temporarily registered OLE automation server running in the other instance of Visual Basic—if the test client application is compiled at this time, it would reference the OLE automation server's temporary registration, which would become invalid when the instance running in Visual Basic is stopped. Refer to Chapter 5, "Controlling OLE Objects," for a discussion of controlling OLE automation servers.

Fig. 6.5
Visual Basic
References
dialog box.

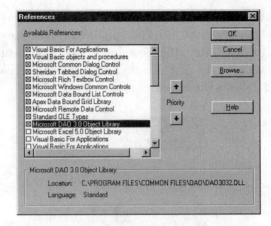

Now that you have a reference to the OLE automation server, you can begin to develop the client procedures that test the interfaces of the server. The following three aspects of the OLE automation server need to be tested:

- Creation of the OLE automation server's externally creatable objects

- Access to the methods exposed by each object

- Termination of the object references

Testing Object Creation

The GetObject button on the client application tests the capability to create an instance of the OLE automation server's externally creatable object. If the object is successfully instantiated, a message is displayed on the client form.

```
Private Sub cmdGetObject_Click()

'so we get to step through w/out remembering break points
Stop

Set CustomerMgr = CreateObject("CustMgr.Application")
CustomerMgr.Initialize UserId:="MyUser", Password:="MyPassword"

Print "Got It"


End Sub
```

Now that you have an instance of the externally creatable object, you can test the interfaces that the object provides.

Testing the Object's Methods

The Customer Manager exposes a dependent object that OLE clients can use to maintain customer information in the GOLF System. The Customers collection represents a group of customer entities defined in the GOLF system, exposing a set of properties that describe the customers.

The Customers collection also exposes methods that allows the OLE client application to insert, delete, and update customers in the system. The cmdModifyCustomers button on the test application tests these methods. This code, shown in Listing 6.4, is located in the \CHAP24\GOLF\TIER1\TEST\TCUSTMGR directory, on this book's companion disk.

Listing 6.4   TCUSTMGR.FRM—Prodcedure to test the CustMgr interfaces

```
Private Sub cmdModifyCustomers_Click()

    'Properties/Methods
    Dim NewCustomer As Object

    'remove the second  customer
    CustomerMgr.Customers.Remove 2

    'Modify existing customer 1
    CustomerMgr.Customers.Item(1).Attention = "Steve Lutz"
    CustomerMgr.Customers.Item(1).City = "Louisville"


    'add a new customer
    Set NewCustomer = CustomerMgr.Customers.Add
                        (Name:="Bear Slide", _
                         Street:="1234 Main", _
                         City:="Indianapolis", _
                         State:="IN")

    Print "Modified"
End Sub
```

This procedure uses methods exposed by the Customers collection object to retrieve the first customer object in the collection. After the customer has been updated and a new customer has been added, the LoadCustomers method of the Customers collection is called and the number of customers retrieved is displayed on the form.

Testing OLE Server Termination

The final aspect of an OLE automation server to test is the Termination of the server. When no more references are open to any of the OLE automation servers objects, OLE tells the OLE automation server to terminate and destroy that instance.

II

OLE

The test client verifies that the Customer Manager server terminates properly by allowing the object reference to go out of scope. The test client declares the following variable at the form level, so that it is available to all of the procedures of the test application:

```
Dim CustomerMgr As Object
```

When the application is closed, this form level variable goes out of scope, closing the open reference to the OLE automation server. If an error occurs while the OLE automation server is being destroyed, the client application cannot end properly.

Now, you have a complete test application that you can use while developing your OLE automation server.

Debugging OLE Server Applications

You can debug the OLE automation servers that you create with Visual Basic by using multiple instances of Visual Basic. Use one instance to run the OLE automation server application and the second instance to run the test application. Both Visual Basic instances have full debugging capabilities, just as they do for normal client applications.

Using Multiple Instances of Visual Basic

When using multiple instances of Visual Basic to debug OLE automation server applications, you can place break points in both instances of Visual Basic. Focus switches between the instances of Visual Basic as the code execution changes from instance to instance. When the OLE automation server application code encounters a break point, for example, focus switches to the instance of Visual Basic that is running the OLE automation server.

When debugging OLE automation server applications that employ the Terminate event, remember that this event will fire in the development environment only if the End statement is used. Clicking the Stop button on the toolbar or selecting End or Restart from the Run menu will not cause this event to fire.

Similar to what happens when debugging any Visual Basic applications, artificial changes in focus between the development environment and the application may prevent your code from behaving exactly as you may expect. These artificial changes are especially true when dealing with activate and focus events.

Using Break On Error

The Visual Basic Options dialog provides the capability to alter the manner in which Visual Basic enters break mode when an error occurs within an OLE automation server application. This capability is set by using the Error Trapping option of the Advanced tab on the Options dialog box.

The Advanced tab of the Options dialog, illustrated in figure 6.3, provides the following three options for the level of error trapping that can be set within the development environment:

- Break on All Errors
- Break In Class Module
- Break on Unhandled Errors

These options refer to any error encountered within an OLE automation server application, including errors that the OLE automation server specifically raises using the Err object's `Raise` method. The following section discusses how each setting affects the manner in which Visual Basic enters break mode when errors are encountered in the OLE automation server.

Break On All Errors

When the *Break On All Errors* option is selected and an error occurs within the OLE automation server, the OLE automation server project is given focus and the procedure where the error occurred is displayed, with the line that caused the error highlighted. Visual Basic always enters break mode when an error occurs within the OLE automation server, even if an active error handler exists within the procedure that encountered the error.

Break In Class Module

When an error occurs within the OLE automation server and the *Break In Class Module* option is selected, Visual Basic enters break mode only if no active error handler exists within the procedure that encountered the error. In this situation, the line of code that encountered the error is highlighted.

If an active error handler exists for the procedure that encountered the error, the error handler is invoked, and Visual Basic goes into break mode only if an error is raised within the error handler.

Break On Unhandled Errors

When *Beak On Unhandled Errors* is selected, Visual Basic never enters break mode in the OLE automation server. This occurs because of the manner in which OLE automation servers interact with the controlling application. OLE automation servers are components of the application that controls them—if any error encountered within the OLE automation server does not contain an active error handler, Visual Basic searches back through the active calls list, right into the controlling application. This process automatically passes back the error to the controlling application. Because of this, there never is an Unhandled Error in an OLE automation server. As mentioned previously in this chapter, this is not a recommended way to handle errors within OLE automation server applications.

Visual Basic Development Environment

Now that you have an understanding of how OLE automation server applications are developed, you will take a look at some features of the Visual Basic development environment that pertain specifically to the creation of OLE automation server applications.

Compatible EXE

As you saw in figure 6.2, the Visual Basic Project Options dialog provides a number of options used when creating OLE automation server applications. One option not discussed in the preceding section is the *Compatible OLE automation server* value. The *Compatible OLE server* value points to an existing OLE automation server application (EXE or DLL) with which this OLE automation server needs to remain compatible. Visual Basic uses this value to inform the developer when they are about to make a modification that will render the OLE automation server incompatible with the previous version. This compatibility is based on the OLE version discussed in a following part of this section, not the project version.

This setting helps ensure that the interface of the OLE automation server remains compatible as changes are made to the application, which is important because, as long as the OLE automation server's interface doesn't change, client applications written for previous versions of the OLE automation server will continue to work.

Visual Basic has three levels of OLE automation server version compatibility. The specifics of each level, shown in the following list, are discussed in this section:

- Version Identical
- Version Compatible
- Version Incompatible

Version Identical

A new version of an OLE automation server application is considered *Version Identical* when the objects interface is unchanged. In this case, the modifications made to the OLE automation server do not affect the way in which the controlling applications will interact with the objects.

The OLE automation server can be distributed, and existing controlling applications do not need to be modified or recompiled to work with the new OLE automation server.

Version Compatible

A new version of an OLE automation server application is considered *Version Compatible* when additional object interfaces are added, but the previously existing interfaces remain unchanged. This compatability includes adding new properties and or methods to the object interface.

Again, here, the OLE automation server can be distributed, and existing controlling applications do not need to be modified or recompiled to work with the new OLE automation server. New OLE controller applications developed and compiled with the New version of the OLE automation server work only with the current and later versions. Version compatible is only upwardly compatible.

Version Incompatible

A new version of an OLE automation server application is considered *Version Incompatible* when one or more aspects of its object interface are changed. The following list includes a number of ways in which an OLE automation server can become incompatible with an existing version:

- Changing the project name
- Changing the name of a Public class module
- Removing a Public class module
- Removing or making Private an existing Public property
- Changing the name of a Public variable, procedure, or function
- Changing the name, data type, or order of the parameters to a Public procedure or function

To see the effects of making a version incompatible, open the Customer Manager project in Visual Basic and select the Project Options dialog box. Make sure that the *Compatible OLE Server* value is set to refer to the current OLE server executable file. If so, change the Project Name from CustMgr to

`CustomerMgr` and click OK. Try to create a new executable file. The dialog shown in figure 6.6 is displayed, informing you that the changes you made will make the new OLE server executable Version Incompatible with the previous version.

Fig. 6.6
The Version
Incompatible
message box.

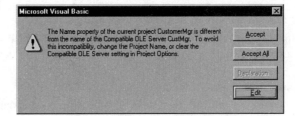

When you need to make modifications that will render the new version incompatible with the previous release of the OLE automation server application, evaluate other alternatives. Often, for example, a modification requires that an additional parameter is passed to a method that wasn't planned for in the initial design. If the modification implements an enhancement and not a bug fix, the modified parameter list can be implemented for a new method, leaving the existing method unchanged.

The *Compatible OLE Server* setting should be set immediately after the first time the OLE automation server is compiled for production. This setting ensures that all modifications made to the OLE automation server application after the production build are either Version Identical or Version Compatible. If a change is made that renders the new version incompatible, Visual Basic notifies the developer of the change that causes the version compatibility problem.

A good rule to use to ensure that future versions of an OLE automation server are always compatible and will not break existing client applications is to always add to the interface and never remove.

The following section discusses some specific ways that OLE uses to determine if a version is compatible and how Visual Basic handles these mechanisms.

Versioning

Versioning plays a large role when developing OLE automation server applications because multiple OLE client applications can use the features of a single OLE automation server. This section discusses the difference between the Project version and the OLE version and also the manner in which Visual Basic and OLE automatically set the *version* of an OLE automation server application.

Project Versus OLE

The Visual Basic project version is specified in the Option dialog in figure 6.7, available by selecting the Options button on the *Make Executable* screen. The Version Number specified on this screen is placed in the executable file that Visual Basic creates. This version number is referred to as the OLE automation server's file version. The file version can be used by the Setup Wizard to determine if a newer version of the OLE automation server is replaced by an older version.

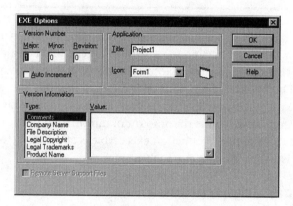

Fig. 6.7
The Visual Basic
EXE options
dialog box.

The OLE version number is completely separate and unrelated to the file version specified in the EXE options. Visual Basic maintains the OLE version number within the type library for the OLE automation server.

OLE uses the type library for the OLE automation server to determine what interfaces, properties, and methods are available to client applications. This library also is where OLE obtains the version number used when a client attempts to instantiate an instance of the object.

OLE client applications that are compiled with a reference to an OLE automation server have the type library version number compiled into its executable. An OLE automation error occurs if the client application attempts to access an OLE automation server with the same name but an incompatible version number.

The type libraries version number is composed of two parts, the major version and the minor version number. OLE uses these numbers to determine the level of version compatibility that exists between two versions of the OLE automation server.

As described in the preceding section, three levels of version compatibility exist for OLE automation server applications. Table 6.2 lists the manner in which the type libraries version number is affected at each compatibility level.

II

OLE

Table 6.2 Type Library Version Update Rules	
Compatibility Level	**Effect on Type Library Version**
Version Identical	The same type library version number is used
Version Compatible	Type library version number is updated, but kept compatible with the prior version
Version Incompatible	New type library version number that is made incompatible with the preceding version

Because the type library version numbers are incremented every time either a version compatible or a version incompatible executable is created, it is recommended that the production executable should be kept separate from the incremental builds. The production OLE automation server executable should be pointed to as the compatible server only when the next production build is being created, which limits the amount of information in the type library and ensures that the new production executable is at the expected compatibility level with the existing executable.

Temporary Registration

For an OLE automation server to be used by a client application, an entry for the OLE automation server first must be made in the Windows registry. To prevent corrupting the Windows registry with multiple entries for OLE automation server applications while they are developed, Visual Basic performs a temporary registration of the OLE object when used in the development environment. This registration only exists while the OLE automation server application is running within an instance of Visual Basic.

Visual Basic makes a permanent entry in the Windows Registry to register the OLE automation server when it makes an executable file by using the *Make EXE File...* option in Visual Basic. The next section describes the other OLE automation related files that are created when an OLE automation server's executable is made.

Runtime Files

Visual Basic creates two runtime files needed for your OLE automation server application when it compiles the executable or DLL by using the *Make EXE File...* option. Specifically, Visual Basic creates a type library file (.TLB) and a Visual Basic registration file (.VBR).

OLE automation server type libraries contain descriptions of the objects and their interfaces that are provided by the OLE automation server application. The type library also contains the OLE version number that will be compiled into any OLE client application that contains a reference to the OLE automation server application.

The Visual Basic registration file is used when an OLE automation server is installed for remote use. Specifically, this file allows the Component Manager to set the remote/local setting of the OLE automation server. This file contains all of the information necessary to update the Windows registry with the references to the Remote Automation Proxy and the network address of the OLE automation server.

Visual Basic Architecture

Now that you are familiar with the methods available for designing and developing OLE automation server applications with Visual Basic, we will look at some of the other options available within Visual Basic that apply specifically to OLE automation servers.

DLLs Versus EXEs OLE Components

Visual Basic can create OLE automation servers that are deployed as .EXE files and servers that are deployed as .DLL files. The deployment method affects the way in which the OLE automation server is instantiated when a create object request is issued by the controlling application.

OLE automation DLLs are instantiated as in-process servers when a request is made from the controller. As this name implies, in-process servers run within the same process as the OLE controlling application that instantiated the object.

OLE automation EXEs are instantiated as out-of-process servers when a request is made from the client application. Again, as the name implies, an out-of-process server runs under a separate process than the client application that requested the reference to the object.

Table 6.3 illustrates the differences between the capabilities of OLE automation servers that are implemented as in-process servers and OLE automation servers that are implemented as out-of-process servers.

II

OLE

Table 6.3 In-Process Versus Out-of-Process Servers

Server Type	Multitask with Controller	Multitask with Other Object Instances	Instances Share Global Memory
In-Process Single-Use	No	Yes	No
Out-Of-Process Single-Use	Yes	Yes	No
Out-Of-Process Multi-Use	Yes	No	Yes

Figure 6.8 demonstrates the scenario of two controller, client applications accessing an OLE automation server, the WidgetMgr. In the first scenario, the WidgetMgr was created as an in-process OLE automation server. In this situation, each controlling application will obtain a reference to its own instance of the OLE automation server that runs within the controlling applications process.

The second scenario demonstrates the same situation, except that the WidgetMgr was created as a Multi-Use out-of-process OLE automation server. In this case, both controlling applications are given a reference to the same instance of the OLE automation server. Because Visual Basic OLE automation servers are single-threaded, the requests from the two controlling applications are processed serially.

The final scenario illustrates two controlling applications accessing the WidgetMgr, which was created as a Single-Use out-of-process OLE automation server. Like the first scenario, each controlling application will be given a reference to its own instance of the OLE automation server. Because the WidgetMgr was created as an out-of-process server, the operating system is capable of multitasking the processes.

In-process servers execute about 20 to 100 times faster than out-of-process servers because of the manner in which OLE handles memory. This increased performance occurs because OLE must perform context switches within memory when passing data between OLE client applications and out-of-process OLE automation servers.

If in-process servers provide such an increase in performance, why implement an out-of-process OLE automation server? There are two instances where implementing an out-of-process server is necessary:

- The OLE automation server is shared by multiple client applications
- The OLE automation server is accessed via Remote Automation

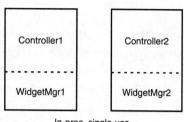

Fig. 6.8
The effect of Single
Use versus Multi-
Use on in-process
and out-of-process
servers.

In-proc, single-use

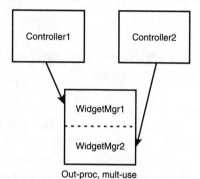

Out-proc, mult-use

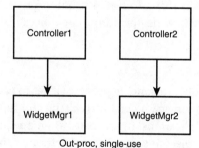

Out-proc, single-use

OLE automation servers that need to provide information to multiple client applications from within the same instance must be implemented as an out-of-process OLE automation server. Because in-process OLE automation servers run within the same process as the OLE client application, other client applications have no visibility to this instance of the server.

Any OLE automation server to be accessed by using Remote Automation must be implemented as an out-of-process OLE automation server. Remote Automation is incapable of supporting in-process OLE automation servers because, as mentioned previously, they run within the same process as the OLE client application. This process isn't running off the machine on which the remote OLE automation server application resides.

II

OLE

Instancing

Instancing refers to how an OLE automation server responds to a request for an object reference from an OLE client application, briefly described in the preceding section. Visual Basic provides the capability to specify the following three ways that an OLE automation server can be created:

- Creatable Single-Use

- Creatable Multi-Use

- Not Creatable

How OLE automation server's objects are created is specified by setting the Instancing property of the class module.

Creatable Single-Use

When the class module's Instancing property is set to `Creatable Single-Use`, instances of the class can be created by the OLE automation server and OLE client applications. When a request is made for a reference to the OLE object, a separate instance of the OLE automation server is started.

OLE automation servers that are created as out-of-process Creatable Single-Use can be multitasked by the operating system because each instance will run in its own process.

Creatable Multi-Use

When the class module's Instancing property is set to `Creatable Multi-Use`, instances of the class can again be created *by* the OLE automation server and also by OLE client applications. In this case, when a request is made for a reference to an OLE object, it's supplied by a currently running copy of the OLE automation server. If no current copy of the OLE automation server is running, one is started to satisfy the request.

As mentioned throughout this chapter, Visual Basic is incapable of creating multithreaded OLE automation applications. When an OLE automation server is defined as Creatable Multi-Use, all requests to the automation server are processed in a serial fashion.

Not Creatable

When the class module's Instancing property is set to `Not Creatable`, instances of the class can be created only by the OLE automation server. OLE clients cannot create an instance of this class.

Not Creatable class modules often are used when creating dependent objects within a hierarchy.

DoEvents

DoEvents is a dangerous function for any application developed with Visual Basic because of the effect that it can have on the execution of the application. DoEvents within OLE automation servers becomes even more complex because multiple controlling applications can access the same instance of an OLE automation server at the same time.

Visual Basic creates single-threaded OLE automation servers, which means that an OLE automation server defined as Creatable Multi-Use will process client requests in a serial manner. When a DoEvents statement is encountered, the operating system is allowed to process additional requests that are pending, which allows the OLE automation server to begin processing the next client request in the queue. If the OLE automation server relies on the values contained within global variables, the results of the server could be altered because multiple client requests are being processed.

Making OLE Server Applications Object Browser Friendly

The OLE Object Browser is a powerful and useful tool when creating applications that make use of OLE automation servers. The Object Browser provides the application developer with the capability to view an OLE automation server's object hierarchy, as well as the properties and methods associated with its objects.

In Chapter 5, "Controlling OLE Objects," you learned about techniques for taking advantage of the Object Browser when developing OLE client applications. This section discusses the methods available within Visual Basic to make your OLE automation server applications more Object Browser friendly.

Visual Basic provides the capability to provide the following information about your OLE automation server application to the Object Browser:

- Description of the OLE automation server

- Descriptions of properties and methods of each object

- Capability to link help file topics associated with objects, properties, and methods

Specifying the Help File

To specify the help file for an OLE automation server developed within Visual Basic, select Options from the Visual Basic Tools menu. Select the Project tab, which displays the Visual Basic project Options dialog, which was shown in figure 6.2.

II

OLE

In the Help File field, specify the name and path of the help file that is associated with this OLE automation server. In the HelpContextID field, specify the context ID for the help topic to display when the user views the OLE automation servers object hierarchy in the Object Browser.

Entering Descriptions and Linking Help Topics

To enter descriptions for the objects and methods within the OLE automation server, open the Visual Basic Object Browser and select the OLE automation server project in the Libraries/Projects combo box. Select an object in the Classes/Modules list and click the Options button. Options displays the Member Options dialog (see fig. 6.9). In the description field, enter the text that describes the selection object. To link a help topic to this object, enter the Help topic ID in the Help Context ID field.

Fig. 6.9

The Object Browser's Member Options dialog, used to link descriptions and help to the object interface.

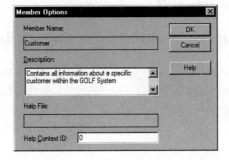

Click OK to return to the Object Browser. Now when you select the object, the description text should appear in the panel at the bottom of the form. Repeat this process for all the objects, properties, and methods exposed by the OLE automation server.

Chapter 15, "Adding Help to an Application," goes into more detail about creating help files that you can use with OLE automation servers.

Implementing Asynchronous Processing

The capability to process long application functions in the background has long been a desirable trait of client applications. The technique that allows the client machine to continue with other tasks while a long running process works in the background often is referred to as *asynchronous processing*. OLE automation provides two mechanisms by which you can achieve asynchronous processing—callbacks and polling.

When an application handles large tasks in an asynchronous fashion, the end-users are given back control of the computer, which allows them to continue working while the task is being completed. Running process in the background and returning control to the client application prevents the user from seeing the infamous hourglass.

Visual Basic 4.0 cannot create multi-threaded OLE automation servers—to implement asynchronous processing, the tasks must be spread across multiple processes. With this approach, the multitasking is handled by the operating system (Windows 95 or Windows NT). Also, the asynchronous processing techniques can be used only with out-of-process servers because in-process OLE automation servers run within the same process as the controlling application.

The following sections discuss techniques for implementing both methods of asynchronous processing.

Implementing Callbacks

Callbacks refers to a technique for implementing asynchronous processing in which the OLE automation server is passed a reference to the client application. The OLE automation server gives control to back to the client application while it processes the client's request. When the OLE automation server is done processing, it calls a method of the client application to complete the request. At a high level, you can implement a callback by taking the following steps:

1. Client application passes an object reference to the OLE automation server, which the server remembers, and then gives control back to the client.

2. The OLE automation server contains a timer that wakes up and calls an agreed-upon method on the client to perform an action.

3. The client's callback method processes the data.

Callbacks can be considered a reversal of roles. The OLE client passes a reference to itself to the OLE automation server. The OLE automation server wakes up and calls a method of the OLE client when data needs to be processed. The client becomes the server, and the server becomes the client.

The client and server in this scenario need to agree on only the name of the callback procedure in the client application.

II

OLE

It's a good idea to use the specific OLE client object type when declaring variables within the OLE callback server, not the generic *Object* datatype. This use ensures that object type errors will be caught at compile time rather than at run time.

If, for example, the OLE automation server is going to place data into a Microsoft Excel worksheet object, it might use the Cells collection of the worksheet object. If the application passes an Excel Workbook object rather than a Worksheet object, an OLE Automation error will occur because no Cells collection of a Workbook object exists. If the specific Excel Worksheet data type is used to declare the parameters and variables, this error will be caught at compile time. If the generic Object data type is used, the error will not be discovered until the application is running.

Visual Basic ships with a sample OLE automation server application that demonstrates this callback technique. The OLE automation server tracks the current time, calling back the client application at the defined interval and giving it the current time. The client application uses the AddObjectReference method of the OLE automation server to both register itself and set up the callback. The OLE automation server uses the TellTime method of the client application to return the current time. An important note: the TellTime procedure must be made Public so that it can be called by the OLE automation server by using the following code, located in the Callbacks sample application supplied with Visual Basic:

```
Public Function AddObjectReference(Caller As Object) As Boolean
    On Error GoTo AddObjectReferenceError

    Set gObjRef = Caller
    frmMain.Timer1.Enabled = True
    AddObjectReference = True
    gbConnected = True
    Exit Function

AddObjectReferenceError:
    MsgBox Error$, vbOKOnly + vbExclamation, "AddObjectReference -
    ➥ Error" & Str$(Err)
    AddObjectReference = False
    Exit Function
End Function

Public Sub TellTime(sCurTime As String)

    frmCBCli.lblTime.Caption = sCurTime
End Sub
```

Polling

The second method for implementing asynchronous processing in an OLE application is to use a *polling mechanism*. In this scenario, the OLE automation server contains a property value that indicates when data exists to be processed. The client application will contain a timer that wakes up and checks the value of the OLE automation server's property. If the property indicates that data is to be processed, the client application retrieves it; if not, it goes back to sleep.

This technique is similar to the callback process; the OLE automation server stops processing and wakes up by using a timer event and does more processing. The difference between these two techniques is that, when the server is done processing, it sets a flag or updates a state variable rather than issuing a callback to indicate that it is done processing—the client application is required to proactively check the state variable to determine if the OLE automation server has completed the task.

This technique's main advantages are that there doesn't have to be an agreed-upon method name established in the client application and in the remote automation environment, and that the Remote Automation Manager doesn't have to be run on both the client workstation and the server. Because this technique doesn't require the client application to create an object for the OLE automation server to call, it works with client applications that cannot create their own objects, such as Excel VBA applications.

The main disadvantage of this technique is that the client application is responsible for checking the status indicator. In this case, the polling logic must be placed in the client application and, therefore, cannot be changed as easily.

From Here...

This chapter described how to use Visual Basic to design and develop OLE automation servers. For more information about the common aspects of creating OLE automation servers, review the following chapters:

- Chapter 5, "Controlling OLE Objects," for more information about using the Object Browser.

- Chapter 14, "Architecting Error Processing," for more information on handling and returning errors from OLE automation servers.

- Chapter 15,"Adding Help to an Application," for more information about creating help files that you can use with your OLE automation servers.

## Chapter 7

Managing OLE Objects

Chapters 5, "Controlling OLE Objects," and 6, "Creating OLE Objects," showed how to control and create OLE objects. This chapter shows how to manage OLE objects within the context of the Visual Basic Enterprise.

OLE is sometimes difficult to configure, often requiring in-depth understanding and the use of additional tools. In this chapter, you learn how to use:

- The registry
- The Registry Editor
- The Component Manager
- Remote automation
- The Remote Automation Connection Manager
- Additional OLE management techniques

The Registry and OLE

Data is stored in the *registry*, in the form of hierarchical trees. Each node in the tree is known as a key. The registry hierarchy is analogous to a file system—each key can contain both subkeys (analogous to directories) and data entries (analogous to files).

Applications use the registry in Windows 95 and Windows NT much in the way they use .INI files—as a centrally located database where information about the computer is stored.

Each key has zero or more values associated with it. Values have the following multiple attributes:

II

OLE

■ **Name**—Identifies the value

■ **Type**—Defines the type of data stored in the particular value, such as string, binary, or DWORD

■ **Data**—Specifies the data associated with the value

The registry has a number of pre-defined entry or top-level points, known as *hives*. OLE class information, for example, is contained subordinate to the HKEY_CLASSES_ROOT hive. This handle is actually an alias for HHEY_LOCAL_MACHINE\Software\Classes.

Registry Configuration Files

There are many types of files that relate to the registry: .VBR, .REG, .OLB, .TLB, .EXE, .DLL, and .OCX files.

EXE and DLL files can be OLE automation servers. EXE files are out-of-process servers (they operate in a different process as the controlling application), and DLL files are in-process servers (they operate in the same process as the controlling application). Often, these files are all you need to register the server in the registry—they contain the special registry resource information. An EXE file, for example, is often self registering, and a DLL file often can be added as a reference to the Object Browser. Likewise, OCX files also may contain interface information.

A REG file is a text file that contains information about what entries need to be written to the registry. When you run a REG file as a command-line argument with REGEDIT, it reads this "script" to determine what entries it should make to the registration database. Most applications no longer use REG files, because they can "self-register" at startup. An example of self-registering apps are OLE automation servers created with VB, Office 95 applications, and MFC OLE applications written with the AppWizard.

OLB and TLB files are type libraries. These files describe the object's interface without actually requiring the object to be present on the system. VBR files are special types of REG files that are used for Remote Automation.

For more information on OLE and the registry, see the following reference materials:

■ Microsoft Developer's Network (MSDN), which contains *Inside OLE 2*

■ The *OLE Programmer's Reference* from Microsoft

Browsing OLE Registry Entries

This section gives you a feel for what goes on in the registry when an OLE automation server is registered. It isn't comprehensive—instead, this section is intended as a starting point for debugging OLE server registry entries.

Most of the information relating to OLE automation servers is contained in they HKEY_CLASSES_ROOT key. Under this key all the registered classes on the computer are listed, as well as three special keys: *CLSID*, *Interface*, and *TypeLib*.

Interface and TypeLib keys aren't particularly useful for the VB developer, but the CLSID key is.

You can find the CLSID entry for a particular object class by selecting the object class in the registry editor, looking at its CLSID value, and then finding this key in the HKEY_CLASSES_ROOT\CLSID section. All kinds of registration information relating to the class is stored here, such as remote-automation authentication level, the associated TypeLib, and the remote-automation protocol.

Registering Objects

When you register an object, you place the appropriate information on the object into the registry. This information addresses questions such as the following:

- Where is the object file located?

- Should the object be executed locally or remotely?

- If executed remotely, what protocol and security should it use?

- Where to find interface information about the class?

Conversely, the process of unregistering a class is removing the class information from the registry.

Usually, components are registered automatically, either when the component is executed, when it is installed from a setup application, or with some of the utilities, like the Component Manager, described in this chapter. Components also should be unregistered with these tools.

Sometimes, however, and errant program may cause the registry to become corrupted. The registry, for example, might contain duplicate CLSID entries or CLSID entries with no class parent. In these cases, you can use the registry editor to debug and correct the situation.

Registry Editor

The registry database stores information regarding the way in which the computer is configured. In particular, the registry database maintains information regarding OLE object configuration.

The Registry Editor (RE) is a tool that enables you to manually change settings in a computer's system registry. You usually should not need to edit a computer's system registry manually with the Registry Editor. Most application programs read from and write to the registry automatically.

The RE is useful for the following two procedures:

■ To view existing registry settings for debugging purposes

■ To change registry entries that have become corrupted

This section is presented early in this chapter to help you gain familiarity with the Registry Editor for the first reason. With this information, you can examine how the registry entries change as OLE objects are managed. After you are familiar with the RE, for example, you can use it to see the differences in registry entries for a local versus remote automation servers.

The second reason for using the Registry Editor is less common. Usually, an application and the operating system maintains registry entries correctly. Occasionally, however, registry entries become corrupt or are left in an inconsistent state. If the application or operating system can't correct the situation, you may need to go into the Registry Editor to fix the problem manually.

You shouldn't manually edit the registry unless absolutely necessary. Careless changes made to the registry can render the computer non-functional. Take extreme care when editing registry entries.

Registry Editor Overview

This chapter focuses its discussion and examples on the Windows 95 registry and Registry Editor. At the end of the chapter, you explore the differences between Win16 and WinNT registries and Registry Editors.

The registry is stored in two files—SYSTEM.DAT and USER.DAT. The Registry Editor is an application named REGEDIT.EXE, located in your Windows directory (WINDOWS). REGEDIT.EXE isn't automatically placed in the Start Menu by Windows Setup because it is an advanced utility. Users who don't know what they are doing can easily put their machine out of commission.

When you execute the RE, you are automatically editing both USER.DAT and SYSTEM.DAT. When the Registry Editor starts up, you see two panes—the key pane on the left and the value pane on the right. Much like Explorer or File Manager, the key pane on the left allows you to navigate a hierarchical list of keys (see fig. 7.1).

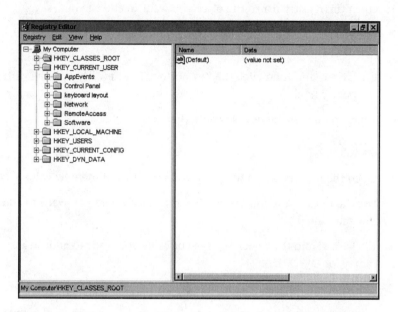

Fig. 7.1
The Win95 Registry Editor. A hierarchical list of keys is navigated in the left pane, and their values appear in the right pane.

Keys are analogous to Folders in the Explorer. Keys contain either values or other keys. Values, analogous to files in the Explorer, are the entities that the keys store.

Each value is composed of two parts, a *value name* and *value data*. The value name is the identifier of the piece of information; the value data is the value assigned to the value name.

At the top level of the key pane are the hive keys. Examples of hive keys are HKEY_CURRENT_USER and HKEY_LOCAL_MACHINE. All OLE class configuration can be found under the HKEY_CLASSES_ROOT hive key.

Changing Keys and Values

Navigating and changing keys and values with the Registry Editor is similar to the Explorer.

Adding

You add keys and values when you need to add registry entries—for example, when an entry is accidentally deleted.

To add a key:

1. Open the registry list to the place you want to add the new key.

2. Use your right mouse button to click the place you want to add the new key.

3. Click New, and then click the Key button. The new key appears with a temporary name.

4. Type a name for the new key, and then press Enter.

To add a value:

1. Open the registry list to the place you want to add the new value.

2. Use the right mouse button to click the place where you want to add the new value.

3. Click New, and then click the type of value you want to add: string, binary, or DWORD.

4. The new value appears with a temporary name.

5. Type a name for the new value, and then press Enter. The value data can be entered by completing the following "To change value data" set of instructions.

Deleting

You delete registry keys and values when you need to delete registry entries. You usually will delete these entries, for example, when they have become old and out-of-date.

To delete a key or value, take the following steps:

1. Find the key or value you want to delete. You do not need to open it.

2. Use the right mouse button to click the key or value, and then click Delete.

3. When asked to confirm the delete, click the Yes button.

Changing

You change registry keys and values when you need to change registry entries. You usually change registry keys and values, for example, when you want to change configuration values.

To rename a key or change a value name, take these steps:

1. Find the key or value you want to rename. You do not need to open it.

2. Use your right mouse button to click the key or value that you want to rename, and then click Rename.

3. Type the new name, and then press Enter.

To change value data, take these steps:

1. Double-click the value you want to change.

2. In the Value Data box, type the new data for the value.

3. Click the Ok button.

Importing and Exporting Registry Entries

The Registry Editor can import and export registry entries to a text file that you can edit with any text editor, which is helpful for backing up portions of the registry before you edit it. It's always a good idea to back up before editing the registry with the RE because mistakes can cause your system to malfunction.

Importing and exporting registry entries also helps when you are copying registry sections from one machine to another. Additionally, you can examine an exported registry file off-line for debugging.

An exported registry file is only a special text file with a .REG extension. It can be edited with any text editor, such as Notepad. Listing 7.1 shows a registry export file from the OrderMgr application class, on the companion disk included with this book:

Listing 7.1   Sample Registry Editor Export Output

```
[HKEY_LOCAL_MACHINE\SOFTWARE\Classes\CLSID\
➡{DBE93A5E-BDD2-11CE-94E2-444553540000}]
@=" "

[HKEY_LOCAL_MACHINE\SOFTWARE\Classes\CLSID\
➡{DBE93A5E-BDD2-11CE-94E2-444553540000}\ProgID]
@="OrderMgr.Application"
```

(continues)

Listing 7.1 Continued

```
[HKEY_LOCAL_MACHINE\SOFTWARE\Classes\CLSID\
➥{DBE93A5E-BDD2-11CE-94E2-444553540000}\LocalServer32]
@="C:\\CHAP23\\CODE\\SAMPLE\\ORDMGR\\ORDMGR.EXE"

[HKEY_LOCAL_MACHINE\SOFTWARE\Classes\CLSID\
➥{DBE93A5E-BDD2-11CE-94E2-444553540000}\InprocHandler32]
@="OLE32.DLL"

[HKEY_LOCAL_MACHINE\SOFTWARE\Classes\CLSID\
➥{DBE93A5E-BDD2-11CE-94E2-444553540000}\TypeLib]
@="{BF15A894-BBB7-11CE-94E2-444553540000}"
```

To export all or part of the registry to a text file, take these steps:

1. On the Registry menu, click Export Registry File.

2. In the Export Range area, click the All button to back up your entire registry or click Selected Branch to back up only a particular branch of the registry tree.

3. Select the .REG file.

To import some or all of the registry, take these steps:

1. Click Registry, and then click Import Registry File.

2. Select the .REG file.

3. Click the Open button.

Backing Up and Restoring the Registry

The registry contains all the information that the operating system knows about the computer. If the registry becomes corrupt, the computer may not function. It's a good idea, therefore, to periodically back up your registry, just as it's a good idea to back up your data files.

As mentioned previously, the registry is stored in two files—SYSTEM.DAT and USER.DAT. Whenever you successfully log on to your computer, the system automatically makes a backup of these files in the WINDOWS directory, named SYSTEM.DA0 and USER.DA0, respectively.

If a computer appears to have problems with the registry and you don't have a backup that you created, you can restore the registry to the state it was in when a user last logged on successfully by taking the following steps:

1. Click the Start button, and then click Shut Down. Click Restart The Computer In MS-DOS Mode, and then click Yes. This operation must be performed in MS-DOS mode because the files to replace are always in use while Windows is active.

2. Change to your Windows directory. If your Windows directory is C:\WINDOWS, for example, type the following:

   ```
   cd c:\windows
   ```

3. Copy the backup files over the corrupt files. You need to use the ATTRIB command because the files are marked as System, Hidden, and Read-Only, and files with these attributes cannot be copied. Type the following commands, pressing Enter after each command. Note that System.da0 and User.da0 contain the number zero.

   ```
   attrib -h -r -s system.dat
   attrib -h -r -s system.da0
   copy system.da0 system.dat
   attrib -h -r -s user.dat
   attrib -h -r -s user.da0
   copy user.da0 user.dat
   ```

4. Restart your computer.

Windows NT

Just like Windows 95, Windows NT and Windows 3.1 also have registry databases.

In Windows NT, the registry files are stored in the WINDOWS\SYSTEM32\CONFIG directory. The Windows NT Registry Editor is in the WINDOWS\SYSTEM32 directory and is named REGEDT32.EXE.

The WinNT Registry Editor is similar to Win 95's (see fig. 7.2). The primary difference is that the WinNT RE is a multiple-document interface application, and has a separate child form for each hive key.

You accomplish adding, deleting, and changing keys and values in WinNT by selecting the appropriate command from the Edit menu. Please see your Windows NT documentation for further information on the Windows NT registry.

II

OLE

Fig. 7.2

The WinNT Registry Editor. A hierarchical list of keys is navigated in the left pane of each hive key child window, and their values are displayed in the right pane.

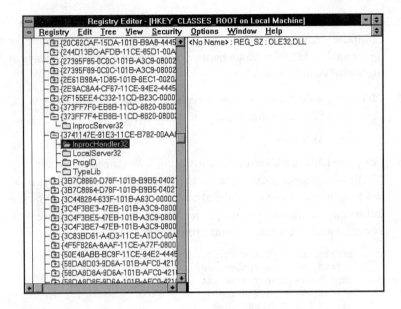

Windows 3.x

The Win16 registry database only contains OLE-related information. It is stored in a single file, REG.DAT. It can be edited and viewed by executing REGEDIT.EXE /V, which starts the registry editor in verbose mode.

Please see your Windows 3.x documentation for further information on the Windows 3.x registry.

Component Manager

One primary benefit of the three-tier architecture is code reuse at the component level. Multiple client applications, for example, should be able to reuse an Order Manager business component.

In complex systems with many components, the developer and end-user needs to be able to locate and install the various components that make up a system. The Component Manager, a tool that ships with VB Enterprise Edition, addresses this need.

The Component Manager (CM) and its associated Component Catalog databases are the central, shareable repository that manage distributed components. Use the Component Manager to manage all OLE server components, not just components created in Visual Basic.

The CM uses a Component Catalog database to store this information. A Component Catalog (CC) is just a set of tables that resides in a database. The database can be either a Microsoft Access .MDB file or an ODBC data source, such as SQL Server or Oracle.

A single CM application can maintain references to multiple Component Catalogs. A user, for example, may want to keep references to two catalogs when running the CM—an order processing CC that contains Order Manager, Product Manager, and Customer Manager component references; and a purchasing catalog that contains Vendor Manager and Inventory Manager component references.

The Component Manager application is stored in the \CLISVR directory of the VB directory. The file name is CMPGR32.EXE.

Why Use the Component Manager?

Before discussing exactly how to use the CM, this section covers a little bit about why the Component Manager is useful and how it relates to other, similar tools. A number of other tools do the same things as the CM. For example:

- The Object Browser allows a user to browse the interface of an object.

- The Remote Automation connection manager allows a user to switch between local and remote automation servers.

- Setup applications install OLE components automatically.

- The command line utilities CLIREG32.EXE, REGSVR32.EXE, REGOCX32.EXE, and the components themselves enable you to register and unregister components in your registry.

The Component Manager is a "one-stop shopping" tool that accomplishes all these functions. It also addresses an important function that none of these other tools provide: the capability to catalog, organize, search, and assign properties to components.

For example, some of the references that the Component Manager can maintain include the following:

- Location anywhere on the network

- Associated files and documentation for the component

- Sample client code

- Detailed description of the component

II

OLE

- Component version information

- Custom property tags that can be searched and sorted

- Registration files

- Licensing issues

- Run-time information

As a developer, then, you can use the Component Manager for organizing and categorizing the many components that will make up complex three-tier client/server application.

To the end user, the Component Manager is useful for browsing and installing an organization's available business objects for automation with tools such as Microsoft Excel.

Browsing Components

Before discussing how to maintain and modify a Component Catalog with the Component Manager, this section walks through exactly how to use an existing CM Component Catalog.

The CM is divided into three main panes (see fig. 7.3). The *Scope* pane on the left shows the Component Catalog databases the application currently references. The *Criteria* pane on the top shows which components for the selected CC are currently displayed. The *Results* pane on the right shows the components in the currently selected CC in the Scope pane that match the criteria last searched in the Criteria pane.

Fig. 7.3

The three main panes of the Component Manager: the Scope pane on the left, the Results pane on the right, and the Criteria pane on the top.

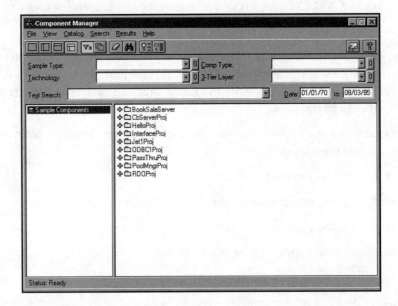

When the CM is executed for the first time after VB is installed, for example, the *Scope* pane shows only one CC—the *Sample Components* CC. By default, the *Tags* in the Criteria pane are empty. Because the Criteria pane is empty, and thus no filter criteria was set, the Results pane shows all the components in the *Sample Components* CC.

Surfing the Results Pane

The Results pane displays a list of the available components in the selected CC in the Scope pane. For components created in VB, the component name corresponds to the VB project name.

Under each component (accessed by double-clicking the component name) is a list of available classes. For components created in VB, the class name corresponds to the name of the public class module.

Under each class is the interface of the class: the properties, methods, member objects, and collections.

The outline, then, is hierarchically structured like the following example:

```
Component item
    Class item
         Interface item
Component item
    Class item
         Interface item
         Interface item
    Class item
         Interface item
         Interface item
```

To view the properties of a component, class, or interface item highlight the item, click the right mouse button, and select *Properties*. You also can select the *Results...Properties* menu item.

A property sheet for the select item appears. The property sheet contains four tabs of property information on the item: *Description*, *Property Tags*, *Details*, and *Associated Files*.

Like any property sheet, each tab has an Update and Close button. The Update button immediately saves all changes made. The Close button closes the property sheet without saving changes.

Description. The *Description* tab is used to view or change descriptive information about the selected item (see fig. 7.4).

Fig. 7.4
The Description tab of an item's property sheet, showing the BookSaleServer sample component.

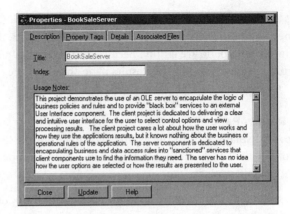

The *Title* box displays the name of the selected item. This field is read-only because the Component Manager cannot change the interface of a component.

The *Help Index* number of the selected item is used for invoking context-sensitive help of the selected item. This field is read-only. It applies only to a class item or an interface item.

The *Usage Notes* contains any text an administrator wants to share with users, such as the purpose of the item, its usage constraints, its author, and so on. You can highlight and copy text to the clipboard with the standard Windows hot keys.

Property Tags. You use the *Property Tags* tab to view or change the property tags of the selected item and its children (see fig. 7.5).

Fig. 7.5
The Property Tags tab of an item's property sheet. This example shows the BookSaleServer sample component.

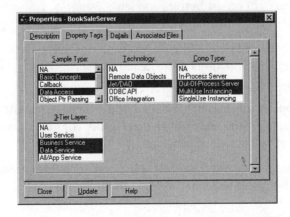

Each Component Catalog has a set of properties for its items, and each item has a valid list of tags or property values associated with it. This tab allows you to browse and change the property tags of an item.

Property tags are used for filtering and searching components. As described in a following section of this chapter, you can create your own property tags for your component catalog that will appear in this dialog. Custom property tags enable you to filter and categorize components as is best suited for your organization. The sample component catalog ships with four sample property tags: Sample Types, Technology, Comp Type, and 3-Tier Layer.

The scrollable list boxes list all the available properties of a component catalog and their enumerated values, and indicate which values apply to the selected item. When you change the tag for an item, the tags for all items subordinate to it also change. So, if you change the tag of a class item, all of its interface items are also affected.

Details. The *Details* tab is used to view or change detail information of the selected item. It's a confusing tab, because fields may or may not be applicable, depending on the type of item that was selected in the Results pane (see fig. 7.6).

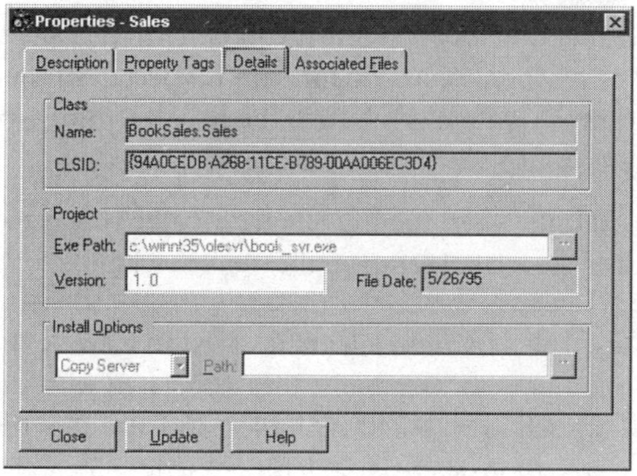

Fig. 7.6
The Details tab of an item's property sheet. This example shows the BookSaleServer sample component's Sales class.

The following list explains the different elements on the Details tab:

- **Class Name**—Shows the name of the component if a component item is selected, the class name if a class item is selected, or the class name of the parent class if an interface item is selected. This field is read-only.

- **CLSID**—Shows zero if a component item is selected, the OLE class ID if a class item is selected, or the OLE class ID of the parent class if an interface item is selected. This field is read-only.

- **Project EXE Path**—Shows the path of the associated component's file. This element is read-only (determined when the component was added to the catalog).

- **Project Version** and **File Date**—Show, respectively, the version and file date of the component's file. It is read-only (determined when the component was added to the catalog).

- **Install Options**—Best explained by describing its three possible values:

  None. Specifies that users aren't allowed to install this server; they can only browse it. Use when you don't want other users to be able to install this particular OLE server; you just want to provide information about it.

  Copy Server. Specifies that the CM installs a copy of the selected OLE server to the user's local machine and registers it. The server is copied by default into the user's WINDOWS\OLESVR directory.

  Use Setup App. Specifies that the CM will launch a setup application program that you provide. This is useful when the OLE server requires additional files to operate correctly, or when the files need to be located in specific locations.

  Because *Install Options* applies to a component, its values can be changed only when a component item is selected in the Results pane. If a class or interface item is selected, the Install Options for the parent component is displayed, but is read-only.

- *Path* is used only when the *Use Setup App* value is selected. This should be set to the associated setup application executable for the component.

Associated Files. The *Associated Files* tab is used to view or change files associated with the component. Generally, files associated with the component are interface files, such as .TLB and .VBR files, and also files the component depends on for execution, such as .DLL files (see fig. 7.7).

The Associated Files tab applies only if a component item was selected in the Results pane.

Files can be added and removed with the Add and Remove buttons.

Filtering and Searching Components

Now that you know how to browse the results pane, you're ready to learn how to manipulate the components, classes, and interface items that are displayed in the Results pane.

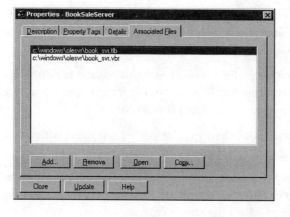

Fig. 7.7
The Associated Files tab of an item's property sheet. This example shows the BookSaleServer sample component.

This knowledge is useful because, as components proliferate in your organization, a typical component catalog may contain hundreds of components and associated classes. Because business rules are never repeated, you may need to search through hundreds of components to find the exact piece of business functionality you need.

The Criteria pane at the top is used to filter, sort, and find specific components (see fig. 7.8).

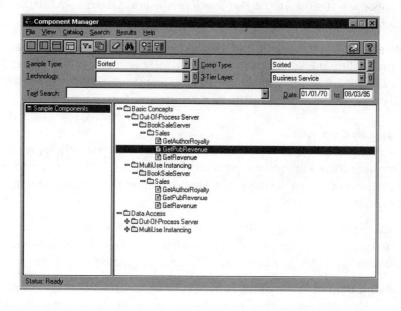

Fig. 7.8
The results of a find and sort specified in the Criteria pane on the Sample Components CC.

The Criteria pane lists the properties of the currently selected CC in the Scope pane. The *Sample Components* CC, for example, has four properties: *Sample Type*, *Technology*, *Comp Type*, and *3-Tier Layer*.

Each of these properties combo boxes can be used to either filter or sort on the associated property. To select a filter for a property, chose a property tag from the property's drop-down combo box.

To sort by a particular property, select the sort order with the numeric buttons next to the property combo box.

After the property filter and sort criteria is chosen, pressing the *Find Result Now* button or choosing the *Search..Find Results Now* menu item updates the Results pane to reflect the search criteria.

For each level of sort criteria specified, the Results pane adds a level corresponding to the sort criteria. If you specify to sort, for example, by *Comp Type* and *3-Tier Layer*, two levels are added on top of the component, class, and interface hierarchies—one for each sort criteria. Because these layers are not components, classes, or interfaces, you cannot view their properties.

The Component Manager also lets you specify a filter on the item's full text or file date. To filter on the item's full text *Usage Notes* (described previously), specify the text string in the *Text Search* combo box. Likewise, to filter on the component's file date, specify a date range in the *Date* text boxes.

Often, you want to erase the last applied filter and sort criteria and reload the entire CC into the Results pane. You can quickly accomplish this by pressing the *Clear Search Criteria* button or selecting *Search... Clear Search Criteria* from the menu, and then pressing the Find Results Now button again.

Grouping Components

Within a Component Catalog you may find that you frequently apply the same filter criteria to obtain a list of related components. Or you may find that all you ever use is a single class from a complicated component that contains many classes.

The Component Manager allows you to create predefined groups of component, class, and interface items. In the CM, these are referred to as *Named Collections* (not to be confused with OLE object collections).

Viewing Named Collections. To view a list of predefined Named Collections, select the *Show Collection Lists* button or choose *View... Show Collection Lists* from the menu. The Criteria pane changes to the Named Collections pane. Like the Criteria pane, the Named Collections pane allows you to change the items displayed in the Results pane.

A list of predefined Named Collections is displayed in the list box. Selecting a item in the list box changes the Results pane to reflect the items in the Named Collection.

Adding Named Collections. To create a new group of components, click the right mouse button on the Named Collections text box and select Add from the menu.

A dialog box prompts for a new collection name. Enter the name of the new named collection. After you finish, the new empty named collection appears in the list of named collections.

Modifying Named Collections. To modify the items contained in a named collection, select the collection, click the right mouse button, and then choose Edit from the pop-up menu. The Edit Named Collections window appears (see fig. 7.9).

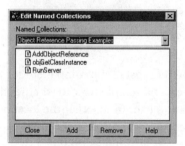

Fig. 7.9
The Edit Named Collections window, where items within a named collection and be added and removed.

This window is not a dialog. That is, it's not modal—it is related back to the Component Manager's main window.

To add an item to the named collection, select the item you want to add from the Component Manager's Results pane. Remember, because the Edit Named Collections window isn't modal, you can browse the Results pane while it remains open—even applying new filters. After the proper item is selected, switch back to the Edit Named Collections window and press the Add button.

Alternatively, you can drag-and-drop the items from the Results pane into the Edit Named Collections window.

To remove an item from the named collection, select the item in the Edit Named Collections window and press the Remove button.

Remember, named collections are just logical groupings of components in the component catalog. When an item is removed from a named collection, it isn't removed from the component catalog.

Installing Components

Now that you're familiar with how to maneuver through the Component Manager and find the appropriate component, you're ready to learn how to install the component.

To install a component, first select a component in the Results pane. Make sure that you select a component, not a class item, interface item, or sort grouping item. Click the right mouse button and select Install.

A dialog similar to figure 7.10 should appear.

Fig. 7.10

Installing a component.

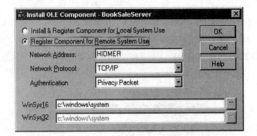

The CM allows you to either install the component for local use or remote use. In this context, local and remote refer to whether the component will execute on the workstation (run from either the local hard disk or on a network share), or whether the component will run on another machine via remote automation, such as an application server over the network.

Don't confuse this local and remote terminology with the location of the component catalog. You can install a component for remote use from a local catalog, just as you can install a component for local use from a remote catalog.

The WinSys16 text box specifies the path to the 16-bit Windows system directory, if one is installed on the machine. If it is in the same directory as the 32-bit system directory, specify the 32-bit system path.

The WinSys32 text box specifies the path to the 32-bit Windows system directory, if one is installed on the machine.

The 16-bit and 32-bit paths have different behaviors, depending on whether or not you're running the 16-bit or 32-bit version of the Component Manager. You will first walk through the 32-bit Component Manager scenario, and then you will see how the 16-bit scenario relates.

The 16-bit path tells the 32-bit version of the Component Manager where to find the path to the 16-bit proxy stub (which cannot reliably be found programmatically). If the 16-bit path is specified, the 32-bit Component Manager registers the server for access by both 16-bit and 32-bit apps. If 16-bit path is isn't specified, the 32-bit Component Manager only registers the server for access by 32-bit clients. The 32-bit path is automatically filled in by the 32-bit Component Manager and cannot be changed by the user.

The 16-bit Component Manager works analogously to the 32-bit version just described—just reverse 16-bit and 32-bit in the preceding description.

Local Installation

To select the component for local use, select the top radio button. When selected, the remote component is copied to the local system. The component and its related files, by default, are placed in the WINDOWS\OLSVR directory. The registry is updated to point all references to the OLE server to the local copy.

This option is appropriate in a number of scenarios:

- For performance reasons, the OLE server needs to be run locally.

- The OLE server is an in-process server that cannot be run via remote automation.

- The OLE server is a user service and, usually, user services are physically deployed on the client workstation.

- The user is a disconnected laptop user who needs to run all three tiers on the same laptop CPU.

Remote Installation

To select the component for remote use (via remote automation), select the bottom radio button. When selected, the registry is updated to point to the remote server—no files are copied locally because no additional process needs to execute on the client workstation.

You need to specify a few additional parameters when installing a component for remote use, so that the client can find and communicate with the remote server over the network:

- **Network Address**—The network address of the system where the server component is located. You can enter the name of the remote server with or without preceding backslashes (\\). For example, you can enter either \\MYSERVER or MYSERVER. In addition, you can specify an IP address for TCP/IP connections.

II

OLE

- **Network Protocol**—The network protocol that the client and server systems use to communicate with each other.

- **Authentication**—The RPC (remote procedure call) authentication to use for communication. Authentication is a tool used to ensure data privacy and integrity.

Remote automation is covered in detail in a following section of this chapter.

Remote installation is appropriate in a number of scenarios:

- You want to lock up and deploy business servers on powerful server machines.

- Client PCs don't have the resources to execute more than user services.

- You want to offer services over the Internet.

Switching Between Local and Remote

Being able to switch between local and remote components frequently may be helpful. For example, you may want to develop servers locally, but frequently test them remotely—the way you will deploy them in production.

The CM can safely reinstall components on top of each other. Therefore, to switch between local and remote you need only reinstall the component with the appropriate settings.

Modifying Components

At this point, you should understand how to navigate and install OLE components within a Component Catalog. This section shows how to change which components are stored in a component catalog.

Adding Components

The Component Catalog doesn't store the actual component—it stores the registry information of the component, as well as a pointer to where the physical component resides on the network.

Adding a component to a CC, therefore, actually just adds this reference information to the CC database.

To add a component, select the component catalog in the Scope pane to which you want to add the component. Then, from the Results pane, click the right mouse button and select Add OLE Components. A dialog box similar to figure 7.11 should appear.

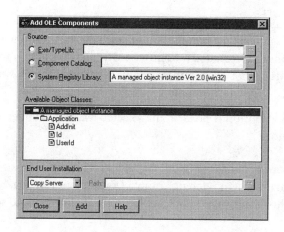

Fig. 7.11
Adding an OLE
component
reference to a
Component
Catalog.

As the dialog implies, there are three places that the Component Manager can find the information it needs to place a reference to the component into the Component Catalog:

■ The EXE or Type Library

■ Another component catalog

■ The registry of a computer that has already installed the component

Exe/TypeLib allows you to select executable (.EXE, .DLL) or TypeLib (.TLB, .OLB) files. Clicking the browse button displays a dialog box that enables you to browse for these kinds of files.

Not all OLE components store OLE information in their .EXE or .DLL files. Some OLE components store data in an external TypeLib file. If you want to add such a component, select the .TLB or .OLB file in the File Browse dialog box. The related .EXE file automatically loads, along with the TypeLib file.

Likewise, not all .EXE and .DLL files are OLE servers. As such, you see an error if you try to add an .EXE file that isn't an OLE server to a component catalog.

Component Catalog allows you to open a local or remote component catalog from which you can select OLE component descriptions.

System Registry Library allows you to select an OLE component listed in the local system registry.

After you select component with one of the three methods, its class and interface items are displayed in the Available Object Classes box. You can either select the entire component or individual classes to add to the catalog.

As the "Details" section of the "Browsing Components" section discussed, the *End User Installation* and *Path* options enable you to determine if and how each component is installed if users try to install it locally on their machines. These options do not affect remote component installations. See the "Details" section for additional information.

When the Add button is pressed, the selected classes are added to your component catalog.

Deleting Components

To delete a component reference from a Component Catalog, select the component in the Results pane, click the right mouse button, and select Delete.

Modifying Component Catalogs

You learned how to view and change the components within a component catalog. Sometimes, you may want to work with multiple component catalogs. This section discusses how to change the component catalogs in the Scope pane.

Adding

To add a CC to the list of CCs in the Component Manager, select the Scope pane, click the right mouse button and select Add Catalog. At this point you are shown a dialog similar to figure 7.12.

Fig. 7.12
Three ways to add a Component Catalog to the Component Manager.

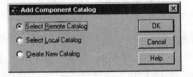

The Component Manager presents the following three options:

■ Select a local catalog

■ Create a new local catalog

■ Select a remote catalog

Select a Local Catalog. A local catalog is just a Microsoft Access .MDB file. When this option is selected, you are prompted to select the appropriate file.

The file can be located on your local hard disk or on a network file server.

Create New Catalog. The *Create New Catalog* option allows you to create a new local catalog. A local catalog is just a Microsoft Access database. After you specify a catalog title, preferred language, and file name the catalog file is created and the reference is added to the Component Manager.

Select a Remote Catalog. When you select a remote catalog, the CM displays a list of ODBC data sources. A component catalog can be placed on any DBMS that supports ODBC. To create a new catalog, the database user must have privileges to create new database tables. After a valid catalog is selected or created, its reference is displayed every time the Component Manager starts up.

Removing

To remove a component catalog reference from the CM, select the appropriate CC from Scope pane, click the right mouse button, and select Remove Catalog.

Note that removing a component catalog reference from the Component Manager just removes the reference to the CC, not the CC itself. If the CC is local, for example, the Access database is not deleted. Likewise, if the CC is remote, the tables will still exist in the ODBC data source.

Changing Properties

Two types of properties apply to a CC that you can change—the name of the CC and its search and filter tags. To change a CC's properties, click the CC in the Scope pane, click the right mouse button, and select Properties. A dialog similar to figure 7.13 is displayed on-screen.

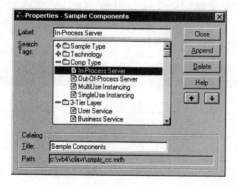

Fig. 7.13
A Component Catalog's properties.

To change the name of the CC, just change the entry in the Title text box.

The top of the dialog box displays the properties global to the component catalog and the valid enumerated values that apply to each property.

You've seen these property values before, in the following two places:

- When you searched and filtered components in the Criteria pane, you did so with the properties and valid values defined here.
- When you viewed the properties of component, class, and interface items in the Results pane, you were able to tag the items with valid values defined here.

To add a new property, select an existing property and click the Append button. The new property then can be renamed with the text box at the top Label text box.

To add a new property value (tag), select an existing value and click the Append button. The new tag can then be renamed with the text box at the top.

To delete a property or tag, select it, and then click the Delete button.

To move a tag, select it, and then press the appropriate Up and Down arrows. Tags appear in other parts of the Component Manager in the order that they are defined in this dialog.

OLESVR

When a component is installed for local use, the EXE, TLB, VBR, and related files are copied by the Component Manager into the \OLESVR directory off of the Windows directory.

When a component is installed for remote use, only the TLB and the VBR files are installed in the \OLESVR directory.

Database Layout

A component catalog can be stored either in an Access database or in an ODBC data source. A component catalog is a collection of tables that describes the components (see Table 7.1).

Table 7.1 Component Catalog Tables

Table	Table
Data_AssocFilePaths	Data_ItemToProp2
Data_CollectionList	Data_ItemToProp3
Data_CollectionMembers	Data_QueryList
Data_ItemDescDetails	Def_CatalogInfo
Data_ItemDescMaster	Def_CatalogProperties
Data_ItemToProp0	Def_PropertyValues
Data_ItemToProp1	

When the Component Manager creates a new component catalog, these tables are installed. Users who have only SELECT privileges on these tables are allowed to modify the component catalog (add components, change properties, and so on).

By changing the column values in these tables, you can alter the component catalog without using the Component Manager. If, for example, a component has changed location on the network, an administrator can modify the appropriate tables in the component catalog to point to a new path name.

When adding files that exist on network file server to a catalog, a UNC file name is created automatically and added to the path of the file. If, for example, you add the component F:\COMPONENTS\ORDERMGR.EXE and F is a network drive mapped to the share \\SERVER\PUBLIC , the component is added into the database as \\SERVER\PUBLIC\COMPONENTS\ORDERMGR.EXE. This UNC name is useful for drive independence; workstations don't need to have their drive F mapped in exactly the same way as the administrator who originally added the component did.

"Drive:" paths are only used when a file is added from the local machine. So, in general, a component's file name should be placed in the catalog from network drives, so all users of the component can access it by UNC name, without regard to drive mappings.

Remote Automation

The ability to easily deploy reusable components across the organization's network has been the principle deterrent to the proliferation of three-tier client/server architectures.

Remote automation addresses this problem by allowing Visual Basic applications to transparently access OLE automation servers across a network just as if they were physically located on the same machine.

Remote automation is truly transparent. The client application doesn't need to be recompiled to point to a remote server (as you saw in the previous section, "Component Manager").

With the release of Visual Basic 4, remote automation servers can be deployed on either Windows 95 or Windows NT workstations. Client workstations can be Windows 3.x, Windows 95, or Windows NT.

With Windows 95 and Windows NT, the remote procedure call (RPC) mechanisms that remote automation runs on top of are included with the operating system. With Windows 3.x client, RPC16 must be installed manually in addition to the remote automation pieces. You can find RPC16 on the REMAUTO\RPC.16 directory, off of the VB directory on the VB4EE CD-ROM.

Remote Automation under the Covers

Before you look at how remote automation works, take a look at how local automation works. When two processes communicate via OLE automation, they do so through a proxy/stub combination. This is known as *single machine remoting* (see fig. 7.14).

Fig. 7.14
The architecture of single machine remoting or "local OLE automation."

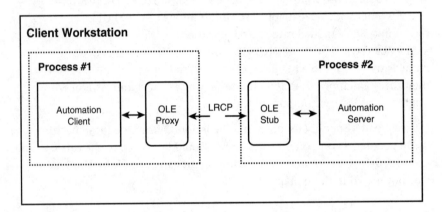

Remote automation introduces an additional component, the remote Automation Manager, which replaces the original proxy/stub combinations with the capability to communicate over a network. This is referred to as *cross machine remoting* (see fig. 7.15).

Fig. 7.15
The architecture of cross machine remoting or "remote OLE automation."

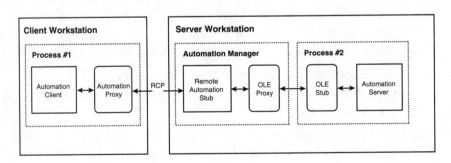

The automation proxy replaces the standard OLE proxy on the client machine. The Automation Manager that resides on the server marshals requests across the network—it manages RPC calls for the OLE stub. Neither the client controller nor the OLE server are aware that the communication is being remoted.

Remote automation is handled by several files (see Table 7.2).

Table 7.2	Remote Automation Files
File	**Description**
AUTMGR32.EXE	Automation Manager
AUTPRX32.DLL	32-bit remote automation proxy
AUTPRX16.DLL	16-bit remote automation proxy for Windows 95 and Windows NT
AUTPRX.DLL	16-bit remote automation proxy for Windows 3.x

These files are installed into the \WINDOWS\SYSTEM directory when VB4EE is installed.

The OLE automation relationship is a client/server relationship. The controlling application, or client, makes requests of the server. These requests are in the form of standard OLE automation interface calls, such as properties, methods, and collections. The OLE server, in turn, processes these interface requests.

This relationship also can be reversed. The client application, for example, can expose its own properties and methods that the server can invoke. This relationship is often known as a *callback*. Application A (the client), for example, may invoke a method on application B (the server) that searches the Internet for a document. When application B finds the document, it invokes a method on application A. This invocation reverses the relationship—application B is acting as the OLE client, and application A is acting as the OLE automation server.

The registry setting on the client computer determines whether the client uses the standard OLE proxy or the remote automation proxy. Although the proxy and stub are handled automatically by OLE, the Automation Manager must first be running on the server machine before clients can instantiate objects.

II

OLE

Applications written for remote automation will continue to run unmodified when remote automation is superseded by the Distributed Component Object model (DCOM).

Performance Issues of Remote Automation

Although an object reacts identically—whether controlled locally or across the network—remote automation introduces several performance considerations. If an object is to be used remotely, then, reality dictates that you consider performance issues when designing the OLE server.

A lengthy in-process OLE call for example, may take <0.1 second. A lengthy out-of-process call, which adds context switching, may take a full second. A lengthy remote OLE automation call, which adds network RPC overhead, may take up to three seconds.

These numbers aren't scientific, they're just presented to give you a feel for the performance differences between in-process, out-of-process, and remote OLE automation calls.

As you may guess, then, the biggest impact on performance in a three-tier system is remote automation calls. Each OLE "dot" operation is an OLE automation call. Therefore, each "dot" operation makes a request across the network.

OLE automation objects that are going to be deployed remotely, then, should be designed to be used with minimal dot operations. Likewise, client applications should be designed so that they minimize the use of the server's dot operations.

The following design techniques can improve the speed of remote automation. These techniques also are useful for local out-of-process servers.

Methods Versus Properties

Setting a property represents an OLE call and, therefore, an RPC call. Commonly, client applications need to set multiple properties. If several properties must be set, creating a special method capable of taking multiple property values and setting them internally is often useful.

Likewise, controllers often need to read multiple property values. A special method that takes multiple optional parameters can be implemented in the server that enables clients to read multiple property values.

If, for example, an object has three properties—*customer*, *product*, and *quantity*—rather than making three separate property set calls, the server can implement a PropertySet procedure that takes optional customer, product, and quantity parameters.

Every server object in the GOLF system implements a special PropertyGet and PropertySet method that enables controlling applications to set and get multiple property values with a single method call.

Return Arrays

OLE servers often expose collections of objects. If a client application needs to access many or all property elements of the object, it needs to make an OLE automation call for each element.

An *Order* object, for example, may expose a collection of *LineItem* objects. The client application commonly needs to read all the line items at once, for example, to place in a grid control. Rather than making an OLE call to read each line item object's properties (such as the PropertyGet example mentioned previously), the LineItems collection (not object) can implement a CollectionGet method that takes a two-dimensional array as a parameter, and returns an array of property values for the entire collection with a single OLE call.

Instance Managers

Techniques for pooling object instance on the server can improve performance of remote automation. Servers, for example, that need to communicate with other servers can be designed in-process to each other. Chapter 23, "Sample Application #2: An Instance Manager," covers the details of instance managers and their benefits.

Avoid ByRef

A parameter passed by reference in an in-process call operates very quickly because only a pointer to the data is passed.

In an out-of-process or remote automation call, the server machine cannot directly access the address space of the controller. So, when a parameter is passed by reference to a server, OLE copies the value and passes it across the network.

When the method is finished, OLE must pass the entire value back across the network, just in case the value was modified. The parameter data passes over the network twice, and the call incurs double the overhead.

Parameters passed by value, however, pass over the network only once—from controller to server.

Parameters should be passed only by reference, therefore, if the OLE server needs to modify the value. If the server method doesn't need to modify its parameters, define its parameters explicitly as *ByVal*.

Property Buffers

Occasionally, several methods all require the same data or parameter values. A business server, for example, may require a user ID and password to access a special data service, such as the Internet. Each parameter adds to the packet size of the RPC call.

OLE servers can intelligently buffer these commonly passed parameters as property values. After the property is set, every method that once took its value as a parameter can now look internally at the property value, shrinking the size of the method's packet size.

Native 32-Bit Applications

Although a 16-bit OLE automation server can be built in VB and deployed remotely on a 32-bit operating system, automation servers operate much more efficiently if they are built as 32-bit applications. The only reason you would ever want to build a 16-bit OLE automation server is if you wanted to deploy it locally on a 16-bit operating system.

Network Protocols

Remote automation can work over several network protocols, including IPX/SPX, TCP/IP, and NETBEUI. Some protocols and tuning methods, however, may be better suited for carrying your application's packets.

Additionally, the authentication level (described in a following section of this chapter) effects performance. A configuration that has no authentication, for example, performs better than a similar configuration that is performing packet encryption.

Network performance tuning is beyond the scope of this book, but you should know that it can have an impact on remote automation performance.

Automation Manager

The Automation Manager manages the RPC connection on the remote automation server. The program is installed in the WINDOWS\SYSTEM directory and is AUTMGR32.EXE.

The Automation Manager is a multi-threaded application, so the single Automation Manager application process can service multiple clients simultaneously. Although it is multi-threaded, however, OLE servers created in Visual Basic are single-threaded. So, if you need multiple clients to be simultaneously served by the same OLE object, consider the instancing of this object. The object, for example, should be Creatable Single-Use, so that a separate process is created for each OLE server instance. Chapter 23, "Sample Application #2: An Instance Manager," discusses in detail multitasking issues with remote automation.

The Automation Manager adds little overhead beyond OLE and RPC. It doesn't start up in response to a client request, so on a server machine, it usually should be configured to start up when the machine boots.

If your application implements asynchronous notification or call-backs to the client machine (described in Chapter 12, "Advanced Coding techniques"), the client machine automatically starts the Automation Manager to handle these kinds of requests. Under this scenario in Windows 95, the Automation Manager runs invisibly.

Remote Automation Connection Manager

The Remote Automation Connection Manager (RACM) is a utility that ships with Visual Basic 4 to help manage remote automation configuration. RACM accomplishes the following two tasks:

- Enables the controller to switch between pointing to local or remote servers

- Configures the server security options

The RACM is somewhat confusing because it is useful for administering both server machines and client machines.

So, when should the RACM be used? On a client machine, it is used to point to either a local or remote server. On the server machine, it is used to determine what OLE servers can be automated remotely, and by whom.

The difference between the Component Manager and the RACM is that the Component Manager is used for installing and managing component catalogs, and the RACM is used only *after* the server has been installed. Additionally, the RACM can set server security options.

II

OLE

When the Remote Automation Connection Manager is started, you see two main panes. On the left, you see an OLE Classes pane, which lists all the OLE classes currently in the registry; on the right, you see the Client Access and Server Connection tabs, used to administer servers and clients, respectively.

Server Connection

The Server Connection tab is used to administer the way clients point to servers (see fig. 7.16).

Fig. 7.16

The Remote Automation Manager's Server Connection tab.

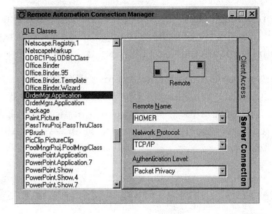

On the left, the OLE Classes drop-down list box enables you to select a previously installed class to administer. The OLE classes listed come from the machine's registry. As classes are selected on the left side, their configurations are displayed on the right side.

The icon at the top indicates whether the currently selected class is installed for remote or local use. To change the installation between remote and local use, move the mouse pointer over the OLE class item, click the right mouse button, and click the Remote or Local menu items.

When the class is installed remotely, the right pane indicates how the client connects to the server. The three options, *Remote Name*, *Network Protocol*, and *Authentication Level* are identical to the options in the Component Manager, described in the preceding section. Authentication is described in detail in Chapter 13, "Architecting Security."

Client Access

The Client Access tab is used to administer the way clients are allowed to access the server (see fig. 7.17).

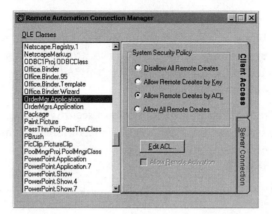

Fig. 7.17
The Remote
Automation
Manager's Client
Access tab.

The *System Security Policy* radio buttons administer the way security is applied to all classes on the server. Specifically, this security system enforces which classes can or cannot be instantiated by controlling applications. Some security policies allow more granularity than others.

Allow All Remote Creates

This policy allows any client machine to instantiate *any* class on the server. *Allow All Remote Creates* isn't a recommended configuration because it essentially gives others free reign to run applications on the server. It can be useful, however, in a test or development environment.

Disallow Remote Creates

This policy prohibits all client applications from instantiating objects on the server machine. This is useful for machines that aren't going to be remote automation servers and is the default setting.

Allow Remote Creates by Key

This policy enables you to selectively turn on remote automation by key. When this policy is set, the *Allow Remote Activation* check box is enabled. As classes are selected in the list box on the left, this check box indicates whether or not the class supports remote automation.

Allow Remote Creates by Key is useful in an open, unsecured environment, when the server wants to make only certain classes public. Microsoft Office OLE servers such as Excel, for example, should not allow remote automation.

This policy also is useful in a non-integrated Windows NT security environment—if, for example, users don't log onto an NT domain.

Allow Remote Creates by ACL

This policy enables you to enable remote automation by user, for each class. When this policy is set, the edit ACL (access control list) button is enabled. As classes are selected in the list box on the left, this button allows you to assign access by user and group.

Allow Remote Creates by ACL is the most robust security method, but it requires that the server run on a Windows NT machine. This is most useful in a production environment, where you need to selectively assign different users different class permissions.

Chapter 13, "Architecting Security," covers remote automation security in detail.

A workstation can be both a remote automation client and a server—a workstation can reference objects on other machines while other machines are referencing its objects.

Client Registration Utility

The Client Registration Utility (CRU) basically is a command line version of the Remote Automation Manager that also allows you to install and uninstall a remote automation class in the registry. This utility is located in the \CLISVR directory off the VB directory and is named CLIREG32.EXE.

The CRU is used by the VB Setup Toolkit to register servers for remote use. It also can be helpful for organizations that need to install servers in batch or as a part of their own custom setup applications.

It utility uses the Remote Support (.VBR) and Type Library (.TLB) files that Visual Basic produces when it compiles the OLE server's .EXE file and the Remote Server Support Files check box is selected.

The complete syntax is shown in the following lines:

```
CLIREG[32][.EXE] vbrfile -s {s} ¦ -p {p} ¦ -a {a} ¦ -t {t} ¦ -u ¦ -
q ¦ -l ¦ -nologo ¦ -[h ¦ ?]
```

Table 7.2 describes these command-line parameters.

Table 7.2 **Client Registration Utility Command-Line Parameters**	
Option	**Description**
–s {s}	Specify network address {s}
–p {p}	Specify network protocol {p}
–a {a}	Specify security authentication level {a}; valid range is from 0 to 6
–t {t}	Specify TypeLib file {t}
–u	Quiet mode: no information dialogs or error messages
–l	Log error information to file, CLIREG.LOG
–nologo	Do not display copyright information
–[h	?]	Display the Help dialog box that presents command line options

Other Ways to Register OLE Objects

You saw two ways to register objects in the registry—the Component Manager and Client Registration Utility for remote registration, and the Component Manager for local registration.

There also are command-line methods for local object registration for OLE EXEs, DLLs, and OCXes.

Out-of-process OLE server .EXEs created in Visual Basic are self registering; every time they are executed, they register themselves. To just register an .EXE without running it, execute the application with the /REGSERVER command-line parameter. To unregister the .EXE, execute the application with the /UNREGSERVER command-line parameter.

Because DLLs and OCXes cannot execute themselves, there are two utilities included with Visual Basic that enable you to register these OLE objects on the command line.

REGSVR32.EXE and REGOCX32.EXE enable registration of, respectively, .DLL and .OCX OLE objects. To register an OLE object, execute the appropriate utility with the name of the OLE file as a single parameter. To unregister an OLE object, execute the appropriate utility followed by a /u command-line parameter, followed by the name of the OLE file.

Remote Automation Debugging

Setting up remote automation for the first time can overwhelm you, especially if things don't work. There are a lot of pieces that need to work together. Usually, the errors aren't specific enough to identify the location of the problem.

The following methodical installation and debugging procedure will help you isolate where problems occur. The philosophy behind this method is that before remote automation can work, local automation needs to work. These procedures outline a manual approach that enables you to identify exactly where the problem lies.

In these steps the *client workstation* is the workstation on which you intend to run the remote automation controller, and the *server workstation* is the workstation on which you intend to run the OLE server. The *controlling application* is the OLE test client, and the *OLE server* is the OLE server application.

Step 1: Unregister Components

You should install the server into fresh registry entries. So first, unregister the OLE server with the /**UNREGSERVER** command-line parameters. You should execute this unregistering on both the client workstation and the server workstation.

If an error occurs on the client or server, there is a problem with the registry; it may be corrupt. You may need to go into the registry with the Registry Editor or another utility and try to clean up the corrupt registry entries.

Step 2: Register Components

Next, register the OLE sever component for local use on both the machines. To do so, run the OLE server with the /**REGSERVER** command-line parameter on both the client workstation and the server workstation.

Make sure that you are using the exact same .EXE. Compiling from the same OLE server project isn't good enough: when you compile the OLE server project, a different CLSID may be generated. It isn't good enough to have just the same class names registered on the client workstation and server workstation, they also must have the same CLSIDs. The safest way to insure this compatibility is to register the components from the same OLE server EXE.

If a problem occurs in this step, the registry or OLE server EXE may be corrupt.

Step 3: Test Local

Before you switch to remote automation, you need to make sure local automation of the OLE server works on both the client workstation and the server workstation.

To test this, run the controlling application once on the client workstation and once on the server workstation.

If an error occurs in this step, it must be related to the way in which the controlling application and OLE server communicate.

Step 4: Configure Server Workstation for Remote Automation

The server needs to be prepared for remote automation requests. First, make sure security won't hinder the connection. To check, run the Remote Automation Connection Manager on the server workstation. Set the security policy to Allow All Remote Creates. This should be only a temporary setting, for debugging purposes.

Now, execute the Automation Manager so that the server workstation is prepared to marshal client requests.

If an error occurs in this step, you may have a problem with your server workstation network configuration.

Step 5: Configure Client Workstation for Remote Automation

Now that the server workstation is ready to receive requests and you have verified that the OLE server runs locally on both machines, you are ready to point the client workstation's controlling application to the server workstation's OLE server.

To do so, execute the Remote Automation Connection Manager on the client workstation. Select the OLE server class you are testing. Type the server name, select the appropriate protocol, and select No Authentication.

Step 6: Test Remote

Everything should be set up at this point. Execute the controlling application on the client workstation.

If OLE automation fails at this point, the problem most likely is with the network connection. Make sure that the client workstation has visibility to the server workstation through other services. Test, for example, to see if the client workstation can access a file share on the server workstation.

II

OLE

You can also try experimenting with other protocols, accessing the server from another workstation, or even reversing the client/server relationship.

If all works well, try reimplementing security on the server workstation and authentication on the client workstation.

As you become more familiar with remote automation, you will start to recognize and associate common errors with common configuration problems.

You may conclude from reading this section that it's always a good idea to have a simple test controlling application for every remotely deployed OLE server, just for these kinds of debugging scenarios.

The Internet

Remote automation works over TCP/IP. The Internet is just a large TCP/IP-based network. Therefore, a remote automation client can transparently control a remote automation server over the Internet.

To specify an Internet server, enter the name of the Internet IP address (such as 144.158.155.12) or the Internet domain name (such as homer.claritycnslt.com) when installing the component on the client with the Component Manager, Remote Automation Manager, or Client Registration Utility.

Remote automation over the Internet opens up a number of possibilities. With remote automation, you can create distributed applications across the Internet without having to learn how to use Windows sockets or special custom controls. Just as servers on the Internet expose FTP, WWW, or Gopher interfaces, they now also can expose OLE interfaces.

RegClean

The RegClean utility is useful for cleaning up corrupted or out-of-date registry entries. You can find the file, REGCLEAN.EXE, in the \TOOLS\PSS directory of the Visual Basic CD-ROM (see fig. 7.18).

RegClean is fairly straightforward. When started, it prompts to either report, correct automatically, or prompts to correct corrupt registry entries. You should use RegClean periodically on machines that frequently register and unregister components—machines that are used to create OLE components with VB and are subject to many OLE registrations and file copies and good candidates for RegClean.

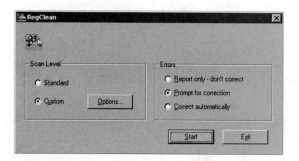

Fig. 7.18
RegClean's
opening window.

From Here...

This chapter provided an overview of managing OLE objects. For more information related to topics covered in this chapter, see the following:

■ For more information on remote automation, see *VB4—OLE Remote Automation*, by Ken Spencer, from Prentice Hall.

■ Chapter 13, "Architecting Security," shows how to use the setup kit for distributing applications, including OLE objects.

■ Chapter 16, "Distributing Applications," shows how to install local and remote OLE automation servers in customer setup applications.

■ Chapter 23, "Sample Application #2: An Instance Manager," details how to use an instance manager to manage remote OLE objects.

II

OLE

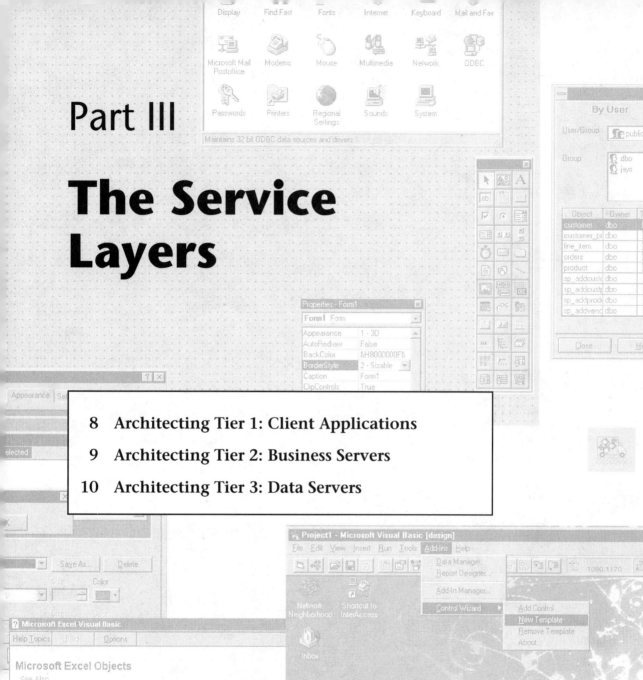

Part III

The Service Layers

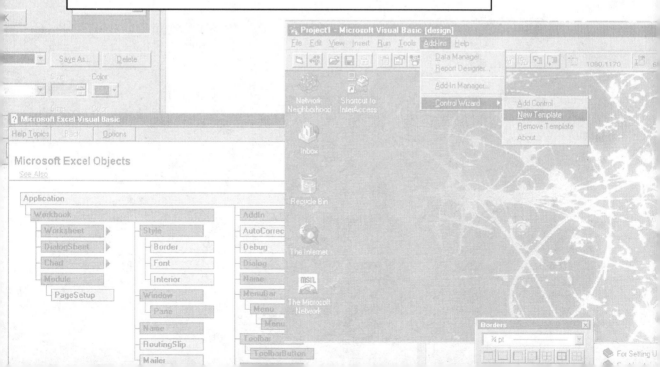

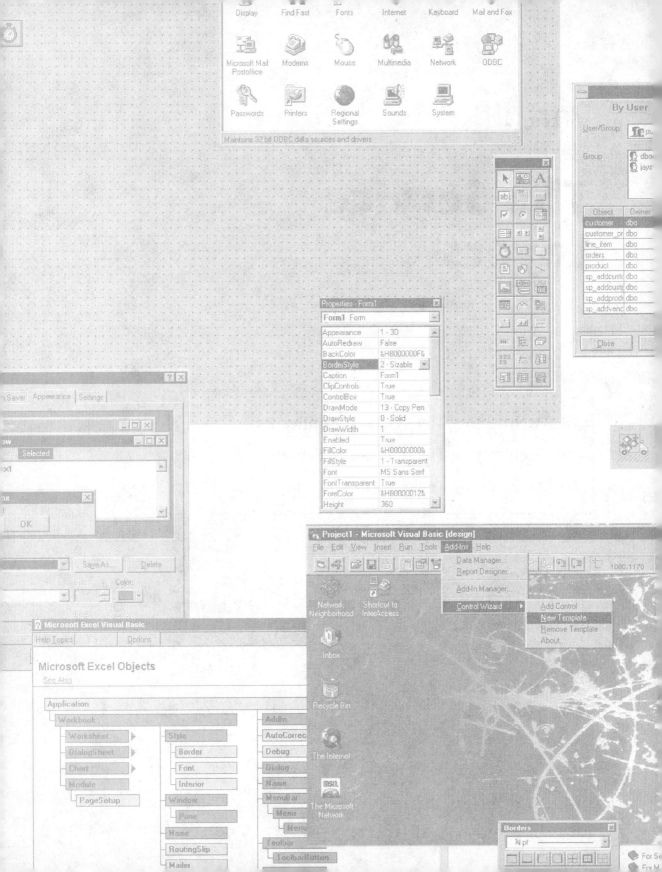

## Chapter 8

Architecting Tier 1: Client Applications

You learned in Chapter 2, "Application Architecture," that each layer of a three-tier client/server system has a specific function within the application architecture. This chapter explores the first tier, user services, in detail. As explained in previous chapters, this book uses the terms "users' services" and "client applications" synonymously to describe components that live within the first tier of a three-tier client/server architecture.

This chapter explains the following:

- The role of client applications in the three-tier architecture

- Deciding between 32-bit and 16-bit applications

- Accessing other user services from the client application

- Accessing business services from the client application

- User interface recommendations

- Creating client applications with tools other than Visual Basic

The Role of Client Applications

Understanding the role that client applications play in the three-tier architecture is critical in designing an effective interface. This section expands on this client application role, as summarized in Chapter 2.

The following list shows the key concepts that you should keep in mind when developing the client application:

III

The Service Layers

- The client application should act as a presentation layer, providing a graphical interface for gathering data and displaying information.

- The design of the client application should be user-driven.

- The client application should contain no business logic. Client applications should pass the "litmus test" of business logic. As described in a following section, the litmus test will determine if any business logic has been placed into the user services tier.

- Client applications that are developed by the Information Technology (IT) group within your organization can serve as the core user interface, but the end users also should be allowed to create custom front ends to business services.

These concepts are important to building the framework of a client application. The remainder of this section explains each of these items in detail.

Providing a Presentation Layer

The overall function of the *client application* is to provide the user with a graphical interface for gathering data and presenting information from the business services. This interface should perform the following functions:

- Clearly display the data delivered by business services

- Allow the users to understand the business services in its entirety

- Permit the users to easily navigate the business services

In following sections of this chapter, we discuss techniques useful when designing a user interface, incorporating controls in your client application, understanding the importance of design standards, and making use of the new functions provided by the Windows 95 operating system.

User-Driven Design

Because the client application provides the sole user interface to the business services, its development should be driven by the users. Only end users can determine when an application is simple enough to permit them to easily understand and properly navigate the business services.

Users should be involved in the requirements and design phases of the client application. In the initial phase of client application development, analysts should watch the end users work with the systems that have been deployed throughout the enterprise.

The current system may not be automated. Sales representatives, for example, may need to initiate orders by writing down on an invoice sheet the number and the quantity of product that a customer wants to order. This sheet might be sent to the central warehouse, where the order is assembled by hand. After an order is sent, a confirmation sheet may be sent back to the sales representative.

Whether or not the system is automated, the current business process will serve as a model for the new system. Observing the system presently in use allows you to focus on areas for improvement.

Several aspects of an existing system should be observed when watching users complete their work. Analysts should note areas of the client application that require users to perform the following tasks:

- **Perform manual tasks.** The client application should automate tasks that users must currently complete manually. For example, the client application may automatically look up the address, city, and state of a customer when the customer's name is entered into a text box.

- **Regularly perform repetitive functions.** The client application should simplify all tasks that the users repeat regularly. For example, if the business process requires a user to create a confirmation letter each time an order is sent, the client application should prompt the user to create this letter and complete as much of the letter as possible.

- **Require users to duplicate work.** The client application should eliminate duplicate work. For example, if the business process requires three customer names and addresses, the client application should populate the second and third fields automatically, after the first field is filled in.

Although these tasks seem obvious choices for areas of improvement, they should be consciously considered by the developer.

In each of the preceding cases, the nature of tasks performed by end users and the ways in which the end users complete those task are the prime factors in the design of the new client application. Developers should not assume, without first consulting end users, that they know the best way to perform a task.

III

The Service Layers

The developer should also consider how job roles dictate how users perform similar tasks in different ways. A sales representative in the field, for example, may enter two or three orders per day, while the customer-service representative will enter two or three hundred orders each day. Both users perform the same task, entering orders, and both will use the same business server, but each user may require two different client applications to facilitate ease of entry.

End-user input can help you develop a client application that requires users to have no knowledge of the rules involved in completing a business process. As was noted in the preceding section's example, placing an order with an order-processing application, should require that the user know only the following information:

- Name, Address, or ID of customer ordering the product

- Name or ID of product being ordered

- Quantity of product being ordered

In this example, the user should not have to know how to adjust inventory on hand. This is a business rule process and should be encapsulated in a business service.

Developing a Core Application

When building a client application, the IT staff should concentrate on creating a front end that includes the functionality required by a majority of users to complete their daily tasks. In an order-processing application, for example, most sales representatives in the field will input single orders placed daily by many customers. Therefore, the functionality needed to complete a single order should be included in the IT-developed client application.

What about the sales representatives that have customers who place a regular bimonthly order? Are these users out of luck? Must they continue to enter the same order on the first and fifteenth of every month?

In two-tier systems, IT departments often had to turn down requests for this type of functionality due to time and budget constraints. Essentially, sales representatives were out of luck; they would continue to spend time to perform a repetitive task. Businesses could not justify dedicating IT resources just to create a piece of functionality that would be used by only one user in the enterprise.

The three-tier architecture enables end users to create their own specialized front ends to perform functions such as automate repetitive tasks. Because the business services of the second tier will expose their objects to any OLE client application, any application that supports OLE automation, such as Excel, can be used to create custom front ends.

Allowing end users to create custom client applications simplifies their work without tying up valuable IT resources. IT can remain focused on building applications that provide the greatest benefit to an organization as a whole, and end users can augment these client applications with their own, more specialized client applications.

Coding the Client Application

When writing code for a client application, developers should remember to keep the first-tier devoid of all business rules utilized by the application. These rules should be located in the business services of the second tier.

By removing business rules from the first-tier, you provide the following benefits to the system:

- Making changes to business rules doesn't require a redeployment of client applications.

- Removing business rules from the traditional *fat clients* of the two-tier architecture allows other, customized front ends to utilize them.

The client application need only include code necessary to create a clear and logical graphical interface for the user.

Several good litmus tests exist that you can use to help determine whether your user and business logic is properly partitioned.

Test #1: Creating a New Application without Adding Business Logic

If you are unable to create a new client application without using logic contained in the original client application, that logic most likely is business logic.

For example, creating an order may involve determining what account should be billed for the product ordered. Often, companies that place orders have a billing address that differs from the address to which the product will be shipped.

In this case, it is the responsibility of the business services to determine if the business address of the customer differs from the shipping address. If the logic required to handle this task were placed in the client application, it would have to be rewritten each time a new client application was created. In other words, it would fail our test.

Test #2: Allowing End Users to Create Applications

When the client application is complete, ask yourself, "Would I, as an IT member, allow a user to create a custom front end in Excel that accesses the business services? If not, why not?"

If you answer "no" to this question, that particular piece of functionality (that prevents you from feeling comfortable with letting a user create a custom front end) is most likely business logic.

For example, you may answer "no" because a user-developed application may not properly log and audit user activity. If such logging and auditing is an organizational requirement, however, it is a business rule and should be incorporated into the business services tier.

Selecting a Controlling Application

Although the client application is capable of interacting with other applications in the user services tier, you typically will create one application that functions as the *controlling client application* for all other services in the first tier. The controlling client application will provide the primary user interface and coordination of other user services. The controlling client application does not have to be an OLE server because it generally is not controlled by other applications. The controlling client application, however, generally controls and coordinates other OLE servers, such as OLE controls, OLE automation servers, and OLE documents.

For example, an Order Entry client application may contain a single controlling client application developed in VB. This VB application, however, may make use of several other user services such as:

■ A common logon form implemented as an in-process OLE automation server

■ A spreadsheet OLE custom control for order detail display

■ Microsoft Excel for report printing

You may ask the question "Which development tool is best suited for the controlling application?" A controlling application should satisfy the following criteria:

- Provides the capability to interact with other components in the user services tier and business services tier, such as OLE automation servers and OLE controls

- Allows a developer to create a simple-yet-elegant user interface

- Employs a standard development language

Visual Basic satisfies all of these criteria. Developers can quickly and easily create an elegant front end, can interact with other components of the user-services tier as well as components in the business services tier. VB supports the integration of third-party tools, and uses a standard development language: Visual Basic. This makes Visual Basic an excellent choice for developing controlling applications.

Desktop tools such as Excel can make suitable controlling client applications in some scenarios, such as client applications created by end users' prototypes and applications with short life spans. But, for applications that require multiple developers, complex GUI interaction, and life spans measured in years, VB is the better choice. It permits better version control, supports team development tools, doesn't make source code available to users, is faster than VBA macros, and so on.

Choosing 16-Bit or 32-Bit Client Applications

Visual Basic 4.0 provides developers the ability to create both 16- and 32-bit applications from the same source code. 32-bit applications provide several benefits over 16-bit applications, however, including performance benefits and an enhanced API set under Windows NT and Windows 95.

32-bit applications require a 32-bit operating system to run. Although 32-bit Visual Basic offers many advantages over 16-bit, 32-bit operating systems may not be available to all end users.

This section outlines the following areas:

- Conditional Compilation, which eases development of both 16- and 32-bit applications from a single set of source code

- Advantages of 32-bit client applications

III

The Service Layers

Conditional Compilation

Developing both 16- and 32-bit client applications from a single set of source code is difficult because 16-bit client applications are unable to natively make calls to the 32-bit API set—they call only 16-bit APIs. Therefore, a call to a 32-bit API cannot be included in a compiled .EXE file. This call causes an error at runtime.

How, then, can 16-bit and 32-bit applications be developed from a single set of source code? Visual Basic provides a feature known as *conditional compilation* to overcome this obstacle.

Conditional compilation allows you to include only certain lines of code in your compiled .EXE file by creating *compilation constants*. When you compile your application, Visual Basic checks the values of these constants and, based on a coding construct defined in a following part of this section, includes only the lines of source code that you specify to include in the .EXE file.

The following two steps are necessary to conditionally compile your code:

- Declaring compiler constants

- Specifying lines of code to be conditionally compiled

Compiler constants are declared on the Advanced tab of the Options folder. These constants are global in scope—they apply everywhere in a project.

To declare a compiler constant, follow these steps:

1. From Visual Basic's Tools menu, select Options. The Options folder appears on-screen.

2. Click the Advanced tab on the options folder.

3. In the Conditional Compilation Arguments text box, enter the compiler constant that you are declaring and assign a value to the constant. For example, you can enter the following line:

   ```
   OSSystem = 1
   ```

   This creates the compiler constant *OSSystem* and sets it equal to 1.

Besides the compiler constants you define, Visual Basic defines constants for exclusive use with the #If...Then...#Else directive (explained in the following part of this section).

Table 8.1 defines the compiler constants on 16-bit development platforms.

Table 8.1   16-Bit Development Platforms Compiler Constants

Constant	Value	Description
Win16	True	Indicates that the development environment is 16-bit
Win32	False	Indicates that the development environment is not 32-bit

On 32-bit development platforms, the compiler constant Win32 has a value of True, and Win16 has a value of False.

To specify lines of code that should be conditionally compiled, you use the *#If...Then...#Else* directive. The behavior of the #If...Then...#Else compiler directive is the same behavior as the run-time If...Then...Else statement, except that the #If, #Else, #Else If, and #End If directives must appear on their own lines (no other code can appear on the same line as any of the directives).

In addition, the #If...#Then..#Else directive is evaluated at compile time. When you create an .EXE file, the compiler evaluates the directive once and includes only the appropriate code in the executable file. In contrast, the If...Then...Else statement is evaluated at runtime. Each time a call is made to a function that contains an If...Then...Else statement, the statement is evaluated.

The GetSubMenu API function, for example, has a 32-bit and 16-bit version. If you use the GetSubMenu API function in an application that will be compiled into both 16- and 32-bit versions, you can use the following code:

```
# If Win32 Then    ' 32-bit VB uses this Declare.
Declare Function GetSubMenu Lib "User32" (ByVal hMenu As Integer,
➥ByVal nPos As Integer) As Integer
# Else    ' 16-bit VB uses this Declare.
   Declare Function GetSubMenu Lib "User" (ByVal hMenu As Integer,
   ➥ByVal nPos As Integer) As Integer
# End If
```

When you compile the preceding code, using the 32-bit version of Visual Basic, the value of the conditional compilation constant Win32 is True, and the 32-bit declaration of the GetSubMenu is used. If you could peek inside the compiled code, you could imagine that you no longer would see the #If...Then...#Else directive, you would see only the following line:

```
Declare Function GetSubMenu Lib "User32" (ByVal hMenu As Integer,
➥ByVal nPos As Integer) As Integer
```

III

The Service Layers

When you compile the same source code by using the 16-bit version of Visual Basic, the value of the conditional compilation constant Win32 is False and, therefore, compiles with the 16-bit declaration. In this case, if you could see the compiled code, you would see only the following line:

```
Declare Function GetSubMenu Lib "User" (ByVal hMenu As Integer,
➥ ByVal nPos As Integer) As Integer
```

It's worthwhile to note that conditional compilation need not be used just to facilitate multi-platform development. Conditional compilation can be used in other useful ways—for example, to exclude debugging code from a production executable, which enables the developer to maintain both a debugging and run-time version of the application from the same source code.

Code excluded during conditional compilation is completely omitted from the final executable file, so it has no size or performance effect.

Benefits of 32-Bit Applications

32-bit applications offer several advantages over 16-bit applications including the following:

- Improved execution speed
- Better management of resources
- Increased stability
- Preemptive multitasking

Each of these advantages is explained in detail in the following text.

Improved Execution Speed

32-bit applications can make full use of the increased performance of 32-bit operating systems. These 32-bit applications will generally run faster than 16-bit applications in the same environment.

Better Management of Resources

32-bit applications do a better job of cleaning up after themselves after execution has completed. They are more apt to unload any DLLs that were loaded and release memory that the application used during run time.

32-bit applications and operating systems aren't limited by conventional DOS memory constraints.

Increased Stability

Because 32-bit applications run in their own address space, they are less likely to bring down other applications or the entire operating system if they crash. Under Windows 3.1, 16-bit applications shared address spaces in memory. Therefore, when an application that was sharing address space crashes, it also can bring down other applications that share this address space. This brings about a cascading effect, and eventually the whole operating system might crash.

16-bit applications continue to share address space in Window 95. Because of this, 16-bit applications still pose the problem of bringing down other 16-bit applications.

An important piece of a three-tier architecture, remote automation, is better supported in a 32-bit environment. Windows 95 and Windows NT have remote procedure call (RPC) mechanisms required by remote automation built in.

Preemptive Multitasking

Preemptive multitasking in 32-bit applications improves a system's responsiveness by allowing users to run multiple applications simultaneously. Preemptive multitasking also provides users the ability to integrate several business-critical applications in a smooth manner.

Conversely, under Windows 95, if one 16-bit application is busy, all 16-bit applications are busy and cannot be accessed until the busy application has completed its processing tasks. 32-bit applications running under Windows 95 are not subject to this type of blocking.

Recommend Using 32-Bit Code

Although it was noted previously in this chapter that not all users in the enterprise may have access to 32-bit operating systems, this book recommends focusing client application development on 32-bit platforms. The performance benefits of 32-bit code outlined previously in this chapter, along with the enhanced 32-bit API set included with the Windows NT and Windows 95 operating systems, are compelling reasons to move away from the 16-bit environments.

If 16-bit applications must be deployed in the enterprise, they should be generated from the same source code used to create the 32-bit client applications. You can accomplish this by using conditional compilation. Using the same source code eliminates the burden of managing multiple source code sets.

Accessing Other User Services

As mentioned in Chapter 2 and in the previous examples in this chapter, a client application is capable of using other services within the user services tier. In this scenario, the Visual Basic client application may tie together other components to create the user's interface.

The client application, for example, may be required to graph data obtained from a business server. Rather than writing the code to create a graph in the client application, this graph can be generated through OLE by using the Chart component of Microsoft Excel. In this case, Excel logically resides in the first-tier as well. Excel provides display and presentation functionality and physically resides on the end-user's workstation.

Several components exist in the first tier that will be used by the client application. These components include the following examples:

- OLE controls (OCXes)
- OLE automation servers
- OLE documents
- DLLs

Each component type can play a role within user services. This section explains how to access each component from your client application, and when these types of components should be used.

Typically, the client application is created by using Visual Basic. The application ties together the other components in the first tier. Figure 8.1 shows what a typical first tier of an order-processing application might look like.

In this system, the client application uses three additional components in the first tier: a Word compound document, an Excel pivot table automation object, and a MAPI DLL. Notice that the client application sits at the center, acting as the "glue" for the interoperable components.

The client application uses an Excel pivot table to display data to the user. The user can enter comments about the data in a compound Word document, then send the message by way of e-mail to a coworker. The sending of e-mail is accomplished through the MAPI.DLL.

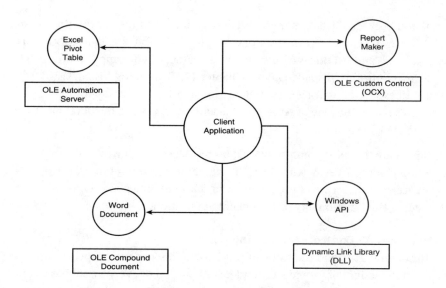

While users may create applications using other desktop front ends, such as Excel, this book recommends that you use Visual Basic to develop all applications that you plan to deploy enterprise-wide. Visual Basic's advanced features, flexibility, and improved speed of performance over applications such as Excel make it the best choice.

OLE Custom Controls

OLE Custom Controls (OCX) are the latest addition to Visual Basic. These controls provide the benefit of drop-in components, like VBXs did in previous versions of Visual Basic, combined with OLE technology. OCXes were described in detail in Chapter 5, "Controlling OLE Objects."

When an OCX is added to a Visual Basic project, it can be added to a form. After the control is added, you can call the control's methods and properties just as you can call any OLE object.

The Enterprise version of Visual Basic ships with several standard OCXes, including the TextBox and ListBox controls, as well as the RichTextBox control. OCXes provide benefit to the client application by shortening development time. The coding is already done for you.

For example, you can purchase an OCX that allows your application to perform spell checking on text entered in a text control. You also can purchase an OCX that allows a Visual Basic application to connect to legacy mainframe systems.

As you begin to develop more client applications, you may notice that certain OCXes will be used repeatedly. For example, aside from standard controls like text boxes and list boxes, you may notice that all of your applications include a Grid control for displaying data. Chapter 17, "Extending Visual Basic," describes several useful OCXes that are frequently used in applications. OCXes make this type of reuse possible without requiring the developer to generate large amounts of code.

OCXes are the most commonly used user-services component. Their ability to integrate seamlessly with the GUI, their high speed in terms of performance, and their ease of implementation make them a good choice for extending the functionality of your client application.

Windows 95 Controls and Techniques

Although it's beyond the scope of this book to discuss every aspect of user-interface design, or provide a complete description of every Visual Basic control in detail, discussing the first tier without mentioning these areas would be incomplete.

This section focuses on several control types and techniques that are useful to the enterprise developer. The topics discussed are shown in the following list:

- Common Dialogs

- The TreeView control

- Drag and Drop techniques

- Grid/Spreadsheet controls

Common Dialogs

Common Dialogs are modal response windows provided by the Windows operating system. These dialogs provide a common interface for operations, such as saving files, opening files, and printing files.

The CommonDialog control provides an interface between Visual Basic and the routines in the Microsoft Windows dynamic-link library COMMDLG.DLL. The routines in the DLL display the types of Common Dialogs shown in Table 8.2.

Table 8.2   The Common Dialog Boxes Available in Visual Basic 4.0

Common Dialog	Function
Color	Displays the Color Common Dialog. From the dialog box, a system color can be selected.
Font	Displays the Font Common Dialog. From the dialog box, a system font and size can be selected.
Open	Display the Open Common Dialog. From the dialog, a user can select the location and name of a file.
Printer	Displays the Printer Common Dialog. From the dialog, a user can choose a destination printer, set properties for a printer, or determine the number of copies to be printed.
Save	Displays the Save Common Dialog. From the dialog, a user can choose a name and location of the file to be saved.

If your client application requires a user to Open, Save, or Print a file, or if the user needs to select a color or font, you can use Common Dialogs to aid in performing these operations.

Common Dialogs save time because the interface required to handle operations was created for you. Additionally, as their name implies, the interfaces are common and consistent from application to application.

Using Common Dialogs simplifies tasks for the user. When users learn how to use the Open Common Dialog, for example, they will be able to open a file in any application that uses the Open Common Dialog.

After the CommonDialog control is added to a form, you can choose one of the Show methods of the CommonDialog object to display the appropriate common dialog. Table 8.3 lists the CommonDialog methods and the Common Dialogs that each method displays.

Table 8.3   The CommonDialog Control's Methods

Method	Dialog Box Displayed
ShowColor	Color
ShowFont	Font
ShowOpen	Open
ShowPrinter	Printer
ShowSave	Save

III

The Service Layers

The following code displays the Save Common Dialog box. The same code can be used to display any of the dialog boxes mentioned in the preceding table by changing the method ShowSave to the method associated with the dialog box that you want to display.

```
' Display the Save common dialog
cdgCommonDialog.ShowSave
```

The TreeView Control

Several new controls in Visual Basic are provided by the Windows 95 operating system. Because Windows 95 uses OLE objects to display things like Tab Sheets and Status Bars, Visual Basic is capable of using these controls.

The TreeView control, one of the new Windows 95 controls, is similar in function to the Outline control in previous versions of Visual Basic. You can use TreeView to display hierarchical data, and each entry in the control can have a small icon placed next to it. This visual cue helps users understand the type of data that is being displayed.

For example, the TreeView control can be used to display the contents of the computer's hard drive. To the left of each directory and sub-directory, a small picture of a folder appears. To the left of each picture, files associated with an application—such as Word documents—a picture of the application's icon appears. Files not associated with an application display a default picture.

The Windows 95 Explorer makes use of a TreeView control. The Explorer is a replacement to the File Manager application in Windows 3.1. Explorer-like applications are used throughout Windows 95, such as the Control Panel and the InBox. Third-party applications will also use Explorer-like interfaces. Using the TreeView control helps users become familiar with the Explorer type of control, which in turn helps them to better navigate the operating system. Conversely, users already familiar with the Explorer control will find the TreeView control familiar and easy to use.

Drag and Drop

Drag and drop is an important technique that client applications should include. Drag and drop allows a user to click an object, and, while holding down the left mouse button, drag the object to another space on the desktop. The user can then drop the object onto another control or onto the desktop (in some cases).

The File Manager application in Windows version 3.1 used drag and drop for copying and moving files. By clicking and holding down the mouse button on a file name, and then dragging it to a new directory, File Manager copied or moved the file. In an order-processing application, you might use drag and drop to simplify the order process. You can display a list of products in a list box. When a user clicks on a product listing and holds down the left mouse button, the user can drag the product listing onto an invoice sheet. When the product listing is dropped on the invoice, the Product ID, Product Description, and quantity columns are automatically populated. Customer service representatives will need to change only the quantity for the ordered item to complete the order.

In a document-management application, you might use drag and drop to allow users to drag a document from the Explorer and drop it into your application. When the document is dropped, the toolbars of your application merge with the toolbars of the application that was used to create the document.

Drag and drop is a useful, time-saving technique. By implementing drag and drop in your client application, you aid users in becoming more adept at navigating the operating system as a whole.

The Grid Control

The Grid control included with Visual Basic enables you to display data in a columnar format. Often, the clearest way to present data to a user is in the column format.

For example, when returning the results of a product search, the Grid control allows you to easily place the data into columns. Product ID, Product Name, and Quantity in Inventory each might be columns in the Grid.

Although the Visual Basic Grid control is sufficient for basic data display requirements, many third-party companies often enhanced Grid controls as VBXs and OCXes. Chapter 17, "Extending Visual Basic," examines some of these Grid controls in detail.

OLE Automation Servers

A second type of component a controlling application may access are OLE automation servers. Applications such as Excel, Word and Project all are OLE automation servers.

OLE automation servers provide powerful methods and properties that can be used by a Visual Basic application. Functions such as spell checking and chart creation can be accomplished through OLE automation. Chapters 5 through 7 detail controlling, creating, and managing OLE automation servers.

III

The Service Layers

How might an OLE automation server be used with the client application? You could create an OLE automation server that displays a system logon dialog window. The client application would display the dialog window that prompts a user for a name and password. When a user enters a name and password, the OLE automation server would pass this information to the business server for validation, then pass a success/fail message back to the client application. The GOLF order processing system demonstrates a system logon dialog window, implemented as in-process OLE automation server. See Chapter 24, "Sample Application #3: A Three-Tier Order Processing System," for more information.

Excel exposes many OLE automation servers. Excel's pivot tables are interactive worksheet tables, used to summarize data from an existing list or table. For example, you can use a pivot table to create a summarization of a sales representative's sales, per region and per quarter. Logically, the pivot table would look like the example in figure 8.2.

Fig. 8.2

A logical representation of an OLE automation server—the Pivot Table.

Sum of Sales	Quarter	Region		First Quarter Total	Grand Total
	First Quarter				
Sales Rep	NW	S	SE		
J. Adams	100	0	150	250	250
J. Best	200	0	0	200	200
J. Davis	0	0	250	250	250
L. Jones	0	100	0	100	100
Grand Total	300	100	400	800	800

If you wanted a different view of the data, a pivot table allows you to drag and drop columns to create different views.

In a client application, you may want to use a pivot table to hold data that was retrieved from a table. You may want to employ the pivot table's flexibility, but you don't need to display the pivot table to the user. OLE automation allows you to create a pivot table from Visual Basic, populate it, and modify it, all without displaying the pivot table to a user.

Users of the client application will be either local (which means the user has access to the network at all times), or remote (the user can only access the network at certain times). Both local and remote users have access to files on their desktop or laptop machines at all times. For this reason, user servers are usually distributed with the client application and reside locally—not on a network file server. Placing helper user services on a remote network will leave the remote user unable to run the client application at certain times.

When creating OLE automation servers for the first tier, create them as out-of-process servers (see Chapter 3, "Understanding OLE," for more information about in-process and out-of-process servers). Out-of-process servers operate up to 20 times faster than in-process servers. You will want this increased performance in the client application to ensure that end users don't have a long wait for OLE automation operations to complete.

Out-of-process servers must be local—you include a copy of the server on each end-user's desktop, which creates more work if updates to the server are made because you have to redistribute the server to all end users. The problem of redeployment is outweighed by the performance benefits of an out-of-process server.

OLE automation allows you to employ the powerful functions of specialized applications, such as spreadsheet and word-processing programs, without you spending the time or effort developing this functionality. Additionally, when internal changes are made to the OLE automation servers, your client applications receive the benefits of the enhancements without requiring you to re-deploy the actual client application.

For more information on OLE automation, see Chapter 5, "Controlling OLE Objects."

OLE Documents

Visual Basic's OLE container control allows you to create documents within an application. A full description of OLE documents is provided in Chapter 5, "Controlling OLE Objects."

In the user services tier, OLE documents are almost always implemented as out-of-process servers. These servers are provided by applications such as Excel and Word.

You can use OLE documents to present read-only data within your client application. An Excel spreadsheet, for example, can be inserted into your Visual Basic client application, and data retrieved from the business server can be displayed within it. You can use all of Excel's formatting, charting, and computational features to create a professional-looking display.

OLE documents also are useful when an application permits freeform input. In a workflow application, for example, users might generate e-mail messages to each other. An OLE document can provide all the formatting capabilities associated with the parent application.

OLE documents are not very well suited for structured data input. A timesheet entry program, for example, requires that the spreadsheet that is used for time entry has a specific layout. The days of the week may need to reside at the top of the form, time may need to be entered within a defined cell range, billing codes may need to be listed in a certain area of the sheet, and the employee's billable rate may need to be entered in a specific cell.

III

The Service Layers

This layout could be created in two ways—using Excel to create a template spreadsheet and distributing it along with the client application, or using OLE automation to create the sheet each time the application is run.

Because certain fields on the spreadsheet change periodically—such as the days of the week and billing codes—creating a spreadsheet in Excel requires a lot of work and may require that the spreadsheet is updated periodically. Redistributing the updated spreadsheet to all end users can prove quite a chore.

Creating the spreadsheet through OLE automation requires a large amount of code. Because the format of the timesheet may change regularly, you would need to redistribute the application to all end users as updates occur.

Additionally, several fields on the timesheet may require validation. The client application may require that data on the sheet is entered in a specific format, such as *mm/dd/yy*.

It is difficult to programmatically enforce rules such as validation in an OLE document. Users have access to too much functionality that a developer cannot account for.

DLLs

DLLs are groups of external procedures contained in files outside of your Visual Basic application. These procedures can perform many operations that VB cannot natively perform: displaying other windows in special states (such as a floating toolbar); performing complex calculations; or providing information about the operating system (such as how many milliseconds have elapsed since the operating system was started). The Windows API is an example of functionality that is accessible through DLLs.

Visual Basic is incapable of creating standard DLLs, but it can make calls to these procedures. To call a procedure in a DLL, you must know the following four things:

- The name of the procedure within the DLL you want to access

- The name of the DLL file which contains the procedure

- The number and data types of the arguments that are passed to the procedure as parameters

- The data type of the return argument if the procedure returns a value

After these four pieces of information are known, you can prepare your Visual Basic application to access the procedure.

The syntax for accessing DLLs from within Visual Basic is described in detail in Chapter 17, "Extending Visual Basic."

When would you use DLLs with a client application? The Windows API is a comprehensive set of functions that allows you to perform standard Windows operations, such as reading the contents of an application's .INI file, that cannot be handled inherently by Visual Basic.

Some third-party vendors release their APIs only in a DLL form. Many OCXes and VBXs have powerful functions that enhance the visual aspects of the control, such as spreadsheet sorting or spell checking. These functions often are implemented as APIs and packaged in a DLL included with the control.

Developers should be aware of several difficulties they may encounter when using DLLs with the client application. DLLs are tied to the operating system—16-bit operating systems use 16-bit DLLs, and 32-bit operating systems are capable of using 32-bit DLLs. If you deploy your application on both 16-bit and 32-bit platforms, you need to make sure that your application uses the proper version of the DLL.

All DLLs that an application accesses must be deployed with the application. Some DLLs are quite large. If you plan on using floppy disks to distribute your application, be sure to take into account the space required by DLLs.

Building a client application around procedures bundled in DLLs has its advantages. When changes are made to DLLs, a redeployment of the client application is not required—only the DLL component needs to be updated.

Remember that the first tier does not refer to a physical location, it refers to a grouping—components of the first tier, such as DLLs and OLE Automation Objects, do not need to reside in the same physical location. Placing all the DLLs accessed by client applications in a single location, a network file server for example, aids in simplifying the redeployment process.

Accessing Business Services from the Client Application

We have learned that the main role of the client application is gathering and presenting data to end users. Because the client application has no direct contact with the data services in a three-tier architecture, all data must pass through the business services of the second tier.

Business services are usually implemented as OLE automation servers. Unlike automation servers such as Word & Excel, business servers will often be without a graphical interface. They are used to enforce the business rules of the enterprise, retrieve data from databases, or manage instances of OLE automation servers.

Client applications access business services in the same way they access OLE automation servers in the first tier. First, a business object is assigned to an object variable, then the objects method and properties are affected by the client application. Usually, however, business services are located on a centralized server, where user services typically are places in the client application workstation.

The following chapter discusses the architecture of business services in detail, but before you can understand how client applications access business services, you need an understanding of a typical business server's interface. For a better understanding of the way business services work with the client application, we will examine a hypothetical order-processing application.

A sales representative in the field is placing an order for a customer. When the sales representative supplies the client application with the pertinent order information—such as customer ID, product ID, and quantity of product to order—the client application passes this information to the business server through OLE automation. The following code fragment shows what this action might look like in Visual Basic code:

```
Public Sub PlaceOrderTest ()
    'Procedure creates an order
    ' Create an OLE object for the order manager
    Dim loOrderMgr as Object
    Set loOrderMgr = CreateObject("OrdrMgr.Application")
    ' The Customer ID, Product ID and Order Quantity all
    ' reside in form level variables
    ' name fiCustomerID, fiProductID, and fiQuantity, respectively
    ' Invoke the PlaceOrder method of the NewOrder object and pass
    ' the order Information to it
    loOrderMgr.PlaceOrder Customer := fiCustomerID, Product :=
    ➥ fiProductID, Quantity := fiQuantity
End Sub
```

You can see from this example how simple interaction between the client application and business server is in a three-tier architecture. Because all business logic is contained in the second tier, the first tier does not require a large amount of code to process incoming data. It only needs to supply the information that the business server requires.

In this example, the business server encapsulated all kinds of complex business rules: after the order is placed, the business server deducts the quantity of product ordered, prepares an invoice for the shipment, or holds the order until items not in inventory can be located. This work is isolated from the client application, which is concerned only with presentation and process flow.

To continue with our order-processing example, suppose three weeks have passed since the original order was placed, and the customer has called to inquire about the status of the order. The client application needs to query the business services to determine the status of the order. The code required to do this might look like the following:

```
Public Sub OrderStatusTest ()
    '
    '
    Dim loOrderMgr as Object
    Dim liOrderStatus as Integer
    Set loOrderMgr = CreateObject("OrdrMgr.Application")
    '
    '
    '
    '
    liOrderStatus = loOrderMgr.GetOrderStatus(OrderID :=
    ➥fiOrderID)
    ' Code to display message box
End Sub
```

Again you can see how simple these kinds of tasks become when OLE automation servers are used.

What happens if the order process changes? The old method of ordering required all items in an order to be in inventory before an order could be shipped—if a customer ordered 20 units of a product, and only 16 units existed in inventory, the entire order would be held until the additional 4 units could be located.

Management has decided that this policy is making too many customers unhappy, and that the company will ship any portion of the order currently in inventory—16 units in this case, and send the remaining 4 units at a later date.

No adjustments would have to be made to the code that was used to place a new order. Changes would be made in the business services, eliminating the need redeploy client applications to all users.

Creating a Graphical Interface

Thus far, we have spent most of this chapter discussing the theory behind the role of the client application, methods for accessing other components in the user services tier, and accessing business services. This section focuses on creating the graphical interface that will be used to gather and display data to the end users. This section discusses the following areas:

III

The Service Layers

- Creating MDI applications

- Creating SDI applications

- Using Visual Basic controls

- Controlling system colors and fonts

While the remainder of this section details each aspect of the user interface outlined previously, you should observe several rules when creating a user interface.

First, the goal of any user interface should be clarity and restraint—the user should have maximum usability of the interface with a minimum amount of learning time. Controls, menu options, and toolbar buttons should be clear in their function and discoverable to the user.

The product you are creating should be efficient and functional but also should be attractive and easy to use. Graphic design should be used in an interface to increase usability, and not for decoration. A screen cluttered with controls, icons, and text makes it look difficult to use.

Using standard sizes for controls such as command buttons, aligning all controls on a screen, and using color sparingly all contribute to a neater, crisper interface that is clearer in design.

User feedback is critical during the design phase of your interface. Solicit as much feedback from end users as possible about the appearance and ease-of-use of your interface. No matter how perfect you think your design is, remember that you are not a typical user, and only a typical user can determine the quality of the interface.

The design of your application should be consistent with both the operating system's visual appearance and the interfaces of other applications that appear on the end user's desktop. This prevents users from having to relearn the function of controls such as the command button or the Help menu.

Using these design recommendations will help your client application result in both a more professional-looking application interface and an interface that allows users to easily discover the full power of the application and the functionality contained within it.

Creating MDI Applications

Visual Basic allows you to create *Multiple Document Interface* (MDI) applications. Word and Excel are examples of MDI applications. MDI applications have a single, *MDI Parent* form that is displayed in the background at all times. *MDI Child* forms are displayed in the foreground of the application, and are always contained within the MDI Parent.

MDI applications provide the following advantages over non-MDI applications:

- In an MDI application, all forms are contained within the MDI parent providing an easy-to-navigate application "package." Forms in non-MDI applications can appear anywhere on the screen, which makes it difficult for an inexperienced user to navigate between them.

- MDI Parent forms provide a place to create menus and toolbars that can be viewed by a user at all times. Even with several MDI child forms open at that same time, users can easily relocate themselves by using the toolbar. In non-MDI applications, users may bury the toolbar under several layers of forms, making it difficult for less experienced users to find.

The following sections outline features that are common to most MDI applications.

Examples of MDI Applications

Many applications developed for the Windows 3.1, Windows for Workgroups, and Windows NT platforms are MDI applications. As you learned in a previous section, MDI applications are characterized by their capability to display multiple documents within a single parent form and allow a user to navigate between the documents without leaving the application.

MDI applications place an emphasis on the parent form. The parent form usually contains controls that are common to all child forms displayed within it. Often, the child forms are devoid of any type of control or menu. Microsoft Word 6.0 is an example of a MDI application. All documents are displayed as MDI child documents within an MDI parent frame. The MDI child allows you to type text onto the child, but all formatting operations and functions that affect text are all performed via the MDI parent's toolbar.

Microsoft Excel 5.0 is another example of an MDI application. Excel allows you to load MDI child forms, referred to as worksheets. You can type text and formulas into the cells of a worksheet, but to format the text or add controls to a sheet, you must access commands provided by the MDI parent's toolbars.

Components of an MDI Application

MDI applications often feature several common components:

III

The Service Layers

- MDI Child forms

- Toolbars

- Menus

The following sections discuss each of these MDI components and explain their functions within the application.

MDI Child Forms

MDI Child forms, as the name implies, are forms that will be contained within the bounds of the MDI Parent form. Word uses MDI Child forms. When you open a new Word document, you cannot move the document outside the confines of the MDI Parent form.

The area in which MDI child forms are displayed is known as the *MDI client area*. Child forms are restricted to the MDI client area; they cannot be moved outside of it. The MDI client area extends beyond the bottom, left, and right margins of a display screen. If you move a portion of an MDI child form off of the left, right, or bottom edges of the screen, scroll bars appear around the MDI client area, allowing you to scroll the MDI child document into view.

MDI children allow you to display multiple copies of a form at one time. Each copy of a form maintains its own set of data. A word-processing application allows you to work on many documents at the same time. An order-processing application may allow you to view the contents of several different orders at the same time, each within its own MDI child window.

Many MDI child forms lack any type of toolbar or menu control. Rather than duplicating a menu or toolbar for each form, the MDI parent contains a single toolbar and menu that can be used to affect the MDI child forms. The MDI parent toolbar and menu contains all of the functions that are used to manipulate information within the document, as well as manipulate the document. The MDI parent toolbar and menu are explained in following sections.

Toolbars

Toolbars in MDI applications are included to provide quick access to commonly used functions. For example, most MDI apps include toolbar buttons that enable a user to quickly open a document, save a document, or create a new child document. The toolbar buttons prevent a user from having to access the applications menu or to press a hotkey combination.

Usually, only the MDI parent form contains a toolbar. All toolbar buttons used in the application are placed on the MDI parent's toolbar and not on the MDI children because the MDI parent is the focus of control in an MDI application.

The MDI toolbar buttons not only perform menu operations *against* the document—such as opening it, closing it, or saving it—but they also perform functions *within* the document, such as changing the color of the document's text, performing spell-check operations or copying text from the document onto the clipboard. As you will learn in the following section of this chapter, this is a major difference between SDI applications and MDI applications.

Because all forms used by an MDI application are contained within the parent, the parent's toolbars are often free to float around the MDI parent frame. Many MDI application's allow you to drag a section of the toolbar and drop it into the MDI client area. The floating toolbar can then be "docked" back onto the main toolbar.

Usually, these floating toolbars are grouped by function. For example, Excel allows you to hide and display a formatting toolbar that contains toolbar buttons specific to Excel's formatting functions. You can float the toolbar about the MDI client. This allows you to move the toolbar close to the area of the worksheet you are formatting. In addition, you do not have to search the main toolbar to find the formatting function you need to use. All formatting functions will be contained in the floating toolbar.

In previous versions of Visual Basic, toolbars were often created by placing a picture box control onto the MDI form. The picture box control had an Align property that allowed it to be placed directly onto the client area of an MDI parent form. You could then place command buttons onto the picture box control, thus creating toolbar buttons.

Windows 95 now provides a Toolbar control, which allows you to quickly create a toolbar that contains buttons.

Menus

In addition to toolbars, most MDI applications will include a menu on the MDI parent form. The menu, like the toolbar, contains commands that affect the MDI child forms. In addition, the menu will contain commands that affect the entire application, such as default fonts for new documents, the option to display and hide pieces of the MDI parent toolbar, and options to exit the application.

III

The Service Layers

A standard MDI parent menu includes the following menu items:

- **File**—The File menu item contains commands that directly affect the MDI child document, such as New, Open, Save, Close, and Print. The File menu also contains commands to Exit the application.

- **Edit**—The Edit menu contains commands that allow a user to Copy, Cut, and Paste text to and from the Windows clipboard. The Edit menu may also contain Find and Replace commands that allow users to locate and/or change specific text items within MDI child documents.

- **Tools**—The Tools menu contains commands that perform utility functions on MDI child documents, such as spell checking or word-count functions. The Tools menu usually contains an Options command, which allows users to set global options for the application, such as default fonts, default directories, and information about the user of the application.

- **Window**—The Window contains commands such as Arrange and Tile that enable you to arrange the MDI child windows displayed within the MDI parent form. The Window menu also contains a list of all MDI child documents currently displayed. By selecting the name of the child document, a user can move directly to it.

- **Help**—The Help menu provides users with direct access to an applications Help file. The Help menu contains commands such as Contents, which displays a Help file's contents screen and Search for Help on, which displays a Help file's index screen. For more information on Help files and the Help menu, see Chapter 15, "Adding Help to an Application."

Including these standard menu items in an MDI application helps make it more recognizable to a user. After users learn how to Close an MDI child document by using menu commands, they should be able to Close a document in any MDI application.

Notice that, like the MDI toolbar, the MDI menu contains commands that operate within the MDI child document, such as Edit, Copy, and Paste. You will see in the following section that this is a major difference between MDI and SDI applications.

Creating SDI Applications

With the release of Windows 95, Microsoft has indicated a new direction in client application interface: Single Document Interfaces (SDI). In sharp contrast to MDI applications, SDI applications stress control over individual documents. A single controlling window is used to launch separate document windows. These individual document windows aren't bounded by the controlling window, as are MDI applications. The document windows, as you will see later in the chapter, are more self-encompassing than MDI child forms. They contain their own version of a toolbar and menu.

Microsoft has indicated that newer versions of Windows will be *document centric*—users will be able to run and save OLE documents within the context of the operating system. The user may have no idea as to what controlling application was used to create the document. For example, a user might create an Excel chart, populate it with data, and save the chart to disk as an object. A second user then can locate the chart object on the hard drive and launch it with no knowledge of the application that was used to create it.

In many respects, SDI is very similar to MDI. Both designs use a parent/child relationship metaphor. With MDI, the parent is an application such as Word or Excel. With SDI, the parent is not an application, but is *the operating system*. For example, users can switch between SDI documents in Windows 95, using the Taskbar. When an e-mail document is opened, the document is displayed in its own document window. The e-mail document window is listed on the Taskbar, just as an MDI child document is displayed at the bottom of the MDI parent frame. A user can display many e-mail document windows at one time, just as a user can display many MDI child documents within the context of the MDI parent frame.

You can see that the emphasis in SDI applications is on the document, and not on the application used to create or view it. This helps SDI applications fit neatly into the document-centric view. Developing SDI applications now will help to prepare your business for future operating systems. The remainder of this section outlines common components found in SDI applications and how you can use Visual Basic to successfully create and implement these components.

Examples of SDI Applications

Many of the applications new to Windows 95 are implemented by using an SDI interface. The Microsoft Exchange InBox is an example of an SDI application. When you double-click the InBox icon on the desktop, the InBox controlling window, shown in figure 8.3, is displayed:

Fig. 8.3
The Windows 95 InBox controlling window.

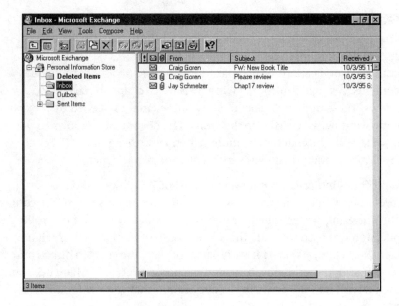

Components of an SDI Application

Like MDI applications, SDI applications generally include the following common elements:

- A controlling window

- TreeView and ListView controls

- Controlling window toolbars

- Controlling window menus

- Document windows

- Document-window toolbars

- Document-window menus

The next few sections cover each of these components in detail and explain the role each plays in the SDI interface.

Controlling Window

The controlling window of an application is the logical equivalent of an MDI parent form in an MDI application. When you execute an application by double-clicking it, the controlling window is displayed. Figure 8.3 shows the Windows 95 InBox controlling window.

An SDI application's controlling window usually displays a list of all documents that were created or otherwise associated with the SDI application. For example, the InBox controlling window displays all mail documents that were created by a user as well as all mail documents that were sent to the user via e-mail or fax. Later in this chapter, we discuss the Windows 95 control used to display the controlling application's associated documents.

The controlling window also contains a toolbar and a menu. However, the SDI controlling window's menu and toolbar are distinctively different from an MDI parent form's toolbar and menu. As you will see later in this section, an SDI application divides its menu and toolbar contents between the controlling window and the document window.

Where the MDI parent form contains a client area in which MDI child forms are displayed, the SDI controlling window has none. SDI document windows are displayed outside of the SDI controlling application. Note, however, that SDI child documents cannot be viewed or loaded without also running the SDI controlling window. For example, you can double-click a mail document that you have saved to disk. The mail document is saved as a standalone file, existing outside of the controlling window. However, when the mail document is double-clicked, not only is the saved mail document displayed, the controlling window—in this case the InBox—also is loaded by Windows. This process may help you to think in terms of a controlling window and a document window.

To help understand each of the components used in the SDI application interface, the following sections will explain the components in greater detail.

TreeView and ListView Controls

TreeView and ListView controls, which were explained previously in this chapter, are used extensively in the SDI controlling application. Returning to the InBox controlling window that was shown in figure 8.3, you can see that the left portion of the window uses a TreeView control to display a hierarchical list of a user's Personal Information Store. The Information Store is a group of folders used to organize documents within the InBox, similar to the way you might organize all of your files within the Explorer.

The right portion of the controlling window uses a ListView control to display all the documents contained within a folder in the Personal Information Store. The ListView control allows you to sort the documents contained within it by name, date received, subject, and various other criteria.

III

The Service Layers

The ListView control can display icons within a row, which allows you to provide an additional visual cue as to the type or types of documents that you are listing. For example, the InBox's ListView control displays a small envelope next to each e-mail document. The ListView control also indicates e-mail files with attachments by showing a paper clip to the left of the document's *From* field.

In a document-centric operating system, these two controls will be used extensively. Throughout Windows 95, you can see other applications using the two controls such as the Windows Explorer. Incorporating these controls into your SDI applications helps users become more efficient at navigating the application. After they learn the basics of ListView and TreeView operation, they will be prepared to manipulate almost any interface that contains the two controls.

Controlling Window Toolbars

Several times in this chapter, we discussed the difference between the toolbars in an MDI application and an SDI application. The main difference between the two toolbars can be summed up in two sentences: The MDI toolbar provides access to commands that can directly affect the internal contents of a document. The SDI toolbar does not.

For example, Word 6.0's toolbar contains buttons that allow you to Cut and Paste text within a document. You also can change font style and sizes from the toolbar. If you look at the InBox's toolbar, shown in figure 8.3, you see no such buttons. The SDI interface of the InBox's controlling window allows you to open, close, and save mail documents; create new e-mail documents; and retrieve or send e-mail. The toolbar does not allow you to affect the internal contents of an e-mail message. That, as you will see later in the chapter, is accomplished through the SDI document window.

Like an MDI parent form's toolbar, an SDI controlling window's toolbar generally has several standard toolbar buttons, which are shown in the following list:

- **Open**—Opens an existing document. Clicking the button causes an SDI document window to be displayed outside of the SDI controlling application.

- **New**—Creates a new instance of a document. Clicking the button causes a new document window to be displayed outside of the controlling window.

- **Directory hierarchy navigation buttons**—This button, or group of buttons, helps a user navigate the hierarchical structure of the TreeView or ListView control in the controlling window. At least one button is usually included, allowing a user to navigate up to the next highest directory level.

- **Print**—Prints the currently selected document.

- **Delete**—Deletes the currently selected document.

When developing and SDI application, you probably will include several toolbar buttons with functionality specific to your application.

Controlling Window Menus

You learned in the previous section that MDI parent form toolbar's differ from SDI controlling windows in that functionality specific to the internal contents of a document is not represented on the SDI toolbar. The same rule holds true for SDI controlling window menus.

The SDI controlling window's menus will contain commands that enable you to act upon a document *as a whole*, such as deleting the document or saving the document to a file. You will not find commands on a controlling window's menu that allow you to affect the internal contents of a document. The MDI parent form's Edit menu, for example, contains the Copy, Cut, and Paste commands, which users can use to modify the internal contents of a document displayed in an MDI child form. The SDI controlling window's Edit menu contains commands, such as Mark as Read, which modifies the appearance of a document's icon in the SDI ListView control to visually indicate to a user that the document was read.

Just as the controlling window has standard toolbar controls, most SD controlling window menus will contain the following menu items:

- **File**—This item contains commands such as Open, Move, Copy, or Print. These commands perform actions on an entire document. For example, the Copy command will not copy the contents of a document, but does create a copy of the document. The Open command opens an existing document in its own document window. The File menu also should contain an Exit command, which is used to Exit the application.

- **Edit**—The Edit menu contains commands that affect the visual display of the ListView or TreeView controls on the controlling window. For example, we discussed the Mark as Read option previously in this section.

■ **Tools**—The Tools menu contains commands that can be used to affect a document as a whole, such as the Deliver command in the InBox's menu. The Tools menu usually contains an Options command that allows a user to set global options for an application, such as the default display font used.

■ **Help**—The controlling window's Help menu usually contains the commands described in Chapter 15, "Adding Help to an Application."

Document Windows

SDI document windows are the logical equivalent of MDI child forms in an MDI application. Like MDI child forms, SDI document windows are used to display documents that are associated with the SDI application. The Windows 95 InBox, for example, displays SDI document windows that contain e-mail or fax documents.

Document windows differ from MDI child forms in the following aspects:

■ SDI document windows are not contained by a client, as MDI child forms are.

■ SDI document windows contain their own toolbars and menus. MDI child forms, however, either lack menus and toolbars or have menus and toolbars that merge with the MDI parent menus and toolbars.

■ When displayed or minimized, SDI documents are represented on the Windows 95 Taskbar with an icon and title. With MDI, however, only the MDI parent form is displayed on the Taskbar. MDI child forms are displayed as minimized icons within the MDI client area.

Usually, SDI document windows are implemented as createable OLE automation servers.

Similar to other types of forms and windows discussed in this chapter, document windows generally contain several common interface components. These components are discussed in the following sections.

Document Window Toolbars

Document window toolbars are identical to all other toolbars we have discussed so far. The document window toolbars differ only in content. In addition to containing toolbar buttons that affect the application as a whole—such as buttons for navigating the hierarchical document directory—the document window toolbar contains toolbar buttons that affect the content of the document being displayed.

For example, the document window of the InBox (see fig 8.4), contains tool-bar buttons that allow you to format the text within the document being displayed. The toolbar also contains a Print toolbar button, a Delete toolbar button, and a Help toolbar button.

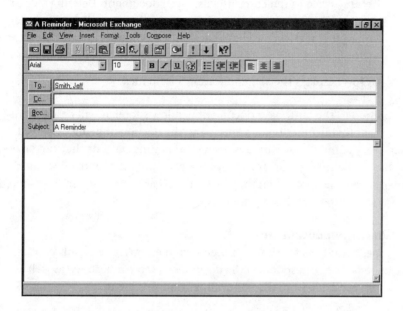

Fig. 8.4
The InBox's
document window.

In a previous section, we discussed that a document window cannot be displayed without its controlling window also being loaded. This allows the document window to maintain a link to the application information stored in the controlling window. For example, the InBox document window displays a single document. When reading through your e-mail, it may become tedious to have to access the ListView control in the controlling window, double-click the document you want to read, read the document in a document window, close the document window, and return to the controlling application to select a new document from the ListView control.

Rather than requiring all of the preceding steps, the document window uses its link to the controlling window and presents two buttons, placed near the center of the toolbar. These two buttons have arrow icons that point up and down. By clicking the down arrow button, you can move to the next document in the ListView list. The document currently displayed in the document window is replaced with the next document in the controlling window's list. Likewise, clicking the up arrow button replaces the currently displayed document with the previous document in the controlling application's list. These two buttons save the user from a large amount of additional work.

III

The Service Layers

An SDI document window generally contains the following standard toolbar buttons:

- **Print**—Prints the currently displayed document.

- **Delete**—Deletes the currently displayed document. Deleting a document doesn't mean that control returns to the controlling window. Rather, the next document in the control window's document list may be displayed.

- **Help**—Displays the SDI application's Help file.

In addition to the buttons, a document window's toolbar will contain buttons that provide functionality specific to the document being displayed. For example, the InBox also displays several formatting buttons that can be used to change the style, color, and size of the text contained in the document. An order processing application may include toolbar buttons for adding an item to an order or performing a price check.

Document Window Menus

Document windows also contain their own menus. These menus contain commands that correspond to the document's toolbar buttons, as well as functions available from the controlling window's menu.

For example, the InBox document window's menu contains an Edit menu item that displays commands that allow you to Cut, Copy, or Paste text within an e-mail document. The document window's Tools menu item contains an Options command that corresponds to the Option command in the controlling window's Tools menu.

Like the document window's toolbar, the main difference between a controlling window's menu and the document window's menu is that the document window's menu will contain commands that can directly affect the internal contents of the document being displayed. The items in the following list are commonly found on a document window's menu:

- **File**—The File menu item contains commands that affect the entire SDI document, such as Save and Print. The File menu will also contain a Close command, which closes the currently displayed document.

- **Edit**—The Edit menu contains commands that allow a user to Copy, Cut, and Paste text to and from the Windows clipboard. The Edit menu may also contain Find and Replace commands that allow users to locate and/or change specific text items within a document.

- **View**—The View menu allows a user to adjust the document window's interface. From here, users may choose to hide and display toolbars or select the next or previous document in a list.

- **Tools**—The Tools menu contains commands that perform utility functions on the document, such as spell-checking or word-count functions. The Tools menu generally contains an Options command, which allows users to set global options for the application, such as default fonts, default directories, and information about the user of the application.

- **Help**—The Help menu provides users with direct access to an application's Help file. The Help menu contains commands such as Contents, which displays a Help file's contents screen, and Search for Help on, which displays a Help file's index screen. For more information about Help files and the Help menu, see Chapter 15, "Adding Help to an Application."

Other Types of Forms

In both SDI and MDI applications, forms should appear on-screen as MDI children, SDI document windows or *modal response forms*. Modal response forms are simple, modal windows that halt application execution until a user responds to a question.

Modal response windows are used to ask a question before committing an action. In a word-processing application, for example, if a user makes changes to a document, and then attempts to close the document before saving it. Figure 8.5 shows the Microsoft Word modal response window that appears when this situation occurs.

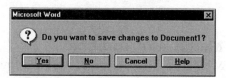

Fig. 8.5
A modal response window, prompting a response before action can continue in an application.

The application cannot continue to execute until the user saves the document (Yes), closes the document without saving (No), or cancels the close operation and returns to editing the document (Cancel).

Modal response forms also can be used to solicit information from a user that is critical to the completion of a process. For example, when a word-processing document is saved for the first time, a modal response form, shown in figure 8.6, appears, asking the user for the name and location of the file to which the document will be saved. Without this information, the save process cannot continue.

Fig. 8.6

A modal response form in Word.

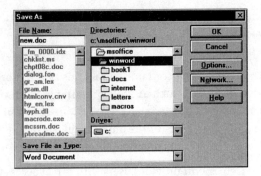

The modal response window in the preceding example is a special type of window known as a *Common Dialog*. Common Dialogs are standard response windows used in operations such as saving, opening, or printing files. Common Dialogs were discussed in more detail in previous sections of this chapter.

Only one copy of a modal response can be displayed at a time. When the form is displayed, the application halts execution until the form is unloaded. To display a form modally in Visual Basic, use the *Modal* style with the *Show* keyword.

The following code shows how to display a modal response window:

```
Sub DisplayModalForm ()
    '
    ' Declare a constant for the MODAL style
    CONST MODAL = 1

    ' Display a form
    frmFormToShow.Show MODAL
    '
    '
End Sub
```

Negotiating Menus and Toolbars

Toolbar and *Menu Negotiation* is the process of active documents in an application sharing the menu and toolbar space on the MDI Parent form. When a menu is added to a MDI Child form, for example, and the MDI Child form is activated in the application, the child form's menu appears at the top of the MDI Parent form instead of the MDI Parent's menu. The same holds true for Toolbars.

Negotiation becomes important when OLE documents are displayed in an MDI application. If you allow your users to open Word documents from within your application, you will want them to have all the functionality that Word provides. Negotiation allows you to display the commands and toolbar buttons that Word uses, within the context of your MDI application.

You accomplish Toolbar and Menu negotiation by setting the NegotiateToolbar property of an MDI form to True. This property is set in the Properties Window. By default, the NegotiateMenus property of the MDI Parent form is set to True. Because of the added functionality and ease of use that negotiation provides, this book recommends that all MDI Parent menus and toolbars are made negotiable.

Selecting Border Sizes and Window Controls

A forms border style is controlled by setting the BorderStyle property of the form. Figure 8.7 shows the BorderStyle property, as it appears in the Properties Window.

Fig. 8.7
A form's BorderStyle property.

Although Visual Basic provides several choices for a form's BorderStyle, most forms use only one of two settings.

The Sizable setting allows user to resize the form when it is displayed in the running application. Excel worksheets are an example of sizable forms.

When the Sizable setting is selected, Visual Basic sets the *MaxButton* and *MinButton* properties to true. The MaxButton property, when set to true, displays a maximize button in the upper right corner of the form. When clicked, an MDI Child form fills the entire child area of the MDI Parent. If the form is a document window, it fills the entire desktop. Figure 8.8 shows a form in a maximized state.

III

The Service Layers

Fig. 8.8
A maximized Word document. When maximized, MDI Child forms such as this one occupy the entire MDI Parent screen.

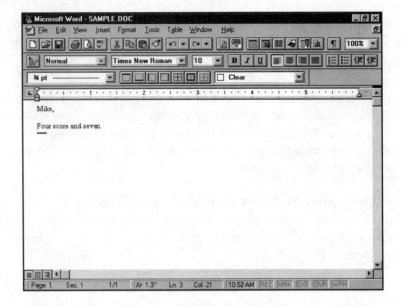

If the maximize button is clicked when the form is in its maximized state, the form returns to the size it was before the user clicked the maximize button the first time.

The MinButton property, when set to true, displays a minimize button in the upper right corner of the form. When the minimize button is clicked, an MDI Child form is displayed as a minimized icon at the bottom of the MDI Parent. If the form is a document window, it is displayed in the Taskbar. Figure 8.9 shows a minimized MDI Child form.

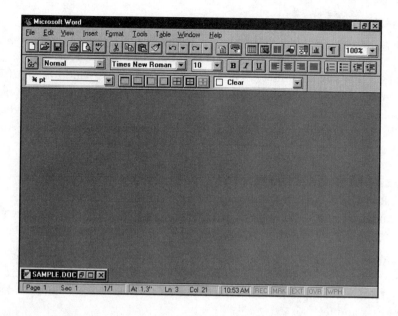

Fig. 8.9
A minimized
Word document.
The document
appears in the
lower left corner
of the screen.

Controlling System Settings under Windows 95

Several properties and controls that were part of Visual Basic 3.0 moved to the operating system in Windows 95, which means that you, as a developer, no longer will change properties like the background color of forms or the color of text on command buttons from within Visual Basic.

Instead, these kinds of properties are defined as global standards by a user through the Control Panel. Among the properties controlled by Windows 95 are the following:

- The Appearance property

- The BackColor property

- The ForeColor property

III

The Service Layers

Appearance

The Appearance property of a Visual Basic OLE control has two settings—3-D and Flat. This setting was added to allow a developer to give a 3-D look to controls that will be running in environments other than Windows 95. Under Windows 95, all controls have a 3-D look, which makes the Flat option obsolete. For consistency, the Appearance property of all controls should be set to 3D, which ensures that all controls have the same appearance if the application is run under a different version of Windows.

BackColor and ForeColor

The BackColor and ForeColor properties of a control determine the background color and the color of the text displayed in the control, respectively. Changing the settings of these properties has no effect under Windows 95.

The settings for background color and text color are controlled under the Control Panel's Display Window, shown in figure 8.10. These settings help to ensure that all applications running under Windows 95 have a more consistent look and feel.

Fig. 8.10

The Appearance Tab of the Display folder.

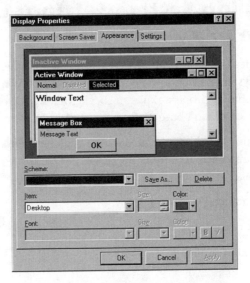

Note that, although the color of text cannot be changed from Visual Basic, the Font property of a control still allows you to change the style and size of the text.

Implementing Coding Guidelines

When you develop client applications, implementing the coding guidelines early in the development life cycle is an important step. *Coding guidelines* are conventions that are used when naming controls, declaring variables, and writing procedures.

Guidelines are important to development, especially in a team environment. Guidelines allow different developers to create code of similar form and function. This, in turn, allows other developers who may review the code to quickly understand its intended function of the code, and not waste time trying to decipher it.

For example, prefixing variables to indicate the scope and data type of the variable is a coding guideline. This guideline allows other developers to look at a variable and immediately understand the variable's scope and data type.

A thorough discussion of coding and development guideline can be found in Chapter 20, "Creating Development Guidelines."

An Approach to Developing Client Applications

Now that you have an understanding of the role of the client application, using 32-bit applications, creating MDI forms, using other components in the first tier, accessing business services, and the types of controls and forms used in client applications, you can begin developing the application.

Before any code is written or any forms drawn, a development approach first should be laid out. The approach discussed in this section is a phased design and development approach:

1. Gather client application requirements.
2. Design the client application.
3. Prototype the application.
4. Obtain user feedback.
5. Refine the application.
6. Repeat steps 4 and 5 until finished.

III

The Service Layers

Step 1: Gathering Requirements

The first step, gathering requirements, requires that you find the answers to questions. How many people will use the application? How often will they perform certain functions such as entering an order? Obtaining the answers to these questions usually involves interviewing potential users.

Take notes during the requirements phase. These notes do not need to be formal, but they should be detailed enough to use as a reference during the design phase.

Also, remember to keep an open mind when gathering requirements. Do not predispose yourself to a certain design. Listen carefully to what the end users need, and then build a design around these needs.

Step 2: Application Design

The next step, designing the application, should be done not with your development tool, but with pen, paper, and whiteboard. Plan what each screen will look like, how these screens will interact with the business services, and how the screens will flow between one another.

Application design is based on the requirements of the end users. Requirements of an order-processing system may include the ability to create, edit, and delete orders. Requirements of a document-management application may include the ability to create, edit, save, and delete documents. It often helps to create flowcharts that graphically illustrate how screens relate to each other and how the processes involved in the application relate to screens. The diagrams will help you look at, and improve on, the overall design of the client application. These diagrams also make it easier to explain the design to end users.

The diagrams you create don't have to be formal. They can be created with pen and paper or a freeform diagram tool like Visio. The diagrams may be entity-relationship diagrams, data-flow diagrams, or process-flow diagrams. Generating diagrams may seem like tedious work, but it is difficult to create even the first prototype of a complicated system without having a high-level picture laid out before you.

If the client application is replacing or enhancing an existing production system, it helps to create "before" and "after" diagrams. The before diagram should show the current processes and how these processes map to screens in the existing system. The after diagram will show not only the flow of the new system but also how the new system improves on the existing application. Again, this kind of diagram is beneficial when explaining your application design to end users.

Step 3: Prototyping the Application

After you form a solid design plan, you can start prototyping the application. *Prototyping* involves creating each screen in a development tool with a minimal amount of code behind it. The main role of a prototype is to give end users an idea of how the final application will look and feel.

Prototyping differs from a traditional development approach in that you focus design efforts on the presentation aspect of the client application. Little code is written during the prototype phase. The code that is written is used for demonstration purposes or for form navigation.

In the past, Visual Basic often was identified as a tool to be used only for prototyping applications. These prototypes would be scrapped in the development phase and the application would be rewritten in C++ or some other low-level language, mostly because Visual Basic lacked many of the features found in other development tools, such as the capability to create components such as OLE servers.

Visual Basic now is a suitable tool for developing both the prototype and production client application. The client application development life cycle, therefore, should take this into account by minimizing "throw-away" code, which saves time during the development phase because you simply continue to build on the existing prototype.

The prototype should be completed quickly, usually in a few weeks. Because of this time frame, it usually isn't possible to include all functionality that will be present in the final version of the application in this first prototype. Attempt, however, to lay the framework for what will become the production client application.

This means that the ideal prototype includes all screens that will be present in the final version of the client application. Additionally, the prototype should demonstrate how a user moves from one screen to another.

Step 4: Obtaining User Feedback

After the prototype is complete, meet with the end users and demonstrate to them your screen flow. You probably will receive ideas from the end users about some ways to improve the prototype. These ideas can be incorporated as you refine the application.

Remember that the only person who can validate the simplicity and flow of your design is a typical user. You, as a developer, are not a typical user. Note what your user base has to say about the application interface. Pleasing users and simplifying their jobs should be a high priority of any project.

III

The Service Layers

Step 5: Refining the Application

After the end users provide feedback on the first prototype, you can begin the next phase: refining the application. Because the first prototype laid out the visual elements of the application, the next phases should focus on putting code behind each window and refining the original user interface design.

Approaching client application development with this phased approach results in a cleaner design that is driven by the end users. It also saves development time because the prototype you create is not discarded, but built upon during the refinement phases.

This section serves as an overview of the phased development approach. Chapter 21, "Organizing the Development Approach," describes this process in detail.

Using Non-Visual Basic Client Applications

One benefit of the three-tier architecture is that end users can create customized front ends. With all business logic packaged in the business services, users need to learn only a few coding constructs.

Although you can encourage users to create custom client applications, it may not be realistic to assume that every end user has access to Visual Basic or that every user feels comfortable using Visual Basic to create client applications.

Because business services are OLE automation servers, they can be accessed from any application capable of acting as an OLE automation client. Several tools exist today that can act as OLE automation clients, including the following:

■ Microsoft Excel 5

■ PowerSoft's PowerBuilder 4

Excel is an easy-to-use application that uses Visual Basic Applications Edition as its internal macro language—client application code written in Visual Basic 4.0 can literally be cut-and-pasted into Excel macros. Excel's ease of development, and that it already may exist on the majority of your end-users' desktops, makes it an excellent choice for creating custom client applications.

PowerSoft's PowerBuilder development tool also can access the OLE business servers through OLE automation. Although the actual keywords and coding constructs that are used to access the servers may differ, the concept of OLE automation is the same.

The syntax needed to create OLE objects in PowerBuilder and assign them to an object variable differ slightly from the equivalent code in Visual Basic, but the syntax used to invoke properties and methods of the objects is identical. So, you actually can create client applications in PowerBuilder that use business services created in Visual Basic.

Because users may create client applications, it is a good idea for IT to provide sample code templates. These templates can contain sample blocks of code that users place directly into their client applications.

Code templates can help the user create and assign objects to object variables, invoke methods and properties, and release connections to business objects when finished. The templates also should include an explanation of what the code is doing, and also any arguments that must be passed as parameters to an object's method.

For example, the code in Listing 8.1 may represent a code template, used to connect to an Order Manager business object to place an order. You can find this code on the companion disk, in the directory \CHAP08.

Listing 8.1 CODE01.TXT—A sample code template

```
' Code Template for connecting to Order Manager and Placing an Order
' The code creates a NewOrder object and calls the PlaceOrder method.
' The PlaceOrder method takes the arguments CustomerID, ProductID
and ' ProductQuantity as parameters
Dim loOrderMgr as Object
Dim liCustomerID As Integer, liProductID As Integer,
➥liProductQuantity As Integer ' Dim argument variables
Set loOrderMgr = CreateObject ("OrderMgr.NewOrder") 'Assign object
➥to variable
' Insert code to assign Customer ID, Product ID, and Quantity
' ordered to local variables here
'..
'..
' Call the PlaceOrder method to place the order
OrderMgr.PlaceOrder Customer := liCustomerID, Product :=
➥ liProductID, Quantity := liProductQuantity
' Destroy the object variable
Set loOrderMgr = Nothing
```

Once tested in Visual Basic, this code can be saved as a text file. It can then be copied and pasted directly into an Excel module.

III

The Service Layers

From Here...

In this chapter, you learned about the role of user servers in the three-tier client/server model. You should now understand the development process of a client application, how to select a controlling application, the differences between MDI and SDI applications, and common components of the user services tier.

For further information related to topics covered in this chapter, see the following chapters:

- Chapter 5, "Controlling OLE Objects," explains the methods used to control the various implementations of OLE objects from Visual Basic applications.

- Chapter 6, "Creating OLE Objects," details the creation of OLE Objects and the standard methods and properties that are included with them.

- Chapter 15, "Adding Help to an Application," details the creation of Windows Help files and Help menus within an application.

- Chapter 20, "Creating Development Guidelines," for information on creating development guidelines for a project.

- Chapter 21, "Organizing the Development Approach," provides information on setting up and carrying out a development plan.

- Chapter 22, "Sample Application #1: An OLE Document Manager," to see a sample SDI application.

- Chapter 24, "Sample Application #3: A Three-Tier Order Processing System," for more information on creating and accessing in-process OLE automation servers.

Chapter 9

Architecting Tier 2: Business Servers

In Chapter 6, "Creating OLE Objects," you learned how to design and develop OLE automation servers with Visual Basic. OLE automation servers provide a means of encapsulating common functionality and making it available to multiple-controlling applications.

This chapter discusses a special type of OLE automation object, the *business server object*. After reading this chapter, you'll have an understanding of the techniques used to design and develop business servers, using Visual Basic and remote automation in the context of a three-tiered client/server application.

This chapter isn't intended as a final authority on business object design. Rather, it walks you through specific design goals and provides examples and suggestions on how to meet these goals with Visual Basic. Logical business object design still is far more immature than relational database design, and the physical design is even more immature. As a result, few tools on the market today assist in the design of business objects. Presently, no "right" way—or even commonly accepted way—exists to design a business object in Visual Basic. The reality of physical constraints, such as network performance, may dictate the logical design of your business objects.

As always, consider your organization's specific needs and apply these techniques to meet them where appropriate, but do not hesitate to abandon techniques that are less useful to your organization.

In this chapter, you learn about the following areas of business server development:

- The definition of a business object

- How to design and develop a business server

- Business server deployment issues

To understand how to develop and design a business server, you first must understand exactly what the terms *business server* and *business object* mean.

What Is a Business Object?

Think of a business object as a specialized application object. An *application object* is a self-contained piece of functionality that is accessible from other applications. A business object therefore, is a self-contained piece of your organization's business model. In the services model of the three-tier architecture, business objects map to the second tier, the tier that houses the organization's business rules.

Types of Business Objects

Two types of business entities exist within an organization:

- Tangible or Intangible objects

- Business events

After a discussion of the differences between these entities, we will explore how they map to specific VB constructs.

Defining Tangible Versus Intangible Objects

Tangible objects consist of the physical elements of a business. These objects include paper-based items such as invoices, purchase orders, complaint reports, and so on. Any aspect of the business that can be physically touched, or represented is considered a tangible business object.

Intangible objects on the other hand consist of the elements of a business that cannot be physically touched or represented. These intangible aspects of a business include the processes and relationships that exist within the organization. Intangible business objects include such things as placing an order, issuing a credit, and so on.

Defining Business Events

Business events are activities that occur as a result of a change to an object or another action that requires an action to be taken on behalf of the organization. Events include activities like an end-of-day close, end-of-month processing, and so on.

The combination of tangible and intangible objects and business events makes up the day-to-day operations of the business.

Understanding a Business' Granularity

Each of the types of business objects described in the preceding section can be created at different levels of granularity. Simply put, an enterprise can be made up of a large number of small, simple business objects, or a smaller number of very large, immensely complicated business objects.

The advantages and disadvantages of each of these objects is discussed in following sections of this chapter. For the present, you just need to understand what levels can exist.

At its simplest level, a business object performs an action based on the user's input. This input is taken, processed, and a result is returned to the user.

Using the credit check as an example, the client application might pass a customer number to the OLE automation server. The OLE automation server takes this information and determines if the customer's credit limit has been exceeded, and passes back an indicator to the controlling application.

At a more complex level, a business object may contain other business objects. In this case, the business server employs several objects that are dependent upon a parent object.

The GOLF System's *OrderMgr* object is an excellent example of a business server of this type. The *OrderMgr* exposes an *Order* object which, in turn, exposes a collection of LineItem objects that pertain to each order. The *OrderMgr* itself contains all of the business logic and business rules that apply to both the *Order* object and the *LineItem* object.

Benefits of Business Objects

Implementing the logic and rules of an organization in the form of business objects provides a number of benefits. Some of the benefits include the following:

- Reusability
- Scalability
- Maintenance
- Flexibility
- Departmental expertise, shared throughout the enterprise
- Business services are invokable from end-user tools
- Well-defined interface to the business objects

The following sections describe in greater detail the benefits of implementing these rules and logic.

Reusability

Business objects provide the capability for pieces of business logic within an enterprise to be developed once. This business object then can be used within many different applications.

For example, after the GOLF System's *OrderMgr* is developed, multiple applications can make use of its functionality. The customer service representatives may require a robust application to perform their job, while the account executives may need a less feature-rich application. Because all of the business logic pertaining to the creation of an order is encapsulated within the OrderMgr, both applications can employ this functionality without making the developers reinvent the wheel.

Scalability

Business objects allow applications to be moved to a three-tier application architecture that better uses the processing power of the client and server machines. The business logic of the enterprise now will execute on a powerful server machine rather than on the less-powerful client machines. This new capability leaves the client machine available to handle presentation of the data.

Maintenance

Business objects are centrally located and maintainable applications—the business logic of the enterprise is located in one location, rather than being spread across multiple client machines. Centrally located business logic is much easier to update and secure.

In the OrderMgr example discussed previously, if a change needed to be made to the way an order was created, both the customer service and account executive applications would need to be changed. Because each of these applications reside on the user's desktop, this change would have to be made to tens or hundreds of computers simultaneously. With a business object, this change is made in only one location.

Flexibility

Business objects provide added flexibility in application design. No longer are application developers forced to create "fat" client applications. These large applications can now be broken into smaller components—business objects.

Shared Departmental Expertise

Encapsulating departmental knowledge into business services that can be shared throughout the enterprise allows the departments to leverage each other's knowledge.

An example of this is the Credit department, creating a series of OLE automation servers that encapsulate the process of approving a line of credit increase for a customer. With these business objects in place, other departments can include the credit approval process within their applications, without having to know all the organization's business rules that are associated with the process.

Invokable from End-User Tools

OLE automation servers that are created with Visual Basic operate just like other OLE automation server applications. So, business objects that you create can be accessed with end-user tools and other programming languages that support OLE automation.

Using the credit approval business example described in the preceding section as an example, the enterprise developers can create custom applications using Visual Basic, Powerbuilder, C, or C++ that employ the functionality of the credit object. Power users and developers also can reference the credit object when creating custom applications in end-user tools like Microsoft Excel or Microsoft Access.

Defined Interface to Business Objects

As discussed in Chapter 6, "Creating OLE Objects," a controlling application interacts with an OLE automation server through its interface. The object's interface is determined by the developer of the OLE automation server; controlling applications can interact only with the business object in the manner intended. The controlling application also isn't required to have knowledge of the inner workings of the business servers functionality in order to use it.

It's this clearly defined interface to the business objects that facilitates client application development for the power user using desktop applications.

Types of Business Services

In general, business objects provide two types of services:

- Batch business services
- Interactive business services

III

The Service Layers

These two types of services can reside in the same physical business object, or they can reside in different business objects. Because they differ in design requirements, an organization usually finds that it is best suited to implement a particular business entity's batch and interactive interface in two separate objects.

The GOLF System, for example, has two separate components to manage the order business entity. OrderMgr object is instantiated multiple times to service individual controlling applications, usually run by end users, but OrderMgr object also has an OrderBatch business object that is always instantiated on the server, it just lives in the background, waiting to perform batch processing. The only time a client-application instantiates this object is when an administrator needs to modify or check the status of the batch order processing.

Batch Business Systems

As mentioned in Chapter 2, "Application Architecture," limits on interactive processing power usually means that an organization probably cannot get away from some forms of batch processing. System design should strive to eliminate the need for batch systems but often, there are times when their use is appropriate.

A batch process can be invoked in the following two ways:

- The batch business server can run constantly and "wake up" when an action needs to be performed.

- A batch operation can be scheduled to start-up at certain times of the day by way of a system scheduler.

Either way, the business server probably will process transactions that accumulated since the last time it was run.

The controlling application in the first scenario is a simple application that manipulates the always-instantiated object's properties to set parameters, such as start time.

In the second scenario, the controlling application most likely is a scheduling package that invokes the methods on-the-fly, according to its schedule.

The GOLF System contains a batch business server that handles the shipment of orders. This business server is implemented, using the second scenario. Each night, a scheduler starts the OrderBatch business server, executing its ShipOrders method, which ships all orders that have a status of "O," denoting an open order. The ShipOrders method contains all of the business logic and rules that apply to shipping an order.

Interactive Business Servers

Interactive business servers also are instantiated on the server, but these usually interact with multiple-client applications, running on users' desktops. These probably are the most common types of business servers. As discussed in following sections, business servers must be designed carefully if they are to be deployed across the network.

For example, Business servers usually will be deployed across a network and controlled by a client application by way of remote automation. In this situation, it's important that the business server not display any GUI elements. Remote Automation doesn't support the capability to pass these GUI elements to the controlling application. If a business server displays a modal dialog or message box, it will be displayed at the server machine, where the business object resides. The controlling application has no knowledge of this modal form and is hung while the business server waits for a response.

A following section in this chapter, "Handling Errors," discusses this aspect in greater detail when dealing with run-time and business errors that can occur within the business servers.

Designing Business Servers

Now that you have an understanding for what business servers are and how they fit into the three-tier application architecture, we can begin to discuss the design of these application components. In the three-tier world, a solid business server design becomes just as important as a solid database design. Business objects are the interface that application developers will manipulate when creating client applications. The business object's interface must provide all of the functionality necessary to build useful client applications.

This section looks at techniques for modeling the enterprise with OLE automation business servers. After determining what business objects exist within our environment, you will look at ways of encapsulating the business rules that exist and incorporating them into the application. We will finish our design by discussing some of the standard properties and methods that should be present in all business objects.

Modeling the Business Servers

Before sitting down and coding the business servers in Visual Basic, however, give careful thought to the logical design of the organization's business entities.

This process is analogous to what has been time-tested in the relational database world—before implementing tables, triggers and other DBMS objects, the database first should be modeled and thought given to object relations. The same applies to business objects created in VB—all business objects should be identified and categorized, and then each object's interface should be designed before a single line of code is written.

There are four design steps, shown in the following list, to defining the business servers that you should follow:

- Identify logical business entities

- Identify logical business entity groupings

- Identify physical components

- Develop an object hierarchy and interface for each business server

Taking the time to develop these object models ensures that all the business requirements are satisfied by the business server's interfaces.

The tools you use for this purpose are irrelevant; the work can be accomplished with tools not specifically designed for the task, such as Excel and Visio. More likely, however, the world will begin to see object modeling tools that integrate with the VB environment, and even create Visual Basic OLE automation server code.

This chapter discusses OLE automation object modeling in very generic terms, without regard to any specific tool.

Identify Logical Business Entities

The first step in modeling the enterprise is to identify the logical business entities that exist within the organization. Business entities are the nouns that make up the activities of the enterprise. Business entities can include such areas as an order, customer, and product. These entities eventually will become members of the object hierarchies of individual business servers.

After defining all the business entities that exist within an organization, you need to take a first cut at identifying all the attributes and business functions associated with these entities. An entities attributes are defined by the adjectives that are used when referring to an entity. An order entity, for example, has customer, order date, order status, and line item attributes. As the order example illustrates, an orders attributes can consist of other dependent entities, the line item entity.

In addition to attributes, business entities often have business functions associated with them. An order entity, for example, may have associated create, update, and print invoice functions.

The next step is to define the relationships that exist between these objects. These relationships correspond to the verbs of a business. These verbs include things such as a "customer places an order," "an order is shipped," and so on.

The attributes and business functions that are defined during this step loosely corresponds to the properties and methods of the business objects that will be developed later. Figure 9.1 shows the business entities that were defined in the design phase of the GOLF System.

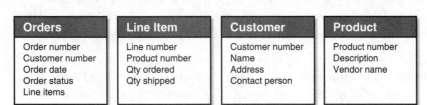

Fig. 9.1
GOLF System's business entities.

Identify Logical Entity Groupings

After all the business entities and their attributes and functions are defined, you need to logically group these entities so that you can later determine how to best partition them into physical components. In the GOLF System for example, the Orders and Line Items are organized into a business group named Order Processing. Figure 9.2 shows how these logical groupings will be used to create the physical business servers that exist within the GOLF System.

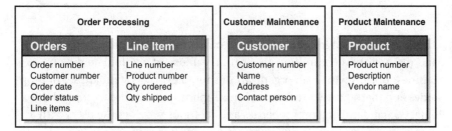

Fig. 9.2
The GOLF System's logical business entity groupings.

Identify Physical Components

The easiest way to consider business object partitioning is to think about your organization's logical business entities, defined in the previous steps. These groupings also become apparent when you start to group your database tables by subject matter. For example, most organizations use similar entity dimensions: orders, products, customers, vendors, employees, and so on.

You can use object modeling tools, such as Asymetrix's InfoModeler, to create the conceptual enterprise object model. These tools also will assist in the definition of the database structure that needs to exist to support the objects. In the future, expect these tools to work better within the business tier, and to actually create Visual Basic code.

Define Object Hierarchy

The concept of an object hierarchy is not new. You have seen object hierarchies in OLE applications like Microsoft Excel for some time. When referring to an enterprise, the object hierarchy is a physical representation of the business objects that are present within an organization. This hierarchy not only identifies each of these objects, it also illustrates the relationships between them.

Figure 9.3 illustrates the object hierarchy that exists for the GOLF System's business servers. This model depicts three business objects, the Customer Manager, Product Manager, and Order Manager, which are associated with customer, product, and order maintenance, respectively.

Fig. 9.3
The GOLF System's business server object hierarchies.

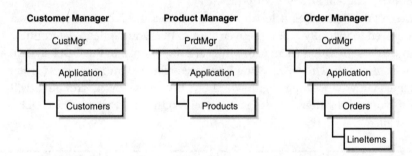

The objects defined in the applications object hierarchy contain properties and methods that controlling application can use to manipulate the object. Business objects within an organization should expose a standard set of properties and methods that the controlling applications can use to control the objects. Standardizing on properties and methods provides the users with a common interface across the organization's business objects.

Defining the object hierarchy defines the business server's object interfaces. Controlling applications and other business entities will use these interfaces to interact with the business server. It's important that the interface is defined first, before any business server development is started.

When defining the business server interface, it's important to ensure that all requirements of the object are met. A good way to do this is to ask the question, "If I were an end user, how would I want this entities interface to look?"

The business objects defined in this process should be universal so that they can accommodate the entire organization. Even if the business object isn't going to serve the entire organization initially, it should be designed so that, eventually, it can accommodate the entire organization without breaking existing systems.

Encapsulating Business Rules

The business rules that exist within the enterprise should be encapsulated within the business objects. These business rules are implemented through a combination of object properties and methods.

Figure 9.4 shows the interface of the GOLF System's OrderMgr. The business rules that apply to activities such as creating an order, for example, are encapsulated within a single method, `Orders.Add`. In this figure, the elements of the object interface are broken into three categories, properties, methods, and performance methods. Methods and performance methods are essentially the same, but were broken out to demonstrate the deviations from standard object design that are often necessary for performance and implementation reasons. Each of these categories is discussed in detail in following sections of this chapter.

Objects

Order Mgr

Fig. 9.4
The OrderMgr's object interface.

	Application	Orders	Order	LineItems	LineItem
Collections:	Orders		LineItems		
Member objects:		Item		Item	Parent
Properties:	Id	Count	OrderID	Count	LineID
	Userid		CustomerID		ProductID
	Password		OrderDate		OrderQty
			ShippedFlag		ShipQty
			RemovedFlag		
Methods:	Initialize	LoadOrders		Add	
		UpdateOrders		Remove	
		Add			
		Remove			
(Performance tuning):		CollectionGet	PropertyGet	CollectionGet	PropertyGet
		CollectionSet	PropertySet	CollectionSet	PropertySet
Data Tier:		sp_Get_Orders	sp_Add_Order		sp_Add_LineItem
			sp_Delete_Order		

III

The Service Layers

Methods

Methods represent actions that the OLE automation server can take on behalf of the controlling application. Methods usually perform an action of the business object with which they are associated.

The OrderMgr's Orders object, for example, has a Remove method that takes the order out of the system. In this case, Remove provides an interface for controlling applications to delete orders without being aware of any business rules that apply to the process of deleting orders.

Properties

Properties represent characteristics of the OLE automation server object that are meaningful to the user, the object, or both. Often, there are times when the OLE automation server itself needs a property value, but the controlling application shouldn't be allowed to alter the value. These are known as *read-only* properties.

Properties are often used to determine which action should occur when a certain method is called. Therefore, it's important to minimize the number of calls a controlling application must make to set the properties that it needs. For example, to allow a controlling application to modify an existing order in the GOLF System, it first must set the property values of the Order object that are to change. If multiple aspects of the order need to be modified, the controlling application needs to make multiple OLE calls to set the property values. After setting these properties, the controlling application then calls the Update method of the Orders collection.

To minimize the number of calls needed to set the object's properties, methods should be provided that allow the controlling application to update and retrieve multiple property values at the same time. The need to reduce the number of OLE calls required of the controlling application is discussed in detail in the section "Business Server Performance Tuning," which appears later in this chapter.

Developing Business Servers

Now that we have defined the objects that make up the business, defined their attributes and relationships, grouped them into logic business servers, and defined their physical interfaces, you can begin to look at how to develop the actual business services.

This section discusses the techniques that you can use to create business servers within Visual Basic. We start by discussing the use of a test application.

After the test application is defined, we will discuss techniques for controlling the interaction between objects, working with data sources, and handling errors.

Developing a Test Application

When developing the business servers—or any OLE automation server for that matter—it is important to start at the most basic level. Although the business servers may be accessed through an instance manager, these services should not be used during the initial development of the business servers. These layers should be included only after the business servers are developed and tested by using a test application.

The OrderMgr was developed and tested by using a simple test application that provides no more than a hard-coded interface into the business server's properties and methods. The test application should be complete, manipulating all aspects of the object. The more complete the test application, the easier it becomes to develop the final controlling applications.

In a production environment, as you will see, a controlling application may go through multiple objects, such as a logon or pool manager object, to obtain a reference to a business server. It is easier to debug an application that has a client requesting services from a single object than to debug an application that has a client requesting services from an object that must pass through two or more other objects.

To gain a better understanding of the usefulness and design of a test client application, this chapter discusses two of the procedures used in the OrderMgr Test Client. In the test application, each of these procedures is associated with a command button on the test form. The goal of the test application is to test all aspects of interaction with the business server's objects and methods, not to provide a dynamic client application. Chapter 24, "Sample Application #3: A Three-Tier Order Processing System," goes into detail about the test applications used to develop the GOLF system.

GetObject

Before a controlling application can use a business server, it must obtain a reference to one. The *cmdGetObject_Click* procedure tests the capability to instantiate the OrderMgr object. The following code instantiates the object in one of the two methods available in the previously discussed architecture—direct object creation and object creation by using the instance manager. This code also shows how you can test, in an incremental manner, all the levels of access to the business objects. The code in Listing 9.1 provides a simple interface for debugging object instantiation. You can find his code on the companion disk, in the \CHAP24\GOLF\TIER1\TEST\TORDMGR directory.

Listing 9.1   TORDMGR.FRM—Code to test the capability to instantiate OrderMgr

```
Private Sub cmdGetObject_Click()

Dim OrderMgrs As Object
Dim LogonMgr As Object


'basic logon
Set OrderMgr = CreateObject("OrderMgr.Application")
OrderMgr.Initialize UserId:="sa", Password:=""

'logon w/LogonMgr (which uses instance mgr behind the scenes)
'Set LogonMgr = CreateObject("LogonMgr.Application")
'Set OrderMgr = LogonMgr.GetInstance("OrderMgr.Application")


If OrderMgr Is Nothing Then
    Print "Did not get it"
Else
    Print "Got it"
End If

End Sub
```

The levels of object instantiation should be increased only after all the other means of manipulating the objects are tested.

ModifyOrders

Controlling application also need to manipulate the object's properties and methods. The *cmdModifyOrders_Click* procedure tests the capability to populate the OrderMgr's Orders collection and access its properties and methods.

The procedure in Listing 9.2 passes hard-coded values to the OrderMgr's Orders methods to test the capability to connect to and use them. There is no need for the test application to develop a fancy user interface and dynamically accept values. Remember, the goal of the test client is to validate that the business servers work correctly, without requiring a great deal of time to set up. The output from the results of the following test is displayed directly on the client form. You can find this code on the companion disk, in the \CHAP24\GOLF\TIER1\TEST\TORDMGR directory.

Listing 9.2   TORDMGR.FRM—Procedure to test the manipulation of the Orders object

```
Private Sub cmdModifyOrders_Click()

'-------------------------
```

```
'Properties/methods
'------------------------

Dim NextOrder As Object

'remove second order
OrderMgr.Orders.Remove 2

'modify existing line items for 1st order
OrderMgr.Orders.Item(1).LineItems.Item(3).Productid = 867867
OrderMgr.Orders.Item(1).LineItems.Item(3).OrderQty = 111
OrderMgr.Orders.Item(1).LineItems.Item(3).ShipQty = 222

'add new order w/3 identical line items
NextOrder = OrderMgr.Orders.Add(CustomerId:=543265564)
NextOrder.LineItems.Add Productid:=867867, _
                OrderQty:=333, ShipQty:=444
NextOrder.LineItems.Add Productid:=867867, _
                OrderQty:=333, ShipQty:=444
NextOrder.LineItems.Add Productid:=867867, _
                OrderQty:=333, ShipQty:=444

Print "Modified"

End Sub
```

The test application should begin by unit testing basic business object functionality. After unit testing is successful, you then can incorporate more complex business server interface aspects.

When the test application can move through the various test procedures previously defined, the additional levels of object instantiation should be tested. The levels should be built up to include the Instance managers. Starting from the most basic level and incrementally adding complexity will make it easier to debug problems that occur.

After the test application tests the business object's validity, creating the controlling application now is just a matter of defining the presentation logic.

Another technique for business object creation is to develop and unit test the object's locally, even if they are intended for remote deployment. Remote Automation adds additional complexities that can cause endless nightmares during the development process. Business objects should be system-tested via remote automation before deployment to the production environment, even if they were developed and unit tested with just local automation.

Component Size

As discussed previously in this chapter, business server components' size and persistence generally follow two patterns:

III

The Service Layers

- Small non-persistent components
- Larger persistent components

Small Non-Persistent Components

Smaller business servers usually implement a single piece of functionality. An example of this type of business object is a Credit object that exposes a GetCredit method. The GetCredit method takes a customer number parameter and returns the customer's credit limit. These small components, don't need to remember anything between client requests, which makes the component non-persistent because it remembers no information specific to a client.

Non-persistent components act like remote-procedure or stored-procedure calls. The controlling application passes parameters to the object's methods, and the method returns a result based on the parameters. A single instance of a non-persistent object can be easily re-used by different controlling applications because there is no need to "remember" anything between calls.

Larger Persistent Components

Larger business servers usually are richer and more complex objects that contain persistent data. The GOLF System's OrderMgr object is a persistent component because it remembers property values like UserID, OrderNum, and so on between client interactions. Because of this, a single instance of the OrderMgr cannot be shared between different controlling applications, each controlling application must reference its own instance of the business server.

Persistent business objects provide powerful mechanisms that aren't available with RPC and stored procedure calls. The OrderMgr object, for example, maintains a rich collection of orders and line items on the server that the object's methods can reference. This allows persistent objects to perform multiple actions, using the same object property values across multiple method calls without passing the same information across the network multiple times.

How Objects Interact

The services model is based on the interaction of different services. In Chapter 4, "Visual Basic Application Architecture," the interaction between the various services within the three tiers of the services model was discussed. Each tier can interact with services located in the tier above and below the server, as well as other services located within the same tier.

This intra-tier interaction is necessary to satisfy one design goal for the business servers—business rules should be located in only one location. To make this goal possible, functions performed by multiple business servers must be encapsulated within an object that can be referenced by other business servers.

The GOLF System's OrderMgr might make use of this intra-tier functionality by employing a credit check object to ensure that the new order doesn't put the customer over their credit limit. By using another business server to perform the credit check, the business rules associated with checking a customer's credit level are located in one location, rather than being placed in multiple business servers.

Working with Data Services

In order for a business server to perform its job, it must interact with the data that makes up the enterprise. The role of the user services is to present data to the user, and allow them to maintain it. This section discusses, at a high level, the types of data services that can be used by business servers.

Chapter 10, "Architecting Tier 3: Data Servers," and Chapter 11, "Remote Data Objects," go into more detail about the design and development of RDBMS and other data services, respectively.

Relational Database Management Systems

When working with an RDBMS data service, business servers should use the functionality provided by the specific database server. Most DBMS servers provide the capability to access the server via stored procedures.

A *stored procedure* is a set of SQL statements that were pre-compiled by the database server and have a pre-determined execution plan. Stored procedures provide a number of benefits over embedded SQL in business servers, such as tighter control over the database and increased performance.

The use of stored procedures is discussed in detail in Chapter 10, "Architecting Tier 3: Data Servers."

At this point, however, it is important to understand that all of the business logic should reside within the business server, not spread between the business and data servers. For this reason, stored procedures should be used for elementary data functions: to retrieve and update the data needed for a specific transaction, not to manage the actual transaction.

Listing 9.3 demonstrates the OrderMgr's UpdateOrder method that uses multiple elementary stored procedures to retrieve the data that is needed to

III

The Service Layers

update an existing order. You can find this code on the companion disk, in the \CHAP24\GOLF\TIER2\ORDMGR directory.

Listing 9.3   ORDERS.CLS —Method to udpate changes to the Orders collection

```
Public Sub UpdateOrders()

Dim qryDeleteOrder As rdoPreparedStatement
Dim qryAddOrder As rdoPreparedStatement
Dim qryAddLineItem As rdoPreparedStatement

Dim OrderIdx As Long
Dim LineItemIdx As Long
Dim NextLineItem As LineItem

'1) Delete all orders and line item keys in the original collection
'2) Insert all orders and line items in current collection,
'    ignoring those orders marked RemoveFlag="Y"


db.BeginTrans

'open a handle to the delete orders stored procedure
Set qryDeleteOrder = db.CreatePreparedStatement( _
                    "sp_Delete_OrderHdr", _
                    "{call sp_Delete_OrderHdr (?)}")
'delete orders
OrderIdx = 0
Do
    OrderIdx = OrderIdx + 1
    qryDeleteOrder.rdoParameters(0).Value = _
    Me.Item(OrderIdx).OrderID
    qryDeleteOrder.Execute
Loop Until OrderIdx >= Me.Count

'close the delete orders PreparedStatement handle
qryDeleteOrder.Close


'open a handle to the add order stored procedure
Set qryAddOrder = db.CreatePreparedStatement( _
                    "sp_Add_OrderHdr", _
                    "{call sp_Add_OrderHdr (?, ?, ?, ?)}")
qryAddOrder.rdoParameters(0).Direction = rdParamInputOutput
qryAddOrder.rdoParameters(1).Direction = rdParamInput
qryAddOrder.rdoParameters(2).Direction = rdParamInput
qryAddOrder.rdoParameters(3).Direction = rdParamInput

'open a handle to the add line item stored procedure
Set qryAddLineItem = db.CreatePreparedStatement( _
                    "sp_Add_LineItem", _
                    "{call sp_Add_LineItem (?, ?, ?, ?, ?)}")
```

```
'reload all of the order currently in the orders collection
OrderIdx = 0
Do
    OrderIdx = OrderIdx + 1
    'only add if not marked for removal
    If Me.Item(OrderIdx).RemovedFlag = "N" Then
      With Me.Item(OrderIdx)
          qryAddOrder.rdoParameters(0).Value = .OrderID
          qryAddOrder.rdoParameters(1).Value = .CustomerID
          qryAddOrder.rdoParameters(2).Value = .OrderDate
          qryAddOrder.rdoParameters(3).Value = CStr(.ShippedFlag)
          qryAddOrder.Execute

          'update order id which was set by SP
          Me.Item(OrderIdx).OrderID = qryAddOrder.rdoParameters(0). Value
      End With

      'add the line items
      LineItemIdx = 0
      Do
          LineItemIdx = LineItemIdx + 1
          Set NextLineItem = Me.Item(OrderIdx).LineItems.Item _
              (LineItemIdx) With NextLineItem
              qryAddLineItem.rdoParameters(0).Value = Me.Item _
              (OrderIdx).OrderID
              qryAddLineItem.rdoParameters(1).Value = LineItemIdx
              qryAddLineItem.rdoParameters(2).Value = .ProductId
              qryAddLineItem.rdoParameters(3).Value = .OrderQty
              qryAddLineItem.rdoParameters(4).Value = .ShipQty
              qryAddLineItem.Execute
          End With
      Loop Until LineItemIdx >= Me.Item(OrderIdx).LineItems.Count
    End If

Loop Until OrderIdx >= Me.Count

'close the PreparedStatement handles
qryAddOrder.Close
qryAddLineItem.Close

'commit the transaction
db.CommitTrans

Set prvOrders = Nothing


End Sub
```

In the preceding procedure, the sp_delete_orders stored procedure is called to delete the current order from the database. The sp_add_OrdHdr and sp_add_LineItem stored procedures then are called to insert the order back into the database, using the current property settings. In this example, all the

III

The Service Layers

business logic related to updating orders is contained within the business server. The stored procedures simply perform the basic delete and insert data functions.

Connecting to RDBMS Services

When creating a three-tier relational database application, you should look for the following four features in a database connectivity interface:

- Object based access

- Solid performance

- Support for advanced database features

- Ability to operate against multiple DBMSs

It's important that the connectivity method supports the advanced features of the DBMS, which include using stored procedures, bound parameters, error processing, concurrency control, and record-locking control. Using a connection method that meets the these goals ensures that the business servers make use of the functionality of the data service.

Remote Data Objects—The RDBMS Connectivity Answer

With Visual Basic 4.0 Enterprise Edition, only remote data objects (RDO) satisfies all four connectivity goals. Therefore, this book focuses solely on using RDO to connect to RDBMS data services. Chapter 11, "Remote Data Objects," goes into detail about the use of RDO.

The remote data control also provides a majority of the goals but does not work with the services model. In the services model, only the business services will interact with the DBMS. Because business services cannot have GUI controls, the remote data control is irrelevant and, therefore, is not discussed in this book.

Other Data Service Interfaces

Other data services will provide their own interfaces to the data that they supply. Although RDBMS data services can be accessed through an OLE interface by using Remote Data Objects, other data services may not provide a similar OLE interface. As you will see in Chapter 11, "Remote Data Objects," there are two possible approaches to accessing these data services:

- Use the native API

- Wrap the native API

Use the Native API

Most data services provide a native API that can be used to access the data it provides. Applications can use Winsock, for example, to access the Internet, APPC or HLAPPI for 3270 emulation, and proprietary APIs for imaging and multidimensional DBMS services.

Using a native API doesn't present a severe problem because only the business servers will interact with the data services, which means that only the developers working on the actual business servers need to understand these native APIs. The controlling application developers only need to understand how to interact with the business servers, the same as they would for RDBMS data services.

Wrap the Native API

Another approach is to develop a custom OLE interface to the native APIs. This approach requires that a small number of developers learn the native API, and that they create an OLE automation server that exposes the API's functionality to the business servers.

For complex API sets, this approach significantly reduces the learning curve for the business server developers. The native API will be exposed in an object model that is easy to understand and use.

Chapter 10, "Architecting Tier 3: Data Servers," goes into detail about developing three-tier applications that use non-RDBMS data services.

Business Server Development Techniques

Now that you understand how to design a business server, we can take a look at some specific techniques for implementing this design.

This section examines techniques that implement the objects, properties, and methods that are common in business servers.

Creating the Application Object

A good design for complex business objects is to have each object expose a single class, the *Application* class. The *Application* class is instantiated and passed to the controlling application when the object is created. This class provides the controlling application with the visibility to additional classes and collections that make up the business service. These other objects depend on the *Application* object; they cannot be instantiated by themselves.

III

The Service Layers

The *Application* object provides a single entrance and instantiation point for the controlling application. This single entry point eliminates the confusion often associated with object hierarchies, which provide multiple external objects. It also is useful when managing server resources—a few large instantiated objects are more manageable than many small objects that provide the same functionality.

As you learned in Chapter 6, "Creating OLE Objects," each object exposed by an OLE automation server created with Visual Basic is associated with a *Public* class module in the Visual Basic project. To create an *Application* class, add a new class module to your project. Set the class modules name property to `Application`, its Public property to `True`, and its Instancing property to `Creatable SingleUse`.

This section details some suggestions and recommendations for your business server's *Application* object design. The *Application* class should contain a number of common interface attributes.

Application Object Properties

The *Application* class should contain read-only properties that store information about the current instance of the business server. These read-only properties are implemented as private variables in the *Application* class module.

The *Application* class's read-only properties include UserId, Password, Id, and Parent. Some of these properties may not be used right away, but they do provide information that can be used for advanced security features in the future.

The UserId and Password properties should be "write-once" properties. When an instance of the business server is created, these properties should be set, and they should not be changed during the life of the object. Controlling applications should be allowed to only read the UserId property. The Business server uses these values when connecting to the data sources.

The Id and Parent properties are useful when the object is stored in a collection, such as an Instance Manager. The Id servers as the key within the collection, and the Parent indicates the Parent object in the collection. Refer to the "Methods" section for the specifics of this implementation.

Listing 9.4, located in the declarations section of the OrderMgr's *Application* class module, shows the implementation of the read-only properties. You can find this code on the companion floppy disk, in the \CHAP24\GOLF\TIER2\ ORDMGR directory.

Listing 9.4   APP.CLS—Code to implement read-only properties

```
'All business server's should have these objects.

'The UserId and Id property are read-only by the client application,
'the others are neither read nor write by the client application.

'Private copy of client application's user id
'This is read-only to the client application, because it might
'be helpful for debugging
Private prvUserId As String

'Private copy of client application's password
'It is neither read nor write by the client application because
'no one should ever be able to read a password
Private prvPassword As String

'Id and Parent are optional, and only make sense
'if the object is instantiated by an instance manager.

'Private copy of this instance's ID
'This is read-only to the client application, because it might
'be helpful for debugging
Private prvId As String

'Private copy of the parent object.
'It is neither read nor write by the client application because
'the client application has no reason to reference the
'Instance Manager
Private prvParent As Object
```

Application Object Collections and Dependent Objects

The *Application* class also will contain properties that store references to the dependent objects and collections that the controlling application can access. These properties are implemented as public variables in the *Application* class module.

Usually, the *Application* object has dependent objects and collections that correspond to the business entities that the business server manages. The GOLF System's OrderMgr, for example, exposes a single collection—the Orders collection. The following code, located in the declarations of the OrderMgr's *Application* class module, shows the implementation of these dependent objects and collections:

```
'Declare the order objects
Public Orders As New Orders
```

Application Object Methods

The business server's *Application* class can expose an Initialize method that handles the housekeeping needed when an instance of the business server is created.

III

The Service Layers

The Initialize method is used after the object is instantiated to set the write-once properties: UserId, Password, Id, and Parent. You also can use this method to perform actions, such as establishing a connection to the data server for persistent business objects.

Listing 9.5 shows the Initialize method of the OrderMgr's *Application* object. This method updates the read-only properties of the *Application* class discussed in the previous section and establishes a connection to the data service. You can find this code on this book's companion disk, in the \CHAP24\GOLF\TIER2\ORDMGR directory.

Listing 9.5   APP.CLS—OrdMgr's initialization method

```
Sub Initialize(UserId As String, _
               Password As String, _
               Optional Id As Variant, _
               Optional Parent As Variant)

'This procedure is called once when the server is instantiated.

'If it is instantiated by an Instance Manager, the object Id and
'Parent will be passed by the Instance Manager.

'If it is instantiated by a client application, the client probably
'has no need to pass an Id or Parent.

'This shows how this generic object shell can be used in an Instance
'Manager environment or in an environment where the client
'application is allowed to instantiate the object directly.

'...............................................................
'make sure procedure is only called once
'...............................................................

Static Initialized As Boolean
'only allow one initialization
If Initialized Then Exit Sub
Initialized = True

'...............................................................
'Assign the initialized object values
'...............................................................

prvUserId = UserId
prvPassword = Password
If IsMissing(Id) Then 'optional parm
    prvId = "<None>"
Else
    prvId = Id
End If
If IsMissing(Parent) Then 'optional parm
```

```
        Set prvParent = Nothing
    Else
        Set prvParent = Parent
    End If


    'set up default environment
    rdoEngine.rdoDefaultUser = UserId
    rdoEngine.rdoDefaultPassword = Password
    'open a connection to the database
    Set db = rdoEngine.rdoEnvironments(0).OpenConnection( _
                DATA_SOURCE, _
                rdDriverNoPrompt, _
                False)


End Sub
```

Creating Dependent Business Server Objects

Dependent objects that are part of the business server are implemented as class modules within the Visual Basic project. These dependent objects will contain properties and methods associated with the attributes identified during the business-server design phase.

To prevent controlling applications from being able to create an instance of these dependent objects separate from the Application object instance, the Instancing property of the class module must be set to Not Creatable. The class module's *Public* property should be set to *True* to allow the object to be accessible from the controlling application.

The business server's dependent objects can be specific objects, or they can be collections of objects. Dependent collections are specialized OLE automation server objects that are capable of containing multiple objects. Collections also are implemented as class modules within the Visual Basic project. A collection object is defined as a new collection, rather than as a new object.

The following line of code, for example, is used in the Order class module to define the LineItems collection that is a dependent collection object:

```
    Public LineItems As New LineItems
```

Like the Application object, dependent objects will expose their own properties, methods, dependent objects, and collections.

Chapter 6, "Creating OLE Objects," discussed the specifics of creating OLE automation server applications, using Visual Basic. Refer to Chapter 6 for the specifics of implementing dependent object, properties, and methods of an OLE automation server application.

III

The Service Layers

Handling Errors

Business servers provide both additional capabilities for handling errors encountered by the application and introduce new issues that need to be accounted for.

Business Errors

Business servers provide the capability to return consistent and meaningful error messages to the controlling applications. Business servers should take advantage of this capability by always passing "business errors" to the controlling application, rather than run-time and data-specific errors common in two-tier applications. Figure 9.5 shows the manner in which the business server can redefine data and run-time errors that are encountered, passing a business error to the controlling application.

Fig. 9.5
All errors encountered by the business server are passed as business errors.

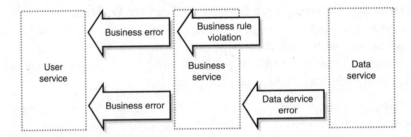

Because all access to the application data sources is provided through business servers, data-specific errors should be translated and presented to the user as business errors. The OrderMgr, for example, may translate a referential integrity error that occurs when the controlling application attempts to create an order with an unknown customer number to a more meaningful business error message such as, Can't insert an order for a customer that does not exist.

> **Note**
>
> These translations of data to business errors can be handled once by the business server, rather than requiring that each controlling application make the translations. These translations also ensure that controlling applications display consistent error messages, rather than messages that provide data errors and others that provide business errors.

Other business errors may be unrelated to an error discovered by the data service. For example, the GOLF system's OrderMgr might return an error if the user attempts to update an order that already shipped. This error isn't generated by any constraints defined within the data services. The error is specific to a business rule that exists.

Chapter 14, "Architecting Error Processing," discusses the specific ways in which business servers can implement this type of error handling.

Event Logging

Business servers usually will be deployed on a server machine that runs the Windows NT operating system. This deployment means that business servers can take advantage of the extensive error logging and alerting provided by Windows NT.

Business servers, and any application running on a server, not only should alter the controlling application that an error occurred, they also should have the capability to alert system administrators to the error. Simply informing the client and expecting the end user to notify the system administrator usually is not enough.

Window NT provides the Event Log, where applications can write information pertinent to an application event. These events can include both errors and events that occur during normal program execution. Using the event logs makes it easier for system administrators to remotely administer the business servers.

Chapter 14, "Architecting Error Processing," discusses event logging in greater detail.

Passing Errors to the Controlling Applications

Business servers are often deployed on remote machines—any form or dialog box displayed by the business server is displayed on the remote machine, not on the machine where the controlling application is executing. Therefore, it's not enough to trap a run-time error within a business server, display a message box, and end the application. All unrecoverable errors that occur must be trapped and passed back to the controlling application.

Business servers should make every possible attempt to anticipate and recover from errors that can occur during their execution. Errors that cannot be anticipated or that are unrecoverable should be reassigned to an error number associated with the business server and passed back to the controlling application.

Visual Basic provides the vbError constant that should be used when assigning new error values. Using this constant ensures that the error number doesn't conflict with a pre-defined internal Visual Basic error.

III

The Service Layers

Chapter 14, "Architecting Error Processing," goes into greater detail about the process of handling errors within business servers and also the other services layers of a three-tier application.

Business Server Performance Tuning

Just as good design of business servers is now as important as the design of relational database tables, performance tuning of the business servers also is just as important as performance tuning of the relational data services.

All controlling application requests for data will make use of properties and methods of the business servers, which means the performance of a controlling application is directly tied to the performance of the business server. Generally, OLE automation servers that are intended to be deployed for remote automation—such as business servers—require different design considerations than servers that are just deployed locally.

This section concentrates on performance issues as they relate to remote OLE automation calls. You will find that these performance techniques also improve the performance of all OLE automation servers. You also will look at the memory considerations involved when dealing with OLE automation servers.

Minimize OLE Calls

As mentioned in the performance tuning section of Chapter 7, "Managing OLE Objects," each remote OLE automation call equates to a remote procedure call. This means that when business servers are deployed remotely, the object's interface should provide features that minimize the number of OLE calls—OLE dot operations—that controlling applications are required to make. For example, an operation that requires the controlling application to make 50 OLE automation calls to the business server performs 50 times faster if the business server is designed in a manner that allows the operation to be performed by using a single OLE automation call.

Methods Versus Properties

Setting a property represents an OLE call. Often, controlling applications need to set multiple properties. Therefore, it's often useful to create a special method that can take multiple property values and set them internally.

Controlling applications often need to read the values of multiple properties. A special method that takes multiple optional parameters can be implemented in the business server that enables clients to read and write multiple property values with a single dot operation.

The following sections demonstrate the `PropertyGet` and `PropertySet` methods' procedures that were designed to provide the controlling application with a mechanism for setting or retrieving all the object properties with a single OLE automation call.

PropertyGet

A `PropertyGet` method should be implemented for all dependent objects of the OLE automation server. It allows the controlling application to retrieve the current values of all the properties that the OLE object makes available with a single dot operation. `PropertyGet` contains an optional parameter list that accepts all the property values that the OLE object has chosen to make accessible to the controlling application.

The procedure in Listing 9.6 uses the `IsMissing` function to determine which parameters the controlling application passed in. These parameters then are populated with the current value in the associated object property. You can find this file on the companion disk, in the \CHAP24\GOLF\TIER2\ ORDMGR directory.

Listing 9.6   ORDER.CLS—The Order objects PropertyGet method

```
Public Sub PropertyGet(Optional OrderID As Variant, _
                       Optional OrderDate As Variant, _
                       Optional CustomerID As Variant, _
                       Optional ShippedFlag As Variant, _
                       Optional RemovedFlag As Variant)

If IsMissing(OrderID) = False Then
    OrderID = prvOrderID
End If
If IsMissing(OrderDate) = False Then
    OrderDate = prvOrderDate
End If
If IsMissing(CustomerID) = False Then
    CustomerID = prvCustomerID
End If
If IsMissing(ShippedFlag) = False Then
    ShippedFlag = prvShippedFlag
End If
If IsMissing(RemovedFlag) = False Then
    RemovedFlag = prvRemovedFlag
End If

End Sub
```

PropertySet

A `PropertySet` method also should be implemented for all dependent objects. `PropertySet` enables the controlling application to set all the property values associated with a dependent object, using a single OLE dot operation.

III

The Service Layers

Like `PropertyGet`, the `PropertySet` method uses the `IsMissing` function to determine which property values the controlling application is trying to set. The procedure then updates the private variables that are associated with the specified parameters. The procedure in Listing 9.7 demonstrates the PropertySet procedure that is exposed by the GOLF System's Order object. You can find this code in the \CHAP24\GOLF\TIER2\ORDMGR directory of this book's companion floppy disk.

Listing 9.7   ORDER.CLS—Order object's PropertySet method

```
Public Sub PropertySet(Optional OrderDate As Variant, _
                       Optional CustomerID As Variant, _
                       Optional RemovedFlag As Variant)

    If IsMissing(OrderDate) = False Then
        prvOrderDate = OrderDate
    End If
    If IsMissing(CustomerID) = False Then
        prvCustomerID = CustomerID
    End If
    If IsMissing(RemovedFlag) = False Then
        prvRemovedFlag = RemovedFlag
    End If


    End Sub
```

Using these methods, all five Order properties can be updated or retrieved with only one procedure call. Without this procedure, five individual calls are needed to obtain all the information.

Return Arrays

OLE automation servers often expose collections of objects, like the Orders collection of the GOLF System's OrderMgr. Just as setting and retrieving multiple properties values at the same time is a common operation, retrieving and updating multiple members of a collection is also common. Like working with property values, each time a member of a collection is accessed, an OLE automation call is required.

To improve the performance of these requests and updates of collection information, a method must be developed that allows the business server and controlling application to pass large amounts of data back and forth quickly and easily. Multiple OLE dot operations won't do it because of the network overhead associated with them.

Objects are passed by reference from an OLE automation server to the controlling application. In the user-services tier, the client and in-process OLE automation server applications can simply pass a copy of the object to each other. A remote business server, on the other hand, lacks the capability to pass a copy of an object to a controlling application across the network, nor can the controlling application pass a copy of an object to the server.

As noted in the preceding section, large amounts of data can be passed between the client and server applications, using parameters. This technique works well when the amount of data that needs to be passed is a known quantity but doesn't address the need to pass the unknown amounts of data (such as data associated with a collection object), which can be handled by passing Variant arrays. Variant arrays, not arrays of strings or integers, are needed because OLE automation server cannot support parameters of user defined types. Variant arrays, however, do support multiple datatypes within the same array.

To improve performance of accessing collections, business servers should expose methods as part of their interface that allow the controlling application to update and retrieve all the members of a collection, using a single OLE automation call. Because this adds complexity to the object's interface, the standard properties and methods still should exist. By keeping the standard interfaces, end users still can create their own custom applications using the simple business server interface. The application developers, however, will be able to use these more advanced methods to increase the performance of their applications.

CollectionGet

Similar to the `PropertyGet` method, the `CollectionGet` method allows the controlling application to retrieve all of the members of a collection by making a single OLE call. To accomplish this bulk transfer of data, the business server exposes a method that accepts an array of variants as its only parameter.

Listing 9.8 demonstrates the `CollectionGet` method that is exposed by the OrderMgr. You can find this code in the \CHAP24\GOLF\TIER2\ORDMGR directory of this book's companion disk.

Listing 9.8   ORDERS.CLS—The Orders CollectionGet method

```
Function CollectionGet() As Variant

Dim OrderIdx As Integer
Dim OrderArray As Variant
Dim NextLineItemArray As Variant
```

(continues)

```
Listing 9.8   Continued

Dim OrderID As Variant
Dim CustomerID As Variant
Dim OrderDate As Variant
Dim RemovedFlag As Variant
Dim ShippedFlag As Variant

'redimension the OrderArray to contain make enough room
'for all the members of the collection
ReDim OrderArray(1 To ordMaxAttribute, 1 To Me.Count)

'loop through the collection elements
Do
    OrderIdx = OrderIdx + 1

    'get the order object properties
    Me.Item(OrderIdx).PropertyGet OrderID:=OrderID, _
                               CustomerID:=CustomerID, _
                               OrderDate:=OrderDate, _
                               RemovedFlag:=RemovedFlag, _
                               ShippedFlag:=ShippedFlag

    OrderArray(ordOrderID, OrderIdx) = OrderID
    OrderArray(ordCustomerID, OrderIdx) = CustomerID
    OrderArray(ordOrderDate, OrderIdx) = OrderDate
    OrderArray(ordRemovedFlag, OrderIdx) = RemovedFlag
    OrderArray(ordShippedFlag, OrderIdx) = ShippedFlag
    'get the line items of order
    NextLineItemArray = Me.Item(OrderIdx).LineItems.CollectionGet
    OrderArray(ordLineItems, OrderIdx) = NextLineItemArray

Loop Until OrderIdx >= Me.Count

'return the OrderArray
CollectionGet = OrderArray

End Function
```

CollectionSet

Similar to the PropertySet method, the CollectionSet method allows the controlling application to update all the members of a collection by making one OLE call. Like the CollectionGet method, this is accomplished by exposing a method that uses an array of variants to update the collection's information.

Listing 9.9 demonstrates the CollectionSet method that is exposed by the OrderMgr. This code can be found on the companion disk, in the \CHAP24\GOLF\TIER2\ORDMGR directory.

Listing 9.9   ORDERS.CLS—The Orders CollectionSet method

```
Public Sub CollectionSet(OrderArray As Variant)

Dim OrderIdx As Integer
Dim NextLineItemArray As Variant

'Delete private orders collection (note: this is different
'to what happens with the .Remove method)
Set prvOrders = Nothing

'update the orders collection with the information passed from the
'client application
OrderIdx = 0
Do
    'loop through the OrderArray
    OrderIdx = OrderIdx + 1

    'get the order information
    Me.Add OrderID:=(OrderArray(ordOrderID, OrderIdx)), _
           CustomerID:=(OrderArray(ordCustomerID, OrderIdx)), _
           OrderDate:=(OrderArray(ordOrderDate, OrderIdx)), _
           RemovedFlag:=(OrderArray(ordRemovedFlag, OrderIdx)), _
           ShippedFlag:=(OrderArray(ordShippedFlag, OrderIdx))

    'get the line items of order
    NextLineItemArray = OrderArray(ordLineItems, OrderIdx)
    Me.Item(OrderIdx).LineItems.CollectionSet NextLineItemArray

Loop Until OrderIdx >= UBound(OrderArray, 2)

End Sub
```

Creating a Client Application Wrapper

The addition of the CollectionSet and CollectionGet methods add complexity to the manner in which data is retrieved and updated in the controlling application. To prevent the application developer from having to understand the manner in which the variant arrays are created, a wrapper procedure can be developed and included within the controlling application.

This wrapper procedure should handle reading values from the variant array, as well as re-creating the variant array to pass back to the business server's CollectionGet method. This procedure can be developed as a set of Visual Basic procedures that are added to the project or as an in-process OLE automation server that resides on the client machine.

Avoiding ByRef

As discussed in Chapter 7, "Managing OLE Objects," passing parameters ByRef to out-of-process OLE automation servers requires OLE to copy the value and pass it across the network. When the OLE automation server's

III

The Service Layers

method completes, the value must be copied back across the network, in case it was modified.

Passing parameters ByVal instead eliminates need to pass the parameter's value back to the client after the method finishes executing because the server is not allowed to update its value. To accomplish this condition, the methods of the business server always should be declared by using the ByVal keyword for its parameters.

In this case, the parameter values that are passed to the method don't need to be updated by the business server, so they are declared by using the ByVal keyword. This ensures that their values are not passed back to the controlling application. The following example illustrates the function declaration for the Add method of the OrderMgr's Orders collection:

```
Public Function Add(Optional ByVal CustomerID As Variant, _
                     Optional ByVal OrderID As Variant, _
                     Optional ByVal OrderDate As Variant, _
                     Optional ByVal RemovedFlag As Variant, _
                     Optional ByVal ShippedFlag As Variant) As _
                     Object
```

Memory Considerations

Memory resources on the server that contains the business services is another important consideration when looking at the performance of OLE automation business servers. As mentioned in Chapter 6, "Creating OLE Objects," each instance of an out-of-process OLE object deployed on a remote server requires 500K of memory on the remote server. This memory demand is important to remember when creating business servers that will be accessed by multiple-controlling applications.

In-Process Versus Out-Of-Process OLE Servers

In-process OLE automation servers run within the same process as the OLE controlling application that references them. Therefore, the 500K overhead is not incurred when instantiating an in-process server. In-process servers cannot be run directly via remote automation because they must run in-process of the Remote Automation Manager, which for reasons of stability, doesn't allow in-process server instantiation. In-process servers, however, can be instantiated and accessed via remote automation if they are instantiated by an already-running, out-of-process server on the remote machine.

Out-of-process OLE automation servers, on the other hand, run in their own process. This means that each instance of an out-of-process server requires 500K of the server machine's memory.

Single-Use Versus Multi-Use OLE Servers

When an OLE automation server is defined as Creatable Single-Use, a new instance of the OLE automation server is created for each object request made by a controlling application.

When an OLE automation server is defined as Creatable Multi-Use, a single instance of the OLE automation server can handle the requests of multiple-controlling applications. These requests are handled serially, on a first come, first served basis.

Because Creatable Single-Use OLE automation servers are created for each request, it's important to make use of techniques such as instance managers, discussed in Chapter 23, "Sample Application #2: An Instance Manager," to limit the number of OLE automation server instances are allowed to be running.

Managing Connections

A DBMS data service governs and manages client connections. Likewise, a business server deployed for remote automation also must manage its connections.

As mentioned in the preceding section, Visual Basic provides the capability to create OLE automation servers as creatable single use, whereby a new instance of the server is created in its own process for every client create request, or as creatable multi-use, whereby a single instance of the server is created and all client requests are processed serially by the single OLE automation server process.

OLE automation servers created with Visual Basic are single-threaded. To allow multiple instances of an OLE automation server created with Visual Basic to multitask, they must be created so that they live in different processes. The operating system then handles the multitasking of the processes.

TP Monitors

A new buzz word phrase that has come about as part of the three-tier architecture is "Transaction Processing Monitor." The concept of a TP Monitor is nothing new: they have, for example, existed in the mainframe environment for years.

Transaction Processing Monitors manage the connections between clients and servers. This is accomplished by providing the following features:

III

The Service Layers

- Transaction management capabilities

- Load balancing

- Error recovery and transaction restart capabilities

- Transaction routing

- Guaranteed data consistency

In the services model of the three-tier application architecture, TP Monitors functionality can be implemented in business and data servers. A well-designed business server, as described in this chapter, provides all of the functionality associated with a TP monitor, with the exception of load balancing.

Load balancing, however, also can be accomplished by using a special type of business server that is discussed briefly in the following section, the pool manager or instance manager.

Instance Manager

One method to manage the business server connections is to develop an instance or pool manager that manages the available business server connections. This method provides the following features that assist in the management of business servers:

- **Pre-loads object instances**—Client doesn't have to wait for the server to create the new object instance on demand.

- **Multitasking instances**—Allows OLE automation server to be created as creatable single-use, allowing the operating system to multitask the processes.

- **Governing process**—Instance manager can be set to limit the number of instances that can be created, which ensures that the servers resources are not depleted.

- **Load balance across machines**—Instance manager can create OLE automation server instances across multiple machines, transparently to the client machine.

- **Reuse object instances**—When controlling applications are handled with an instance, the instance manager can attempt to reclaim the old instance for the next client request.

The creation of instance managers is discussed in detail in Chapter 23, "Sample Application #2: An Instance Manager." It is important, however, that the developers creating business servers are aware of the issues related to the management of business server instances and client connections, and the ability to manage them by using an instance manager.

Deploying Business Services

Now that the business servers are developed and tested, it's time to discuss some techniques for deploying the business servers.

The following sections discuss a deployment strategy that can be used and examines other important deployment considerations, such as security.

Physical Deployment

OLE automation business servers can be deployed either locally or remotely with respect to the controlling application. Usually, however, business servers are deployed on a remote NT machine to take advantage of the 3-tier's architecture's scalability, security, and management capabilities.

Deploy on a Windows NT Machine

OLE business servers created with Visual Basic should be created as 32-bit applications and deployed on a server that runs Windows NT, version 3.51 or later, which allows the business server to take advantage of all the functionality provided by Visual Basic's OLE features. These added features include OLE automation server security and error-logging capabilities.

Deploy as a Windows NT Service

Business servers should be deployed in a manner that meets the following goals:

- Automatically starts when the server machine boots
- Runs under a power user's security context, not the administrator's
- Doesn't require interaction with the server's console
- Can be administered remotely

When business servers are deployed under a Windows NT environment, they can be installed as Windows NT services. OLE automation servers created with Visual Basic cannot be natively installed as Windows NT services. But the Windows NT Resource Kit provides a utility, SRVANY.EXE, that allows 32-bit applications to be run as Windows NT services.

For example, the OrderMgrs instance manager can be installed as a Windows NT service, using the following steps.

III

The Service Layers

1. Install the Windows NT 3.5 Resource Kit and copy the SRVANY.EXE file to the server machine's \\WINNT35\SYSTEM32\ directory.

2. Install SRVANY.EXE as a service by using the command, `INSTSR OrderMgrs \\WINNT35\SYSTEM32\SRVANY.EXE`.

3. Use the Control Panel's Services applet to set the user account that will be used when the service is started.

4. With Registry Editor, REGEDIT32.EXE, create a "Parameters" key, under HKEY_LOCAL_MACHINE\SYSTEM\CurrentControlSet\Services\OrderMgrs.

5. Under the Parameters key, create an "Application" value of type REG_SZ and enter the path of the executable (including the extension), `\\GOLF\TIER2\ORDMGRS\OrdMgrs.EXE`.

When the server is next rebooted, the OrderMgrs business server will start automatically under the specified ID, without a user logging onto the machine.

The AppParameters and AppDirectory optional values can be created under the Parameters key. These values specify the command line parameter and current directory used by the application, respectively.

SRVANY.EXE can be installed multiple times on a server by specifying distinct service names for each instance. This allows all the GOLF System's instance managers to be installed as Windows NT services.

Moreover, the Automation Manager is a prime candidate to install as a service, using the technique just described. Running the Automation Manager as a service ensures that controlling applications will continue to have access to the business servers, even if a system administrator must log in and log off the server machine. Applications installed as services will continue to run, even after a user logs off the machine.

Security

Three-tier application security is discussed in detail in Chapter 13, "Architecting Security." It is important at this point, however, to realize that application security should reside within both the business servers and the data servers—you want to secure the business objects and processes, not just their underlying data.

The goals of the application security architecture are to make security an administrative task, not a development or programming task. This should be done by using the security features available within the business services tier.

Visual Basic ships with the Remote Automation Connection Manager utility. This utility provides the capability to set the security levels for each OLE automation server.

From Here...

This chapter described the design and creation of the business services tier of a three-tier application. For more information about some common aspects of business servers, review the following chapters:

- Chapter 6, "Creating OLE Objects," for more information on creating OLE servers in Visual Basic.

- Chapter 8, "Architecting Tier 1: Client Applications," for more information about how to create OLE client applications.

- Chapter 10, "Architecting Tier 3: Data Servers," for more information about creating the back data services.

- Chapter 13, "Architecting Security," for more information about implementing security within a three-tier applications.

- Chapter 14, "Architecting Error Processing," for more information about how to handle errors within business servers.

- Chapter 16, "Distributing Applications," for more information about distributing business servers.

- Chapter 23, "Sample Application #2: An Instance Manager," for more information about creating instance managers.

Chapter 10
Architecting Tier 3: Data Servers

Data services manage the enterprise information. This information is a collection of data used by the business services layer to make decisions and enforce business rules. Data services implement the data storage and relationships that map the business objects onto physical data store.

Data services support data definition, management, access, and updating. Definition is the database schema—the logical design. Management encompasses administration, security, and backup utilities. Access encompasses query execution methods. Updating encompasses transaction processing and database consistency, including the support of elementary data functions.

This data doesn't have to be stored in just database management systems. It can reside in mainframes, imaging servers, the Internet, or other sources.

In the three-tier services model, these additional data sources should be encapsulated, just as with a DBMS data source. As technology improves, we will begin to see these rich, nontraditional data sources gain popularity in large organizations.

This chapter provides an architectural overview of the more popular data sources. It provides detail on the most common data source: the DBMS. It is beyond the scope of this book, however, to provide detail on all other possible data sources. But this chapter does provide an overview of how these other data sources might be used in your organization and where to find additional information.

Please keep in mind that products are constantly changing. This book names certain products for sake of clarity and provides real-world examples, but the authors do not endorse these particular products over other products. Nor should this chapter be thought of as presenting an exhaustive list of data sources. Instead, this chapter is intended to show how data sources should be thought of in the three-tier architecture. The beauty of three tier, however, is that when you "discover" a new data source, it can be quickly incorporated into the architecture and easily managed.

In this chapter, we will cover:

- The popular data services available
- How to design and implement DBMS data services

DBMS Data Services

In this section, we look at the specifics of designing and implementing a relational database within the three-tier application architecture. First, we briefly talk about the definitions and theory behind the relational database model before going into detail about the design and implementation process.

Throughout this section, we refer to the process that was followed when developing the SQL server database used by the GOLF System sample application.

Explaining Database Terminology

Before we can begin to talk about the design and implementation of an enterprise database, we must first understand some of the terminology used when referring to a database, which is defined in the following list:

- **Database**—A shared collection of data that is logically related and designed to meet the needs of multiple users.
- **Database management system (DBMS)**—a software application that is used to create, maintain, and provide controlled access to the information stored within a database.
- **relational database**—A database that consists of data that is represented by a collection of relationships, or tables.

The Relational Database Model

The relational database model was developed in 1970 by Dr. E. F. Codd. This model was originally built upon the network and hierarchical database designs that were then common, replacing record pointers (which were used to associate records) with relationships between table attributes. In the relational database model, a relationship is a link between two records, in two separate tables, that have the same column or attribute values.

The removal of record pointers to link tables makes a relational database and its data DBMS independent. The data from one relational database can be exported in its entirety and imported into a database using a different DBMS and work the same way.

To establish these relationships, or links, a relational database requires that some data be duplicated among tables. Although this method requires duplication across tables in the form of primary and foreign keys, which is discussed later in this chapter, it does not allow data to be duplicated within the tables. A link between two tables creates a primary and dependent table relationship. A dependent table is a table or entity that cannot be fully identified or defined without obtaining information from its primary table.

The relational database model defines the following list defines three types of relationships that can exist between tables:

- **One-to-One**—Requires that only one record in the dependent table relate to one and only one record in the primary table.

- **One-to-Many**—Requires that one or more records in the dependent table relate to one, and only one, record in the primary table.

- **Many-to-Many**—Allows one or more records in the dependent table to relate to one or more records in the primary table. This is not a true relationship because, as you will see, a many-to-many relationship requires an additional relation table to maintain database integrity.

Properly defining the relationships between database tables by creating the correct primary and foreign keys provides the foundation for an effective relational database implementation.

Designing a Database

Now that you have an understanding of the relational model and what a relational database is, you can begin to design the application's database. The process of designing a database involves a number of steps. You begin the design phase by modeling the data that will be maintained by the application within the database. This process is similar in concept—and actually builds upon—the modeling we did when designing our business servers in Chapter 9, "Architecting Tier 2: Business Servers."

After the database has been modeled and organized into database tables, you must normalize the data by removing unnecessary duplicate information.

The extent to which this is done will vary, depending upon the type of application being developed. A decision support system, for example, will often contain a higher level of redundant data in the form of summary tables to increase the performance of the system. Online transaction processing systems, however, will often need to be fully normalized to provide the quick-hit performance they require.

After the data is normalized and the new table definitions are created, the relationships—referred to as *database referential integrity*—must be established by defining primary and foreign keys. The final step in designing the database is to define the initial indexes that will be needed to achieve the desired level of performance.

Modeling the Database

Two approaches can be taken when modeling the data that will reside within the database:

- **Bottom-Up**—This approach looks at data requirements from an application perspective, determining what information is required and how this information needs to be stored to support the applications.

- **Top-Down**—This approach looks at the data of the enterprise as a whole. The contents of the database then determine what information the applications can utilize.

The modeling approach that is used depends upon the long-term goals of the database. Often, organizations will use the bottom-up approach, and then find out that, a couple of months or years down the road, the database no longer can support the application's changing needs. For this reason, it is recommended that databases be designed in a top-down fashion to ensure that the requirements of the enterprise are being met, rather than just the requirements of the current application.

When we were designing our business servers in Chapter 9, we went through a number of modeling exercises to determine the entities that existed within the enterprise. After these entities were identified, we grouped them and defined attributes, or properties, of each that the application was interested in. These entities and their attributes provide you the starting point when modeling the database.

Each business entity will map to one or more of the physical database tables that will be kept in the DBMS. Taking the entities defined previously in Chapter 9, "Architecting Tier 2: Business Servers" (refer to fig. 9.1), we can begin to formulate the relational database model that will support this application.

In a database, data is stored in tables. Tables are collections of information about a particular topic or entity. When determining what attributes, or columns, should be present in a table, keep in mind the topic or entity that the table is representing. This process of associating attributes to tables is similar to the process of defining properties of the business servers. After all the business entities and their attributes have been mapped to database tables and columns, we can begin the process of normalizing the data.

Normalization

Normalization is the process of eliminating redundant data within the database by grouping attributes into well-structured relationships. The goal of database normalization is to allow applications to insert, delete, and update records within a table without producing errors or inconsistencies, referred to as data anomalies.

Pure normalization is done in six stages, where each stage represents a normal form. The term, *normal form*, refers to a state of a relation that corresponds to the dependencies that remain. The six stages of normal forms are defined in the following steps:

1. **First Normal Form** (**1NF**)—Repeating groups are removed, leaving a single value at the intersection of a row and a column.

2. **Second Normal Form** (**2NF**)—Partial functional dependencies are removed. Each row is uniquely identified by the table's primary key.

3. **Third Normal Form** (**3NF**)—Transitive dependencies are removed. All non-key fields are dependent upon the primary key but independent of each other, so that a change in a non-key field does not affect another non-key field.

4. **Boyce-Codd Normal Form** (**BCNF**)—Remaining anomalies resulting from functional dependencies are removed.

5. **Fourth Normal Form** (**4NF**)—Multi-valued dependencies are removed.

6. **Fifth Normal Form** (**5NF**)—Remaining anomalies are removed.

When designing a database, most developers stop at third normal form because at this point, most of the major data anomalies—the anomalies caused by inserts, updates, and deletes—have been removed. Taking the normalization process further often creates performance problems because a select from

III

The Service Layers

a single table in 3NF can become a select from a multi-table join in a 4NF database.

Boyce-Codd normal form is the only other level that is, in most cases, worth achieving. Often, people group the Boyce-Codd normal form level into their specification of 3NF. When a database is in third normal form, it is possible for anomalies to still exist as a result of functional dependencies. This occurs mainly when multiple candidate keys are present for a table. A candidate key represents an option that can be selected to create the table's primary key.

Take a fictitious company where an employee can work in multiple departments and has a supervisor in each department. A supervisor, however, can only supervise one department. In the process of creating a 3NF design, a table was established with a primary key of employee_ID, department, supervisor. This relation is 3NF because no functional or transitive dependencies exist, but anomalies are still present. In this design, we cannot add a supervisor until there is at least one employee working in that department. To solve this problem and place the design in Boyce-Codd normal form, the table is decomposed into two tables—one table with a primary key of employee_ID, department and the other with a primary key of department, supervisor.

Transaction Processing

The DBMS must allow business services to process modifications to the database in a consistent and reliable fashion. A commonly accepted and well-understood protocol associated with this process is ACID, which stands for atomicity, consistency, isolation, and durability. The following list defines the letters of the ACID acronym:

- **Atomicity**—A transaction's changes to the database are atomic, either all happen or none happens.

- **Consistency**—The actions of a transaction taken as a group do not violate any of the integrity constraints associated with the database.

- **Isolation**—Although multiple transactions execute at the same time, each transaction appears to occur serially.

- **Durability**—After a transaction completes successfully, its changes to the database are permanent.

The system architect should understand the ACID protocol and ensure that the business and data services do not violate the terms of the protocol.

Referential Integrity

Referential integrity refers to the process of ensuring that the relationships defined during the normalization process are kept intact when data is inserted into, updated in, or deleted from the database. This data integrity is maintained by using primary and foreign keys.

We already briefly mentioned the concept of a primary key while talking about normalization. The primary key of a table consists of the column or group of columns that uniquely identifies a record in the table. For example, a record in the LineItem table of the GOLF database can be uniquely identified by using the order_num and line_num columns.

Foreign keys ensure the integrity of the dependency relationships that exist between different database tables. The foreign key consists of the column or group of columns in the dependent table that uniquely identifies a record in the primary table. As this definition implies, the foreign key columns are associated with the primary table's primary key. For example, in the GOLF database, the OrdHdr table has a foreign key relationship with both the Product and the Customer tables. The customer_ID column in the OrdHdr table serves as a foreign key to the Customer table, and the product_ID column in the OrdHdr table serves as a foreign key to the Product table.

By defining primary and foreign key relationships in the database, you can ensure that an error will result if an application attempts to make a change that will violate the referential integrity of the data. For example, with the foreign key relationships mentioned previously, if an application attempts to create an order for a customer or a product that does not exist, an integrity error results and the order will not be inserted into the database.

When we defined our business entities, the tools we used did not really matter, as long as we could present the entities in a logical and understandable fashion. When modeling a relational database, however, there are a number of advantages to using one of the many database modeling tools that exist today. These tools not only allow us to define the tables and relationships that exist within the database, but also can generate the SQL (pronounced "sequel") scripts that we can use to create the actual database and enforce its relationships.

Indexes

Indexes are used to increase the performance of a database, by reducing the time it takes to locate a specific record within a database table. An index is a database object that contains the location of a record. Indexes, like tables, are created by using a key to identify an entry in the index table.

The most common example of an index key is the primary key of a table. Most relational database management systems (RDMSs) automatically create a unique index on the primary key of a table. When this occurs, an index object is created that contains the same key as the table's primary key and a pointer to the location of the actual record within the table.

Indexes reduce the time needed to retrieve a record because the database engine can search the index object, which is stored in a sequential fashion, for the location of the record within the table, rather than searching the entire database table. The nature of the relational database model is that the actual data doesn't need to be stored in any particular order. Because of this, a database engine often must scan the entire table area to locate a specific record, if a suitable index is unavailable to help the search.

It may be tempting to index every possible column that an application may use when selecting a record, but it is not usually feasible. Indexes require space on the machine where the database is located, because they store data that is redundant to the index's associated table. Although they greatly improve the ability to select records from a table, indexes degrade the performance of inserts, updates, and deletes from the table, because the changes need to be made not only to the physical table data but also to any index values.

For this reason, it is often recommended that during the initial design phase for a database, indexes should be created only for the primary and foreign keys that exist. These keys are safe to index because they will frequently be used to select data and join tables. Additional indexes should be added only after performance problems are identified. Before additional indexes are added, they should be system tested to ensure that they do not lead to a severe degradation of performance on aspects of the system that will be modifying the data.

Implementing the Design

After the database has been designed, it is time to begin the actual development and implementation of the database. In this section, we look at some components (available in most relational database management systems) that can be used to implement the design aspects discussed in the preceding section.

In addition to looking at the features of the database engine itself, we also address some other aspects of database development that should be considered before an application can be placed in production. We conclude this section by giving you a look at some basic performance-tuning techniques used to ensure that the database is operating in the most efficient manner possible.

Server Components

SQL database engines provide a number of database objects that can be used to assist in the implementation of a relational database. In this section we look at some of these objects and discuss how they can be used to assist in the development and maintenance of the enterprise data services.

Tables. As mentioned in the previous sections, tables are the core component of a relational database. It is the tables of a database that actually store the information being maintained in the database.

Database tables are created using Data Definition Language (DDL) scripts. The following example, Listing 10.1, shows the script that was used to create the OrderHdr table in the GOLF database, including its referential integrity constraints. You can find this code on the companion disk, in the \CHAP10 directory.

Listing 10.1   CODE01.TXT—DDL script used to create the OrderHdr table

```
CREATE TABLE OrderHdr
(
     OrderID int NOT NULL ,
     OrderDate datetime NULL ,
     ShippedFlag char (1) NULL ,
     CustomerID int NULL ,
     CONSTRAINT PK_OrderHdr_1__13 PRIMARY KEY  CLUSTERED
     (
          OrderID
     ),
     CONSTRAINT FK_OrderHdr_2__13 FOREIGN KEY
     (
          CustomerID
     ) REFERENCES dbo.Customer (
          CustomerID
     )
)
```

The options available when creating the physical database tables vary, depending upon the database engine. Most RDBMSs allow for: (1) the specification of the physical location of the table's data files on the hard disks, and (2) parameters to specify the sizing constraints of the table. The capability to specify the location of the table allows for flexibility when performance tuning large databases that reside on multiprocessor machines. When supported by the database engine, moving data around can provide performance increases because the database engine will be able to break up queries into multiple steps. These steps then can be executed simultaneously, using different processors and accessing different disk drives on the server.

III

The Service Layers

When determining the physical layout of the database, become familiar with the capabilities and options provided by the database engine to ensure that the engine is being used to its fullest.

Triggers. A *trigger* is a section of SQL code that is executed automatically whenever an application makes a specified change to the database. Triggers are executed based on events that occur within the database. In most RDBMSs, triggers can be defined that will execute when an update, insert, or delete is attempted against a table.

When not supported inherently by the database engine, triggers provide a mechanism by which the database can prevent primary key values from being updated and can implement cascading deletes against the dependent tables when a record is removed from the primary table. In addition, triggers allow the database to ensure that a primary table record exists when an insert is made into a dependent table.

Most RDBMSs today support the concept of declarative referential integrity, whereby the maintenance of the integrity constraints is handled automatically by the database engine. For systems in which this is not the case, triggers provide the best mechanism for enforcing integrity.

In the three-tier application architecture, triggers should only be used to handle data operations. Business rules should no longer be implemented using triggers, but instead should be placed in the business servers.

Rules. Rules are another mechanism for ensuring the integrity of the data. Rules go beyond the concept of referential integrity by allowing checks on the specific aspects of the data being placed into the table.

For a table that contains a phone number, a database rule may be placed on the area-code column to ensure that the first position of the area code is not a 1 or a zero. In many cases, such constraints to limit the valid values for a database column can be implemented as "lookup" tables, but there are situations in which this kind of lookup table does not make sense. In the previous example, it is easier to place a rule on the column than to create an additional table that contains all the valid area-code numbers that can be used.

Defaults. In a relational database, every column of a table must contain a value, even if the value is Null. A default allows the database to place a standard value into a column that is not populated when a new record is inserted into the database.

For example, for a database that contains transaction records that are received throughout the day from a legacy system and are processed on set intervals by a batch business server, we might have a status column of the record to indicate whether the record has been processed by the system. To ensure that the status column is set properly, a default indicating a status of not processed could be assigned by the database whenever a record is inserted into the table without a specified status value.

Stored Procedures. A stored procedure is a pre-compiled set of SQL statements that is stored as part of the database. Stored procedures provide a performance increase over embedded SQL calls because they have already been compiled by the database engine and have a query plan established.

In the two-tier application environment, stored procedures were often used as a means of placing the business logic in a central location, on the database server. The move to a three-tier architecture moves these business rules from the data services into the business services tier, and out of stored procedures. In this new architecture, stored procedures are used to handle the basic data manipulation tasks that are needed by the business server. Transaction management and business logic are thus moved into the business servers.

The following example, Listing 10.2, demonstrates a stored procedure that is used by the GOLF System's OrderMgr when creating a new order. The stored procedure simply places the data into the OrderHdr table, leaving the transaction management functions to the business server. You can find this code in the \CHAP24\GOLF\TIER3 directory on this book's companion disk.

> **Listing 10.2   ORDER01.SQL—Procedure to add a new order header record**

```
create procedure sp_Add_OrderHdr
@OrderID int = 0 OUTPUT,
@CustomerID int,
@OrderDate varchar(25) ,
@ShippedFlag char(1) = "N"

as

begin

/* Get the next order number if none passed */
if @OrderID = 0
begin
     select @OrderID = max(OrderID) + 1 from OrderHdr
end

/* for the first order check for the null */
if @OrderID = NULL
     select @OrderID = 100000000
```

(continues)

III

The Service Layers

Listing 10.2 Continued

```
insert into OrderHdr (OrderID, OrderDate, ShippedFlag, CustomerID)
values(
@OrderID,
@OrderDate,
@ShippedFlag,
@CustomerID)

end
```

Record Locking

When implementing a relational database, it is important to examine the method by which database records will be locked while being updated. The purpose of record locking is to ensure that two application users are not attempting to make a change to the same record at the same time.

RDBMSs implement record locking differently, and many provide the option to specify the level of record locking to be used. For example, many database engines read data from the tables in chunks, such as a page at a time. By default, these engines also place a lock on the page or pages being read, as opposed to locking the specific record being used. The size of a page varies among the database engines but usually will contain more than one record. This means that when a record is being updated, the other records on this page are also locked by the database and are not available to other users. For this reason, the manner in which the database locks records needs to be determined.

The choice of locking schemes to use depends mostly on the characteristics of the applications that will access the database. For example, an online transaction processing system is often characterized as making a large number of updates and inserts into the database. This means the application will continually be acquiring and freeing locks on the database tables. Decision support systems, however, are characterized as having large read-only queries against the database, in which case only shared locks are used.

Two record-locking schemes are available in most relational database management systems—pessimistic and optimistic record locking.

Optimistic Record Locking. With optimistic record locking, the record being updated is locked only while the actual update is taking place. This lock is released after the update process is completed.

The advantage of optimistic record locking is that the record, or database page, is locked for only a short time: the time it takes to actually update the record. This scheme reduces the chance that another user will be blocked while attempting to access a record on the same data page.

The disadvantage of this method is that it's possible for another user to make a change to the record between the time the record is selected and the time the change is actually attempted. If optimistic record locking is the method chosen, the manner in which this situation is trapped and handled needs to be determined.

Pessimistic Record Locking. Pessimistic record locking places a lock on the record or data page when it is determined that an edit will be made. This lock is released after the actual update has been completed.

This method prevents another user from making a change to the record between the time the record is selected for update and the time the change is actually submitted to the database. The disadvantage is that the record or data page is locked for a longer period. This increases the probability that another user will be blocked while attempting to access this or another record located on the same data page.

Under most situations, optimistic record locking is the best choice because the chances of someone else attempting to modify the same record are a lot lower than the chances of someone attempting to access another record located on the same physical data page. A number of techniques also can be used to test the current value of the data before an update is made to ensure that the data has not been changed since the user selected it.

Data Access Characteristics

Database applications fall into one of two classifications—transaction processing systems or decision support systems. A system is classified based on the types of transactions or queries that are run against the database. Each application class requires a different approach for designing and implementing the database.

Decision support systems are characterized by large read-only requests against a vast amount of historical data. In the decision support world, the user is manipulating data to answer questions and make decisions about the performance of the business. These systems usually provide users with the ability to create their own *ad hoc* queries against the database.

Transaction processing systems, on the other hand, are characterized by a large number of small, quick-hit actions that modify the data, through inserts, updates, and deletes. Transaction processing systems support the day-to-day operations of the organization. For example, the GOLF System would be classified as a transaction processing system because its purpose is to allow the user to maintain information about the entities of the business: customers, products, and orders.

Because of the differences between these two classes, it is recommended that, when both types are required within the enterprise, they are physically separated into two distinct databases, which are often placed on two separate server machines. Doing this prevents the data requests from the decision support applications from interfering with the day-to-day operations of the transactional processing systems. The term *data warehouse* is commonly used to refer to the historical and summary data that provides the foundation for the decision support environment.

Environments that support both transaction processing systems (to maintain the daily operations of the enterprise) and decision support applications (for analysis and strategic decision making) often employ distributed databases to update the data between the two systems.

Distributed Databases

The term *distributed database* refers to a logical database that is physically spread across multiple database servers, which can be geographically dispersed. The database servers that make up a distributed database are connected by a network, either a LAN or a WAN.

Distributed databases provide a number of benefits:

- Improved data availability.

- Improved performance, because workload can be distributed across servers, and reduction in network traffic to a central database.

- A flexible and scalable model.

Two methods are used to create and maintain distributed databases: two-phased commit and replication. The choice of methods is often driven by the requirements of the timeliness of the data that is present on each database server.

Two-Phased Commit. A *two-phased commit* describes the way in which an atomic transaction occurs and is coordinated across multiple servers. The two-phased commit implementation ensures that transactions that are successfully applied to one server are successfully applied to all servers in the distributed database. If the transaction fails on one server, the transaction is rolled back on all servers.

Two-phased commits are implemented internally much as the name implies. When a transaction is performed against one database participating in the distributed system, the transaction also must be applied to all other databases that are part of the distributed system. To ensure that the data remains in sync, what can be thought of as a global transaction is started when the first server applies the transaction. If all the database servers successfully apply the transaction, this transaction is committed by also committing the global transaction. If one database server fails to complete the transaction, the global transaction is rolled back, thus rolling back the transaction on any of the database servers where it completed.

This method ensures that the data is 100 percent in sync among all servers 100 percent of the time. The two-phased commit approach is often used in distributed transaction processing systems, where a tight consistency between the original data and its copies must exist.

Replication of Database Data. The other method of implementing a distributed database is the process of *replication*. Replication is designed for cases in which the data is not required to be 100 percent synchronized across all the database servers 100 percent of the time. The replication method is often used to move data from the transaction processing system to the decision support data warehouse on a nightly basis.

RDBMSs that support replication often use some variation of a publisher-and-subscriber metaphor. Using this metaphor, the publishing database makes available information in the form of tables, views, or databases of which the subscribers can receive copies. Often in this relationship, the publishing database maintains the source, updatable copy of the information, and the subscribers receive read-only copies of the data. Although it is usually not a requirement that the subscriber's data be treated as read-only, this relationship is often only one way. This means that changes made to the subscriber's copy of the data will not be replicated back to the publishing database.

Expanding on this metaphor, there are four publisher-subscriber models that can be implemented:

- **Single publisher to multiple subscribers**—A single publisher distributes data to multiple servers. All data maintenance occurs in the publisher database and is replicated to the subscribers.

- **Single publisher using distribution server**—This is similar to the single-publisher-to-multi-subscriber model, except that distribution is handled by a separate machine. The distribution server acts both as a subscriber to the publisher's database and as a publisher to the other subscriber databases.

III

The Service Layers

- **Multiple publishers to single subscriber**—A single database subscriber receives publications from multiple publishing databases. This is often used to replicate data back to a central location.

- **Multiple publishers to multiple subscribers**—Each server acts as both a publisher and subscriber, making its data available to the other servers and receiving copies of the other servers' data. In this scenario, each server has a complete copy of the data but maintains only the data that it publishes.

The replication method of distributing data is time-driven, in that data is replicated at defined intervals, such as weekly, daily, or hourly. Because of this, the replication method only provides a picture in time of what exists on the publishing server. As mentioned previously, replication is most commonly used to move data from the transaction processing database to the decision support database, or to the data warehouse, on a nightly basis.

Database Performance Tuning

Database *performance tuning* is more of an art than a science. To effectively performance tune a database, you must have an understanding of both the way the database engine operates and how the application makes use of the data.

Indexes, discussed earlier in this chapter, are the primary tools for performance tuning an application. Although it may be easy to throw an additional index on a table to speed up a select query, it is not a recommended practice. With each index attached to a table comes the added overhead of maintaining that index during inserts, updates, and deletes.

The following list offers starting points regarding performance tuning a relational database through the use of indexes:

- Index foreign keys that are used to join to other tables.

- Ensure that composite primary key indexes are created in a manner that provides the most flexibility. Most database engines can utilize partial index keys only when working in from the first key value.

- Index short codes, as opposed to long test strings.

- Indexes on numeric values usually perform better than those using character values.

> **Note**
>
> In addition to the indexing of the database, the file operations being performed by the database engine will often provide clues to the cause of a performance problem. For example, if two queries are attempting to retrieve data from different tables residing on the same hard drive, a bottleneck will form.

Database management systems usually include a number of administrative utilities that can assist in the performance-tuning process. These tools provide information about the inner workings of the database engine itself, related to the reading and writing of data from the physical database files.

Most RDBMSs also contain a query optimizer that examines the syntax of a SQL statement and determines the best method of performing the requested action. The optimizers can also provide a detailed plan to the proposed execution method that can be used to isolate performance problems, and can provide clues to the candidates for additional indexes.

Using SQL to Access the Database

Now that we created and tuned the relational database, this section discusses the method for working with the data provided. The data within a relational database is accessed using variations of the Structured Query Language (SQL).

SQL syntax variants are divided into two types of functionality—the SQL syntax that manipulates and defines the structure of the underlying database and syntax that is used to manipulate the actual data contained within the database. This section examines both aspects of SQL, concentrating on the commonly used data manipulation constructs.

Data Definition Language

SQL data definition language (DDL) is the scripting language used when creating or modifying the structure of tables, columns, indexes, and other aspects of a relational database. Although the exact syntax employed to perform these actions will vary—based on the database server that is being used—each action will provide the following basic statements for each creatable database object.

- **CREATE**—Creates a new table, index, view, or other object in the database.

- **ALTER**—Modifies the current definition of an existing table, index, view, or other object within the database.

III

The Service Layers

■ **DROP**—Removes an existing table, index, view, or other object from the database.

An example of a SQL DDL script that creates a new table was included previously in this chapter, during the discussion of database tables. For specific details about the use of SQL DDL, refer to the manuals provided with the database engine being implemented.

Data Manipulation Language

The SQL syntax used to work with or manipulate the data contained within a relational database is referred to as the data manipulation language. The main components of the SQL data manipulation language can be divided into two main groups—components that allow an application to retrieve data from the database, and those that allow an application to update or change the data in the database.

SELECT Statement. The SQL SELECT statement retrieves data from a relational database. The syntax of the SELECT statement determines what data will be returned. The general syntax of the SELECT statement is shown in the following example:

```
SELECT [predicate] fieldlist FROM tablelist
    [table relations] [range options]
    [group options] [sort options]
```

The predicate of the SELECT statement is used to specify the uniqueness of the field list retrieved. For example, to retrieve only one occurrence of a customer number from the GOLF System's OrderHdr table, the DISTINCT predicate could be used, as in the following example:

```
SELECT DISTINCT customer_id FROM orderhdr;
```

As illustrated preceding, the *fieldlist* argument of the SELECT list specifies the actual data elements that will be retrieved by the SELECT statement. This list can include any number of columns present in the FROM tables, aggregate functions, or a wild card. For example, to retrieve all the column information from the OrderHdr table, either of the following SELECT statements can be used:

```
SELECT * FROM orderhdr;
```

or

```
SELECT
    order_num,
    order_dt,
    customer_id,
    order_sts
FROM
    orderhdr;
```

Although both of these SELECT statements produce the same results, it is recommended that all of the specific column names are specified when creating SELECT statements that will be retrieving data to be sent to an application. This way, if a column is added to the table, the application will not stop working because it suddenly is getting an extra column that it was not expecting.

The FROM clause, as we have seen, specifies the table or tables from which the data is being retrieved. When multiple tables are present in the FROM clause, they must be joined using the optional table relations clause. Failure to properly join tables in the FROM clause results in what is known as a Cartesian product, whereby the field list is returned once for every combination of the FROM table primary keys.

The following example, shown in Listing 10.3, illustrates the use of the FROM clause to obtain information from more than one table in a single SELECT statement. In this example, the table relations are defined in the WHERE clause, which is discussed later in this chapter. This example also demonstrates the use of table aliases to specify the table from which the column is to be selected. Often, when two tables are being joined, the columns by which the join occurs have the same name. For the database engine to determine which column to use, the column name must be prefixed by either the full table name or a table alias. You can find this code in the \CHAP10 directory, on this book's companion disk.

Listing 10.3   CODE02.TXT—Example of a SELECT statement

```
SELECT
      oh.order_num,
      oh.order_dt,
      c.cust_name
FROM
      orderhdr oh,
      customer c
WHERE
      oh.customer_id = c.customer_id;
```

In addition to joining multiple tables in the FROM clause, the WHERE clause can be used to limit, or filter, the number of rows returned by the SELECT statement. When used in this manner, the WHERE clause specifies the optional range for the SELECT statement.

III

The Service Layers

Using the previous example again, let's limit the number of rows returned to only those orders that have a status of open, or 0. In this example, shown in Listing 10.4, the filter is placed in the WHERE clause to limit the number of rows returned. This code can also be found on the companion disk, in the /CHAP10 directory.

Listing 10.4 CODE03.TXT—Using the WHERE clause to filter results

```
SELECT
      oh.order_num,
      oh.order_dt,
      c.cust_name
FROM
      orderhdr oh,
      customer c
WHERE
      oh.customer_id = c.customer_id and
      oh.order_sts = '0';
```

It is often necessary to obtain summary or aggregate information from a table. This is done using the group options of the SELECT statement.

Again building on the previous example, let's retrieve the number of open orders and the order date of the oldest open order for each customer. To accomplish this, we can use the SQL GROUP BY clause to aggregate the selection, as shown in Listing 10.5. We will also use the built-in aggregate COUNT and MIN functions to summarize the data. This code is located in the \CHAP10 directory of this book's companion disk.

Listing 10.5 CODE03.TXT—Aggregating results using the SQL GROUP BY clause

```
SELECT
      c.cust_name,
      MIN(oh.order_dt),
      COUNT(oh.order_num)
FROM
      orderhdr oh,
      customer c
WHERE
      oh.customer_id = c.customer_id and
      oh.order_sts = '0'
GROUP BY
      c.cust_name;
```

The result of this query will be one record per customer that has open orders in the database.

Data stored within a relational database is not kept in any specific order, which means that unless specified, the data will not come back sorted in any given way. To retrieve data in a specific order, the desired order must be specified in the SELECT statement using the ORDER BY clause.

Building again on the previous example, suppose that you need to retrieve the customer open-order counts in ascending order by oldest order, and then by alphabetical order based on customer name within the same order dates. To do this, the ORDER BY clause is used, with multiple sort columns specified. The sort will occur in the order that the columns are specified. Listing 10.6 is located in the \CHAP10 directory of the companion disk.

Listing 10.6   CODE05.TXT—Using ORDER BY to sort the results

```
SELECT
      MIN(oh.order_dt),
      c.cust_name,
      COUNT(oh.order_num)
FROM
      orderhdr oh,
      customer c
WHERE
      oh.customer_id = c.customer_id and
      oh.order_sts = 'O'
GROUP BY
      c.cust_name
ORDER BY
      1, c.cust_name;
```

In the preceding example, we also demonstrate the use of an ordinal column number and a column name to specify the ORDER BY columns. Most database servers will allow the ORDER BY and GROUP BY clauses to be specified using either the ordinal value of the column in the select list, or the column name itself.

The SELECT statements demonstrated here illustrate the basics of data retrieval using SQL. Most implementations of SQL provide the ability to union SELECT statements into a single result. Typical SQL implementations also allow sub-SELECTs, which are SELECT statements within SELECT statements, both in the WHERE clause and as members of the SELECT list.

III

The Service Layers

UPDATE Statement. Now that you can retrieve data from the database, the only thing left to do is change the data that exists by inserting, deleting, and updating the database. The SQL UPDATE and DELETE statements provide a lot of the same features as the SELECT statement. The main difference between the capabilities of the UPDATE and DELETE statements and the INSERT statement is the capability to use multiple tables in the WHERE clause.

The SQL UPDATE statement is used to change the data of existing records within the database. As with the SELECT statement, an UPDATE can be performed on an entire table or only on a limited number of rows by specifying selection criteria within the WHERE clause. The general syntax of the UPDATE statement is shown in the following line:

```
UPDATE tablename SET field = value [WHERE clause]
```

The *tablename* specifies the table that is being updated, and *field* indicates the specific columns within this table that are being affected.

The following example illustrates an SQL UPDATE statement that could be used to change the Order_Sts value of all orders in the OrderHdr table to Shipped when the current value is Open. Just as with the retrieval of records by using the SELECT statement, the UPDATE statement uses the WHERE clause to limit the number of rows affected by the action being performed.

```
UPDATE orderhdr
SET
    order_sts = 'S'
WHERE
    order_sts = 'O';
```

The UPDATE statement supports the ability to limit the affected rows based on values that exist in a related table. Most often this limiting is done by specifying a sub-SELECT within the WHERE clause.

DELETE Statement. The SQL DELETE statement is used to remove records from a relational database. Unlike the other SQL data manipulation statements, the DELETE statement does not contain a field or column list because only entire rows can be deleted from the database tables.

The general syntax of the DELETE statement is:

```
DELETE FROM tablename [WHERE clause]
```

Like the UPDATE statement, the DELETE statement can be applied to an entire table or to remove only limited rows by specifying criteria in the WHERE clause. The DELETE statement is dangerous because, after a record is deleted from the database, that record is gone, unless the delete happened within a transaction that has not yet been committed.

Again using the GOLF System's OrderHdr table, the following example will delete from the table all the orders that currently have a status of Paid. Like all SQL statements that limit the rows affected, the DELETE statement uses the WHERE clause to specify the criteria for rows that are to be removed from the database.

```
DELETE FROM
     orderhdr
WHERE
     order_sts = 'P';
```

Like the UPDATE statement, the DELETE statement can operate based on the values contained within other database tables by using a sub-SELECT within the statement's WHERE clause.

INSERT Statement. The final SQL data manipulation statement that is commonly used is the INSERT statement. The INSERT statement, as the name implies, allows an application to add a record into a database table. Most database systems support two general syntaxes for an INSERT statement. One syntax employs a SELECT statement and the other does not:

```
INSERT INTO tablename (column list) VALUES (values)
```

and

```
INSERT INTO tablename SELECT remainder of standard select statement
```

The following example demonstrates how a record could be inserted into the GOLF System's OrderHdr table using the first syntax. In this case, the inserted values are hard coded, but in a production application these values would likely be substituted with parameter values:

```
INSERT INTO orderhdr (order_num, order_dt, order_sts, customer_id)
VALUES(
     '100202',
     '07/03/95',
     '0',
     '9900203');
```

Although the exact syntax for the SQL statements mentioned in this section will vary, depending upon the relational database management system in which they are being implemented, all databases will provide these SQL statements at a minimum.

At this point, you are ready to being developing a three-tier client/server application that makes use of a relational database to supply the data services to the remainder of the application.

III

The Service Layers

Host and Mainframe

The bulk of corporate data exists in host-based systems. Almost every large organization's transaction processing environment consists at least partly of mainframe and midrange systems. Thousands of lines of COBOL code are the "meat and potatoes" of an organization's Information Technology (IT) infrastructure. These systems have kept the business humming.

The three-tier architecture suggests that these legacy systems have a place in a client/server environment. The choice between a host-based system and client/server is no longer a mutually exclusive, black-or-white decision. In a well-planned three-tier architecture, existing host-based systems can be leveraged by GUI user services and reengineered business services.

There are two main approaches to incorporating host-based information into a three-tier Visual Basic client/server environment:

- Access the data directly
- Access the existing host-based applications and transactions that manipulate the data

Each approach carries advantages and disadvantages.

If host-based systems are encapsulated into the services model, users can see an intuitive, reengineered interface that may incorporate multiple, complex host systems.

Host-Based Data Access

A host such as an IBM mainframe 3090 or midrange AS/400 is capable of providing services similar to those provided by other database servers such as Oracle and SQL Server. IBM's DB2 relational database is a robust, powerful database management system that runs well on IBM's largest mainframes. DB2 can be accessed by a PC-based business server like any other RDBMS product. Even nonrelational flat file and record-based host data such as VSAM and IMS files can be accessed by PC-based business servers with gateway products. Figure 10.1 shows how this data service fits into the services model.

If a host does not allow direct data access, this access can often be accomplished with a gateway product. Gateway products usually make host-based data look like a more common PC-based data service. For example, MicroDecisionware's MDI Gateway makes a DB2 database look like a SQL Server database to a PC-based client.

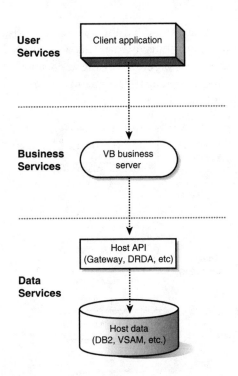

Fig. 10.1
An architecture
that incorporates a
host-based data
service.

Host-Based Transaction Access

Sometimes it is not possible or desirable to access host data directly. Many lines of COBOL business rule code may be tightly intertwined with the underlying data. An organization migrating to client/server may wish to leverage this business code, which has stood the test of time and run well in a production environment, and which may not be well documented.

In this situation, the client/server developer may want to access just the host transaction and not necessarily the underlying data. Such COBOL applications can be thought of as business servers encapsulating business rules. Figure 10.2 shows how this architecture fits into the three-tier services model.

The COBOL application incorporates a subset of the business rules of the service-based system. For example, an organization may have a complex host-based order-processing system that doesn't incorporate customer credit checks. The company may decide to reengineer its order-processing system in a client/server environment, but may not find it cost-effective to replace the existing mainframe order-processing logic. Instead, existing mainframe order-processing applications are "wrapped" in richer Visual Basic OLE automation business servers. The client application accesses the business server via remote automation, just as with any other business server. The Visual Basic business server, however, isn't talking directly to a database: instead, it's communicating with a legacy mainframe order-processing application. Although the legacy order-processing system doesn't implement a credit-check mechanism, the "wrapper" VB application can.

Fig. 10.2
An architecture that incorporates both host-based transactions and data.

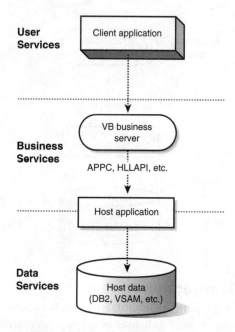

Note, too, that the VB client application has no knowledge that a mainframe application is being used by the business server—it is simply interfacing with the business object via OLE automation, just like any other business object. This example demonstrates the flexibility of the three-tier services model: if later you decide to rip out the plumbing of the mainframe application and replace it with a different platform (such as Oracle on UNIX), the client application need not be modified.

Many tools are available that allow a VB application to talk to a mainframe. Such a dialog between a VB application and a mainframe application is often called "screen scraping," because the VB application is automating the "screens" of the mainframe application. Because screen scraping is sensitive to trivial changes to the mainframe application (such as an edit field that changes screen position), such applications are often difficult to support and maintain. In the services model, however, business objects encapsulating such terminal screens may be centrally located and more easily managed.

Several application programming interfaces (APIs) can be used to help a PC communicate with a host-based system. IBM's High Level Language Application Programming Interface (HLLAPI) helps a PC emulate multiple terminal sessions. Extended HLLAPI (EHLLAPI) is a subset of HLLAPI. Advanced Program to Program Communication (APPC) is a peer-to-peer protocol more advanced than HLLAPI. Finally, some vendors offer remote procedure call (RPC) mechanisms that enable a PC to run mainframe applications through a proprietary API or through an SQL emulation mode.

Many vendors, such as Attachmate and Wall Data, provide VB-to-host transaction access.

Information Access Systems

Strictly speaking, *information access*, such as reporting, spans all three tiers: user, business, and data services. Because the focus of this book, however, is on developing transaction processing systems; because reports generally leverage tools other than VB; and because these tools don't yet generally implement a three-tier architecture, they are covered in this chapter.

In this context, *information access system* (IAS) refers to any type of system designed strictly to provide information to the end user. So, for example, a lookup system, a reporting system, an executive information system (EIS), or a decision support system (DSS) is also an IAS.

Traditional corporate reporting is undergoing significant changes. Typically, users have worked with the transaction processing system—entering orders, changing customer profiles, or altering pricing contracts—to enter data. When users needed to look at aggregations of this data, they turned to batch reports that ran during regular intervals such as nightly or monthly.

Lookup Systems, Reporting Systems, Executive Information Systems, and Decision Support Systems

Users have several ways to get at data in a client/server environment. Information access can be classified into the following main categories:

- Lookup Systems
- Reporting Systems
- Executive Information Systems (EIS)
- Decision Support Systems (DSS)

III

The Service Layers

Sometimes, there isn't a clear line separating these categories, and vendors who are constantly adding functionality to their tools contribute to this ambiguity. The following sections discuss the characteristics of each category, the tools that are used, and how each fits into the services model.

Lookup

In a GUI environment, the online transaction processing (OLTP) system offers much of the "batch report" functionality both online and real-time. Most GUI maintenance systems have "lookup" and print capability. For example, an order-processing system may allow users to list orders by customer and to output the list to a printer.

Lookup systems are generally built with tools like VB using spreadsheet controls, and usually are incorporated right into the OLTP application. Lookup systems tend to answer questions against the live, OLTP data. They generally do not aggregate data.

Reporting Systems

Reporting systems display information in a form most similar to traditional reports. In a client/server environment, however, reports generally can be made available both in hard-copy (printed) and electronic (displayed) form. For example, the latest version of Crystal Reports enables users to save a report's data along with its layout so the report can be archived, distributed, or viewed later.

Reports can be batched to run at regular intervals or run on demand. They can operate against OLTP data or against specialized data-warehouse data (see the "Data Repository" that follows in this chapter).

Reporting systems tend to answer recurring questions over a standard period. An operational report might be a list of all unshipped orders from the previous day that require a customer-apology phone call. A data-warehouse report might be a sales commission report by sales representative.

Executive Information Systems

Executive information systems (EIS) tend to operate against data-warehouse data, not transactional data. The name comes from the fact that these systems usually are used by senior management to answer questions. An EIS is an online system that usually defines a series of "drill-downs" that enable the user to selectively peer deeper and deeper into information detail.

EISs should be uncluttered and easy to use. They are designed for the way the end user asks recurring questions. They should incorporate both graph and table views. EISs are either custom developed with tools such as VB or built with specialized, off-the-shelf EIS applications.

Decision Support Systems

Like EISs, decision support systems (DSS) tend to operate against data-warehouse data, not transactional data. Unlike EIS, however, DSS applications don't pre-define access paths into the data. They are designed to answer questions that the developer never anticipated.

DSS applications can be thought of as robust ad hoc tools that don't require the user to understand SQL and that incorporate complex analysis and sophisticated presentation capabilities. They tend to be used by analysts because they are so open-ended and flexible. They should be "meta-data" driven. *Meta-data* is data about the data. Meta-data driven means the application should dynamically change as the underlying data structure changes.

Unlike EIS applications, DSS applications are often too complex to custom build and maintain. Tools such as DSS Agent by MicroStrategy are more capable and flexible than applications that IT shops can build themselves.

Data Repository

Data repositories and *data warehousing* are buzzwords often related to information access. There is no strict definition of what is and what is not a data warehouse. In general, however, a data warehouse is an aggregation of operational data in a single, logical database separate from the operational database.

A data repository (DR) is a relational picture of the data residing in the organization's online transaction processing (OLTP) systems. A DR is stored in a physical database separate from the OLTP systems and refreshed at regular intervals (usually nightly). It should evolve into a consistent, centralized view of the enterprise.

A number of benefits can be gained from operating IAS applications against a data repository versus the OLTP system.

The OLTP system is shielded from the often intensive resource utilization of the IAS applications. Because it is refreshed at regular intervals, the DR presents a consistent view of data in time that doesn't change throughout the day. This is often a requirement of IAS applications.

Tables can be designed specifically for IAS applications, whose needs are often different from those of OLTP applications. For example, IAS database access is characterized by long-running SELECT queries that acquire shared locks on

III

The Service Layers

many records, whereas OLTP database access is characterized by short UPDATE, INSERT, and DELETE queries that acquire exclusive locks on only a few records. For performance reasons, IAS tables are usually summarized and heavily indexed on non-key fields. Historical information can be kept without affecting the OLTP table sizes.

The data repository should contain two logical layers: the data warehouse layer and the data mart layer. Each layer may contain any number of tables (see fig. 10.3).

Fig. 10.3
A data repository contains two logical layers: the data warehouse and the data mart.

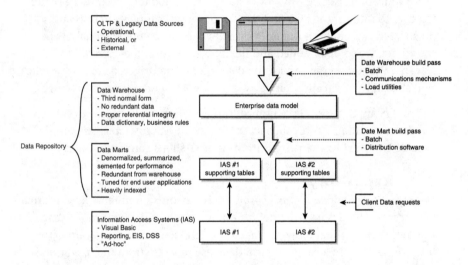

Physically, each layer can reside on any number of servers including the OLTP servers. In practice, it usually makes the most sense to dedicate a DBMS server, separate from the OLTP server, and store both layers on this new server.

The new data repository doesn't have to be created all at once. Instead, the data repository requirements for the next three to five years should be designed and the data repository should evolve, driven by the prioritized needs of the end-user applications.

A great deal of care should go into the design of the data repository. It should be architected to accommodate the inevitable changes in your organization's business model. For example, it should contain proper primary and foreign key relationships. The power of SQL directly correlates to proper relational database design.

Data Warehouse

The *data warehouse* layer contains a normalized picture of the enterprise's data for a given period. It is called the data warehouse because, like a wholesaler, it is the one source of detail bulk data for the data mart and other services.

The data warehouse contains consolidated business entities and is not tuned for specific end-user applications. It should be refreshed in batch at regular intervals. Because the data may come from many different sources, the data-warehouse build pass should rigorously convert the data to a consistent, enterprise-wide view. This may involve intensive normalization and validation of denormalized data.

The data-warehouse build pass will be specific to your environment. Often, specialized gateway products (MDI Gateway or Microsoft SNA Server) or custom server-based applications are required to migrate data from legacy production environments to the data warehouse.

Data Mart

The *data mart* is built from the data warehouse in subsequent batch passes. The data marts are designed for specific end-user applications; often they are designed as a single-table, "one-stop shopping" data source. This section of the database is called a data mart because, like a retailer, it provides data packaged the way the accessing applications would like to see it.

For example, where an application request for data might involve a four-table join against the data warehouse, the same request might involve only a single data-mart table.

Three-Tier and Information Access

In general, reporting, DSS, and EIS tools don't fit into the services model very well because their functionality spans logical layers: the user, business, and data services layers. Lookup systems, which often are incorporated in the transaction processing system, do fit well. This functionality is best illustrated by an example.

It should be clear that reporting, EIS, and DSS tools encompass the user services tier: their primary purpose is to display information in an intuitive format. What may be less obvious is that these tools also incorporate business rules. Suppose that users are interested in looking at delinquent customer information with a reporting, EIS, or DSS tool. The definition of exactly what constitutes *delinquent* is a business rule. Is a customer delinquent when it has more than $100,000 in receivables 90 days past, or is a customer delinquent when it has *any* receivables 90 days past? To tell the user that a customer is delinquent, a reporting system, EIS, or DSS needs to have knowledge of this rule. This usually means that the rule must be defined in the reporting engine, as opposed to being defined in a common, centralized business engine.

Ideally, a reporting, EIS, or DSS tool should be able to leverage your centrally defined business rules. Realistically, this capability isn't going to appear for a while. Reporting, EIS, and DSS tools will, for the near future, remain two-tier and talk directly to the DBMS. We are beginning to see reporting, EIS, and DSS tools that logically separate the business and presentation rules in their own environment, however.

For example, an excellent DSS tool by MicroStrategy, named DSS Agent, works within a three-tier data warehousing environment. DSS Agent also has a "query engine" analogous to a business server that can be deployed anywhere on the network and accessed by a client application.

Three-Tier Reporting

Although it's difficult to fit IAS applications into the strict three-tier model when using commercial, off-the-shelf products such as reporting tools, your custom reporting applications can be built in the three-tier architecture.

One extremely useful paradigm is a *reporting server* that creates reports at the request of end users. These reports can be created by the server in a spreadsheet tool, such as Microsoft Excel. Here's how the reporting server process can work:

1. A client application makes a request for a report to a reporting server that runs across the network via OLE automation.

2. The reporting server acknowledges the request and asks the data service for the appropriate data.

3. The reporting server launches Microsoft Excel and, using OLE automation, builds a custom report.

4. The reporting server completes, notifying the client that it is done, and either printing or passing to the client the finished report.

This architecture is useful not only for standard reports, but also for operational printed output, such as packing slips and invoices. In this architecture the client application is unaware of how an invoice should look. It simply makes a request for an invoice and the reporting server takes care of everything else, incorporating rich presentation elements such as logos and rich text. The report server also may produce *smart reports*, incorporating pivot tables and auto-formatting. Very few OLE controls can match Excel's charting and display capabilities. Reports created in Excel can also be manipulated by end users, just like any other Excel spreadsheet.

Messaging

In the three-tier world, *messaging* should be thought of as a data service. Examples of messaging services include Microsoft Exchange, Microsoft Mail, Lotus Notes, and Lotus cc:Mail.

Messaging services are analogous to DBMS data services. Their similarities include the following areas:

- A DBMS is accessed through an API, usually RDO or ODBC. Likewise, a messaging service is accessed through an API, such as MAPI (Messaging API), VIM (Vendor Independent Messaging), or MHS (Message Handling System).

- A DBMS stores data, such as relational columns and rows. Likewise, a messaging service stores data, such as documents and rich text.

- A DBMS can be file-based or client/server. Likewise, a messaging service can be file-based (like Microsoft Mail) or client/server (like Lotus Notes).

There are differences between the two types of services, however. A DBMS is good at providing access to structured data, whereas a messaging service is better suited to providing access to free-form data.

A DBMS is designed to provide real-time, connection-oriented access to structured data. For example, a DBMS user must maintain a live connection to the database while the user is interacting with the system. Users generally ask for a transaction to be performed, and then must wait for the transaction to complete. A messaging service, on the other hand, is designed to provide the connectionless and store-and-forward data services. *Connectionless* means the system can support off-line work—work that is performed while the user is not logged into the service. *Store-and-forward* means that a user transaction request (such as sending an e-mail message) occurs without the user having to wait for the transaction to be complete or even care whether the transaction is complete.

These characteristics make messaging services ideal for e-mail and "disconnected clients," such as laptop users who are on the road.

III

The Service Layers

Electronic Mail

Electronic mail systems can be leveraged by Visual Basic applications. Electronic mail is a useful transport mechanism for off-line documents, such as time sheets and expense reports. MAPI is the WOSA standard for access to electronic mail systems.

Visual Basic includes two OLE controls that enable VB to access MAPI data services. The MAPI session control both establishes a MAPI session and signs off from a MAPI session. The MAPI messages control enables you to perform a variety of messaging systems functions, after a messaging session is established. These functions include sending and receiving messages, displaying the address-book dialog boxes, accessing attachments, resolving recipient address names, and performing reply and delete actions on messages.

For these controls to work, MAPI services must be present on the computer. MAPI services are provided in MAPI-compliant electronic mail systems such as Microsoft Exchange. Most electronic mail vendors support MAPI.

Groupware

The term *groupware* is used to describe message-based electronic bulletin boards that enable groups of users to simultaneously work on documents or hold discussions.

The most popular groupware package at the time of this writing is Lotus Notes. Lotus Notes enables groups of users to store, access, and edit rich data. A common type of Lotus Notes application is a sales tracking system that enables salespeople to track customer contact information.

The key piece of functionality Notes provides is replication. Notes' replication facility enables users to work on their own, local database and to seamlessly synchronize it with another database, such as a centralized database. For example, a group of 50 sales reps could work off-line on laptops on their own copy of a customer tracking database. When they plug into a modem and replicate, all of their changes are posted to the centralized database, and all changes made to the centralized database by other users since they last replicated are sent down to their local database copy.

The Notes product encompasses not only the database and replication functionality, but also front-end application development functionality. Notes provides an archaic macro-based development environment. There are several products, however, from both Lotus and third parties that enable VB applications to access the Notes database engine. So, for example, in a three-tier environment a standard OLE business server built in VB could use the Notes database engine.

Workflow

The term, *workflow*, describes a service that automates dependent human tasks. You can view many business processes as a series of tasks that proceed from user to user. For example, a transaction such as the government creating a new passport may have to go through a series of steps that span departments and users, such as a background check, payment processing, printing, and shipping.

The flow of such work generally is slow and prone to mistakes. The goal of business process reengineering is to eliminate these kinds of dependencies and steps. In reality, however, these types of business process steps will always be around to some degree. Workflow software helps automate, speed up, and track these kinds of workflow.

Because such manual processes are based on paper forms and work queues (a user processing a form on a first-come, first-served basis), their underlying transport is messaging. E-mail supports workflow well because it interfaces directly with users, can "carry" rich documents such as forms, and supports queuing. The database is used to store the state of the workflow and related information, whereas the e-mail system is used to support the end-user interface and tracking.

Workflow systems often sit on top of messaging and database systems. For example, several commercial workflow packages sit on top of Lotus Notes. Likewise, there are commercial software packages that sit on top of Microsoft SQL Sever and Exchange, such as Action Technologies' ActionWorkflow.

The Internet

The Internet is a data source. The Internet contains an unimaginable amount of data. Although the popularity of the Internet can be attributed to its openness and flexibility, we need to take a more rigorous view of the Internet for business OLTP applications.

The Internet provides two main services that raise it beyond the level of other types of data services:

- Instant access to computers all over the world (the service)

- An enormous amount of information (the data)

The first point, instant access, describes the way in which you access the data, or the protocol. The second point, the amount of data available, describes the data itself.

III

The Service Layers

In terms of protocols, there are several ways that computers can communicate over the Internet. They all operate by using a network protocol named TCP/IP, or "Transmission Control Protocol/Internet Protocol." Some of the more popular services that operate on top of TCP/IP include:

WWW (World Wide Web)—Describes how rich-text and hypertext documents can be navigated across the network.

FTP (File Transfer Protocol)—Specifies how files can be exchanged across the network.

Telnet—Specifies how one computer can be operated by another computer across the network.

These services provide all kinds of data. The WWW has search engines, company information, and online catalogs. FTP servers provide software and data files. Telnet enables you to access data from applications that are running on other machines.

In the three-tier OLTP environment, the Internet can be thought of a couple of ways. The Internet is just a large TCP/IP network, so services should be able to communicate seamlessly over it. For example, Chapter 7, "Managing OLE Objects," shows you how a client application can transparently automate an OLE business server over the Internet.

But as with mainframe and messaging data sources, the data that resides on the Internet can also be made available to business servers through the services such as WWW, FTP, and Telnet.

Imaging

As technology advances, you will see imaging systems gain in popularity. Imaging systems are specially designed databases that contain graphical information, such as photographs or scanned forms. Imaging systems that store this kind of data have needs different from the needs of a DBMS. Imaging systems need to hold large quantities of data, so they require a lot of network bandwidth and disk space.

Specialized imaging systems, like a DBMS, are just another data service in the three-tier architecture.

Telephony

At the time of this writing, PC-based telephony products are just starting to take off. Products such as VB Voice from Pronexus enable VB developers to use sophisticated telephony equipment, incorporating voice-mail, touch-tone response, caller ID, and call transfer. Programming interfaces such as Microsoft's TAPI (Telephony API) are enabling hardware vendors to work together.

In the three-tier environment, telephony applications can be incorporated into data services and user services layers. An example of a user service would be a touch-tone-telephone front end into a banking organization's account-balance business rules.

From Here...

This chapter should have made clear that data services are not just DBMS data sources. As technology progresses, these non-DBMS options will proliferate. By separating user and business services from data services, the three-tier architecture ensures that as data-service technology changes rapidly, applications also can change rapidly (see fig. 10.4).

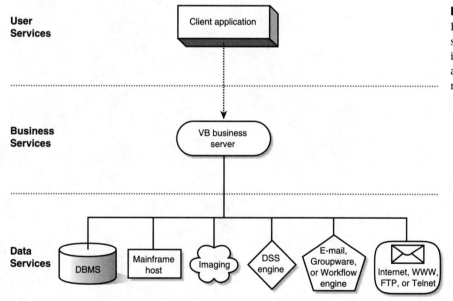

Fig. 10.4
How all the data services can fit into the three-tier architecture model.

III

The Service Layers

For information relating to data services, see the following chapters:

- Chapter 9, "Architecting Tier 2: Business Servers," for more information on how business servers access data servers.

- Chapter 11, "Remote Data Objects," for more information about accessing DBMS data services with RDO.

Part IV

Application Enhancements

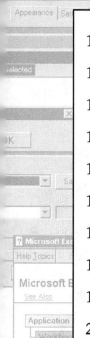

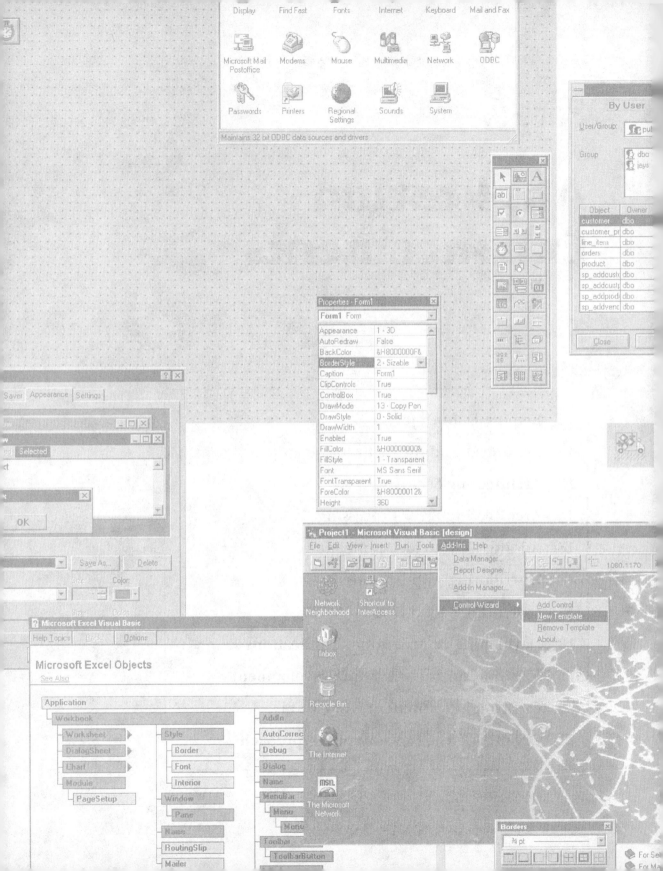

Chapter 11

Remote Data Objects

Chapter 10 discussed the architecture and development of the data services tier using relational database management systems (RDBMS) and other data services. In this chapter, we look specifically at the process of connecting to RDBMS data services.

First, this chapter covers the criteria that should be followed when selecting a method for accessing the remote DBMS data services. After you have an understanding of what to look for in the data access method, we review some of the common ways that are available to Visual Basic applications to gain access to the data services. After reviewing the options, we look at the underlying architecture and the details of connecting to RDBMSs using the most robust of the access methods, Visual Basic's *Remote Data Objects*.

In this chapter, you will learn:

- How to select the appropriate data access methods

- The underlying architecture of ODBC upon which many data access methods are built

- How to use Visual Basic's Remove Data Objects

Selecting the Appropriate Data Access Methods

The three-tier application architecture relies on the capability of the business services to connect to and manipulate the data provided by the data services tier. A distinguishing aspect of Visual Basic is that it provides a number of options for establishing this connection.

Taking the time to select the appropriate data access method for the application will pay off in the long run. In addition to the criteria discussed in the next section, be sure to take into account the full life cycle of the application. Don't make the common mistake of choosing a data access method without thinking about the long-term position of the application being developed.

Too often, an application that starts with a user base of 5 people can balloon into an application that needs to support 50 to 100 users. If the method chosen to access the data in the initial version does not support this increase in volume, or cannot be easily modified to do so, the application must be rewritten.

Data Access Criteria

When choosing a method to access the enterprise data services, you should look for the following four main characteristics:

- **Object-based access**—It is easier for application developers to learn an object hierarchy and its interfaces than to learn an API.

- **Solid performance**—Providing the throughput that is required by the application now and into the future.

- **Support for advanced database features**—Providing support for server-based cursors and so on.

- **DBMS Independence**—Capability to operate against multiple DBMSs.

As we see in the next section, only one data access method is available to Visual Basic that provides all these features in a manner that can be employed within a three-tier application.

Popular Data Access Methods

In contrast to many development tools on the market, Visual Basic's open environment has allowed third-party vendors to develop mechanisms to access data sources from within a Visual Basic application. Although this provides for a flexible development environment, it also makes for a difficult decision when choosing an enterprise data access method.

In this section, we look at some of the common ways to access data from within a Visual Basic application and consider the advantages and disadvantages of each.

Microsoft JET Database Engine

The Microsoft Jet database engine and its Data Access Objects (DAO) is probably the most common method for accessing relational data from Visual

Basic. The Jet engine ships with Visual Basic and also is the database engine used in Microsoft Access.

DAO, as the name implies, provides an easy-to-understand, object-based interface for accessing relational data. The application developer retrieves and updates data by setting object properties and executing their methods. By leveraging ODBC, Jet/DAO can also provide access to multiple DBMSs ranging from personal productivity database systems such as dBASE and Paradox to larger enterprise databases such as Oracle and SQL Server. When using ODBC to connect to a data source, Jet requires a great deal of information about the data source itself. This information is requested each time a query is submitted, which adds a lot of overhead and decreases performance.

One downfall of Jet/DAO comes in terms of performance and support for large systems with multiple concurrent users. Because DAO is based on the Jet database engine, regardless of the actual back-end database, the application will still rely on Jet's capability to process the query.

Data and Bound Controls

The Visual Basic data bound control is by far the simplest means for accessing data from within a Visual Basic application. This method has improved over the data control in version 3.0, through performance increases and additional data bound controls.

Using the data control in conjunction with bound controls reduces the amount of application code required. Aspects such as moving from one record to another through the result set are handled for you by the control. These advantages do not come without some limitations.

Not all of the data manipulation procedures are handled inherently by the data control. For example, there is no support for adding or deleting records using the data control. The data control also makes it difficult to specify the manner in which transactions are processed because the record edit and update process is handled automatically.

Although data bound controls work well in small applications, developers often run into problems when the application is suddenly supporting 50 users across the network. One problem that is frequently encountered is an increase in record contention due to the locking mechanism used by the data control.

Although the data control provides access to multiple back-end data sources through the use of ODBC, a performance hit usually occurs. This hit in performance is a result of the fact that the data control still uses Jet to access the ODBC data source, adding an application layer.

Data bound controls are also designed to work with an end user, requiring that GUI controls be present. In the three-tier environment, all data access is handled through the business servers, which do not possess any GUI elements. This aspect alone eliminates the data control as an option when developing three-tier applications.

VBSQL/DB-LIB

The Programmer's Toolkit for SQL Server, also known as VBSQL, provides Visual Basic application developers with the ability to utilize SQL Server's call-level interface, DB-LIB. DB-LIB is a set of C APIs that handle opening connections, formatting and submitting queries, executing stored procedures, and other operations that can be performed against a Microsoft SQL Server database.

VBSQL offers good performance when working with SQL Server databases because it provides a direct route to the data. Rather than going through Jet or some other layer to get at the data, VBSQL talks directly with the SQL Server API. VBSQL also provides a custom control that can be used so developers don't have to learn the actual API. Although this is not as easy as learning an object model, it certainly is not as difficult as learning the API itself.

VBSQL provides access to SQL Server specific features, such as its BCP utility, but it doesn't match the flexibility of other options. VBSQL only provides access to database servers that support the DB-LIB API—Microsoft and Sybase SQL Server. This means that VBSQL is an option only in an environment that exclusively utilizes SQL Server databases.

Oracle Objects

As part of its Workgroup/2000 suite of client/server development tools, Oracle has provided Oracle Objects for OLE, a mechanism for accessing data residing in an Oracle database. Oracle Objects exposes a data-access object hierarchy that is similar to the DAO objects exposed by the Jet database engine. A developer familiar with DAO will not have a problem coming up to speed using Oracle Objects.

Oracle Objects provides connectivity across multiple network protocols using its built-in SQL Net technology, as well as providing access to the advanced features of the Oracle 7 database server. It, however, does not provide the capability to access back-end data sources other than Oracle.

Like VBSQL for SQL Server, Oracle Objects provides a solid mechanism for developing applications that will work exclusively with an Oracle database server, but is not an option for organizations that must support multiple database back ends.

Open Database Connectivity API

Microsoft's Open Database Connectivity (ODBC) API provides the capability to access multiple DBMS back ends and the capability to exploit the advanced features of independent database back ends, as well as providing solid data access performance. Microsoft's goal when creating ODBC was to provide a standard mechanism by which applications could operate against multiple back-end databases without requiring front-end coding changes.

The ODBC API provides a lot of flexibility because it is a low-level API. Its support for multiple database back ends makes it a good solution for applications that require portability. Because ODBC talks directly to the data source, the data access operations are fast.

The downside of ODBC has always been the fact that developers must learn a low-level API and often have to create wrapper procedures to limit the number of API calls they make. The ODBC API has lacked an object-based interface that developers can use to access enterprise data, until now.

Remote Data Objects

Visual Basic 4 introduces a new data access method that combines the performance and multiple database support of ODBC with the easy-to-learn object interface of Jet's Data Access Objects. Visual Basic's Remote Data Objects (RDO) is an object interface layer that is similar to the existing DAO objects and that sits on top of the existing ODBC architecture. This thin application layer exposes the features of the ODBC API to application developers without requiring that developers have an intimate knowledge of ODBC. In the next section of this chapter, you will look at the underlying ODBC architecture in more detail.

RDO's main advantage over DAO is that the former does not rely on Jet, which makes the database engine part of the application. Instead, RDO uses the ODBC API to pass the data requests to an ODBC data source.

RDO provides all the desired characteristics of an enterprise data access method. Because of this, it is the focus of the remainder of this chapter. We start by developing a high-level understanding of the underlying ODBC architecture, and then go into the details of developing a three-tier application, using RDO.

Open Database Connectivity

Open Database Connectivity (ODBC) is a key component of Microsoft's Windows Open Services API architecture. Windows Open Services API (WOSA) is a set of standard application interfaces for accessing all aspects of an enterprise, from data services to electronic mail. Since its introduction, ODBC has started to become the *de facto* standard for cross-vendor database access mechanisms.

ODBC is the framework upon which many of the data access methods mentioned in the previous section of this chapter are built. This section discusses both the basic architecture that ODBC employs and the process of defining an ODBC data source.

ODBC Architecture Overview

The ODBC architecture is divided into three levels that work together to provide the application with access to information contained in the data source. These layers consist of the ODBC driver manager, the ODBC driver, and the physical data source, as shown in figure 11.1.

Fig. 11.1
Layers of the ODBC architecture.

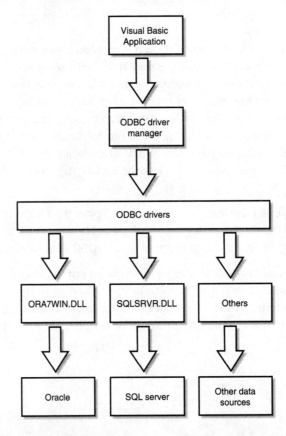

When an application requests data or submits a query, the ODBC driver manager takes the request and communicates with the specific ODBC driver associated with the data source. The ODBC driver then reformats the request so it can be handled by the database (this process is discussed in more detail in a following section of the chapter). The result of the request, referred to as a result set, or the query completion status, is returned to the ODBC driver, which in turn passes it to the driver manager. The driver manager takes the results and passes them back to the client application.

Most of the work to submit a request is handled by the ODBC driver. All ODBC drivers provide the following two basic types of functionality:

- Capability to install, set up, and remove ODBC data sources, the named connections used by applications.

- Capability to manage the queries and SQL statements from client applications to database servers, the return of result sets and completion status from the database server to the client application, and the return of error messages generated in the data source or ODBC driver to the client application.

ODBC implements SQL by using a standard set of functions that translate the ANSI SQL queries submitted to the ODBC driver manager into the SQL dialect used by the specific RDBMS. This translation from ANSI SQL to DBMS-specific syntax is handled by the ODBC driver. ODBC also provides the capability to pass SQL statements already written to the RDBMS dialect directly, without translation, through the use of the SQLPassThrough method.

All ODBC drivers are classified as being a member of one of two categories:

- **Single-tier**—Drivers developed for DBMSs that do not have the capability to process SQL statements themselves. These drivers translate the SQL operation into the low-level instructions necessary to operate directly on the database files. Microsoft Access, FoxPro, and Paradox are examples of single-tier ODBC drivers.

- **Multiple-tier**—Drivers developed for DBMSs that have a query engine capable of processing SQL statements. These drivers translate the SQL operation into the dialect supported by the database server and then pass the operation along to the server to process. Oracle and Microsoft SQL Server are examples of multiple-tier ODBC drivers.

In addition to falling into one of these two levels of classification, each ODBC driver also adheres to one of the three ODBC conformance levels:

- **Core**—Driver provides the capability to connect to the database, prepare and execute SQL statements, retrieve query result sets, support transaction processing by using commit and rollback, and retrieve error messages.

- **Level 1**—Driver provides all the features available in the Core level, plus connectivity by using driver-specific dialogs, get and set connection options, and the capability to obtain driver and data source capabilities.

- **Level 2**—Driver provides all the features available in Level 1 drivers plus the capability to list and browse connections and to retrieve query results in any format. The driver also implements scrollable cursors.

Most ODBC drivers conform to the Level 1 specification and many add aspects of Level 2, such as scrollable cursors.

Setting Up an ODBC Data Source

As mentioned in the previous section, for an application to connect to a database using ODBC, the appropriate ODBC driver must be installed on the machine and a data source must be defined. ODBC drivers and data sources can be created manually by using the ODBC Manager applet installed in the Windows Control Panel group (see fig. 11.2), or programmatically by using the data access methods. The programmatic creation of an ODBC data source is discussed later in this chapter.

Fig. 11.2
ODBC Manager, located in the Control Panel.

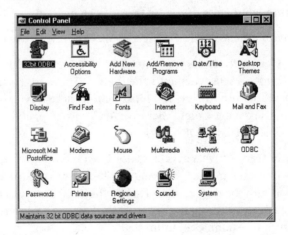

The ODBC Manager applet found in the Control Panel provides the capability to install new ODBC drivers as well as create new data sources. When the ODBC Manager is started, the Data Sources dialog box, shown in figure 11.3, is displayed. From this dialog box you can add, remove, or modify data sources, as well as add or remove ODBC drivers.

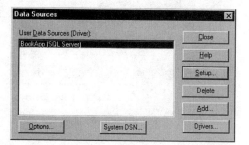

Fig. 11.3
ODBC Data
Sources dialog box.

To install or remove an ODBC driver, select the Drivers button from the Data Sources dialog box. This will bring up the Drivers dialog box, shown in figure 11.4, which displays all the ODBC drivers currently installed on the machine.

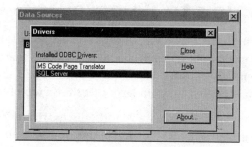

Fig. 11.4
The ODBC Drivers
dialog box.

To create a new ODBC data source, select the Add button from the Data Sources dialog box. This button brings up the Add Data Sources dialog box, which contains a list of the ODBC drivers currently installed. Select the driver that should be used for the new data source. To create the data source used by the GOLF system, select the SQL Server driver. After selecting the ODBC driver, click the OK button, which brings up the ODBC SQL Server Setup dialog box shown in figure 11.5.

The Setup dialog box is specific to the ODBC driver being used. Figure 11.5 shows the SQL Server Setup dialog. In the Setup dialog, specify the data source name and the name of the SQL server. Use the Options button to display the login and other optional information that can be specified when creating an ODBC data source.

At this point, your ODBC driver is installed, and the data source is defined. You are now ready to access the database using ODBC or an ODBC-compliant data access method, such as RDO.

Fig. 11.5
ODBC Setup
dialog box.

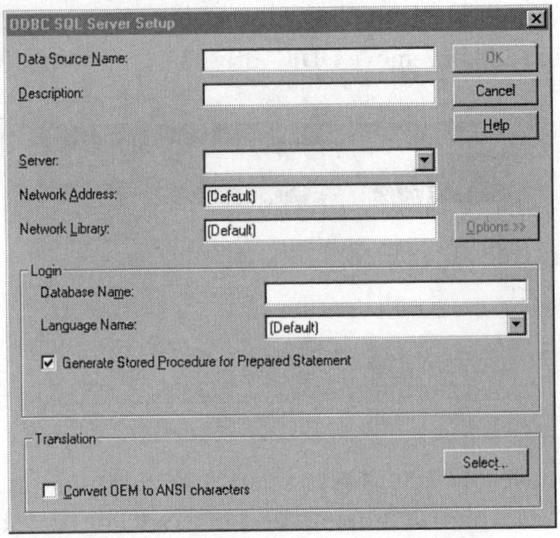

Introduction to Remote Data Objects

This section discusses the new method of data access provided by Visual Basic 4, the Remote Data Object (RDO). RDO is a set of objects that provide the capability for applications to access remote data stored in a variety of databases. RDO is implemented as a thin layer that sits on top of the ODBC API.

To get an understanding of RDO, we will first discuss the functionality that is supported and the object model it exposes. After you have an understanding of the features of RDO, this section then discusses the specifics of the individual objects and how they can be used to access data from within a Visual Basic application.

Features of RDO

RDO supports the data access features desirable in a robust data access method. These include:

- Access to ODBC data sources

- Support for server-specific functionality

- Asynchronous query execution

- Minimal memory requirements

- Object model access to data

Access to ODBC Data

Because RDO is implemented as a layer on top of the ODBC API, RDO provides the capability to access any ODBC-compliant data source using the same client application code. This includes server-based RDBMSs such as Microsoft SQL Server and Oracle as well as file-based DBMSs such as Microsoft Access and Borland's Paradox.

When accessing a server-based database, RDO will utilize the server's query engine to increase the performance of remote queries. From a performance perspective, RDO is rivaled only by the ODBC API itself, or by the database-specific API such as the DB-LIB API for Microsoft SQL Server.

Server-Specific Functionality

Because RDO is built upon ODBC, it also supports server-specific functionality, including stored procedures, multiple result sets, and the limiting of result-set size.

Stored Procedure Support. RDO provides applications with the capability to access stored procedures when this facility is supported by the RDBMS. The support for stored procedures works for database server stored procedures such as those found in Microsoft SQL Server and Oracle, as well as for stored queries found in file-based database systems such as Microsoft Access.

The functionality that can be placed within the stored procedures depends on the database engine. For example, Microsoft SQL Server supports returning result sets from stored procedures whereas Oracle only supports the capability to return a single row through the use of output parameters. When developing applications that will support multiple back-end databases, it is important to consider the functionality of all supported engines. For example, an application that uses SQL Server stored procedures to retrieve result sets will not work against an Oracle database without requiring modifications to the application's code.

Multiple Result Set Support. When multiple result sets are supported by the database server and the ODBC driver, RDO allows applications to manage multiple result sets from a single query. This provides an increase in performance because a single query can obtain the information needed to populate multiple lists in the client application.

Governing Result Size. Often it is desirable to limit the number of rows the client application is allowed to retrieve. RDO provides a query governor that can limit the amount of data returned to the client application. This allows the developer to better manage the resources of the server and workstations.

Server-Side Cursor Support. Many server database engines, such as SQL Server and Oracle, support the capability to create cursors on the server rather than on the client workstation. Creating cursors on the server can greatly improve performance because the cursor's key does not have to be sent to and from the client workstation.

RDO provides the ability to specify ODBC library cursors, created on the client workstation, server-side cursors, and driver-dependent cursors (which create server-side cursors when supported by the ODBC data source and ODBC library cursors when they are not supported).

Asynchronous Query Support

When executing a query that takes a long time to complete, the application should have the capability to either perform other functions or cancel the query. RDO provides an asynchronous query option that allows applications to do just that.

When a query is executed using the asynchronous option, RDO returns control back to the client application while the query is executing. This allows the application to perform other tasks or to cancel a query that has not yet completed.

Minimal Memory Requirements

The machine running the client application often has a limited amount of RAM. Because of this, RDO was developed to use a smaller amount of RAM and workstation resources than other data access methods that are available. For example, RDO does not require local memory or disk space to implement its lowest-level cursors.

Object-Model Data Access

RDO provides client applications with access to the data stored within the database system using an easy-to-understand object model. The specifics of the RDO object model are discussed in the next section.

RDO Object Model

As the name of the model implies, RDO provides a series of objects that allow applications to access data stored in relational databases. Before we can develop applications using RDO, we must have an understanding for the objects that exist. Figure 11.6 shows the RDO object hierarchy.

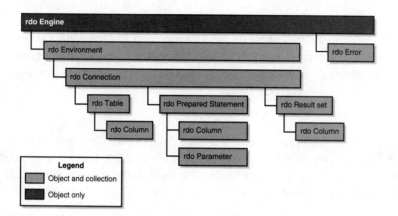

Fig. 11.6
The RDO object
model.

The RDO object hierarchy is the framework that applications use to manipulate aspects of a remote ODBC database. The relationships between the objects represent the logical structure of the database. The object hierarchy used by RDO is similar to the DAO object hierarchy exposed by Jet. This similarity makes it easier for application developers who have used DAO to make the transition.

The RDO framework consists of two series of objects:

- Objects that manage the connections to the remote data sources

- Objects that allow the application to interact with and manipulate the data provided by the data sources

An application uses the rdoEngine and rdoEnvironment objects to set up the properties of the rdoConnection. The rdoConnection represents the physical link to the database where the objects that provide access to the data are exposed. The connection allows the application to create rdoResultset and rdoPreparedStatement objects, which return and manipulate the data.

The next sections of this chapter describe in detail the objects that are exposed by RDO and how they are used in developing an application that will access a relational database.

Connecting through RDO

Now that you have an understanding of the functionality provided by RDO, and of the architecture upon which it is built, you are ready to look at the specific objects within the RDO object hierarchy that are used when establishing a connection to a remote data source. To use RDO with Visual Basic, a reference must first be established using the Tools References dialog box.

As with any data access method, before it can retrieve and update data from the remote data source, the application must first establish a connection to the data source. With RDO, this is done using the rdoEngine, rdoEnvironment, and rdoConnection objects. This section goes into the details of how these objects are used.

rdoEngine

The rdoEngine object represents a remote data source. This object is created automatically the first time a reference is made to RDO. Because rdoEngine is the top-level object in the RDO object hierarchy, all the other objects and collections are exposed by it.

This does not, however, mean that all RDO objects must be specified in application code using the rdoEngine object. For example, the following statements will produce the same results:

```
Print rdoEngine.rdoVersion
Print rdoVersion
```

Because rdoEngine is a pre-defined object that is created automatically when RDO is referenced, an application is not allowed to create an additional instance of the object. The rdoEngine object is used to set the data source parameters, as well as the parameters that define the default rdoEnvironment settings.

Table 11.1 lists the properties exposed by the rdoEngine object and a description of what each property represents.

Table 11.1 Properties of the rdoEngine Object	
Property	**Description**
rdoDefaultCursorDriver	Type of cursor to be created: ODBC; server-side; server-side if supported, else ODBC.
rdoDefaultErrorThreshold	Value of the ErrorThreshold property used by rdoPreparedStatement objects.
rdoDefaultLoginTimeout	Number of seconds ODBC driver waits when attempting to connect to a data source. This property is the default for all connections but is overridden if a value is specified in the LoginTimeout property of the rdoEnvironment object.
rdoDefaultPassword	Password used when creating a new rdoEnvironment if no password is supplied.
rdoDefaultUser	UserId used when creating a new rdoEnvironment if no userid is supplied.
rdoVersion	Five-character RDO library version number.

The rdoDefault properties are used when creating a new rdoEnvironment or rdoConnection object, if the corresponding arguments of the methods are not specified.

Table 11.2 lists the methods exposed by the rdoEngine object and a description of each method's function.

Table 11.2 Methods of the rdoEngine Object	
Method	**Description**
rdoCreateEnvironment	Creates a new connection to the remote data source and an rdoEnvironment object.
rdoRegisterDataSource	Registers data source connection information into the Windows Registry.

When the rdoEngine object is created, it automatically creates the default environment, rdoEnvironment(0), using the rdoDefault parameters. When the application requires settings other than those specified in the default properties, it can change the default values of rdoEnvironment(0) or rdoEngine before creating the connection.

Although the rdoEngine object is shared by the applications that use it, the default properties of the rdoEngine are not shared. Each instance of the application has its own default values that do not affect any other applications using RDO.

As mentioned previously, ODBC data sources can be defined programmatically by using the rdoEngine's rdoRegisterDataSource method. This method needs to be executed only once to create the data source. Setup applications can use this method to create the ODBC data source the application will expect.

The rdoRegisterDataSource method takes four arguments:

- *dsName*—Name used in the OpenConnection method. The name that will be used when referring to the recently created data source.

- *driver*—Name of the ODBC driver, not the ODBC DLL file.

- *silent*—Boolean value, indicating whether the ODBC dialog box that prompts for driver-specific information should be displayed.

- *attributes*—String listing the keywords that are added to the ODBC.INI file.

rdoEnvironment

The rdoEnvironment object represents a set of database connections for a specific UserId. The rdoEnvironment object has a logical correspondence to an ODBC environment. A single rdoEnvironment object can support multiple database connections. Because ODBC supports only one environment handle per application, actual ODBC connections occur only when an rdoConnection object is opened.

When multiple connections are made using a single environment, the rdoEnvironment properties such as *UserName* and *Password* are shared between the connections. As mentioned in the previous section, to open a connection using a different *UserName*, a new rdoEnvironment object must be created and added to the collection.

rdoEnvironment objects are created using the `rdoCreateEnvironment` method of the rdoEngine object. For example, the following code could be used to create an additional connection to the database used by the GOLF System. In the following example, the rdoEngine object is not specified because this object is assumed when referring to one of its methods or collections:

```
Dim objEnv as rdoEnvironment
Set objEnv = rdoCreateEnvironment("Golf1", "MyUser", "MyPassword")
```

Within an application, the rdoEnvironment object can manage the transactions being performed. When transactions are managed at the environment level, executing the `CommitTrans` method will commit the pending transactions in all open rdoConnections associated with that rdoEnvironment object. This type of commit should not be confused with what is referred to as a two-phase commit operation. The rdoEnvironment's `CommitTrans` simply informs all pending transactions to commit, regardless of the success of each individual connection.

Managing transactions at the environment level links all transactions occurring within the same environment. This includes transactions occurring in different connections, even in different databases. To process multiple transactions independently of one another, the application must create a separate rdoEnvironment object.

ODBC and RDO do not support nested transactions. This means that within an rdoEnvironment object, a second `BeginTrans` cannot be issued until the initial transaction is either committed or rolled back. However, SQL statements can be used to implement nested transactions when this facility is supported by the data source.

Table 11.3 describes all the properties exposed by the rdoEnvironment object.

Table 11.3 Properties of the rdoEnvironment Object

Property	Description
Count	Number of rdoEnvironment objects that exist within the collection.
CursorDriver	Type of cursors that can be created: ODBC or server-side, dependent on ODBC driver support.
hEnv	ODBC environment handle that can be passed to the ODBC API.
LoginTimeout	Number of seconds the ODBC driver manager waits before timeout occurs when establishing a connection.
Name	Name associated with the rdoEnvironment.
Password	Write-once property, containing password used to create the rdoEnvironment.
UserName	Write-once property, containing the user name of the rdoEnvironment object user.

Table 11.4 lists all the methods associated with the rdoEnvironment object and a description of each method's functionality.

Table 11.4 Methods of the rdoEnvironment Object

Method	Description
BeginTrans	Begins a new transaction
Close	Closes an rdoEnvironment and any open rdoConnections, rolling back any pending transactions
CommitTrans	Completes current transactions, saving any changes that were made
Item	Returns the specified member of the rdoEnvironment's collection
OpenConnection	Opens a connection to an ODBC data source, returning an object representing that database
RollbackTrans	Completes the current transactions, undoing any changes that were made

The OpenConnection method is used to establish the actual connection to the data source. This method has the following four arguments:

- *dsName*—Specifies the name of the registered data source being connected to.

- *prompt*—Specifies whether the user is allowed to supply additional arguments through the ODBC connect dialogs. Specifying rdDriverNoPrompt prevents the user from seeing the ODBC dialogs.

- *readonly*—Specifies whether the user expects to update data when using this connection.

- *connect*—String that specifies parameters to the ODBC driver manager. These parameters differ between data sources.

The example in listing 11.1 demonstrates how the GOLF System's OrderMgr uses the OpenConnection method to establish a connection to the data services. In the following example, the application uses integrated security, so there is no requirement for additional *connect* information. This code can be found on the companion disk, in the \CHAP24\GOLF\TIER2\ORDMGR directory.

Listing 11.1   APP.CLS—Using the OpenConnection method to connect to the data source

```
'set up default environment
rdoEngine.rdoDefaultUser = UserId
rdoEngine.rdoDefaultPassword = Password
'open a connection to the database
Set db = rdoEngine.rdoEnvironments(0).OpenConnection( _
             DATA_SOURCE, _
             rdDriverNoPrompt, _
             False)
```

When using integrated or mixed security, it is important to leave the userid and password parameters of the connect argument blank, as in the preceding example. Under this security model, Windows NT will pass the user's NT logon ID and password to the data source. This eliminates the need for the application to have any knowledge of the current userid and password when connecting to the data sources.

rdoConnection

The rdoConnection object represents a physical link to the data source. An rdoConnection object is created as the result of the rdoEnvironment.OpenConnection method discussed in the preceding section.

Table 11.5 describes the properties exposed by the rdoConnection object.

Table 11.5 Properties of the rdoConnection Object

Property	Description
AsyncCheckInterval	Number of milliseconds RDO waits before checking the completion status of an asynchronous query.
Connect	Read-only string containing the ODBC connect-string value used with the OpenConnection method.
Count	Number of rdoConnection objects currently in the collection.
hDbc	The ODBC connection handle corresponding to this rdoConnection object.
Name	Data source name used for the connection.
QueryTimeout	Number of seconds the ODBC driver manager will wait before causing a timeout error during query execution.
RowsAffected	Number of rows affected by the most recent Execute method.
StillExecuting	Boolean, indicating whether the query is still running.
Transactions	Boolean, indicating whether the rdoConnection object supports transactions.
Updatable	Boolean, indicating whether changes can be made to the object.
Version	Version of the data source associated with this object.

Transactions also can be managed at the connection level. In this implementation, the commit or rollback of a transaction only affects the current connection, not all connections within the rdoEnvironment. A transaction statement issued at the environment level, however, will still affect a transaction specified at the connection level.

Table 11.6 lists all the methods exposed by the rdoConnection object and describes each method's functionality.

Table 11.6 Methods of the rdoConnection Object

Method	Description
BeginTrans	Begins a new transaction.
Cancel	Cancels a query that is running in asynchronous mode.

(continues)

Table 11.6 Continued	
Method	**Description**
Close	Closes the specific connection.
CommitTrans	Ends the current transaction, saving the changes.
CreatePreparedStatement	Creates a new rdoPreparedStatement object.
Execute	Runs an action query or SQL statement that does not return any rows.
Item	Returns a member of the rdoConnections collection.
OpenResultSet	Creates a new rdoResultset object. Used to execute queries and SQL statements that will return data.
RollbackTrans	Ends the current transaction, undoing any changes.

All the objects, methods, and properties used to manipulate data within the data source are exposed by the rdoConnection object. The remainder of this chapter discusses how these objects can be used to access and update application data.

Accessing Data

Now that you understand how to establish a connection to the remote data source by using RDO objects, you can look at the objects exposed by the rdoConnection object that allow an application to manipulate the data. RDO supports data access through rdoResultset objects, as well as the use of stored procedures. This section focuses on the result set objects and using cursors, saving stored procedure discussions for the next section.

rdoTable

The rdoTable object represents the definition of a table or view within the database. The rdoTables collection contains information on all the rdoTable objects that exist within the database. For performance reasons, the rdoTables collection is not populated automatically when a connection is made to the database. The collection must be populated using the .Refresh method before any individual rdoTable objects can be used.

The rdoTable object provides applications with the capability to examine the definition/characteristics of a table within the database. The definition is read-only and cannot be changed through RDO. To modify the definition of a database table or to add a table definition, the application must generate the SQL statements necessary to do so.

The rdoTable object exposes an rdoColumns collection that contains the definition of each individual column of the specified table. The rdoColumn object is discussed in more detail in a following section of this chapter.

Table 11.7 lists all the properties exposed by the rdoTable object.

Table 11.7   Properties of the rdoTable Object

Property	Description
Count	The number of rdoTable objects present in the collection.
Name	The database table name associated with the rdoTable object.
RowCount	The number of rows that exist within the database table.
Type	String that represents the object type: table, view, alias, and so on.
Updatable	Boolean indicating whether the table can be changed. Currently, no changes are allowed.

The rdoTable object exposes an OpenResultSet method that allows the application to create an rdoResultset object based on all the rows within the table. Because this method does not provide any means for filtering the results, it is not the recommended way to create a result set.

Table 11.8 lists all the methods exposed by the rdoTable object.

Table 11.8   Methods of the rdoTable Object

Method	Description
Item	Returns a specific member of the rdoTables collection
OpenResultSet	Creates a new rdoResultset object containing all rows from the rdoTable object
Refresh	Retrieves the list of table names from the database and repopulates the rdoTables collection

rdoResultset

When a query or SQL statement is run that returns records from the database, these records are stored in an rdoResultset object. The rdoResultset represents all the rows that were returned from the select query or statement. The rdoResultset collection contains all the open rdoResultset objects associated with a specific rdoConnection.

Resultset objects are comprised of rows and columns just like database tables. The rows represent each record that satisfies the selection criteria and the columns correspond to the elements of the select list.

The rdoResultset object supports multiple result sets through the use of the MoreResults method. When a select query returns multiple result sets, they must be processed in a serial manner, meaning that the first result set contained in the rdoResultset object must be processed before the second result set can be used. The MoreResults method will discard the rows associated with the current result set and activate the next rdoResultset. This procedure can be repeated until the MoreResults method returns false, signaling that there are no more results sets to process.

With a result set, the current row is positioned at the first row of the rdoResultset object when the object is created, assuming that rows were returned. If no rows are returned, the *RowCount* property is set to zero, and the *BOF* and *EOF* properties are both set to True. The Move methods—MoveFirst, MoveLast, MoveNext, and MovePrevious—of the rdoResutset object can be used to change row positions within the result set.

When creating a new rdoResultset object, you will use the type argument of the OpenResultset method to specify the type of result-set object to be created. Specifically, the type argument specifies the type of cursor created to access the data. The four type options are:

■ **Forward-Only**—Rows of the result set can be accessed and updated by using a row pointer that can move only toward the end of the result set. A forward-only result set is not a cursor.

■ **Static-Type**—A copy of the rows in the result set is used. Static result sets can be updatable when using ODBC or server-side cursors, depending on the ODBC driver and data source support.

■ **Keyset-Type**—A dynamic result set that can be used to add, update, or delete rows from the database tables. Specifying keyset type allows unrestricted movement through the result set. The rows that belong to the result set are fixed.

■ **Dynamic-Type**—A dynamic result set that can be used to add, update, or delete rows from the database tables. The rows that belong to the result set are not fixed.

Table 11.9 shows the main differences between the features supported by each rdoResultset object type. This table compares the ability to move between the rows contained in the cursor, the visibility to cursor data, the ability to update the cursor's data, and the ability to refresh the cursor selection.

Table 11.9   Feature Comparision of rdoResultset Object Types

rdoResultset Type	Updatable	Record Selection	Row Visibility	Movement
Forward-only	Driver Dependent	Fixed	One	Forward
Static	Driver Dependent	Fixed	All	Anywhere
Keyset	Yes	Fixed	All	Anywhere
Dynamic	Yes	Dynamic	All	Anywhere

In some cases, the capability to update records within the cursor depends on the functionality of the data source or on the ODBC driver being used.

Table 11.10 lists the properties exposed by the rdoResultset object.

Table 11.10   Properties of the rdoResultset Object

Property	Description
AbsolutePosition	Zero-based value, indicating the ordinal position within the keyset, dynamic, or static rdoResultSet. Can be used to move to the specific location or to determine the current location within the result set.
BOF	Boolean value, indicating whether the current row is the first row in the result set.
Bookmark	Returns/sets a bookmark that identifies the current row within the result set. Used to quickly move to a specific row.
Bookmarkable	Boolean value, indicating whether the rdoResultset object supports bookmarks.
Count	Returns the number of rdoResultset objects in the collection.
EOF	Boolean value, indicating if the current row is the last row in the result set.
hStmt	Corresponds to an ODBC statement handle.
LastModified	Returns a bookmark to the last modified or changed row.
LockEdits	Boolean value, indicating the type of locking used during editing.
Name	String containing the first 256 characters of the SQL query used to populate the result set.

(continues)

Table 11.10 Continued	
Property	**Description**
PercentPosition	Indicates or changes the approximate location of the current row based on the number of rows in the result set. To ensure that the rdoResultset is fully populated, use the MoveLast method before accessing this property.
Restartable	Boolean value indicating whether the rdoResultset object supports the Requery method.
RowCount	Number of rows accessed in the result set.
StillExecuting	When created using rdAsyncEnable, Boolean value, indicating whether the query has finished processing the results. The rdoResultset object cannot be accessed until the property is set to False.
Transactions	Boolean value, indicating whether the rdoResultset supports transactions.
Type	Read-only value, indicating the Type argument that was specified when creating the rdoResultset object.
Updatable	Boolean value, indicating whether the result set contains updatable rows.

Table 11.11 lists all the methods exposed by the rdoResultset object.

Table 11.11 Methods of the rdoResultset Object	
Method	**Description**
AddNew	Prepares a new row that can be edited and added to the database, for updatable result sets. Changes are saved using the Update method. Moving to a new row without issuing an Update causes all changes to be lost.
Cancel	Cancels all pending results associated with the rdoResultset object.
CancelUpdate	Cancels all pending updates to the rdoResultset object by clearing its copy buffer.
Close	Removes the rdoResultset object from the rdoResultsets collection.
Delete	Deletes the current row from an updatable result set. The delete occurs immediately in the database, and the current row pointer must be moved to a new location before it can be accessed again.
Edit	Places a copy of the current row of an updatable result set into the copy buffer, where editing can occur. Changes are not saved until the Update method is called.

Method	Description
GetRows	Copies multiple rows from a result set into a two-dimensional array.
Item	Returns a specific rdoResultset object from the rdoResultsets collection.
MoreResults	Prepares the next result set for processing, clearing the previous result set.
Move	Positions the current row *Rows* records from the *Start* row. If *Rows* is positive the current position is moved forward; if it's negative, the current position is moved backward.
MoveFirst	Places the current row pointer at the first row in the result set.
MoveLast	Places the current row pointer at the last row in the result set.
MoveNext	Places the current row pointer at the next row in the result set.
MovePrevious	Places the current row pointer at the previous row in the result set.
Requery	Re-executes the query used to create the result set, repopulating the rdoResultset object.
Update	Saves the changes that are present in the copy buffer to the current row.

rdoColumn

The rdoColumn object represents a column of data present in a database table. The rdoColumn object's properties contain the specifications that were used to create the table in the database and also the value that is present for the current row.

The rdoColumn object exposed by the rdoResultset and rdoPreparedStatement objects is used to obtain and update the values of the data columns of the current row. The rdoColumn object exposed by the rdoTable object provides only the definition of the data column within the database. This information can be used to view the structure of the database table but cannot be updated through RDO properties and methods.

The rdoColumn object can be referenced within the rdoColumns collection using its Name property. This name is the same as the column name that was specified during the creation of the table, or the SQL query that produced the result set.

When exposed by an rdoResultset object, the data for the current row is accessible in the rdoColumn objects Value property. Because the rdoColumns collection is the default collection of the rdoResultset object, the collection often is not referenced directly.

The example in Listing 11.2 from the OrderMgr's LoadOrders method illustrates the use of the rdoColumns collection to retrieve data from a result set. In this example, the rdoResultset object qryAddOrder contains all the order information retrieved from a previous query. This information, shown in the following code, is placed into the Orders collection. This code can be found on the companion disk, in the \CHAP24\GOLF\TIER2\ORDMGR directory.

Listing 11.2 ORDERS.CLS—Example use of the rdoColumns collection of the rdoResultset object

```
'reload all of the order currently in the orders collection
OrderIdx = 0
Do
    OrderIdx = OrderIdx + 1
    'only add if not marked for removal
    If Me.Item(OrderIdx).RemovedFlag = "N" Then
        With Me.Item(OrderIdx)
            qryAddOrder.rdoParameters(0).Value = .OrderID
            qryAddOrder.rdoParameters(1).Value = .CustomerID
            qryAddOrder.rdoParameters(2).Value = .OrderDate
            qryAddOrder.rdoParameters(3).Value = CStr(.ShippedFlag)
            qryAddOrder.Execute

            'update order id which was set by SP
            Me.Item(OrderIdx).OrderID = qryAddOrder.rdoParameters
            ➥(0).Value
        End With

    End If

Loop Until OrderIdx >= Me.Count
```

Table 11.12 lists all the properties and methods exposed by the rdoColumn object.

Table 11.12 Methods of the rdoColumn Object

Property/Method	Description
AllowZeroLength	Property, indicating whether a zero-length string is valid for the Value property of the column. If set to false, zero-length strings must be inserted as NULLS.

Property/Method	Description
Attributes	Property, indicating characteristics of the column such as fixed length, auto increment, updatable, and so on.
ChunkRequired	Property, indicating whether or not the GetChunk method must be used to retrieve data from this column.
Count	Property, indicating the number of rdoColumn objects that exist in the collection.
Name	Property that contains the database column name.
OrdinalPosition	Property that returns the ordinal position within the rdoColumns collection.
Required	Boolean property value, indicating whether this column requires a non-NULL value.
Size	Property that indicates the maximum number of characters the column will accept for string columns and the maximum number of bytes the column will accept for numeric columns.
SourceColumn	Property, containing the name of the column that is the original source of the data in the column object.
SourceTable	Property, containing the name of the table that is the original source of the data in the column object.
Type	Property, containing the data type of the column object.
Updatable	Boolean property value, indicating whether the value of the column can be changed.
Value	Property that represents the current data held in the column object.
AppendChunk	Method that appends data to a column of type rdTypeLONGVARBINARY or rdTypeLONGVARCHAR.
ColumnSize	Method, returning the number of bytes in an rdoColumn object that requires AppendChunk/ GetChunk to access its value.
GetChunk	Method that returns all or part of an rdoColumn object with the ChunkRequired property set to True.

Using Stored Procedures

The capability to use stored procedures to interact with the data source provides applications with a performance increase over the use of embedded SQL statements. This increase in performance comes about because stored procedures are pre-compiled SQL statements for which the database engine has already created an execution plan.

RDO provides a series of objects that allow an application to utilize stored procedures when working with a remote data source.

rdoPreparedStatement

The rdoPreparedStatement object represents a stored query definition. The rdoPreparedStatements collection contains all the rdoPreparedStatements that exist within a given rdoConnection.

The rdoPreparedStatement object provides a means for the application to store a query definition that will be used repeatedly throughout the application. This includes embedded SQL statements and database stored procedures.

To facilitate this, the rdoPreparedStatement object supports both static SQL statements and what are often referred to as *parameter queries*. A parameter query allows the application to create an SQL procedure that accepts values at runtime that affect the actions of the query. The use of the parameter object is discussed later in this chapter.

rdoPreparedStatements create temporary stored procedures. This means they can be used to implement actual stored procedures that permanently reside in the data source, or they can be procedures created at runtime that only exist for the life of the rdoPreparedStatement object. Because a prepared statement is compiled only once by the database server, it provides a performance increase over the use of the same embedded SQL statement over and over.

Table 11.13 lists all the properties associated with the rdoPreparedStatement object.

Table 11.13	Properties of the rdoPreparedStatement Object
Property	**Description**
BindThreshold	Largest column that will be automatically bound under ODBC, thus not requiring the GetChunk/AppendChunk functions.
Connect	Read-only string that contains connection information used to create the rdoConnection object.
Count	Number of rdoPreparedStatement objects that exist within the rdoPreparedStatements collection.

Property	Description
ErrorThreshold	Determines the severity level that triggers a fatal error.
hStmt	ODBC statement handle.
KeysetSize	Specifies the number of rows in the keyset buffer.
LockType	Indicates the type of record concurrency handling to be used.
LogMessages	Location of the ODBC trace file used by the ODBC driver to record its operations.
MaxRows	Maximum number of rows that can be returned by a query. A value of –1 sets no limit on the number of rows returned.
Name	Name used in the `CreatePreparedStatement` method for this object.
QueryTimeout	Number of seconds the ODBC driver waits before generating a timeout error while waiting for a query to complete.
RowsAffected	Number of rows affected by the last `Execute` method.
RowsetSize	Number of rows of the keyset cursor that will be buffered by the application.
SQL	SQL statement used to define the query that is executed.
StillExecuting	Boolean value, indicating whether a query run with the rdAsyncEnable option has completed.
Type	Indicates whether the query is a select, action, or procedural query.
Updatable	Indicates whether the result set being created is updatable.

A prepared statement is executed by using one of two methods. When the statement returns a result set, the `OpenResultSet` method must be used to create the rdoResultset object to hold the results. Action queries that do not return a result set are executed by using the `Execute` method of the rdoPreparedStatement object.

Table 11.14 lists all the methods exposed by the rdoPreparedStatement object.

Table 11.14   Methods of the rdoPreparedStatement Object

Method	Description
Cancel	Cancels an asynchronous query.
Close	Removes the rdoPreparedStatement object from the collection.
Execute	Executes a query or SQL statement that returns no rows.
Item	Returns a specific rdoPreparedStatement object from the collection.
OpenResultSet	Creates a new rdoResultset object that is appended to the rdoResultsets collection.

As previously mentioned, prepared statements can be used with database stored procedures and embedded SQL statements. This means that applications that employ the same SQL statement multiple times within the application can create an rdoPreparedStatement object for the SQL statement, allowing it to be accessed using a more meaningful name.

A set of prepared statements therefore, can define all of the elementary data functions of the data service, whether they are actually stored procedures or dynamic SQL statements. The preparation of the prepared statements can be encapsulated in an OLE automation server or class module that takes an rdoConnection as a parameter. This allows multiple business servers to dynamically link to the elementary data functions provided.

rdoParameter

The rdoParameter object provides the mechanism by which the application developer can set query parameters before running the query. This requires that the rdoPreparedStatement be defined using parameter markers.

For example, the GOLF System's OrderMgr uses parameter queries when retrieving orders to populate the Order collection. In Listing 11.3, taken from the LoadOrders method of the OrderMgr, the sp_Get_Orders procedure is defined to accept two parameters. The rdoParameter object's Value property is used to set the parameter. You can find this code on the companion disk, in the \CHAP24\GOLF\TIER2\ORDMGR directory.

Listing 11.3   ORDERS.CLS—Demonstration of a parameter query

```
Set qryGetOrders = db.CreatePreparedStatement( _
                          "sp_Get_Orders", _
                          "{call sp_Get_Orders (?, ?)}")
qryGetOrders.rdoParameters(0).Value = CustomerID
qryGetOrders.rdoParameters(1).Value = ShippedFlag
Set rstGetOrders = qryGetOrders.OpenResultset(rdOpenForwardOnly, _
                          rdConcurReadOnly)
```

You can see that, as with all RDO collection objects, the ordinal position of the collection begins with zero.

RDO supports both input and output parameters. The rdoParameter's Direction property is used to determine whether the parameter is an input, output, input/output, or return value. Output parameters are common when working with data sources such as Oracle that do not support the capability to return result sets from a stored procedure.

When a procedure uses a return value to pass data back to the calling application, the rdoParameter's Direction should be set to rdParamReturnValue. Although using rdParamOutput does work, to ensure compatibility with future versions of RDO it's recommended that the more specific directional indicator be used.

When working with parameters that have a direction of anything other than rdParamInput, which is the default, the Direction property must be set before the procedure is executed. This ensures that the ODBC driver will handle the parameter correctly.

Table 11.15 lists all the properties associated with the rdoParameter object.

Table 11.15   Properties of the rdoParameter Object

Property	Description
Count	Returns the number of rdoParameter objects present in the collection.
Direction	Indicates how the parameter is used by the query.
Name	Name assigned to the parameter.
Type	Data type expected by the parameter.
Value	The default property that specified the value of the parameter.

Cursors

RDO implements cursors when an rdoResultset object is created. The Type argument of the OpenResultset method determines the type of cursor/result set that is created. The different cursor implementations and result-set types primarily affect the manner in which the application is allowed to move through the cursor and how often the data within the cursor is updated.

When working with cursors, choosing the right type of cursors for your application can impact the performance of the application. This section examines the different options available when creating cursors using RDO and the types of applications for which each cursor is best suited.

Although forward-only rdoResultset objects do not actually create a cursor, they act like a cursor and provide increased performance over an actual cursor because they eliminate the overhead associated with creating a cursor. Creating a forward-only result set works well when the application needs to quickly retrieve data and see only one row at a time. If the application needs the capability to move around within the cursor, the forward-only result set will not provide the required functionality.

Static cursors are similar to the Jet snapshot object, in that a static cursor's data appears to be static. The rows contained within the cursor, and the order and values in the result set, are set when the cursor is opened. Any updates, deletions, or inserts to the database are not visible to the cursor or the result set until they are closed and reopened.

Keyset cursors, like static cursors, remain unchanged from the time the cursor is opened. A keyset cursor contains the key value for each row contained within the cursor. When the application requests a row, the key value is used to obtain the remaining data from the data source. Keyset cursors can be set up to build the cursor on the client, an ODBC library cursor, or on the server, a server-side cursor. The ability to create server-side cursors is dictated by the features of the data source.

Dynamic cursors' performance differs from those previously mentioned and also results in the greatest amount of overhead. A dynamic cursor is created in the same manner as a keyset cursor, except that it constantly checks the data source to ensure that all rows that meet the selection criteria are included in the cursor. For example, if another application changes the data to where an additional record now meets the criteria of the cursor, a dynamic cursor will pick up the additional record. Keyset and static cursors, on the other hand, pick up the additional record only if the cursor is closed and reopened. Although this creates a large amount of overhead, dynamic cursors are faster than keyset cursors at the initial build of the cursor.

The type of cursor you use depends upon the functionality of the application being developed. For example, the GOLF System's OrderMgr uses forward-only result sets because of their speed and the fact that the business server only needs to see one row of the result set at a time. Other applications, however, may need to move forward and backward through the result set and may require updated information. In the latter case, a dynamic cursor, though slower than a forward-only result set, provides the functionality necessary without the application developer writing additional code.

When creating cursors, it is important to recognize that the location of the cursor also impacts its performance. Server-side cursors generally operate faster because they are located on the more powerful server machine and are not required to load all the cursor information down to the client machine. The ability to create a server-side cursor depends on the data source used.

The rdoDefaultCursorDriver property of the rdoEngine, or the rdoEnvironment's CursorDriver property, allows the application to specify the type of cursor to be created. As mentioned earlier in the chapter, these properties can be set to create ODBC cursors, server-side cursors, or driver-dependent cursors, meaning that a server-side cursor is created if the ODBC driver supports it.

Handling Transactions

A transaction refers to an operation performed against the database. Transaction management is the process of grouping these transactions into logical units of work whereby either all operations are completed or none of them is completed. When the GOLF System's OrderMgr creates an order, for example, it first inserts a record into the Order Header table, and then inserts the individual line items into the Line Items table. This entire operation must be one transaction. If the line items fail, then the order header should be removed from the table.

RDO provides a series of methods for the rdoConnection and rdoEnvironment objects that allow applications to manage transactions.

To mark the start of a transaction, the application calls the BeginTrans method. After this method is called, all database operations that are performed become part of this transaction. To signal the end of a transaction, the application calls either the CommitTrans or the RollbackTrans method.

The CommitTrans method is called after the operations that make up the transaction have completed successfully. CommitTrans saves all changes made to the database and ends the transaction.

The RollbackTrans method, however, is used when an error has occurred during one of the operations within the transaction. This method also ends the transaction but undoes all changes that were made to the database since the BeginTrans method was executed. In this case, the database is returned to the state it was in at the time the BeginTrans method was issued.

The following example from the GOLF System's OrderMgr, shown in Listing 11.3, shows the implementation of a transaction that is used while updating orders. In this example, the existing orders are first deleted, and the current values contained in the Order objects are inserted into the tables. If for some reason the inserts do not work, the transaction needs to be rolled back, replacing the old order information. You can find this code on the companion disk, in the \CHAP24\GOLF\TIER2\ORDMGR directory.

Listing 11.3   ORDERS.CLS—Example of implementing a transaction

```
Public Sub UpdateOrders()

Dim qryDeleteOrder As rdoPreparedStatement
Dim qryAddOrder As rdoPreparedStatement
Dim qryAddLineItem As rdoPreparedStatement

Dim OrderIdx As Long
Dim LineItemIdx As Long
Dim NextLineItem As LineItem

'1) Delete all orders and line item keys in the original collection
'2) Insert all orders and line items in current collection,
'    ignoring those orders marked RemoveFlag="Y"


db.BeginTrans

'open a handle to the delete orders stored procedure
Set qryDeleteOrder = db.CreatePreparedStatement( _
                       "sp_Delete_OrderHdr", _
                       "{call sp_Delete_OrderHdr (?)}")
'delete orders
OrderIdx = 0
Do
    OrderIdx = OrderIdx + 1
    qryDeleteOrder.rdoParameters(0).Value = Me.Item(OrderIdx).OrderID
    qryDeleteOrder.Execute
Loop Until OrderIdx >= Me.Count

'close the delete orders PreparedStatement handle
qryDeleteOrder.Close
```

```
'open a handle to the add order stored procedure
Set qryAddOrder = db.CreatePreparedStatement( _
                     "sp_Add_OrderHdr", _
                     "{call sp_Add_OrderHdr (?, ?, ?, ?)}")
qryAddOrder.rdoParameters(0).Direction = rdParamInputOutput
qryAddOrder.rdoParameters(1).Direction = rdParamInput
qryAddOrder.rdoParameters(2).Direction = rdParamInput
qryAddOrder.rdoParameters(3).Direction = rdParamInput

'open a handle to the add line item stored procedure
Set qryAddLineItem = db.CreatePreparedStatement( _
                     "sp_Add_LineItem", _
                     "{call sp_Add_LineItem (?, ?, ?, ?, ?)}")

'reload all of the order currently in the orders collection
OrderIdx = 0
Do
   OrderIdx = OrderIdx + 1
   'only add if not marked for removal
    If Me.Item(OrderIdx).RemovedFlag = "N" Then
     With Me.Item(OrderIdx)
        qryAddOrder.rdoParameters(0).Value = .OrderID
        qryAddOrder.rdoParameters(1).Value = .CustomerID
        qryAddOrder.rdoParameters(2).Value = .OrderDate
        qryAddOrder.rdoParameters(3).Value = CStr(.ShippedFlag)
        qryAddOrder.Execute

        'update order id which was set by SP
     Me.Item(OrderIdx).OrderID =qryAddOrder.rdoParameters(0).Value
   End With

     'add the line items
     LineItemIdx = 0
     Do
        LineItemIdx = LineItemIdx + 1
        Set NextLineItem =Me.Item(OrderIdx).LineItems.Item(LineItemIdx)
        With NextLineItem
           qryAddLineItem.rdoParameters(0).Value =Me.Item(OrderIdx).OrderID
           qryAddLineItem.rdoParameters(1).Value = LineItemIdx
           qryAddLineItem.rdoParameters(2).Value = .ProductId
           qryAddLineItem.rdoParameters(3).Value = .OrderQty
           qryAddLineItem.rdoParameters(4).Value = .ShipQty
           qryAddLineItem.Execute
        End With
     Loop Until LineItemIdx >= Me.Item(OrderIdx).LineItems.Count
  End If

Loop Until OrderIdx >= Me.Count

'close the PreparedStatement handles
qryAddOrder.Close
qryAddLineItem.Close
```

(continues)

Listing 11.3 Continued

```
'commit the transaction
db.CommitTrans

Set prvOrders = Nothing


End Sub
```

Another aspect of transactions that needs to be understood is the concept of locking records. RDO supports the two types of record locking that are found in most data sources—pessimistic and optimistic.

Under pessimistic locking, the database page containing the record being updated is locked and no other user is allowed to access this page from the time it is selected until the changes have been committed to the database. Optimistic record locking, however, locks the database page containing the record to be updated only while the actual update is taking place. Other users are allowed to access the record after it has been selected and before the update takes place.

The type of record locking is specified using the LockEdits property of the rdoResultset object. When LockEdits is set to True, the default, pessimistic locking, is used. This means the database page is unavailable to other users from the time the record is placed in edit mode by using the Edit method until the Update method has been executed.

Setting LockEdits equal to False uses optimistic record locking. In this case, the database page is still available to other users when the record is placed in edit mode. The database page is unavailable only while the Update method is being executed.

The type of record locking used for an application depends on the number of concurrent updates that will be taking place within the system.

Asynchronous Queries

RDO provides the rdAsyncEnable option to allow applications to process queries in an asynchronous fashion. When this option is specified, RDO initiates the query and immediately returns control to the calling application before the result set is built or before the action is complete. The rdAsyncEnable option is available when creating a result set using the OpenResultset method or when running an action query, using the Execute method.

During an asynchronous operation, the application is allowed to perform other tasks that do not involve the result set that was requested. The application is responsible for checking the StillExecuting property to determine when the query has completed. During these kinds of operations, RDO will check to determine whether the query has finished. The AsyncCheckInterval property determines the interval at which RDO checks for completion.

When rdAsyncEnable is used while creating an rdoResultset object, the result set is not available until the StillExecuting property has been set to False.

Asynchronous queries can be stopped by using the `Cancel` method of the object. This method stops the execution of the query, including all aspects of the query that may have already returned data.

When the rdAsyncEnable option is not used, Visual Basic does not allow any other tasks to be performed within the application until the first row of the result set has been retrieved. Only the current Visual Basic application is blocked. Other Windows applications are allowed to continue execution.

Handling Errors

Any statement that uses RDO can cause an error or multiple errors to occur. The rdoError object and rdoErrors collection provide the information about all errors associated with the most recent RDO operation.

Each rdoError object within the collection represents a specific error that occurred during the operation. Unlike most collections, the rdoError objects are not appended to the collection, but instead are added based on their severity or detail.

For example, if an application attempts to create a result set and an ODBC error occurs, the first object in the rdoErrors collection will contain the most specific, or lowest-level, ODBC error. The remaining errors in the collection represent the ODBC errors that were generated in the other layers of ODBC, such as the driver manager and driver.

To determine the cause of an error, the application can examine the rdoErrors(0) object because it contains the lowest-level error.

When an error occurs during an RDO operation, the rdoErrors collection is cleared, and all the errors that result from the operation are placed into the collection. Each error that occurs is represented by an individual rdoError object within the rdoErrors collection.

The rdoDefaultErrorThreshold setting determines whether or not the error is severe enough to generate a run-time error within the application. When a runtime error is generated, the application execution will fork into the error-handling routine. Using the properties listed in Table 11.16, the error handler can determine what action should be taken.

Table 11.16 Properties and Methods of the rdoError Object

Property/Method	Description
Count	Property containing the number of errors currently in the rdoErrors collection.
Description	Property containing the text message that describes the error.
HelpContext	Property value that holds the Windows Help file context ID associated with the error code.
HelpFile	Property value specifying the path to the Windows Help file.
Number	Property containing the error number.
Source	Property value that indicates the source of the error, often the object class where the error occurred.
SQLRetCode	Property values that contains the status code from the last RDO operation that indicates completion status: rdSQLSuccess, rdSQLError, and so on.
SQLState	String property that corresponds to the X/Open and SQL Access Group SQL error standard, containing the error class and subclass values.
Clear	Method that resets the rdoErrors collection.
Item	Method that returns a specific rdoError object from within the rdoErrors collection.

From Here...

In this chapter, you learned the characteristics to look for when selecting a data access method and how to use the powerful new data access method provided with Visual Basic 4, RDO. For more information on designing and developing data access applications, refer to the following chapters:

- Chapter 9, "Architecting Tier 2: Business Servers," for more information about creating business servers

- Chapter 10, "Architecting Tier 3: Data Servers," for information about creating relational databases.

Chapter 12

Advanced Coding Techniques

So far in this book, we have discussed the creation, implementation, and management of Visual Basic applications by making use of many of Visual Basic's new features. This chapter examines some advanced coding techniques that will help enhance your three-tier Visual Basic applications by applying some of these features. For each technique, you'll learn the basic principles behind it, how to implement each technique in Visual Basic, and issues to be aware of when using the technique in a production application.

By the end of this chapter, you will know how to:

- Create a "black box" function
- Use Visual Basic forms as OLE objects
- Read and write OLE documents to and from a database
- Use collections of objects
- Use the DoEvents() function effectively
- Create a multithreaded application in Visual Basic

Creating a "Black Box" Function

During development, you'll often create a function that can prove useful to an application other than your own. For example, you may create a function that converts a Julian date into a Cartesian date. After creating it, you may want to share the code with other developers.

We already know that Visual Basic makes this possible. You can create the date conversion function and place it in a code module. This code module can then be placed in a common area where developers creating new applications can retrieve it and drop it into their projects. This will help decrease development time in the future, as other programmers won't have to spend time rewriting code that you've already created.

Although this example of a date conversion function is simple, it is an example of one of Visual Basic's strongest features: reusable code. This code module can be thought of as an object. As with any other object, you need to pay particular attention to its design.

Creating a Function's Interface

In Chapter 6, "Creating OLE Objects," you learned that the first step in designing an object is to lay out its interface. An object's interface is comprised of the object's methods, properties, and events. The interface should be created in such a manner that anyone using the object's properties or methods need not understand the inner workings of the object. A good interface makes an object easier for other developers, as well as end users, to use.

The same principles of interface design should hold true for all functions in your Visual Basic applications. The interface you create for your common functions should be simple enough that a developer without an understanding of the inner workings of the function can still use it. This is where the term *black boxing* of functions stems from.

Black box functions are functions that expose a simple, generic interface to a user, but contain complex logic. Black box implies that the user knows what goes into the function and what comes out, but has no visibility to what went on inside.

Visual Basic's `MsgBox()` function can be thought of as a black box function. To a developer, the function appears simple, due to its simple interface design. You pass it several arguments: a prompt, constants indicating buttons and icons, a title, a help file name, and a help context ID. Behind the scenes, the function displays and aligns the message dialog box, includes the appropriate prompt and title, displays the appropriate buttons or icons, and incorporates context-sensitive help. All this occurs without you, the developer, having any specific knowledge of the inner workings of the function.

The Role of Black Box Functions

Black box functions play an important role in the enterprise. Because the person who develops a function may not be available to support the function later in the application's life cycle, a generic function allows developers to continue to use the function without having to understand the logic used to create it.

For example, a developer may create a function that reads and writes OLE documents to a database. A second developer may be required to perform this action in a new application, but he or she may not fully understand the process required. If the functions needed to read and write the OLE documents to a database are encapsulated in a function, the second developer can use these encapsulated functions without having an intimate knowledge of the code required to complete the operation. This saves valuable development time and effort, while at the same time ensuring that a common method of reading and writing OLE documents to the database is implemented.

In three-tiered systems, end users are encouraged to develop their own client applications. Often, the end users will not be experienced Visual Basic programmers. They may not have the time to learn the programming techniques required to implement certain pieces of functionality within their programs. If you spend the time to develop black box functions, these less-experienced developers will then be able to create powerful client applications without having to understand the functions' inner workings.

Why not Use OLE Objects?

When we discussed three-tiered architecture previously in this book, you learned that complex logic shared through the enterprise should be encapsulated in OLE objects. These objects can then be placed in a common location, making them easily accessible to all developers and end users who choose to develop their own applications. Why, then, do we ever need to create a black box function and place it in a code module? Why can't we place all our functions in OLE objects?

Although powerful, OLE objects have some limitations. For example, you can't pass a control as an argument to a remote OLE object. Often during development, you will create a function that performs some cosmetic feature, such as aligning text in a list box or sorting entries in a TreeView control. Without the capability to pass the control to method, you will have to extract all the text from the control, pass it to an OLE object, and then re-enter the text into the control. This can prove to be quite difficult and inefficient.

Code modules, on the other hand, allow you to pass controls as arguments. This makes them ideal candidates for functions used in client applications for display purposes. If you want to create a sorting function for a TreeView control, you can pass the control as an argument, have the function perform the complex sorting routine, and display the newly sorted results. The end user doesn't need any knowledge of the inner workings of the function.

Distributing a Black Box Function

After you have developed your function, you will want to encapsulate it in such a manner that it can easily be inserted into other Visual Basic projects. You can do so by placing all the functions called by your new function—as well as the function itself—into a single Visual Basic code module. You will also want to make sure that you have declared all constants and variables used by the functions within your code module's general declarations section.

After placing all the code, constants, and variables required by the function into a code module, you need to place the code module in a common location where other developers will have access to it. You may want to use a source code control utility, such as Visual SourceSafe, to track revisions of the module. This helps ensure that changes to the module are communicated to other developers.

Using Visual Basic Forms as Objects

You generally use Visual Basic forms to create the visual interface for an application. But forms are also objects, which means that forms can have methods and properties that other modules in your application can access and modify. The major difference between a form and a class or code module is that a form can have a visible interface, whereas a class or code module can't.

Any form created in Visual Basic has a number of pre-defined methods and properties. For example, the Show method of a form allows you to make a form visible to a user. A form's Caption property controls the text that's displayed in the form's title bar.

You can also create your own custom methods and properties for a form. Because a form is simply an object with a visible interface, the same techniques you used to create methods and properties for class modules also can be used to create methods and properties for forms. These methods and properties can then be called from other forms, code modules, or class modules.

Creating Custom Methods and Properties

In previous versions of Visual Basic, it was often difficult to share data between forms. Suppose that you had an application that required a user to enter a value, a product number, and a quantity, and then the application displayed a second form, where the user entered a shipping address for the order. Your application required you to pass the product information that was entered on the first form to the second form. To make this happen, you had several options, none of which were very efficient.

If the product quantity form was displayed modally, you could pass the order information to the second form by using a global variable. If the forms were not displayed modally, however, managing a global variable could become difficult. As a second option, you could create several invisible label controls on the second form. When a user entered the product information on the first form, you could enter the values for the product number and the quantity into the label controls on the second form. This is also an inefficient method, which requires that you create and manage invisible controls. Another developer who later edits your application may not realize what the invisible label controls are used for and delete them.

Visual Basic 4.0 allows you to create custom methods and properties for forms that aid in overcoming these types of problems. Custom methods and properties are created by using the Public keyword. By declaring a procedure with the Public keyword, you create a method that's accessible by all other forms, code modules, and class modules in your Visual Basic project. For example, place the following code in the general declarations section of Form1 to create the `DisplayMessage` method for the form:

```
Public Function DisplayMessage (asPrompt as String) as Integer

     ' Function displays a message box and returns users response
DisplayMessage = MsgBox (asPrompt, vbOKCancel)
End Function
```

To call the `DisplayMessage` method from another form, you would use the following code:

```
Form1.DisplayMessage "Display this text"
```

To create a new property for a form, you declare a variable but again use the Public keyword, this time in place of the Dim statement. For example, place the following code in the general declarations section of Form1 to create a property, named **FormNumber**, for Form1:

```
Public FormNumber as Integer
```

You can set this property from another form with the following code:

```
Form1.FormNumber = 3
```

You also can retrieve the value of the FormNumber property from another form. To perform this step, you would use the following code:

```
liSomeVariable = Form1.FormNumber
```

Creating Custom Properties by Using Property Get, Let, and Set

You can also create properties for a form by using *property procedures*. You create property procedure using the Property Get, Property Let, and Property Set statements when declaring procedures within the form. Property procedures are used when you want an action to occur when a property of a form, or any object, is changed.

For example, you might want to create a *FormText* property that allows a user to change the text that appears in a label on a form. Because you want to ensure that all text in the label is visible to a user, you may have to resize the form if a large amount of text needs to be displayed. With property procedures, you can create a *FormText* property that responds by adjusting the size of the form to accommodate the label.

For more information on the Property Get, Let, and Set statements, see Chapter 6, "Creating OLE Objects."

Memory Considerations

Although 32-bit operating systems, such as Windows 95 and Windows NT, overcome many of the memory limitations of earlier versions of Windows, designing applications that minimize the use of system resources will help your programs to run both faster and cleaner.

Each control and variable in a Visual Basic application uses system resources. In previous versions of Visual Basic, accessing a control on a form that was not currently loaded caused the form to be loaded. For example, the following line of code would cause Visual Basic to first load Form1 (leaving it hidden), and then change the Caption property of the label:

```
Form1.Label.Caption = "Hello"
```

In Visual Basic 4.0, you can access a Public variable, call a custom method, or set a custom property on a form without loading the form. In a previous example, we created the *FormNumber* property of Form1. If Form1 hasn't been loaded before this statement, Form1 will remain unloaded. We still have full visibility of the FormNumber property from any other form or module in the application.

Using the Initialize and Terminate Events

Similar to a Visual Basic class module, a form has Initialize and Terminate events. When a form is loaded, the form's Initialize event is fired, and then the form's Load event is triggered. This gives you an opportunity to create instances of other classes, connect to a data access object, and set values of variables before the Form_Load event occurs.

The `Terminate` event is triggered after a form's `Unload` event. This gives you the opportunity to perform any final tasks before the form is unloaded from memory.

Using Custom Properties and Methods in Code

A form's properties and methods allow you to perform several useful functions in your code that previously required a more significant effort. For example, they help eliminate the need to pass global variables as "holders" for values retrieved in modal dialog boxes.

You probably performed this type of operation before. Often in an application, you need to perform an operation that requires a user to supply a piece of information before processing can continue. For example, in an order-processing application, you may require a user to enter a customer's ID number before a new order can be created. This was generally accomplished by creating a global variable, displaying a modal dialog box, setting the value of the global variable equal to the value of the user's input, unloading the form, and reading the value.

With custom properties of a form, this is no longer necessary. To accomplish the same task, you can create a property for the form, display the form modally, set the value of the form's property to the value of the user's input, hide the form, and then read the value that the user entered from the form's property.

Reading and Writing OLE Documents to a Database

You learned about the OLE container control in Chapter 5, "Controlling OLE Objects." The OLE container control allows you to display and edit OLE documents from within your Visual Basic application. This can be a valuable aid if you plan to create applications that allow users to create word-processing documents, charts, or spreadsheets. With the OLE container control, you can use the functionality of other applications, such as Word or Excel, to create professional-looking documents within your own application.

Several database engines, such as Access and Microsoft's SQL Server, will allow you to store OLE objects, including OLE documents, within the database. With these engines, you can create applications that not only can create OLE documents and objects, but can store them to a database.

Storing an OLE Document to a Database

For specific details on inserting OLE documents into the OLE container control or for information on the OLE container control itself, see Chapter 5, "Controlling OLE Objects." This section assumes that you're already familiar with the functions and methods used to insert an OLE document into the OLE container control. This section also assumes that you already created an ODBC-compliant database, with at least one table that contains a column capable of storing an OLE object. In Access, this datatype is OLE Object. In SQL Server, the Image datatype is used.

After an OLE document is inserted into an OLE container control, saving the document to a database requires two steps: saving the OLE document in the container control to a binary file and then using Visual Basic's AppendChunk method to read the data stored in the file to a database.

Saving an OLE Document to a File

To save an OLE document to a file, you use the OLE container control's SaveToFile method. The SaveToFile method saves an OLE object to an open binary file. To open a binary file, you use the following code:

```
Dim liFileNumber as Integer
liFileNumber = FreeFile
Open "OLEFILE.TMP" for Binary as liFileNumber
```

The Open statement opens a file for input or output. Before you can perform actions on a file in Visual Basic, you must Open it. Because the OLE document must be saved in binary format, we use the *Binary* keyword in our Open statement. This ensures that data written to the file by Visual Basic is stored in binary format and not as ASCII text. If the file you specify in the Open statement—in the example, OLEFILE.TMP—currently doesn't exist, the Open statement creates the file.

When you open a file, you also specify a file number. In the example, we used the file number, liFileNumber. First, we assigned the value of FreeFile() to liFileNumber. The FreeFile() function returns the next file number available for use by the Open statement. You use the FreeFile() function to ensure that the file number you will use in the Open statement isn't already in use. The file number you specify in an Open statement is used to perform subsequent actions on the open file, such as reading and writing data, as well as close it.

After the file is opened for binary input, you need to save the OLE document with the SaveToFile method. The SaveToFile method has the following syntax:

```
object.SaveToFile filenumber
```

Here, `object` is the name of the OLE container control, and `filenumber` is the file number used in the Open statement. Continuing with the example, you use the following code to save the OLE document to a file:

```
OLEContainer.SaveTiFile liFileNumber
```

After saving the OLE document, you'll need to close the file by using the Close statement. To do so, use the following code:

```
Close liFileNumber
```

Referencing an rdoColumn Object

After the OLE Document is saved to a binary file, you use Visual Basic's `AppendChunk` method to store the OLE document to the database. Our example will use Remote Data Objects (RDO) to store the document to an ODBC database. You also can use Jet Data Access Objects (DAO) to store the document to an Access database.

The `AppendChunk` method is actually a method of an rdoColumn object. Therefore, the next step in saving your OLE document is creating a reference to an rdoColumn object. This is done by creating an RDO connection to your database, creating an rdoResultSet object, and finally creating a reference to the OLE Object column you created.

To create an RDO connection, use the `OpenConnection` method of the rdoEnvironment object. You can use the default rdoEnvironment object supplied by Visual Basic. For more information on RDO, see Chapter 11, "Remote Data Objects."

To create a connection, you use the following code:

```
Dim lenvDataEnviron as rdoEnvironment
Dim lconConnection as rdoConnection
Set lenvDataEnviron = rdoEnvironments(0)
Set lconConnection = lenvDataEnviron.OpenConnection("Document _
Manager Database", True, False, "UID=admin;")
```

The first variable, lenvDataEnviron, is used to reference the default environment object supplied by Visual Basic, rdoEnvironments(0). The second variable, lconConnection, is used to maintain a reference to the database connection that we will create.

The `OpenConnection` method of the rdoEnvironment object has the following syntax:

```
Set connection = environment.OpenConnection _
(dsName[, prompt[, read- _
only[, connect]]])
```

The OpenConnection method syntax has these parts:

- **connection**–A variable of an rdoConnection object data type that represents the rdoConnection object you're opening.

- **environment**–A variable of an rdoEnvironment object data type that represents the existing rdoEnvironment object that will contain the database.

- **dsName**–A string expression that is the name of a registered ODBC data source name. Some considerations apply when using dsName:

  If it doesn't refer to a valid ODBC data source name, an error occurs, or if prompt is true, the user is prompted to pick from a list of registered data source names.

  If it's a zero-length string ("") and prompt is true, a dialog box listing all registered ODBC data source names is displayed so the user can select a database.

- **prompt**–Based on the value of the prompt argument, the ODBC driver manager prompts the user for connection information, such as user ID and password. Use one of the following Integer constants to define how the user should be prompted:

Integer Constant	Purpose
rdDriverNoPrompt	(Default) The driver manager uses the connection string provided in connect. If sufficient information isn't provided, the OpenConnection method returns a trappable error.
rdDriverPrompt	The driver manager displays the ODBC Data Sources dialog box. The connection string used to establish the connection is constructed from the Data Source Name (DSN) selected and completed by the user via the dialogs or, if no DSN is chosen and the DataSourceName property is empty (in the case of the RemoteData control), the default DSN is used.
rdDriverComplete	If the connection string provided includes the DSN keyword, the driver manager uses the string as provided in connect; otherwise, it behaves as it does when rdDriverPrompt is specified.
rdDriverCompleteRequired	Behaves like rdDriverComplete, except the driver disables the controls for any information not required to complete the connection.

■ **read-only**–A Boolean value that's true if the connection is to be opened for read-only access and false if the connection is to be opened for read/write access. If you omit this argument, the connection is opened for read/write access.

■ **connect**–A string expression used for opening the database. This string constitutes the ODBC connect arguments. If the connect argument is " " (an empty string), the user ID and password are taken from the UserName and Password properties.

In this example, we're using the OpenConnection method to connect to an ODBC data source, Document Manager Database. We also specified that we don't want to display a prompt to the user, and that we don't want to open the database in read-only mode.

When the connection is created, we can use the rdoConnection object to create a reference to a table in the rdoTables collection object. The rdoTables collection is a dependent object of the rdoConnection object. This means that the rdoTables collection object can't be created directly by an external application; it must be referenced through an existing rdoConnection object. The rdoTables collection contains all the stored tables in the database. Because all rdoTable objects are read-only, we must use the newly created table object to create a result set. The result set will contain an updatable reference to the table used to store the OLE document.

For our example, we will assume that the name of the table that will store the OLE document is OLE_DOC_TABLE. To create the result set object, use the following code:

```
Dim lrstResultSet As rdoResultset
Dim ltbTable As rdoTable

Set ltbTable = lconConnection.rdoTables("OLE_DOC_TABLE")
Set lrstResultSet = ltbTable.OpenResultset(rdOpenKeyset, _
    rdConcurLock)
```

This code first creates a reference to OLE_DOC_TABLE by using the rdoTables collection, and then uses this reference to create an updatable result set object by using the table object's OpenResultset method. (For more information on the OpenResultset method, see the documentation included with Visual Basic.)

For this example, we'll add a new record to OLE_DOC_TABLE. We can do so by using the AddNew method of the result set we just created. The following code creates a new record in the result set and makes it the current record:

```
lrstResultSet.AddNew
```

After adding the new record, we can use it to create a reference to the column that's used to store the OLE document. The rdoColumns collection is a dependent object of the rdoTables collection that contains all the columns in a table. Figure 12.1 graphically depicts the rdoConnection/rdoTables/rdoColumns relationship.

Fig. 12.1

The rdoConnection object hierarchy. When an rdoConnection object is created, you can view both the tables and the columns within those tables, contained in the database.

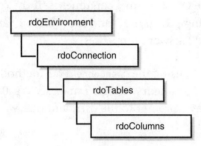

To create a reference to the OLE Object column, you use the following code:

```
Set rdoColumn = rdoResultset.rdoColumns(OLEColumn)
```

Here, *rdoColumn* is an rdoColumn object, *rdoResultSet* is a previously created rdoResultSet object, and *OLEColumn* is a string that contains the name of the column in a database table, for example, *OLETable* declared as type OLE Object.

For the example, assume that the name of the OLE Object column within table OLE_DOC_TABLE is OLE_DOC_COLUMN. To create a reference to the OLE document column, you would use the following code:

```
Dim lcolOLEColumn as rdoColumn
Set lcolOLEColumn = lrstResultSet.rdoColumns("OLE_DOC_COLUMN")
```

Now that we have a reference to an OLE Object column, we can use the AppendChunk method to retrieve the OLE document from the binary file we created previously.

Using the AppendChunk Method

An rdoColumn object's AppendChunk method can be used to append string data from a string expression to an OLE Object data column. We've already created a reference to the OLE Object column. Now we must create a Byte array expression that contains the OLE document's data. To do so, we'll use the binary file OLEFILE.TMP, which we saved earlier.

In previous versions of Visual Basic, the AppendChunk method required that you divide your binary data into chunks, and then append each chunk to the database. For example, a large file may require several calls to the AppendChunk method. This was because no variable type existed in Visual Basic that could store more than 64K worth of string data. String variable types created using the 32-bit version of Visual Basic can now contain more than one gigabyte of data, but the handling of strings in Visual Basic 4 has been changed. Information stored in string variables is immediately converted to Unicode, which means that retrieving information from a binary file into a string data type will result in the information being converted to Unicode. Unicode strings cannot be appended to the OLE column properly.

Visual Basic now uses the Byte data type to store binary information. To properly append the binary data from an OLE file into the database, we can use an array of Byte variables, and read the information from the file a single Byte at a time. The Byte array also can be written into a Variant data type without harming the binary data. This makes passing the binary data to other functions simple.

To store the data in the database, you'll first retrieve it from the binary file into a Byte array, and then store it locally in a Variant variable. To do this, we first need to declare the Byte array and Variant variables that will be used to hold the data:

```
Dim eError As Integer
Dim b() As Byte
Dim lvChunkHolder as Variant
```

Because we're using the Open statement to open the binary file, you also will need to declare an integer to hold the file number:

```
Dim liFileNumber As Integer
```

Next, we will open the binary file, using the Open statement. We also will use the FreeFile() function to retrieve a number for the next available file:

```
liFileNumber = FreeFile
lsPathName = "OLEFILE.TMP"
'Create temp
Open lsPathName For Binary As liFileNumberSeek liFileNumber, 1
```

The previous block of code also used the Seek statement to move to the first position in the open binary file. The Seek statement takes two arguments: the number of an open file and the position in the file to which you want to move. Because we want to move to the beginning of the file, we pass the value 1 as our position.

As a precautionary step, we set the value of the rdoColumn object to an empty string. Because we created a new record in the result set, this step isn't required. This step is purely precautionary. When you apply the Edit method to an rdoResultSet object as we did previously in this section, the first time the AppendChunk method is used on an rdoColumn object within the rdoResultset, the column is automatically cleared. Subsequent calls to the AppendChunk method will append new data to the "end" of the column. To clear the column, use the following code:

```
' Set the column's value to an empty string
lcolColumn = ""
```

We're now ready to retrieve the data stored in the binary file into the Byte array that we declared as b(). To do this, you use the Get statement. The Get statement retrieves information from an open file into a variable. The following code retrieves the data:

```
'get entire file into byte array
ReDim b(LOF(liFileNumber))
Get liFileNumber, 1, b

'now we can assign to variant of VarType = vbByte + vbArra
lvChunkHolder = b
```

When using the Get statement, the number of bytes read equals the number of characters already in the string. Because we want to read all the data in the open file into the variable, we first use the LOF() functions to dimension the Byte array equal in size to the length of the data file. We can then use the Get statement to retrieve all data, without having to redimension the array. After the information has been retrieved in the Byte array, we pass the information to the lvChunkHolder Variant variable.

The following section of code uses the AppendChunk method to add the OLE document's binary data to the database:

```
' Append info. to file
lcolColumn.AppendChunk (lvChunkHolder)
```

We finished loading the data, so you should close the file and delete it by using the Close and Kill statements:

```
'Close file and delete it
Close liFileNumber
Kill lsPathName
```

To commit the new record to the database, use the Update method of the result set:

```
' Commit new record to database
lrstResultset.Update
```

Reading an OLE Document from a Database

After you save your document to a database, you can retrieve and display it in an OLE container control. You learned in Chapter 5, "Controlling OLE Objects," that the OLE container control's ReadFromFile method can be used to insert an OLE document from a binary file. Because the method must read data from a binary file, you must programmatically extract data stored in the database and write it to a binary file before you can read it into the container control.

Extracting the data and writing it to a file is a process similar to storing an OLE document to a database. You first must read the data from the database by using the GetChunk method of an rdoColumn object. This data is stored in a Byte array variable and then written to a binary file with the Put statement. Finally, you use the ReadFromFile method to insert the OLE document into an OLE container control.

Referencing an rdoColumn Object

As you learned previously, GetChunk is a method of an rdoColumn object. To use it, we must first create a reference to the column that contains the OLE object.

To create a reference to the rdoColumn that contains the OLE document, we'll use techniques similar to techniques we used to store the OLE document. First, we'll create a connection, and then use this connection to create a reference to an rdoTable object. We then can create a result set from the rdoTable object, and finally create a reference to an rdoColumn by using the result set.

When we stored an OLE document to the database, we had to use the rdoTable object to create a result set object because the table object was read-only. Because we won't be updating any information in the database, only reading it, why don't we use the table object to create the column reference?

We don't use the table because you'll most likely be using a result set when you read OLE objects in a production application. The rdoTable object doesn't support any type of find or seek method. This makes it very difficult to move to a specific record in a table by using only the rdoTable object. You would have to create a For...Next loop and cycle through each record until you found the one you wanted. Instead, you'll probably use a stored procedure or dynamic SQL to move directly to the record you're interested in. In the case of a stored procedure or dynamic SQL, you will use a result set. Therefore, the example in this book demonstrates using a result set to create a reference to an rdoColumn.

Remember that the following code can be used to create a connection to an ODBC database:

```
Dim lenvDataEnviron as rdoEnvironment
Dim lconConnection as rdoConnection
```

```
Set lenvDataEnviron = rdoEnvironments(0)
Set lconConnection = lenvDataEnviron.OpenConnection("Document _
    Manager Database", True, False, "UID=admin;")
```

This code uses the OpenConnection method of the default rdoEnvironment object to create the new rdoConnection object. We can use this connection object to create a reference to OLE_DOC_TABLE as we did in the previous example:

```
Dim lrstResultSet As rdoResultset
Dim ltbTable As rdoTable

Set ltbTable = lconConnection.rdoTables("OLE_DOC_TABLE")
Set lrstResultSet = ltbTable.OpenResultset(rdOpenKeyset, _
    rdConcurLock)
```

Finally, we can create a reference to the column containing the OLE object:

```
Dim lcolOLEColumn as rdoColumn
Set lcolOLEColumn = lrstResultSet.rdoColumns("OLE_DOC_COLUMN")
```

Now that we have a reference to the OLE document's column, we can use the GetChunk method to retrieve its contents.

Using the GetChunk method

Visual Basic's GetChunk method can be used to retrieve data from a database column into a local variable. After the data is retrieved, we can write the data to a binary file.

The GetChunk method uses the following syntax:

```
OLEDataArray = column.GetChunk(numbytes)
```

The GetChunk method syntax has these parts:

- **OLEDataArray**–The name of a Byte array or a Variant that holds a Byte array that receives the data from the rdoColumn object named by a column.

- **column**–The name of an rdoColumn object whose Type property is set to rdMemo (Memo), rdLongBinary (OLE Object), or the equivalent.

- **numbytes**–A numeric expression that's the number of bytes you want to return.

Previous versions of Visual Basic required you to read data from a database column in chunks because no data type was available in Visual Basic to hold more than 64K of binary data. We now can use a Byte variable to retrieve all of the data into a single array. We are still required to make multiple calls to the GetChunk method, but this is because we are unsure of the amount of data stored in the database column.

To retrieve the data, you'll first retrieve it from the database and store it in a Byte array variable. To do this, we need to declare the Byte variable that's used to hold the data:

```
Dim b() As Byte
```

Because we're using the Open statement to open a binary file, you need to declare an integer to hold the file number:

```
Dim liFileNumber As Integer
```

We can now open a binary file that's used to store the OLE document until we retrieve it into the OLE container control. To do this, we use the Open statement just as when we stored an OLE document to the database. The following code opens a binary file using the file number returned by the FreeFile() function:

```
liFileNumber = FreeFile
Open "OLEFILE.TMP" For Binary As liFileNumber
```

Next, we'll use the GetChunk method to retrieve the data stored in the rdoColumn object into the Byte variable, b(). Because we are unsure of the amount of data in the column, we make multiple calls to the GetData method. Each call to the GetData method will return the amount of data, in bytes, that we ask for. In this example, if you ask for too much data—if you ask for 50 bytes of data and only 25 bytes are present in the column—the GetChunk method will only return 25 bytes of data. If you ask for data and no data exists in the column, an error is generated. The following code demonstrates how to use the GetChunk method to retrieve data into a Byte array:

```
On Error Resume Next
'put chunk into file until receive a Null back (which will
'generate a type mismatch error when trying to assign to b() )
Do
    b = lcolColumn.GetChunk(50)
    Put liFileNumber, , b
Loop While Err = 0
```

Notice how we used the On Error Resume Next statement to continue to retrieve data until we receive an error from the GetChunk method. When the error is generated, the code exits the loop.

The Put statement is used to transfer data stored in a local variable into an open file. The Put statement has the following syntax:

```
Put [#]filenumber, [recnumber], varname
```

The Put statement syntax has these parts:

■ **filenumber**–Any valid file number.

- **recnumber**–Record number (Random mode files) or byte number (Binary mode files) at which writing begins.

- **varname**–Name of variable containing data to be written to disk.

We created the `filenumber` argument when we opened the binary file. Because the file is a new file, we don't need to pass the `recnumber` argument; we're writing our data to the first position in the file. We passed the Byte array variable b() as the `varname` argument.

After the data is written to the open binary file, we can close it with the Close statement:

```
Close liFileNumber
```

You're now ready to load the data into the OLE container control.

Reading an OLE Document from a File

In Chapter 5, "Controlling OLE Objects," you learned how to insert an OLE document in the OLE container control by using the `ReadFromFile` method. To load the data stored in our binary file into the OLE container control, we use the following code:

```
liFileNumber = FreeFile
Open "OLEFILE.TMP" For Binary As liFileNumber
OLEContainer.ReadFromFile liFileNumber
Close liFileNumber
Kill "OLEFILE.TMP"
```

As you've seen in other functions, you can open the binary file that holds the object data with the Open statement. The `filenumber` argument of the Open statement is retrieved from the `FreeFile()` function. After opening the file, we load the OLE document into the OLE container control with the `ReadFromFile` method. We then close the binary file with the Close statement, and delete the file with the Kill statement. For more information on the `ReadFromFile` method, see Chapter 5 or the documentation included with Visual Basic.

Encapsulating the Read/Write Functions

Previously in this chapter, you learned about encapsulating and creating "black box" functions, which contain complex logic but expose a simple interface. Now that you've learned about reading and writing OLE documents to and from a database, you should see how the complex logic these operations require make them a good candidate for encapsulation. A simple interface to these complex functions will allow other developers to use them.

Although the logic behind reading and writing is somewhat complex, the operations are carried out using three basic components: an OLE container control, an OLE column in a database, and a temporary binary file. From a system point of view, the end user doesn't need to have any knowledge of the temporary file. The function takes care of creating the file, reading or writing from it, and deleting it when finished. It isn't required as a parameter. If a user were to supply the handle of an OLE container control and the location of the OLE object column in a database, you could create a function that reads or writes the OLE document contained in the control to or from the database.

Figure 12.2 shows what the black box OLE read/write functions look like conceptually from a user's point of view.

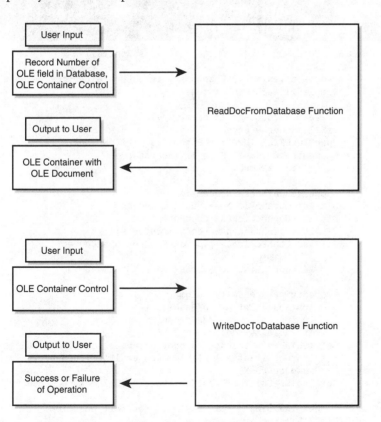

Fig. 12.2
A conceptual diagram of the OLE read/write functions.

In both cases, a user needs only to pass in an OLE container control and a value identifying the OLE document in the database (in this case, a record ID). In the write function, the result is that the document contained in the

OLE container control is written to the database. Because the write function inserts a new record, the record ID doesn't need to be specified. In the read function, the result is that the OLE document contained in the record specified is inserted into the OLE container control passed to the function.

From a developer's perspective, the call to the write function may look like

```
WriteDocToDatabase (OLEContainer)
```

where OLEContainer is the name of an OLE container control. The WriteDocToDatabase black box procedure may look like the code in Listing 12.1. You can find this code on the companion disk, in the \CHAP12 directory.

Listing 12.1 CODE01.TXT—Sample code that can be used to insert on OLE object into a database

```
Sub WriteDocToDatabase (OLEContainer as Control)

' Procedure saves the OLE document in OLEContainer to the database
    Dim liFileNumber as Integer

    'Save OLE document to binary file
    liFileNumber = FreeFile
    Open "OLEFILE.TMP" for Binary as liFileNumber
    OLEContainer.SaveTiFile liFileNumber
    Close liFileNumber

    ' Create database connection
    Dim lenvDataEnviron as rdoEnvironment
    Dim lconConnection as rdoConnection
    Set lenvDataEnviron = rdoEnvironments(0)
    Set lconConnection = lenvDataEnviron.OpenConnection _
        ("Document
        Manager Database", True, False, "UID=admin;")

    ' Create reference to column
    Dim lrstResultSet As rdoResultset
    Dim lcolOLEColumn as rdoColumn
    Dim ltbTable As rdoTable
    Set ltbTable = lconConnection.rdoTables("OLE_DOC_TABLE")
    Set lrstResultSet = ltbTable.OpenResultset(rdOpenKeyset, _
        rdConcurLock)
    Set lcolOLEColumn = lrstResultSet.rdoColumns("OLE_DOC_COLUMN")

    ' Open the binary file and move to first position
    Dim liFileNumber As Integer
    liFileNumber = FreeFile
    Open "OLEFILE.TMP" For Binary As liFileNumber
    Seek liFileNumber, 1

    ' Set the column's value to an empty string
```

```
            lcolColumn = ""
            Dim lvChunkHolder as Variant
            Dim b() as Byte

            ' get entire file into byte array
            ReDim b(LOF(liFileNumber))
            Get liFileNumber, 1, b

            ' now we can assign to variant of VarType = vbByte + vbArra
            lvChunkHolder = b
            ' Append info. to file
            lcolColumn.AppendChunk (lvChunkHolder)
            ' Close file and delete it
            Close liFileNumber
            Kill "OLEFILE.TMP"
        ' Commit new record to database
        lrstResultset.Update
    End Sub
```

You can see the benefit of a black box function. Developers who need to use the function are shielded from the complex logic of the code required to carry the function out. If the method for saving an OLE object to a database becomes simpler in the future, a developer could adjust the inner workings of the WriteDocToDatabase procedure without affecting the program calling the procedure.

Using Collections of Objects Instead of Arrays of User-Defined Data Types

Visual Basic provides several methods for storing elements of data in a single construct. Among these are user-defined data types and objects. The following sections examine both storage methods, as well as techniques used to store large numbers of each type.

Using User-Defined Data Types

Before version 4 of Visual Basic, user-defined data types were the only way developers could store pieces of related data in a common structure. For example, in an order processing application, when you retrieve an order from the database, you'll most likely retrieve several pieces of data: a customer's ID, name, and address; an order ID, date, and total cost; and the current status of the order. You could create a user-defined data type named **OrderInfo** to store these elements in a single variable type. Within the type, you could store all the elements that make up the order: customer ID, name, and address; order ID, date, and total cost; and status. To do so, you would use the code shown in Listing 12.2. You can find this file on the companion disk, in the \CHAP12 directory.

Listing 12.2   CODE02.TXT—A sample declaration of a user-defined structure

```
Type OrderInfo
        CustomerID as Long
        CustomerName as String
        CustomerAddress as String
        OrderID as Long
        OrderDate as Date
        OrderTotal as Currency
        OrderStatus as Integer
End Type
```

You then could dimension a variable of type OrderInfo and populate it with the following syntax:

```
OrderInfo.element = value
```

Here, *element* is one of the elements you defined for the OrderInfo type. Assuming that you had already retrieved the value of the order's customer ID from the database into a long variable named **llCustomerID**, you could use the following code to store the value into OrderInfo's CustomerID element:

```
Dim lstrCurrentOrder as OrderInfo
lstrCurrentOrder.CustomerID = llCustomerID
```

Using Objects

Visual Basic 4.0 provides a new method for storing data elements in a common unit: objects. As you learned in Chapter 6, "Creating OLE Objects," an object created with Visual Basic is composed of properties and methods. Through properties, you can create a object that's similar to a user-defined data type. If you want to store the same order information that you stored in the user-defined OrderInfo variable, for example, you can create an Order class with similar properties. To do this, add a class module to your Visual Basic project, name the module **Order**, and add the following code to the general declarations section:

```
Public CustomerID as Long
Public CustomerName as String
Public CustomerAddress as String
Public OrderID as Long
Public OrderDate as Date
Public OrderTotal as Currency
Public OrderStatus as Integer
```

You then can dimension a new object of type Order and populate it:

```
Dim loleCurrentOrder as New Order
loleCurrentOrder.CustomerID = llCustomerID
loleCurrentOrder.OrderDate = #11/19/95#
```

> **Note**
>
> Notice that the syntax used to populate the Order object is identical to that used to populate the OrderInfo type structure.

Object classes provide several benefits over user-defined types. You can implement methods in classes that can be used to perform functions. In the Order object example, we can create a method called `PlaceOrder`, which stores the Order's data in the database. You also can create property procedures that execute a function when a property of an object is changed. If you changed the OrderTotal property of an order, for example, you may want a new invoice generated and sent to the customer, notifying that customer of the change. Property procedures allow you to do this.

In addition to providing property procedures and methods, objects can be placed centrally in a three-tiered system, allowing them to be easily managed. For example, you may find a need to add a new property to your Order object. If you had implemented it as a user-defined type, you would have to redistribute the client application to all end users. However, because you can place the Order class in an OLE server located on a network, you can add the new property without the need to redistribute your code to end users.

Using Collections of Objects

Suppose that you need to retrieve 10 orders from the database and store them in your application. Visual Basic allows you to create arrays of user-defined types just as you can create arrays of any other data type. To create an array of OrderInfo structures, you use the following code:

```
Dim lstrCurrentOrder(10) as OrderInfo
```

You can then populate each element of the array:

```
lsrtCurrentOrder(1).CustomerID = llCustomerID
lstrCurrentOrder(2).OrderID = llOrderID
```

Populating elements of an existing array is straightforward. But what about adding new elements or deleting existing elements? If you want to add an eleventh element to your array, you need to `ReDim` the entire array and then populate the new element. If you want to remove the third item from the array, you can't easily do so. You need to create a new array, transfer all elements except the third one into the new array, and then delete the old array.

What about locating a specific object in an array? Aside from using the index, which can only be a long integer, to specify an element in the array, there's no way to move directly to an element. You can designate a field in your user-defined type as a key to the array. In the OrderInfo type structure, for example, OrderID is unique for each order and can be used as a unique key. Even with the creation of a unique key, you still need to move through the array to find an element. You can create a For...Next loop that cycles through each element in the array, examines the element's OrderID setting, and executes some code when it finds the element you were looking for. The code to do so may look like the code you see in Listing 12.3. You can find this file on the disk, in the \CHAP12 directory.

Listing 12.3   CODE03.TXT—Sample code that can be used to search for information in an array

```
Dim llOrderToLookFor as Long
Dim llCounter as Long
llOrderToLookFor = 12334
For llCounter = 0 to UBound(lstrCurrentOrder)
    If lstCurrentOrder(llCounter).OrderID = llOrderToLookFor Then
    ' Execute some code
    ..

    ..
    ' Exit the loop
    Exit For
    End If
Next llCounter
```

This can affect the performance of your application, if the size of your array is large.

Visual Basic 4.0 provides a construct similar to an array called a *collection*. (Collections are explained in detail in Chapter 5, "Controlling OLE Objects.") Collections are much more flexible than arrays. A collection object exposes methods that can be used to add or remove members without requiring you to ReDim the collection. Suppose that you had created an Order object and set all of its properties. To add the object, you would use the following syntax:

```
collection.Add(item, key, before, after)
```

Here, *collection* is the name of a collection object you declared previously, and *item* is the new object or expression that you want to add to the collection.

Although each member in the collection has an index value that's similar to the index value of an array, you also can specify a *key* for the member. A member's key is a string that uniquely identifies it within the collection. We will see later in this section how a member's key can be used to immediately locate the member within the collection.

You also can add new members at a specific point in the collection. This is done by including the *before* or *after* argument in a call to the Add method. The *before* and *after* arguments are either valid index values of an existing member in the collection, or valid keys. (For more information on the Add method, see the documentation included with Visual Basic.)

If you've previously declared a collection named **gcolOrderCollection**, you can add a new order object to it by using the following code:

```
gcolOrderCollection.Add (loleNewOrder, CStr(llOrderID))
```

Here, we added a new order object to the collection (loleNewOrder) and set the new member's key to llOrderID. If we later want to examine the order object's CustomerID property, we can do so by using a collection Item method. The Item method has the following syntax:

```
collection.Item(index)
```

Here, *collection* is the name of a collection object, and *index* is either a member's index value in the collection or a string that specifies a member's key value. To access the member we added in the previous example, use the following code:

```
gcolOrderCollection.Item(CStr(llOrderID)).CustomerID
```

Note

You can directly access any member in the collection by using the Item method and the Order object's key value. You don't have to use a For...Next loop to examine each member's OrderID property, as we did with the array.

Although we used as a key value the Order object's OrderID, which we defined as a long integer, remember that a member's key can be any string value. For example, your OrderID may require you to include alphabetic characters in addition to numbers. Collections allow you to provide a descript key that helps developers more easily locate specific members of a collection later.

For example, the rdoPreparedStatements collection, described in detail in Chapter 11, "Remote Data Objects," is a collection of stored procedures or dynamic SQL statements that you, as a developer, can create. Your database administrator may require that all stored procedures in the database are named according to a convention. These stored procedure names may or may not be easily understood by the developer who created them. The name, sp_retrv_cust_info, may be descriptive enough to remind the developer who wrote the procedure of its function, but another developer may not understand for what the procedure is used. When the stored procedure is added to the rdoPreparedStatements collection, you can provide a descriptive key. A developer could assign a key value of "GetCustomerAddressInfo" to the sp_retrv_cust stored procedure. This allows other developers to refer to the more descript collection key when referencing the stored procedure.

When using an array, we noted that it was difficult to remove elements. This isn't true with a collection. The Remove method of a collection allows you to remove any member of the collection without requiring you to redimension the collection. For example, if we want to remove the Order object that we added in the preceding example, we can use the following code:

```
gcolOrderCollection.Remove (CStr(llOrderID))
```

As with the Item method, you specify which member you want to remove from the collection by passing a member's index or a member's key value to the Remove method.

Using the DoEvents() Function

The DoEvents() function in Visual Basic causes your application to temporarily yield control to the operating system. This allows Windows to process events in the queue and all keys in the SendKeys queue before returning control to your application.

The following sections will show how to use DoEvents() to perform two actions:

- Provide processor time for user events
- Determine when a shelled process has terminated

After explaining these two techniques, the discussion will outline precautions that should be taken when using the DoEvents() function in Visual Basic applications.

Providing Processor Time for User Events

In 16-bit operating systems, programs aren't inherently multitasked—if a program takes up a large amount of processing time to complete an operation, no other code can be executed within the application, nor can any other application be activated until the process is complete. Multitasking in 32-bit operating systems allows the processor to be shared among applications when a lengthy process is executing, but it doesn't permit additional code to be executed within the application running the process.

If portions of your Visual Basic code take up large amounts of processor time, you periodically may want to give control to users so that they can perform other actions in the application. For example, you may create a routine that copies files from one directory to another. During the copy routine, you may want to give users a chance to cancel the copying.

The DoEvents() function can aid you in implementing this type of functionality. Typically, DoEvents() is used to give up processor time in a For...Next loop. For example, if you placed the following block of code in an application, your program would have to wait until the loop completed all 1 million cycles until any other code could be executed:

```
For llcounter = 0 to 1000000
    ..
    ' Statements
    ..
Next llCounter
```

The code in Listing 12.4 would cause execution of the application to yield to the processor once every 1,000 iterations of the loop. You can find this code on the companion disk, in the \CHAP12 directory.

Listing 12.4 CODE04.TXT—Code used to shell out processor time to other events

```
For llCounter = 0 to 1000000
    ..
    Statements
    ..
    If llCounter Mod 1000 = 0 Then
        DoEvents()
    End If
Next llCounter
```

Previously, we discussed the example of a function that copied files between directories on a user's machine. If the user is copying a large number of files, he or she may want to cancel the copy process before it is completed.

The code in Listing 12.5 uses DoEvents() to check to see whether the user has clicked a Cancel button periodically during the copy routine. You can find this code on the companion disk, in the \CHAP12 directory.

Listing 12.5 CODE05.TXT—Code used to determine when a user has clicked the Cancel button

```
' For every file selected by user, copy to new destination
For llCounter = 1 to liFileCount
    ' Copy the next file
    ..
    ' Check if user clicked cancel button
    DoEvents()
    If fbCancelClicked = True Then
        ' When user clicks cancel button, a form
        ' level variable is set to true.
        ' User clicked cancel, undo copy
        ..
        Statements
        ..
        Exit For
        ..
    End If
Next llCounter
```

If a user clicks the Cancel button during the copy routine, a form-level variable, fbCancelClicked, is set to true. The loop checks the value of fbCancelClicked, and when it's set to true, it deletes any files that have been copied and exits the loop. DoEvents() allows Windows to process the Cancel button click, although Visual Basic is executing the copy loop.

Determining When a Shelled Process Has Terminated

You may require your Visual Basic application to shell out to a DOS program or an application that hasn't yet been implemented as an OLE server, such as WORDPAD.EXE. To do so, you use Visual Basic's Shell() function. Shell() starts another executable program asynchronously and returns control to your Visual Basic application. The shelled program will continue to run in-definitely until the user closes it. Terminating your Visual Basic application won't end the shelled application.

You can use the DoEvents() function with the GetModuleUsage() API to cause your application to wait until the shelled program has finished execut-ing. This can be useful if your application requires the user to complete an operation in another application before execution can continue.

Using the GetModuleUsage() API

The GetModuleUsage() API is used to determine how many instances of an application is running. Each time an application loads, its module count is increased by one. Likewise, when an application is terminated, its module count is decreased by one. When you call GetModuleUsage(), the API returns the current reference count of the module specified by the window handle.

To declare the GetModuleUsage() API, add the following code to the general declarations section of a form or code module:

```
Declare Function GetModuleUsage Lib "Kernel"
➥ (ByVal hModule As Long) As Long
```

Using the Shell() function

Visual Basic's Shell() function has the following syntax:

```
Shell(pathname[, windowstyle])
```

The Shell function syntax has these named arguments:

■ ***pathname***–The name of the program to execute and any required arguments or command-line switches; may include directory and drive. May also be the name of a document that has been associated with an executable program.

■ ***windowstyle***–The number corresponding to the style of the window in which the program is to be run. If *windowstyle* is omitted, the program is started minimized with focus.

The Shell() function returns a unique handle to the application or DOS session that was started in the Shell() call. The following code can be added to the click event of a command button. It starts an instance of the WORDPAD.EXE application:

```
Dim llWinHandle as Long
llWinHandle = Shell("WORDPAD.EXE")
```

Determining Whether an Application Is Running

By adding the following code immediately after your call to the Shell() function, you will cause Visual Basic to remain in a continuous loop until the application executed with the Shell() function has been terminated:

```
While GetModuleUsage(llCounter) > 0 Then
    ' If Shelled process had finished, GetModuleUsage equals 0
    DoEvents()
Wend
```

As long as an instance of the shelled application is running, the `GetModuleUsage()` function will return a number greater than zero, and the While...Wend loop continues to iterate. `DoEvents()` prevents the Visual Basic application from blocking the shelled application.

Limitations of the DoEvents() Function

Several things should be kept in mind when you use the `DoEvents()` function in a Visual Basic application. Because instructions aren't serialized by Visual Basic, you'll need to programmatically manage situations that may not occur otherwise.

For example, if you use `DoEvents()` to provide processor time to user events, you'll need to make sure that the procedure that has given up control with `DoEvents()` isn't executed again from a different part of your code before the first `DoEvents()` call returns. This can cause unpredictable results in your code. Also, you shouldn't use the `DoEvents()` function if other applications can potentially interact with your procedure during the time you have yielded control.

Creating a Multithreaded Application

Multithreading is the capability of an application to carry out processes in more than one thread of execution. In an application, a *thread* is a path of execution. Each thread consists of a memory stack, the state of CPU registers, and an entry in the execution list of the system scheduler.

A process consists of one or more threads and the code, data, and other resources of a program in memory. Typical resources are open files, semaphores, and dynamically allocated memory. A program is executed when the operating system gives one of the application's threads control of execution. When threads are being executed, a low-priority thread may have to wait while higher priority threads complete execution. On multiprocessor machines, a scheduler can move individual threads to different processors to balance the CPU load.

Multithreading can provide added stability to an application. If one thread is interrupted, all may not go down. This helps ensure that processes initiated in your application will run to completion even if an error in another process occurs. Also, multithreading provides increased performance to your application. Processes must no longer be executed synchronously. Threads can be executed in parallel, which allows the process as a whole to be completed more quickly.

Windows 95 and Windows NT implement preemptive multitasking. *Multitasking* is the capability of an operating system to permit an executable to continue to receive CPU cycles while other background operations continue. In a multithreaded application, execution is really a thread. Therefore, a multitasking operating system permits multiple threads to be executed simultaneously. Multitasking doesn't necessarily mean that an application you develop—even a multithreaded one—will behave differently, only that users can continue to do other work while your application performs some operation.

You can't yet create multithreaded applications in Visual Basic. Each process in a Visual Basic application is carried out, using a single thread of execution. However, you can multitask work by having a single-threaded application, such as Visual Basic, ask another application process to perform tasks, for example, as an out-of-process OLE server. In a multitasking environment, such as Windows 95, this type of application executes in a multithreaded-like fashion.

Methods of Creating Multi-Processing Applications

There are two methods by which multitasking applications can be implemented in Visual Basic—OLE callbacks and polling.

OLE callbacks are a method by which an OLE client registers itself with an OLE automation server. The server can subsequently invoke the controller's methods, thereby reversing the client/server relationship. This is done by calling a registration method in the OLE automation server. The method registers the client and then returns control to the client. A timer event in the OLE server checks the registered clients and executes a function. When the function has completed execution, the OLE server calls a notification method in the OLE server.

Polling is another method by which multitasking applications can be created. In the polling scenario, an OLE client also registers itself with an OLE server by calling a registration method. The OLE server uses a timer event to periodically check the registered clients and execute a function. However, when execution of the function is completed, the OLE server doesn't call a method of the OLE client, but instead changes the value of a property within itself. It's then the responsibility of the client application to periodically poll the OLE server to determine whether execution of the process has completed.

The remainder of this section explains the OLE callback and polling methods in detail and provides examples for implementing both in a Visual Basic application.

OLE Callbacks

As you learned in the preceding section, the OLE callback method of multitasking requires the OLE client to call a method of the OLE server. The OLE server periodically checks to see which OLE clients have queued up requests and executes a process. After completing the process, the OLE server will call a method of the OLE client that notifies the client of completion. To accomplish this, the OLE client and the OLE server must each have a specific makeup. The OLE server must handle the following processes:

- Define the tasks the OLE server will perform

- Implement an externally creatable class in the OLE automation server that enables the controller to notify the server that it would like work queued

- Define a mechanism for tracking controllers that have requested the OLE automation server to perform work

- Define a method the OLE controller must implement to receive OLE server callbacks

- Define a timed event that will periodically check the awaiting tasks and execute them

The OLE controller must handle the following processes:

- Implement a method that's called by the server application to indicate that the server task is complete. This method should conform to the parameters defined by the OLE server.

- Request the OLE automation server to perform some work and tell the server which object to use to perform the callback method.

Defining a Task

The first step in creating your multitasking system is to define the task that you want to execute asynchronously. This is often a query to a data service, an insertion to a database table, or any other operation that would have forced the end user to wait for a long time without being able to interact with the client application.

Creating a Notification Method

After you determine the task to be executed, you can create a class in an OLE server that includes a method that will allow controlling applications to notify the server that they're awaiting execution of the task. To help explain the method used to receive notifications in an OLE server, we will examine the code included with the Callback example that ships with Visual Basic. The code shown in Listing 12.6 makes up the AddObjectReference method in the Callback application's OLE automation server. You can find this code in the \CHAP12 directory on the companion disk.

Listing 12.6 CODE06.TXT—A sample notification routine used by an OLE callback application's OLE automation server

```
Public Function AddObjectReference(Caller As Object) As Boolean
    On Error GoTo AddObjectReferenceError

    Set gObjRef = Caller
    frmMain.Timer1.Enabled = True
    AddObjectReference = True
    gbConnected = True
    Exit Function

AddObjectReferenceError:
    MsgBox Error$, vbOKOnly + vbExclamation,_
    "AddObjectReference - Error" & Str$(Err)
    AddObjectReference = False
    Exit Function

End Function
```

The AddObjectReference method requires a single parameter: an instance of the controlling application's callback class. The controlling application's callback class exposes a method that will be called by the server application when a task is complete. We discuss the Callback method in detail in a following section of this chapter, "Creating a Callback Method." You may want to pass additional parameters to the AddObjectReference method, such as the frequency at which you want the task to be executed or the maximum number of times you want to retry the task before returning an error message.

The method also enables a timer control and sets the value of a global variable, *gbConnected*, to True. The timer control, explained later in this section, periodically checks for registered controlling applications. If the timer determines that a controller was registered, a task is executed. Using a timer control allows you to control when tasks are carried. For example, if the controlling application is requesting a particularly lengthy task or a task that may affect overall performance of the data services, you may want the task to be carried late in the evening. Using a timer control allows you to control the frequency at which these tasks are executed.

The class that contains the AddObjectReference method should be implemented as a Creatable—Single Use object. This causes a new instance of the class that contains the method to be instantiated each time the AddObjectReference method is called by a controller. While instantiating a new instance of the class each time the method is called may require more overhead than using a Creatable—Multi Use automation server, it does allow multiple processes to be executed concurrently. If a MultiUse server were used, controlling applications would be blocked from registering new events if the OLE automation server was executing tasks previously registered.

Creating the Timer Event

The execution of a task in an asynchronous server occurs in the Timer event of a timer control located in the OLE automation server. The Timer event periodically checks to see if a controlling application has registered itself with the callback server. If a controller is registered, a task will be executed and the controller is subsequently notified of the success or failure of the task.

To implement the timer procedure, you'll need to add a form to your OLE server. This can be done by selecting Form from Visual Basic's Insert menu. In the callback example included with Visual Basic, this form is named **frmMain**, but you can select any name you want. After creating the form, you can place a timer control on it. In the callback server example included with Visual Basic, the timer control is named **Timer1**. Again, you can give the timer control any valid name. Figure 12.3 shows a form with a timer control on it.

Fig. 12.3

The timer form with a timer control.

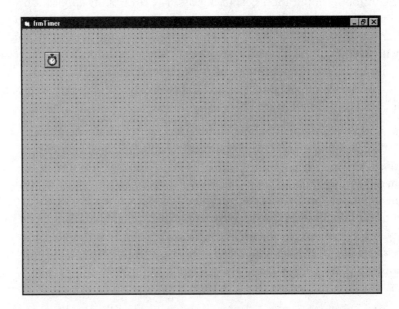

The code segment in Listing 12.7 shows what the timer control's Timer event looks like in the callback example provided with Visual Basic. You can find this code in the \CHAP12 directory on this book's companion disk.

Listing 12.7 CODE07.TXT—A sample timer event for the callback server

```
Private Sub Timer1_Timer()
    If gbConnected Then
        sCurTime = Time
        lblTime.Caption = sCurTime
        gObjRef.TellTime (sCurTime)
    End If
End Sub
```

The Timer1 control's Timer event first checks to see if a controller is registered by checking the value of the *gbConnected* variable. Remember from this section's previous discussion of the callback method that the gbConnected variable is set to True when a controlling application registers itself with the callback server. If a controlling application is registered, the Timer1 control's Timer event retrieves the current system time, using Visual Basic's Time() function. It then calls the TellTime method of the controlling application. The TellTime method is explained in the next section, "Creating a Callback Method." After calling the TellTime method, execution of the task is complete.

Creating a Callback Method

As a quick review, so far we created a notification class in an OLE automation server, which we have referred to as the callback server, that allows controlling applications to register themselves when they wish to execute a task asynchronously. Within the callback server, we have seen how to implement a Timer control with a Timer event that periodically checks to see if controlling applications have been registered. If a controlling app has been registered, the Timer event carries out a task and notifies the controller of the task's completion by calling a method within the controlling application.

In this section, we discuss the method called by the callback server when a task has been completed. Remember from the previous section that the method used to notify the controller when the callback server had retrieved the current system time is called TellTime. Listing 12.8 shows the code that comprises the controlling application's TellTime method. You can find this code on the companion disk, in the \CHAP12 directory.

IV

Application Enhancements

Listing 12.8   CODE08.TXT—Sample code for the controlling application's TellTime method

```
Public Sub TellTime(sCurTime As String)
      'This is the *public* method the server calls to update the
      'client's time. In a real scenario, the server would typically
      'be doing something much more substantial... such as delivering
      'stock quotes, user requested news articles, or business reports.
      'Note, if this sub were not marked as public, the server
      'could not call it.
      frmCBCli.lblTime.Caption = sCurTime
End Sub
```

The TellTime method only sets the caption of label to the current time. As the comments in the TellTime method indicate, a callback server will generally be used to carry out more substantial processing, such as retrieving stock quotes or business reports.

The TellTime method is located in a class module named CbClientClass. The CbClientClass module is a Creatable—Single Use class module that is registered when a call is made to the OLE automation server's notify method. Because the controlling application registers the entire class with the server, you are free to give the class module any valid name.

Calling the OLE Server's Notify Method

Now that the required controlling application and OLE server classes have been created, you can create functions that use the asynchronous callback method of multitasking. To call the OLE server's notify method, you first need to create an instance of the OLE controlling application's callback class. Remember that the sample callback application included with Visual Basic names the class module that contains the callback method CbClientClass:

```
Dim loleCallback as New CbClientClass
```

Next, you create a reference to the OLE server's notification class:

```
Dim loleNotification as Object
Set loleNotification = CreateObject ("OLEAPP.Notify")
```

Remember that "Notify" is the name of the class module in the OLE automation server that contains the notification method. The class module can have any valid Visual Basic name. For this example, we named the class module **Notify**.

Finally, you register your request by calling the Notification class's `AddObjectReference` method and passing your newly created reference to the callback class:

```
loleNotification.AddObjectReference   loleCallback
```

Polling

The asynchronous callback method of multitasking requires that the OLE automation server have knowledge of the specific callback method name and parameters. Typically, OLE automation servers that implement such callbacks will be business services. Because business services service many types of controlling applications, such as Microsoft Excel, it is not always a safe assumption that the controlling applications can support an OLE callback. Microsoft Excel, for example, cannot create its own OLE objects.

The polling method allows you to create a multitasking application without requiring the controlling application to support a specific callback method. Rather than use a callback to the controlling application, the OLE server changes a property when a task has been completed. It's then the responsibility of the controlling application to periodically poll the OLE automation server to determine when a process has completed.

The disadvantage of the polling approach is that the controlling application must procedurally check the state of the OLE automation server at regular intervals. The callback approach, on the other hand, is event-driven.

As with the asynchronous notification method of multitasking, an application using the polling method must have an OLE client and an OLE server. Each component will have a specific makeup. The OLE server must:

- Define the tasks the OLE server will perform

- Implement an externally creatable notification class that enables the controller to notify the OLE automation server that it would like work to be carried out

- Define a mechanism for tracking controllers that have requested the OLE automation server to perform work

- Define a timed event that will periodically check the awaiting tasks and execute them

- Supply a read-only completed property, which can be polled periodically by the OLE controller to determine whether a process has been completed

The OLE controller must:

- Periodically check the OLE automation server's completed property

- Conform to the parameters defined by the OLE server

- Request the OLE automation server to perform some work

You should notice that the makeup of the OLE server and the OLE controller used in the polling method resemble the OLE server and OLE controller used in the asynchronous callback method.

The rest of this section explains the makeup of the OLE controller and the OLE server in an application using the polling method of multitasking.

Creating a Notification Method

The notification method you need to create for a polling application is nearly identical to the one you created using the asynchronous callback method of multitasking. You again need to create a class module that contains a method that will be called by a controlling application to indicate that some work should be performed. In the callback server, this method was the AddObjectReference method. For the polling server, we will also create the AddObjectReference method, with one minor change. Listing 12.9 shows what the AddObjectReference method of a polling application might look like. CODE09.TXT can be found in the \CHAP12 directory, on this book's companion disk.

Listing 12.9   CODE09.TXT—A sample AddObjectReference method in a polling server

```
Public Function AddObjectReference() As Boolean
    On Error GoTo AddObjectReferenceError

    frmMain.Timer1.Enabled = True
    AddObjectReference = True
    gbConnected = True
    gbCompleted = False
    Exit Function

AddObjectReferenceError:
    MsgBox Error$, vbOKOnly + vbExclamation, _
    "AddObjectReference - Error" & Str$(Err)
    AddObjectReference = False
    Exit Function

End Function
```

Only three differences exist between the polling server's and callback server's `AddObjectReference` methods. The first difference is found in the following statement:

```
gbCompleted = False
```

This code fragment sets a global variable, gbProcessComplete, to False. This variable will be used by the polling server to indicate to the controller application when a process has been completed.

Also, the polling server's `AddObjectReference` no longer requires an argument. This is because the polling server will not be calling a method of the controlling application to indicate the completion of a task. Subsequently, there is no need to assign the passed object to a form level variable, as we did in the callback example.

You'll also need to create a new property that allows controlling applications to check the status of registered tasks. For our example, we will create a new property, named **Completed**. Remember that you can give the property any valid Visual Basic name.

To implement the Completed property, you first declare a form level variable that will be used by the `Timer` event to indicate when a process has been completed. To do this, add the following code to the general declarations section of the class module that contains the `AddObjectReference` method:

```
Private gbCompleted as Boolean
```

In a following section of this chapter, you will see how the gbCompleted variable is used to set the Completed property of the polling server after a task has been completed.

Creating the Timer Event Procedure

Just as the `AddObjectReference` method of the polling server was similar to the `AddObjectReference` method of the asynchronous callback server, the Timer event in both servers are nearly identical. When you create a polling server, you'll need to add a form with a timer control just as you did in the asynchronous callback example. You should also add code to the timer event to carry out your task. For example, the code in Listing 12.10 shows code that might appear in the Timer control's Timer event. This code file, CODE10.TXT, is located on this book's companion disk, in the \CHAP12 directory.

Listing 12.10   CODE10.TXT—A sample Timer event in a polling server

```
Private Sub Timer1_Timer()
    If gbConnected Then
        sCurTime = Time
        lblTime.Caption = sCurTime
        gbCompleted = True
    End If
End Sub
```

Note similarity between the polling server's Timer event and the callback server's Timer event (refer to Listing 12.7). This code ensures that the timer is activated. As noted in the asynchronous callback example, setting the value of the timer control's interval to a constant is a good idea. This allows you to easily tune the parameter after the server is put into production.

The Timer event carries out the task, in this case we check the current system time, and sets the gbCompleted variable to True. In the following section, you will see how the gbCompleted variable is used by the polling server to indicate to the controlling application that a task is complete.

Creating a Read-Only Completed Property

You've already created a variable, gbCompleted, which is set in the Timer event of the polling server's Timer control to indicate that a task is complete. Remember that we declared this variable as *Private*, which prevents the controlling application from directly accessing this variable to determine when the task is complete. We did this because we do not want the controlling application to change the property. We only want to read the property.

How, then, do we make this property available to the client application? We can make it available through a *property procedure*. Property procedures, discussed in detail in Chapter 6, "Creating OLE Objects," are used in place of Public variables when you have code that must be executed when a property value of an object is set or read. You can create read-only property procedures by using the Property Get statement.

Our property procedure will return the value of the Completed property to the controlling application. The code to do this might look like the code in Listing 12.11. As with the other files, this code file, CODE11.TXT, is located on the companion disk's \CHAP12 directory.

Listing 12.11 CODE11.TXT—A sample property procedure for the polling server

```
Public Property Get Complete () As Boolean

    ' Process determines is a process has been completed
    ' If process is complete, gbCompleted is true
    ' Otherwise, value is false
    Complete = gbCompleted
End Property
```

The Completed property returns the value of the gbCompleted variable to the controlling. Until the `Timer` event has executed its code, the gbCompleted variable is set to False. Calls to the Complete property also will return False. When the task has been completed, the value of gbCompleted is set to True. Calls to the Complete property will also return True.

This code should be added to the class module that contains the `AddObjectReference` method. You will see in a following section of this chapter how the controlling application accesses the Complete property to determine whether a task has finished.

Calling the Polling Server's AddObjectReference Method

To call the polling server's `AddObjectReference` method, you don't need to create an instance of a callback class as you did in the asynchronous notification method. Instead, you simply create a reference to the polling server's notification class, as in the following example:

```
Dim foleNotification as Object
Set foleNotification = CreateObject ("OLEAPP.Notification")
```

Recall that the class name in this example, Notification, is arbitrary. You can give the class module that contains the `AddObjectReference` method any valid Visual Basic name. You do want to declare the object variable, in a form level variable, that is used to reference the Notification object. This will allow a separate procedure to check the state of the task.

After creating a reference to a notification class, you can register your request by calling the notification class's `AddObjectReference` method:

```
foleNotification.AddObjectReference
```

The task now has been initiated. In the following section, you will learn how to check the polling server's Complete property to determine if a task has finished processing.

Creating the Polling Timer

After a task is registered with the task server, you'll want to periodically check the server to determine if your task has been completed. To do this, you will implement a polling mechanism, much like the one used by the task server, to execute registered requests.

You need to add a timer to a form in your Visual Basic project. You will place code in the timer control's Timer event that will check the polling server's Complete property to determine whether the requested process has finished.

You should make sure that the timer is enabled when a request is registered, just as we did with the timer control in the OLE sever. You also need to make sure that the Interval property of the timer is set to a value other than 0. How often your polling timer checks for the completion of a process depends on many factors. You don't want your users to have to wait a long time before a result set is returned. Remember, however, that each call to the OLE server will block the execution of the controlling application, thereby preventing the user from performing any other work until control is returned. You also should consider how long the registered task will take in a normal situation. If the task generally takes 5 seconds to complete, polling the server every 5 milliseconds may be excessive.

Listing 12.12 shows a sample timer event for a controlling application. You can find the file that contains this code, CODE12.TXT, on this book's companion disk, in the \CHAP12 directory. This event allows the controller to determine when a task has been completed.

Listing 12.12   CODE12.TXT—Sample timer event for the polling controlling application

```
Private Sub Timer1_Timer()

    ' Check the value of the polling server's
    ' Complete property to determine if a task
    ' is finished

    If foleNotification.Complete = True Then
        ' Code for completed event
        ..
        ..
        ..
    Else
        ' Process is not completed
        ' Add code to make sure that timer continues to check
        ' for completion of process
        ..
        ..
```

```
        End If

        Set foleNotification = Nothing
    End Sub
```

If the value of the polling server's Complete property is True, the task has been completed. You can process the results of the task and disable the `Timer` event. If the property is False, the task hasn't yet been completed, and your application will need to continue to poll the task server.

By setting the value of foleNotification to Nothing, you uninstantiate the polling server. Your application is now ready to register another task.

From Here...

This chapter described some of the advanced coding techniques that can be used in Visual Basic applications. For more information on specific items mentioned in this chapter, review the following chapters:

- Chapter 5, "Controlling OLE Objects," for more information on using collections.

- Chapter 6, "Creating OLE Objects," for information on creating OLE objects in Visual Basic.

- Chapter 8, "Architecting Tier 1: Client Applications," for information on creating client applications that may use the callback or polling methods of multitasking.

- Chapter 10, "Architecting Tier 3: Data Servers," for more information about accessing data servers.

Chapter 13

Architecting Security

The introduction of the three-tier client-server environment adds greater flexibility to the creation of a secure application environment. This flexibility, however, increases the complexity of the architecture decision.

This chapter discusses the goals of a three-tier security architecture, the long-term security direction of the three-tier environment, what security features are currently available, and how these features are implemented.

Security is a set of business policies that define who can do what in the system. It usually involves authentication, proving who you are with a username/password combination, and authorization, determining if your security context has authority to do something. The list of a user's privileges is often referred to as the user's credentials. The list of what an object can have done to it is known as the object's *Access Control List (ACL)*. These terms are used throughout this chapter.

This chapter discusses the following aspects of an enterprise security architecture:

- Differences between traditional and three-tier security architectures
- The goals of a three-tier security architecture
- How security is implemented in Remote Automation
- Approaches to securing components

Traditional Security Architectures

Before you can understand the issues that face three-tier security architectures, you need to understand the decisions of the past, understand their weaknesses, and learn why their strengths may no longer be applicable.

Security in a Centralized Environment

In the centralized mainframe environment, users' access to programs was determined by the menus available. If users were given access to a menu, they had access to the programs associated with that menu. This architecture worked well because programs and data were married. In the mainframe environment, there was no way to bypass a program to get at the data.

The centralized mainframe environment is very secure but, as you learn from reading this book, there are many disadvantages to the 100-percent secure environment. These disadvantages include a lack of development tools, character-based user interface, and scalability.

Security in a Two-Tier Environment

The two-tier environment separated the client application from the server that stores the data. Users still logged into the database, but were not limited to the client application when accessing the database. Users have the ability to log into the database with tools such as Microsoft Excel, instead of the client application.

In two-tier applications, security was either enforced in the back-end database, using the DBMS's security features, or by the front-end client application, which required additional application development.

Most DBMSs provide the capability to secure tables, views, stored procedures, and other database objects. Managing security for all of these objects can be a difficult and confusing task. In addition, this approach only secures the actual data by defining who has access to it; it does not secure the way in which the data can be changed.

This limitation has a work-around, limiting access to the data through the use of stored procedures. This in turn, means that all the business logic must be placed in stored procedures. For example, when an order processing system ships an order, the inventory for that product needs to be decreased by the quantity on the order. A complex stored procedure can be created that updates the status of the order, and decreases the inventory, all within one database transaction.

Often, business logic is too complex to be handled entirely within stored procedures because they require server-based applications to use many smaller procedures to process the business rule. For example, the process of creating an order cannot usually be contained within a single stored procedure.

Security can also be enforced by the front-end application, using a series of custom application roles to determine if a user should have access to a particular piece of functionality. This locks up the business logic but leaves the back door wide open. Using an application like Excel, users can completely bypass the security rules built into the front end. All the user needs to know is the login name used to gain access to the database. After they are logged in, they will have access to all of the data because the security was built into the front-end application.

In the two-tier environment, systems were often less secure than the centralized mainframe. Specifically, data objects were often secure but the way in which data was manipulated was not secure. As you see in the following section, the goals of the three-tier architecture are to provide the same level of security as the centralized environment, but with the flexibility of two-tier environments.

Security Architecture Goals

There are a number of goals that the security architecture should strive to accomplish. The security architecture should:

- Be administered on the business objects
- Leverage the operating system security features
- Be purely an administrative task

Security as an Administrative Task

Application developers should not need to spend a lot of time putting security into their applications. Securing the application and its data should be an administrative task. For example, an application developer should not have to make an operating system call, such as the LANManager IsGroupMember API, to determine if the user should have access to functionality in the application. In this case, if the groups security definitions change or additional groups are added, the application will need to be recompiled and redistributed to accommodate the change.

By removing the responsibility of securing the application from the developer, access to application objects can be more easily changed. Changing security permissions in the applications themselves usually involves a code change and recompiling the application.

A good litmus test to determine if your security policy is an administrative task is to determine if the security policy can be completely revamped without one line of application code being changed. If so, you've passed the test.

Securing All Application Services

The security architecture must ensure that access to all objects used within an application are secured. It's no longer sufficient to simply ensure that the client application is secure, leaving the data services open for anyone to access.

Securing Data Services

The logic behind this lax security policy—security by ignorance—was based on the assumption that application end-users could not understand the manner in which application data was stored and retrieved. It was assumed that the end-user of an application lacked the knowledge to access an application's objects with any tools other than the application itself. This assumption is no longer true because almost every off-the-shelf desktop application ships with the capability to access server data through easily used front-end query builders.

Securing application objects is not limited to simply securing the access to those objects. The security architecture needs to also ensure that the application's data is left in a consistent state at all times. The architecture should protect the application against well-meaning and malicious users.

Securing the Business Services

In the three-tier environment, the business services become the enforcers of the security policies. It is at this level that all of the organization's business rules and logic are kept. Think of security as another one of the organization's business policies. Therefore, it is at this level, that security administration should take place.

By enforcing security on the business server, the client application does not have to be allowed direct access to the data services. This ensures that the business rules remain secure because the only means a client application has to access the database is through the business server.

Securing the User Services

As you will see, securing user services is no longer a major concern in the three-tier architecture. In three-tier applications, the business logic and rules that are important to secure are moved to the business-services tier. Only the presentation logic is accessible on the desktop.

To take full advantage of the three-tier architecture, the security architecture never should count on user services being secure. With business services secure, it doesn't matter what user service or front end (custom application, Excel, Access) the user employs to talk to the business services.

There may be situations, however, in which an organization may want to lock up user services. This action will be appropriate if the mere presentation flow—not just the data and business processes—is considered sensitive or confidential.

We go into more detail about securing each level later in the chapter.

Use the Operating System's Security Features

To fully understand the methods by which application objects can be and are secured, it's important to understand the operating system's security features. This allows the application developer to leverage the authentication procedures of the operating system rather than to implement their own user id and password authentication.

Because the business servers will be deployed on Windows NT machines, we discuss some specific security features provided by the Microsoft Windows NT operating system in the next section.

The NT Security Model

The Windows NT operating system was designed with security in mind. Consequently, it exposes the features that are used for securing the objects in a three-tier application.

Access Control Lists

The Access Control List (ACL) specifies the level of access that users and groups are granted for an individual object. The ACL is made up of many Access Control Entries (ACE) that actually specify object-access levels at a user and group level.

When a user or application requests an object, the Windows NT security subsystem searches through the ACEs in the ACL to determine if access to the object should be granted. The order in which the ACEs are defined in an ACL is important because of the way permissions are determined. When an object is requested, the ACEs are checked until either enough permission has been accumulated, an entry is encountered that explicitly denies access, or access is implicitly denied because the end of the ACL was reached.

For users that are members of multiple groups, the order in which the ACEs appear can be important. For example, if User A requests an instance of Object_1, the security subsystem will begin to search the object's ACL for User A to determine if access should be granted. Figure 13.1 illustrates Object_1's ACL. User A is the member of two groups, Managers and Reps. The Managers group has access to create an instance of Object_1, but the Reps group does not. If the ACEs were ordered like they are in figure 13.1, the Reps group's ACE would be encountered first. User A would be denied access to the object because the security subsystem found an explicit access denial, even though the next ACE gives explicit access to the object.

Fig. 13.1
Example ACL permissions check performed by the Windows NT security subsystem.

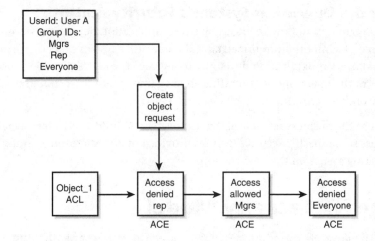

The Windows NT security subsystem performs this security check each time a user requests access to any secured object.

Using Windows NT Impersonation

Now that you have an understanding of the method the security subsystem uses to determine if access should be granted, we can look at the method used to determine which users security token should be referenced. Windows NT uses impersonation to determine the security context of a process.

Impersonation is a process's capability to inherit the security context or attributes of another process. In Windows NT, the server process takes on the security context of the client process on behalf of which it is working. This process ensures that an application started by a user does not have more access to objects than the user running the application.

The identity of a user is stored in what is referred to as a *security token*. This token defines the security groups to which the user belongs. The information stored in the access token defines the security context of the user and all processes started as that user.

When a process requests access to an object, the security token associated with the process is checked to determine its security context. The requested object's ACL is then checked to determine if the process can be granted access to the object.

Impersonation is a key operating system feature that is used in securing three-tier applications.

Security and Remote Automation

Before you can evaluate and design a security architecture, you need to not only understand the operating system, but you also need to understand to what extend Visual Basic and remote automation make use of the operating system.

Remote Automation Connection Manager

The Remote Automation Connection Manager is a utility that provides the application developer, or security administrator with the ability to specify the types of access remote clients have to OLE server objects, as well as the data authentication required during the RPC calls.

How these two security features fit into the overall security architecture is discussed later in the chapter. First, however, you need an understanding of the different levels of security that are supported.

Assigning Security to Classes

Figure 13.2 shows the Client Access tab of the Remote Automation Connection Manager, where the access control option for an OLE object is set.

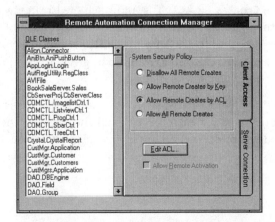

Fig. 13.2
The Remote Automation Connection Manager dialog box's Client Access Tab, used when setting object security.

The options specified in the System Security Policy group affect the OLE classes listed on the left. These options do not necessarily affect only the selected object; some are global to all objects. The following sections will discuss each of these options in detail.

Allow All Remote Creates. The Allow All Remote Creates option allows every remote client complete access to all objects. When this option is set, authentication is never performed. The only time this option should be used is to take the security checks out of the picture in a development environment. It should not be used for a production environment.

Disallow All Remote Creates. The Disallow All Remote Creates option sets the RemoteActivationPolicy entry to CreateNone. This setting prevents a remote client computer from creating an instance of any class. The option applies to any remote user that attempts to create an instance of any object. Essentially, remote automation is turned off for the machine.

Disallow All Remote Creates does not, however, prevent the computer (where the object is located) from passing a reference of the object to another computer. The developer needs to be aware of this so that users are not accidentally given access to objects through other objects.

Allow Remote Creates by Key. This option allows remote automation to be selectively turned on or off for a specific class. This is done by setting the AllowRemoteActivation setting in the registry to Y for objects accessed by remote clients. This option applies to all remote users who attempt to create an instance of the object.

The CLSID of a remote OLE object is set to *not creatable* by default. When the subkey has a value other than Y, or the subkey does not exist, the class cannot be created, and an Access is denied error message is returned to the client application.

Allow Remote Creates by ACL. The Allow Remote Creates by ACL option requires that the user id associated with the security context of the requesting application be present in the ACL for the CLSID within the Windows Registry. This allows selected users and groups to be given access to create an object remotely.

Clicking the Edit ACL button displays the Remote Class Permissions dialog box shown in figure 13.3, which is used to update the users and groups that have access to this object. This option is available only for Windows NT computers.

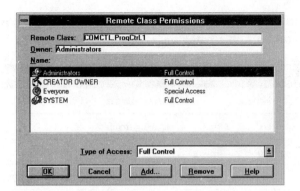

Fig. 13.3
The Remote Class Permissions dialog box.

When the Allow Remote Creates by ACL option is selected, permission to create objects can be granted to specific users. In this case, the Automation Manager uses impersonation when attempting to create the object. The security is actually on the CLSID key in the Registry. If the impersonated user can read the registry key, they are given permission to create the object.

Again, this security only applies to the creation of new objects. After an application has created a remote OLE server object, it can be passed to any component, whether or not it has permission to create it.

Authenticating Data

The second way the Remote Automation Connection Manager allows objects to be secured is by specifying the way data, which is passed to the remote OLE server, is authenticated. The Authentication Level list box on the Server Connection tab (see fig. 13.4) is used to set the level of data validation that is performed during Remote Process Communication (RPC) calls.

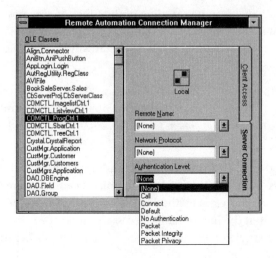

Fig. 13.4
The Remote Automation Data Authentication specification options.

Table 13.1 lists the seven levels of data authentication available for remote OLE servers running on a Windows NT machine.

Table 13.1	Remote Automation Data Authentication Options	
Value	**Name**	**Description**
0	Default	Network default
1	None	No authentication
2	Connect	Authenticates connection to the server
3	Call	Authenticates the beginning of each RPC
4	Packet	Verifies all packet data is from the expected client
5	Packet Integrity	Verifies that no data in the client-to-server transmission has been modified
6	Packet Privacy	Verifies all previous levels, and encrypts argument values

Data authentication is specified at the class level of OLE servers, which allows the level of checking to vary between servers. As the level of RPC authentication increases, performance declines. It is important that the need for authentication be carefully evaluated because of its performance implications.

Security and the Distributed Component Object Model

Now that you have an understanding of the functionality provided by the operating system and remote automation, you are ready to read this section, which discusses the security mechanisms that will be available when OLE matures.

As discussed in a Chapter 3, "Understanding OLE," the *Component Object Model (COM)* is the mechanism that allows objects to communicate with each other. The *Distributed Component Object Model (DCOM)* extends COM across the network.

The introduction of DCOM will provide additional security features for application objects. With DCOM, application objects can be secured at the individual object property and method level. This means that one object can be created with all of the functionality necessary, and access to its functionality can be given to individual users on a functional basis, rather than to the object as a whole.

DCOM also extends the reaches of impersonation through all objects. This means that security impersonation will chain through all objects. *Chaining* refers to the process by which OLE server objects are created under the security context of the object that has requested them.

For example, when User1 accesses a remote OLE server object, Server A, User1's security permissions are referenced to determine if the user has authority to create the object. The object is then created under User1's security context. This means that if Server A references another OLE server object (Server B), that object will be created under Server A's security context, which is the same as User1's. Here, impersonation is chained back to the original end user of the client application.

Security Features Available Today

Remote automation impersonation is not capable of the chaining process previously described. Figure 13.5 illustrates the reach of impersonation in today's Remote Automation and DCOM. As you can see in this illustration, impersonation stops at the point of object creation. All objects that are created with Remote Automation are created under the security context of the Remote Automation Manager. We discuss this process in greater detail in the following section.

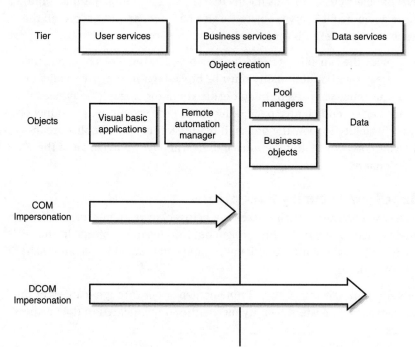

Fig. 13.5
Scope of impersonation in Remote Automation versus DCOM.

This following section discusses the specifics of the security features available today, and how they can be used to implement an application security architecture.

Impersonation to the Object

Remote Automation provides security impersonation to the point of initial object creation. Impersonation chaining is not possible in Remote Automation.

Using the example from the preceding section, Remote Automation will handle the request for the object in the following way. User1 accesses a remote OLE server object, Server A. User1's security context is used to determine if this user has permission to create an instance of the object. Server A will then be created, using the security context of the remote automation manager on the machine where Server A resides. In most cases, this will be the local system account of the Windows NT machine. If Server A then accesses another remote OLE server object (Server B), Server A's security context will be used, not User1's, to determine if access to the application should be granted.

Security at the Object Level

Remote Automation doesn't provide security for remote objects beyond the level of object creation. This means that if a user is granted permission to create a remote OLE server object, he also has permission to access all the properties and methods associated with that object.

To provide the capability to discriminate between the levels of access that users are granted, functionality must be broken out into many smaller objects. Customer service reps in an organization, for example, may need the ability to view and change open orders, while the warehouse personnel only need the ability to view the orders. If both pieces of functionality are included in one object, both groups of users will have access to all of the functionality.

Handling Security Exceptions

Even when functionality is broken out across objects, there still will be cases where functionality cannot be broken out into separate objects. In these cases, additional security functionality can be developed to accommodate these exceptions.

This additional security can be implemented either through features of the data service, or a custom security mechanism implemented in the business servers.

The Security Model

Now that you have an understanding of the security features provided by the operating system and object model, we can discuss how to develop a security architecture that will both secure our system and position the system to leverage future operating-system and object-model security features.

This chapter presents a thought-out policy. You should study the recommendations and approach and adjust it to suit your environment.

Which Tier Enforces Security?

Figure 13.6 shows the three-tier architecture again, to illustrate one of the first questions that needs to be asked when developing the three-tier application security architecture. Which tier should enforce the majority of the application's security policies?

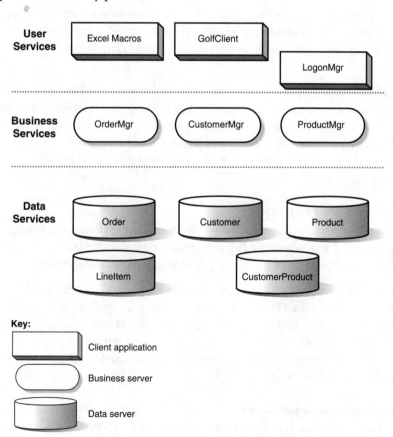

Fig. 13.6
Three-tier application architecture.

Looking at the diagram in figure 13.6, you see that one point exists through which all applications must go to leverage the maximum application reusability—the business services layer.

To allow the system's power users to create their own applications using the functionality of the business servers, the system's security policies must be enforced in a tier below the user services.

In two-tier applications, security can be placed in the client application without too much concern because the users are not able to create their own applications. Users would have been required to have the same knowledge as the application developers about the business rules and the way data was stored. The introduction of business servers allows the data storage and business rules to be hidden and exposed in the form of more understandable properties and methods.

The business services are the keepers of all the enterprise business policies. Think of security as one of the business policies, differing only in the fact that it changes more frequently and enforces many of the other business policies.

Because security impersonation doesn't extend beyond the Remote Automation Manager, you need to pass credentials to the business server by passing a userid and password to the business server when it is created. All business services may not require a userid and password, but it's good practice to include them—in case there is a need for them in the future and for consistency.

The Logon Manager

Included with this book is an OLE server object we developed, the Logon Manager. The purpose of the Logon Manager is to create objects with a common userid and password, without prompting the user more than once.

The Logon Manager handles asking the user for a userid and password, and then passing it to the object being created. When an application needs to reference an object, an instance manager or an object itself, the Login Manager should be used to create the object. This object returns an object reference to the calling procedure, and ensures that the userid and password are supplied to the OLE server object.

How Logon Manager Works

The Logon Manager is an in-process, OLE automation server application that resides in the user services tier, most likely on the same machine as the client application. When an application starts up, it creates a reference to the Logon

Manager and keeps it until the application terminates. When the application needs to reference an OLE server object, it uses the Logon Manager's `GetInstance` method to create a reference to the object.

The `GetInstance` method uses the following syntax:

```
LoginMgrObject.GetInstance(ObjVar as Object, _
                           ObjName As String[, _
                           InstMgr As String]) As Variant
```

Only the first two of the parameters are required. The third parameter, *InstMgr*, is used to create objects that make use of an instance manager. Instance managers are described in detail in Chapter 23, "Sample Application #2: An Instance Manager."

The parameters are string values that contain the class of the object that is being created, or the class of the instance manager that is being used to create the object. The Logon Manager assumes that the complete class is specified. When an instance manager is used, Logon Manager also assumes that the object adheres to the instance managers standards discussed in Chapter 23. Specifically, it requires that the method used to obtain an object reference is named `GetInstance`, and that it accepts UserId and Password parameters.

The example shown in Listing 13.1 demonstrates the use of LogonMgr and its `GetInstance` method. In the GOLF System, the user can update the information pertaining to a customer. This procedure requests a reference to the CustMgr object, and uses its `Modify` method to update the customer record. In this example, the InstMgr parameter is passed the value, CustMgrs.Application. You can find this code in the \CHAP13 directory of the companion floppy disk.

Listing 13.1   CODE01.TXT—An example of using the Logon Manager to obtain an object reference

```
Private Sub cmdOK_Click()
    Dim liRtnCd As Variant
    Screen.MousePointer = 11

    'Use the Login Manager to obtain a reference to the
    'CustMgr object. Passing the PoolMgr parameter specifies
    'that we want to use the CustMgr Instance Manager (CustMgrs)
    'to obtain a reference.

    liRtnCd = LoginObj.GetInstance(CustMgr, _
              InstMgr:=CustomerClassName)

    'make sure that we got one
    If CustMgr Is Nothing Then
```

(continues)

Listing 13.1 Continued

```
        Screen.MousePointer = 0
        MsgBox "There are no CustomerManager objects available"
        Exit Sub
    End If

    'update the customer
    CustMgr.ModifyCust

    Screen.MousePointer = 0

End Sub
```

When the GetInstance method is referenced, it will check LogonMgr's memory cache to determine if it already has a UserId and Password to pass to the object. If it does not, the login dialog box in figure 13.7 is displayed to obtain this information from the user.

Fig. 13.7

The OLE Login Manager login dialog box.

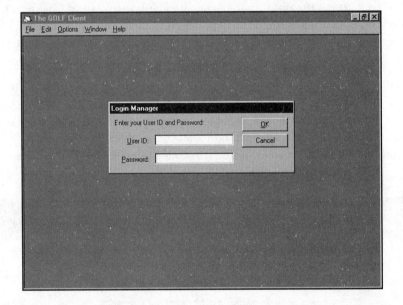

The GetInstance method then determines what type of object is being requested based on the parameter that was passed. An instance of the object is then created, and a reference is passed back to the client application.

The procedure in Listing 13.2 performs the actions of the GetInstance method. This method can be modified to add additional functionality that is business server-specific. These enhancements can include things such as notification when the user does not have permission to access an object, or a list of the methods and procedures of the object that are available to the user. The following code is located in the \CHAP13 directory on the companion disk.

Listing 13.2   CODE02.TXT—An example code from the Logon Manager

```
Public Function GetInstance(ObjName As Object, _
                        Optional ObjName As Variant, _
                        Optional PoolMgr As Variant) As Variant
    'function will return the handle to the object that the calling
    'function has requested.  If this is the first time that
    'AccessObject has been called the login dialog box will be
    'displayed and the user will be prompted for a userid
    'and password.

    Static UserId As String
    Static Pwd As String

    'if the UserId and password are empty, display the login dialog
    If Len(Trim(UserId)) = 0 Then
        frmLogin.Show vbModal
        If giCancel Then
            Exit Function
        End If

        'update the static variables
        UserId = gsUserId
        Pwd = gsPwd
    End If

    'make sure that at least one of the parameters was passed
    If IsMissing(PoolMgr) And IsMissing(ObjName) Then
        'we need at least one of these to create an object
        MsgBox "Must specify either an Instance Manager or _
                Specific Object.", vbExclamation, _
                "Object Creation Error"

    GetInstance = False
        Exit Function
    End If

    'get an instance of the object being requested
    If IsMissing(PoolMgr) Then
        'get an instance of the object
        Set ObjName = CreateObject(ObjName)

    Else
        'ask the pool manager for an instance
        Dim objPoolMgr As Object
```

(continues)

```
Listing 13.2  Continued
        Set objPoolMgr = CreateObject(PoolMgr)
        Set ObjName = objPoolMgr.GetInstance(UserId, Pwd)
    End If

    GetInstance = True

End Function
```

Installing the Logon Manager

The Logon Manager, as mentioned in the previous section, is an in-process, OLE automation server. Because the object manages the user's ID and password, and is an in-process server the object must execute on the same machine as the client application that will access it.

Because the Logon Manager is an OLE automation object, it must be registered on the client machine so that OLE knows where to find it. The Logon Manager can be registered by executing it with the /**REGSERVER** command-line parameter.

Securing the Components

Now that you have an understanding of the security features of the operating system and object models, you are ready for this section, which discusses the specifics of securing three-tier applications in Visual Basic. This section then discusses the methods for securing each level of the three-tier application.

Implementing Security for the User Services

The User Services tier is the first security point of an application and one that requires careful attention. This is where the users should be informed of the activities they can or cannot perform. There are two security aspects that need to be considered when securing the user services.

- Securing access to the client application.

- Notifying the users of their access to functionality within the application.

The following section discusses both aspects of securing the user services tier. It also presents some possible means of implementing this security.

Securing Access to the Application

Securing access to the client application is the most well-understood aspect of application security. The goal is to prevent users from accessing the application if they have not been given security to do so.

The most common method of securing the client application is to leverage security features of the network operating system. In this case, the application files are placed on the network, and only users that have been given access to the network share where the application is located have the ability to run the application. This method is sufficient in most cases.

The developer always should assume that the client application is going to be used by someone who does not have access to it. For this reason, the application should be secured to protect any presentation logic that may be considered confidential.

Notifying the User of Access to Application Functionality

The business services layer secures the objects that contain the business logic. Even though the client application does not enforce security, it still needs to react to the security policies that are being enforced by the business server.

Often, many different classes of users exist that need access to different pieces of an application. The client application needs to determine how it should inform the user of the pieces of functionality that are available.

A user-friendly application tells the user which functions in the application he has access to before he attempts to use them. This is accomplished by enabling the controls that correspond to the available functionality, and disabling the controls that correspond to the functionality to which the user does not have access.

Implementing Security for the Business Services

As previously mentioned, in the three-tier client-server environment, the business server should enforce the security policies. Security is implemented by assigning and removing privileges to the business objects. Depending upon the level of security needed, a number of approaches can be taken.

So far in this chapter, we discussed the future of security in the three-tier world, and the security features available today. This section discusses the methods for implementing security in the business objects with the tools currently available. This is done by positioning the architecture to take advantage of the additional features that will be present in the future.

The Remote Automation Connection Manager utility that ships with Visual Basic provides the capability to administer security for remote OLE servers. Chapter 7, "Managing OLE Objects," discusses the use of the Remote Automation Connection Manager in more detail. The tool provides the capability to define the following two types of security for remote objects:

- Access control

- Data authentication

The Remote Automation Connection Manager, as the name implies, is a tool for securing remote access to server objects.

Table 13.2 describes the four levels of access control that the Remote Automation Connection Manager provides for 32-bit network computers that are running remote OLE servers.

Table 13.2 Levels of Access Control		
Value	**Name**	**Description**
0	CreateNone	No object may be created by remote clients.
1	CreateAll	Any object may be created by all remote clients.
2	CreateIfKey	Objects are created only if its CLSID in the Windows Registry has the subkey setting: **AllowRemoteActivation=Y**
3	CreateIfAcl	Objects are created if the ACL in the Windows Registry includes the requesting user.

The following access control option is stored in the Registry:

```
HKEY_LOCAL_MACHINE\SOFTWARE\Microsoft\Automation Manager
➡\RemoteActivationPolicy=
```

Implementing Security for the Data Services

Securing the application's data services is an important part of the security architecture. As mentioned previously in this chapter, the user ignorance method of data security is a thing of the past. Off-the-shelf desktop applications like Microsoft Excel ship with the capability to access enterprise data, using easy-to-use graphical query builders. The security architecture must protect the application data's integrity against both well-meaning and malicious users.

The data services does not only refer to a Relational Database Management Systems (RDBMS). This layer includes other types of data servers such as imaging servers, document management servers, and the Internet. Each of these data servers requires special security considerations.

A general data services security approach is to leverage the security features provided by the data services, if it is not available via impersonation from the operating system. As described previously, the business server can then query the data service to determine what level of security the current user was granted.

The following section discusses some specifics of the most common data service used in enterprise applications—RDBMS servers.

RDBMS Security

Relational Database Management systems like Microsoft SQL Server and Oracle provide security features that can be leveraged to ensure the integrity of the data and authenticate users' access to the data.

Both Microsoft SQL Server and Oracle allow for the integration of user security with the host operating system. Microsoft SQL Server refers to this as the *integrated security option* because users are defined in the Windows NT operating system and assigned to groups. These users and groups are then granted access permissions within the SQL Server environment.

RDBMSs provide the following two powerful features that can be leveraged for securing the data that resides in them:

■ User privileges

■ Custom database views

Privileges. Although each RDBMS has its own name for this capability, most RDBMS packages provide the capability to limit the access to the database objects on a per user basis. This allows applications to be developed, while ensuring that users cannot gain access to data they are not supposed to view, or modify.

Think of privileges as the Microsoft SQL Server implementation of the ACL. Users are granted privileges that determine what level of access the user has to the objects within the database.

Most DBMSs implement the following five main privileges that users can be granted for most database objects:

Privilege	Description
Select	Provides read-only access to a table, view, or column
Update	Alters a table, view, or column
Insert	Adds a new record to a table or view
Delete	Removes a record from a table or view
Execute	Calls a stored procedure

Granting and Assigning Permissions

Most DBMSs have a DDL or a utility to define security. For example, Microsoft SQL Server 6.0 provides two methods for granting object permissions for users. The Database Administrator (DBA) can either write TransactSQL statements to grant to objects using the following syntax:

```
GRANT {ALL ¦ permission_list}
ON {table_name[(column_list)]¦
    view_name[(column_list)]¦
    stored_procedure_name}
TO {PUBLIC ¦ name_list}
```

Or, you can use the SQL Enterprise Manager's graphical user interface. The Enterprise Manager allows the DBA to perform all of the grants with an easily used interface, and then produce the TransactSQL statements that were actually used to perform the grants. These scripts then can be placed under version control with the remainder of the database creation scripts so that the database can be rebuilt to the proper version.

Figures 13.8 and 13.9 illustrate the two levels at which the SQL Enterprise Manager allows object permissions to be granted. Figure 13.8 shows the Object Permissions By User tab, which allows permissions to be assigned for all objects based on the users or groups defined.

Figure 13.9 shows the Object Permissions By Object tab, which allows permissions to be set for all available users and groups on an object-by-object basis. Both of these interfaces provide the capability to assign the same permissions. They differ only in the manner in which the objects are organized and presented.

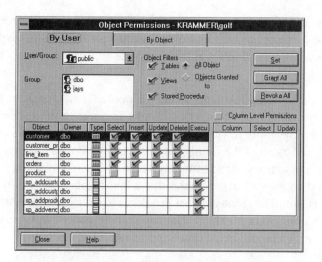

Fig. 13.8
SQL server Object
Permission, By
User tab.

IV

Application Enhancements

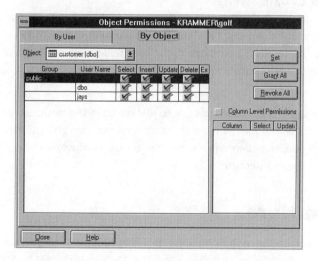

Fig. 13.9
SQL server Object
Permissions
assignment, By
Object tab.

Views. *Views* provide another technique of looking at data from one or more
tables. Views are derived from one or more *base tables* or other views. To the
user or application developer, a view looks like any other database table to
which he or she has access. There are few restrictions when accessing or
modifying the data within a view.

Views provide an additional layer of security because they can limit the rows
that are visible based on specified criteria. A view is created by using a standard SQL statement, so any selection that can be done with a TransactSQL
statement also can be done when creating a view.

As you learned in the preceding section, privileges can restrict access to objects, and for table objects, can limit access to specific columns within the table. Views allow you to get at the next level of security—the actual rows the user can see.

An example of where row-level security is needed is an organization that handles transactions for competing clients. The organization wants to give each client the ability to view their data, which resides in the transaction tables shared by all of the clients. The clients should not, however, be able to view the transactions of the company's other clients. In this case, views can be created on the transaction tables that allow clients to view only their data. All clients would be granted access privileges to only their views and not the base tables used to create them. The same functionality can be accomplished by using stored procedures if they support returning result sets.

Non-RDBMS Data Services

When working with data servers other than RDBMS products, the developer should attempt to leverage the authentication features provided by the operating system. If this is unavailable, the business server can implement a custom security authentication process like the one previously described in the chapter.

For this reason, it's a good practice to always have the business server carry the user name and password; if the data server is changed and the information is needed, the client applications will not require any change to work with the new architecture.

From Here...

This chapter presented an overview of the options available when developing a security architecture, as well as the basic goals that should be accomplished. For more information about related subjects, refer to:

- Chapter 9, "Architecting Tier 2: Business Servers," for more information about creating applications that reside in the business servers tier.

- Chapter 10, "Architecting Tier 3: Data Servers," for more information about creating the data services layer.

Chapter 14

Architecting Error Processing

Error processing is an often-overlooked aspect of application design. The introduction of the three-tier client/server environment requires a different approach to error processing than the two-tiered environment. In the three-tier environment, applications are partitioned into many pieces, all of which must work together to trap, log, and recover from errors.

In this chapter, we discuss the goals of a good three-tier client/server error-processing architecture. The following list names these goals, which are to

- Trap all types of errors
- Properly notify the end user or administrator
- Gracefully recover or clean up and terminate the application

After gaining a good understanding of these goals, we will discuss the specific facilities available within Visual Basic 4.0 that can be leveraged to create a solid error-processing architecture.

After you become familiar with the error-processing features of Visual Basic, we will then discuss some specific implementation strategies for handling errors in each type of application that make up the layers of a three-tier client-server application.

Types of Errors to Handle

In the three-tier client/server architecture, you need to account for the following three basic types of errors:

- Run-time errors that occur within client applications

- Run-time errors that occur within OLE object applications, which can be client applications, business servers, or data servers

- Run-time errors passed along by OLE applications referenced within client applications, business servers, or data servers

Each error type is discussed in detail in following sections of this chapter. The first sections, however, review the mechanisms available within Visual Basic to handle run-time errors encountered by your applications.

Handling Errors in Visual Basic

Visual Basic provides a number of programming constructs that assist in providing a solid error-processing architecture. These constructs provide the developer with the tools necessary to identify and react to run-time errors encountered within their applications.

Creating Error Handlers

By default, when Visual Basic encounters a run-time error, it displays an error message and ends the program. The application doesn't have the opportunity to attempt to recover from the error or gracefully shut down. This sudden termination of the application can result in data inconsistencies, client-side memory problems, and end-user frustrations.

To alleviate these problems, Visual Basic allows you to create "error handlers" within your code. When Visual Basic encounters an error, it searches for an enabled error handler in the code and continues execution from there.

You need to trap all errors so that you can meet the three previously mentioned goals of the error-processing architecture: *trap all errors*, *notify the end user or administrator*, and *recover or gracefully shut down the application*.

To ensure that all run-time errors are properly trapped, every application event should contain an enabled error handler, which prevents a run-time error from being handled unknowingly by an error handler further up the active calls list and causing unexpected results. The calls list contains all of the procedures within the application that were started but were not completed.

Procedure calls are placed in the calls list in the order in which they are called by the application. In event-driven applications, such as applications developed by using Visual Basic, application code is triggered by an event caused by a user. Looking at the active Calls list shows these events at the top of the calls list. Placing an error handler in every event that contains application code ensures that an error occurring anywhere in the application is trapped when Visual Basic searches back through the Calls list.

Error handlers also can be placed within user-defined procedures. Placing error handlers within these procedures adds additional layers to the error-handler hierarchy because most procedures are accessible to many events and procedures. In this case, there may be situations in which the calling procedures will need the capability to handle the error differently. In other situations, it makes sense for common procedures to handle the error.

An application that opens document files often, for example, may contain a FileOpen procedure that is called by multiple events and procedures throughout the application. Rather than requiring every event or procedure that will call the FileOpen procedure to handle the run-time errors associated with opening a file, the FileOpen procedure itself can contain an error handler to catch these situations. This process is discussed in more detail in a following section of this chapter.

Event and procedure error handlers are defined with any valid Visual Basic label. A good naming convention is to use the event or procedure name, followed by an _ErrHndlr suffix. This naming convention ensures that no two error handlers within a form or module have the same name. Using this naming convention, the error handler for the click event of an OK command button would look like the following example:

```
Private Sub cmdOK_Click()
On Error GoTo cmdOK_Click_ErrHndlr

    '

    'your event code

    '

    Exit Sub

'Define error handler
cmdOK_Click_ErrHndlr:
    '

    'your error handler code

    '

End Sub
```

The specifics of this example are discussed in following sections.

Within the error handler for each event or procedure, the application should anticipate all errors likely to occur and attempt to recover from them. In a procedure that opens a file, for example, the error handler needs to account for invalid file names, invalid drive specifications, and all other errors that can occur when attempting to access a file.

For errors that cannot be anticipated, you should develop a generic error handler that displays a notification to the end user and gracefully ends the application, performing all necessary clean up.

Listing 14.1, for example, displays a generic run-time error message to the user that describes the error, and then ends the application (you can find this code on the companion disk, in directory \CHAP14):

Listing 14.1 CODE01.TXT—An example procedure that handles an unexpected run-time error

```
Sub HandleFatalError(ErrObj As Object)
'This procedure will display a message to the user describing the
'run-time error that occurred, and the exit the application.

    Dim lsMsg As String

    'set the Message text
    lsMsg = "The following run-time error has occurred:"
    lsMsg = lsMsg & Chr(10) & Chr(10) & ErrObj.Number & " -
➥" & ErrObj.Description
    lsMsg = lsMsg & Chr(10) & Chr(10) & "Your last operation may
➥not have been successful.  Contact your system administrator
➥for assistance."

    'Display the message box
    MsgBox lsMsg, 16, "Fatal Run-Time Error"

    End

End Sub
```

Using On Error Goto

The most common means of trapping run-time errors within Visual Basic is by using the On Error Goto statement. When a run-time error is encountered in a Visual Basic procedure with an enabled On Error Goto statement, an exception is raised and the program execution jumps to the error handler designated by the Goto statement. This switching allows the application to react to run-time errors, such as File Not Found, without the application abruptly terminating.

For On Error Goto to raise an exception when a run-time error occurs, it first must be enabled. This occurs when the On Error Goto statement is executed. The statement is followed by a valid label located in the current procedure, as in the following example:

```
On Error Goto cmdOK_Click_ErrHndlr
```

Optionally, the Resume Next clause can be used in place of a `Goto` `<label>`. This option instructs Visual Basic to proceed to the statement immediately following the one that encountered the error, as opposed to jumping to an error handler or stopping code execution. On Error Resume Next often is used when implementing a technique known as *in-line* error processing, which is discussed in detail in a following section of this chapter.

The On Error Goto construct also can be disabled within a procedure by using the following syntax:

```
On Error Goto 0
```

The following procedure saves an Excel workbook to the file name passed into the procedure. Before attempting to save the file, the procedure first deletes an existing file, if there is one. The Kill statement produces a run-time error if the *asFileName* file doesn't exist. In this example, the error doesn't present a problem, and we want our procedure to continue its execution. The following procedure shows an example where disabling the error handler in the middle of the procedure may make sense:

```
Sub SaveFile(ByVal asFileName As String)
On Error GoTo SaveFile_ErrHndlr
    'For this example, assume that CurrentWorkBook is
    'as global Excel WorkBook object.

    '
    'initial save processing
    '

    'disable error handler in case no previous
    'file exists, ignore the error.
    On Error GoTo 0

    'Delete any previous file with this name
    Kill asFileName

    'enable error handler
    On Error GoTo SaveFile_ErrHndlr

    'save the file
    CurrentWorkBook.SaveAs asFileName

    Exit Sub

'Define error handler
SaveFile_ErrHndlr:
    '
    'Error Handler Code
    '
    Resume Next

End Sub
```

It's important to remember that On Error Goto uses a label to indicate where program execution should jump. This label is like any other you might use in your Visual Basic application. It's common practice to place the error handler after an *Exit Sub*, *Exit Function*, or *Exit Property* statement within a subroutine, function, or property procedure respectively—which separates the normal program code from the error-handler code and ensures that the error handler isn't inadvertently used during normal program execution.

Using Resume

After an error handler is invoked from a run-time error, the Resume statement is used to continue program execution after the error is dealt with. There are three basic methods in which Resume is used:

- **Resume** Continues execution with the statement that produced the run-time error.

- **Resume Next** Continues execution with the statement immediately following the line that produced the run-time error.

- **Resume <*label*>** Continues program execution on the line indicated by <*label*>.

The Resume statement allows the application to make some modifications or to inform the user of the error, and then to jump back to normal program execution (to attempt to perform the action again, for example).

The Resume Next method allows the application to skip the action that caused the error and continue with normal program execution on the line of code following the line that caused the error.

The Resume <*label*> method enables the application to jump to any part of the procedure (to skip the original action, for example).

Handling Errors in Procedures

So far, this chapter has only discussed handling errors within events. Although placing an error handler in every event with code is recommended to ensure that all run-time errors are properly handled, there may be times when handling errors within one of the called procedures is more desirable because this attack provides a finer level of granularity as to where the error actually occurred. Implementing error handling in this manner, however, introduces additional complexities. You should understand the manner in which the Visual Basic Resume statement handles search backs through the active calls list.

When a Visual Basic application encounters a run-time error, it first looks for an enabled error handler located within the current procedure. If one is not found, Visual Basic begins to search backward though the active calls list and executes the first enabled error handler it encounters. If no enabled error handler is found, a message is displayed and program execution ends.

If an enabled error handler is located, execution continues in this routine as if the error that was encountered within this routine affects the manner in which the Resume statements operate. Table 14.1 describes how Resume operates when the active calls list is searched and the first error handler found is in a different routine than the routine that caused the error.

Table 14.1	Resume Statement Categories
Statement	**Description of Action**
Resume	Continues normal program execution on the procedure in the calls-list where Visual Basic just found an enabled error handler. It doesn't necessarily execute the specific statement that caused the error because this statement may have been lower in the calls list.
Resume Next	Continues normal program execution on the statement immediately following the call to the procedure that Visual Basic just searched. It doesn't necessarily execute the statement immediately following the specific statement that caused the error because this statement may have been lower in the calls list.

This confusing concept is best illustrated by an example. Figure 14.1 illustrates an example of a run-time error that searches back through the active calls list to find an enabled error handler.

In figure 14.1, if an error occurs *in Procedure_3*, which doesn't have an enabled error handler, Visual Basic begins to search back through the active calls list. This search goes through *Procedure_2*, which also doesn't have an enabled error handler, and then *Procedure_1*, where it finds an error handler. Figure 14.2 shows the active Calls list dialog box that can be obtained by pressing Ctrl+L in the debugging environment. Notice how in Visual Basic's event-driven model, an event always is at the top of the calls list. Therefore, as mentioned previously, having an error handler in all events with code ensures that all errors are trapped.

Fig. 14.1
Example of Visual
Basic, searching
through the active
Calls list.

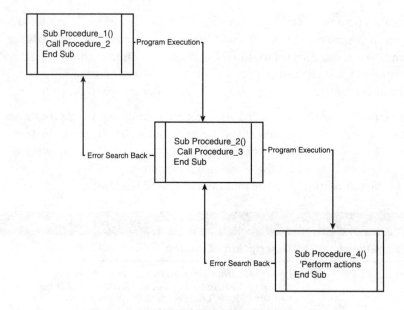

Fig. 14.2
The Calls dialog
box, showing the
active Calls list.

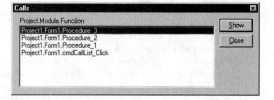

At this point, the program execution continues in Procedure_1's error-handler
routine. Assume that Procedure_1's error handler looks like Listing 14.2 example found on the companion disk, in directory \CHAP14.

**Listing 14.2   CODE02.TXT—Using Resume within the Visual Basic
Calls list**

```
Sub Procedure_1()
On Error GoTo Procedure_1_ErrHndr
    'declare the return code variable

    Dim liRtnCd As Integer

    liRtnCd = Procedure_2()

    MsgBox "Procedure 2 returned: " & liRtnCd

    Exit Sub
```

```
'Define Error Handler
Procedure_1_ErrHndlr:
    '
    'error processing code
    '

    'Resume execution at the next statement
    Resume

End Sub
```

In this example, after the error handler performs its action, program execution then proceeds to the statement that calls the procedure that was last searched. In this example, the call to Procedure_2 will be executed again. This isn't the statement that originally caused the run-time error because we know, based on the example, that the error occurred within Procedure_3.

Look at the effect on the program execution of changing the error handler in Procedure_1 to use a Resume Next statement rather than the Resume, using Listing 14.3, found on the companion disk, in directory \CHAP14.

Listing 14.3   CODE03.TXT—Using Resume Next within the Calls list

```
Sub Procedure_1()
On Error GoTo Procedure_1_ErrHndr
    'declare the return code variable

    Dim liRtnCd As Integer

    liRtnCd = Procedure_2()

    MsgBox "Procedure 2 returned: " & liRtnCd

    Exit Sub

'Define Error Handler
Procedure_1_ErrHndlr:
    '
    'error processing code
    '

    'Resume execution at the next statement
    Resume Next

End Sub
```

In this case, program execution continues with the statement immediately following the call to Procedure_2. The MsgBox statement is executed and produces a result that may not be expected.

As you can see, allowing Visual Basic to search back through the active call list to find an enabled error handler increases the complexity of your error processing. In some situations, this type of error processing makes sense—when a procedure is being called by multiple events and procedures, for example, and each needs to react to a run-time error in a slightly different manner.

The Visual Basic Error Object (Err)

Visual Basic 4.0 introduces a new object for use in error processing, the Err object. To fully exploit this new object, you must understand all the properties and methods associated with it.

Err Object Methods

Table 14.2 describes the methods associated with the Visual Basic Error (Err) object.

Table 14.2	Methods of the Err Object
Method	**Action**
Clear	Clears all property settings for the object. The method is called by default whenever a *Resume, Resume Next, Exit,* or *On Error* statement is encountered.
Raise	Generates a run-time error programmatically. Useful for creating user-defined errors and when generating errors from within OLE Automation server objects. Provides the capability to identify the actual source of the error, and the capability to link help topics to the error.

The Raise method of the Err object has a number of optional parameters. If this method is called without these parameters, the current property values of the Err object are used for the raised error.

Err Object Properties

Table 14.3 describes the properties of the Err object.

Table 14.3	Properties of the Err Object
Property	**Description**
Description	Returns or sets descriptive text associated with an error. If a description isn't supplied, and the error number associates to a predefined Visual Basic error, the text associated with the most recent error (the same as is returned by the Error function) is contained in this property.

Property	Description
HelpContext	Returns or sets the context ID for a help file. Uses the value of the HelpFile property to determine the location of the help file to be referenced. If an error occurs and this property isn't set, the error number is checked and, if it associates to a Visual Basic error, the HelpContext that is associated with this error is placed in this property.
HelpFile	Returns or sets path to a Windows help file. The help file specified is called when the user clicks the Help button on an error message box. If the HelpContext property is set, that topic is displayed. If the HelpFile property isn't set, the Visual Basic help file is displayed.
LastDLLError	Available only for 32-bit Windows systems. Returns system error code produced by a call to a dynamic link library.
Number	Err object's default property. Returns or sets the numeric value associated with an error.
Source	Returns or sets the name of the application or object that encountered the error.

When programming other objects, using the HelpContext property to associate errors with the object's help file enhances the features of your application's error handling.

Visual Basic Error Functions

Visual Basic also includes a number of functions that can be used for error processing. Table 14.4 describes these functions.

Table 14.4   Visual Basic Error-Processing Functions

Function	Description
CVErr	Creates user-defined errors that you associate with application specific errors.
IsError	Indicates whether or not an expression evaluates to an error. Only meaningful for variants of *VarType vbError*.
Stop	Stops execution of the application. In the Visual Basic development environment, Stop performs like a breakpoint. In the run-time environment, Stop performs like the End function.

In-Line Error Handling

As you can see from the preceding sections, Visual Basic has a fairly robust exception-handling mechanism.

Many of today's programming languages, such as generic C, do not support error processing through the use of exceptions—the interruption of execution when an error is encountered. These languages instead implement an in-line process of handling errors, where success of each procedure call is checked after execution to ensure that no errors occurred.

In Visual Basic, implementing in-line error handling is essentially the same as bypassing the error handler and manually checking for errors after each statement.

The most common example of in-line error handling in Visual Basic occurs in applications that employ calls to external DLL functions or APIs. If a Visual Basic program employs the functionality provided by the Windows API, for example, errors that occur within these external functions are discovered by checking the return value of the call.

There are three main approaches to implementing in-line error handling within Visual Basic:

- Develop functions and statements that return values indicating successful execution or that a specific error has occurred

- Allow Visual Basic to raise an error in the procedure where the error occurred, and handle it in an in-line manner

- Develop functions that return a variant value to indicate to the calling procedure that an error occurred

When in-line error handling is used, the exact statement or function call that generated the error is known. Exception-based error handling, as we have seen, allows the application to determine which procedure or event encountered the run-time error, but you don't always know the exact statement that generated the error. The ability to know the specific statement can help you when dealing with OLE Automation objects, because a more meaningful error handler or message may be created.

Using Function Return Values

The first technique for implementing in-line error handling is to have all functions and statements trap errors and return a value that indicates the result of its execution. This technique works well when you are developing functions and procedures that will be called from multiple procedures and events. The method ensures that all run-time errors are trapped within the procedure but gives the calling procedure the flexibility to react to the error as it sees appropriate.

In this case, the called procedure's error handler traps the error, and the calling procedure's error handler never sees an error until it checks the return value.

The example in Listing 14.4 demonstrates in-line error processing using function return values. In this example, the function DivideNumbers accepts three parameters, the numerator for the division, the denominator for the division, and a place to store the result. The function returns –1 to indicate the division was successful. If a run-time error is encountered, the error number associated with the error is returned. The following example can be found on the companion disk, in directory \CHAP14.

Listing 14.4   CODE04.TXT—Inline error handling, using return values

```
Const SUCCESS = -1
Const FAIL = 0

Function DivideNumbers(aiNumerator As Integer,
➥aiDenominator As Integer,_
 ByRef adResult As Double) As Integer
On Error GoTo DivideNumbers_ErrHndlr

    adResult = aiNumerator / aiDenominator

    'return status of success
    DivideNumbers = SUCCESS

    Exit Function

' Define Error Handler
DivideNumbers_ErrHndlr:
    'return the error
    DivideNumbers = Err.Number
End Function

Dim liResult As Integer
Dim ldAnswer As Double

liResult = DivideNumbers(1, 0, ldAnswer)
If liResult <> SUCCESS Then
    '
    ' Handle the error
    '
End If

'continue application
```

Visual Basic Exception Handling

The second technique of implementing in-line error handling uses some of the Visual Basic error-processing facilities previously discussed.

In the example in Listing 14.5, the On Error Resume Next statement is used to tell Visual Basic to ignore any raised error and proceed immediately to the next statement in the procedure. This is an in-line error handler because, when a run-time error occurs, an exception is raised but the program execution doesn't jump to an error handler. To determine if an error has occurred, the program must continually check the value of the Err object's number property. To find this code, go to the directory \CHAP14, on this book's companion disk.

Listing 14.5   CODE05.TXT—Inline error handling, using On Error Resume Next

```
Const SUCCESS = 0
Const FAIL = 1

Function DivideNumbers(aiNumerator As Integer,
➥ aiDenominator As Integer) As Double

    'divide the numbers and return the result
    DivideNumbers = aiNumerator / aiDenominator

End Function
Dim ldAnswer As Double

'if an error occurs proceed to the next statement
On Error Resume Next

ldAnswer = DivideNumbers(1, 0)
If Err.Number <> SUCCESS Then
    '
    ' Handle the error
    '
End If

'continue applications
```

Returning Variants

The third technique of implementing in-line error handling also uses the error-processing facilities available in Visual Basic. The Visual Basic *Variant* data type has a tag that indicates the type of data actually contained within the variable. By using the error-processing functions discussed previously, you can set the tag of a variant to indicate that it is a Visual Basic error code.

This allows you to develop procedures that use the return code to pass back either the result of the function or an error code.

In Listing 14.6, Visual Basic's CvErr() function is used to return a user-defined error to the calling procedure. The DivideNumbers function accepts a numerator and denominator as arguments and returns a variant value that represents either the result of the division, or the error that occurred. The CVErr function is used to tag the variant as an error value. The calling procedure uses the IsError function to determine if the returned value represents the result, or a run-time error. You can find this code on this book's companion disk, in directory \CHAP14.

Listing 14.6   CODE06.TXT—Inline error handling, using the Variant error tag

```
Function DivideNumbers(aiNumerator As Integer,
➥ aiDenominator As Integer) As Variant
On Error GoTo DivideNumbers_ErrHnldr

    'divide the numbers and return the result
    DivideNumbers = aiNumerator / aiDenominator

    Exit Function

DivideNumbers_ErrHndlr:
    'convert the error code to a tagged variant
    DivideNumbers = CVErr(Err.Number)
End Function
Dim lvAnswer As Variant

lvAnswer = DivideNumbers(1, 0)
If IsError(lvAnswer) Then
    '
    ' Handle the error
    '
End If

'continue application specific code
```

Handling Errors in Client Applications

When developing client applications, there are two major categories of errors that need to be handled:

■ Run-time errors that occur within the client application.

■ OLE Automation errors that are returned from OLE objects referenced by the client application.

Client applications are responsible for handling several activities when one of the preceding types of errors occur:

1. Notify the end user of the error and any corrective action that they can take.

2. Gracefully handle unexpected errors that cannot be corrected.

3. Gracefully terminate the application for fatal errors.

End-User Notification

When a client application encounters an error, an attempt should be made to recover from the error. If it is determined that the error cannot be handled internally, the application should inform the end user of the error encountered. When appropriate, users should be given information about corrective actions that they can take to help the application in recovering from the error.

The information displayed to the user should be meaningful. For example, if an application tries to read a file from a floppy disk and receives a media error—indicating that a disk may not be in the drive—the user should be told and given an opportunity to correct the problem. Here, the user is more likely to recover if given a message like the example shown in figure 14.3.

Fig. 14.3
An informative
error message.

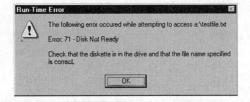

Unlike figure 14.3, figure 14.4 displays a more technical message.

Fig. 14.4
A technical error
message.

Graceful Application Recovery

Unfortunately, the client application often cannot recover from a run-time error, even with the assistance of the end user. In these situations, the application still is responsible for proper "cleanup."

The following section looks at some tasks that should be performed to ensure that the application terminates gracefully in the event of an unrecoverable run-time error.

Closing Referenced Object Applications

During normal termination, an application that references an OLE Automation object exposed by another application will release all references to that object. Abnormal termination of the application should attempt to do the same.

This process often can be accomplished with the creation of a special *CleanUp* or close procedure that is called from every error handler before the application terminates. The following example demonstrates this process for an application that has accessed a Microsoft Excel Worksheet object.

In Listing 14.7 the CloseAppObj function performs all the OLE Automation cleanup needed when our application terminates. If during execution of the application, the WorkBookShow procedure encounters a run-time error, the user first is given the chance to try to correct the situation. If the user cannot help, the application terminates after calling the CloseAppObj procedure to handle OLE Automation cleanup. You can find the code on this book's companion disk, in directory \CHAP14:

Listing 14.7   CODE07.TXT—Sample OLE Automation cleanup procedure

```
Sub CloseAppObj ()
'Closes the application object found in the global AppObj variable
'Shuts down the instance of Excel if there are
'no other workbooks open.

On Error Resume Next

    'clear clipboard to avoid Excel "save large clipboard" msg
    clipboard.Clear

    'Close excel if no workbooks are present
    If AppObj.workbooks.Count < 1 Then
        AppObj.Quit
    End If
```

(continues)

Listing 14.7 Continued

```
        Set AppObj = Nothing

End Sub

Sub WorkBookShow (workbook As Object)

'Prepares a workbook for VB OLE manipulation.
Dim ResCode As Integer

On Error GoTo WorkBookShow_Error

    WorkBookShow_Try:

    'disallow user interaction
    workbook.application.interactive = False

    workbook.Windows(1).activate
    workbook.Windows(1).Visible = True

Exit Sub

'ole automation error. Give the user a chance to help us out.
WorkBookShow_Error:

    ResCode = MsgBox("Cannot access Microsoft Excel. _
            Please make sure Excel isn't displaying any dialog _
            boxes or editing any cells. (" & CStr(Err) & _
            ")", vbRetyrCancel + vbExclamation, _
            "OLE Automation Problem")

    If ResCode = vbCancel Then
        'user hit the cancel button so give up
        Call CloseAppObj
        End
    Else
        'the user wants to retry.
        Resume WorkBookShow_Try
    End If

End Sub
```

Closing Your Application

Besides closing all references to external OLE Automation objects, the application also is responsible for ensuring that it properly closes itself down. When a run-time error is encountered from which the application cannot recover, the application should gracefully end at this point to ensure that further harm is not done.

Again, the termination of the application is best handled by making modifications to the CleanUp procedure, described in the previous section. These additions should include actions necessary to ensure that the integrity of the application and its data are maintained.

The following example demonstrates modifications that may be needed for the Excel example previously described (see Listing 14.8). In this case, the application also has accessed a Microsoft Access database. To ensure that our database doesn't become corrupt, it is important to properly close all open connections to it before terminating the application. The code that follows is on this book's companion disk, in directory \CHAP14.

Listing 14.8 CODE08.TXT—Sample application data access cleanup procedure

```
Sub CloseAppObj ()
'Closes the application object found in the global AppObj variable
'Closes the connection to the database found in the global CurDB
'variable. Shuts down the instance of Excel if there are no other
'workbooks open.
On Error Resume Next

    'clear clipboard to avoid Excel "save large clipboard" msg
    clipboard.Clear

    'Close excel if no workbooks are present
    If AppObj.workbooks.Count < 1 Then
        AppObj.Quit
    End If

    Set AppObj = Nothing

    'Close the database
    CurDB.Close

End Sub

Sub WorkBookShow (workbook As Object)

'Prepares a workbook for VB OLE manipulation.
 Dim ResCode As Integer

On Error GoTo WorkBookShow_Error

    WorkBookShow_Try:

    'disallow user interaction
    workbook.application.interactive = False

    workbook.Windows(1).activate
    workbook.Windows(1).Visible = True
```

(continues)

```
  Listing 14.8   Continued

    Exit Sub

    'ole automation error. Give the user a chance to help us out.
    WorkBookShow_Error:

        ResCode = MsgBox("Cannot access Microsoft Excel. _
                    Please make sure Excel isn't displaying any _
                    dialog boxes or editing any cells.
                    (" & CStr(Err) & ")", vbRetyrCancel + vbExclamation, _
                     "OLE Automation Problem")

        If ResCode = vbCancel Then
            'user hit the cancel button so give up
            Call CloseAppObj
            End
        Else
            'the user wants to retry.
            Resume WorkBookShow_Try
        End If

    End Sub
```

Handling Errors in OLE Server Applications

As discussed in detail in Chapters 6, "Creating OLE Objects," and 8, "Architecting Tier 1: Client Applications," Visual Basic 4.0 provides the capability to create OLE Automation servers.

Now that Visual Basic can create reusable OLE objects, you need to know how to handle a new class of applications errors—object errors that will be passed back to a calling application.

The types of errors that will be encountered, shown in the following list, are similar to those found in Visual Basic client applications:

- Run-time errors which occur within your OLE applications.

- OLE Automation errors that are returned from OLE objects referenced by your application.

- Business Logic errors that occur in OLE business servers.

OLE Automation server objects encounter run-time errors (such as operating system or remote data object errors), just like client applications do. These objects have the same basic responsibilities in regard to error processing as client applications. The main difference is that the "end user" of an OLE Automation server object is a controlling application, not a person.

This distinction means that OLE Automation servers need to take additional care in the manner in which they identify errors, pass them to the calling procedure, and alert the controlling application to the problem.

The OLE server should map each error type to an error that is passed back to the controlling application. Table 14.5 describes how errors should be mapped when passed back to the controlling application.

Table 14.5   Mapping Errors from OLE Automation Servers

Type of Error	Error Mapping
Error encountered in server application	Application-specific error code raised to controlling application
Run-time error	Internal error constant and the actual run-time error
OLE Automation error	Internal error constant and the OLE automation error (always 440)
Business error	Application-specific business error constant

Business error values and constants defined to represent application internal errors values must be greater than 600. Visual Basic uses the values 0 to 600 to define its internal errors.

Run-time and OLE Automation errors that are encountered within an OLE server should return error values as descriptive as possible to the controlling applications. This process provides the controlling application developers with more understanding of the error that occurred and allows them to more easily debug the error.

While the *Err.Number* property should be reassigned to indicate that the error came from the OLE server, the other Err object properties (description, source, and so on) should be left as they are. Leaving these values intact gives the controlling application developer additional information when debugging the error.

Object-Specific Run-Time Errors

When an OLE Automation server encounters a standard run-time error such as File Not Found, it should be passed back to the calling function as an internal error. This technique assists developers who are incorporating this object into other applications to determine where the error actually occurred.

Listing 14.9 demonstrates how an OLE Automation server might handle an unexpected error by first assigning a generic "Internal Error" number to it, while keeping the text of the original error. At a minimum, the Visual Basic constant, vbObjectError, should be added to the internal error constant to indicate that the error was generated from within a VB object. You can find this code on the companion disk, in directory \CHAP14.

Listing 14.9   CODE09.TXT—An example of redefining a run-time error within an OLE Automation server

```
Sub FileOpen(ByVal lsFileName As String)
'this procedure attempts to open a file within a OLE server
On Error GoTo FileOpen_ErrHnldr:


    '
    'perform operations of file
    '


    Exit Sub

FileOpen_ErrHndlr:
'determine what type or error occurred
Select Case Err.Number
    Case 53 ' File not found
        '
        'attempt to recover from an expected error
        '
    Case Else
        'remap the error code
        Err.Raise Number:=vbObjectError + ERR_INTERNAL
End Select
'Clear the error object
Err.Clear

Resume Next

End Sub
```

OLE Automation Error Received from Referenced Objects

OLE Automation servers can reference other OLE Automation servers to perform tasks, such as custom created business objects or RDO objects. This means that OLE Servers, such as business servers, need to handle errors encountered within referenced objects.

To remain consistent with the method of passing errors from OLE automation servers to the controlling applications, errors encountered within an OLE Automation server that are the result of a referenced object should be remapped and passed to the controlling applications.

The remapping of the error, as described previously, should include the assignment of a generic "Internal Error" number, which allows the calling application to handle the error without needing to know too much about where the error occurred. The error description should contain the details of the error, including an indication of the problem encountered by the referenced object.

Returning Business Errors

Business server objects that you create by definition introduce another type of error that needs to be accounted for, the violation of "business rules." These rules consist of organization-specific rules, such as the following:

- Order cannot be created if inventory isn't currently in stock.

- Order cannot be canceled if it has already been shipped.

- Customer may not order products for which they do not have a pricing contract on file.

In these situations, the object should return a business error to the calling application. *Business errors* look like any other error to the calling application, but they don't necessarily correspond to a run-time error within the OLE object.

Defining custom business errors specific to the business server object allows many of the advanced error-processing features to be leveraged. Context help can be associated with a business error that allows the user to get a better understanding of the error that occurred and the actions to take to correct it.

To implement context-sensitive help, both the HelpFile and HelpContext properties of the Err object must be set. If both properties are set, the user can press F1 and the help topic associated with the context ID appears on-screen. Some host applications, such as Microsoft Excel, add a *Help* button to the message box by default. Clicking the Help button produces the same result as using the F1 key.

Chapter 15, "Adding Help to an Application," goes into the details of associating a help file with error messages returned by an OLE automation server.

Listing 14.10 demonstrates the concept of a custom business error that you may find in an order processing application. In this example, the CancelOrder procedure tries to change the status of a specific order to *Canceled*. The procedure first checks the current status of the order to ensure that it was not already shipped. If the order was shipped, the business rules state that it cannot be canceled. This results in the generation of a custom business error. This code can be found on the companion disk, in directory \CHAP14.

Listing 14.10   CODE10.TXT—Example of returning a custom business error

```
Sub CancelOrder(ByVal OrderNum As Integer)
'Procedure will attempt to cancel the order specified by
'the OrderNum argument.

Dim liRtnCode As Integer     'Holds procedure return code

'check to ensure that the order has not already shipped
liRtnCode = IsOrderShipped(OrderNum)
If liRtnCode Then
    'the order has already shipped, cannot be canceled.
    Err.Raise Number:=ERR_ORDER_SHIPPED, Description:=
    ➥"Cannot Cancel a shipped order."
    Exit Sub
Else
    'the order has not shipped, continue with cancel.
    Call UpdateOrderStatus(STATUS_CANCEL)
End If

End Sub
```

Handling Fatal Errors

OLE Servers, like client applications, encounter unrecoverable "fatal runtime" errors that require the object instance to terminate. A fatal error is a run-time error that the developer never anticipated, and therefore didn't provide specific code to handle.

OLE automation servers have the same fatal error cleanup responsibilities as a client application with the additional responsibility for cleaning up connections to all additional clients.

OLE automation servers that accommodate multiple controlling applications need to ensure that when an unrecoverable error occurs, all clients with active references are informed, and connections are closed without damaging the integrity of the controlling applications.

Reusable Code: Error Logging Class

OLE business and data servers usually reside on a server machine—never directly seen by an end user. The visibility to errors that occur within these objects is dependent upon the manner in which the errors are passed back to the controlling application and the way the controlling application then handles them.

But a business or data server should not rely exclusively on the controlling application to handle its internal errors. End users don't administer servers, IT does. So IT should have visibility to server errors.

To ensure that all the information about a particular error isn't lost, OLE automation servers should include a mechanism that logs the information about all errors encountered. This could be as simple a creating a flat file that contains the pertinent information, or a more complex solution that leverages the features of the operating system on which it resides.

Provided with the sample code is an error-logging class module that implements the first method of error logging previously mentioned—writing to a log file. Table 14.6 describes the functions available within this class module. A similar module could be developed that allows 32-bit applications to place events in the Windows NT event log.

Table 14.6 **Error Logging Functions in VBLogErr**	
Function	**Description**
Event_LogMsg	Writes a message to the error file
Event_LogFatalErr	Writes a message to the error file that describes the error that occurred, and triggers the application to end

From Here...

This chapter covered the various ways to handle errors encountered within a Visual Basic application. This chapter covered using specific features of Visual Basic, such as the On Error Goto construct, as well as more traditional error-handling methods, such as in-line error handling. As you can see, taking time to design a solid error-processing architecture that can be used by all developers results in more solid and maintainable applications.

For further information related to topics covered in this chapter, see the following:

- Chapter 6, "Creating OLE Objects," provides more information about creating an OLE Automation server.

- Chapter 9, "Architecting Tier 2: Business Servers," provides more information about designing and creating a business server.

- Chapter 15, "Adding Help to an Application," provides details about associating a help file with your application.

Chapter 15

Adding Help to an Application

As client applications become more and more feature-rich, they increase in complexity. With this increase in complexity comes a necessity for easily accessible on-line documentation that clearly describes the use of these client applications.

The goals of this chapter are to:

- Show how to effectively design and create a Windows help file

- Show how to link the help file to your application

- Detail a type of help that is often overlooked during application development—inline commenting of code

The Elements of On-Line Help

Like paper documentation, on-line help files provide a valuable aid to users by accomplishing the following goals:

- Offering "How to" instruction

- Explaining terms, commands, and procedures used within the context of an application

- Providing real-life demos and examples

- Clearly and concisely defining and making accessible key terms

Figure 15.1 shows a Windows help file.

Fig. 15.1
A Windows help
file.

Many applications now ship with on-line documentation in place of printed manuals. Help files can aide in support of an application by providing answers to technical questions previously answered by help desk personnel.

Just as standards for Windows applications have developed over the years, standards for help systems also have appeared. Users have come to expect help files to accompany client applications.

Creating a Help File

On-line help can be as simple as a form created in Visual Basic, displayed when a user clicks a help button.

Most applications developed for the enterprise, however, require a more robust, full-featured help system. To manage and display these advanced help files, Windows includes its help engine, WinHelp (WINHELP.EXE and/or WINHELP32.EXE). This application can manage help files that contain multiple fonts and colors, and provide indexing and search capabilities. Most commercial applications use the Windows help engine to display help files.

Understanding these tools is important, but providing complete instructions on using these tools is beyond the scope of this book. This chapter focuses on how to develop a Window help file, rather than how to use these tools.

Using the New Help Features in Windows 95

Windows 95 adds several features to the Windows help engine and improves on features in the Windows 3.1 help engine. These features make help easier for all users to access.

The most notable new features in Windows 95 are the help Contents screen shown in Figure 15.1, which now has an Explorer-type look and feel, and the Index/Find window shown in figure 15.2. The Index/Find system replaces the Search window used in previous versions of Windows help systems.

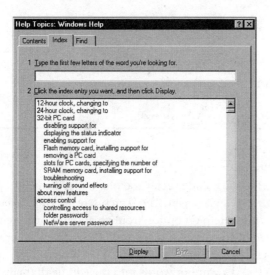

Fig. 15.2
The Windows 95 Index/Find screen.

Each new feature is discussed in this chapter. Additionally, because of the improvements offered by the Windows 95 help engine, this chapter focuses on building and manipulating help files by using the new engine, and discusses Windows 3.1 help files only when necessary.

Help files created under Windows 3.1 are converted automatically to Windows 95 help files the first time they are accessed. Help files compiled under the WIN31.EXE help compiler, however, retain the Windows 3.1-style Contents screen shown in figure 15.3. The search window is updated to the Windows 95 Index window style.

Fig. 15.3

The Contents screen of a Window help file, created with the Windows 3.1 help compiler.

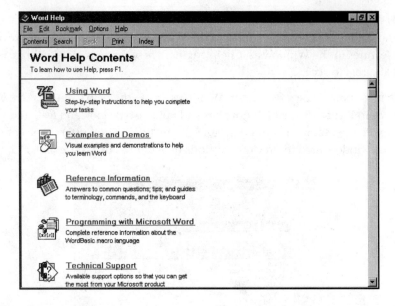

The Index Window

In Windows 3.1x, you could quickly look for a specific help topic within a help file using the Search screen. The Search screen is displayed if you selected the Search for Help on option from an application's Help menu. This option consisted of an edit field at the top of the screen, where you could type the subject you were looking for, and a list box near the center of the screen. As you typed a word or words into the edit field, the list box would display help topics that matched these words. You could select a help topic from the list box, and move immediately to it in the Help file.

In Windows 95, a similar technique is used. The Index screen displays a list of all index entries contained within the compiled Help file. You can type a word or words in the edit box at the top of the Index screen. As you type, the list box at the bottom portion of the screen displays index entries that match any words you type in the edit box. When you click an entry in the list box, the Help file displays a help topic or a list of help topics that correspond to the index entry you select.

The Index screen provides a simple way for a user to quickly find and move to a help topic. When you compile a help file, the elements that make up the Index screen are automatically created.

The Find Window

A second useful feature of the Windows 95 Help engine is the Find screen. As in the Index screen, you can use the Find screen to move directly to a specific help topic that you select. However, the Find screen doesn't limit you to words that are found in the Help file's Index.

When you access a Help file's find screen for the first time, the Help file runs the Find Setup Wizard. You use the Find Setup Wizard to create a database containing all the words that are contained within the Help file. The database allows you to search for Help topics by typing using words and phrases. You are not limited to entries that were made in the Help file's index.

You have three options when creating the database. You can create a database of minimum size, which enables you to perform searches with words and phrases, but you may not find every match for the information you entered.

You can choose to maximize your search capabilities, which causes the Find Setup Wizard to create a large, inclusive list of help topics. When you perform subsequent finds, your query probably will return the maximum number of help topics related to the words or phrases that you type. A Find database built for maximized search capabilities allows you to search for all of the items shown in Table 15.1.

Finally, you can customize the build of your Find database. The Find Setup Wizard takes you through the steps needed to build the Find database. You can choose the options outlined in Table 15.1.

Table 15.1 Options Available When Creating a Custom Find Database	
Option	**Description**
File To Include	If the application uses multiple Help files, you can select which file to include in the Find database.
Untitled Topics	Many Help files include untitled topics. These usually are pop-up definitions that do not include titles because the author of the Help file did not want them displayed in the Index list. These help topics may be of little use.
Phrase Searching	Allows you to search for complete phrases in the Help file, for example, to search for a person's first and last name.
Display Phrases	Instructs the Find screen to display matching phrases as you begin to type them. This feature is similar to the type-ahead feature of the edit box on the Index screen.
Similarity Search	Allows you to mark found items in the database. You can later search the database for information related to the marked items.

You use the Find screen much like the Index screen. In the edit box, *Type the word(s) you want to find*. The Help engine then searches through the Find database and lists help topics that match your criteria in the list box, *Click a topic, then click Display*. If you select one of the help topics listed in this box and click Display, the help topic you selected is displayed.

You can select keywords listed in the *Select some matching words to narrow your search* list box to limit the number of help topics displayed. You also can click the checkbox to the left of help topic, then click the Find Similar button to display help topics that nearly match the help topic you selected.

The Find screen is a powerful addition to the Windows Help engine, and all of its features are available without additional programming from a Help file developer.

Tools You Need to Create a Help File

To create a help file that the Windows help engine can interpret, you need a help compiler. Visual Basic includes a help compiler (HC.EXE), which you use to compile text documents into help files. These compiled files are in turn interpreted by the Windows help engine and accessed from Visual Basic applications. The Visual Basic SETUP program places the compiler in the \HC subdirectory of the Visual Basic directory. This directory contains all files that the help Compiler requires.

Besides a help compiler, you need an application that can create and save documents in Rich Text Format (RTF). When a file is saved in RTF, its formatting is converted to instructions that other applications, including the Windows help Compiler, can read and interpret. Many word processors, such as Microsoft Word and WordPerfect, support RTF.

Third-party help authoring tools, which are discussed in following sections of this chapter, allow you to create help files by using standard Microsoft Word file formats rather than RTF files. When the files are ready to be compiled, the authoring tools translate the standard format files into RTF files.

Designing the Help File

After you have the necessary tools, you can begin the next step in help file development—planning your help system. As with any application, careful planning up front saves development time and results in a higher quality product.

Understanding the Audience

The first step in planning a help file is understanding the types of users who will use it. Help file users can be placed into one of the following four categories:

- **New to computers.** This user has little or no experience with computers or Windows applications. The user requires a step-by-step help approach. Definitions of key words and terms must be defined within help topics so that the user is not required to extensively navigate the help system.

- **New to application.** This user is familiar with Windows applications but is new to this specific application. This user also benefits from a step-by-step approach, but will focus on using the help system to understand new terms and techniques.

- **Experienced with application.** This user has some experience with the application. The user will avoid the step-by-step approach in favor of directly accessing detailed information about unfamiliar terms and techniques.

- **Expert with application.** This user has extensive experience with computers and the application. The user employs the help system to learn about new features of the product. The on-line help system allows this user type to locate information faster than paper-based documentation.

Most applications have users that fit into several of these categories. The key to a well-designed help system is satisfying the needs of all of these users, which includes providing quick access to help for the more experienced user while providing intuitive, step-by-step features for the novice user. Both of these needs can be accomplished with a single help file through careful planning.

Planning the Contents of a Help System

Once the client application audience is understood, the next step in designing the help file is planning its contents. This planning includes the following:

- Determining which help Categories appear on the Contents screen

- Determining help Topics

- Determining Search Criteria

To understand how to properly plan a help file, you need to understand the standard methods of help file navigation and the terms used to describe the various elements of the Help system. After laying out the terms, this chapter discusses how to assemble the Help file.

When a help file is run from Visual Basic, the help file's *Contents* screen appears. Figure 15.1 showed a Windows help file's Contents screen.

A *help topic* is a document or collection of documents that answers a specific question about the application such as, "How do I save a file?" or "What does the OK button do?"

When an item in the Contents Window displays a book icon to the left of its text, it contains additional help topics below it. Double-clicking the item displays the items *subtopics*, or collection of related topics.

The lowest level of the help file hierarchy is indicated by a help topic with a question mark icon. Figure 15.4 shows the complete help file hierarchy.

Fig. 15.4

The complete Windows help file hierarchy.

When a user double-clicks the lowest level help topic, a help document with detailed information on the help topic appears outside of the Contents window. Figure 15.5 shows the lowest-level help document. Besides text, this window may contain references to related help topics, which can be accessed directly from the window.

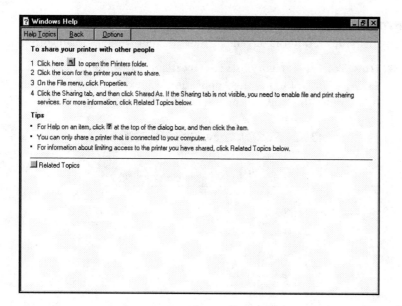

IV

Application Enhancements

Fig. 15.5
The lowest level help document provides detailed information about a selected help topic. Clicking on Related Topics displays a list of associated details.

Selecting the Help Categories

As you learned previously in this chapter, help categories are logical group-ings of help topics contained in the help file. Help categories can be listed on the Contents screen in any order but generally are displayed either alphabeti-cally or categorically.

Because experienced users usually bypass the Contents screen when using help in favor of more advanced help navigation methods, the best choice is to develop a Contents screen that suits novice and less experienced users.

Arranging the categories on the Contents screen by function, rather than alphabetically, provides new users with a more intuitive overview of the help file. Because your help system also will include a search screen and an index, more experienced users can search the help topics alphabetically.

The new Windows 95 Contents screen is consistent with other drill-down search windows in Windows 95, such as the Explorer window. The benefit of this consistency is that after users understand how to use a drill-down search window, they understand how to use the many search windows employed by Windows 95.

Additionally, the Windows 95 Contents screen improves over Windows 3.1 Contents screen by allowing a user to examine the help topics under many categories at once. Under Windows 3.1, it was only possible to drill-down through a single help category at a time.

Sample Help Categories

Many help files' Contents screens include the following four categories:

- **How To.** This category lists step-by-step instruction topics, such as Saving a File or Exiting the Application. Figure 15.6 shows the topics listed under the How To category of the Windows 95 help file.

Fig. 15.6
Sample topics of the How To help category.

- **Reference.** This category lists help topics that describe how specific controls in the application work, such as the help Menu or the Save button, and also topics that define terms used in the application, such as *alignment* or *data source*.

- **Tips.** This category lists topics that users find useful for simplifying everyday tasks in the application, such as an explanation on viewing the status of a print job. Figure 15.7 shows some sample topics for the Tips category.

- **Technical Support.** This category will contain a list of persons to contact for assistance with the application. Optionally, this list may be categorized by application area.

Because these categories should allow for virtually any help topic to be added below one of them, they should be included in every help file. Doing so minimizes the need to add additional help categories.

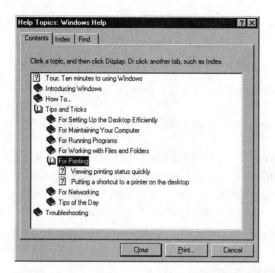

Fig. 15.7
Sample topics for
the Tips help
category.

Creating a large number of help categories makes it difficult for inexperienced users to locate the help topic that they need to find. Making use of
these four categories provides the most benefit to less experienced users by
simplifying the Contents screen.

Selecting the Help Topics

After selecting your help categories, it is useful to create an outline that shows
which help topics will appear beneath each category and which subtopics
appear beneath each of these topics. A well-designed outline simplifies the
process of creating the text for your help topics later. Figure 15.8 shows a
sample help topic outline, using the some of the categories defined in the
previous section.

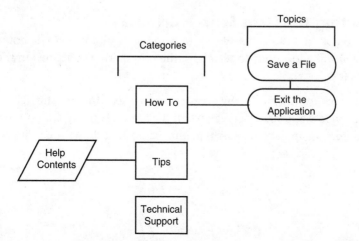

Fig. 15.8
A sample topic
outline.

When creating your help topic outline, you need to determine the following information:

- What topics to include

- What information the user is permitted to search on

These two items complete the planning phase of your help file.

Building the Topic Hierarchy

By determining what topics appear beneath each category in your help file, you build a Topic Hierarchy. As you can see in figure 15.8, the Topic Hierarchy you are creating resembles the Contents screen of a Windows help file.

You should create new topics to explain any procedures regularly completed by the user (such as exiting the application and saving files); to define key terms used in the application ("What is a widget?"); or to explain the functions of the application's menu items and controls (Help Menu, OK button, and so on).

Although you usually shouldn't add new categories to the Topic Hierarchy, you should add subtopic groupings (topics within topics) to the help outline if you create two or more help topics that can be easily grouped together. If you create the new topic, for example, "Opening a Single File," and a second topic, "Opening Multiple Files," then creating a new topic, "Opening Files," and placing the other two as subtopics below this new topic in the outline makes sense.

Because most novice users can easily access help through the *Contents* screen and traverse down the topic hierarchy, you should limit the number of levels below a category to no more than three. This limit prevents these users from getting lost in the hierarchy.

Selecting the Help Search Criteria

After you outline the various levels of help topics, you need to determine how you will allow users to search for the information contained in the help topic's text.

Users search for help topics by accessing the Index window. The help file's Index window appears on-screen when the Search For help On option is selected from an application's help menu. Figure 15.9 shows the Index window.

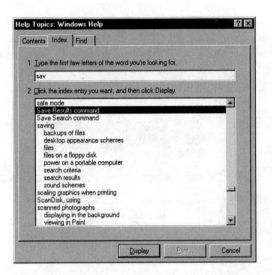

Fig. 15.9
The Windows 95
help Index
window.

This window contains two main controls: a text box at the top of the screen for entering keywords and a list box at the center of the control that displays the keywords that make up the help file's Index. As a user types a word in the search criteria text box, the Index window locates the entry in the help index that alphabetically matches what the user types. When a user clicks on an Index entry in the list portion of the search window, the help topic or topics associated with the entry are displayed. As users become more familiar with navigating the help file, they may choose to access help topics directly through the Index window, rather than moving the Contents screen's categories and subtopics.

When planning search criteria and building your applications index, look at the topics in the help outline and determine which words a user might search for to access a topic. These words are known as *keywords*.

For example, when trying to determine how to save a file to disk, a user probably would search for the word, *Save*. So, Save is an obvious choice for a keyword. But, a user also might search by using the words, *Store* or *Disk*. You should include each of these words as search criteria that leads a user to the help topic *Save*.

Keywords become part of your search criteria by including them in your help file's Index. For details on creating an Index in a help file, see your help authoring tool's documentation or your Visual Basic help documentation.

An additional search feature provided by Windows 95 is the Find feature. The Find window is displayed by clicking the Find folder tab on the Index window. Figure 15.10 shows the Find window.

Fig. 15.10
The Window's
Help File Find
window.

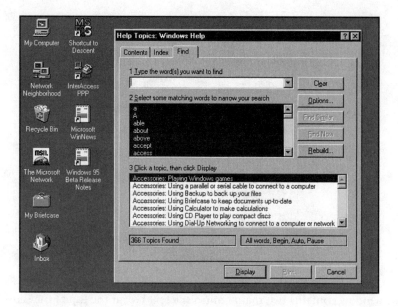

The Find feature allows a user to search for words or phrases within a help topic. The word or phrase may appear anywhere within the help topic, not just in the title. The database that the Find feature uses is built the first time a user accesses the Find window. This list is built from the topics you include in your help file. No additional development is required to use the Find feature under Windows 95.

The Help Browse Sequence

The Windows 3.1 help engine provided users with the option to read through the help file from beginning to end. This option was accomplished by implementing a *browse sequence* within the file. Because of the many new search features that were added to the Windows 95 help engine and the improved Contents screen, which allows a user to view several help topics simultaneously, browsing no longer is necessary in files compiled with the Windows 95 help compiler.

For backwards compatibility, help files created with the Windows 3.1 help compiler still display a browse sequence under Windows 95.

Adding Context-Sensitive Help

Experienced users expect to be able to access help on a control by pressing F1. This is known as *context-sensitive help*. For example, when the user presses F1 while a "customer" list box has the focus, the user expects a help screen on the "customer" list to appear.

Context-sensitive help allows the user to jump to an appropriate help topic with only one keystroke. If context-sensitive help is not included with an application, a user must access all help information by selecting items from the Help menu, and then manually search for the appropriate help topic.

Implementing context-sensitive help requires that each topic in the help file be assigned a *help context ID*. A help context ID is a number associated with each topic that is unique within the help file. Most third-party help authoring tools automatically assign each topic a unique ID. If you decide to author your help file with an RTF text editor, you must assign these IDs manually. The technique used to implement context-sensitive help in a Visual Basic application is detailed in a following part this chapter.

Although context-sensitive help saves time for end users, it requires more maintenance by developers. Help files need to be rewritten, recompiled and redistributed along with enhancements to the application. If a help topic, for example, is removed from the help file, the helpContextID of the associated control needs to be cleared.

Because context-sensitive help is not an apparent feature in Visual Basic programs, many novice end users don't realize that this powerful feature exists. When creating a help menu, you may want to create an additional item labeled "How to Use Context-Sensitive Help," which explains to the user how to use the F1 function key for context-sensitive help.

Compiling the Help File

Now that you carefully planned the design of your help file, you are ready to create and compile it. To create the text for each help topic you use a word processor program. The Windows help Compiler compiles only files that are saved in *Rich Text Format* (RTF). Word-processing applications such as Microsoft Word can save files in this format.

Much like Visual Basic code, the Windows help Compiler requires you to use special keywords and symbols when creating the RTF files. Figure 15.11 shows a typical RTF file.

Fig. 15.11

A sample RTF help
file.

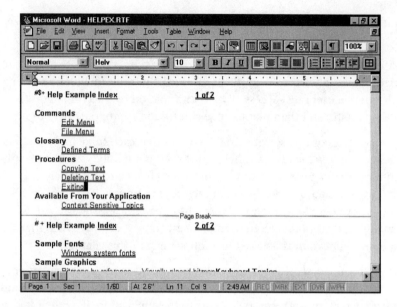

The specifics of formatting RTF help files are not discussed in this book. The
Visual Basic Professional Features manual devotes several chapters to help-file
creation. The information detailed therein is beyond the scope of this chapter. For details on the codes used when creating a compiled help file, see the
documentation included with Visual Basic.

Although you can create help files with an RTF text editor and the help compiler, it is strongly recommended that you use a third-party help authoring
tool. These add-ons to the help compiler speed and simplify help system
development, and they are worth their cost. A help authoring tool usually
works in conjunction with a word processor and allows you to create help
files, using standard word-processing commands and formats rather than
help compiler codes and RTF documents. These tools make it easy to accomplish tasks such as inserting graphics, creating an Index file, and assigning
context Ids. Additionally, most third-party tools compile the help file.

Preparing an Application to Access Help

After a help file is designed and created, you need to take the following several steps so the client application can access it:

1. Create a help menu for the application.

2. Specify the application's help file.

3. Specify the Windows help file.

4. Assign helpContextIDs for controls that will utilize context-sensitive help.

Creating a Help Menu

In all client applications, an item labeled help should be included in the main menu. The help menu item should appear at the right end of the menu bar and be assigned the H key as the *mnemonic accelerator* (or hot key). The help menu should contain five submenu items: Contents, Index, Search For help On, How to use help, and About. These items have the following functions:

Menu Item	Function
Contents	Displays the Contents screen of the help file. Should appear at the top of the help menu.
Search for Help on	Displays the WinHelp Search dialog box.
Index	Displays the help files Index, an alphabetical list of all help topics included in the file.
How To Use help	Displays a standard Windows help file that provides instructions on navigating a Windows help file.
About	Displays an About box, providing information about the version number and release date of the application. Should appear as the last item under the help menu and be separated from other items on the menu by a separator bar.

Figure 15.12 shows a standard help menu.

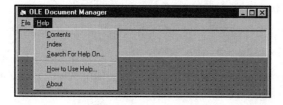

Fig. 15.12
A standard Help menu.

You use Visual Basic's Menu Editor to create the help menu. To build a standard help menu, perform the following steps:

1. Open the Menu Editor by selecting the Menu Editor option under Visual Basic's Tools menu. Figure 15.13 shows the Menu Editor.

Fig. 15.13
Visual Basic's
Menu editor.

2. Create the main menu title by typing **&Help** in the Caption text box and typing **mnuHelp** as the Name. Leave all other properties with the default settings.

3. Click the Next button.

4. Create the Contents submenu, typing **&Contents** as the Caption and **mnuContents** as the Name.

5. Create the Index submenu, typing **&Index** as the Caption and **mnuIndex** as the Name.

6. Create the Search sub menu, using **&Search** For help On... as the Caption and **mnuSearch** as the Name.

7. Insert a separator into the menu by typing - (a hyphen) for the Caption. Name this separator **sepOne**.

8. Create the How To Use help submenu, using **&How to Use help** as the Caption and **mnuHowTo** as the Name.

9. Insert a separator into the menu by typing - (a hyphen) for the Caption. Name this separator **sepTwo**.

10. Create the About menu sub-item, using **&About...** as the Caption and **mnuAbout** as the Name.

11. After you have finished, click OK.

Your finished help menu should resemble figure 15.14.

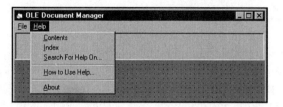

Fig. 15.14
The final help menu.

Specifying the Help File

To access the help file, you must inform the application which help file WINHELP.EXE should load when one of the items on the help menu is selected. To specify the help file to use, follow these steps:

1. Select Options from the Tools menu. The Options folder, shown in figure 15.15, appears on-screen.

2. Click the Project tab on the Options folder.

3. Enter the name of the help File into the help File text box or click the ellipsis to the right of the text box to browse for the file.

4. After you select the help file, click OK.

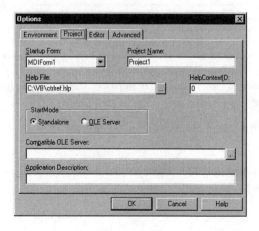

Fig. 15.15
The Project tab of Visual Basic's Options folder.

Enabling Your Application to Execute WinHelp

In previous versions of Visual Basic, you had to declare the WinHelp function, a Windows Application Programming Interface (API) library function, to allow your application to run WINHELP.EXE and display help properly. Additionally, you needed to declare several help constants, and write a significant amount of code to display the help file when a user chose an option from the help menu.

In Visual Basic 4.0, much of the effort required to launch help from application now is integrated and simplified. The ShowHelp method is now used to display various help file screens. ShowMethod is a method of the *CommonDialog* object. By assigning a value to the HelpCommand property of the CommonDialog object and calling the ShowHelp method of the object, a help file is displayed.

Help constants have been declared for you in VB 4.0—they are intrinsic. Table 15.2 lists the help constants used by the OLE Document Manager sample application and their functions, when assigned to the helpCommand property of the CommonDialog object.

Table 15.2 The Visual Basic Constants Used When Accessing Help from an Application

Constant	Function
Context	Displays help for particular topic
Index	Displays the index of the specified help file
Contents	Displays the contents screen of the current help file
HelpOnHelp	Displays help for using the help application
PartialKey	Calls the search engine in Windows help

A complete listing of the Visual Basic help constants can be found by searching for "Visual Basic Constants" in the Visual Basic 4.0 on-line help file.

To enable help for the menu created in the preceding section, follow these steps:

1. Place a CommonDialog object on the form for which a help menu has previously been created.

The CommonDialog object cannot be placed directly on an MDI form. If you create the help menu on an MDI form, you first need to add a control capable of being placed directly on the MDI form, such as a PictureBox control, and place the CommonDialog object within the PictureBox.)

Figure 15.16 shows a PictureBox control, with a CommonDialog object placed within it.

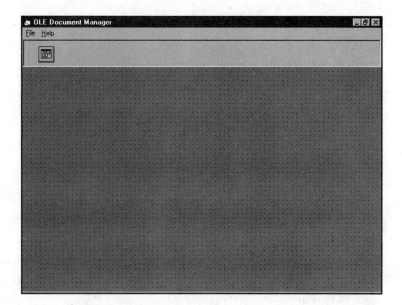

Fig. 15.16
A form with a common dialog control.

2. Set the Name property of the CommonDialog object to cdgHelpDialog.

3. Open the code window for the <u>C</u>ontents help menu item (by selecting the Contents item from the help menu in design mode), and select the *Click* procedure. Figure 15.17 shows the Contents menu item's code window.

4. Add the following two lines of code to the Click event:

```
cdgHelpDialog.HelpCommand = Contents
cdgHelpDialog.ShowHelp
```

Fig. 15.17
The Contents
Menu item's code
window.

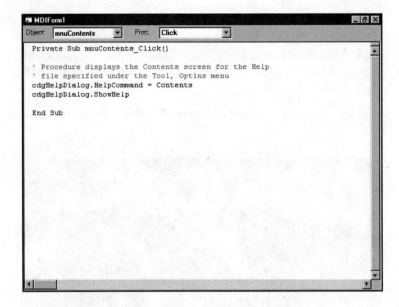

```
MDIForm1
Object: mnuContents          Proc: Click

Private Sub mnuContents_Click()

' Procedure displays the Contents screen for the Help
' file specified under the Tool, Optins menu
cdgHelpDialog.HelpCommand = Contents
cdgHelpDialog.ShowHelp

End Sub
```

The first line of code prepares the CommonDialog object's
helpCommand property to display the help file's Contents screen. The
second line calls the CommonDialog object's ShowHelp method, which
carries out the helpCommand.

5. If a help file has been associated with the application and the Contents
   item is selected from the help menu, the Contents screen of the help
   file is displayed.

Notice that, in the preceding example, it was unnecessary to declare any
functions or constants to incorporate help into an application and display it
from the help menu.

To add other help functions to an application, such as displaying the How to
Use help screen or displaying the help search screen, follow the preceding
example, but use the help Constants described in Table 15.2.

To display the help file's Index, add the following code to the mnuIndex
object's Click event:

```
cdgHelpDialog.HelpCommand = Index
cdgHelpDialog.ShowHelp
```

To display the help file's Index/Find window, add the following code to the
mnuSearch objects Click event:

```
cdgHelpDialog.HelpCommand = PartialKey
cdgHelpDialog.ShowHelp
```

To display the Window help on Using help's Contents screen, add the following code to the mnuHowTo objects `Click` event:

```
cdgHelpDialog.HelpCommand = helponHelp
cdgHelpDialog.ShowHelp
```

Implementing Context-Sensitive Help

To allow a user to access the specific help topic associated with a control on a Visual Basic form, assign the unique help context ID of the topic in the help file to the control's helpContextID property. When the user gives this control focus and presses the F1 key, the control's help topic is displayed. Figure 15.18 shows the helpContextID property of a CommandButton object.

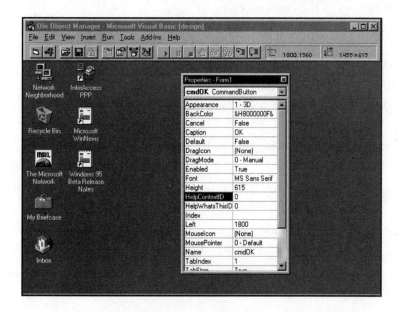

Fig. 15.18
The helpContextID property in a CommandButton object's property window.

Certain Visual Basic controls are not capable of using context-sensitive help because they don't have a helpContextID property. The line and label controls, for example, cannot receive the focus and therefore do not have the helpContextID property needed to display context-sensitive help.

Most third-party help authoring tools assign a unique context ID to each topic in your help file. If you choose to generate your own help file by using a text editor, you must assign an ID for each topic you will access. For example, Wex-Tech's Doc-To-Help and Blue Sky Software's Robohelp both include this feature.

If a help file was specified in the application (see the previous section called "Specifying a Help File"), Visual Basic automatically displays the help topic associated with a control when the control has focus and the F1 key is pressed. No additional programming is needed.

Adding Help to an OLE Automation Server

Beyond being able to create context-sensitive help for forms and controls, Visual Basic also lets you create context-sensitive help for OLE automation servers. Context-sensitive help for OLE servers allows you to display a short piece of information to the user when a server is viewed through the Object Browser. You also can instruct Visual Basic to display a Help file when the Object Browser's Help button is pushed.

Help for OLE automation servers can be a beneficial enhancement to your application when it is deployed throughout the enterprise. When end users begin to develop applications, the context-sensitive help will help users understand the function of the OLE automation server. This makes incorporating the OLE automation server into a customized application easier for the end user.

To add context-sensitive help to an OLE automation server, follow these steps:

1. Activate Visual Basic's Object Browser by selecting the Object Browser command from Visual Basic's View menu.

2. From the Classes/Modules list box on the Object Browser, select the OLE Server for which you want to add context-sensitive help.

   For more information on the Object Browser and displaying OLE Servers within it, see Chapter 5, "Controlling OLE Objects."

   When you select the OLE Server, the Options button becomes enabled. You can add Help only to OLE automation servers that you created in Visual Basic. If the Options button doesn't become enabled when the server is selected, you cannot add Help to it.

3. Click the Options button.

   Visual Basic displays the Member Options dialog box. From the Member Options dialog, you can enter the following information:

   - **Description**—Allows you to enter a brief description of the server. This description is displayed in the lower portion of the Object Browser when you select the OLE server from the Classes/Modules list.

- **Help File** (non-editable)—If a Help file was declared for the application, the name and path of the file is displayed in this edit box.

- **Help Context ID**—the unique context ID that identifies the help topic you want to associate with the OLE server. When you assign a context ID, a user can click the question mark (?) button on the Object Browser to view the specified help topic.

4. Click the OK button.

You also can add context-sensitive help for each property and method within an OLE automation server that you created in Visual Basic. The steps needed to create context-sensitive help for a property or method are exactly the same as the steps used to create context-sensitive help for an OLE automation server, except that, rather than selecting an OLE automation server in step 2, you select a property or method from the Object Broswer's Methods/Properties list box. You then click the Options button and add a help context ID for the property or method you selected.

Adding "What's This" Help

Windows 95 adds a new type of help, known as *What's This* Help. What's This help is activated by dragging the questions mark (?) icon that appears in the upper right corner of a Visual Basic form, with its WhatsThisHelpButton property set to True and its WhatsThisHelp property set to True over a control that has its WhatsThisHelpID set to a value equal to a help context ID in the application's help file.

What's This Help is similar to context-sensitive help. The main difference lies in the ways the two are invoked. Context-sensitive help is activated when a control receives focus and the user presses the F1 key. As you saw previously, What's This Help is activated when a user drags the question mark icon over a control with a WhatsThisHelpID set to a value help context ID.

You also can invoke What's This Help programmatically. Controls capable of displaying What's This Help have a ShowWhatsThis method. This method can be called in code. It displays the help topic associated with the control's WhatsThisHelpID.

Although users may initially be more familiar with using the F1 key to invoke context-sensitive help, more and more applications will begin to use What's This help. Including What's This Help in application's you deploy gives your apps a professional look and feel. What's This Help also will be more obvious to a new user. The question mark icon is easily associated with help, indicating to a user that this is where to look for guidance.

Creating What's This Help requires minimal additional coding. Because you will be including help context IDs with your controls, you just have to include What's This Help by placing the help context ID value in two places—the control's HelpContextID property and the control's WhatsThisHelpID property.

To make sure that your application's have a consistent look and feel, it's a good idea to always display a form's What's This button (set the forms WhatsThisHelpButton property to True) rather than invoke WhatsThisHelp programmatically by calling the ShowWhatsThis method. This technique gives users a consistent place to look for help and requires them to learn only one method of invoking it.

Commenting Code

One overlooked aspect of developing applications is *inline documentation* of code. But commenting code adds to development time. So why do it?

Consider commented code as on-line help for other developers and you. This section explains good code-documentation and commenting techniques.

Why Comment Your Code?

While most people consider comments as purely for the benefit of others, commented code also provides you with many benefits. Comments can produce the following results:

- Help other developers better understand the code that makes up your application

- Help you develop better code

- Help you recall the purpose of functions, procedures, and variables

So, what does commenting code have to do with enterprise development? Well-commented code is an investment in the future. It enables an organization to more easily evolve its applications to the changing business environment. A little investment up front pays off in time savings in the future.

Helping Other Developers Understand Your Code

The most compelling reason for documenting your code is to provide an aide to other developers who may examine the code. Every developer has a unique style of programming. There is no single correct way to program an application. Code that seems obvious to you may seem murky to others.

Inline commenting allows developers to examine each others' code and understand what the code is doing.

In a corporate environment, applications need to be enhanced periodically. Unlike a software house, where code is revised and examined continuously, in a corporate environment applications often are released and then remain unmodified for several years. In this scenario, poorly documented code is either difficult or impossible to modify.

To help understand how much easier commented code is to comprehend, consider the following example:

```
For liCounter = 1 to 100
    If gbWasSuccesful(llRow, llCol) = True Then
        giNoHits = giNoHits + 1
        gbReset = True
    End If
Next liCounter
```

The function of the preceding code fragment is far less clear than this example:

```
' Run test loop to determine if the row and column selected
' hold a character
For liCounter = 1 to 100
    ' Call function to look for character
    If gbWasSuccesful(llRow, llCol) = True Then
        ' Update global hit counter
        giNoHits = giNoHits + 1
        ' Reset globe test case indicator
        gbReset = True
    End If
Next liCounter
```

Helping Yourself Design Efficient Code

Aiding other developers is not the only reason for documenting code. While you are developing, good documentation encourages you to think carefully about the code you are writing. You may glance back at the comments you just added and think, "This code is not doing what I said it is doing."

Likewise, commenting as you develop encourages efficient coding. Comments help you answer the question, "What is the simplest, most efficient code that I can write to accomplish the description of this procedure?"

As you comment your code, you begin to create an outline within your procedures and functions. You can use this outline to determine if you are writing your code as efficiently as possible.

Comments Do not Affect the Size of the Executable

What about the size of the compiled executable? Visual Basic comments do not contribute to the size of the final executable. The comments are stripped out during the p-code generation process, which allows developers to include any number of comments that they choose, without affecting executable size.

Inline Comments: Another Form of Help

Although it may not appear so at first, inline commenting of code is simply another form of help. Looking at a preceding section in this chapter and examining our definition of help, you see that commenting provides an aid to its users—in this case, analyst developers.

Understanding Your Audience

As in help file development, developers should understand both their user base and the scope of their inline comments. The user base usually includes three types of users:

- You

- Users who haven't seen your code

- Users who have seen your code

When commenting code, you must assume the least common denominator: that someday, your audience will be a user who has neither seen your code nor was involved in the original project.

Therefore, comments should enable developers from all the categories in the preceding list to understand your code because your application may be maintained years from now by other developers.

Commenting Techniques

Now that you understand the benefits of using comments, you need to look at what exactly should be commented.

There is no right or wrong way of commenting code just as there is no right or wrong amount of comments. Developers generally agree on the more useful commenting techniques. This section describes these techniques, as applied to Visual Basic, and proposes some standards.

In general, commenting should focus on describing pieces of functionality (blocks of code) rather than individual lines of code. Only extremely complicated algorithms need to be commented in detail, by line of code.

Developers who understand Visual Basic should be able to look at a single line of code and understand what the line does, but it is more difficult to understand what thousands of lines of code are trying to accomplish as a group without comments.

The Benefits of Coding Standards

Adhering to good development standards (see Chapter 20, "Creating Development Guidelines") complements the benefits of commenting. For example. consistently prefixing the names of functions and procedures helps developers understand what is being accomplished within them. A well-thought-out function name will prove as valuable in disclosing the purpose of the function as any amount of inline commenting.

Besides procedure and function names, variable naming standards assist in communicating the purpose, scope, and type of a variable without requiring a developer to provide inline comments. The variable name, TotalAttachments, for example, provides some useful information but the name, giNumberOfAttachments, is more useful, describing the use purpose, scope, and variable type.

Commenting Procedures and Functions

Commenting procedures and functions is important. For the purpose of the following explanation, the term *procedure* refers to both procedures and functions.

Well-designed procedures should be thought of as "Black Boxes"—other developers should be able to use your procedures without having intimate knowledge of the specific processes that occur with the procedure. The developers need to be aware only of the information that the procedure requires as input (number of parameters, types of parameters) and what information the procedure returns (the procedure's interface).

A well-commented procedure should disclose this information at the top through comments. This disclosure allows other developers to understand and use the procedure without reading through all of the code.

The beginning of every procedure and function within a Visual Basic project should contain the following information:

- A description of the action that this particular subprogram is accomplishing

- A description of the parameters that are passed to the function or procedure as arguments

■ If the subprogram is a function, a description of the return value of the function

■ The person who originally wrote this function, the date it was written, and the date and name of the person who last modified this procedure or function

This inline documentation allows a developer to look at only the first several lines of the function and understand the following information:

■ What this function accomplishes

■ What each argument in the function or procedure is used for

■ What result the function is returning

■ Who should be contacted for information about the original makeup of the function

■ Who has since made changes to the function

The code fragment in Listing 15.1 shows a typical header for a Visual Basic function. You can find this code in the \CHAP15 directory on the companion disk.

Listing 15.1   CODE01.TXT—A sample function header

```
Function fiUpdateUserInfo (aiUserID as Integer, astrUserInfo as
Structure) as Integer

''''''''''''''''''''''''''''''''''''''''''''''''''''''''''''''''''''''''''''''''''
'
'       Function updates a Users Name, Address, City, State or Phone Number
'       Parameters:
'           aiUserID - uniquie ID identifying a user
'           astrUserInfo - a structure containing the users Name, address
'                           Phone Number
'       Return Value: Returns True (-1) if successful, False (0) otherwise
'       Written By: JDS          Date: 06/06/95
'       Last Edit By: JDS          Date: 6/16/95
''''''''''''''''''''''''''''''''''''''''''''''''''''''''''''''''''''''''''''''''''
```

Within procedures and functions, larger or complex code blocks should include comments that describe what the block of code is accomplishing.

Commenting If..End If Constructs

When creating a block of code that contains many nested If..End If loops, it is a good idea to comment each End If statement to indicate which If statement is being closed, as in the following example:

```
If liCounter > 5 Then
    ..
    If fiEndOfFile (lsFileName) = False Then
        ..
        If liFileLength > MAX_FILE_LENGTH Then
            ..
        End If  ' liFileLength > MAX
    End If  'fiEndOfFile
End If  'liCounter
```

Commenting Variable Declarations

Variable declarations are more understandable when preceded by a brief comment that describes the use for each variable. Commented variables are useful when re-examining code at a later date. Comments are needed, even with good variable naming conventions because even the most thoughtful variable name may not remind you of its purpose in the application:

```
' Boolean to indicate when a file is no longer in use
gbNoLongerUsing
```

Commenting Updates to Code

When updating your code to a new version after it is released, comment the changes/updates. These comments allow you to easily identify low-level revisions and their effect on the enhancements, as well as enabling a team of developers to easily track who made changes to what code. The following example shows comments included with updated code:

```
'Determine if the user has made any changes to document
If fiDocDirty = True Then
    ' Prompt user for save
    liResponse = MsgBox (MSG_MESSAGE_HEADER, "Do you want to save
    ➡changes?")
    If liResponse = RESPONSE_OK Then
        ' Save the file
        ' Code changed 6/31 by JDS. Bug fix
        ..
    End If ' liResponse
End If 'Form is dirty
```

What Shouldn't Be Commented

The goal of commenting is to make computer code more readable. If you think a line of code is difficult to understand, comment it. When in doubt, add the comment.

As a rule, simple Visual Basic constructs don't need to be commented. The following line of code, for example, probably does not merit its own comment:

```
MsgBox (MSG_MESSAGE_HEADER, "There was an error that occurred",
➥ICON_EXCLAMATION)
```

A complex string manipulation like the following, however, probably does:

```
MidWords = Mid(MyString, InStr(4, SearchString, SearchChar, 1),
➥Len(MyString))
```

Comments don't have to be works of art, however. They don't have to be complete sentences or grammatically correct, they just have to fulfill their purpose—to communicate to a human what the code is doing.

Comments Should Be Descriptive

Comments should not simply restate what Visual Basic is doing. Rather, they should describe the *purpose* of a line of code. For example, when assigning a value to a variable, the following code isn't very descriptive:

```
' Assign a value of 3 to the variable giHitCount
giHitCount = 3
```

The preceding code, even though the first comment was longer, is in fact actually much less descriptive than the following example:

```
' Record number of hits
giHitCount = 3
```

From Here...

This chapter provided information on designing a help system for your Visual Basic application. It also demonstrated several techniques useful for creating a special type of help—in-line code comments. You should now feel comfortable with the steps needed to create on-line help and understand the importance of commenting your code.

For further information related to topics covered in this chapter, see the following:

- Chapter 5, "Controlling OLE Objects," for information on the Object Browser and the functionality it provides.

- Chapter 21, "Organizing the Development Approach," for more information on assembling a project team and assigning roles to team members.

IV

Application Enhancements

Chapter 16

Distributing Applications

After you develop an application, you will want to distribute it to the users. This chapter details the definition of application distribution, the components that should be included in the distribution files, and the tools available in Visual Basic for creating a distribution application.

In this chapter, you learn the following techniques for effective application distribution:

- Using the SetupWizard to create an installation
- Creating a custom setup application
- Preparing your application for distribution

Defining the Components of an Application

In three-tier systems, distributing an application involves more than making copies of the application's .EXE file and placing it on a user's machine. In addition to the .EXE file, the program's support files, such as .INI files and OLE Controls (OCXes); operating system files; and OLE servers will need to be copied to each user's desktop. The OLE automation servers that make up an application's business services may be installed onto one or more network file servers. The OLE automation servers comprising an application's data services may be installed onto one or more database servers.

Because applications often will be dependent upon a specific version of a Dynamic Link Library (DLL) or OCX, you need to take steps to ensure that newer versions of DLLs and OCXes are not replaced by older versions that you may distribute. Additionally, you will not want to place two versions of the same DLL or OCX on a user's desktop. Doing so can lead to compatibility problems with other applications in the future. DLLs and OCXes that are used by many applications should be placed in a user's system directory. Generally, the directory in which you place these files is \WINDOWS\SYSTEM. In a network environment, however, users may share a system directory, and these files will need to be copied to a different location.

After you install OLE servers, they need to be registered. OLE servers that are used by the client application need to be registered locally as well as any remote OLE automation servers that will be accessed. Business services need to register their OLE servers as well.

Choosing a Distribution Method

What is the best method for distributing your application to the end users? Several options exist. You could walk to each user's desk, copy the files necessary to run the application, register the OLE servers, and create icons or Start Menu links to the .EXE files. This works well if all users work in the same office as you, but what if some users work in another city or another state? Making trips to each remote office may prove costly and impractical.

You could place all the files required by a user to run your application on a set of floppy disks, write a script that explains which files need to be copied to which directory and how to register OLE servers, and then send out the package to the end users. Visual Basic includes the Component Manager, which is capable of registering both client and server OLE automation servers.

Although some users may install the application without problems, other users may require support during setup. Still other users may set up the application incorrectly and corrupt other applications on their desktop. You should not rely on end users to determine file dependencies. The Component Manager may be too difficult for end users to understand.

The easiest way to distribute an application to all end users and ensure proper setup is to create a setup program capable of the following actions:

- Installing an application's files onto a user's machine

- Installing files into the appropriate directories, regardless of the names of the directories on the user's machine

- Enabling the installation of both VB Remote and Local OLE Automation servers on both the client and the server sides

- Removing files after an aborted installation

- Determining whether newer versions of DLLs and OCXes should be copied to a user's machine

- Creating Windows Program Manager groups and icons or Start Menu links for your application

A setup application will allow programs to be installed at remote locations. A setup application also ensures that files upon which your application depends are installed to their proper directories. Besides providing a simpler initial installation, a setup program will ease future upgrades. If you leave the project on which you currently are working, a new employee can continue to make use of your application and set up the application on new users' machines.

Visual Basic provides two methods in order to create an installation program capable of these functions—the Visual Basic SetupWizard and the Visual Basic Setup Toolkit. The remainder of this chapter will both outline the features of these two installation tools and describe how you can use them to create a setup application for your user services, business services, and data services.

Using the Visual Basic SetupWizard

The Visual Basic SetupWizard, included with both the Professional and the Enterprise editions of Visual Basic 4.0, allows you to easily create distribution disks or a distribution directory for your Visual Basic application. The SetupWizard performs the following tasks:

- Creates a Setup program

- Builds an executable file for a Visual Basic project you specify

- Determines your application's file dependencies

- Compresses files and assigns them to a disk layout

- Notifies you of the number of blank formatted disks that you will need to hold your application and all of its dependency files

- Copies all of the distribution files to blank formatted disks

- Optionally copies the distribution disks to your hard disk. These disk images then can be copied onto a shared server for network distribution or for transfer to a CD-ROM

Creating an installation application by using the SetupWizard is a seven-step process. The remainder of this section details each step.

Step 1: Selecting a Visual Basic Project File

When the SetupWizard's icon is double-clicked, the SetupWizard's Step 1 dialog box appears, as shown in figure 16.1.

Fig. 16.1

The SetupWizard's Step 1 dialog box.

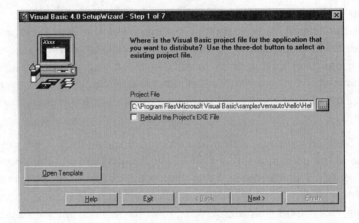

In the Project File text box, enter the path and filename for the .VBP file of the application you want to distribute. To browse project files on your hard disk, click the browse (...) button to the right of the Project File text box.

The SetupWizard can be used to distribute both .EXE and .DLL files, which makes it possible to create a setup application for both stand-alone executable files, as well as for OLE servers. To create a setup application for an OLE server, select the VBP file of the OLE automation server as you would any Visual Basic project file.

If an executable file or in-process dynamic link library does not exist for the specified project file, the SetupWizard will automatically build one. To force the SetupWizard to rebuild the application's executable file or dynamic link library, click the Rebuild Project's .EXE File check box.

If you previously have created a distribution template, and now you want to use it to create a new setup application, click the Open Template command button. You may find a template useful if only a few files in a project have changed or if you decide to create a new set of distribution files. A distribution template can be created after you have completed all steps in the SetupWizard.

After you select a project file or a previously saved distribution template, click the Next button to continue.

Step 2: Selecting Data Access Engines

If your application uses a data control or any of the data access objects, the Step 2 dialog box appears. The Step 2 dialog box is shown in figure 16.2. If your application does not use the data control or data access objects, the Step 3 dialog box, shown in figure 16.3, will appear.

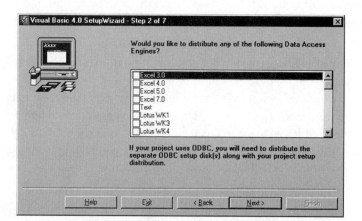

Fig. 16.2
The SetupWizard's Step 2 dialog box.

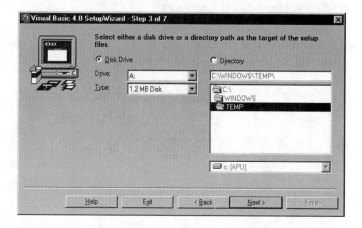

Fig. 16.3
The SetupWizard's Step 3 dialog box.

From this dialog box you can select any of the data access drivers your application uses. To select an engine, click the check box to the left of the engine name. If your application does not use data access objects or the data control and the Step 2 dialog box appears, you can remove the Data Access Objects reference in the References dialog box.

If you are using the Remote Data Control or Remote Data Objects in your application, you need to include the ODBC installation disk with your setup disks. An image of the ODBC setup disk is included on the Visual Basic CD-ROM.

After you have selected a database driver, click the Next button to continue.

Step 3: Selecting a Destination for the Setup Application

Step 3 of the SetupWizard requires that you select the target of the setup files. If you are creating distribution disks, select the Disk Drive option button and select the disk drive on which you want to create your disks. You also should choose the type of floppy disks you will use.

To build the setup directory to a local hard drive or to a network drive, select the Directory option button, and then select the destination drive and directory into which you want to copy the distribution files. The files that will be copied to this directory can be used to set up the application over a network. Remember that if you want to create distribution disks, you can copy the files placed in the installation directory to floppies. If you plan on distributing your application on CD-ROM, you can copy the distribution files to a "CD-ROM generation" system.

After you select a destination directory, click the Next button to continue.

Step 4: Selecting OLE Servers

After completing Step 3, the SetupWizard will attempt to determine which OLE servers will be used by your application. The OLE servers that it detects will be listed in the Step 4 dialog box, as shown in figure 16.4.

Fig. 16.4
The SetupWizard's
Step 4 dialog box.

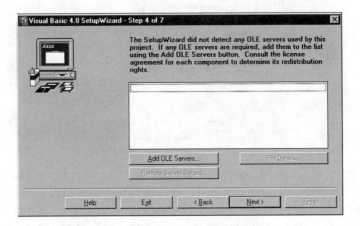

If your application references an OLE server that does not appear in the list in the Step 4 dialog box, you can add this server by clicking the Add OLE Servers button. Any added OLE servers must be .EXE or .DLL files capable of self-registration. The SetupWizard will search through the OLE server's file version information for the keyword, *OLESelfRegister*. When you create an OLE server by using Visual Basic, this keyword is automatically placed in the version information of the compiled .DLL or .EXE file.

Because OLE servers might not be placed in the same directory as the .EXE file when they are distributed, it is extremely important that the servers are able to function independent of their location. The OLE server's files will be placed in the \OLESVR directory, which is a subdirectory of the \WINDOWS directory under Windows NT and a subdirectory of the \PROGRAM FILES\COMMON FILES directory under Windows 95.

The Step 4 dialog box is the only place where OLE servers and Remote Support files can be added to the distribution application. If an OLE server or Remote Support file is added through the Add Files button in Step 7, it will not be installed as an OLE server or remote OLE automation server, but as an additional file.

If you select a Remote Support file (.VBR file) by using the Add OLE Servers button, the SetupWizard will display the Remote OLE Server Details dialog box shown in figure 16.5.

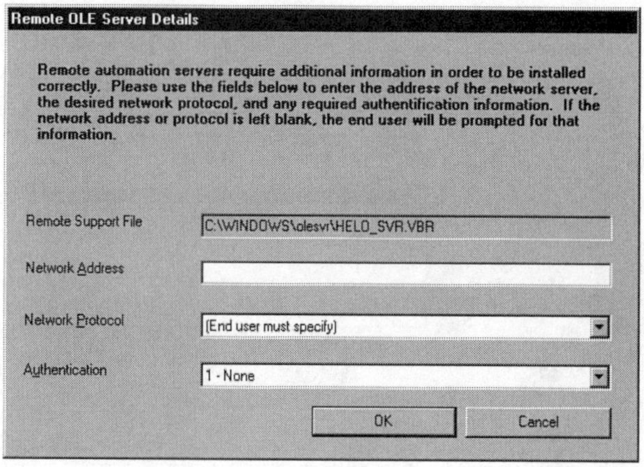

Fig. 16.5
The Remote OLE Server Details dialog box.

In the Remote OLE Server Details dialog box, you should enter the network address, the network protocol, and the authentication information that is required for the OLE component to work correctly.

The *Network Address field* refers to the name of the server on which the OLE Automation Server resides. The *Network Protocol* setting refers to the type of network protocol used for communication between the OLE client and the

OLE server. If the Network Protocol is set to End user must specify, the user will have to choose the network protocol at run time. The *Authentication* setting refers to the method by which an OLE server authenticates an OLE client.

To accept the Remote OLE Server settings, click the OK button. If you click the Cancel button, the dialog box disappears, and the .VBR file appears, unchecked, in the OLE servers list. Clicking the Remote Server Details button brings up the Remote OLE Server Details dialog box again.

The SetupWizard uses the OLE servers that you select in the References dialog box under the Tools menu. If you included references to remote or local OLE servers that your application does not use, these servers are displayed in the Setup 4 dialog box. If you do not want the SetupWizard to include an OLE server, deselect the check box to the left of the OLE server's name.

Step 5: Determining File Dependencies

The SetupWizard's Step 5 dialog box, shown in figure 16.6, displays a list of files or objects that are referenced in your Visual Basic project. You can easily add or remove files in the list by selecting or clearing the check box next to each file name.

Fig. 16.6
The SetupWizard's
Step 5 dialog box.

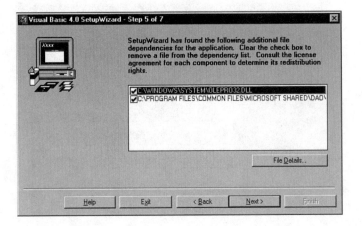

Even if you know that a file that is included in the list already exists on an end user's machine, it is a good idea to still include the file. Including this kind of file helps to eliminate any possible version compatibility problems. You should remove all the files from the list for which you do not have distribution rights. The files listed on this screen should be included in your release notes so that users can verify that they have all the files needed to run the application in place.

After you finish adding and removing files, click the Next button to continue.

Step 6: Selecting a Deployment Mode

You must now choose the deployment mode for your application. The Step 6 dialog box is shown in figure 16.7.

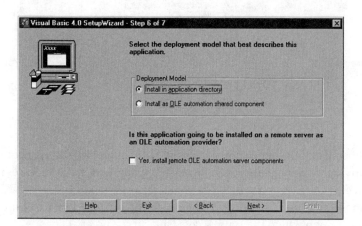

Fig. 16.7
The SetupWizard's Step 6 dialog box.

If the application is a stand-alone .EXE file, select the first option, *Install in application directory*. This option installs the application into the directory specified by a user during setup. If the application will be a shared OLE automation server, select the *Install as OLE automation shared component* option. This will install the OLE component to the shared components directory (the \OLESVR directory).

If the OLE Automation Provider check box is checked, the Automation manager support files will be added to the file list. This check box will appear only if you are using the 32-bit Enterprise Edition of the SetupWizard because remote OLE Automation servers can be installed only on 32-bit operating systems.

After you have selected a deployment mode, click the Next button to continue.

Step 7: Selecting Files to Install

The SetupWizard's Step 7 dialog box displays a list of all of the files that are required for your application to function properly. Figure 16.8 shows the Step 7 dialog box.

Fig. 16.8

The SetupWizard's
Step 7 dialog box.

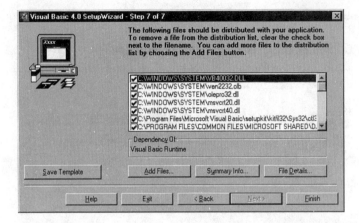

The Dependency Of frame shows which file or files are dependent upon the currently selected file. This screen differs from Step 5 in that it includes files upon which the files you selected in Step 5 are dependent. For example, if your application uses Data Access Objects, the Step 7 dialog box will show all of the files upon which the Data Access Object type library depends.

You can add files to the distribution list by clicking the Add Files button. The SetupWizard does not permit duplicate file names in the distribution list. If you try to add duplicate files, you will be prompted to change the name of the duplicate file.

To see the total number of files that were selected for installation and the storage size of these files, click the Summary Info button. Clicking the File Details button displays the size, date, version information, current location, and install destination of the files that are currently selected in the distribution list. From the File Details dialog box, which is shown in figure 16.9, you can change the destination directory of a file.

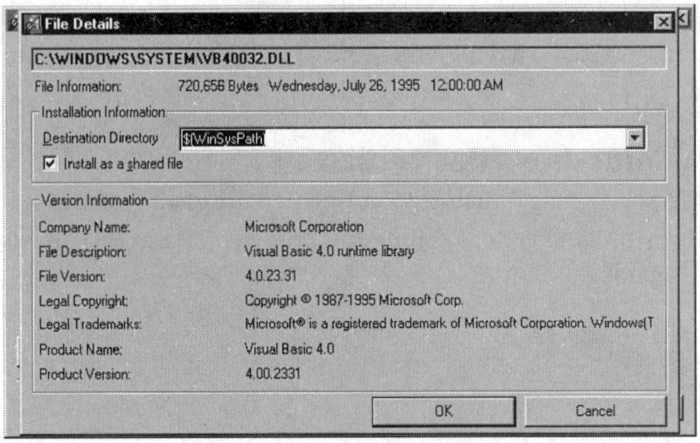

Fig. 16.9

The SetupWizard's
File Details dialog
box.

Changing the destination directory of an OLE server or shared file should be done with caution because it could cause problems. If two OLE servers with the same name exist in two different directories, removing one server may result in the removal of registry information required to make both files accessible. This removal will leave the remaining server inaccessible.

The Save Template button in the Step 7 dialog box allows you to save your setup configuration to a template file (.VBZ file). This allows you to return to your work later, using the Open Template button in the Step 1 dialog box.

After you finish adding and removing files, click the Finish button to continue.

Step 8: Creating Distribution Disks

If you chose a directory path as the destination of your setup files, the SetupWizard will begin copying the compressed setup files to the directory you specified. Before copying, however, the SetupWizard will ask whether you want to delete any existing files in the destination directory.

As the SetupWizard compresses each file in your setup application, the Compressing Files progress screen, which is shown in figure 16.10, indicates which file is currently being compressed as well as all the files that already have been compressed.

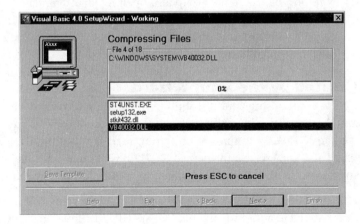

Fig. 16.10

The SetupWizard's Compressing Files progress screen.

When all files have been compressed, the SetupWizard will display the Copying Files progress screen shown in figure 16.11.

Fig. 16.11
The SetupWizard's
Copying Files
progress screen.

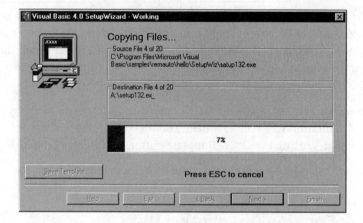

If you chose to copy the distribution files to floppy disks, the Copying Files progress screen will prompt you to insert the disks. If you chose to copy the distribution files to a directory path, the progress screen will show you which files are being copied to the directory you selected.

When copying is complete, the SetupWizard displays the Finished screen.

From the Finished screen, you can save a template of your distribution setup. After the template is saved, you can create additional copies of your distribution disks by rerunning the SetupWizard and opening your template. You also can click the Back button to return to Step 8, and then click the Finish button to re-create your distribution disks. If you have finished, click the Exit button to leave the SetupWizard.

Files Created by the SetupWizard

In addition to compressing your distribution files, the SetupWizard will include several other files on your distribution disks. Most of the files are those required by any Visual Basic application to run, such as VB43200.DLL. The SetupWizard also will create a file named SETUP.EXE. You use this file to install any bootstrap files that your installation application may require.

The SETUP.LST file created by the SetupWizard lists all files that will be installed or registered in a user's machine. The SETUP.LST file can be viewed with any text editor. The SETUP.LST file is explained in detail in a following section of this chapter.

The SetupWizard also creates and compresses a file named SETUP132.EX_ if you are creating a 32-bit installation application or SETUP1.EX_ if you are creating a 16-bit installation application. This file is launched by the SETUP.EXE program and performs functions that were outlined previously as being necessary for an installation application.

For example, SETUP132.EXE will check a user's machine for necessary disk space before installing files. This setup application also will compare file dates and versions before overwriting an existing file. The SETUP132.EXE application will create Program Manager icons or Start menu links for the new application. If installation is aborted, processes in the SETUP132.EXE will delete files that were copied by the installation program. The SetupWizard automatically includes this functionality when you create distribution disks. The SETUP132.EXE application is explained in greater detail in a following section of this chapter.

As you will see in the following section, the source code for SETUP132.EXE is included with the Setup Toolkit. By modifying this source code, you can create a customized setup application.

Creating a Custom Setup Program, Using the Setup Toolkit

Although the SetupWizard is capable of creating a basic installation program, you may want to provide more options to a user. For example, if your application includes Help files, a more advanced user may not want to install all of these files. A user who is short on disk space may want to install only the files necessary to run the program and leave out the sample files. The SetupWizard is not capable of offering these kinds of options.

Visual Basic includes a Setup Toolkit capable of creating a setup program with such custom installation options. All of the tools required to run the Setup Toolkit are included in the \SETUPKIT\SETUP1 directory.

The Setup Toolkit will allow you to perform the following custom options:

- Compress your application's files

- Pre-install files that are required by your setup program

- Create a customized "look and feel" for your setup program

- Install your application's files on a user's machine

- Enable the installation of VB Remote OLE Automation servers on client and server sides

- Uninstall files during setup (32-bit Enterprise Edition only)

- Determine whether a file should be replaced with a newer version

- Create Windows Program Manager groups and icons under Windows NT or Windows 3.x, or create Start menu links with Windows 95

The remainder of this section describes the features of the Setup Toolkit and how you can use these features to create a customized setup application.

Files Included with the Setup Toolkit

The \SETUPKIT\SETUP1 directory contains several DLLs and utility applications that will help in creating a setup program. The main component of the Setup Toolkit is a sample Setup program written in Visual Basic. This sample program is the same program used by the SetupWizard when it creates a setup application for you. The SetupWizard modifies several of the sample program's files, creates a copy, and then places the modified Setup program on your distribution disks.

The following list describes the files located in the \SETUPKIT\SETUP1 directory:

- **SETUP.EXE**—A program generated by both the Setup Toolkit and the SetupWizard. The SETUP.EXE program is used to pre-install your customized setup application, and then run it.

- **SETUP132.EXE**—The customized Setup program you create. This program is compressed with your other distribution files and placed on your installation disks. The 16-bit version of Visual Basic generates a program named SETUP1.EXE.

- **SETUP.LST**—The text file that lists all files to be installed on the user's machine.

- **SETUP1.VBP**—The Setup Toolkit project file used to write your Setup program.

- **SETUP1.BAS**—A collection of Visual Basic functions. These functions are used in SETUP1.VBP to perform the tasks required by a Setup program.

- **ST4UNST.EXE** (32-bit)—An application-removal utility, for use with the Visual Basic Setup Toolkit.

- **VER.DLL** (16-bit)—Calls LZEXPAND.DLL, which copies and decompresses files. VER.DLL also can detect the version of a file that has a Microsoft Windows version stamp. VER.DLL is used only for 16-bit setup applications.

- **CLIREG32.EXE** (32-bit)—A 32-bit Remote OLE Automation client registration utility. This utility is used by the setup application to register Remote OLE Automation servers on a client machine.

- **CLIREG16.EXE** (16-bit)—A 16-bit Remote OLE Automation client registration utility. This utility is employed by the setup application to register Remote OLE Automation servers on a client machine.

Because this book focuses on 32-bit application development, the remainder of this section refers to SETUP132.EXE and CLIREG32.EXE.

Using the Setup Toolkit

The Setup Toolkit includes the source code of the installation application used by the SetupWizard. By modifying this code, you can create a custom setup application. The Setup Toolkit also includes the utilities used by the SetupWizard to compress files, expand the files during installation, and register OLE servers. These utilities are accessible to Visual Basic programs. Although the Setup Toolkit can be used to create a Setup program from scratch, it's always a good idea to use the Setup Toolkit in conjunction with the SetupWizard. This section describes the creation of a custom Setup program that is built from the standard Setup program created by the SetupWizard.

> **Note**
>
> The SetupWizard does a good job of determining which files should be distributed with your application and which files should be used even when creating a custom setup application. This helps to ensure that you do not forget to include one or more files with your distribution disks.

The SetupWizard provides several other benefits. Although you can use the COMPRESS.EXE program included with the Setup Toolkit to compress your distribution files, COMPRESS.EXE is not capable of spanning a file across multiple disks—if your application requires that you distribute a file larger than 1.44M when compressed, you will have to manually split the file. Conversely, the SetupWizard is capable of creating compressed files that span multiple disks. The sample setup application includes a function that can reassemble these files.

The SetupWizard also can create a copy of the sample setup application included with the Visual Basic Setup Toolkit. You can modify this Setup program to include custom setup options. This saves you time in development because you will not have to create a setup application from scratch.

Understanding Useful Functions in the Setup Toolkit

Before you begin to modify the sample setup application included with the Visual Basic Setup Toolkit, you should understand several key functions used by the program. These functions and variables are used to start the setup application and display the appropriate user prompts, to determine the application's destination directory, to determine a user's \WINDOWS and \WINDOWS\SYSTEM directory and make it available to the rest of the setup application, to calculate free disk space on a user's machine and the space required to install the application, to copy and expand the distribution files from your installation disks to a user's hard drive, to register OLE servers you may have included, and to create Program Manager icons or Start menu links.

In addition, if a user aborts the installation or the installation process is interrupted due to an error, the 32-bit Enterprise Edition of the Setup program will automatically uninstall any files copied to the user's machine. This is accomplished by creating a log file of all files that have been copied and invoking the ST4UNST.EXE utility program. When installation is complete, this log file will be copied to the user's \WINDOWS\SYSTEM directory. This permits the user to uninstall the application using Windows 95's Add/Remove program facility.

The Startup Form

The frmSetup1 form is the startup form for the installation application project. The form is shown in figure 16.12.

Fig. 16.12
The Setup Toolkit sample application's frmSetup1 form.

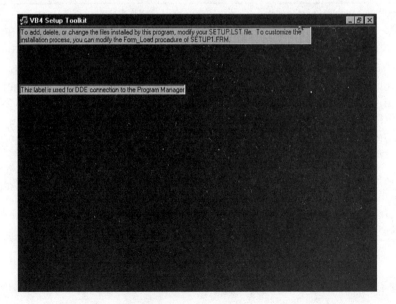

When you start the setup application, frmSetup1's Form_Load event is triggered. The Form_Load event displays several other forms that prompt the user to specify where the application should be installed, calls functions to determine the location of the \WINDOWS and \WINDOWS\SYSTEM directories on the user's machine, calculates the disk space that is available on the user's hard drive, expands and copies the distribution files, registers local and remote OLE servers, and creates Program Manager icons and Start menu links.

Most modifications to the sample setup application will occur in the Form_Load event of frmSetup1.

Displaying User Prompts

The sample setup application includes a prompt that asks the user for the destination directory of the application.

This directory is stored in a variable and made available to the rest of the setup application's procedures. The code used to display the prompt is shown below:

```
'Read default destination directory.  If the name specified
'conflicts
'with the name of a file, then prompt for a new default directory
'
'gstrDestDir = ResolveDestDir(ReadIniFile(gstrSetupInfoFile, _
'gstrINI_SETUP, gstrINI_APPDIR))
'While FileExists(gstrDestDir) = True Or gstrDestDir = gstrNULL
    'If MsgError(ResolveResString(resBADDEFDIR), MB_OKCANCEL Or _
    'MB_ICONQUESTION, gstrSETMSG) = IDCANCEL Then
        'ExitSetup Me, gintRET_FATAL
    'End If
    'ShowPathDialog gstrDIR_DEST
'Wend
```

If the directory the user selects as a destination is not present on the user's drive, the Setup program asks the user if he or she would like to create that directory. After a user selects a valid destination directory, this directory is stored in the gstrDestDir global variable. This variable will be used later in the application to determine where the main program files should be installed on a user's machine.

One feature absent from the setup application generated by the SetupWizard is the capability to install only a portion of the entire application. If you plan to distribute Help files with your application, for example, more advanced users may forgo the installation of Help files in favor of conserving disk space. To allow for this, you will need to display a dialog box that asks the users what portions of the application they may want to install.

Many off-the-shelf applications include these types of setup prompts. Many will include choices of Typical, Complete, and Custom setup options. This type of flexibility may not be necessary in your application. You may want to offer options such as Complete, Minimal, or Laptop installation.

The Setup application includes an area where you will want to insert the code used to display a setup options prompt. This area is marked by the following commented code:

```
'
'This would be a good place to display an option dialog,
'allowing the user
'a chance to select installation options: samples, docs,
'help files, etc.
'Results of this dialog would be checked in the loop below
'
```

Displaying a custom prompt is explained in detail in a following section of this chapter.

Determining the \WINDOWS and \WINDOWS\SYSTEM Directories

The sample setup application includes a function that will locate the \WINDOWS and \WINDOWS\SYSTEM directories of the machine on which the application is being installed. As you learned in a previous section ("Using the Visual Basic SetupWizard"), you will often want to install files that will be shared by many applications to a user's \WINDOWS\SYSTEM directory. An application's .INI files should be placed in the \WINDOWS directory.

The functions GetWindowsDir and GetWindowsSysDir are used to locate the \WINDOWS and \WINDOWS\SYSTEM directories, respectively. These functions are located in the setup application's basCommon code module. The two functions make use of Windows APIs to determine the location of the two directories. As you will see later in this chapter, you do not need to make modifications to these two functions, but you will employ them when you create your customized application.

Calculating Disk Space Required and Disk Space Available

The sample setup application includes a function that can calculate the disk space required to fully install your application. The function, named CalcDiskSpace, is located in the basSetup1 code module. CalcDiskSpace determines which files will be installed to a user's hard drive and the amount of disk space that these files require.

The CalcDiskSpace function makes adjustments to the amount of disk space required for a special case. If one of the files that the Setup program will copy to a user's hard drive already exists on that drive, the amount of space required by the Setup program is decreased. CalcDiskSpace adjusts the disk space required accordingly. This kind of adjustment ensures that you get an accurate reading of space required.

The CheckDiskSpace function, also located in the basSetup1 code module, determines how much disk space a user has available. If the user's hard disk doesn't have enough free disk space to permit the installation of the application, the Setup program alerts the user and asks him or her to either choose a new destination directory or free some disk space.

Copying and Expanding Distribution Files

After a destination directory has been selected and the setup application has determined that enough free space exists on the destination drive to permit the installation of the application, the Form_Load event calls the CopySection function. The CopySection function reads through each File section on the SETUP.LST file and copies the files named there to the destination directory. A more detailed explanation of the SETUP.LST file is provided in a following section of this chapter.

The CopySection function determines whether the file included on the distribution disks is newer than an existing file on the user's hard drive. The function first attempts to compare version numbers between the two files. If the file on the distribution disks is a more recent version than the existing file, the existing file will be replaced. Otherwise, the existing file will not be overwritten.

If no version information exists, file dates are compared. If the file on the distribution disks has an older file date than the existing file, the distributed file will not be copied. If the distributed file has a more recent file date, the distributed file will replace the existing file.

The CopySection function also takes care of reassembling files that were split by the SetupWizard. When a new installation disk is required by the setup application, the CopySection function prompts the user to insert the next disk.

Registering OLE Servers

After copying files, the Form_Load event calls the RegisterFiles function, which is located in the basSetup1 code module. This function registers the local and remote OLE servers that were copied to a user's drive by the CopySection function.

The registration of local OLE servers is accomplished by making a call to the REGSERV utility included with the Visual Basic Setup Toolkit. To register remote servers, the RegisterFiles function calls the CLIREG32.EXE utility.

Displaying Setup Status

The Setup program displays a form to indicate the current file being copied as well as to indicate what percentage of files has been copied.

The ShowCopyDialog function displays the Copy dialog form, named *frmCopy*. Each time a file is copied using the CopySection function, the name of the file being copied is displayed on the Copy dialog form, and the graph on the Copy dialog form is updated.

Creating Program Manager Icons and Start Menu Links

After all distribution files have been copied and registered, the setup application will create program groups or Start menu links for the application being installed. This is accomplished through the CreateOSFolder and CreateOSLinks functions in the basSetup1 code module.

The CreateOSFolder function is called first in the Form_Load event of the startup form. This function will determine the current operating system (Windows NT, Windows 95, or Windows for Workgroups). Then the CreateOSFolder function will create a new Program Manager program group under Windows NT or Windows for Workgroups or a new folder under the Start menu in Windows 95.

When the application's program group or folder has been created, the startup form calls the CreateOSLinks function. This function again determines the current operating system and creates either a new program item, in the case of Windows NT or Windows for Workgroups, or a new link under Windows 95. The links created are determined by settings in the SETUP.LST file. We examine the SETUP.LST file in detail in a following section of this chapter.

Creating a Log File and Uninstalling Copied Files

Whenever the Setup program copies a file to a user's hard drive or registers an OLE server, the NewAction function is called. This function marks the beginning of an action such as copying a file. When the action has been completed successfully, the CommitAction function is called. The CommitAction function marks the action as complete, and then outputs the action to a log file.

If an action is not completed successfully, the AbortAction function is called. This function determines whether the error was serious enough to require the application to shut down. If the application must cease, the ST4UNST.EXE is invoked and any files copied to the destination drive are removed.

Understanding the SETUP.LST File

The SETUP.LST file is the file that lists all the files to be installed on a user's machine. The SetupWizard creates the SETUP.LST file and includes information such as file size, file date, and other file attributes. SETUP.LST also describes the layout of the distribution disks.

The SETUP.LST file is divided into three sections:

- The [BOOTSTRAP] section

- The [FILES] section

- The [SETUP] section

The remainder of this section describes each file component in detail.

The [BOOTSTRAP] Section

The [BOOTSTRAP] section lists all files that must be loaded onto a user's machine before the application can load. These files are referred to as *bootstrap* files. The bootstrap files include files required by any Visual Basic application to run, such as VB40032.DLL, as well as any files that are required by SETUP1.EXE. The SETUP.EXE application that you create will install these files before running SETUP1.EXE.

The [FILES] Section

The [FILES] section contains all other files required by your application, such as the compressed .EXE file that you will be installing, data files, initialization files, dependency files, and OLE servers. After it is installed by the SETUP.EXE program, SETUP1.EXE continues to copy and decompress the files listed in this section.

All files listed in the [FILES] section, as well as the files listed in the [BOOTSTRAP] section, comply with the following format:

> **File**x=y**[SPLIT]**,*file,install,path,register*,date,shared,size,[*version*]

File is a keyword that must appear at the beginning of each file description line.

x is a sequence number, starting at 1 in each section. For example, the [BOOTSTRAP] section starts with 1, and the [FILES] section will also begin with 1. The numbering sequence must be in order and it cannot skip any values.

y is the number of the disk on which the file will be distributed. If you are distributing to a network server or CD-ROM, this number is always 1.

SPLIT is an optional flag indicating that this file is not the last part of a segmented file. For subsequent file names that are part of this same file, you should not repeat the fields following *install*. The last piece of the same file will not have the **SPLIT** keyword. A segmented file might be represented like this:

```
File1=1,SPLIT,SUPPORT.DL1,SUPPORT.DLL,$(WinPath),,8/2/95,112233
File2=2,SPLIT,SUPPORT.DL2,SUPPORT.DLL
File3=3,SPLIT,SUPPORT.DL3,SUPPORT.DLL
```

file is the name of the file as it is distributed.

install is the name of the file that is used during installation. Usually, the file name may be different from *file*, such as when you create the media using compressed files where the last character of the filename is an underscore and you want to install the file onto a user's machine with the original character replacing the underscore.

path is the path of where the file should be installed. The setup application recognizes several macros, listed in the following table, that should be used in place of the actual path name.

Macro	Description
$(WinSysPath)	Installs a file in the \WINDOWS\SYSTEM subdirectory. A user's \WINDOWS\SYSTEM directory is determined by the GetWindowsSysDir function of the setup application.
$(WinPath)	Installs a file in the \WINDOWS directory. A user's \WINDOWS directory is determined by the GetWindowsDir function of the setup application.
$(AppPath)	Installs a file in the application directory specified by the user, or in the DefaultDir value specified in the [SETUP] section.
$(AppPath)\SAMPLES	Installs a file in the \SAMPLES directory below the application directory.
c:\path	Installs a file in the directory identified by *path* (not recommended).
$(CommonFiles)	The common directory to which shared files will be installed, such as: C:\PROGRAM FILES\COMMON FILES\ (Windows 95) C:\WINDOWS (Windows NT, Windows for Workgroups)
$(ProgramFiles)	The initial directory to which the application will be installed: C:\PROGRAM FILES (Windows 95) C:\ (Windows NT, Windows for Workgroups)

In the [BOOTSTRAP] section, no file may be installed by using the $(AppPath), $(CommonFiles), or $(ProgramFiles) macros.

Register is a key that indicates how the file is to be included in the user's system registry. The four possible keys are listed in the following table.

Key	Description
(no key)	This file does not contain linked or embedded objects and does not need to be registered on the user's machine.
$(DLLSelfRegister)	Use this key if the file is a self-registering DLL, .OCX control, or any other file with self-registering information.
$(EXESelfRegister)	Use this key if the file is an object application created in Visual Basic.
$(Remote)	This key indicates that the file is a Remote Support file (.VBR).
appname.REG	Use this key for any component you distribute that needs to be registered but does not provide self-registration. This key contains the information that updates the system registry.

Remote# is a line written to SETUP.LST using the information from the Remote Server Details dialog box at Step 4 of the Setup Wizard. This line contains the command line information used by the Client Registration utility to register the Remote OLE Automation server. This information consists of the server address, network protocol, and authentication information, separated by commas. The # corresponds to the File# that contains the $(Remote) key. The following is an example of the Remote# implementation.

```
File1=1,,Remote.VB_,Remote.VBR,$(CommonFiles)\OLESVR,$(Remote),
➥$(Shared),8/2/95,1111
Remote1="\\APPSVR1","ncan_ip_tcp",1
```

$(Shared) is a keyword automatically added to the list entry of any file installed to \WINDOWS, \WINDOWS\SYSTEM, or $(CommonFiles). This keyword can be either $(Shared), indicating that it is a shared file and is registered to the registry, or blank, indicating that it is a private file.

Date and *size* are the same as the last date modified and the file size, as it would appear in File Manager or the Explorer. The date information is used when the CopySection function compares dates of existing files. Size is used by SETUP1.EXE to calculate how much disk space your application requires on a user's machine.

Version is an optional internal version number of the file. You can determine the version number of a file by clicking the File Details button in Step 7 of the SetupWizard. This number is not necessarily the same number as the display version number you see by checking File Properties in File Manager.

It should be noted that the [FILES] section is the default section created by the SetupWizard when setting up your distribution disks. You will see in following sections of this chapter how you can add your own sections to create a custom setup application.

The [SETUP] Section

The final section of the SETUP.LST file, the [SETUP] section, contains the information used by functions within the Setup program. This section is the equivalent of most applications' .INI files.

The following list describes the components of the [SETUP] section:

Component	Description
Title	The name of the application that will appear in the splash screen during installation. This name also will be used for the Program Manager icon group and icon name.
DefaultDir	The directory to which the application will be installed, unless the user enters a different destination directory during the Setup program.
Setup	The name of the Setup program file. By default, it is SETUP1.EXE. If you rename the SETUP1.EXE file, make sure that you also change the name here. You can give your setup application any name except SETUP.EXE.
Btrieve	Should be set to a non-zero value if you include Btrieve drivers in the distribution files.
AppPath	Application-specific PATH variable used by Windows 95 to find any additional files needed for application execution.
AppEXE	Should be set to the name of the application being installed.

You will probably make adjustments to the Title and DefaultDir entries only. You may want to change the name of your installation application to something other than SETUP132.EXE. If you do, remember to change the Setup entry. Remember that SETUP132.EXE is not directly executed by the user. Rather, it is the Setup program created by the SetupWizard or the custom setup application created by you. The file SETUP.EXE is run by the user. In turn, SETUP.EXE launches SETUP132.EXE. It is an accepted standard to give the application that is launched by the user the name, SETUP.EXE.

Building a Custom Setup Application

Now that you have an understanding of the various components of the setup application and the functions the application uses to copy files, you are ready to see how a customized setup application is created. The process of creating a Setup program can be divided into the following four discrete steps:

- Using the SetupWizard to determine the files you need to create and distribute a SETUP.LST file

- Modifying the SETUP.LST file to support custom setup options

- Modifying the Visual Basic sample setup application to include custom setup options

- Recompressing the modified Setup program and creating distribution disks

The first step requires that you use the SetupWizard to assemble all the files that will be installed by your setup application. The SetupWizard will also generate a SETUP.LST file for you. You will modify this file later.

The second step involves adding custom prompts to the Form_Load event of the frmSetup1 form. In the following example, you will add a prompt that asks the user whether he or she would like to use the setup application to install all files to the machine or only the files necessary to run the application.

The third step of modifying the setup application involves editing the SETUP.LST file created by the SetupWizard. You will add a new section, similar to the [FILES] section created by the SetupWizard. By doing this, you can create a custom installation option that will allow a user to install only a portion of the distribution files.

After you modify the SETUP.LST file, you will complete your customized setup application by compiling and recompressing the customized setup program, and then creating your distribution disks.

The following few sections describe how to carry out each step required to create a custom Setup program.

Step 1: Using the SetupWizard to Determine Distribution Files

When determining which files should be distributed, you can use the SetupWizard. As described in the previous section, the SetupWizard is capable of determining which data, text, and initialization files should be included with your application; OCXes and VBXs that are referenced by your application; shared files such as DLLs that your application requires; and local and remote OLE servers that are referenced by your application. This can prove to be a time-consuming and difficult task if done manually.

To use the SetupWizard, follow the steps which were described in a previous section in this chapter, "Using the Visual Basic SetupWizard." That section guides you through the actions that are required to determine which files will be distributed with your setup application.

After the SetupWizard has determined which files should be distributed, SetupWizard will lay out the distribution disks and compress the distribution files for you. Because you will modify several of the files that the SetupWizard has compressed, it is a good idea to have the SetupWizard create a distribution directory instead of copying the distribution files to floppy disks. When you have finished modifying the setup application and the distribution files, you can compress the modified files manually and create your own set of distribution disks.

The SetupWizard will also create a SETUP.LST file, which includes the name, file size, file date, version number, and destination directory of all the files distributed with your application. You also can create the SETUP.LST file manually. However, creating the entire file by hand and modifying it may prove extremely time-consuming and prone to mistakes. Using the SetupWizard to create the SETUP.LST file will save you valuable development time.

Finally, the SetupWizard will create a copy of the sample installation application project that is included with the Setup Toolkit. You will modify this copy of the sample application at a later point. Note that the SetupWizard will make a copy of the setup project that is located in the \SETUPKIT\SETUP1 directory. If you modify the project located in this directory and save it, all subsequent Setup programs created by the SetupWizard will include these changes. To avoid this condition, you should always make a copy of the file that is contained in \SETUPKIT\SETUP1 before making any changes.

In this example, we will use the SetupWizard to create distribution files for the HELLO sample project included with Visual Basic. This project can be found in the \SAMPLES\REMAUTO\HELLO directory. The HELLO sample project uses OLE automation to display a message box. We will create distribution disks that install both the client files and the server files.

To experience the features of the SetupWizard and the Setup Toolkit, we will make several modifications to the HELLO project before creating a Setup program. You will want to make a copy of the HELLO project and place it in a new directory before modifying this project.

Follow these steps to create distribution files for the HELLO sample application:

1. Open the HELLO server sample project. This project file is named HELO_SVR.VBP. From the File menu, choose Make EXE File. Name the .EXE file HELO_SVR.EXE and save it to the same directory as the project file. This will create and register the OLE server component on your machine.

2. Save the HELO_SVR.VBP project and close it.

3. Open the HELO_CLI.VBP project. Under the Tools menu, select Reference.

4. The freshly created HELO_SVR OLE automation server appears near the bottom of the Libraries/Projects list. Note that HELO_CLI also appears on the list. Make sure that you select the HELO_SVR.EXE file. Create a reference to this file by selecting the check box to the left of the file name.

5. Close the References dialog box and select Make EXE File from the File menu. Name the .EXE file HELO_CLI.EXE and save it to the same directory as the project file. After you have created the .EXE file, save the HELO_CLI.VBP project and close it.

6. Start the SetupWizard. In the Step 1 dialog box, select the HELO_CLI.VBP Visual Basic project as your project file. Because you just created the project's .EXE file, you do not need to select the Rebuild the Project's EXE File check box. Click the Next button to continue. The SetupWizard will begin to process the HELO_CLI.VBP project file.

7. Because the HELO_CLI project does not use any type of database access, the Step 2 dialog box is not displayed. Instead, the SetupWizard moves directly to the Step 3 dialog box. In the Step 3 dialog box, choose a destination directory for the distribution files by clicking the Directory option button. Choose the directory in which you want to place your distribution files and click the Next button to continue.

8. The Step 4 dialog box appears. Because the HELO_CLI project references the HELO_SVR OLE automation server, the Step 4 dialog box lists HELO_SVR.EXE as a dependent file. To see information about the HELO_SVR.EXE OLE server, select the file in the list and click the File Details button. Click the Next button to continue.

9. The Step 5 dialog box indicates the HELO_CLI project has another dependent file, OLEPRO32.DLL. This file will be included with your distribution files. Click the Next button to continue.

10. In the Step 6 dialog box, select `Install in application directory` as your deployment model. Do not select the `Install remote OLE automation server components` check box. Click the Next button to continue.

11. The Step 7 dialog box lists all other files required by the HELO_CLI project to operate on a user's machine. To see the dependencies of each file, select a file from the list and look in the Dependency Of group box.

12. Click the Add Files button. You will add Visual Basic's Help file to the distribution files. To do this, locate the Help file. You can find the Help file in the same directory in which you installed the Visual Basic main executable file. Click the OK button to return to the Step 7 dialog box.

13. Click the Finish button to continue. The SetupWizard begins compressing and copying the distribution files to the destination directory you specified in step 7 of this example.

The SetupWizard has placed compressed copies of your distribution files into the directory you specified in step 3. You can use a text editor to open SETUP.LST and review all of the files that are included. Notice how the SETUP.LST file lists the name of each file, its file date, its size, and several other attributes.

The SetupWizard also created a file named SETUP.EXE and a file named SETUP132.EXE. The SETUP.EXE file is used to load the Setup program's bootstrap files and to launch the installation program. The SETUP132.EXE file is a compiled version of the SETUP1 sample installation program. You will replace the SETUP132.EXE file after you modify it.

Step 2: Modifying the SETUP.LST File

You learned previously in this chapter that the `CalcDiskSpace` and `CopySection` functions use file section headings in the SETUP.LST file to calculate the disk space required by a file section and to copy files to a user's machine. For example, the following statement will copy all files listed under the [FILES] section of the SETUP.LST file:

```
CopySection "Files"
```

This statement makes the CopySection function extremely powerful. By adding or removing sections from the SETUP.LST file, you can create custom setup options.

In this example, you want to give your users the option to install all files or only the files that are necessary to run the executable file. To do this, you need two file sections. For the first section, you will use the [FILES] section created by the SetupWizard. The [FILES] section should contain the following list of files:

```
[Files]
File1=1,,OLEPRO32.DL_,OLEPRO32.DLL,$(WinSysPath),$(DLLSelfRegister),
➥$(Shared),6/15/1995,74240,4.0.0.5135
File2=1,,Helo_svr.ex_,Helo_svr.exe,$(CommonFiles)\OleSvr,$(EXESelfRegister)
➥,$(Shared),8/3/1995,11264,1.0.0.2212
File3=1,,Helo_cli.ex_,Helo_cli.exe,$(AppPath),
➥$(EXESelfRegister),,8/3/1995,9216,1.0.0.0
File4=1,,VB.HL_,VB.HLP,$(AppPath),,,6/15/1995,3634571
```

Remember to make all changes to the SETUP.LST file located in the directory in which the SetupWizard placed your distribution files.

For the second section, you need to create a section named [HELP]. In it you will add only the Visual Basic Help file. You should add the following two lines to the SETUP.LST file:

```
[HELP]
File4=1,,VB.HL_,VB.HLP,$(AppPath),,,6/15/1995,3634571
```

Finally you should remove the following line from the [FILES] section:

```
File4=1,,VB.HL_,VB.HLP,$(AppPath),,,6/15/1995,3634571
```

In the following section, we will make modifications to the setup application that will permit it to copy only the files that are listed in the [FILES] section if a user selects the Minimal installation option or to copy the files in the [FILES] and [HELP] sections if a user selects the Complete installation option.

Step 3: Modifying the Sample Setup Application

After the SetupWizard has determined the file dependencies of your application and created an executable version of the sample setup application, you can begin to modify the sample setup application to include your new installation options. You can add to the Setup program any kind of option that is programmatically possible through Visual Basic. For example, you may want to incorporate a custom compression mechanism to compress and extract the distribution files. You may want to create a splash screen that reminds users to register their copy of the application. This section explains how to create a setup option that allows a user to choose between two setup options—Minimal and Complete.

The Minimal installation option will install only the program files that are necessary to run the application. In this case, the only file in the system not required by the application is the Visual Basic Help file. The Complete installation option will copy all files to a user's machine, including the Visual Basic Help file.

We will need to make several changes to the sample installation project. First, we will add a dialog box that asks the user which installation option he or she prefers. Second, we will adjust the Form_Load event to copy all the files (in the case of a Complete installation) or all the files, except the Help file (which is the case when you are providing a Minimal installation).

Before you make any changes to the sample setup project, you should copy the contents of the SETUP1 directory to a new directory. Remember that the SetupWizard will use the project in the SETUP1 directory to create the SETUP132.EXE application. If you modify the project in the SETUP1 directory, these changes will appear in all subsequent SETUP132.EXE files generated by the SetupWizard.

The floppy disk included with this book contains a dialog box that you can add to the sample Setup program. You can find the Install Options dialog box, named frmInstallOptions, in the \SAMPLES\SETUP directory, which is saved under the file name, INSTOPS.FRM. Add this form to the sample Setup program by selecting the Add File option from Visual Basic's File menu. The Install Options dialog box is shown in figure 16.13.

Fig. 16.13
The Install Options dialog box.

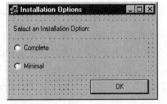

You will also need to add some code to the Setup form's Form_Load event and the basSetup code module. In the basSetup code module, add the following variable declarations:

```
'Return value for installation options
Global Const INSTALL_COMPLETE = 0
Global Const INSTALL_MINIMAL = 1
Global giInstallOption As Integer
```

In the frmSetup1 form, add the following lines of code to the Form_Load event:

```
Const strHELP_FILES$ = "Help"
Dim liInstallOption As Integer
```

You will also add the following block of code to frmSetup1. This addition will create the ShowOptionsDialog procedure, which is used to display the Install Options form.

```
Sub ShowOptionsDialog(ByRef aiInstallOption As Integer)

    ' Procedure displays the options dialog
    ' form which prompts a user to select one
    ' of two installation options

    giInstallOption = 0
    frmInstallOptions.Show 1
    aiInstallOption = giInstallOption

End Sub
```

You will need to make two more additions to the Setup form's Form_Load event. The first addition will call the ShowOptionsDialog function and display the Install Options dialog box. The sample setup application includes a place holder, indicating where this line of code should appear. You will need to scroll through the Form_Load event until you find the following block of comments:

```
'This would be a good place to display an option dialog,
'allowing the user a chance to select installation options:
'samples, docs, help files, etc. Results of this dialog would
'be checked in the loop below.
'ShowOptionsDialog (Function you could write with _
                    option check boxes, etc.)
    '
```

Replace the ShowOptionsDialog line with the following code:

```
'ShowOptionsDialog liInstallOption
```

This new line of code will call the ShowOptionsDialog function and display the Install Options form. When the user makes a selection regarding which type of installation he or she wants, Complete or Minimal, this choice is stored in the variable, liInstallOption. You will add two more blocks of code to the Form_Load event that will employ the user's installation-option selection to calculate the amount of disk space that is required by the installation and to copy the appropriate files.

Continue to scroll down through the Form_Load event until you find this block of code:

```
'If chkInstallSamples.Value = TRUE then
'    CalcDiskSpace "Samples"
'End If
```

Replace it with the following code:

```
If liInstallOption = INSTALL_COMPLETE Then
    CalcDiskSpace strHELP_FILES
End If
```

You learned in a previous section that the CalcDiskSpace function calculates the amount of disk space that is required by the application. If the user chooses the Complete installation option, this block of code will cause the Setup program to include the Help files after it determines the amount of space that is required by the application. If the user chooses the Minimal installation option, the Help files will not be included by the Setup program.

To make the final adjustment to the Form_Load event, scroll down until you find this block of code:

```
'If chkInstallSamples.Value = TRUE then
'    CopySection "Samples"
'End If
'
```

Replace it with the following code:

```
If liInstallOption = INSTALL_COMPLETE Then
    CopySection strHELP_FILES
End If
```

You learned previously in this chapter that the CopySection function reads the SETUP.LST file, and then copies the files under each section heading. In this case, the Setup program copies the files under the Help section of the SETUP.LST file, if the user chooses the Complete installation option. If the user chooses the Minimal installation option, the Help file is ignored.

Your changes to the sample setup application are now complete. The next section describes how to recompress the modified file and copy it to your distribution disks.

Step 4: Recompressing the Modified Setup Program and Creating Distribution Disks

Now that you have finished modifying the Setup program, you need to recompress this program, and then place it onto the distribution disks with the rest of your distribution files. First, you should re-create your application's .EXE file by selecting the Make EXE File option from Visual Basic's File menu. You can name the .EXE file anything you want, but if you change the name to something other than SETUP132.EXE you will need to update the Setup entry of your SETUP.LST file.

To compress the file, you will use the COMPRESS.EXE file located in the \SETUPKIT\KITFILES directory. COMPRESS.EXE is a DOS program, so you will need to go to an MS-DOS prompt to run the utility. To compress the SETUP132.EXE file, enter the following command at the DOS prompt:

```
compress -r SETUP132.EXE
```

The **-r** switch automatically replaces the last character of the compressed file with an underscore character.

You now can copy the compressed SETUP132.EX_ file to the directory in which the rest of your installation files reside. You should replace the existing SETUP132.EX_ file.

Now, you are ready to copy your distribution files to floppy disks. Because the compressed installation files for the customized Setup program require only one disk, you can copy all of the files onto a single floppy. If the project required more than one disk, you would need to read the SETUP.LST file in order to determine the location of each file.

After all of the distribution files have been copied to the floppy disks, you can install the HELO_CLI application by inserting the disk into your A: drive and by running the SETUP.EXE program.

Developing Service-Specific Installation Programs

In a distributed computing environment, you may have user services that must reside on one machine and business or data services that must reside across a network. How does this "cross environment" file distribution affect a distribution application? It means that you will not have to distribute every file every time you perform an installation. For example, if your application accesses a remote OLE server, you may need to install only the OLE server once to a file server on the LAN, and then simply register the remote server at each user's workstation.

You also may need to address the laptop-versus-LAN user requirement. Users with access to the LAN will be able to share files located on a file server. This means that you can place a single copy of many OLE servers, DLLs, or other shared files onto the file server. Laptop users, however, will be able to access the shared files on the LAN. To rectify this difficulty, you will need a separate installation option that installs all files to a user's laptop machine.

When distributing an application in the enterprise, you will need to develop an installation application for each of the following components:

- User services
- Business services
- Data services
- Laptop users

The remainder of this section describes the requirements of the setup application for each component.

User Services

The user services installation application will be similar to the sample setup application that you developed in this chapter. The user services installation application will install the main application's .EXE file to a user's machine along with any DLLs, local OLE servers, or other dependency files required by the application. It also will register both local and remote OLE servers.

Although the user services installation application will register remote OLE servers, it will not install them. This installation is accomplished by the business services installation application. The user services application will install no other shared files, such as DLLs used by the business services or any other files that may be accessed from multiple user machines. Again, these files will be installed by the business services installation application.

The user services installation application may offer several types of installation options, such as complete or minimal installations that will install all files or only the files necessary to run the application, respectively. The setup application will also perform some additional actions that will not appear in the business services or data services installations, such as the creation of Program Manager icons or Start menu links.

Business Services

The business services installation application will install the OLE servers that comprise the business services tier of the application. This installation includes the OLE servers that will be accessed by remote clients and any dependency files required by the business servers, as well as any local OLE servers used by the business servers. The installation application will also register the OLE servers.

Because users will share most of the files that comprise the business services, this installation application will probably be run fewer times than the user services installation application. Because of this, it may seem to make more sense to just manually copy the files to a file server. As we discussed previously in the chapter, it is generally worth the time and effort to create an installation program for business services. Because you probably will leave a project eventually, the installation application ensures that persons without an intimate knowledge of the files that comprise the business services will be able to install them without your support.

Data Services

The data services installation application will be much like the business services application, installing files that will be shared by most users over the network. The data services installation program may copy the script files that are used to create a database as well as populate the database tables and create stored procedures used with the application.

As with the business services installation application, the data services Setup program will be run less often than the user services installation application. It is still an important program, however, because it will allow someone without a detailed understanding of the files that comprise the data services to install them.

Laptop Users

Laptop or remote users present special situations that may require a modified version of your installation routine. For simplicity, the remainder of this section uses the term, *laptop user*, to refer to all users who do not have direct, full-time access to the LAN.

Because laptop users may not have access to the LAN at all times, you may need to develop an installation application that installs all of the files of the user, business, and data services tiers onto the user's machine. This installation will allow laptop users to run the application, even when they are not "connected." You may require a special version of the application—one that is able to determine whether it is being run in a laptop environment or a normal environment. In the laptop environment, the application might write data to a local database instead of a database server. The application might require access through an RAS connection rather than a direct network connection. As you will see, the files that are copied during this installation may not be the same files as the files that are used in a non-laptop installation.

For example, a laptop installation may use an Access database rather than a SQL Server database. This will require a different set of files—the Access database itself—to be installed with the data services tier. The laptop installation also may not always be able to access remote OLE servers. This can mean that all OLE servers must be installed and registered as local OLE servers.

You do not necessarily need to create a unique installation program for the laptop users. You may want to include **Laptop** as an option in your Setup program, in addition to the **Complete** and **Minimal** setup options. If you plan on distributing setup disks to a large number of users, and the laptop setup requires several additional floppy disks, you may find that creating a special Setup program for laptop users—rather than distributing the additional disks—is the most economical and efficient solution.

The main point to remember when creating an installation program is to consider not only the files that are required to run your application but also the files that are required to run the application in different user environments. Remembering this point will help you to create a setup application that is capable of installing your program files for both the local and the laptop users.

Testing Your Distribution Application

Just as with any other application, your distribution application should be tested. Aside from following the normal debugging measures that need to be taken with a production application, you will also need to ensure that the Setup program contains all the files that are necessary to run your executable file properly. To test the distribution application, you should run it and install the application you will be distributing. After installation, run the distributed application. If the application fails because it is unable to locate a DLL or some similar type of dependency file, you will need to find and include the missing file with your setup application.

From Here...

This chapter described the Visual Basic SetupWizard and how you can use it create setup applications. After reading this chapter, you should understand the basic features and functionality of the SetupWizard, how to create a setup program by using the SetupWizard, and how to create your own customized installation applications.

For more information on specific items mentioned in this chapter, review the following chapters:

- Chapter 6, "Creating OLE Objects," for more information about creating OLE objects.

- Chapter 7, "Managing OLE Objects," for more information about remote OLE automation.

- Chapter 8, "Architecting Tier 1: Client Applications," for more information about creating a Visual Basic application.

- Chapter 17, "Extending Visual Basic," for information about including DLLs and other files with your Visual Basic applications.

IV

Application Enhancements

Extending Visual Basic

One feature that distinguishes Visual Basic from other development environments is the ease in which Visual Basic can be extended. This chapter discusses the ways in which you can extend Visual Basic beyond what comes in the box.

In this chapter, we will look at options such as:

- Third-party custom controls

- Using the Windows Application Programming Interface (API) to perform native Windows operations

- Extending the Visual Basic integrated development environment, using Add-Ins

- Using other API sets to perform Remote Access and Telephony operations

After discussing each option at a high level, this chapter goes into some specifics of implementing each mechanism and discusses some extensions that are commonly found in Visual Basic applications.

Ways to Extend VB

Visual Basic provides three main mechanisms for extending the development environment:

- Use of third-party custom controls

- Calls to external DLLs, including the Windows API

- Visual Basic add-in components

In the following section, we discuss each of these mechanisms in detail.

Using OCXes and VBXs

OCXes and VBXs are the most common means of extending the Visual Basic programming environment. VBXs (Visual Basic Custom Controls) and OCXes (OLE Custom Controls) are reusable code modules that you can include in a Visual Basic application to provide features such as a spreadsheet control or an electronic-mail interface. Hundreds of third-party custom controls are available for Visual Basic.

VBX is the original custom control specification designed for Visual Basic. These controls usually are developed by using a programming language such as C. VBX custom controls were designed specifically for 16-bit Windows, and cannot be used by a 32-bit Visual Basic application.

OCX is the new custom control specification that works in both the 16-bit and 32-bit Windows environments. These "controls" actually are OLE objects that you can include as part of your project. As 32-bit Windows OLE development becomes the standard, the major VBX vendors will shift their existing VBX controls over to the OCX format. OLE controls operate as in-process OLE objects for fast performance.

Custom controls expose a series of properties, events, and methods that the Visual Basic developer can manipulate. A spreadsheet custom control, for example, might expose a *Sort* method and *Column* property to identify the columns to sort by and the sort order, which allows the developer to sort the spreadsheet by simply setting the property values and calling the sort method, rather than implementing a sorting algorithm in Visual Basic code.

Custom controls enable Visual Basic developers to buy, rather than build, functionality from scratch. These custom controls provide a majority of the functionality that is common across applications.

Using the Windows API

Visual Basic provides the capability for applications developers to develop Windows applications without needing to have an intimate knowledge of the inner workings of the Windows operating system. At the same time, Visual Basic also provides the developer with the capability to access a majority of the native Windows APIs (Application Programming Interfaces) to perform standard Windows operations that cannot be handled inherently within Visual Basic.

This chapter discusses how to access the Windows API from within Visual Basic and demonstrate some of its more common uses. This chapter also focuses on the Windows APIs, but the concepts discussed can be applied to any external function within a DLL (Dynamic-link Library).

First, we discuss the manner in which external procedures are declared within Visual Basic, the ways that parameters can be passed to these procedures, and how to map the data types, usually defined for the C programming language, to datatypes available within Visual Basic. After understanding how to declare the external procedures you want to use, this chapter discusses the differences between the 16-bit and 32-bit Windows operating systems and how these differences effect the use of DLL procedures.

Declaring Functions

For a DLL procedure to be used by Visual Basic, it first must be defined, using the *Declare* statement within the declarations section of a form, standard module or class module. DLL procedure declarations adhere to the same scoping rules that exist for normal Visual Basic procedures and variables. When a DLL procedure is declared in a standard module, its scope is public and accessible from anywhere within the application. When declaring a DLL procedure in the declarations section of a form or class module, the Private keyword must be included.

DLL procedures that return a value are declared as Functions, using the following syntax:

```
Declare Function publicname Lib libname [Alias "alias"]
➥[([ByVal]variable [As Type] [, _...])] As Type
```
Procedures that do not return a value are declared as Sub procedures using the following syntax:

```
Declare Sub publicname Lib libname [Alias "alias"][(ByVal]
➥variable [As Type] [,...])]
```

Table 17.1 explains each element of the Visual Basic Declare statement.

Table 17.1 Elements of the Visual Basic Declare Statement	
Statement Element	**Description**
PublicName	Procedure name to be used by the Visual Basic applications and the actual DLL procedure name, if the alias clause is not used.
LibName	Library or DLL where the function is located. Can contain a fully qualified path.

(continues)

Table 17.1 Continued	
Statement Element	**Description**
Alias	Name of the procedure within the DLL being declared (discussed in detail in a following section of this chapter).
VariableList	A list of parameters that is being passed to the procedure and the data types that are expected.

When the complete path isn't included in the *LibName*, Visual Basic searches for the file in the following locations, in the following order:

1. Currently loaded in memory.

2. The directory containing the .EXE file.

3. The current directory.

4. The Windows 32-bit system directory, if present (usually \WINDOWS\SYSTEM32).

5. The Windows 16-bit system directory (usually \WINDOWS\SYSTEM).

6. The Windows directory (usually \WINDOWS).

7. The PATH environment variable.

When using the Windows API, the DLLs that are referenced are located in the \WINDOWS or \WINDOWS\SYSTEM directory. DLLs shared by multiple applications also should be placed in the \WINDOWS\SYSTEM directory, so that all of the applications can use them. DLLs that provide functionality that is used by only one application usually reside in the same directory as the .EXE file, which allows the application to be easily uninstalled without leaving DLL files scattered around the machine.

Standard Declarations

The standard Visual Basic DLL procedure declaration uses the public name defined within the DLL as the procedure name used within the application.

The following example demonstrates the declaration and use of a DLL function that returns a value. In this example, the GetWindowsDirectory procedure located in the Windows "Kernal" library is used to retrieve the directory where Windows is installed. The specifics of this example are discussed in following sections of the chapter.

```
Declare Function GetWindowsDirectory Lib "Kernal"(ByVal lpBuffer
➥As String, ByVal nSize As Integer) As Integer
Function FindWinDir() As String
    'Get the users Windows directory
    Dim lsWinDir As String
    Dim liRtnCd As Integer
    Const PATH_SIZE = 255
    'initialize the local variable
    lsWinDir = Space(PATH_SIZE)
    liRtnCd = GetWindowsDirectory(lsWinDir, PATH_SIZE)
    'return the Windows directory
    FindWinDir = Left$(Trim$(lsWinDir))
End Function
```

The following example demonstrates the declaration and use of a DLL procedure that doesn't return a value. This example uses the UpdateWindows API to immediately refresh a window, redrawing any areas of the window that were previously not visible:

```
Declare Sub UpdateWindows Lib "User" (ByVal hWnd As Integer)
Sub RefreshWin(hWnd As Integer)
    'Refresh the window identified by the hWnd window handle
    Call UpdateWindow(hWnd)
End Sub
```

Using Alias

The preceding section demonstrated the standard and most common way of declaring DLL procedures within Visual Basic. There are times, however, when you need to declare the public name for a DLL procedure used by Visual Basic as something other than the procedure name found in the DLL itself, which is helpful in the following situations:

- When the DLL procedure name contains a value that makes it an illegal identifier within Visual Basic

- When developing shared code modules that use common API declarations to avoid a conflict

- When a DLL procedure needs to be declared many times with different parameter data types instead of using As Any.

In these situations, the Alias clause of the Declare statement can be used to define the public_name for the procedure as something other than the DLL procedure name.

In the following example, the DLL's procedure name is not a valid Visual Basic identifier because it begins with an underscore. The following Declare statement will allow the application to use this procedure by aliasing it with a public_name that is a legal identifier.

```
Declare Function LCreateFile Lib "Kernal" Alias "_lcreat"(ByVal
➥lpFileName As String, ByVal nAttribute As Integer) As Integer
```

In the following example, which you can find on the companion disk in the
\CHAP17 directory, the error-processing function writes to a log file located
in the users Windows directory (see Listing 17.1). Because the Windows API
to retrieve the Windows directory is commonly used, the alias clause is used
to ensure that a duplicate declaration doesn't occur when other applications
include this procedure.

Listing 17.1   CODE01.TXT—Aliasing a commonly used Windows API

```
Declare Function ERRPROC_GetWinDir Lib "Kernal" Alias _
    "GetWindowsDirectory" (ByVal lpBuffer As String, _
                    ByVal nSize As Integer) As Integer


Sub LogMsg (ByVal vsProcName As String, _
            ByVal vsMsgText1 As String, _
            ByVal vsMsgText2 As String)
    'this procedure will write a message to the
    ' error log that is located in the users windows directory.
    Dim lsWinDir As String
    Dim lsFileName As String
    Dim liRtnCd As Integer
    Dim lsStr1 As String
    Dim lsStr2 As String
    Dim lsStr3 As String
    Const PATH_SIZE = 255
    'get the windows directory
    lsWinDir = Space(PATH_SIZE)
    liRtnCd = ERRPROC_GetWinDir(lsWinDir, PATH_SIZE)
    lsWinDir = Left$(Trim$(lsWinDir))
    'get the file name
    lsFileName = lsWinDir & "\" & App.EXEName & ".log"
    'format the strings to be logged
    If Len(vsProcName) <> 0 Then lsStr1 = " Procedure: " &
    ➥Trim(vsProcName)
    If Len(vsMsgText1) <> 0 Then lsStr2 = " Data 1: " &
    ➥Trim(vsMsgText1)
    If Len(vsMsgText2) <> 0 Then lsStr3 = " Data 2: " &
    ➥Trim(vsMsgText2)
    'open the file for append so that if it does not exist it
    'will be created
    'otherwise this entry will be placed at the end of the file.
    Open lsFileName For Append As 1
    'add the new message line to the file
    Print #1, Format$(Now, "General Date") & lsStr1 & lsStr2 &
    ➥lsStr3
    'close the file
    Close 1
End Sub
```

Call by Reference Versus by Value

Like procedures written in Visual Basic, most DLL procedures need data to be passed into the procedure and often return data to the calling procedure.

For a DLL procedure to update the value of the parameter it is passed, it must be given the address of the parameter. This is known as *passing the parameter by reference*. When a parameter is passed by reference, the procedure is given a pointer to the actual memory location that contains the variable. When Visual Basic passes a parameter to a procedure, the default process is to pass the parameter by reference. To force the parameter to be passed by value, it must be specified in the procedure's declaration. When the DLL procedure does not need to update the parameters value—it usually expects the value of the parameter, not a reference to its location. To pass a variable by value in Visual Basic, the Declare statement for the procedure should define the parameter, as is shown in the following example:

```
Declare procedurename Lib libname (ByVal variablename As datatype)
```

The string data type is an exception to this rule because of how Visual Basic handles strings internally. We discuss these exceptions in detail in following sections the chapter.

Specifying Parameter Data Types

The Declare statement used in Visual Basic contains an optional parameter list for the DLL procedure. Specifying the parameters for a procedure allows Visual Basic to check the statement used to call the procedure to ensure that the values being passed match what is expected.

Most DLL procedures accessed from Visual Basic were written in C. Therefore, most of the documentation for these procedures is written for a C developer. To successfully call a procedure in a DLL, you must pass the proper parameters to the procedure, which requires that the C data types in the documentation be translated into data types available within Visual Basic.

Table 17.2 lists the common data types used for DLL parameters, and their Visual Basic equivalents.

Table 17.2 Common C Datatypes and their Visual Basic Equivalents

C Data Type	Declare as	VB Data Type
BOOL	ByVal *var* As Boolean	Boolean
LPSTR (pointer to a string)	ByVal *var* As String	String

(continues)

Table 17.2	Continued	
C Data Type	**Declare as**	**VB Data Type**
LPDWORD (pointer to a long integer)	*var* As Long	Long
DWORD, LONG	ByVal *var* As Long	Long
WORD	ByVal *var* As Long	Long
Pointer to Void	*var* As Any	Any variable (must use ByVal for strings)
NULL	As Any or ByVal *var* As Long	ByVal Nothing or ByVal &0 or vbNullString
char	ByVal *var* As Byte	Byte
Pointer to char	*var* As Byte	Byte
Null Pointer	ByVal *var* As String	vbNullString

For many of these data types, special considerations must be taken into account to ensure that the procedure is called correctly and that a General Protection Fault (GPF) is not generated from an incorrect calling method. A GPF can occur when an application accesses a location in memory and encounters invalid data or data that has been modified, which can occur if the DLL procedure is called with parameters of the wrong data type. The following section discusses these considerations.

Strings

You need to give special attention to DLLs that expect string parameters and understand the following three aspects of using strings:

- Passing strings to DLLs

- Passing strings to procedures that modify the string

- Passing strings to OLE Automation DLLs

Passing Strings

Visual Basic uses a data type defined by OLE Automation which is known as a BSTR to represent a string. Data stored in a BSTR variable contains a header with information that is used by Visual Basic. The BSTR acts like a pointer to the first byte of a null-terminated string, this is the first position after the header information.

Most DLL procedures, including the Windows APIs, use LPSTR strings, which act as pointers to standard null-terminated C strings, and do not have the header prefix. Because Visual Basic defaults to passing parameters by reference, a BSTR variable within a Visual Basic application is passed as a pointer to a pointer that contains the first element of the null-terminated string. Passing a BSTR variable by value—using the ByVal clause—passes a pointer to the first element of the null-terminated string (the area after the header), which, when passed to a DLL procedure, makes the BSTR variable look like an LPSTR variable.

To ensure that strings are handled correctly when calling a DLL procedure, they always should be passed by value, even if the DLL is going to modify the data. Strings can be passed by reference only if the DLL procedure was written to handle the OLE Automation BSTR data type.

Passing Strings that Will Be Modified

DLL procedures can modify the string parameters that they receive as arguments. A DLL procedure has no means to determine the length of a string parameter. If the return value is longer than the parameter that is passed in, the procedure simply continues to write beyond the end of the string, potentially overwriting other application data.

To avoid this, pass fixed length string variables to the parameters that will be modified, and set the string length to the largest possible value of the return string. These variables can be declared as strings using the following syntax, which declares the variable as a fixed length string:

```
Dim variable As String * length
```

They also can be initialized with the String() or Space() functions as in the following examples:

```
variable = String(length, character)
```

or

```
variable = Space(length)
```

These functions initialize the variable to a blank string with *length* elements. When using the Windows API, procedures usually do not return strings longer than 255 characters.

Initializing string variables before passing them to DLLs also ensures that the return string will contain only the correct data, not data from a previous call to the function. When a DLL procedure updates the value of a string parameter with data that is shorter than the length of the given string, the data that previously existed in the string will remain.

Passing Strings to OLE Automation DLLs

Some DLLs that are written specifically for OLE Automation use the OLE Automation data types, such as BSTR. Because Visual Basic uses the OLE Automation data types as its internal data types, arguments can be passed by reference to any of these DLL procedures. If a DLL procedure expects an OLE Automation string as an argument, the declare statement does not need to specify the **ByVal** clause for this argument. The ByVal clause is needed only if the procedure expects the argument to be passed by value.

User-Defined Types

Some DLL procedures expect a user-defined type, or structure, as an argument. The individual elements of a user-defined type can be passed to procedures just like ordinary variable parameters. To pass the entire structure to the procedure as a single argument, simply pass it by reference.

This process works because Visual Basic passes the address of the first element of the user-defined type to the procedure. The remaining elements are stored in memory following this first element. User-defined types cannot be passed by value.

The Listing 17.2 example uses the GetCursorPos API to determine the location of the mouse pointer on-screen. This procedure expects a user-defined type POINTAPI as an argument. The following user-defined data type contains two elements that correspond to the X and Y coordinates of the mouse pointer. This example is located in the \CHAP17 directory on the companion disk.

Listing 17.2   CODE02.TXT—Passing user defined types to DLL procedures

```
'Windows API function declarations
Declare Sub GetCursorPos Lib "User" (lpPoint As POINTAPI)
'Type used by the GetCursorPos() API
Type POINTAPI
    x As Integer
    Y As Integer
End Type

Sub GetMousePosition(lpPoint As POINTAPI)
'return the current mouse pointer position
    'get the current mouseposition
    Call GetCursorPos(lpPoint)
End Sub
```

User-defined types can contain elements of any data type, including BSTR strings, objects, and arrays. User-defined types that contain strings, which are fixed length, look like a LPSTR string when passed to a DLL procedure. Variable-length strings however, are passed as a pointer to the string data.

Passing Properties

Properties can be passed only by value. If the DLL procedure argument is declared by using By Val, the property can be passed directly.

Properties cannot be passed by reference. If you want a DLL procedure to update the value of a property, you must use an intermediate variable.

DLL Calls from 16-Bit Versus 32-Bit Applications

This book focuses mainly on the techniques needed to develop 32-bit applications. There are, however, times when an application needs to be written to work in both 16- and 32-bit environments which ideally should be accomplished by using one set of source code and Visual Basic's conditional compilation.

Special consideration must be given to the way DLL procedures are called from 16-bit versus 32-bit applications. To remain backward-compatible, the Windows 3.1 API calls are included in both Windows 95 and Windows NT.

Declaring Procedures

In the 16-bit environment, DLL procedure calls aren't case-sensitive, so TestProcedure and TESTPROCEDURE both refer to the same DLL procedure. In 32-bit environments however, DLL procedure calls are case-sensitive. The preceding example will produce a run-time error because TESTPROCEDURE isn't an existing procedure name.

The 16-bit environment also differs in how it searches for the procedure libraries when not given a fully qualified path in the Declare statement. In a 16-bit environment Visual Basic will search these locations for the DLL in the following
order:

1. The current directory

2. The Windows directory (often \WINDOWS)

3. The Windows system directory (often \WINDOWS\SYSTEM)

4. The directory containing the executable (.EXE) file

5. The PATH environment variable

Data Type Differences

Arguments passed to DLL procedures in the 16- and 32-bit environments use the same data types except in the following instances:

- In 32-bit environments the C integer data type always should be passed as a Visual Basic Long. In the 16-bit environment, a Visual Basic Integer should be used.

- In 32-bit environments, the Window handles (hWnd) are passed as a Visual Basic Long. In the 16-bit environment, an Integer is used.

Unicode Versus ANSI

16-bit Visual Basic applications use ANSI to store and manipulate strings. The 32-bit version uses Unicode to deal with strings. The conversions between these two string formats are for the most part hidden, but it is important to understand what goes on behind the screens.

ANSI is a character set in which each character is represented by a single byte. The Unicode character set, however, represents each character by using two bytes, which provides the capability to cover 65,000 unique characters, where the ANSI character set can represent only 256 characters.

Table 17.3 describes the character set used by the Windows operating system and development environments.

Table 17.3   Character Sets Used By the Windows Operating Systems

Environment	Character set
Windows 3.1 API	ANSI
Windows 95 API	ANSI
Windows NT API	Unicode
16-bit Visual Basic	ANSI
32-bit Visual Basic	Unicode
16-bit object libraries	ANSI
32-bit object libraries	Unicode
Windows 95 OLE Automation	Unicode
Windows NT OLE Automation	Unicode

Using Byte Versus String

When dealing with binary data in Visual Basic programs, it is important to store this data by using the Byte data type. The Byte data type allows access to the data on a byte-by-byte basis. which ensures that the application works the same way with ANSI strings as it does with Unicode strings. Visual Basic string functions such as Get and Put work the same way on Byte and String data types.

This kind of storage allows string data to be handled the same way when an application is operating in a 16-bit or 32-bit environment.

Using OLE Objects

You can use a common code base for 16-bit and 32-bit Visual Basic applications—even if one application type uses ANSI and the other Unicode character strings—because most conversions are made automatically. Visual Basic developers need to think about the following two issues when they work with OLE Automation objects across 16-bit and 32-bit environments:

- 16-bit Visual Basic applications running in a 32-bit environment with 16- and 32-bit OLE servers available will use the 16-bit version if the Server is a DLL (in-process server), and the 32-bit version if it is an .EXE (out-of-process server). The OLE interpretability layer handles the conversion of strings between Unicode and ANSI as needed.

- When 32-bit Visual Basic applications request 16-bit OLE Automation objects the OLE interpretability layer handles the conversion of Unicode to ANSI when strings are passed, and the conversion back to Unicode when strings are returned. The 32-bit OLE Servers may use ANSI internally, but Unicode is exposed externally.

Conditional Compilation

When you are developing an application that must run on both 16- and 32-bit environments, it is important that you use the DLL procedure declaration designed for the appropriate environment. This alleviates the need to worry about many of the conversion and compatibility issues that were discussed in previous sections.

To allow applications to be developed for both environments using one common code base, Visual Basic provides the capability to conditionally compile applications. This topic is discussed in more detail in Chapter 20, "Creating Development Guidelines." We talk about it here only in the context of DLL procedure declarations.

In Listing 17.3, we revisit the **GetCursorPos** API used previously in the chapter. To create a 16- and 32-bit version of this application from a common code base, this procedure must be declared for both environments. The following code, located in the \CHAP17 directory of the disk, demonstrates the use of conditional compilation to accomplish this.

Listing 17.3   CODE03.TXT—Using conditional compilation with Windows APIs

```
'Windows API function declarations
# If Win32 Then
    'declare the API using 32-bit Windows
    Declare Sub GetCursorPos Lib "User32" (lpPoint As POINTAPI)
# Else
    'declare the API using 16-bit Windows
    Declare Sub GetCursorPos Lib "User" (lpPoint As POINTAPI)
# End If
```

The Alias keyword also can be used to create one public procedure name for cases where the 16- and 32-bit DLL procedure names differ.

Visual Basic Add-Ins

Visual Basic provides the application developer with the ability to extend the Visual Basic integrated development environment (IDE) by using Add-Ins. Add-Ins are third-party or custom extensions to Visual Basic that provide support for the application developer. This type of support includes the capability to add functionality like source code control, using the SourceSafe add-in. Add-In creation is possible by accessing exposed Visual Basic objects.

Because a Visual Basic Add-In is just an OLE automation server, you can create Add-Ins with any language capable of creating an OLE Automation server, including C, C++, and Visual Basic.

In this section, we briefly discuss the Visual Basic object hierarchy to better understand the types of objects that Visual Basic exposes. After defining the object hierarchy, we discuss registering and deregistering Visual Basic add-ins.

After you understand the types of Add-Ins that can be created and how to tell Visual Basic that they exist, we go into detail about how to create an Add-In using Visual Basic.

Visual Basic Object Hierarchy

Visual Basic has exposed four types of objects that can be used when creating add-ins. These objects allow an add-in to perform the following tasks:

- Manage the addition and removal of the add-in

- Add menu items to the Visual Basic Add-Ins menu and respond to the selection of the new menu items

- Manage the creation, opening, and closing of files associated with a project

- Manipulate forms in a project and the controls on the forms

These objects, shown in figure 17.1 and described in Table 17.4, make it possible to create add-ins that handle processes such as source-code control and application development wizards.

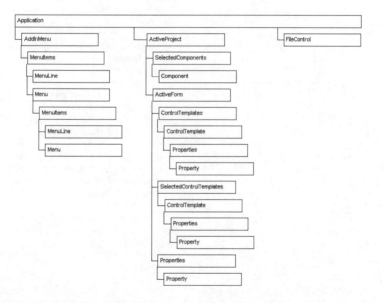

Fig. 17.1
Visual Basic object hierarchy.

Table 17.4 Exposed Visual Basic Objects and Collections

Name	Type	Description
Application	Object	Exposes properties of the current instance of Visual Basic.
Menu	Object	Represents a menu option placed under the Visual Basic Add-Ins menu. Each menu option has associated MenuItems.

(continues)

Table 17.4 Continued

Name	Type	Description
MenuItems	Collection	Represents entries for a particular menu, which may be menu lines or additional submenus.
MenuLine	Object	Represents an entry in the menu that performs an action in the application, which represents the final choice a user makes to initiate the add-in.
FileControl	Object	Handles notification of all activity in Visual Basic that results in the manipulation of files included in a project. Includes saving, renaming, loading, and creating project files.
ProjectTemplate	Object	Represents a Visual Basic project. Provides the ability to add and remove files, forms, references, and toolbox items in the project.
SelectedComponents	Collection	All currently selected components. Allows add-in to perform actions on a set of controls selected by the user.
Componet	Object	Represents a single component (form, module, and so on) in a project. Allows add-in to determine if the component has been modified and saved.
FormTemplate	Object	Represents a form in a project. Allows add-in to access properties of the form and properties of controls on the form, add code to the form module, and add menus to the form.
ControlTemplates	Collection	Represents the controls on the active form. Allows access to all existing controls on a form and the ability to add form controls.
SelectedControlTemplates	Collection	Represents currently selected controls on the active form. Allows add-in the same access as the ControlTemplates collection, but on only the selected set of controls.
ControlTemplate	Object	Represents an individual control. Allows add-in to access all design-time properties of a control, and identify the object that contains the control.

Name	Type	Description
Properties	Collection	Represents design-time properties of a control or form. Allows add-in to read and update these properties.
Property	Object	Represents an individual property. Allows add-in to read or update a property of a control or form.

Some properties and methods of these objects are discussed in more detail in a following section, "Creating Visual Basic Add-Ins." For a complete list of the properties and methods available for each of these objects, refer to the *Creating Extensions with Visual Basic* documentation provided with Visual Basic.

Registering the Add-In

The add-in needs to be notified after it is installed so that it can make itself available. This notification process is handled through the ConnectAddIn event. The ConnectAddIn event is fired when the user selects the add-in from the Add-In Manager Dialog box shown in figure 17.2. At this point, the add-in is added to Visual Basic Add-Ins menu, and the user can access its tools. To display the Add-In Manager Dialog box select Add-In Manager from the Visual Basic Add-Ins Menu.

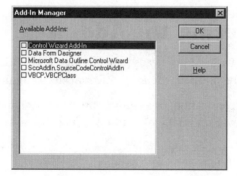

Fig. 17.2
The Visual Basic
Add-In Manager.

All Visual Basic add-ins must define the ConnectAddIn event as part of one of its classes. Visual Basic fires this event when the add-in is installed within an instance of Visual Basic. The event has one parameter that identifies the instance into which the add-in is being installed.

The ConnectAddIn event should handle the initialization of the add-in, which includes adding its menu items to the Visual Basic Add Ins menu, and all other initialization activities that it performs.

Because multiple instances of Visual Basic now can run at the same time, it is possible that an add-in will install into multiple instances. Note that the add-in doesn't assume that only one instance of the class is created.

For Visual Basic to use an add-in, the add-in OLE automation server must be installed to the system registry, and the add-in class added to the VB.INI file. The VB.INI file contains two sections where the add-ins are listed:

```
[Add-Ins16]
[Add-Ins32]
```

These sections contain the list of add-in classes available for the 16-bit and 32-bit versions of Visual Basic. The add-in should place its class name in the section that corresponds to the version it supports.

Visual Basic uses the value associated with each ProgID key in the VB.INI file to determine which add-ins are set to be installed. If the value is 1, the add-in has been installed, a value of 0 indicates that it has not.

When the Visual Basic Add-In Manager is invoked, the list of available Add-Ins is populated, based on the values found in the VB.INI file. The add-in name used is populated with the description of the Connector class, which can be set by using the Object Browser.

Deregistering the Add-In

Just as the Visual Basic add-in needs to be notified when it is installed, the add-in also must be notified when it is disconnected or removed.

To handle the disconnection, one add-in class must contain the DisconnectAddIn event. Visual Basic add-ins can be disconnected in the following two ways:

- Visual Basic is being closed (Mode = 0).

- Add-in is being removed by the Add-In Manager (Mode = 1).

For some add-ins, different actions may be required, dependent upon the method by which the add-in is being removed. To notify the add-in of the disconnect method, the DisconnectAddIn event has a parameter (Mode) that indicates how the disconnect was initiated.

To manually deregister an Add-In, open the Add-In Manager by selecting Add-In Manager from the Visual Basic Add-Ins menu. This displays the Add-In Manager dialog box that was referred to previously. All registered add-ins are checked. To deregister an add-in, uncheck the add-ins check box.

Creating Visual Basic Add-Ins

You can create Visual Basic add-ins with any programming language that is capable of creating an OLE automation server application—even Visual Basic. Now that we have discussed the basic concepts needed to create a Visual Basic add-in and the objects exposed by Visual Basic to do so, we can look at what you really need to do, using Visual Basic, to create a simple add-in. You can use the Control Wizard add-in that is supplied with this book to eliminate many of the tedious tasks that exist when creating applications in Visual Basic. This example add-in demonstrates how to use the Visual Basic objects to create an add-in that eliminates repetitive programming tasks.

Adding Menu Items

As mentioned previously, when a Visual Basic add-in is installed, additional menu options can be added to Visual Basic's Add-Ins menu. These menu options are how the developer interacts with the completed add-in.

The Control Wizard adds a Control Wizard option to Visual Basic's Add-Ins menu, shown in figure 17.3, during the ConnectAddIn event, using the Visual Basic AddInMenu object and its MenuItems collection.

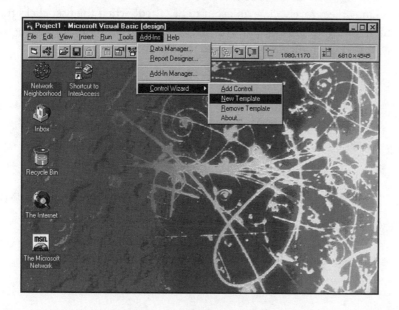

Fig. 17.3
Visual Basic Add-Ins menu, with Control Wizard installed.

The following code adds the menu options, each of which has a submenu that contains the actual actions that the user can select:

```
Sub ConnectAddIn(VBCurInstance as VBIDE.Application)
    '
    'Other connection code
    '
    With VBInstance.AddInMenu.MenuItems
        'Add our Control Wizard Menu and menu lines to the
        'Visual Basic Add-In menu.
        Set WizMenu = .AddMenu("&Control Wizard")
        With WizMenu.MenuItems
            Set MenuLines(Control) = .Add("&Add Control")
            Set MenuLines(Template) = .Add("&New Template")
            Set MenuLines(Remove) = .Add("&Remove Template")
            Set MenuLines(About) = .Add("About...")
        End With
    End With
    '
    ' continue connection processing
    '
End Sub
```

After the add-in menu is added to the Visual Basic menu, the MenuLine objects need to be associated with the procedures that will perform the actions that the user requests. The Control Wizard uses an array to track the connection IDs that will be used when each menu option is called. One event or method is defined for each menu option that is available from the add-in. To determine the exact action taken, the menu sets a property that indicates the selections that the user made.

The following code uses the ConnectEvents method of the Visual Basic MenuLine object to associate an event to be "fired" when the user clicks the menu option. This procedure also initializes the add-in instances, setting the Type property to indicate what the user wants to create:

```
Sub ConnectAddIn(VBCurInstance As VBIDE.Application)
    '
    ' Other connection code
    '
'Connect the corresponding event handler object to the correct
'menu line.
    For i% = Button To Dialog
        'Create a new handler for each option
        Set MenuHandler(i%) = New AllControls
        'Save the ID for each connected event.
        ConnectID(i%) = MenuLines(i%).ConnectEvents(MenuHandler(i%))
        'Pass the VBInstance to the child objects.
        Set MenuHandler(i%).VBInstance = VBInstance
    Next i%
    'Set the AfterClick handler for the about box.
    ConnectID(About) = MenuLines(About).ConnectEvents(Me)
```

```
    'Initialize the directional Align instances.
    MenuHandler(Control).ControlType = Control
    MenuHandler(Template).ControlType = Template
    MenuHandler(Remove).ControlType = Remove
End Sub
```

When the add-in is disconnected from the instance of Visual Basic, the menu items that were added need to be removed. The following procedure is called when the user disconnects the add-in. The MenuItems are removed by using the Remove method of the MenuItems collection. The DisconnectEvents method is used to remove the event association that was created for the MenuLines.

```
Sub DisconnectAddIn(Mode As Integer)
Dim i As Integer
Dim mnuItems As VBIDE.MenuItems
    'Remove control wizard menu items.
    Set mnuItems = WizMenu.MenuItems
    For i% = Button To About
        'Disconnect the event handlers from the menu lines
        MenuLines(i%).DisconnectEvents ConnectID(i%)
        'Remove the menu and menu lines we installed in Visual Basic
        mnuItems.Remove MenuLines(i%)
    Next i%
    'Remove items from Addins menu.
    With VBInstance.AddInMenu.MenuItems
        .Remove WizMenu
    End With
End Sub
```

Adding Forms

When the user selects an option from the add-in that might create a new dialog box, the add-in adds one to the project. The properties from the template are used to set the initial property values of the new form), and then the form is added to the project.

The following procedure uses the AddFormTemplate method of the ProjectTemplate object, to add a new blank form to the current project. The forms properties are set using the values retrieved from the user.

```
Private Sub AddDialogBox()
    'display the dialog box wizard form to get the user selections
    frmDialogWiz.Show vbModal
    If giCancel Then
        'user canceled the operation
        Exit Sub
    End If
    'create the new form
    With VBInstance.ActiveProject
        .AddFormTemplate
        'update the properties of the new form
        With .ActiveForm.Properties
```

```
                    .Item("Name").VALUE = gsFormName
                    .Item("Caption").VALUE = gsFormCaption
                    .Item("BorderStyle").VALUE = 1
            End With
        End With
    End Sub
```

Adding Controls

The default controls specified by the template are then added to the form, using the Add method of the ControlTemplates collection. The classname argument is used to denote the type of control to add.

```
    Private Sub AddButton()
        'this procedure will add a button to the active form
        With VBInstance.ActiveProject.ActiveForm
            'add a command button
            .ControlTemplates.Add "CommandButton"
            'update the controls properties
            With .SelectedControlTemplates.Properties
                .Item("Name").VALUE = "cmdOK"
                .Item("Caption").VALUE = "&OK"
                .Item("Height").VALUE = 350
            End With
        End With
    End Sub
```

Adding Code

Code that is to be placed in the new object can then be added by using the InsertFile method of the FormTemplate object. Visual Basic allows code to be inserted by retrieving the code from a file. To provide this feature, the Control Wizard has to contain text files you can import that contains the procedures needed for each object specified in the template. The add-in would then determine which text files to import, based on the template that was used.

Common Ways to Extend Visual Basic

Now that we discussed the three ways to extend the Visual Basic development environment, we can look at some Visual Basic extensions that are commonly found in custom applications. In the following sections, we will look specifically at ways a Visual Basic application can leverage functionality provided by the operating system and its API sets.

Using the Registry and INI Files

Most applications need access to information specific to the current installation and machine on which it runs. Concerns such as the path to the database or a list of recently accessed files are specific to each user or installation.

In the 16-bit Windows environment this information usually resides in application .INI files. Windows NT and Windows 95 provide a centralized database for storing this application and machine information. This database is known as the *registry*. The registry is the recommended place for storing application specific information in the Windows NT and Windows 95 environments.

Visual Basic provides a set of functions that can be used to manipulate application settings in both the 16-bit and 32-bit windows environments. The functions in the two environments differ in the following ways:

- In 16-bit Windows, the functions work with the SYSTEM.INI file.

- In 32-bit Windows, the functions work with the registry.

GetSetting

The GetSetting function retrieves application settings either one at a time or for an entire section. The GetSetting function has three main parameters: appname, section, and key. A fourth optional parameter, Default, can be used to return a specified value if no entry is found.

The Listing 17.4 example uses the GetSetting function to retrieve the path to the database that the application will use. This code is located in the \CHAP17 directory on the companion disk:

Listing 17.4   CODE04.TXT—Using the Visual Basic GetSetting procedure

```
Private Function GetDBPath() As String
    Dim lsPath As String
    'get the application settings
    lsPath = GetSetting("MyApp", "Environment", "DBPath", "NONE!")
    If lsPath <> "NONE!" Then
        'return the database path
        GetDBPath = lsPath
    Else
        'handle the setting not found.
    End If
End Sub
```

GetAllSettings

The GetAllSettings function returns multiple application settings from the registry or .INI file. The GetAllSettings function has two parameters—appname and section.

The GetAllSettings function returns an array that contains the multiple entries that were found.

The Listing 17.5 example uses the GetAllSettings function to retrieve all the Recently Accessed File entries for the application. This code is located in the \CHAP17 directory on the companion disk.

Listing 17.5   CODE05.TXT— Using the GetAllSettings function

```
Private Sub GetRecentFileList(asFileList() as String)
    Dim arSettings As Varaint
    Dim n As Integer
    ' get the settings
    arSettings = GetAllSettings("MyApp", "RecentFiles")
    'redim the asFileList array
    ReDim asFileList(UBound(arSettings, 1))
    'populate the asFileList array
    For n = 0 to UBound(asFileList)
        asFileList(n) = arSettings(n, 1)
    Next n
End Sub
```

SaveSetting

The SaveSetting function updates or creates application settings. When the SaveSetting function is used, the specified setting is updated if it already exists, or created if it doesn't currently exist. The SaveSetting function has four parameters: appname, section, key, and setting.

The following example uses the SaveSetting function to save the name of the last file that the application accessed into the applications recent files list:

```
Private Sub SaveLastFile(sFile As String)
    'save the file specified in sFile to the registry
    SaveSetting "MyApp", "RecentFiles", "LastUsed", sFile
End Sub
```

DeleteSetting

The DeleteSetting function deletes a setting from the registry or .INI file. The function has three parameters: appname, section, and key. If the key parameter is set to Off when the function is called, all of the settings under the specified section are deleted.

The following example uses the `DeleteSetting` function to delete the recently access file settings:

```
Private Sub DeleteFileList()
    ' remove all of the recently accessed file settings from
    ' the registry
    DeleteSetting "MyApp", "RecentFiles", "LastUsed"
End Sub
```

Microsoft recommends that application settings be kept in the registry, not in .INI files, for the following reasons:

- All application and system information is located in one place and organized in a logical manner. Previously, this information was scattered across multiple .INI files.

- The .INI files have a limit of 64k of storage; the registry can store up to 102M. It is recommended that the registry be kept under 25 percent of the page pool size however.

- Application and system settings are easily shared between applications.

- Information can be stored on a per user, per application, per machine basis.

- Availability of references to environment variables such as %SystemRoot% to refer to the Windows directory.

- The registry allows multiple levels of nesting; .INI files can support only one level.

- With information stored on a per user basis, administrators can easily move a user's information from one machine to another.

Spreadsheet Controls

Often applications need to present data to the user in a spreadsheet format. Often, the user also is allowed to make changes to the data on the spreadsheet and have these changes updated on the back end. This process often is difficult to do with the standard controls provided with Visual Basic. A common attack in this situation is to use a product like Microsoft Excel and in-place activation to provide the spreadsheet. This approach often presents some problems because the application then looses a lot of the control it must have over what the user actually enters.

To combat this problem, a number of third-party custom controls are available that provide spreadsheet interfaces and all of the functionality commonly associated with them. This allows the application developer to provide the user with many of the functions of a spreadsheet application like Microsoft Excel without yielding control of the application.

These types of custom controls are discussed in more detail in Chapter 8, "Architecting Tier 1: Client Applications," because they are applicable only to the user services.

Resize Controls

Another common extension to Visual Basic is the use of third-party resizing controls. These custom controls allow the applications forms to automatically resize themselves when the user resizes the form, or when the application is run under a different screen resolution. This is done without the developer writing any code.

These types of custom controls also are discussed in more detail in Chapter 8 because they are applicable only to the user services.

Mail-Enabled Applications—MAPI

With electronic mail systems becoming as commonplace in the business world as voice mail, more and more applications now must link to these systems. Visual Basic has the capability to access the Messaging Application Programming Interface (MAPI) functions that allow your application to send and receive mail messages over a MAPI-compliant mail system such as Microsoft Mail and Exchange. You also can use Vendor Independent Messaging (VIM) API functions to send and receive mail across systems such as Lotus Notes and cc:Mail.

A number of third-party custom controls (VBXs and OCXes) also are on the market that allow Visual Basic applications to talk to one or both of these API sets without the developer needing to learn the APIs.

Mail-enabling applications allows the user to send spreadsheets and documents that were created by the application to other users, without printing and mailing them a hard-copy version. Mail enabling also is useful when creating workflow applications where another user needs to be notified of an occurrence within the application.

When customers place orders that exceed their credit limit, the order must be approved by the credit department before it can be processed. With a mail-enabled application, an approval request can be sent directly to the credit department, rather than making the user manually switch to another system to make the request. This capability includes applications that allow remote laptop users to interact with transaction-processing systems by initiating message-oriented transactions, such as create order, in the form of e-mail.

You can find a complete list of the available MAPI functions and descriptions in the MAPI SDK Documentation.

Remote Access Service

Remote Access Service (RAS) is Microsoft's solution for connecting mobile users to corporate networks. RAS is optimized to work in the client-server environment, establishing a network connection over standard telephone lines.

RAS provides the following features to remote/mobile users in today's corporate environment:

- Multiple protocol support (IPX/SPX, TCP/IP, NetBEUI)

- Transparent network access

- Reliable security architecture

- Optimized performance for the client-server environment

- Scalability from workgroup to enterprise to global use of the Internet

- Comprehensive wide-area network support (POTS, ISDN, X.25 networks)

- Programmability through the RAS API set

API Functions

RAS provides a set of APIs that allows application developers to implement solutions that take advantage of the RAS architecture. Table 17.5 describes the available APIs. For a detailed description of each API and its function, refer to the *Remote Access Service SDK*.

Table 17.5 RAS API Functions	
API	**Description**
RasDial	Establishes a RAS connection between RAS client and a RAS Server, including callback and user-identification information. Function works asynchronously, the connection status must be checked to determine when connection is established.

(continues)

Table 17.5   Continued

API	Description
RasEnumConnections	Lists all active RAS connections, returning the connection handle and phone-book entry name.
RasEnumEntries	Lists all entry names in the RAS phone book.
RasGetConnectStatus	Retrieves information of the status of the specified connection.
RasGetErrorString	Retrieves error message for a specified RAS error code.
RasGetProjectionInfo	Obtains information about a remote-access projection operation (where client and server negotiate protocol-specific information) for the specified protocol.
RasHangUp	Terminates the specified RAS Session.

The Remote Access APIs also can be made available by using available custom controls (OCXes, VBXs).

How Can RAS Be Used?

RAS allows applications to establish and disconnect remote network connections automatically. For example, the remote client software for an electronic mail system should, by default, establish the network connection that is needed to transfer messages between the client and the mail server when the application starts. When the user exits the application, the connection should be dropped without requiring additional user interaction.

Telephony API

The integration of computers with the telephone network is known as Telephony. The Windows Telephony Application Programming Interface (TAPI) is the set of functions that allow applications to integrate telephone network features with a personal computer in the Microsoft Windows Environment.

The functions that make up TAPI support all aspects of establishing a connection with the telephone network: voice, data and video communication, call-management techniques (conference calls), voice mail, call waiting, and also the support of multiple terminal devices.

TAPI supports a variety of telephone connections including the basic POTS (Plain Old Telephone Service), ISDN, T1/E1, and Switched 56 service. For a detailed description of these services, the additional functionality they provide, and the additional complexities of developing to them, refer to the Windows Telephony SDK documentation.

TAPI was developed to the Windows Open Services Architecture (WOSA)—it works in conjunction with other API sets to develop applications that use the telephone network. TAPI only handles control over the actual phone line and devices, not the data or information being exchanged during the call. To manage the information, or media stream, TAPI works with other Windows-based API sets. For example, an application that manages voice mail messages uses TAPI to establish and monitor the physical phone-line connection over which the voice messages are sent. To work with the voice messages, the application would use the Windows WAV API set.

How Can TAPI Be Used?

As you can see, the TAPI function set provides application developers with a rich set of APIs for managing connections to the telephone network. TAPI can be incorporated with other WOSA APIs to provide applications like the following:

- **Personal-information managers**—Allow users to work with electronic mail and voice mail over telephone lines, as well as provide automatic dialing features from a Windows interface.

- **Conference-call managers**—Allow users to set up conference calls by dragging and dropping names of the people to include into the "conference" area.

- **Multiple-line call managers**—Allows users to screen incoming calls while on another line, without placing anyone on hold. Users could have a prerecorded message for the second caller to hold on for a moment or automatically reroute the call to another person.

- **Information-transfer applications**—Allows users to send data between remote locations by dragging a file icon from one site to another. A user also could specify if the delivery occurs as a file transfer, an e-mail message, or a FAX.

- **Remote-access** and **remote-control applications**—Allow users to log into a remote machine or network over regular phone lines and obtain access to everything, as if they were at the remote location.

Using the techniques described in this chapter, you—as a Visual Basic developer—can create robust applications that will fulfill the user's requirements.

These applications will leverage all of the functionality provided by the operating system and other applications that exist in the corporate environment.

From Here...

In this chapter, we discussed various ways of extending the Visual Basic development environment. Because of its open environment, many third-party vendors have created custom controls and add-ins that allow application developers to go beyond the basic features of Visual Basic. In addition, VB allows developers to access a majority of the internal functions exposed by the operating system.

For further information related to topic covered in this chapter, see the following:

- Chapter 6, "Creating OLE Objects," for more information about creating OLE automation servers.

- Chapter 8, "Architecting Tier 1: Client Applications," for more information about creating client application in Visual Basic.

- Chapter 9, "Architecting Tier 2: Business Servers," for more information about creating business servers.

Chapter 18

Developing International Applications

Overview

As the International market continues to grow, application developers face a new challenge—creating applications that can be used by people of different countries.

Countries differ not only by physical location but also by language and customs. To be useful in other countries, applications must be tailored to these differences.

Creating applications for international use requires more than displaying characters in different languages. As with any application, issues such as interface design and coding standards must be considered, but as we shall see, the global market adds several new considerations.

This chapter covers the following areas:

- Key concepts and definitions for developing international applications

- The localization model

- Advantages of designing an application with a foreign market in mind

- Guidelines for writing flexible code

- Creating, editing, and accessing a resource file

- Special considerations when using the double-byte character set

After reading this chapter, you should understand the steps needed to write a flexible, portable international application.

Key Concepts and Definitions

When developing an application for international use, you need to understand the following four key terms:

- International software
- Locale
- String resources
- Localization

International software is software that is marketable worldwide. Software can be considered international only if it is as functional in a foreign market as it is in its domestic market.

Locale describes a user's environment. Conventions, culture, and language of the users' geographical region all are properties of their environment. A locale consists of a unique combination of a language and a country. Examples of locales are: English/US and Mexico/Spanish.

A language may be spoken in more than one country. Spanish, for example, is spoken in Spain and Mexico. The countries share a common language, but conventions, such as currencies, vary among countries. By our definition, each country is a unique locale—Spanish/Spain and Spanish/Mexico. Some countries have more than one official language. Belgium has three: French, Dutch, and German. By our definition, Belgium has three locales: French/Belgium, Dutch/Belgium, and German/Belgium.

The third term, *string resources*, refers to all the text that appears in an application's user interface, including menus, dialog boxes, and alert and error messages. If an application will be used in a locale other than the one in which it was developed, the meaning of the text in every string resource must be translated.

Finally, *localization* is the process by which an application is adapted to its locale. Localization is the process of translating all string resources in an application. Localization involves more than just a literal translation of words. The *meaning* of each string resource also must be translated.

Architecting an International Application

When creating an international application, no string resources should be present in the Visual Basic code. These resources should be included in the applications *data block*. The data block is a conceptual entity that contains all of an application's string resources, icons, and bitmaps that are localized (non-localized bitmaps and icons do not need to be placed in the resource file). In Visual Basic 4.0, this entity is physically implemented as a *resource file*. A following section in this chapter, "Creating Resource Files," describes resources files.

Although more work, placing all applications string resources in a separate resource file has the following advantages:

- **Efficiency.** Creating a new localized version of the application only involves creating a new resource file. Each version of the application uses the same main .EXE.

- **Security.** If localizing an international version of the application requires you to use an external company, the external company will not need to access your source code. They only need to edit your resource file.

- **More Complete Localization.** By placing all string resources in one file, you decrease the probability of leaving some strings unlocalized.

Besides the data block, a localized application has a second conceptual block—a *code block*. The *localization model* shown in figure 18.1 visually describes the separation of an application's data block and code block. The combination of these two blocks results in a localized application.

Fig. 18.1

A localization model. When combined, the data block and code block make up a localized application.

The data block contains all user-interface string resources and no code. The code block, conversely, contains all the code needed to run the application in all locales, but no string resources. The code block manages the run-time loading and unloading of an application's string resources and locale-specific settings. The section "Handling Locale Specific Formats in Code" later in this chapter describes in detail how to write Visual Basic code that handles locale-specific settings.

The key to successful international-software design is the separation of the code block and the data block. By adhering to the localized model described here, a localized version of an application can be developed by changing only the data block. The code block should require no changes and permit the application to read and write data, regardless of the application's locale.

In the three-tier model, the bulk of localization affects tier one because of the client application's role in the three-tier architecture—graphical presentation. Developers will focus most of their attention on the client application when localizing.

Designing a User Interface

Because of differences in text length and meaning, and the lack of international language standards, several elements of an application's user interface require particular attention. This sections provides guidelines for including the following components in an application:

- Messages
- Controls, menus and dialogs
- Icons and bitmaps

Designing Messages

Messages are the text displayed in an alert, information, or warning message box. Usually, when an application is localized outside of the English/US locale, the text displayed tends to increase in length. Microsoft has drawn data from Visual Basic applications that have undergone localization and computed the average growth rates and included in the VB user documentation. Table 18.1 shows this data.

Table 18.1 The Average Growth for Localized Strings	
English length (characters)	**Additional growth for localized strings**
1 to 4	100%
5 to 10	80%
11 to 20	60%
21 to 30	40%
31 to 50	20%
over 50	10%

When creating messages for your international application, consider these growth rates and allow for text to wrap to more lines as the message gets longer.

Designing Controls, Menus, and Dialog Boxes

Control menus and dialog boxes, like messages, tend to grow when an application is localized. So, extra space should be allocated for text to grow inside these controls. Figure 18.2 shows a command button with text written in English. Figure 18.3 shows the same command button with Spanish text. Notice the difference in length of the text within the controls.

Fig. 18.2
A command button, with English text.

Fig. 18.3
A command button, with Spanish text.

By leaving additional space in the initial version of an application, you decrease the amount of time needed to resize forms and controls when localized versions are developed.

Similarly, increasing the space allotted for a menu item's help caption decreases the amount of effort needed to localize the application.

Using Icons and Bitmaps

Application's generally use icons and bitmaps to graphically depict functionality without using text. Because graphics are understandable across locales, icons and bitmaps provide value to an international application by decreasing the amount of modifications necessary when localizing.

Use the following guidelines when working with icons and bitmaps:

- Avoid using icons and bitmaps that aren't an international standard. A bitmap of a Yield sign in the U.S. may have little or no meaning to users from another locale.

- Avoid using icons and bitmaps that contain text. They need to be redrawn when the application is localized. Moreover, the text may grow in length and cause problems.

- Make sure icons and bitmaps are culturally sensitive. What is acceptable in one locale may be inappropriate in another.

Coding Localized Applications

When developing international software, pay attention to user locales, not just language or specific countries. Code should run regardless of locale and, more important, run the way a user expects it to run. Additionally, the application should be easily transported to different locales.

This section explains how to generate and localize a resource file that simplifies the task of localizing your application. It also provides guidelines for writing code in international applications, with special consideration for the following:

- Locale-specific formats: dates, currencies, numeric values, and separators

- Locale-aware functions

- Sort order and string comparison

- File Input/Output

- Localizing OLE Automation Servers

Using Resource Files in Visual Basic

As noted previously, the easiest way to prepare an application for international use is to separate all string resources from an application's code block. These string resources are stored in an application's resource file.

Besides strings, a resource file can contain locale-specific bitmaps, icons, and other data that must be loaded on demand by the application at run time.

Implementing a resource file requires four steps: creating the file, localizing the file, adding the file to the VB project, and accessing the file through code. The following section describes these four steps in detail.

Creating Resource Files

A resource file is identified by the .RES file extension. A Visual Basic project can have only one resource file. If you try to add more than one resource file, an error is generated.

The resource file contains all string resources, icons, bitmaps, cursors, and sounds to include in your application.

To create a resource file, follow these steps:

1. Create individual files for all icons, bitmaps, cursors, and sounds to include in the resource files.

2. Create a file with a .RC extension. You can create this file, known as a resource-definition file, with any text editor or word processor. In this file, you specify all string resources to be used by your application.

3. Use a resource compiler to convert the source file into a resource file (*.RES). Visual Basic includes a resource compiler (RC.EXE). The SETUP program installs the compiler in the TOOLS\RESOURCE subdirectory (under \RC16 for the 16-bit compiler, or under \RC32 for the 32-bit version).

Resource-Definition Types

A resource-definition file, referred to in the preceding steps, contains two types of instructions: *Statements* (which name and describe resources), and

Directives (which provide information about actions that the resource compiler will perform on the definition file).

Two types of statements are used in a resource-definition file: Single-line resource-definition statements and multiple-line resource-definition statements.

You use *Single-line resource-definition statements* to define bitmaps, icons, sounds and cursors in the resource-definition file. You can use any of the keywords shown in Table 18.2 to begin a single-line statement.

Table 18.2 Available Single-Line Resource-Definition Keywords	
KeyWord	**Description**
BITMAP	Defines a bitmap by naming it and specifying the name of the file that contains it.
ICON	Defines an icon by naming it and specifying the name of the file that contains it.
SOUND	Defines a sound file by naming it and specifying the name of the file that contains it.
CURSOR	Defines a cursor by naming it and specifying the name of the file that contains it.

A *multiple-line resource-definition statement* defines string resources and data resources in a resource-definition file. Data resources can be used to include binary data directly into the executable file. Any of the keywords shown in Table 18.3 can be used.

Table 18.3 Available Multiple-Line Resource-Definition Keywords	
KeyWord	**Description**
STRINGTABLE	Defines string resources. String resources are null-terminated ASCII strings that can be loaded from the executable file.
RCDATA	Defines data resources. Data resources let you include binary data directly into the executable file.

Directives instruct the resource compiler to perform actions or to assign values to names in the resource-definition file. Any of the directive keywords shown in Table 18.4 can be used.

Table 18.4   Resource File Directive Keywords

KeyWord	Description
#define	Defines specified name by assigning it a given value.
#elseif	Marks optional clause of a conditional compilation block.
#else	Marks last optional clause of a conditional compilation block.
#endif	Marks end of a conditional compilation block.
#if	Carries out conditional compilation if a specified expression is true.
#ifdef	Carries out conditional compilation if a specified name is defined.
#ifndef	Carries out conditional compilation if a specified name is not defined.
#include	Copies contents of a file into the resource-definition file before RC processes the latter.
#undef	Removes current definition of the specified name.

Each entry in the resource definition that will be accessed from our application must be assigned a unique ID. This ID can be any integer except the number 1.

In Visual Basic, the resource whose ID is 1 is reserved for the application's icon. Therefore, you cannot have a resource in your .RES file with an ID number of 1. Visual Basic generates an error message if your code attempts to load this resource ID.

Listing 18.1 (the file can be found in the TOOLS/RESOURCE directory) shows a sample resource-definition file:

Listing 18.1   A Sample Resource-Definition File

```
//Resource-definition file for ATM sample.
//
#include "resource.h"
/////////////////////////////////////////////////////////////////////
//
// Bitmap
//
16                      BITMAP  MOVEABLE PURE    "USA.BMP"
144                     BITMAP  MOVEABLE PURE    "SPAIN.BMP"
/////////////////////////////////////////////////////////////////////
```

(continues)

Listing 18.1   Continued

```
/
//
// Sound
//
16                        SOUND    MOVEABLE PURE    "USA.WAV"
48                        SOUND    MOVEABLE PURE    "SPAIN.WAV"
///////////////////////////////////////////////////////////////////////
//
// String Table
//
STRINGTABLE DISCARDABLE
BEGIN
    16        "Welcome"
    17        "Please enter your pin number:"
    18        "Please choose an account:"
    19        "Checking account"
    20        "Savings Account"
    21        "Please enter an amount:"
    22        "OK"
    23        "Your transaction is being processed..."
    24        "Thank you for using our ATM"
    25        "The following amount will be withdraw from your:"
    26        "US Dollars"
END
STRINGTABLE DISCARDABLE
BEGIN
    144       "Bienvenido"
    145       "Por favor, ingrese su n\372mero de
              ➥identificaci\363n secreto:"
    146       "Por favor, elija una cuenta:"
    147       "Conto corrente"
    148       "Cuenta de ahorros"
    149       "Por favor, ingrese un importe:"
    150       "Aceptar"
    151       "Su transacción se está procesando..."
    152       "Le agradecemos que haya usado nuestro cajero
              ➥ autom\341tico"
    153       "La siguiente cantidad será retirada de su:"
    154       "Pesetas"
END
```

Localizing a Resource File

After a resource file has been created, you may want to adjust the file for a specific locale. To localize a resource file, follow these steps:

1. Load the resource file in a resource editor. AppStudio (which ships with Microsoft Visual C++), can be used to edit the entries.

2. After the file is loaded, localize the entries. Create as many language versions of the strings, bitmaps, icons and data as needed.

3. Save the updated resource file.

Including the Resource File in a Project

To add a resource file to your project, follow these steps:

1. From the File menu, choose Add File.

2. In the Add File dialog box, select Resource Files (*.RES) in the Files of Type box.

3. Select the resource file you want to add to the project, and click Open. Use a 16-bit .RES file for 16-bit projects, and a 32-bit .RES file for 32-bit projects.

Visual basic recognizes resource files by the .RES file extension. If your resource file doesn't have the proper extension, Visual Basic will not load it. Conversely, if a file has the .RES extension, Visual Basic assumes that the file is a resource file when it is added to the project. If the file doesn't follow the standard composition of a resource file, using the valid keywords outline previously in this chapter, Visual Basic generates an error the first time you try to access it or when you create a .EXE file.

The View Code and View Form buttons on the Project Window are disabled when the resource file is selected. When you create a .EXE file, Visual Basic compiles all resources in the file into the .EXE file as Windows resources.

Accessing the Resource File from Visual Basic

Visual Basic includes the following three functions for accessing data stored in an application's resource file:

- LoadResString

- LoadResPicture

- LoadResData

LoadResString Function

The LoadResString function allows you to load a string resource from a compiled resource file. When you load a string, you must include the ID of the resource. The following code fragment demonstrates accessing a string resource from a file:

```
Private Sub FillMessageText ()
   Dim lsResourceString as String
   lsResourceString = LoadResString (23)
   MsgBox lsResourceString
End Sub
```

LoadResPicture Function

The LoadResPicture function is used to load a bitmap, icon, or cursor from a resource file. When using the LoadResPicture function, you must specify the ID of the bitmap, icon, or cursor and also the format of the information to load. The types of formats used with the LoadResPicture function are shown in the following table:

Constant	Value	Description
vbResBitmap	0	Bitmap resource
vbResIcon	1	Icon resource
vbResCursor	2	Cursor resource

The following code fragment shows how to load a bitmap from a resource file and assign it to the Picture property of a PictureBox control:

```
Private Sub AssignPicture ()
    picPictureBox.Picture = LoadResPicture (16, vbResBitmap)
End Sub
```

LoadResData Function

Finally, the LoadResData function allows you to load any type of data stored in a resource file into your application.

Like the LoadResPicture function, you must specify both the ID and the format of the data your application will be loading. Some format settings that can be used with the LoadResData function are shown in the following table:

Settings	Description
1	Cursor resource
2	Bitmap resource
3	Icon resource
6	String resource

For a complete list of format settings and their descriptions, see your Visual Basic documentation.

Handling Locale-Specific Formats in Code

As you learned earlier in the chapter, preparing an application for international use requires more than a literal translation of text. locale-specific support for dates, currencies, numeric values, and separators also need to be considered.

Dates

When writing Visual Basic code, never type dates as string literals. To explain why, we will run the following code fragment in two different locales and compare the results:

```
Private Sub PrintDate ()
    ' Procedure shows a date in a message box
    Dim ldStartDate as Date
    Dim ldDateToShow as Date
    ldStartDate = "6/11/95"
    ldDateToShow = CDate(ldStartDate)
    MsgBox ldDateToShow,, "Date Example"
End Sub
```

When the code is run in the English/US locale, it displays the result shown in figure 18.4.

Fig. 18.4
The results of the *PrintDate* procedure in the English/US locale.

When run in the Spanish/Mexico locale, it displays exactly the same result.

The CDate function converts a date into the format of the currently selected operating system locale. This feature may cause errors when you are programming.

To avoid problems, always type dates in your code as *date literals*. In Visual Basic, a date literal is entered by typing a # character before and after the date. **#6/11/95#** is an example of a date literal.

Typing the date as a literal allows Visual Basic to recognize the date you intend. To see how date literals differ from string literals, run the following code fragment under both the English/US and Spanish/Mexico locales:

```
Private Sub PrintDate ()
   ' Procedure shows a date in a message box
   Dim ldStartDate as Date
   Dim ldDateToShow as Date
   ldStartDate = #6/11/95#
   ldDateToShow = CDate(ldStartDate)
   MsgBox ldDateToShow,, "Date Example"
End Sub
```

Under the English/US locale, the code produces the result shown in figure 18.5.

Fig. 18.5

The results of the PrintDate function when a date literal is used under the English/US locale.

Under the Spanish/Mexico locale, the code produces the result shown in Figure 18.6.

Fig. 18.6

The result of the PrintDate function when a date literal is used under the Spanish/Mexico locale.

This time, both dates are displayed in the format the program intended. How did Visual Basic know we wanted to display the date this way?

Visual Basic allows only English/US as a *code locale* when programming. Therefore, when a date literal is used in code, it always is displayed the same, no matter what the locale of the end user. To include specific dates in your Visual Basic code, use the month/day/year format.

Conversely, when displaying a date to a user or receiving input from an input dialog box, Visual Basic uses the *system locale* of the operating system, or the locale of the user who is running the program. In Windows 95, the system locale is set under the Regional icon of the Control Panel.

To help understand system locale, consider the following example. If a user in Mexico enters **6/11/95** into an input box in a Visual Basic application, it is interpreted as November 11, 1995 by the program. If a user in the US enters the same date, it is interpreted as June 6, 1995 by the same program.

Currency

As with dates, avoid typing currencies as strings in your code. For example, the following code fragment causes Visual Basic to produce a Type Mismatch error when run under the Spanish/Mexico locale because the Spanish/Mexico locale doesn't recognize the "$" character as a currency symbol:

```
lcStartMoney = "$1.50"
lcMoneyToShow = CDate(lcStartMoney)
```

To use currencies in Visual Basic code, type the currency as a number, using a period as a decimal separator. The following example can be run under any locale without producing an error:

```
lcStartMoney = 1.50
lcMoneyToShow = CDate(lcStartMoney)
```

Why does the second example not produce an error when run under the Spanish/Mexico locale as the first one did? As with dates, the code locale for Visual Basic is always English/US.

Numeric Values and Separators

The United States uses a period (.) as a decimal separator when writing numbers. In several European countries, however, the comma (,) is used as a decimal separator. The following table shows the decimal formats for several countries:

Country	Decimal Format
United States	1234.1234
France	1234,1234
Austria	1234,1234

Similarly, in the United States, a comma is used as a thousands separator to group digits to the left of the decimal separator. In European countries, a period or space is often used. The following table shows some examples of digit grouping formats:

Country	Digit Grouping Format
United States	12,345
France	12 345
Austria	12.345

The Str and Val functions in Visual Basic use the code locale and always assume a period for a decimal separator.

Localizing OLE Automation Servers

So far in this chapter, you have seen how Visual Basic uses various constructs to allow end users to enter and receive information in a Visual Basic application that is consistent with their locale. For example, you saw how Visual Basic can interpret dates in a locale specific format without requiring you, as a developer, to deploy multiple sets of your code.

In the three-tier model, end users not only enter and receive information to and from applications that were developed for them, they are encouraged to develop their own client applications. This is possible because all business logic should be contained in OLE servers. End users can make calls to the OLE servers with applications such as Microsoft Excel.

Because end users will interact with the OLE automation servers, in an ideal situation you would localize your OLE servers just as you localize any other user-facing component of your application, such as message boxes or labels on text boxes. Remember, users browse OLE automation servers with the Object Browser, which also displays help information.

If, for example, you developed an application in the English/US locale, you might create an OLE automation server and name its class *OrderMgr*. Within the OrderMgr class, you might create a method named AddOrder. When you begin to localize this application for the Spanish/Mexico locale, you would replace all of your English strings that will be displayed to the user with their Spanish equivalents. You already saw how you can use a resource file to do this. But what about your OLE automation servers? When an end user in the Mexico/Spanish locale decides to develop an application, will they understand what the method AddOrder is used for? Will the Spanish equivalent of AddOrder make more sense?

Unfortunately, Visual Basic always uses the English/US locale for its code. This means that OLE automation servers' interface attributes, as well has OLE automation interface help, are always named using the English/US locale. Nothing currently exists that allows you to localize the names of your OLE automation servers and their interface attributes. Future versions of Visual Basic, however, probably will begin to include this kind of functionality.

Locale Aware Functions

As you have seen, different locales have different conventions for displaying dates, currencies, numbers, and other information. When developing an international application in Visual Basic, however, it is not necessary to know all these conventions. Many functions in Visual Basic use the system locale, set in the Control Panel, to determine these conventions at run time. These functions, known as *locale-aware* functions, allow you, as a developer, to use these locale-specific conventions without having firsthand knowledge of them.

Format Function

The Format function can accept format codes but format codes do not take the user's locale into consideration. For example, the following code fragment:

```
ldShortDate = #06/11/95#
Debug.Print ldShortDate
```

always produces the following output, regardless of locale:

```
06/11/95
```

This date format is not appropriate for most European users because it is interpreted as November 6, 1995.

For more flexibility, the Format function provides named formats that do take a users locale into consideration. Additionally, the named format can generate output in the users native language, including the names of months and days of the week. The following code:

```
ldDate = #6/11/95 12:01 AM#
ldDateFormat1 = Format (ldDate, "Short Date")
ldDateFormat2 = Format (ldDate, "Medium Date")
ldDateFormat3 = Format (ldDate, "Long Date")
ldDateFormat4 = Format (ldDate, "General Date")
Debug.Print ldDateFormat1, ldDateFormat2, ldDateFormat3,
➥ldDateFormat4
```

produces the following result in the debug window, when run in the English/ US locale:

```
6/11/95    11-Jun-95       Sunday, June 11, 1995   6/11/95 12:01 AM
```

When run using the Spanish/Mexico, the following results appear in the debug window:

```
11/6/95    11-Jun-95       Domingo, Junio 11, 1995 11/6/95 00:01
```

For more information in the Format function and a complete list of named formats, see your Visual Basic documentation.

Print Function

Visual Basic's Print function uses the system locale when generating output. In the following example, the Print function prints a date in the correct short-date format to the debug window. For the example, we use the following code:

```
ldSampleDate = #12/07/95#
Debug.Print ldSampleDate
```

When the code is run using the English/US locale, the following appears in the debug window:

```
12/07/69
```

When the code is run using the Spanish/Mexico locale, the following appears in the debug window:

```
07/12/69
```

For more information on the Print function, see the documentation included with Visual Basic.

Comparing Strings

Locales may have different rules when comparing stings. The Spanish language, for example, treats the letters "ch" as a single character. Therefore, when comparing strings, all words beginning with "ch" follow all words beginning with the letter "c" when placed in alphabetical order.

Visual Basic provides two functions, Like and StrComp, which take these locale-specific rules into account when comparing strings. Both functions rely on the *Option Compare* statement for proper use.

Using Option Compare When Comparing Strings

The Option Compare statement supports two methods: Binary and Text. If Binary is specified, comparisons are done according to a sort order derived from the internal binary representation of characters. If Text is specified, comparisons are handled according to the case-insensitive textual sort order determined by the user's system locale. The default comparison method is Binary.

The following code fragment compares two words, "apples" and "Oranges:"

```
Private Sub SortWords ()
   Dim lsWordOne as String
   Dim lsWordTwo as String
   lsWordOne = "apples"
   lsWordTwo = "Oranges"
   If lsWordOne < lsWordTwo Then
      MsgBox lsWordOne & " comes before " & lsWordTwo,, "Sort
Example"
```

```
    Else
        MsgBox lsWordTwo & " comes before " & lsWordOne,, "Sort Example"
    End If
End Sub
```

Because a comparison method wasn't specified, the `Binary` comparison method is used in the preceding example. Because the internal binary representation of uppercase letters are smaller than lowercase letters, the conditional statement, `lsWordOne < lsWordTwo`, evaluates to true and Visual Basic produces the result shown in figure 18.7.

Fig. 18.7

The results of the Binary comparison in the English/US locale.

When the same code is run in the Spanish/Mexico locale using the words, "churros" and "colores," the code produces the result shown in figure 18.8.

Fig. 18.8

The results of the Binary comparison in the Spanish/ Mexico locale.

This result isn't what you would expect because in the Spanish alphabet, the letter "c" comes before the letter "ch."

When the *Option Compare Text* statement is added to the form's general declarations section, the result of the following code fragment is shown in figure 18.9:

```
Private Sub SortWords ()
    Dim lsWordOne as String
    Dim lsWordTwo as String
    lsWordOne = "apples"
    lsWordTwo = "Oranges"
    If lsWordOne < lsWordTwo Then
        MsgBox lsWordOne & " comes before " & lsWordTwo,, "Sort Example"
    Else
        MsgBox lsWordTwo & " comes before " & lsWordOne,, "Sort Example"
    End If
End Sub
```

IV

Application Enhancements

Fig. 18.9
The results of a
Text comparison.

When the same code is run in the Spanish/Mexico locale, using the words, "churros" and "colores," and the Option Compare Text statement in the general declarations section, we see the correct result, as shown in figure 18.10.

Fig. 18.10
The results of a
Text comparison
under the Spanish/
Mexico locale.

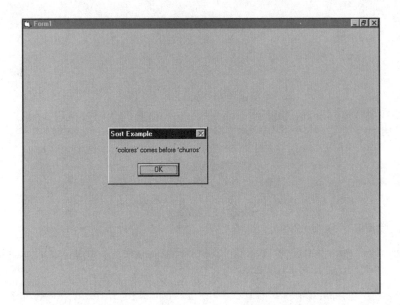

Comparing Strings with the Like Operator

The Like operator compares two strings. Additionally, Like makes use of character ranges when comparing strings. It is critical that you are aware of the comparisons method discussed in the preceding section when using the Like operator.

For example, the following code fragment uses the Option Compare Binary method with the Like operator to compare the word, "apple," to the range, [A-C]:

```
"apple" Like [A-C]
```

This code evaluates to false. The [A-C] range excludes all lowercase characters. Only strings beginning with A, B, and C will evaluate to true.

When the Text method of Option Compare is used with the preceding example, all lowercase characters are included in the [A-C] range and the expression evaluates to true.

For more information on the Like operator, see your Visual Basic documentation.

Comparing Strings with the StrComp Function

The StrComp function also can be used to compare two strings. It returns a value that indicates if one string is less than, equal to, or greater than another string.

Similar to the Like operator, the StrComp function relies on the Option Compare method when comparing strings.

File Input/Output

As you learned previously in the chapter, one of the most important requirements of international software is its capability to read and write data, regardless of locale.

Visual Basic provides the following three functions for reading and writing information to and from data files:

- Input#

- Print#

- Write#

The Input# function is used to read information from a data file. The Print# and Write# statements can be used to write information to data files. As you will see, each function has a distinct purpose and each is described in this section.

Input

The Input # statement is not capable of reading locale-aware data that has been written to a file with the Print # statement. To write locale-independent data, use the Write # statement rather than the Print # statement.

Print

The Print # statement is a locale-aware function that puts data into a file as it is displayed on-screen. For example, the following code fragment places the date, 6/11/95, into a data file, using the following *Short Date* format:

```
Print #filenumber #6/11/95#
```

As indicated in the preceding section, data written to a file with the Print # statement cannot be read by the Input # statement.

Write

You can use the Write # statement, like the Print # statement, to write data to a file. Unlike the Print # statement, however, data written with the Write # statement is written in a fixed format, which insures that the Input # statement can read it.

Dates written with the Write # statement are stored in the universal date format described previously in this chapter.

The code in Listing 18.2 demonstrates how to write data to a file by using the Write # statement and retrieve it by using the Input # statement.

Listing 18.2   CODE04.TXT—A sample function used to read and write data to a binary file. This code will operate independently of locale and is compatable with the DBCS

```
Dim ldDate As Date
Dim ldNewDate As Date
Dim liFileNumber As Integer

' Set values for the date to be written
ldDate = #8/2/67#

' Open the file to which data will be written
' First, retrieve a file number
liFileNumber = FreeFile

Open "DATEFILE" for Output As #liFileNumber

' Write file information
Write # liFileNumber, ldDate
Close # liFileNumber

' Reopen file and read info. from it
' Switch locales in the OS before reopening the file
Open " DATEFILE" for Input As # liFileNumber

' Read info. from file
Input #liFileNumber, ldNewDate

' Print the date to the debug window
Debug.Print Format$(ldNewDate, "Short Date")

' Close the file
Close #liFileNumber
```

If you switch date formats before reopening the file, the file is printed to the Debug window in the correct Short Date format.

Using the Double-Byte Character Set

The *double-byte character set* (DBCS) was created to handle Far Eastern language requirements. Many Far Eastern languages use a character set of more than 256 characters. Characters in DBCS are addressed using a 16-bit notation. With 16-bit notation it is possible to represent 65,536 characters. Most Far East languages use far fewer than this number of characters. The Japanese character sets, for example, use approximately 12,000 characters today.

Locales that use DBCS define both a single-byte and double-byte character set. *Single-byte character sets* are used to conform to the 8-bit national standards for each country and correspond closely to the ASCII character set. Certain ranges in the single-byte character set are designated as lead bytes for DBCS characters. A lead byte and a trail byte paired together represent one double-byte character.

When developing a DBCS-enabled application, you should consider the following goals:

- String manipulation functions

- Displaying fonts correctly

- Processing files, including the double-byte character set

Developing a DBCS-enabled application is a good practice because the code you develop is portable and is a truly international application.

String Manipulation Functions

Although a DBCS character is composed of a lead byte and a trailer byte, it must be treated as a single byte in any operation involving characters and strings. String manipulation functions, such as `Left`, `Len`, `Mid`, `Right`, `Instr`, and `Input`, handle DBCS characters as if they were comprised of a single byte.

For example, the `Mid` function is used to return a specified number of characters from a string. When using DBCS, the number of characters and the number of bytes is not necessarily the same. If the `Mid` function is used on a DBCS character string, only the number of characters specified are returned, not the number of bytes.

It is recommended that you use the character-based functions mentioned previously when manipulating string data because they can be used on both ANSI and DBCS strings.

Many Windows API and DLL functions return the size of strings in bytes, not characters. The return value does include single-byte characters and also double-byte characters—the length of DBCS strings will be reported correctly. However, in 32-bit environments such as Windows NT, the string returned includes the Unicode characters. Therefore, do not rely on the returned value of the string's size.

As was the case under Windows 3.1x, any Windows 95 API that accepts an ANSI string as an argument also accepts DBCS characters.

Displaying DBCS Characters

When a DBCS-enabled application is used with a DBCS version of Windows, the application should display DBCS characters. If a single-byte character set font is used, the DBCS characters may not display correctly. To change the font to display in a DBCS-enabled application, you need to change the FontName property for all controls.

The default setting for the FontName property is MS Sans Serif. This font is not a DBCS-enabled font and should be changed to a setting appropriate for the DBCS environment in which the application will run.

If your system does not have a DBCS-enabled font, or you do not know which font is appropriate for the DBCS locale you will be running in, you can use the System or FixedSys fonts. These fonts reside in every Windows environment.

Processing Files with the DBCS Character Set

In a locale that uses DBCS, data files may include both single-byte and double-byte characters. Because DBCS uses two-bytes to represent a character, a Visual Basic application must avoid splitting a single DBCS character in half when information is read from a file.

To do so, you use an array of Bytes type variables rather than a String type variable. You also will use the Get function to retrieve the data from the file. Using a String data type with the Input function will produce an automatic conversion between DBCS and Unicode. The result: you may split the two-byte DCBS Character.

The following code fragment shows how to load information from a file that contains DBCS characters:

```
' Open the DBCS file for reading
Dim liFileNumber as Integer
liFileNumber = FreeFile
Open "DBCSFILE" For Input as #liFileNumber

' Read a fixed length of data from the file
Dim lbDBCSArray(0 to 100) as Byte
Get #liFileNumber, ,lbDBCSArray
```

DBCS-Enabled Functions and Events

Several function and events in Visual Basic are DBCS-enabled. These include the KeyPress event, the Asc function, the Chr function, and the String function.

In Visual Basic, the KeyPress event of a control has the following format:

```
Sub ControlName_KeyPress (KeyAscii as Integer)
```

Here, ControlName is the name of the control.

The KeyPress event processes a double-byte character as a single event. The higher byte of the KeyAscii parameter represents the lead byte of a DBCS character and the lower byte represents the trailer byte.

Visual Basic's Asc function returns the character code that corresponds to the first character in a string. For example, the statement, Asc("A"), produces the following result:

```
65
```

The Asc function returns a character code regardless of whether the character is single-byte or double-byte.

The Chr function returns a single-byte or a double-byte character associated with an ANSI code. For example, the statement, Chr(65), produces the following result:

```
A
```

The String function is used in Visual Basic to return a repeating character string of a specified length. For example, the code, String (5, "A"), returns the following result:

```
AAAAA
```

The String function returns a repeating character string of the length specified regardless of whether the character is single-byte or double-byte.

From Here...

This chapter provided information on localizing Visual Basic applications. You should now understand how to prepare a product for international use, how to design an application so that only minor changes need to be made when it is localized, and how Visual Basic interprets dates, currencies, and numbers under different locales.

For further information related to topics covered in this chapter, see the following:

- Chapter 4, "Visual Basic Application Architecture," examines the overall design of Visual Basic application.

- Chapter 21, "Organizing the Development Approach," provides more information on organizing and developing Visual Basic Applications.

Chapter 19

Version Control and Team Development

As you begin to use Visual Basic to develop three-tier client/server applications within the enterprise, the size of the project often necessitates that a team of developers work to complete the system. Having more than one person work on a Visual Basic project requires that you manage the following aspects of the system code:

- Source code

- Application and application component version control

Source-code management corresponds to keeping the code that makes up your system safe. You need to ensure that developers do not accidentally delete code, or that two developers do not overwrite each other's changes.

Because your code is constantly changing, version control ensures that you can always create a snapshot of your code at anytime during the development cycle. Versioning becomes important when you debug; you may need to step back to an earlier version of code to determine what changes caused problems.

In this chapter, you learn about the following areas of version control and team development:

- The services that are necessary for good source-code management

- How Visual SourceSafe is used to manage source code

- Specific features and functionality of SourceSafe

- The importance of version control in enterprise development

- OLE server version and executable version management

Source-Code Management

When building applications or the enterprise, keeping your source code safe becomes a serious concern. After months of developing, testing, and tuning, a development team cannot risk the chance that a failed hard drive, for example, will completely undo its work.

This section describes how source-code management can provide many valuable assets to a development project. In addition to keeping the code safe, you see how to accurately track changes to your code, how you can restrict access to certain files, how files can be shared among projects to help minimize duplicate development efforts, and how to administer source-code control to keep your project running smoothly.

Why Do I Need Source-Code Management?

Development teams typically require that developers share code modules and forms within Visual Basic projects. Consider the following situations:

- Developer A and Developer B both want to work on the same form. Developer A makes changes to a local copy while Developer B makes changes to a second local copy. Both developers then copy their forms to a network directory. Developer A copies his form first. As Developer B copies her form, she realizes that she hasn't yet incorporated Developer A's changes. She now has a choice: overwrite Developer A's changes with her own changes, or discard her copy of the form and manually add her changes to Developer A's copy.

- Developer A makes changes to a local copy of a form. Developer B makes changes to a second local copy of the same form. As the end of the day nears, Developer C wants to compile an executable for testing. Which version of the form should Developer C use?

Without source-code control, the first situation requires that one developer's changes are lost. Either Developer B loses her changes, or she overwrites Developer A's changes. With source-code control, however, Developer B can merge her changes with Developer A's changes. This control allows both developers to work concurrently on the same files, and therefore shorten development time.

In the second situation, Developer C runs into a problem when compiling because two copies of the same form exist in the enterprise. With source-code control, however, all code resides in a common location, which helps to ensure that only the most recent version of files is used when creating executable applications.

These situations show only two of many cases where source-code management can help to make your project run smoothly.

Selecting a Source-Code Management Tool

Over the past few years, several source-code management tools that are capable of controlling Visual Basic source code have been introduced. The major problem with these tools was that they lacked true integration within the Visual Basic development environment. Several tools, including InterSolv's PVCS, managed to add menu options to Visual Basic's tools menu that allowed developers to perform limited functions without leaving Visual Basic, but in the end, a vast majority of the code management application features still had to be accessed through a separate application.

Integration with the Visual Basic environment was difficult, if not impossible. The development environment did not effectively open itself to allow integration with other tools. But Visual Basic version 4.0 has changed this limitation. Visual Basic 4 provides an interface that allows true integration with other applications, including source-code management tools.

Visual SourceSafe, which is included with the enterprise edition of Visual Basic, is an example of a source-code management tool that fully integrates with the Visual Basic development environment. Most SourceSafe's features are available from directly within the Visual Basic development environment, and switching to the SourceSafe application is simple. Its close integration with Visual Basic, its powerful source-code management features, and the fact it is included with the Enterprise Edition, make Visual SourceSafe an excellent choice for source-code control.

In the following sections, you will learn how Visual SourceSafe can be used to manage all of your code in the Visual Basic Enterprise. Although this chapter focuses exclusively on Visual SourceSafe, you should note that, because the Visual Basic development environment has been "opened up," in the very near future, other vendors also will begin to develop source-code management tools that will integrate with Visual Basic just as seamlessly as SourceSafe. Because the enterprise may already be using a source-code management tool, such as PVCS, examining tools other than SourceSafe may be the best solution for your corporation.

Roles of Source-Code Management

A typical development team may include programmers, technical writers, technical architects, and managers. As you saw in the previous section, when source-code is shared among developers, the team requires several new services that may not be as familiar. Visual SourceSafe divides these services into the following categories:

- **Library Services**—The library services work to permit users to easily check files in and out.

- **History Services**—History services play a part in keeping a record of all changes made to a file.

- **Security Services**—Security services assume the role of controlling access to source code.

- **Custodial Services**—Custodial services assume the role of providing utilities and ensuring that all aspects of source-code control continue to operate smoothly.

The following sections will outline each of these services and the roles they play in source-code control. You will learn how Visual SourceSafe accomplishes the tasks associated with each service.

Library Services

The most compelling reason for using a source-code control tool during development is to keep your source code safe. "Safe" means that changes to files do not get lost, or that developers do not accidentally overwrite each others changes to forms and modules. The library services in Visual SourceSafe are responsible for keeping your source code safe. When you work with files in Visual SourceSafe, you check them in and out, similar to checking books in and out of the library.

When you keep your files in Visual SourceSafe, the library services provide many important advantages to your source code. Perhaps most important, Visual SourceSafe ensures that no member of the team will accidentally delete information within the files or will accidentally delete the physical files. Files cannot be accidentally deleted because while working with Visual SourceSafe, developers work only with a local copy of a file. A single master copy of each file in the SourceSafe project is stored in a separate database. A following section of this chapter, "Administering a SourceSafe Project," will discuss how you can further ensure that your SourceSafe project is safe.

Visual SourceSafe ensures that the information in files is not lost by saving the changes that you make to a file.

Library services also help you organize your files into a well-ordered hierarchy of projects and subprojects. SourceSafe uses a model similar to the Windows operating system to organize projects. At the highest level exists a project, much like a main directory on your hard drive. Within each project, both files and subprojects exist. Think of a subproject as the equivalent of a subdirectory on your hard drive. Within each subproject, more subprojects and more files can exist. This model allows Visual SourceSafe to provide scalability and flexibility as your project grows, without adding complexity. Both the number of subprojects you can have and the number of different projects you can store are limited only by your machine's hard-disk size.

Visual SourceSafe requires that developers check out files when they want to make changes to them. This checkout is accomplished by clicking a button. After changes are made, you can add comments, describing both what changes were made and what future changes you plan to make to a file. After editing is complete, a developer checks the file back into Visual SourceSafe, allowing other users to retrieve these changes or to check out the file for editing. SourceSafe fully integrates with Visual Basic 4.0, allowing you to check files in and out of a project, without leaving the development environment.

SourceSafe library services permit two developers to share files across projects, platforms, and networks—you do not need to maintain separate copies of your Visual Basic files that are used by multiple projects. A single master copy of each file is stored, and every developer within the project can check out his or her own copy of the master file. This capability permits applications that share files to be developed in parallel and also allows customization of existing source code without affecting other developers who use the same files. Besides sharing files, SourceSafe allows two or more users to check out a single file at the same time. When each user checks his or her copy of the file back in, Visual SourceSafe can merge each developer's changes into a single file.

Visual SourceSafe also can store any file, not just Visual Basic files—Excel spreadsheets, Word documents, Access database, and so on, within SourceSafe. Your development effort will most likely require you to create help files, technical documentation, and project workplans. Visual SourceSafe allows you to store all your project-related files in a single location.

History Services

History services in Visual SourceSafe are responsible for keeping records of changes made to each file. Not only is it important to know what changes were made, it's also important to know when the changes were made, as well as who made them.

SourceSafe keeps only one copy of each file in a project. When a file is checked out and changes are made, SourceSafe stores only a record of the changes, not a new copy of the entire file. This allows you to easily retrieve older versions of a file for modifications.

When a file is checked in, SourceSafe also records the date and time at which the changes occurred, which allows you to create reports detailing file and project activity. You can save these reports to a file or print them. You also can create journal files that record each command a user enters. Visual SourceSafe also allows you to display the differences between two versions of a file.

Security Services

In team development, it is important not only to make sure that files in a project and changes made to the files are saved, but also to control who can access the files. The security services in SourceSafe allow you to limit user access to the files within projects. Access rights can be set by project and by user, providing full flexibility to a development team—you can allow read-only access to certain files while allowing users to freely edit other files within the same project.

Security is maintained through the Visual SourceSafe Administrator application, which is discussed in detail in a following section of this chapter, "Administering a SourceSafe Project."

Custodial Services

You already may have developed a version of an application that uses a different source control tool, such as PVCS or Microsoft Delta. The custodial services of Visual SourceSafe provide utilities that allow you to convert projects stored in both PVCS and Microsoft Delta to Visual SourceSafe projects.

Additionally, SourceSafe provides a command-line interface to all features, which allows you to integrate SourceSafe with applications other than Visual Basic. Through the command-line interface, you also can create batch files that act upon large numbers of Visual SourceSafe files without human intervention. You might, for example, want to create a weekly batch routine.

Definition of Terms

Before discussing how each of the services you learned about is implemented in Visual SourceSafe, it is important to understand several terms that are used recurrently when describing SourceSafe. These terms are shown in the following list:

- Project
- Subproject

■ Files

■ Working directory

The remainder of this section both defines these terms and describes how they relate to Visual SourceSafe.

Projects

A Visual SourceSafe *project* is a collection of files stored in a Visual SourceSafe database. A SourceSafe project is similar to a directory in the Windows operating system. Both can contain files and subprojects (or subdirectories, in the case of a Windows directory). Both are arranged in a hierarchy, starting at the root project or directory.

It is where the similarities between projects and directories end that you begin to see the benefits of source-code management. Although only one file can exist in exactly one directory at any time, for example, a single file can be shared by many projects. Visual SourceSafe's project hierarchy also is operating-system independent. A project can be accessed transparently from MS-DOS, Windows 3.1, Windows 95, Windows NT, or the Macintosh.

Subprojects

Just as projects mirror the directory structure of an operating system, *subprojects* mirror the subdirectory structure. Subprojects can be thought of as projects within a parent project. A subproject can contain files or other subprojects. For simplicity, this chapter uses the terms project and subproject interchangeably.

Files

Files are the binary and text files that are organized within the projects and subprojects stored in a Visual SourceSafe database. A file stored in the project database is referred to as the *master copy*. Only one master copy of any file exists in a project database. When a user makes modifications to a file, only the changes are stored in the database. The master copy remains intact. Because SourceSafe stores each set of changes, a user can obtain a copy of any version of the file.

When users check a file out of Visual SourceSafe, they actually are checking out a copy of the master file. This "second degree of separation" helps to ensure that the master file will always remain safe and free of errors.

IV

Application Enhancements

Working Directories

As you learned in the previous section, when you check files out of a SourceSafe database, you only obtain a copy of the master file. You must have a place to put this copy. This place is referred to as the *working directory* for the file. The working directory can exist on a local hard drive or on a network drive. Only after you have a copy of a master file in a working directory can you make changes to it.

Every file in a Visual SourceSafe project is associated with a working directory. A working directory is assigned on a per project basis, not on a per file basis. This helps to make sure that your SourceSafe project hierarchy will mirror your project's directory hierarchy.

A working directory can be an existing directory on your hard drive. Visual SourceSafe can also create a new directory to be used as a file's working directory. Later in this chapter, you will learn how to create a working directory and check a file out to it.

Project Naming Conventions

Visual SourceSafe uses the following convention when naming projects and files:

```
$/projectname/subprojectname/filename
```

Here, `projectname` is the name of the project, `subprojectname` is the name of the subproject, and `filename` is the name of your file. If, for example, you created a project named *TestProject*, created a subproject for the project named *UserLogin*, and placed a Visual Basic form named *FRMPASSWORD.FRM* in the userlogin subproject, it would be referred to as the following example:

```
$/TestProject/UserLogin/FRMPASSWORD.FRM
```

Throughout this chapter, this same format is used to refer to projects, subprojects, and files and to their locations within a SourceSafe project.

Visual SourceSafe's Interface Components

SourceSafe helps to greatly simplify source-code management by allowing you to manipulate files in a graphical, Windows-like environment. Visual SourceSafe's graphical interface is composed of the following two components:

- The SourceSafe Explorer
- The Administrator

The SourceSafe Explorer is the client application used by developers to perform actions such as checking files in and out of SourceSafe, creating new projects, adding new files to the project, and obtaining information about files. The Administrator is SourceSafe's administrative tool. It is used to add new users to the SourceSafe database and to edit user rights.

To help you better understand how these components are used to maintain source code, the following sections outline the SourceSafe Explorer and the Administrator, and explain the basic features and functions of each component.

Using the SourceSafe Explorer

The SourceSafe Explorer is displayed when you select Visual SourceSafe 4.0 from the Start menu or Program Manager. The SourceSafe Explorer is used primarily by developers to check files in and out of SourceSafe and also obtain information on each of the files.

The SourceSafe Explorer is composed of the following elements:

- The project list
- The file list
- The status bar

The remainder of this section is an overview of the components of the SourceSafe Explorer. In following sections of this chapter, you learn how to use the Explorer to perform functions such as checking files in and out of the database.

Project List

The project list appears on the left side of the Visual SourceSafe Explorer, shown in figure 19.1. The Explorer uses a TreeView control to display a hierarchical list of all projects contained in the Visual SourceSafe database. Each project is displayed as a folder, with its subprojects displayed as folders beneath it in the TreeView hierarchy.

At the top of the tree, also referred to as the root project, a folder is displayed with the name, **$/**. When you select a project, its full path name appears above the file list. When you select the project in the project list, the files contained within this project are displayed in the ListView control, on the right side of the SourceSafe Explorer screen.

Fig. 19.1
The Visual
SourceSafe
Explorer.

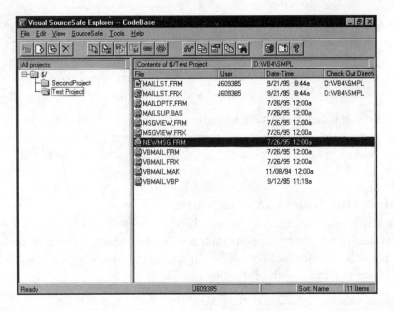

Fig. 19.1
The Visual
SourceSafe
Explorer.

Remember that the project list is a TreeView control—the items in the list can be expanded and collapsed. Just click the plus and minus signs that appear to the left of the project and subproject names to expand and collapse the tree, respectively.

File List

The file list, which appears on the right portion of figure 19.1, displays the files in the currently selected project. The file list also displays the following key pieces of information about each file:

- **File**—The first column displays the name of the SourceSafe file. Immediately to the left of the file name is the file icon, used by many Windows applications. If the file icon appears as a single file, the file appears only in the currently selected project. If the file icon appears as two overlapping files, the file is shared by two or more projects. If the file icon appears to have a pin pushed through it, the file was "pinned." Finally, when the file icon has a check mark in its center, the file has been "checked out."

  Sharing files, pinning files, and checking files in and out of Visual SourceSafe are explained in detail in following sections of this chapter.

- **User**—If the file is checked, the second column displays the name of the user who checked out the file. If ellipses (...) appear after the username, more than one user has the file checked out.

- **Date**—The third column shows the date/time for the file. If the file is currently checked out, the column shows the date and time that the file was checked out. If the file is currently checked in, the column shows the date and time the last change was made to the file.

- **Checkout Directory**—If a file is checked out, this column displays both the directory to which the file was checked out and the name of the computer to which it was checked out.

You also can view the text contained in any file, provided it is saved in ASCII text format, by double-clicking the name of the file in the file list.

Status Bar

The SourceSafe status bar appears at the bottom of figure 19.1. The status bar displays the following information:

In figure 19.1, the status bar shows that SourceSafe is ready to receive a command, the logged-in user is J609385, the current Sort criterion is on the Name column, and the total number of files in the currently selected project is 11. Each of these items is explained in detail in the following paragraphs.

- **State**—Indicates whether or not SourceSafe is ready to accept commands. This area of the status bar also shows a description of a command when the mouse pointer is dragged over a toolbar button or a command in the menu.

- **Logged-in user**—Displays the name of the user logged into the current SourceSafe session.

- **Sort criterion**—Displays the current sort order of the file list. You can change the sort order by selecting the Sort menu item from the View menu.

- **Number of files in project**—Displays the number of files in the currently selected Visual SourceSafe project.

The SourceSafe Administrator

You start the SourceSafe Administrator, the administrative component of Visual SourceSafe, by clicking the Administrator icon from the Windows 95 Start Menu or from the Program Manager. From the administrator, you can perform the following tasks:

- Maintain the user list

- Configure the SourceSafe installation

- Set security

The Administrator is comprised of the user list, a ListView control that displays the names of all users currently added to the SourceSafe database, and the Administrator menu, which contains various options for maintaining users and SourceSafe security.

Later in this chapter, you learn how to use the Administrator to maintain your SourceSafe project.

Creating a Visual SourceSafe Project

The first step is managing your code with Visual SourceSafe is creating a project. Remember that all files in SourceSafe are kept in projects. Think of a project as an object. The project object has certain properties, such as subprojects and files, and certain methods, such as move or copy. Like other objects, the first step in creating a project is design. By spending time up front to create a good design for your project, you help to reduce development time by minimizing the number of changes you may later have to make.

As you learned previously, Visual SourceSafe projects are similar to an operating system directory structure. Logically, the outline of your SourceSafe project should, therefore, follow your Visual Basic directory structure—for each directory you use to hold your Visual Basic files, you should create a SourceSafe project. For each subdirectory within a directory, create a subproject.

Because the number of subdirectories in a project is limited only by the amount of disk space available, organize your project logically between projects and subprojects. If multiple developers are working on a project, each developer may have a subproject that contains the files he or she works on most often. If functional areas of your application comprise more than one file, you may consider placing all the files in a subproject. Although virtually no limit exists to the number of projects and subprojects you can create, be conservative in your use of subprojects. Creating many nested subprojects can make your SourceSafe project difficult to navigate and comprehend.

> **Note**
>
> Make sure that all files needed to build a program are included in one project—not just Visual Basic files, but DLLs, libraries or bitmaps, and any other external files used by the project. This grouping simplifies the creation of an executable version of the project.

Figure 19.2, for example, shows a SourceSafe project with several Visual Basic files, a bitmap file, a Word document, and a .DLL file.

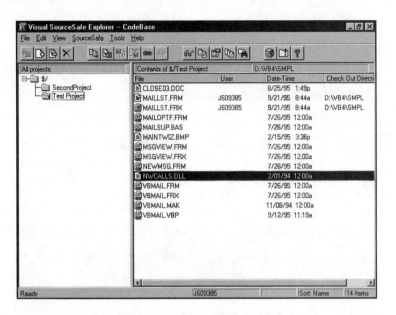

Fig. 19.2
A sample
SourceSafe project.

To create a SourceSafe project, follow these steps:

1. From the File menu in the SourceSafe Explorer, select the Create Project option.

   Visual SourceSafe displays the Create Project dialog box.

2. Type a name and a comment for the project.

   You always should add a comment to describe the Visual SourceSafe action you are performing. It helps others to understand why you performed the action.

3. Click the OK button to add the project.

Adding Files to Projects

To keep your files safe, you need to add them to a SourceSafe database by adding files to a project. After you create a project, you can add your files by using the Add File command.

To add a file to a project, follow these steps:

1. From the project list, select the project or subproject to which you want to add a file.

2. On the Explorer's File menu, select Add Files.

   The Add File dialog box is displayed.

3. From the Add File dialog box, select the file or files you want to add to the project.

4. Click the Add button.

   When you click the Add button, SourceSafe displays the Comment dialog box shown in figure 19.3. On this dialog box, add a comment that describes the new file you are adding to the project.

Fig. 19.3
The Comment dialog box.

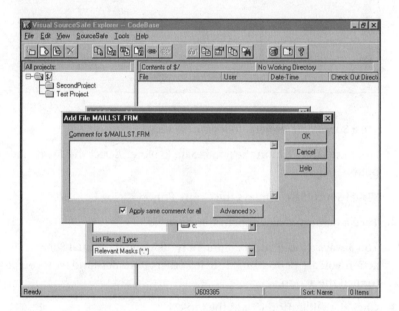

If you are adding more than one file, you can click the Use for All check box to have the same comment for all files you are adding.

After you click the Add button, the file you added no longer will appear on the Add File dialog box because it is already part of the project.

You also can click the Advanced button on the Comment dialog box. This button causes the additional fields to be displayed. By clicking the appropriate check box, you can instruct SourceSafe to do the following:

- **Store only latest version**—Causes SourceSafe to store only the latest version of the file. You no longer have to store changes to the file, making it impossible to return to a previous version. Use this option with care because you are essentially eliminating one benefit of source-code control: version tracking. If you are placing a bitmap file, for example, you probably will not refer to an earlier version of it, and you may want to select this option.

- **Check Out immediately**—This option causes SourceSafe to immediately check out the file as soon as it is added to the project.

- **Remove local copy**—Selecting this option causes SourceSafe to delete the new, added file from your current directory after it is added to the SourceSafe project. Because the file's working directory may not be the same as the file's current directory, selecting this option helps ensure that you do not have two copies of the file on your local machine.

- **File type**—You can select how SourceSafe treats this file: as binary or text, or allow SourceSafe to auto-detect which type of file is being checked in.

You also can add an entire directory to a Visual SourceSafe project. When youadd a directory, SourceSafe creates a new subproject under the parent project you have selected.

To add a directory to a project, follow these steps:

1. Click a project from the project list on the SourceSafe Explorer.

2. From the File menu, click Add Files.

3. SourceSafe displays the Add File dialog box.

4. In the Directories list box, click the directory you want to add to SourceSafe.

5. Click the Add button.

   SourceSafe displays the Add Directory dialog box. This dialog box is identical to the Add File dialog box shown in figure 19.3, with one exception. Rather than the Use for All check box, the Add Directories dialog contains a Recursive check box. Clicking the Recursive check box instructs SourceSafe to add not only the directory you selected and all the files it contains, but also all subdirectories.

6. To select any of the advanced options shown at the bottom of figure 19.3, click the Advanced button. These are the same options you select when you add a file.

7. After selecting all the desired options, click the OK button.

One critical difference between SourceSafe's project hierarchy and an operating system's directory structure is that a file in SourceSafe can exist in more than one project. A file in an operating system can exist in one, and only one, directory (you may place *copies* of files in different directories, but a single instance of a file cannot exist in more than one directory).

In SourceSafe, this is known as *sharing* a file. If a file is shared between more than one project, all changes made to the file are propagated to all projects that share the file. Consider this propagation when designing your project. A file that exists in more than one project (or subproject) should be shared among projects, rather than adding a separate copy of the file to each project. This ensures that all changes made to the file are included in every project. We discuss sharing in detail later in this chapter.

Specifying a Working Directory

To ensure that your source code remains safe, Visual SourceSafe doesn't allow you to edit the master copies of files that are stored in the SourceSafe database. Rather, editing is performed at an operating system level in a directory that you specify to SourceSafe. This directory is known as the *working directory*.

You set a working directory per project, per user. For example, if you have two projects in SourceSafe—$/order/catalog and $/customer/, you have two working directories, one for each project. Likewise, if a second developer was working on the same projects, he or she would have his or her own working directories.

When you set a working directory for a project, you set the working directory for all subprojects under the project. You also can explicitly set a working directory for each subproject.

To set a working directory for a project or subproject, follow these steps:

1. Select a Project or Subproject from the project list.

2. From the Explorer's File menu, select Set Working Directory.

    SourceSafe displays the Working Directory dialog box shown in figure 19.4.

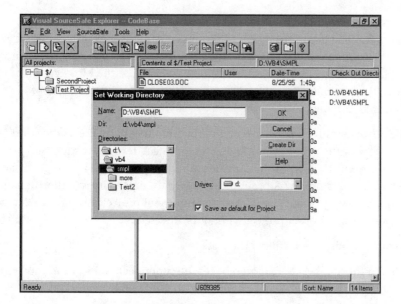

Fig. 19.4
The Working
Directory dialog
box.

3. Enter a directory path for the working directory.

 To create a new directory, click the Create Dir button.

 The Save as Default for Project button is used to instruct SourceSafe to use the working directory you are specifying each time you check out files in the selected project or if you only want to use the working directory for your current session.

 If you want to always use the working directory, check the Save as Default for Project check box. If you only want to use the working directory for your current session, uncheck the box.

4. Click the OK button when you are finished.

SourceSafe's Check Out, Get, and Share commands all require a working directory. If you try to use any of these commands on a file without first specifying a working directory, Visual SourceSafe displays a message box indicating that the files do not have a working directory, and asks if you want to create one.

Moving Projects

At times, you may find that it's necessary to move a subproject to a new location. You can move a subproject by using the Move command. The Move command redefines the project path of the selected subproject and all of its contents.

Suppose that you had a subproject named customermgr whose parent project was order. The full project path of the customermgr subproject would be $/order/customermgr. You then decide that the customermgr subproject should be placed under a new project, customer. You can use the Move command to move the customermgr subproject. The new project path of the subproject then is $/customer/customermgr.

The Move command neither renames the subproject nor affects the contents or history of the subproject. Moving a subproject does affect the history of its former parent project. In the previous example, you would no longer be able to faithfully restore the $/order project. Any attempt to do so will generate a warning message that states the customermgr subproject was moved. Future versions of the $/order project will not be affected.

To move a subproject, follow these steps:

1. In the SourceSafe Explorer, select the subproject you want to move from the project list.

2. From the File menu, click Move Project.

   SourceSafe displays the Move dialog box. The From field displays the current path to the project. Enter the name of the new parent project in the To box.

3. Click OK when you have finished.

Renaming Files and Projects

At some point during development, you may decide that the name you chose for a file or project no longer is indicative of the application. You may have created a new project in SourceSafe for example, and named it $/DevelopmentOne. You have been using this project to hold the files that make up the order processing application you are building. Now that you are in the fourth week of development, you decide to change the name of the project to $/OrderProcessor. You can change the project name by using the Rename command. When you rename a project, its complete history is retained.

You also can rename files stored in Visual SourceSafe by using the rename command. If a file shared by multiple projects is renamed, the file is renamed in all projects sharing the file. Files that have been branched are not re-named. Like a project, when you rename a file, the file's history is retained.

Take great care when renaming files that are part of a Visual Basic project. Remember that renaming a file in Visual SourceSafe requires you to re-add the file to the Visual Basic project. Because the file will be renamed in all files that share the project, all developers that use the file must re-add it to their Visual Basic projects.

To rename a project or file, follow these steps:

1. From the SourceSafe Explorer, select the file or project that you want to rename.

2. Select the Re<u>n</u>ame command from the <u>F</u>ile menu.

   The Rename dialog box is displayed. The project or file that you are about to rename is shown in the From field.

3. Type a new name for the file or project in the To field.

4. Click OK when you are finished.

Retrieving Files

Retrieving files is the act of bringing a copy of a file stored in a Visual SourceSafe database into its working directory. You can retrieve a file as read-only or as a writable version that can be edited. Remember that you must specify a working directory for your project before you can retrieve a file. If you haven't specified a working directory, SourceSafe prompts you to do so when you retrieve a file.

This section describes the three commands that you can use to retrieve files. They are:

■ Get

■ Check Out

■ View

The Get Command

You use the get command to retrieve a read-only copy of a file to the file's working directory. It is a good idea to keep read-only copies of all files that you are not currently editing. These copies help to ensure that you do not inadvertently make changes to a file. They also help make sure that the file is available to all other developers working on the project who may need to make changes to it.

You need to keep your read-only copies of files up to date. The Get command is useful for this updating. When you begin working each day, for example, you will want to make sure that the code with which you are working is up to date. Your co-developers may have made changes to files, and you want these changes to be reflected in your working code. You can use the Get command to retrieve the up-to-date files from the SourceSafe database.

You can use the Get command to retrieve a single file, a number of files, or an entire project. To use the Get command, follow these steps:

1. On the SourceSafe Explorer, select the files or projects you want to get.

2. From the SourceSafe menu, select the Get command. If you set your preferences to display a dialog box for the Get command, the Get dialog box, shown in figure 19.5 is displayed.

Fig. 19.5
The Get dialog box.

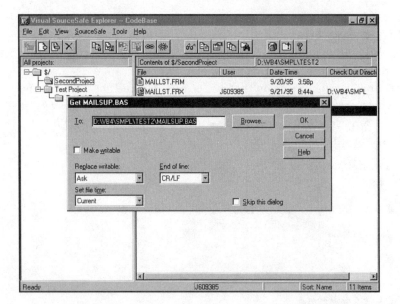

Later in this chapter, we discuss how to adjust the preferences for a SourceSafe project.

The Get dialog box contains the following options:

■ **Recursive**—Click the recursive check box when you want to retrieve all files in the currently selected project as well as all subdirectories. This check box is visible only when you use the Get command on a project.

- **Make Writable**—Selecting this check box causes SourceSafe to place an editable copy of the file you are Getting in the file's working directory, but it doesn't check the file out of the SourceSafe database, so all changes you make to the writable file will not be stored.

- **Skip this dialog**—Causes SourceSafe to not display the Get dialog box when subsequent Get commands are issued.

If you click the Advanced button on the Get dialog box, the following options become available:

- **Replace writable**—You can select Ask, Default, Replace, Skip, or Error. See the later section "Creating a SourceSafe User Environment" for details on these settings.

- **Set file time**—Allows you to choose the time SourceSafe places on the file when getting it for you. The options are Current, Up date, and Modify. See the section later in this chapter, "Creating a SourceSafe User Environment," for details on each of these settings.

- **End of line**—Lets you choose the end-of-line character for a file. The options are Default, CR, LF, CR/LF. See the following section, "Creating a SourceSafe User Environment," for details on these settings.

The Check Out Command

Use the Check Out command to retrieve an editable copy of a Visual SourceSafe file. When you check out a file, you "lock" the file. This locking prevents all other SourceSafe users from checking out the file and making changes to it, unless you have enabled multi-user check out.

Like the Get command, you can use the Check Out command to retrieve one file, a number of files, or an entire subproject. To use the Check Out command, follow these steps:

1. Select the files or project you want to Check Out from the SourceSafe Explorer.

2. Select the Check Out command from the SourceSafe menu.

If you have set your preferences to display the dialog box for the Check Out command, the Check Out dialog box (see fig. 19.6).

Fig. 19.6

The Check Out dialog box.

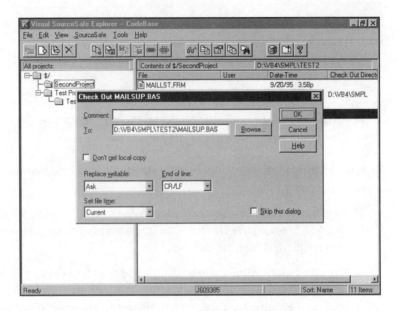

The options presented on the Check Out dialog box are nearly the same as those presented on the Get dialog box. See the previous section for details on these options.

The one option that differs, the Don't get local copy check box, allows you to determine whether or not SourceSafe places a local copy of the file you are checking out into the file's working directory. If you click the check box, SourceSafe marks the file as checked out but doesn't give you a new copy. This can be useful if you made changes to a local file without checking the file out first. By using the Don't get local copy option, you can check the file out of the SourceSafe database without overwriting your local copy, then check your local copy of the file back in to the database, storing your changes.

3. Click the OK button when you have finished.

After checking out a file, you may decide that you no longer need to make changes to the file. When you Check In a file, SourceSafe prompts you for comments and automatically increments the internal version number of the file. The Undo Check Out command allows you to return a file to the SourceSafe database without saving changes, incrementing the internal version number, or requesting you to add comments. This can help to make reviewing the history of a file clearer because the person reviewing the history will not have to wade through comments that indicate a file was checked in without changes.

To undo the checkout of a file, follow these steps:

1. Select a file from the file list that you currently have checked out.

2. From the <u>S</u>ourceSafe menu, select the <u>U</u>ndo Check Out option.

   If the Undo Check Out dialog box is enabled in the preferences section, the Undo Check Out dialog box, shown in figure 19.7, is displayed. Later in this chapter, we discuss how to set the preferences for a project.

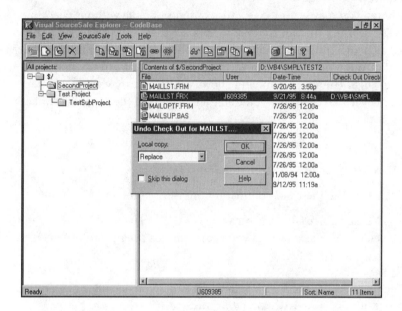

Fig. 19.7
The Undo Check Out dialog box.

The Undo Check Out dialog presents two options. The first is the Local Copy drop-down list box. From this list box, you can choose what SourceSafe does with the local copy of the file after the Check Out is undone. You have the following choices:

- **Replace**—Causes Visual SourceSafe to replace the local copy of the file with a read-only copy.

- **Delete**—Removes the file from your directory after the Check Out has been undone.

- **Leave**—Do nothing to the file after the checkout.

- **Default**—Causes Visual SourceSafe to use the settings specified on the Local Files tab or the settings inherited from a parent project when undoing the check out. This option is used automatically when you select multiple files.

The second option presented on the Undo Check Out dialog box is the Skip this dialog check box. If you select this check box, Visual SourceSafe doesn't present the Undo Check Out dialog box during subsequent Undo Check Out operations.

3. Click the OK button after you have finished.

The View Command

At times, you may want to view the contents of a file without checking out the file or using the Get command. Suppose that your project plan shows that a change is needed in a function in a Visual Basic code module, but you think another developer with which you are working already may have made the change. The View command allows you to quickly view the contents of a file without requiring you to retrieve a copy of the file to its working directory.

To view a file, follow these steps:

1. Select a file to View from the SourceSafe Explorer's file list.

2. Select the View File command from the Edit menu.

   Visual SourceSafe displays a copy of the file, using the file's default editor. You also can view the contents of a file by double-clicking the file in the file list.

Note that because the file you view is not copied to a working directory, you do not need to have a working directory specified.

When you view a file, Visual SourceSafe uses the file's default editor to display it. Remember that Visual SourceSafe can store any type of file, including Word documents or Excel spreadsheets. If you viewed an Excel spreadsheet, SourceSafe will load Excel and display the sheet. You then could read it or print a hard copy of the file. SourceSafe displays a read-only copy of the file; the changes you make to the file are not stored by SourceSafe.

Returning Files to the Database

After you finish editing a file, you will want to return the file to the Visual SourceSafe database. This action allows SourceSafe to save the changes that you have made to the file. It also allows other developers to incorporate your changes into their projects.

To check a file in, you must first have the file checked out. To Check In a file, follow these steps:

1. Click the file in the SourceSafe Explorer's file list you want to Check In.

2. Select the Check In command from the SourceSafe menu.

   The Check In dialog box shown in figure 19.8 is displayed.

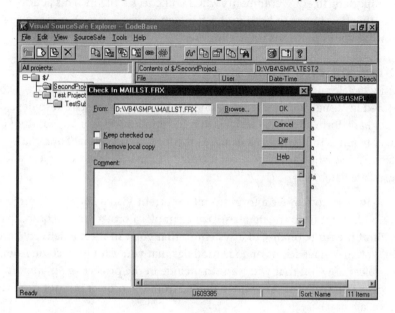

Fig. 19.8
The Check In
dialog box.

The Check In dialog box presents the following options:

- **Keep checked out**—If you select this option, SourceSafe keeps the file checked out to you after the Check In is completed. This option is useful if you plan to continue work on the file but you decided to check the file in for safety purposes or to allow other developers to incorporate your changes.

- **Remove local copy**—If this option is selected, SourceSafe removes the local copy of the file after it was checked in. Remember that a Visual Basic project requires you to have a local copy of all files in the project. If you select the Remove local copy option, you will not be able to load your Visual Basic project.

- **Diff**—Click this button to have Visual SourceSafe display the differences between the version of the file you are about to Check In and the version of the file currently in the Visual SourceSafe database. You can use the Diff command only if you are checking in a single file.

3. Type a comment for the file.

4. Click OK when you are finished.

It is important to enter comments when you check a file in. This action allows other developers to both understand where you made changes in a file and what your intentions for the file are.

Removing and Recovering Files

During development, you may discover that you no longer require a file that is stored in Visual SourceSafe. For example, you may have started to develop a Visual Basic form and then decided that the application you are building no longer requires it. If you already added the form to the Visual SourceSafe database, you will want to remove it from both the SourceSafe project and SourceSafe database.

You may want to remove a form from the current Visual SourceSafe project but not delete it from the database. For example, a project may require that you limit the functionality of a system so that you can meet a delivery date. If so, you may have forms or code modules that you want to exclude from the project now but that you want to include in the project again later. In this case, you will want to remove the file from the project but not from the SourceSafe database.

Visual SourceSafe can accommodate both of these situations. It does so by providing the following commands to remove files:

- Delete
- Destroy
- Purge

When you Delete a file, you remove it from a project. The file still is stored by the Visual SourceSafe database. A deleted file from a project also can be recovered. The Delete command also presents you with the option of Destroying the file. When you Destroy a file, it is permanently removed from the SourceSafe database.

Remember that if you do not Destroy a file when you Delete it, it remains in the SourceSafe database. If, at a later time, you decide that you want to remove the file permanently from the SourceSafe database, use the Purge command.

To Delete a file, follow these steps:

1. Click the file that you want to delete from the SourceSafe database in the Explorer's file list.

2. From the <u>F</u>ile menu, select the <u>D</u>elete command. SourceSafe displays the Delete dialog box.

The Delete dialog box includes the Destroy permanently check box. If you check the Delete box, the file you are deleting not only is removed from the selected project, it also is permanently removed from the Visual SourceSafe database. You will not be able to recover this file.

3. Click the OK button when you have finished.

To Purge a file, follow these steps:

1. Click the project in the SourceSafe Explorer's project list that contains the files you want to Purge.

2. From the <u>F</u>ile menu, select the <u>P</u>roperties command.

SourceSafe displays the Project Properties tabbed dialog box shown in figure 19.9.

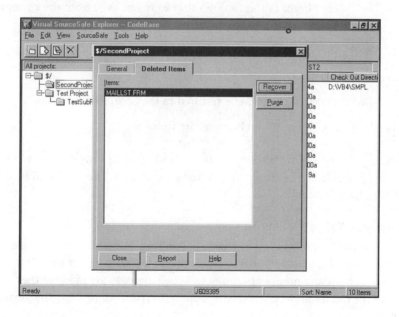

Fig. 19.9
The Project Properties tabbed dialog.

3. Click the Deleted Items tab.

The Deleted Items tab lists files that were removed from the current project by using the Delete command.

4. Select the file or files you want to Purge from the database.

5. Click the Purge button.

   The files you have selected are now permanently removed from the currently selected project.

6. Click the Close button when you have finished.

You can recover a file that is still contained in the Visual SourceSafe database. A SourceSafe project maintains a list of files that were deleted (and not destroyed or purged).

To recover deleted files, follow these steps:

1. Select the project that contains the files you want to recover from the project list on the SourceSafe Explorer.

2. From the File menu, select the Properties command.

   The Project Properties tabbed dialog box shown in figure 19.9 is displayed.

3. Click the Deleted Items tab.

   The Deleted Items tab shows files that were removed from the current project by using the Delete command.

4. Select the file or files you want to recover.

5. Click the Recover button.

   The files you selected will be restored to the SourceSafe database.

6. Click the Close button when you are finished.

If a file is shared among projects, using the Delete or Destroy command removes the file from the currently selected project only. The file remains in all other projects sharing it.

Sharing Files

Visual SourceSafe allows you to share files among many projects. A single, master copy of the file is stored in the SourceSafe database, but the file is accessible from any number of projects. When changes are made to the shared file in any project, the changes are reflected in all projects that share the file.

This section helps you understand when and how to share a file among projects. In a following section of this chapter, "Branching Files," you will read more about a special case of sharing known as *branching*.

When to Share a File

Sharing can help to both decrease development and maximize resource usage by helping to avoid duplicate effort. While building an order processing application, suppose that a team of developers creates a graph builder. This graph builder can accept a group of data points and generate a graph on-screen. The order processing development team uses the graph builder to report on quarterly revenue. Now, suppose that a second group of developers begin to work on a lead-tracking application. It determines that adding graphing capability to this application will make it more usable. Rather than creating a graph builder from scratch, it can use the code that the order processing team has already developed, by sharing the files through Visual SourceSafe.

This type of code sharing has always been available in Visual Basic. So what advantage does sharing offer? Move back to the order processing team. A new developer comes on board and has time to significantly enhance the graph builder. The lead tracking team hears about the enhancements and realizes the benefit of the improvements. What does it need to do to incorporate these changes into its program? Nothing. Because the two development teams are sharing the graph builder code, the changes made by the order processing team are automatically propagated to lead-tracking project.

When sharing files, all development teams should be aware of other teams that may be using the files and avoid placing references to forms, functions, or variables that may not be available to all teams who share the files. If two teams share a file, for example, and Team A makes a reference within the shared form to a global variable that is not present in development Team B's project, Team B will experience an error when attempting to run or compile its project. If a shared file needs to reference a function or variable, try to declare the function or variable within the form itself or within a code module that is shared by all projects.

Sharing the Current Version of a File

When you share a file between projects, you may share either the current version of the file, or any of the previous versions of the file that have been stored in Visual SourceSafe.

Generally, you will share the most current version of a file. The next section discusses instances where you may want to share an older version. To share the most-current version, follow these steps:

1. Select the project into which you want to share a file or files.

2. From the SourceSafe menu, select the Share command.

   SourceSafe displays the Share dialog box shown in figure 19.10.

Fig. 19.10

The Share dialog box.

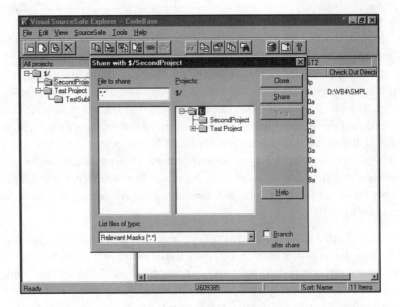

3. From the Projects list box in the Share dialog box, select the project from which the file or files are to be shared.

4. From the Files to Share list box, select the file or files you want to Share.

5. Click the Share button when you have finished.

   The files you selected from the Files to Share list box on the Share dialog box are now shared with the currently selected project.

You also can share a file by dragging and dropping the file into another Visual SourceSafe project or by clicking the Share toolbar button.

Sharing an Older Version of a File

To help you understand why you may want to share an older version of a file, recall the graph builder that was being shared by the order processing team and the lead-tracking team. Suppose that a third development team begins to work on a customer-complaint tracking system. It, too, determines that the graph builder will help to enhance its application. At this time, the order processing team is presently working on a third version of the graph builder that adds many advanced features. The complaint tracking team decides that it does not yet need the advanced version and decides instead to add an older version of the graph builder.

When you share an older version of a file, you do not want to propagate any changes to the file every time that it is updated in a project. You do want to maintain the version of the file that was originally shared. To permit this maintenance process, Visual SourceSafe provides a mechanism known as *pinning*. Pinning allows you to freeze an older version of a file. When a file is pinned, the version of the file that you pinned—and not the most recent version—becomes the version of the file that is shared.

When a file is pinned, you no longer can make changes to the file (which is why this process is called pinning). You are, in effect, sticking a pin into the project, so that the version of the file you chose to share, or pin, with your project remains unchanged.

To pin a specific version of a file by using the Visual SourceSafe Explorer, take the following steps:

1. Select the file you want to pin from the file list in the SourceSafe Explorer.

2. From the Tools menu, select the Show History command. You also can select the History button from the toolbar.

   SourceSafe displays the History of File dialog box shown in figure 19.11.

3. From the History list box, select the version of the file you want to share.

   The version number of a file appears in the Version column. To find more information about a version of a file, such as the version comments, click the Details button.

4. Click the Pin button.

5. Click the Close button when you have finished.

   When you close the History of File dialog box, SourceSafe displays the version number of the file beside the file's name in the file list. This number is a visual cue that a version file has been pinned. In addition, the Icon for the file shows a pushpin.

Fig. 19.11

The History of File dialog box.

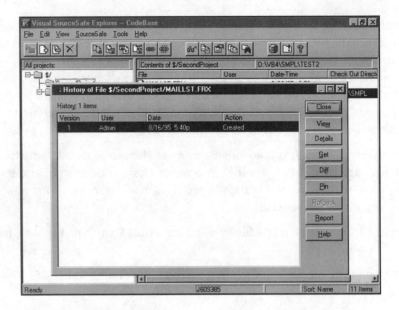

If you later decide that you no longer want to pin a file, you can unpin it. Suppose that the complaint tracking team now decides that it wants to incorporate the updated version of the graph builder into its project. When you unpin a file, you quit sharing the older version of the file and return to the current version of the file.

To unpin a file, follow these steps:

1. Select the file that you want to unpin from the file list.

2. Click the Show History command from the Tools menu.

    The History of File dialog box shown in figure 19.11 is displayed.

3. Click the Unpin button.

    SourceSafe unpins the file and shares the current version of the file with all projects that currently share the file. The caption on the Unpin button changes to Pin.

    To pin a different version of the file to share, you can select another version, and then click the Pin button.

4. Click the Close button when finished.

Rolling Back Files

Visual SourceSafe's Rollback command allows you to reset a file to a previous version. The main difference between pinning and *rolling back* a file is that, after a rollback, you can make changes to the older version of the file, while a pinned file cannot be edited. After you make changes to the rolled back version, it becomes the current version of the file in your project. In effect, you created a separate development path for the rolled back file. Any changes that you make to the file are not reflected in other projects that share the file. Likewise, when a change is made to the file in another project, these changes are not propagated to the rolled back version.

Rolling back a file can be useful in the following development scenario. Moving back to the graph builder example, recall that the order processing team is currently at work on an advanced version of the graph builder. A new development team begins to work on a fourth application—an inventory management tool. The inventory management team decides that graphing capabilities will be helpful, so it decides to include the graph builder. As you learned before, SourceSafe allows it to share the files that make up the graph builder.

In our example, as the order processing team begins to add new features to the graph builder, the inventory management team decides that it will be better off coding its own enhancements. It decides that using an older version of the graph builder is a better idea and continuing its own development path from that point. The inventory management team can easily accomplish this in Visual SourceSafe by using the rollback command.

To rollback to a previous version of a file, take the following steps:

1. From the file list in the SourceSafe Explorer, select the file you want to roll back.

2. Select the Show History command from the Tools menu.

    SourceSafe displays the History of File dialog box shown in figure 19.11.

3. Select the version of the file you want to roll back to in the History of File dialog box.

4. Click the Rollback button.

Branching Files

You just saw how the rollback command can be used to create a separate development path for a file. In SourceSafe, this process is known as *branching*. Branching is the act of creating two or more disparate development paths for a file. You branch a file by first sharing it with a project, and then setting the shared files onto two separate development paths.

Branching is often used to perform parallel development. Suppose that the order processing team released its graph builder, and then discovered that the graph builder contained several bugs. It already plans to create an advanced version of the graph builder, but it realizes that it also has to create a maintenance release. The order processing team can branch the files that make up the graph builder. Now, while one group of developers works on the maintenance release, a second group proceeds with the advanced version of the tool.

Because the graph builder files were branched, all changes made by the maintenance release team will not propagate to the advanced version team. The changes are local to the maintenance release team's branch only. Likewise, changes made by the advanced version team will not be propagated to the maintenance release version.

To create branches, use the Branch command. The Branch command causes the following actions to occur:

- A new version of the file is created in the project from which you executed the branch command. The new branch has a version number that is one number higher than the version from which it was branched.

- The separated file now has an independent history, separate from other versions of the same file in different projects.

- The old link to other projects that share the file is now broken, and a new link to the current project is created.

You can branch files in one of two ways—you can either branch files currently being shared among one or more projects or you can share a file and create a branch in one operation.

To create a branch from a file that is currently being shared, follow these steps:

1. From the file list, select the file or files that you want to branch.

2. From the SourceSafe menu, select Branch. You also can click the Branch button on the toolbar. SourceSafe displays the Branch dialog box.

3. Add a comment for the Branch action. This comment should indicate why you are branching the files.

4. Click the OK button to Branch the files.

To share a file and create a branch in one operation, follow these steps:

1. From the file list, select the file that you want to Share and Branch.

2. From the SourceSafe menu, select the Share command. The File to Share list box is displayed.

3. Select the file you want to share from the File to Share list box.

4. Select the Branch after share check box.

5. Click the Share button.

Merging Branches

In the previous example, the order processing development team used branching to allow the maintenance release sub-team to develop in parallel with the advanced version sub-team. Suppose that the advanced development sub-team completes its enhancements, and the order processing team wants to combine all of the advanced version changes with the bug fixes included in the maintenance release. SourceSafe allows the teams to merge together the branched files.

Merging two files that were previously branched causes changes from one file to be incorporated into a second file. Merges are directional—the changes move from one file to another. If, for example, file A is merged with file B, file A's changes are merged *into* file B. File A remains unchanged. All changes merged in a file immediately become a part of any project that shares this file.

For branched files to be merged, they must satisfy the following conditions:

- The branched files must be ASCII text files

- The files must have a common ancestor at some point in their history (as all branched files should)

After files are merged, all subsequent changes to either file have to be merged again—unless the files are shared—instead of branched, between projects.

To merge files between branched projects, take the following steps:

1. From the file list, select the file into which you want to merge changes.

2. Select the <u>M</u>erge Branches command from the <u>S</u>ourceSafe menu.

   SourceSafe displays the Merge dialog box shown in figure 19.12.

Fig. 19.12
The Merge dialog box.

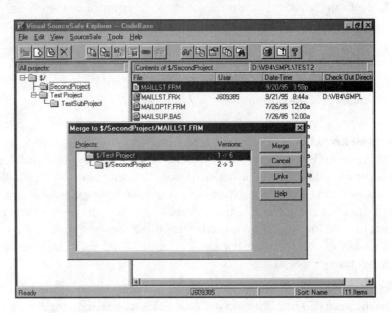

3. In the Merge dialog box, select from the Project list the project that contains the version of the file you want to merge changes from.

4. Click the Merge button.

   The Merge dialog box displays all of the projects that have ever shared the file into which changes are being merged. You can see all the other projects that share this file from the Merge dialog box by clicking the Links button.

Automatic Merging

Visual SourceSafe allows two or more users to check out a single file at the same time. When the users finish editing the files and check them back in, Visual SourceSafe automatically merges together the changes made to both files.

Suppose that the order processing team and the inventory management team both need to modify a file, named GRAPHBLD.FRM, that is used for the graph builder. The SourceSafe Administrator has set the properties of the file to allow multiple users to check it out. The order processing team completes all of its changes and checks the file back into SourceSafe. The inventory management team then completes its changes. When it checks the file back in, one of two situations will occur. If the inventory management team has made changes to lines other than the lines changed by the order processing team, all of the changes are merged.

If, however, the order processing team and the inventory management team have made different changes to the same lines, SourceSafe displays a dialog that informs the inventory management team that a conflict has occurred. The inventory management team now must ease the conflict by editing GRAPHBLD.FRM. Visual SourceSafe automatically places a copy of the file into the inventory management team's working directory and indicates which lines have conflicts (see the following section, "How Visual SourceSafe Indicates Conflicts," for more information). When the inventory management team resolves the conflicts, the file can be checked back in.

How Visual SourceSafe Indicates Conflicts

When two users edit the same file, and then check the file back in, Visual SourceSafe scans the two files for conflicting changes. A conflict occurs when both users have made different changes to the same line of a file.

Visual SourceSafe allows the first person who checks in the file to do so without displaying warning or alert messages. Visual SourceSafe does not allow the second person to check in the file if any conflicts exist. If SourceSafe finds a conflict, it alerts the user with a message box, and then places a copy of the file in the second user's working directory.

Visual SourceSafe adds six consecutive equal signs to the second user's file to indicate which lines are in conflict. SourceSafe refers to the copy of the file placed in the second user's working directory as the local copy of the file, and the copy checked in by the first user as the Visual SourceSafe version of the file.

Visual SourceSafe not only shows which lines are in conflict between the local and SourceSafe versions of the file, but it actually includes both the code that appears in the SourceSafe version and the code that appears in the local version. Suppose that the order processing team and the inventory management team both check out the GRAPHBLD.FRM form. Both teams change the same line of code. The order processing team checks the file back in first. Then, when the inventory management team checks in its version of the file, it receives a warning message that announces that conflicts exist. A copy of the file is then placed in the working directory of the inventory management team. Within this file, the following code appears, indicating the conflict:

```
<<<<<< Visual SourceSafe version
Label1.Caption =  "The order-processing team made this change"
======
Label1.Caption =  "The inventory-management team made this change"
>>>>>> Local version
```

The left angle brackets (<) indicate the Visual SourceSafe version of the code. After the brackets, SourceSafe includes the line or lines of code in conflict. The six equal signs separate the SourceSafe version of the code from the Local version. Finally, right angle brackets (>) indicate both the end of the Local version and the end of the conflict.

When the conflicts are resolved, the inventory management team can check the file back into SourceSafe.

A previous part of this section discussed merging branched files. Remember that branched files are merged into one another. Only one of the files being merged is changed. The other merged file remains unchanged.

When branched files are merged, Visual SourceSafe scans the file being changed for conflicts. If conflicts arise, the merge does not occur until all of the conflicts are resolved. Visual SourceSafe uses a notation similar to the notation used for a file checked out by two users. Rather than naming the files "Visual SourceSafe version" and "Local version," however, SourceSafe uses the names of the two projects that contain the branched versions.

Creating a SourceSafe User Environment

Visual SourceSafe provides many user options to help make performing the daily actions associated with source-code management, such as checking files in and out, easier. By setting these options "up front" for each user, you can make your project run more smoothly. It's also a good idea to make each SourceSafe user aware of these options. They may find a certain setting useful during a particular stage of development.

The SourceSafe Options Settings

Most of these SourceSafe options are set from the SourceSafe Options tabbed dialog, shown in figure 19.13.

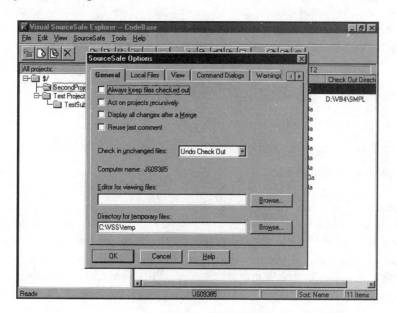

Fig. 19.13
The SourceSafe Options tabbed dialog.

The Options tabbed dialog, which can be displayed by selecting the Options command from SourceSafe's Tools menu, is made up of the following tabs:

- General

- Local Files

- View

- Command Dialogs

- Warnings

- File Types

- Command Line Options

The following sections explain the options that are presented by each folder tab and show how to use the options to help alleviate extra work when managing source code. Due to this book's focus on 32-bit windows development, discussions on the Command Line options tab were omitted. For information on Visual SourceSafe's command line options, see the documentation that is included with the Visual Basic Enterprise Edition.

The General Attributes Tab Settings

The General Attributes folder tab shown in figure 19.13 enables you to choose settings for common tasks such as checking files in and out of the database. The folder tab presents a series of check boxes, drop-down list boxes, and edit boxes that allow you to choose the way in which SourceSafe reacts when you carry out certain actions.

The four check boxes on the tab present the following four options:

- Always keep files checked out
- Act on projects recursively
- Display all changes after merge
- Reuse last comment

The *Always keep files out* check box causes Visual SourceSafe to keep files checked out in the file's working directory, after the file is checked in or a new file is added to a project. Checking this box can be useful if you are constantly working on the same files in a project and you are only using the check-in command to allow other developers to incorporate your changes into their projects.

Remember that if you check this option, any file that you check out of SourceSafe remains checked out by you until you undo the setting. This selection may cause you to inadvertently keep a file checked out, which may force other users to wait for you to check the file in before they can edit it.

The *Act on project recursively* check box causes all actions that act on a project to also act on all subprojects. This setting can save you time by not requiring you to carry out an action, such as Get, for each file in a project. Rather, when you instruct SourceSafe to act recursively, you only need to execute the Get command on a project. SourceSafe will automatically retrieve all files in the project.

The *Display changes after a merge* check box causes Visual SourceSafe to display a dialog box that shows all of the changes that result after a merge, even changes that do not result in conflicts. Although useful, enabling this option causes the dialog box to display every time you merge a file, which may become distracting.

The *Reuse last comment* check box causes Visual SourceSafe to use the most recent comment that you entered as a default for comments when you check in a file. You should use this check box sparingly. When debugging, the comments that are provided by a developer when they check in a file can help you determine which changes to a file are causing problems. Using the same comments for all files you check in can save time, but supplying descriptive comments each time a file is checked is important for the reasons mentioned previously.

The Options tabbed dialog presents a drop-down list box that allows you to select how Visual SourceSafe will handle unchanged files when you check them in. The following choices are displayed:

- Ask

- Undo Checkout

- Check In

If you select the *Ask* option, Visual SourceSafe displays a dialog box that will ask the user whether he or she wants to check in the unchanged file. If an unchanged file is checked in, Visual SourceSafe increments the file's internal version number and prompts the user checking in the file to enter comments. The Ask option is the default option. If the *Undo Checkout* option is selected, Visual SourceSafe cancels the checkout of the unchanged file, does not increase the internal version number and does not prompt a user for a description of the changes that were made. Finally, if the *Check In* option is selected, SourceSafe increases the internal version number, and then prompts a user for comments.

It's always a good idea to leave the unchanged file setting as Ask or Undo Checkout. The Ask setting allows users to decide whether or not they want to include comments with their unchanged files. Adding comments to unchanged files can clutter the history of the file, which can make it difficult to determine when and why changes were made. If you use the Check In setting, you may want to create a standard comment to be entered, indicating that the file was checked back in with no changes.

The General tab dialog also presents two edit boxes at the bottom of the tab. These boxes are labeled `Editor` for viewing files and `Directory` for temporary files.

The Editor for viewing files edit box is used by Visual SourceSafe to determine which editor to use to View files that are not yet assigned a default editor.

Clicking the Browse button displays an Open File dialog box. From here, you can select the Editor.

The Directory for temporary files edit box is used to indicate where to store the temp files that were created by Visual SourceSafe. The default is the TEMP subdirectory, under the directory in which SRCSAFE.INI is stored. Clicking the Browse button to the right of the edit box displays the Select Temporary Directory dialog box. From here, users can select a temporary directory.

The Local Files Tab Settings

The Local Files tab on the Options tabbed dialog, shown in figure 19.14, presents several options that allow you to determine how SourceSafe treats local copies of a file in its working directory.

Fig. 19.14
The Local Files folder tab.

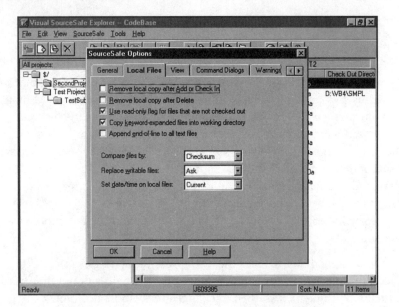

The Local Files tab displays the following check boxes:

- Remove local copy Add or Check In

- Remove local files after Delete

- Use read-only flag on files that are not checked out

- Copy keyword-expanded files into working directory

- Append end-of-line to all text files

When the *Remove local copy Add or Check In* check box is selected, Visual SourceSafe removes the local copy of a file from the file's working directory after you check the file into the SourceSafe database or Add the new file to a SourceSafe project. In most cases, you will not select this option unless you are using Visual SourceSafe to control documents instead of source code. Because Visual Basic requires that you have a local copy of each file in the Visual Basic project before it can be loaded, you will want to keep a read-only copy of the Visual SourceSafe file after you check it in.

If you select the *Remove local files after Delete* check box, SourceSafe deletes the local copy of the SourceSafe file from its working directory after you delete the file from the SourceSafe project. Enabling this setting keeps you from maintaining unnecessary files in your working directory.

The *Use read-only flag on files that are not checked out* check box ensures that files that you are not currently editing are read-only. Enabling this check box helps to ensure that you do not accidentally edit files that you do not have checked out. Although Visual SourceSafe helps to keep your source code safe by not allowing you to check a file into the database that you do not have checked out, accidentally making changes to a local copy of a file can be frustrating. Retrieving a new copy of the changed file can be time-consuming as well.

Selecting the *Copy keyword-expanded files into working directory* check box causes Visual SourceSafe to place a read-only copy of a file containing any expanded keywords it may have. If you do not select the check box, you will see only the keyword—not the information that the keyword supplies—in your local copy. This setting is useful if you frequently scan files for the information that keywords supply, such as version numbers of last edited dates and times.

The *Append end-of-line to all text files* check box causes Visual SourceSafe to append an end-of-line character to all text files that do not currently end with one. Because some compilers require that files are terminated with an end-of-line character, it is always a good idea to have this setting enabled. This setting can help you ensure that your code is as portable as possible.

The Local Files tabbed dialog box also contains several drop-down list boxes:

- Compare files by
- Replace writable files
- Set date/time on local files

The *Compare files by* drop-down list box allows you to control how Visual SourceSafe compares files when the Show Difference command is selected. Your choices are *Contents*, *Time*, and *Checksum*. Selecting Contents instructs Visual SourceSafe to compare the full contents of your local copy of a file to the master copy of the file that is stored in the database. Comparing by Contents is the slowest way to compare files, but it *is* the only method that works in all cases. If you select Time, you instruct Visual SourceSafe to compare the date/time flags of the files. This is the fastest method of comparison, but it also is the most inaccurate because the date and time of local files are determined by the computers they are checked out *to*. The Checksum setting instructs SourceSafe to compare the local and master files based on their checksum values. This method will fail if the two files being compared are different, but have the same checksum.

The *Replace writable files* drop-down list box enables you to control how Visual Basic reacts when a file is checked out and a writable copy of the file already exists in the working directory of the same file. Your choices are *Ask*, *Replace*, *Skip*, and *Error*. If you select Ask, SourceSafe displays a message box, asking if you want to overwrite the file. If you select Replace, Visual SourceSafe automatically overwrites the local writable copy with the copy that is being checked out. The Skip setting causes Visual SourceSafe to skip the checkout of any file for which it finds a local writable copy. The Error setting is similar to the Skip setting, except that it not only skips the checkout, it also reports an error. It is a good idea to select the Ask setting. This setting allows you to overwrite local copies of files, if you choose. It also helps to prevent you from accidentally overwriting local writable copies when you checkout files.

The *Set date/time* on local files drop-down list box enables you to determine how Visual Basic sets the date/time of a file when it's checked out of the Visual SourceSafe database. By default, when a file is checked out to its local directory, Visual SourceSafe sets the date/time of the file to the current time of your computer. The list box allows you to tell SourceSafe to set the date and time of the file to the last modified date of the file (Modification setting) or to the date and time at which the file was last updated (Update).

The View Tab Settings

The View tab, shown in figure 19.15, allows you to adjust the physical appearance of the SourceSafe Explorer. This tab displays several check boxes, which are divided into two group boxes.

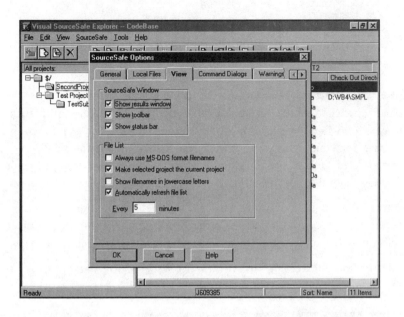

Fig. 19.15
The View folder tab.

IV

Application Enhancements

The first group is labeled SourceSafe Window. It contains the following option boxes:

- Show results window

- Show toolbar

- Show status bar

These three check boxes allow you determine if Visual SourceSafe will display the results window, the toolbar, or the status bar. To hide any of these items, uncheck the appropriate box.

The second group is labeled File List. It contains the following display options, associated specifically with the Explorer's File List component:

- Always use MS-DOS format filenames

- Make selected project the current project

- Show filenames in lowercase letters

- Automatically refresh file list

These check boxes allow you to determine if the File List displays MS-DOS 8.3 format names for files, makes the selected project the current project, shows file names in lowercase, or determines whether the File List will be refreshed.

You can enable or disable each option by checking or unchecking the appropriate box. If you enabled automatic refreshing of the file list, you also can specify the rate of refresh.

The Command Dialogs Tab Settings

Visual SourceSafe can display dialog boxes that prompt for commitment or information when you perform certain actions. When you Get a file from the database, for example, you can have Visual SourceSafe display a dialog box, asking you to confirm the working directory of the file and prompting you to provide a comment for the action.

Command dialogs allow you to gather additional information as to why users are carrying out certain actions in Visual SourceSafe. This can help project leaders to better understand the kinds of changes that are being made.

You can choose the dialog boxes you want Visual SourceSafe to display on the Command Dialogs tab of the Options tabbed dialog box (see fig. 19.16).

Fig. 19.16

The Command Dialogs folder tab.

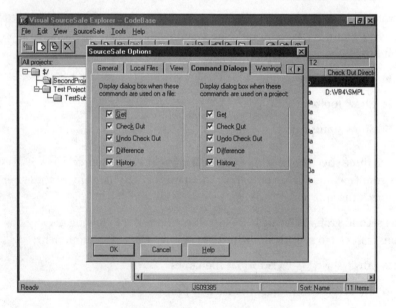

You can choose to display a dialog box when any of the following actions occur:

- Get
- Check out
- Undo check out

- Difference

- History

You instruct SourceSafe to display the dialog box by selecting the check box to the right of the action. For each action, you also can choose whether you want the dialog box displayed when you perform the action on a file, on a project, or on both file and project.

The Warnings Tab Settings

In addition to allowing you to display dialog boxes when SourceSafe commands are executed, SourceSafe allows you to display warning messages when file actions are carried out. These warning messages can help you when they are used in conjunction with commands that can seriously affect the state of a project. When a user, for example, chooses to delete a file from a project, you can instruct Visual SourceSafe to display a warning dialog box that asks the user to confirm the deletion before it is carried out.

Command warning dialogs provide additional security for your project. These dialogs allow users to change their minds before they carry out actions that may adversely affect the SourceSafe project. In addition, command warning dialogs help prevent users from accidentally selecting a different command than the command they intended.

You choose the actions that display warning dialogs from the Warnings tab, shown in figure 19.17, on the Options tabbed dialog.

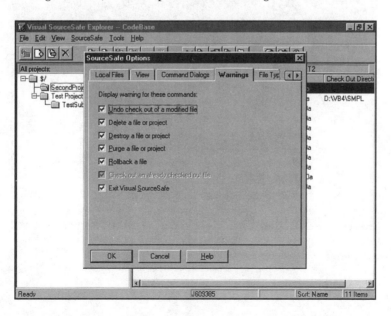

Fig. 19.17
The Warnings
folder tab.

You can choose to display a warning for any of the following actions:

- <u>U</u>ndo checkout on a modified file

- De<u>l</u>ete a file or project

- <u>D</u>estroy a file or project

- <u>P</u>urge a file or project

- <u>R</u>ollback a file

- <u>C</u>heck out an already checked out file (available only if you allow multiple users to check out a single file in a project)

- Exit Visual <u>S</u>ourceSafe

To instruct SourceSafe to display a warning dialog when one of the preceding actions is selected by a user, select the check box to the left of the action.

The File Types Tab Settings

You can use the File Types tab, shown in figure 19.18, to filter the various file lists that are displayed by Visual SourceSafe so that they include only the files with extensions that you specify.

Fig. 19.18
The File Types
folder tab.

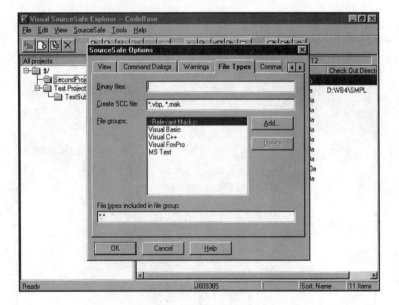

For example, if you plan to use Visual SourceSafe to store Visual Basic files, you can use this tab to filter out files that do not have a .BAS, .CLS, .FRM, .FRX, .RES, .VBP, or .MAK extension.

This tab also lets you override Visual SourceSafe auto-detection of text and binary files. From the Binary file edit box, you can indicate the extensions of files that SourceSafe should always treat as binary.

Showing Differences Between Files

Because Visual SourceSafe stores all changes to files stored in its database, it can readily display the differences between versions of the same file, the differences between different files, and also the differences between the contents of a project and the contents of a working directory.

Determining the differences between versions of a file often helps during the debugging process. Suppose that a group of developers has built a sorting routine. After testing the routine, the developers decide that it is too slow and that they need to performance tune their code. After making several changes to the code, the sort routine stops working properly. Rather than trying to make guesses about where the problem may be arising, they can compare the most recent version of the file to the version of the file that last worked properly. This allows the developers to quickly pinpoint the differences between files and resolve the problem.

To display the difference between two different versions of the same file, take the following steps:

1. From the file list in the SourceSafe Explorer, click a file.

2. From the Tools menu, select the Show History command.

   SourceSafe displays the History of File dialog box.

3. From the History of File dialog box, select the two versions of the file you want to compare.

4. Click the Diff button.

   SourceSafe displays the Differences window shown in figure 19.19. The Differences window shows the difference between the two versions of the file that you selected.

SourceSafe displays the most recent version of the file in the right pane of the window and the oldest version of the file in the left pane. Lines of code that differ between the two versions of the file are displayed in contrasting colors. You also can use the Next Diff and Prev Diff buttons to move to the next and previous difference between the files, respectively.

Fig. 19.19

The Differences window.

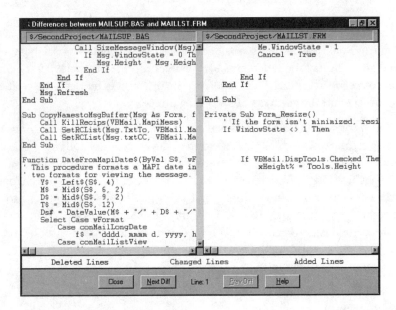

To display the differences between project and working directory contents, follow these steps:

1. In the SourceSafe Explorer project list, select the project for which you want to show differences between files contained in the project and files contained in the working directory.

   SourceSafe displays the Differences dialog box, shown in figure 19.20.

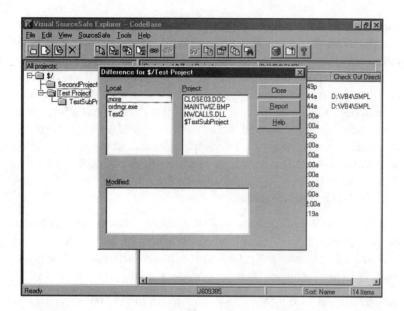

Fig. 19.20
The Differences
dialog box.

When comparing local working directories to the SourceSafe project, SourceSafe doesn't tell you how files differ on a line-by-line basis, it tells you which files are different. The Differences dialog box displays the following three lists:

- Files that exist in the current directory, but not in the project

- Files that exist in the project, but not in the working directory

- Files that differ between the project and the working directory

2. Click Close after you finish reviewing the differences.

You also can click the Report button to send a report of the display to a file, a printer, or the clipboard.

Distinguishing Between Text and Binary Files

Remember that Visual SourceSafe can store any file of any type. The only distinction that SourceSafe draws is whether the file is a text file (it contains only ASCII characters) or a binary file (any other type of file).

Regardless of whether a file is a text or binary file, Visual SourceSafe uses *reverse delta storage* to track differences in file versions. With reverse delta storage, Visual SourceSafe stores only the incremental changes that you make to a file, which allows SourceSafe databases to occupy much less disk space than they do if an additional copy of the file had to be stored every time an update occurred. For example, suppose that you checked out a file, added a few new lines of code to it, and then checked the file back in. SourceSafe would not store a new copy of the file that contains all the lines of code previously entered, in addition to the several new lines. SourceSafe will create only a record of the new lines added to the file. SourceSafe already contains records of the lines previously added.

Visual SourceSafe identifies a file as either text or binary when you add the file to a project. It does so by using the following test: *SourceSafe scans through the file for NULL characters. If it finds such a character, the file must be binary. If no null characters are found, Visual SourceSafe assumes that the file is text.*

Although the test used by SourceSafe was determined to be an accurate test in most cases, it isn't perfect. For this reason, SourceSafe provides a mechanism by which auto-detection can be overridden. You can force Visual SourceSafe to treat a file as either text or binary. The method for doing so is discussed later in this chapter.

When Visual SourceSafe saves changes to a binary file, it stores each change as a small record of which bytes moved where. The record is effective for reconstructing old versions of the file but it is ineffective for displaying the changes to a user. Storing changes for text files is handled differently by SourceSafe because text files consist of distinct lines. Therefore, Visual SourceSafe can not only determine when changes have been made to a text file, it also can display the changes to a user.

The type of file is significant because SourceSafe can perform certain functions, such as `Difference` and `Merge`, on text files only. It's a good idea, if possible, to treat all of the files as text files. This allows you to perform the largest number of SourceSafe functions.

Administering a SourceSafe Project

Administration of a SourceSafe project is carried out from the Administrator application. As you saw in the previous chapter, the Administrator allows you to:

- Maintain SourceSafe users

- Maintain user access rights

- Create a shadow directory

The remainder of this section demonstrates how each function can be carried out through the Administrator.

Maintaining SourceSafe Users

Before users can check files in and out of Visual SourceSafe, these users must be added to the SourceSafe database by using the Administrator application. The Administrator permits you to add new users, edit the rights of existing users, and remove users who no longer require access to SourceSafe. The following sections describe the steps necessary to add, edit, and remove users.

Adding Users

To add a user, select the Add Users command from the Users menu item. The Add User dialog box is displayed.

Type the name and password for the new user. Although Visual SourceSafe allows you to add a user without a password, you should include a password. This helps ensure that your files remain safe.

You can check the Read-only check box on the Add User dialog box to give the new user read-only access to the Visual SourceSafe database. He or she will be able to see all of the files and projects in the database but cannot check out or edit files. If the Read-only check box is unchecked, the new user has read-write privileges, which allows him or her to check out, edit, and view files.

Removing Users

When users no longer need access to the SourceSafe database, you can remove them from the database. This removal prevents them from checking files in or out of the database.

To remove a user, follow these steps:

1. In the Administrator, click a User.

2. From the Users menu, select the Delete User command.

SourceSafe displays a message box, asking you to confirm the deletion.

3. Click Yes to delete the User. Click No to abort the deletion.

Editing Users

After you add a user to the Visual SourceSafe database, you may want to go back and change the user's name or give the user read-only access to the database. You can do so by selecting the Edit Users option from the Users menu. The Edit User dialog box allows you to change a user's name or enable/disable the Read-only rights check box.

To help ensure security, Visual SourceSafe provides no way for any user—even the Administrator—to learn a user's password. The Administrator can, however, change a user's password without knowing the user's original password. Passwords can be changed by using the Change Password dialog box, shown in figure 19.21.

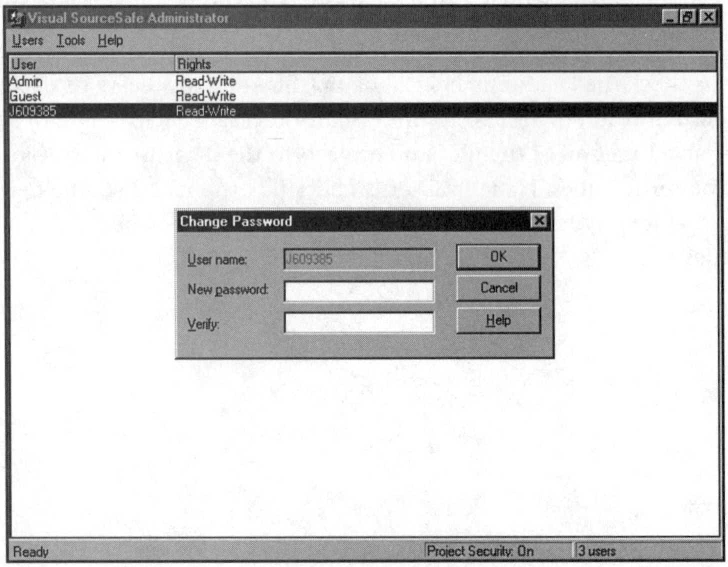

Fig. 19.21
The SourceSafe
Change Password
dialog box.

The Change Password dialog box is displayed by selecting a user in the Admin window and clicking the Change Password option from the Users menu. You can enter a new password for the user and confirm the password.

Maintaining User Access Rights

Visual SourceSafe security is based on security rights. When you install SourceSafe, the default security options are enabled. Through the administrator, you can customize the security rights of users, projects, and the Administrator.

The following sections explain how to maintain security for the SourceSafe application.

Administrator Rights

Any user who has the ability to run the SourceSafe Administrator can change all of the security rights in the Visual SourceSafe application. Additionally, he or she can freely add and delete users. For this reason, it is important that you effectively control access to the Administrator program.

You can limit access to the Administrator in two ways. First, only the Admin user can run the Administrator application. After a new installation, the Admin user has no password—any user entering `Admin` as a user name can run the Administrator. By assigning a password to the Admin user, you can limit access to the Administrator application to only users to whom you choose to give a password.

Second, because the Administrator is a standalone executable file that resides in a directory, you can physically protect the Administrator program by limiting user access to this directory. This limiting prevents unwanted users from accessing the directory from which the Administrator application is run.

User Rights

User rights determine which projects a user can access and which commands a user can execute. By limiting a user's rights, you also limit his or her ability to access projects and execute Visual SourceSafe commands.

User access rights are divided into four categories: Read, Checkout, Add, and Destroy. The following table shows the rights categories and a brief description of the types of actions that are associated with each right:

Right	Description
Read (R)	See, but not change, files by using commands such as View and Get.
Checkout (C)	Modify files by using commands such as Check Out and Check In. Checkout rights include all Read rights.
Add (A)	Modify the file list by using commands such as Add, Delete, and Rename. Add rights include Checkout and Read rights.
Destroy (D)	Destroy files by using commands such as Destroy, Purge, and Rollback. Destroy rights include Add, Checkout, and Read rights.

In the table, notice that each succeeding right includes all rights that precede it. For example, the Checkout right includes all Read rights. Likewise, a user with Add rights also must have Read and Checkout rights.

This four-option security model helps make assigning rights in Visual SourceSafe simple, while ensuring that only the users with the proper authority can carry out destructive operations, such as destroy and purge, or operations that can change the database, such as Check In and Check Out.

When assigning rights to a user, keep in mind the main role or roles that the user will assume in the project. A technical writer or code auditor, for example, probably will not need to make changes to the source code. This kind of user should be assigned only the Read right, which ensures that the user doesn't accidentally make changes to the code but does allow the user to complete the job. If some users aren't assigned the Read right, they may still run the Visual SourceSafe Explorer application, but they will see only a file list that contains no files. The Read right includes the ability to see a list of files in a project.

The Checkout right usually is assigned to all developers. This right enables them to work on source code and make any modifications necessary. Code auditors are not required to make changes to the source code, so they should not receive the Checkout right.

The Add right also is often assigned to all developers, but you may want to assign this right on a project-by-project basis. Allowing only the project leader or team leader the right to Add new files to a project allows one person to inform the rest of the development team when new files are added. If these new files have some common use among the current project or between concurrent projects, the project or team leader can communicate this existence to the other team members. Limiting the Add right also helps to prevent less-experienced users from adding unnecessary files.

If your development team is spread among many physical locations, or if your project leader isn't always on site, not allowing all developers to add files to Visual SourceSafe may hamper development. Usually, in a team development environment it's a good idea to allow all developers to add new files to the Visual SourceSafe database. This helps your project run smoothly and does not require developers to wait until a project leader is present to add a new file. In a worst-case situation, a project leader may have to delete a file that was improperly or inadvertently added to the database.

The Destroy right should be assigned with caution because it allows users to completely remove files from the Visual SourceSafe database. It's a good idea to assign this right to the project or team leader only. This helps ensure that files are not accidentally removed from a project.

Default Security

When an Administrator adds a new user to the Visual SourceSafe database, the Add User dialog box contains a check box, labeled Read-only. The Admin user can use this check box to choose from the following user-rights:

- Read-only rights
- Read-write rights

Read-only rights allow a user to see everything in the Visual SourceSafe database, but the user cannot change anything. Read-write rights are allow users to perform all actions on the database, including adding, deleting, and modifying files in the database. If the Admin user checks the Read-only check box, that user is assigned Read-only rights. Otherwise, the new user receives Read-write rights.

This level of security is referred to as *default security*. It is the simplest level of security to assign and maintain. If your development team is in a situation that demands that very few people work with the code, this simple form of security may work best.

When this level of security rights is enabled, the security-related commands under the Tools menu item are disabled.

Enabling Project Security

To enforce a greater range of access rights than the rights provided by default security, you need to enable *project security*. Project security allows you to assign to each user in the Visual SourceSafe database each of the four security rights mentioned previously in this chapter.

To enable project security, follow these steps:

1. From the Administrator's Tools menu, select Options.

   Visual SourceSafe displays the SourceSafe Options tabbed dialog, shown in figure 19.22.

2. Select the Project Security tab.

3. Click the Enable project security check box to turn on project security.

   You can select Default rights for new users by checking or unchecking the appropriate check boxes in the Default user rights group box.

Fig. 19.22
The SourceSafe Options tabbed dialog.

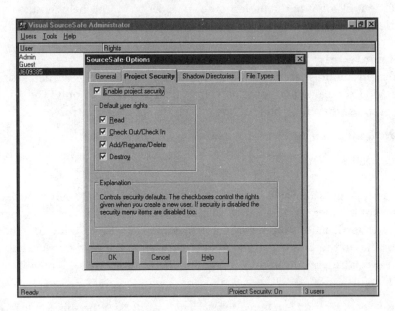

When project security is enabled, the commands under the Tools menu are enabled. These commands allow you to perform the following operations:

- Set rights by project
- Set rights by user

You can set rights by project, by clicking the Rights by project option from the Tools menu. When you click this option, the Project Rights dialog box shown in figure 19.23 is displayed.

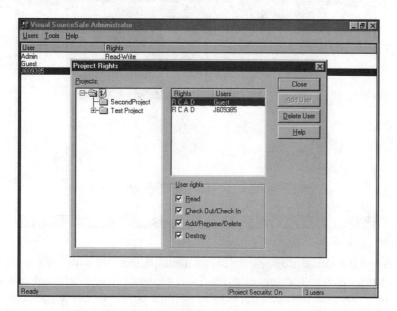

Fig. 19.23
The Project Rights dialog box.

The dialog box shows each project on the left side of the screen and a list of users on the right. When you highlight a project and user, you can set the rights of this user for the selected project. The check boxes at the bottom of this dialog box allow you to assign Read, Checkout, Add, and Destroy rights for each user for each project.

To assign rights for a project to a user that is not yet added to the project, click the Add button. Add brings up a list of users. You can select an additional user from the list. You also can delete a user from the selected project by clicking Delete.

You also can set rights by user. To do so, select the Rights Assignments for Users command from the Tools menu. Then SourceSafe displays the Assign Rights to User dialog box shown in figure 19.24.

Fig. 19.24

The Assign Rights to User dialog box.

The Assign Rights dialog box displays a list of projects for which the user has explicit rights. Projects for which the user has default rights does not appear in the project list. You add rights by selecting a project from the project list, and then checking or unchecking the appropriate check boxes to grant user rights.

To assign rights for a project that doesn't appear on the project list, click Add Assignment, which displays a list of available projects. Select the project to which you want to assign user rights. To remove rights for the user from a project, select the project and click the Delete Assignment button.

Rights Propagation

In the previous sections, you learned how to select default rights for a user and how to assign rights by project. As the name implies, default rights exist for each user in a project, unless these users were assigned explicit project rights. When you assign explicit rights to a user, these rights are propagated down the project tree until a new rights assignment is located.

For example, when you assign read-write rights to some users at the root level ($/), they have read-write rights to all projects in the database and all subprojects within these projects. Now, suppose that you assign read-only rights to the user for the $/OrderMgr project. This read-only assignment blocks the default rights assignment for both the $/OrderMgr project and all subprojects that exist within the OrderMgr project ($/OrderMgr/OrderForm and $/OrderMgr/GraphBuilder). The project $/TestProject is unaffected by these new read-only rights. It maintains full read-write rights.

When users are added to Visual SourceSafe, they have default rights assigned at the root level. The default rights apply to every project until you assign explicit rights.

Using a Shadow Directory

Visual SourceSafe allows you to create a directory on your SourceSafe server that contains the latest version of all the files in a project. This directory is referred to as a *shadow directory*. The shadow directory contains copies of the latest versions of the project's files, not the master copies of the files. This directory provides a single, centralized location to view and compile source code.

You will find a shadow directory useful when you are working in a team development environment. Often, you will perform nightly compiles of your source code to ensure that all files checked into the Visual SourceSafe database can generate a runable program. By creating a shadow directory, you can quickly and easily compile code without having to locate file versions.

Likewise, if you are storing project-related documents in Visual SourceSafe, a shadow directory provides quick access to the files. This access aids in project management because it no longer will be necessary to hunt down the latest version of a project plan or budget worksheets.

To create a shadow directory, follow these steps:

1. From the Administrator Tools menu, select the Options command.

   The SourceSafe Options tabbed dialog, shown in figure 19.25, appears.

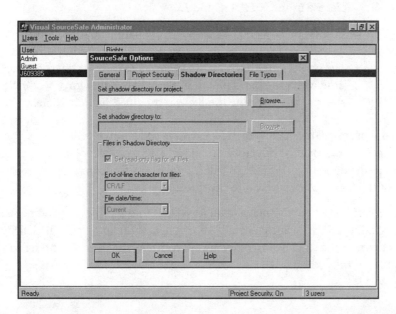

Fig. 19.25
The SourceSafe Options tabbed dialog.

2. Click the Shadow Directories tab.

The Shadows Directories tab opens. This tab contains the following controls:

- **Set shadow directory for project**—In this edit box, type the name of the project to shadow. Clicking the Browse button to the right of the dialog box displays the SourceSafe project tree.

- **Set shadow directory**—Enter the name of the operating system directory to use as the shadow directory. You can click the Browse button to the right of this field to display a directory tree.

The Files in Shadow Directory group box presents the following options:

- **Set read-only flag for all files**—You can select this check box to make all files in the shadow directory read-only. Although modifications to files in the shadow directory do not affect code stored in Visual SourceSafe, it is a good idea to make all files read-only. This setting prevents users from accidentally changing files in the shadow directory.

- **End-of-line character for files**—From this list box, you can select a value to indicate the end-of-line character for reach file in the shadow directory. Because you may use the shadow directory to generate executables, you should be aware of whether or not your compiler requires a specific end-of-line character. If it does, choose from *CR/LF*, *CR*, and *LF*.

- **File date/time**—You can select the date and time from the drop-down list box to use for each file in the shadow directory. The choices are *Current* and *Modification*. Current refers to the time when the file is placed in the shadow directory. Modification refers to the last time the file was modified in SourceSafe.

After you create the shadow directory, you need to initialize it. This is done by opening the shadow directory in the File Manager or Explorer, selecting all files in the directory, and using Visual SourceSafe's Get command to retrieve all of the files in the project into the directory.

From here on, when you make changes to files in the project or add new files, the shadow directory automatically receives all of the updates. This setting ensures that the shadow directory always contains the most recent version of all files in the project.

Using Journal Files

Journal files are files that contain an audit trail, showing all actions that were performed on a file or project. Journal files can be useful for tracking exactly what actions were performed on a file over a period of time. A project leader, for example, may be interested in all development that is occurring in all files that are used by her team. She doesn't have time to talk with each developer to discuss the changes, nor does she have time to scan through the actual source code for changes. The project leader can, however, create a journal file that shows what changes were made to all files in her project.

To create a journal file, you select the Options command from the Tools menu in the Administrator application. When the Options folder appears, the General tab is displayed.

On the General tab, you can enter the name of a journal file in the *Log all actions in journal file* text box. You can either enter the name of an existing file or type the name of a new file where you want SourceSafe to log changes.

Figure 19.26 shows what a sample journal file may look like.

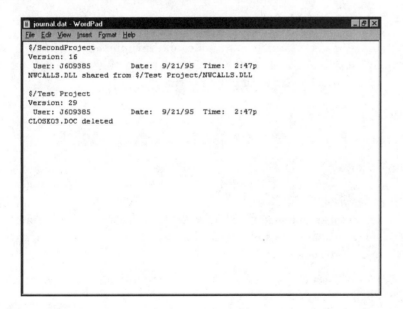

Fig. 19.26
A sample journal file.

Each entry in the journal file shows the project (in the example it's $/project/ test), the version, the name of the user who made changes to the file, the date and time the changes occurred, the activity, and all comments the user supplied when the file was checked. You can see how important comments become. If users fail to make comments regarding their changes, Visual

SourceSafe supplies only a short description of the action. In our example, you can see only that the file was updated. You do not know which part of the file was changed and what effect the changes may have on other projects.

Because a journal file keeps a record of all actions, enabling journal files may slow the performance of Visual SourceSafe.

Backing Up and Restoring Visual SourceSafe

Because you will store all your source code and all other project documents that you need to keep safe within the SourceSafe database, it's important that you always back up the database regularly.

Backing up Visual SourceSafe does not need be a highly complicated process. You should adhere to the following two steps:

- Make regular backups of SourceSafe's DATA directory and all of its subdirectories. This directory contains all the files, all the projects, and the file and project histories. By backing up this directory, your SourceSafe database can be recovered in the event that your system crashes.

- Instruct each user to back up his or her SS.INI file. The SS.INI file contains a user's working directories and environment preferences. By backing up the SS.INI file in addition to the DATA directory, you are in virtually no danger of losing data.

Source-Code Version Control

Visual SourceSafe uses two methods for tracking version of files and projects: Version Number and Labels. *Version Numbers* are internal numbers maintained completely by SourceSafe. Every version of every file in SourceSafe has a version number. These numbers are used exclusively by SourceSafe and are not made available externally. *Labels* are strings that you can apply to any version of a project file.

The following sections will describe how you can use labels to organize versions of your code.

Using Labels

Essentially, a label is a descriptive version number that you choose and apply. A label is used to take a snapshot of your code. A label allows developers to, at any later date, easily locate the snapshot.

Why might you use a label? Suppose that you are working on a development team that created a new application and deployed it throughout the enterprise. You want your team to continue development of the next phase of the application, but you also want to be able to re-create the version that was deployed. A user may report a bug, which you may need to verify before you can fix it. In another scenario, one department may request an enhancement to the application that is applicable to its business unit only. Rather than rework the enhanced version of the application, you can return to the labeled version and begin development from that point.

To create a label for a project, take the following steps:

1. Click a project from the project list in the Visual SourceSafe Explorer.

2. From the File menu, select the Label command.

   SourceSafe displays the Label dialog box.

3. In the Name field, type a name for the label. A label can contain up to 31 characters.

4. Type a comment for the label.

5. Click the OK button when you have finished.

The preceding example showed how to label a project. Although Visual SourceSafe allows you to apply a version label to a file, it's usually good practice to label only projects because whenever a new file is added, you need to create a new version label. Likewise, when a file is deleted or destroyed, all versioning information about the file is lost. You cannot re-create the labeled version. If you label the project instead, even if you add or delete files in the future, you still can faithfully re-create the labeled version.

In general, you want to create a version label every time you release a compiled version of your code to end users. In addition, it is a good idea to label a version every time you reach a significant milestone in your project's lifecycle. This would include prototypes that are released.

Viewing File History

Because Visual SourceSafe tracks all changes that you make to a file, you can use SourceSafe's Show History command to review all the changes that were made to any file checked into the SourceSafe database. The history of files can help you determine when significant changes were made to a file. When debugging, a file's history may help you to track the change in the file that caused the problem.

Visual SourceSafe also allows you to display the history of a project. A project's history includes information such as when new files were added to the project or when new labels were created for the project.

To display the history for a file or project, take the following steps:

1. Select the project or file for which you want to see history from the SourceSafe Explorer.

2. From the Tools menu, select the Show History command.

   If you instructed Visual SourceSafe to display the History Options dialog box, it will be displayed.

   The History dialog box allows you to restrict the history displayed. These choices are described in the following list:

   - **Include files**—If you selected project history, this option displays the history of all files in the project as well as the project itself.

   - **Recursive**—if you are displaying project history, this setting displays all subprojects beneath the selected project.

   - **Labels Only**—displays versions of the selected file or project that have labels assigned to them.

   - **From and To**—restricts the display to range of dates, labels, or version numbers.

   - **User**—restricts the display to the actions of a specific user.

3. You can select any option from the History Options dialog box, or click the OK button to exit without selecting any options.

   Visual SourceSafe displays the History dialog box (see fig. 19.27).

   The History dialog box has two versions—one for projects and one for files. If you are viewing file history, for each row the dialog box lists the file version number, the name of the user who last performed an action on the file, the last date on which a commented action took place, and the action that was taken on the file. When viewing project history, for each row, the dialog box displays the file name or subproject contained in the project, the user who performed the action described in the action column, the date on which the action described in the Action column occurred, and the operation performed on the project or file.

You can perform the following actions from the History dialog box by clicking the appropriate button:

■ **Close**—Closes the dialog box.

■ **Vie_w_**—For history of project, displays additional History of Project dialog box, listing the versions of files in the selected version of the project, or versions of files, if a file is selected. For history of files, displays the contents of the file in an editor.

■ **De_t_ails**—Displays History Details dialog box. Can be used to edit comments and labels for the selected project or file.

■ **_G_et**—Places a read-only copy of the selected file or all files in the selected project, into the file, or project's working directory.

■ **_S_hare**—Shares the selected project with another project.

■ **Diff**—Displays differences between versions of a single file or differences between two selected files.

■ **Pin**—Freezes the selected file at a specific version so it can be shared with another project.

■ **Rollback**—Returns a file to a previous version.

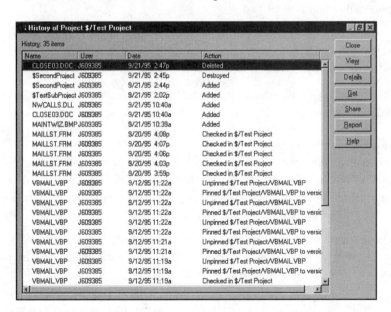

Fig. 19.27
The History dialog box.

Creating Reports

Visual SourceSafe allows you to create reports on the activity of a file or project. To create a report, check the Report check box on any of the following dialog boxes:

- From the Tools menu:

    Show History

    Show Differences

    Files Report

- From Properties on the File menu:

    General (when either a file or a project is selected)

    Deleted Items (when a project is selected)

    Check Out Status (when a file is selected)

    Links (when a file is selected)

    Paths (when a file is selected)

After you select the report check box from one of the preceding dialogs, a Report dialog box is displayed.

The exact contents of the Report dialog vary, depending on which report you are creating. From the report dialog, you can choose to send the report to a file, to a printer, or to the clipboard.

You also can preview each report by clicking Preview on the Report dialog box. A preview of the report is shown in its own dialog window.

Using Keywords

Visual SourceSafe provides the capability to insert information available through standard SourceSafe reports into source-code files. This insertion is accomplished by placing certain keywords, recognized by Visual SourceSafe, into the code that makes up your application.

Suppose that you wanted the developers to place their names at the beginning of every file, each time they made a change. Asking the developers to manually place their names with every change could become very time consuming for both them and you. Additionally, a developer may occasionally forget to place his or her name in the file. You can place a SourceSafe keyword that tells Visual SourceSafe to place, at the beginning of the file, the name of the user who last edited the file.

Keywords use the following syntax:

```
$<keyword>: $
```

For example, to insert the name of the Visual SourceSafe user who last made changes to a file, you use the following syntax:

```
$Author: $
```

The following table shows the keywords, and a brief explanation of each, available in Visual SourceSafe:

Keyword	Purpose
$Archive: $	Visual SourceSafe archive file location, which is used to store the file, such as $/spreadsheet/spell.cpp
$Author: $	User who last changed the file
$Date: $	Date and time of last check-in
$Header: $	Logfile, Revision, Date, Author
$History: $	File history, Visual SourceSafe style
$Log: $	File history, RCS style
$Logfile: $	Same as Archive
$Modtime: $	Date/time of last modification
$Revision: $	Visual SourceSafe version number
$Workfile: $	File name, e.g., HELP.BAS
$Nokeywords: $	Disable expansion for all keywords below it in the file

When you enable keyword expansion, Visual SourceSafe scans your files each time you check them in for the words in the preceding list. If Visual SourceSafe finds one of the keywords, it places the appropriate information within the file. To avoid affecting your code, place keywords within comments. SourceSafe finds the keyword, even if it was commented out.

Because keyword expansion can slow the check-in and add processes, it is disabled by default. To enable expansion, you must change the Keyword_Masks variable in the SRCSAFE.INI file. The variable indicates which files should or should not be scanned for keywords. To tell Visual SourceSafe, for example, to scan all files with the .BAS extension for keywords, set the Keyword_Masks variable to the following:

```
Keyword_Masks = *.BAS
```

It is important to remember that keywords placed in files must match the Visual SourceSafe keywords exactly. Keywords are case-sensitive. If you placed the following line of code in your application, the code would not be recognized as a keyword:

```
$date: $
```

Non-SourceSafe Versioning

Within Visual Basic, several versioning mechanisms exist, including the following:

- OLE server versioning
- Executable versioning

OLE server versioning allows you to assign compatible versions to an OLE server for comparison. This allows you to determine if newer versions of your OLE server are compatible with previous versions. Executable versioning is a method by which you can stamp a version label to a compiled .EXE file, which allows you to track which version of an .EXE is being run by a user. In both cases, these versioning methods can help you to maintain compatibility in your code.

The following sections explain OLE Server versioning and Executable versioning in detail and show you how to use Executable versioning to ensure .EXE compatibility in the enterprise.

OLE Server Versioning

When you deploy an OLE server into the Enterprise, you usually deploy some service, such as a user service or an OLE server in the business or user service tier, that accesses this server.

Suppose that a team of developers deployed an OrderMgr OLE server into the enterprise. This server was deployed when a new order-processing application was deployed. The order-processing application, which is used for entering new orders, accesses the OrderMgr OLE server. The order-processing application relies on a specific interface when accessing the OrderMgr server.

Now, suppose that the development team wanted to make some enhancements to the OrderMgr server. A business rule that deals with ordering has changed, and the OrderMgr OLE server will need to employ additional logic when processing an order. If the developers change a parameter passed to a method with the OrderMgr, or if the developers change the name of one of the OrderMgr properties or methods, the order-processing application no longer can access it. The updated version of the OrderMgr server has become incompatible with earlier versions.

Visual Basic provides you with a way to define a version of an OLE server as a reference to which changes can be compared. This version is referred to as a *compatible OLE server*. If you make a change to an OLE server and compile it, Visual Basic compares your changes to the compatible OLE server and warns you if incompatibilities exist.

To specify a compatible OLE server in Visual Basic, follow these steps:

1. From Visual Basic's Tools menu, select the Options command.

Visual Basic displays the Options tabbed dialog (see fig. 19.28).

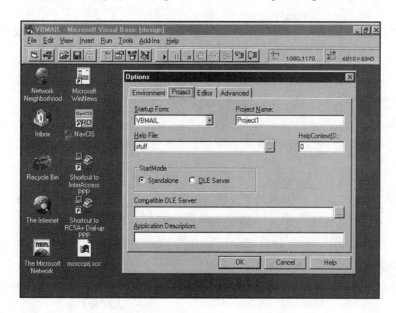

Fig. 19.28
The Options tabbed dialog.

2. Select the Project tab.

3. In the Compatible OLE Server field, enter the full path, and file name of the .EXE file you want to use as the basis for identifying possible version incompatibilities.

4. Click the OK button after you have finished.

When specifying a compatible OLE server, it's good practice to specify a file that differs from the file on which you are currently working. For example, in the previous example, after deploying the OrderMgr OLE server, the development team should place a copy of the server into a directory other than the development directory. When the team specifies compatible versions for the server, it should specify the copy of the file, not the file in the development directory.

If the development team uses the version of the OLE server in the development directory as the compatible server, each time it recompiles the server, the compatible version also will be recompiled. After several recompilations, the development team may not be able to faithfully determine compatibility.

For more information on compatible servers, see Chapter 6, "Creating OLE Objects."

Executable File Versioning

Each time you compile an executable file in Visual Basic, you can opt to assign the file a version number. A version number is an informative stamp that Visual Basic can place within the executable file. Other applications can reference this version number. For example, most setup programs use version numbers to determine if the file being installed is a newer version than an existing file.

Visual Basic allows you to create your own version numbers, but you can set Visual Basic to auto-increment the version number each time you create an executable.

Specify a version number for a file when you select the Make EXE File option from the File menu. When the Make EXE File dialog appears, you can click Options to display the EXE Options dialog box.

The EXE Options dialog box shown in figure 19.29 displays the current version of the file. You can set the version number to any number you like.

Usually, you will assign the first executable file that is deployed into the enterprise a version number of 1.0.0. When you make fixes to the executable, increment the last digit of the version—referred to as the Revision of the version. Suppose that the order-processing development team deployed version 1.0.0 of its order-processing application, and then found a small bug. It fixes the bug and redeploys the application without making any other changes. The team should release the new version as 1.0.1.

Several weeks pass and the development team fixes a number of other bugs and makes a few more changes to the applications interface. It adds additional internal functions to improve performance and remove some previously overlooked unused code. When it deploys this version of the application, it is released as version 1.1.0.

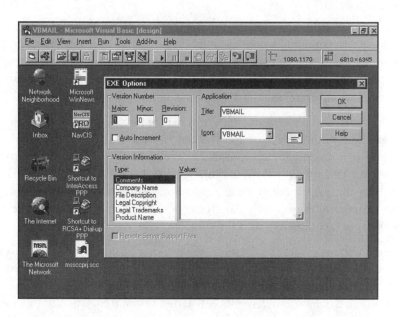

Fig. 19.29
The EXE Options
dialog box.

Several months pass, and the development team implements several changes to the user interface to help increase productivity, adds three new buttons to the application's toolbar, and provides a new feature that allows remote users to place orders over a telephone line. Some of these new features require changes to both the database and the OLE server that is used by the application. These changes make the new version of the application incompatible with the older version of the database. When this version is released, it has a revised version number of 2.0.0.

Maintaining Executable Version Compatibility in the Enterprise

In the previous example, you saw four different versions of the same application deployed throughout the enterprise. The first three versions were different, but they maintained compatibility with the same database. The fourth version of the application required a new database back end and was, therefore, incompatible with earlier versions.

All four versions of the application use an identical method to log on to the database. All versions call a method within an OLE server and pass the same parameters to this method. Although version 1.0.0 of the application cannot submit the proper order information to the database, it still can access the database by way of OLE servers in the business services tier.

What would happen if some users in the enterprise didn't receive version 2.0.0 of the executable? As you have just seen, these users still can log on to the database and potentially corrupt data. How can you prevent this?

You do not want to make changes to the logon method. This method is used by many different applications to attach to many different databases, not just the order-processing database. If you make a change here, you risk making the OLE server that contains the method incompatible to other applications that need to access it.

A solution is to make version-checking a part of logging into the database. For example, within the database, you can create a table that lists compatible versions of front-end applications. For example, in the order-processing application, the table might have four entries: 1.0.0, 1.0.1, 1.1.0, and 2.0.0. Initially, version 1.0.0 is compatible. In addition to the version number, the table contains a compatibility flag that indicates whether or not the executable version is compatible with the database.

When a user logs on to the database, the internal version number of the application is passed with other logon information, such as user ID and password. The logon method checks the version number against the version table in the database and determines whether or not the version number is compatible.

When the application is initially deployed, the version table has a single entry: 1.0.0. Its compatibility flag is set to true. If a user attempts to connect to the database with version 1.0.0, he or she can successfully do so.

When the application moves to version 1.0.1 and 1.1.0, these versions are added to the version table, and their compatibility flags are set to true. You now would have three entries in the table: 1.0.0, 1.0.1, and 1.1.0. All of these entries' compatibility flags would be set to true. Users logging on with version 1.0.0, 1.0.1, and 1.1.0 can successfully connect to the database.

When version 2.0.0 of the application is released, versions 1.0.0, 1.0.1, and 1.1.0 have their compatibility flags set to false. Version 2.0.0 is added to the version table, with its compatibility flag set to true.

When a user tries to connect with a version other than 2.0.0, the connection is refused and the user receives a warning message, stating that his or her version of the executable file is incompatible with the current version of the database.

Integrating SourceSafe with Visual Basic

Visual SourceSafe is integrated with the Visual Basic development environment, providing all the benefits of source-code control without leaving Visual Basic's Integrated Development Environment. Without exiting Visual Basic, you can add new files to the SourceSafe database, check files in and out, and remove files. You gain the power of SourceSafe without adding complexity. This capability makes SourceSafe an excellent choice when deciding which source-code management tool you will use with your project.

Many SourceSafe operations, such as Get, Check Out, Check In, and Undo Check In, are available as commands under Visual Basic's Tools menu. You can access the rest of SourceSafe's functions from the Add-Ins menu item. This section explains how to access Visual SourceSafe's most commonly used features from Visual Basic.

Accessing the SourceSafe Add-In

Visual SourceSafe makes itself available in Visual Basic as an Add-In. An Add-In is an extension to Visual Basic that allows outside applications to integrate their menus with Visual Basic's menus. Visual SourceSafe adds several menu items to Visual Basic's Add-In menu and the Tools menu.

To access an Add-In, you must first reference it through the Add-In Manager. The Add-In Manager is displayed when you select the Add-In Manager command from Visual Basic's Add-Ins menu. The Add-In Manager dialog box shown in figure 19.30 displays the Add-Ins available to Visual Basic. To make the the Visual SourceSafe Add-In available, you first must perform the SourceSafe client install.

To reference an Add-In, check the box to the left of the Add-In's name. To allow the SourceSafe Add-In to add its menu items to Visual Basic, check the box next to the Source Code Control Add In entry. Click OK when you have finished.

When the Add-In Manager dialog box is closed, the Add-In is loaded by Visual Basic. You can view all of the menu items the Add-In includes. Visual SourceSafe adds several menu items to the Tools menu and also adds an entry with several sub-items to the Add-Ins menu.

Fig. 19.30

The Add-In Manager dialog box.

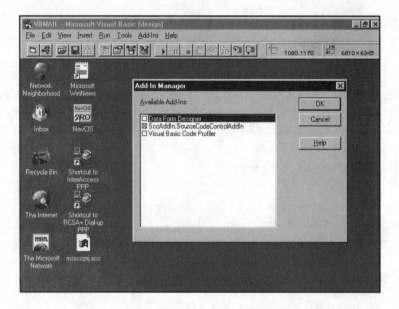

In the following sections, you learn how to access Visual SourceSafe's most common functions from within the Visual Basic interface.

Setting SourceSafe Options

Visual Basic allows you to determine how many of Visual SourceSafe's commands are carried out when they are accessed from Visual Basic. You can configure the way in which Visual SourceSafe responds when you perform actions such as adding new files to your Visual Basic project or closing a Visual Basic project. Configuring the SourceSafe Add-In is similar to setting preferences in the SourceSafe Explorer.

You configure these settings from the Source Code Control Options dialog box that is displayed when you select the Visual SourceSafe option from the Add-Ins menu. This dialog box is displayed in figure 19.31.

The Source Code Control Options dialog box displays several drop-down list boxes that allow you to choose how Visual Basic will respond when certain actions are carried out. For each drop-down list box, you have three choices: Ask, Yes, and No.

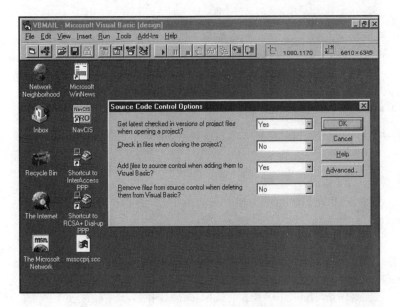

Fig. 19.31
The Source Code
Control Options
dialog box.

The first drop-down list box, *Get latest checked in versions of project files when opening a project?,* causes Visual SourceSafe to retrieve the most recent versions of the files in your project from the Visual SourceSafe database each time you open the project. If you want this action to occur, select Yes from the list box. Selecting Ask causes Visual Basic to display a dialog box, asking if you want to retrieve the files when you open a project. If you do not want Visual Basic to retrieve the latest version of the files, select No. Setting this option to Yes helps ensure that you incorporate other developers' changes to files into your application. This, in turn, helps ensure that your code is compatible with the rest of the Visual Basic project.

The second drop-down list box, *Check in files when closing the project?*, causes Visual Basic to check in all the files that you currently have checked out into the Visual SourceSafe database. As with the first list box, if you want this action to occur, select Yes. If you want SourceSafe to prompt you each time you close a project, click Ask. If you do not want to check in the files when you close a project, select No.

You should check files into the Visual SourceSafe database only when you are sure they will allow you to successfully generate an executable. If errors exist in the file, leave them checked out until you can correct the problems. For this reason, it's a good practice to choose the Ask or No setting for this option. This helps ensure that you do not inadvertently check files into the database before they are ready.

The third drop-down list box, *Add files to source control when adding them to Visual Basic?*, causes Visual SourceSafe to add a new file to the SourceSafe database whenever a new file is added to your SourceSafe project. Selecting Yes for this option helps ensure that your project is synchronized with the SourceSafe database. It also helps eliminate the extra step of adding the file to SourceSafe.

The final option, *Remove files from source control when deleting them from Visual Basic?*, causes a file removed from Visual Basic to also be removed from the Visual SourceSafe database. If you select Yes for this setting, the file will not be removed from the SourceSafe database, only from the current project.

Selecting Yes also requires that a user have Delete privileges for the Visual SourceSafe project. Because it is recommended that only the project or team leader be granted the right to remove files from the database, you should select No for this option. Although your project will not be in sync with the SourceSafe database when files are removed, the No setting ensures that that files are not accidentally removed from the Visual SourceSafe project.

Adding a New Project to SourceSafe from Visual Basic

When you create a new project in Visual Basic, Visual SourceSafe makes an internal note of the new project. You can add the new Visual Basic project to Visual SourceSafe by selecting the Add Project to SourceSafe command from the SourceSafe submenu. SourceSafe displays the Add SourceSafe Project dialog box.

In the Project field, type a new name for the Visual Basic project. When you have entered a name, click the Create button to continue.

SourceSafe creates a new Visual SourceSafe project and displays the Add to SourceSafe dialog box shown in figure 19.32.

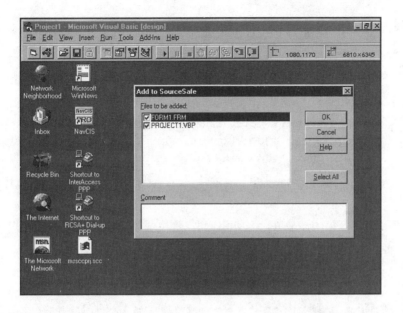

Fig. 19.32
The Add to
SourceSafe
dialog box.

By default, all the files in your Visual Basic project are highlighted when the dialog box is displayed. Click the OK button to add all the files to the SourceSafe database.

Adding an Existing Project to SourceSafe from Visual Basic

You can add an existing project to Visual SourceSafe at any time, without first exiting the project. An existing project is any project that was saved to your local hard disk.

To add an existing project to Visual SourceSafe, take the following steps:

1. From Visual Basic's Add-Ins menu, select the SourceSafe command.

2. From the SourceSafe submenu, select the Add Project to SourceSafe option.

   SourceSafe displays the Add SourceSafe Project dialog box.

3. Type a name for the new Visual SourceSafe project. You should use the same name as the Visual Basic project to ensure that the projects remain synchronized.

4. Click the Create button.

5. Click the OK button.

   SourceSafe displays the Add to SourceSafe dialog box shown in figure 19.32.

6. From the Add to SourceSafe dialog box, select the Visual Basic files that you want to place under Visual SourceSafe control. You should add all files that comprise the Visual Basic project.

   Select which files to add by clicking the check box to the left of each file.

7. Click OK when you have finished.

   Visual Basic displays a SourceSafe status message that indicates whether or not the project add was successful.

Opening a SourceSafe Project from Visual Basic

You can use the Open SourceSafe Project command under the Add-Ins menu to open a project that exists in Visual SourceSafe and doesn't exist on your local hard drive. Selecting this action copies all of the files in the SourceSafe project to your local system and opens the project in Visual Basic.

This function can be useful in the enterprise if your development team discovers that another project team has placed an application in Visual SourceSafe that may contain functionality that your team can use. Rather than Getting each file of interest in the project, you can pull all the files to your local machine by using the Open SourceSafe Project command.

To open an existing Visual SourceSafe project, follow these steps:

1. From Visual Basic's Add-Ins menu, select the SourceSafe option.

2. From the SourceSafe submenu, select the Open New SourceSafe Project option.

   Visual Basic displays the Add SourceSafe Project dialog box.

3. In the Projects list, select a project that you want to open.

4. In the Dir edit box, type the path to the directory in which you want SourceSafe to place the new project. You also can click the Browse button to browse available directories.

5. Click the OK button when you have finished. Visual SourceSafe will use the Get command to copy all of the files in the project to the directory you selected.

After you have opened the project through Visual SourceSafe, you can subsequently open the project using Visual Basic's Open command.

Reading the Project List

Visual Basic's Project List displays important information about files in the Visual SourceSafe database. When you reference the SourceSafe Add-In, the Project List changes slightly to enable Visual SourceSafe to display additional information about each file.

The first thing you will notice about the Project List shown in figure 19.33 is the appearance of a file icon immediately to the left of each entry in the list.

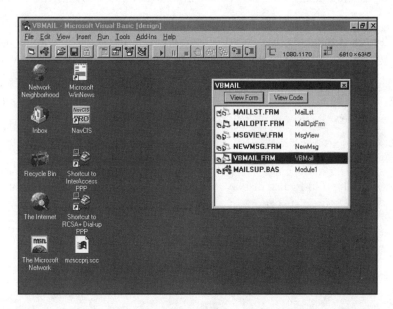

Fig. 19.33
The Project List.

Visual SourceSafe uses this file icon to indicate which files are currently checked in or out by a user. Suppose that the file, MAILLIST.FRM, is checked out. This checked-out status is indicated by the red check that appears on the file icon to the left of the file name.

If a file icon to the left of a file shows two overlapping files, this file is being shared among projects. In this example, the file MSGVIEW.FRM is being shared.

The Project List also displays information about the read-only status of each file. This feature is not added by the SourceSafe Add-In; rather, it is a feature of Visual Basic. When a file is read-only, a small red lock appears next to the icon that identifies a file's type: form, MDI Child, MDI Parent, code module, or class module. In our example, NEWMSG.FRM is read-only, and

MAILLST.FRM is not. Changes made to a read-only file cannot be saved by Visual Basic. The red lock serves as a visual cue to remind you that a file is not editable. Files checked out of SourceSafe should appear as editable.

Checking Out a File through Visual Basic

Just as you can check files in and out of the SourceSafe Explorer, you can check files in and out of the Visual SourceSafe database directly from Visual Basic. To do so, follow these steps:

1. Select the Check Out command from Visual Basic's Tools menu.

   Visual Basic displays the Check Out dialog box shown in figure 19.34.

   The Check Out dialog box displays a list of all files in the Visual Basic project that are not currently checked out of the Visual SourceSafe database. To the left of each file name is a check box. You can check the box next to each file you want to check out of SourceSafe.

2. Enter a comment that indicates the reason why you are checking out the files.

3. After selecting the file that you want to check out, click OK.

   The SourceSafe Add-In checks out each file that you selected from the list. The Add-In also displays a status bar, indicating the current status of the SourceSafe action.

   Notice how the check box to the left of each file that you checked out now is filled with a red check.

Fig. 19.34
The Check Out dialog box.

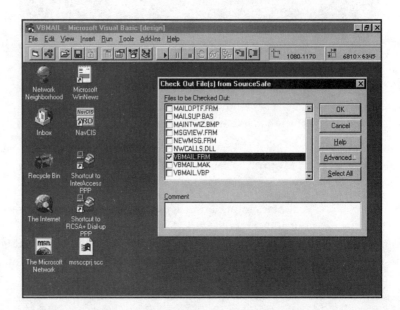

Checking In Files through Visual Basic

Just as you can check out a file in the Visual SourceSafe database from Visual Basic, you also can check a file back in. To check a file in from Visual Basic, take the following steps:

1. From Visual Basic's <u>T</u>ools menu, select the Check <u>I</u>n command.

   Visual Basic displays the Check In dialog box.

   The Check In dialog box displays a list of files that were checked out of the SourceSafe database. Each file has a check box to the left of its file name.

2. From the Check In file list, select the files you want to check into the SourceSafe database by checking the box to the left of its file name.

3. Enter a comment that describes the changes you made to the files you are checking in.

   Because the same comment is used for each file you check in, it's good practice to check files in individually rather than as a group. This allows you to enter a description for each file.

4. Click OK to check in the files that you have selected.

   Notice that the red check mark next to each file you have checked back into the database now has disappeared.

From Here...

This chapter described source-code management and version control in Visual Basic projects. After reading it, you should understand the features and functionality offered by Visual SourceSafe, how to use SourceSafe from the Visual Basic IDE, and the importance of application versioning.

For more information on specific items mentioned in this chapter, see the following chapters:

■ Chapter 6, "Creating OLE Objects," for information on creating OLE objects in Visual Basic and using compatible OLE servers.

■ Chapter 10, "Architecting Tier 3: Data Servers," for more information about accessing data servers.

■ Chapter 17, "Extending Visual Basic," for more information about using Visual Basic Add-Ins.

■ Chapter 21, "Organizing the Development Approach," for more information about how to develop Visual Basic applications for the enterprise in a team environment.

Chapter 20

Creating Development Guidelines

Development guidelines include more than what are commonly referred to as coding standards. Not only should you create a consistent method for the way in which code is written, you should also create guidelines for the environment that developers create applications in as well as methods that should be used when testing and debugging code. Guidelines should be developed for the development, coding, and debugging environments.

In this chapter, you will learn about the following:

- The components of a development environment

- How to use Visual Basic to speed up development time

- How to use Visual Basic to ensure solid, consistent code

Creating a Development Environment

The development environment refers to both the physical appearance of the Visual Basic development tool and the way that Visual Basic interprets and displays your code. Employing development environment guidelines will help reduce errors and make code readable.

Most environment options can be set by selecting the Options command from Visual Basic's Tools menu. Doing so displays the Options tabbed dialog.

From the Options tabbed dialog box, you can select options that affect the following aspects of your Visual Basic project:

- Environment options

- Project options

- Editor options

- Advanced options

The remainder of this section will describe each of these aspects and explain how you can use them to create an environment that will aid in your development effort.

Setting Environment Options

The Environment tab of the Options tabbed dialog, shown in figure 20.1, allows you to set the physical characteristics of the Visual Basic design interface.

Fig. 20.1

The Options tabbed dialog box includes options specific to many of Visual Basic's physical characteristics.

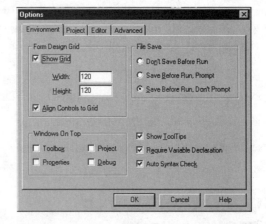

The Environment tab contains the following group boxes:

- Form Design Grid

- File Save

- Windows On Top

It also provides several options for tool tips, variable declarations, and syntax checking. The remainder of this section explains each environment option in detail.

Form Design Grid

The Form Design Grid group box provides several options that allow you to determine how Visual Basic's grid is displayed and how controls behave when they are placed on the grid.

The first option, Show Grid, determines whether or not the grid is displayed on Visual Basic forms. You will want to keep the grid turned on when you are developing because it makes aligning your controls and laying out your form easier. If, however, you need to generate screen shots of forms in your project, and you do not yet have a runnable project, you can turn off the grid and display the form. With the grid off, the form will appear to be in Run mode.

The next set of options, Width and Height, allow you to determine the resolution of the grid. Giving the grid a higher resolution (setting the Width and Height properties to low values) allows you to finely adjust a control's placement on a form. The default setting for Height and Width are 120, 120. If you need finer settings than this, you should try to keep the settings as multiples of 40. For example, 80, 80 is a good setting, as is 40, 40. This ensures that controls you placed on forms before changing the height and width settings will not be misaligned.

The last setting in the Form Design Grid group box, Align Controls to Grid, allows you to determine whether controls will snap to the grid when placed on a form or if the controls will float. Selecting the check box causes controls placed on the form to align themselves with the form's grid. Keeping this box selected helps ensure that all controls placed on your form will be aligned properly. If you allow controls to float and you accidentally move them, you may have a difficult time moving them back to their original position.

File Save

The File Save group box allows you to determine if and when Visual Basic prompts you to save your project before it is run. You have three options:

- Don't Save Before Run

- Save Before Run, Prompt

- Save Before Run, Don't Prompt

Selecting the Don't Save Before Run option causes Visual Basic to run your project without saving it and without prompting you for a save. Avoid this setting because it may cause you to lose your work. If you make changes to a file, and then run it without saving your changes and the program crashes when you are running, you will lose your changes.

The Save Before Run, Prompt option causes Visual Basic to display a message box, asking if you want to save your changes each time you run your project. You have the option of saving changes, which helps you avoid losing work. Save Before Run also gives you the option of not saving your changes. Not saving changes can be useful if you want to make extensive modifications to a project and perform a test run before saving the changes.

Suppose that you thought that changing several lines of code in a function may give your application a boost in performance. You make the changes but before you save them, you want to make sure the code performs as expected. You could choose not to save the code and run the application. If your changes give the desired results, you could save them. If, however, your changes do not work as expected, you can remove the file and then reload it into the project. Because you did not save the file, you do not have to go back and undo your changes.

The final option, Save Before Run, Don't Prompt, causes Visual Basic to save your project every time you run it, without first prompting you. This option helps ensure that you do not lose work because your project has been saved, but it does not allow you to make changes, and then to test these changes without saving them first.

Windows On Top

The Windows On Top group box enables you to instruct Visual Basic to keep one or more windows on top at all times. You can click any of the following four window options:

- The Visual Basic Toolbox
- The Project window
- The Properties window
- The Debug window

If you frequently access any of these windows, making them "always on top" helps you to quickly locate them within a project. If you have many forms open, any one of the previously listed windows may get lost below them. While hot keys allow you to access them, setting them to "always on top" may be easier to manage.

Displaying ToolTips

The Environment tab also gives you the option to display tool tips for the toolbox and toolbar. ToolTips can help the less experienced user and users who are unfamiliar with the toolbar navigate the Visual Basic development environment more easily. To switch ToolTips on, select the Show ToolTips check box at the bottom of the Environment tab.

Setting Variable Declaration Requirements

From the Environment tab, you can determine whether or not Visual Basic requires you to declare all variables used in your project. Checking the Require Variable Declaration check box forces you to declare all the variables that you have used in your application. This process is handled automatically, by using the *Option Explicit* statement within every form, code, or class module you create. The Option Explicit statement requires that every variable be declared with the *Dim*, *Private*, *Public*, *ReDim*, or *Static* statements. If you try to use a variable that has not been declared, an error is generated at compile time.

If you do not require explicit declaration, you can create a new variable in your code by typing it. If you provide no type, Visual Basic assumes that the variable is a *Variant*. With explicit declaration turned off, the following example would be a valid variable declaration:

```
NewVariable
```

Here, NewVariable is interpreted as type Variant and can be used anywhere within the variable's scope.

Requiring explicit variable declaration in each form is an important setting that may save you a great deal of development time. If, for example, you accidentally mistype the name of a variable, an error is generated when you try to run your program or to compile it into an executable. You can change the name of the variable and quickly correct the problem.

If you had not required explicit variable declaration, the mistyped variable would be interpreted by Visual Basic as a new variable of type *Variant*. You may not notice the error until you run the application. You may notice that the value of a variable was not what you expected.

The Require Variable Declaration option automatically inserts an Option Explicit statement in every new form, module, or class module. It does not, however, insert an Option Explicit in existing forms, modules, or class modules. The statement can be manually typed into these files, however.

Setting Auto Syntax Checking

You can also determine whether or not Visual Basic performs syntax checking on a line of code after you have entered it. By default, auto syntax checking is enabled. When you type a line of code and enter a carriage return or use the mouse to move to a new line of code, Visual Basic determines if the syntax of your code is correct. You probably saw this happen if you have ever forgotten to put a *Then* keyword at the end of a line that contains an *If* keyword.

You can disable syntax checking by deselecting the Auto Syntax Check check box. When the feature is disabled, you can enter code without having Visual Basic perform a syntax check.

Setting Project Options

The Project tab of the Options tabbed dialog box, shown in figure 20.2, allows you to control which forms Visual Basic opens when you run your project, which help files your project uses, and several other project options.

Fig. 20.2

The Project tab displays options specific to a Visual Basic project.

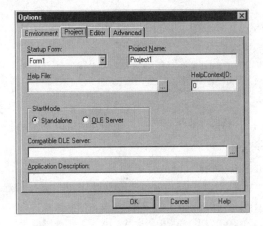

This following sections explain each options in detail and discuss how each option affects your project.

Setting the Startup Form

The Startup Form drop-down list box at the top of the Projects tab enables you to determine which form is displayed when you run your Visual Basic project. This list box shows all forms in the current project. The list box also displays the Sub Main procedure, which also can be used to start a project. To determine which form or procedure will load, select it from the list box.

Choosing a Project Name

You can set a name for the Visual Project through the Project Name text box on the Projects tab. Although usually unused by standalone executable files, the project name is the name that will be displayed in the Object Browser when you create an OLE automation server.

Selecting a Project's Help File

You can select the help file that will be used by your project when a user presses the F1 key or invokes context-sensitive help. This is done by entering the name of your project's help file in the Help File text box on the Projects tab. When selecting the help file, make sure that the help file is located in the same directory as your project or in a directory that you are certain will be on every end user's machine. This ensures that no matter where an end user installs the application, the path to the help file will still be valid.

If your project will be an OLE automation server, you also can specify the Help topic that displays when a user chooses the Question Mark (?) button on the Object Browser while your application's object library is selected. This is done by entering the appropriate help context ID in the HelpContextID field on the Projects tab.

Setting the Start Mode

The StartMode group box allows you to instruct Visual Basic to treat your project as an OLE automation server when debugging. By clicking the OLE Server option button in the StartMode group box, your application will act as though it were a registered OLE automation server when you debug. Additionally, if you plan to compile your project into an OLE server, you will need to make sure that the OLE Server option button is selected.

If you plan to deploy your project as a standalone application, you should click the Standalone option button in the StartMode group box.

Setting a Compatible Server

If you are creating an OLE automation server with Visual Basic, the Projects tab allows you to notify your project of a compatible OLE server. A compatible server is usually an OLE automation server that was already deployed. When you make modifications to the server, you want to make sure that the changes are compatible with the existing version. To have Visual Basic ensure that future changes are compatible, set the compatible server in the Compatible OLE Server text box.

To set the compatible server, enter the full path name of the OLE server's .EXE or .DLL file into the Ole Server text box. You can also search for a compatible server by pressing the ellipses (...) button to the right of the text box.

When you compile your OLE automation server, it will be compared with the OLE automation server you named in the Compatible OLE Server text box. If any method or property's names have changed or are removed, you are notified that the two servers are no longer compatible. If you plan to replace an existing OLE automation server with an incompatible server, you have to make adjustments to the client applications or other OLE automation servers that make use of the new server.

For more information on compatible OLE automation servers, see Chapter 19, "Version Control and Team Development."

Setting a Project Description

Finally, the Projects tab allows you to provide a description about your project. The description can be entered in the Application Description text box. This description will display in the Object Browser and the References dialog box when the application's object library is selected.

This setting can be useful for explaining the functionality of your application to other developers. If you leave a project after developing an OLE automation server, which you most likely will do, other developers can continue to use your server, even if you are not on site to explain its functionality. Additionally, when end users begin to develop their own applications, they can get a brief overview of the functionality contained in your server.

Setting Editor Options

The Editor tab of the Options tabbed dialog box, shown in figure 20.3, allows you to control how your code displays in the Visual Basic development environment.

Fig. 20.3
The Editor tab of the Options tabbed dialog box displays options that pertain to Visual Basic's display of code.

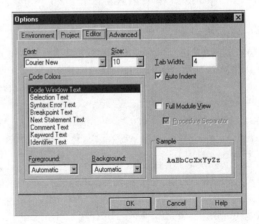

Specifically, you can control the following aspects of your code's appearance:

- Font size, style, and color
- Auto indent and tab width features
- Procedure display style

The remainder of these sections explains each of these features, how they can help enhance the appearance of your code, and how they can aid in simplifying development.

Setting Font Size, Style, and Color

By adjusting settings in the Font and Size drop-down list boxes on the Editor tab, you can control the font used to display your code. Adjusting the size of your code and the font in which it is displayed can be helpful when you display your code to other developers, clients, or end users. During a code walk-through, for example, you may be displaying your code to other team members on an overhead projector. By increasing the size of the font you use to display the code, you can make sure that even the developers seated in the back of the room have a clear view of your application's make-up.

In addition, you can control the colors that Visual Basic uses to display various types of code. The Code Colors list box contains a list box, describing various types of code. Directly below the list box you see two drop-down list boxes, labeled Foreground and Background. You can control the color used to display code by selecting a type of code from the list box and a foreground or background color from the drop-down list boxes. If, for example, you select the Code Window Text item and select Red as the foreground color and Automatic as the background color, and then switch to a code module, you will see your Visual Basic code displayed in red.

You can see how Visual Basic uses different colors to display code without changing any settings. For example, when you comment a block of code, by default Visual Basic displays the commented code in green. In addition, Visual Basic keywords, commands, and identifiers are all displayed in color text.

Using colors to display text can help when you or other developers are reading text. When you know that comments are displayed in green, you can skip over comment sections to more easily locate and view blocks of code. In addition, when you are coding, if you have instructed Visual Basic to display all keywords in the color blue, and you accidentally misspell a keyword, it will not turn blue in color. This provides a visual queue that the keyword is incorrect so that you can correct the mistake.

Generally, you will not need to change the settings of code colors. An exception may be if a development team member has difficulty in interpreting colors or if you feel that some color of code is difficult to see.

Setting Auto Indent and Tab Width Features

Visual Basic allows you to control how it responds when you type one or more tab characters on a line and then enter a carriage return. If you mark the Auto Indent check box on the Editor tab to on, when you enter one or more tab characters on a line of code, each subsequent line is automatically indented by the same amount. This feature is useful within For...Next, If...Then, and With...Each sections of your code. By indenting the first line within one of these sections, you carry the indent throughout the section until you choose to remove the indent. This will clearly identify all statements contained within the loop, making your code more readable.

You can also determine how many spaces Visual Basic moves the cursor when the Tab key is pressed in the code editor window. This is controlled by changing the Tab Width property. Tab width can be any integer value between 1 and 32. Setting Tab Width to a value of four or more will make a tab character most apparent to someone reading your code.

Setting Procedure Display Styles

The Full Module View check box on the Editor tab allows you to control how Visual Basic displays functions and procedures in the code editor window. If the check box is marked, all functions and procedures contained in a module including the general declarations section, will display in a single, scrollable window. An example of the full module view setting is shown in figure 20.4.

Fig. 20.4
A module displayed in Full Module view.

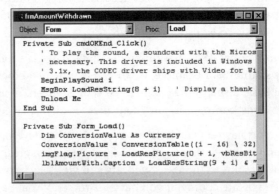

Full module view is the way code is displayed in other applications that use the Visual Basic programming language, such as Excel.

If you select the Full Module View option, the Procedure Separator check box becomes enabled. The Procedure Separator check box allows you to determine whether or not Visual Basic separates functions and procedures with a line when they are displayed in full module view. The code displayed in figure 20.4 shows a procedure separator line. Notice that the break line is similar in appearance to a word processor's page-break line.

If you do not select Full Module View, Visual Basic displays each function or procedure in its own scrollable listing. This is the format used to display functions and procedure in previous versions of Visual Basic.

Regardless of the setting you choose, you select the procedure or function you want to display by selecting the procedure or function's name from the Proc. list box in the Visual Basic code editor window. Enabling the Full Module View may make your code more difficult to read. You may find it more difficult to determine where procedures begin and end, especially if you are scrolling through a long procedure and are using the scroll bars to move through large chunks of code at a time. If you do choose to display your code in full module view, you should also make sure you mark the Procedure Separator check box. This makes reading code simpler.

Setting Advanced Options

The Advanced tab, shown in figure 20.5, allows you to set the following options affecting the Visual Basic environment:

- Project load settings

- Error trapping settings

- Compiler settings

- OLE DLL settings

- Command line arguments

- Conditional compilation arguments

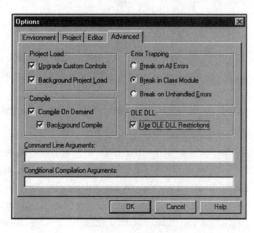

Fig. 20.5
The Advanced Options dialog tab allows you to change several run-time environment settings.

The remainder of these sections explains each of these settings and shows the effect each setting has on your Visual Basic project.

Project Load Settings

The Project Load group box provides two options:

- Upgrade Custom Controls
- Background Project Load

The Upgrade Custom Controls setting determines whether or not Visual Basic attempts to upgrade VBXs in a project to OLE Controls. Upgrades can be accomplished only if a valid replacement OLE Control has been registered in the VB.INI file. Because OLE Controls provide a more open interface than VBXs and because only OLE Controls can be used in 32-bit applications, it's a good idea to always instruct Visual Basic to upgrade controls when they are available. To enable custom control upgrading to occur, select the Upgrade Custom Controls check box.

The Background Project Load check box allows you to choose whether Visual Basic loads code in the background when an application is run in development mode. This allows control to return to a developer more quickly. This setting does not affect how your compiled EXE application is loaded.

Error Trapping Settings

The Error Trapping group box allows you to determine how Visual Basic responds to errors when a project is run in development mode. You can choose any one of the following options:

- Break on All Errors
- Break in Class Module
- Break on Unhandled Errors

The Break on All Errors setting causes Visual Basic to Break mode on all errors regardless of whether or not an error handler is active. Visual Basic also enters Break mode if an error occurs in a class module. This setting gives you an opportunity to see all errors that are being generated when your application is running.

The Break in Class Module setting instructs Visual Basic to enter Break mode if an unhandled error occurs in a class module. It does not affect errors that occur in client applications accessing a class module. This setting is very useful if you are debugging an OLE automation server. In normal mode, when an error occurs in a class module, control returns to the calling application—usually a client application. If, however, you have selected the Break in Class

Module option, the class module will enter Break mode and not return an error message to the calling application. Note that this setting only affects a class module that is running in development mode.

Finally, the Break on Unhandled Errors setting instructs Visual Basic to enter Break mode on any unhandled errors. If an error handler is enabled and an error occurs, Visual Basic will not enter Break mode. If an error occurs in a class module, Visual Basic will cause the project to enter Break mode on the line of code that invoked the method that produced an error in the calling application. This setting is useful when you have created a version of your application that you feel is error free. If you run the application in the break on unhandled errors mode, you will be able to determine the errors that currently are untrapped, and then you can make adjustments accordingly.

Compile Settings

The Compile group box allows you to determine how Visual Basic compiles your program when it is run in development mode. If you select the Compile on Demand check box, your program will compile code only as it is needed—when you run the application, you will receive control back quickly but, as you continue to run the application, you may experience pauses as Visual Basic continues to compile your code. If you do not select this option, all your code will be compiled before the application is run. This means a bigger wait up front, but you will not have to wait for your code to compile again.

If you need to access one area of your code for testing, or if you need to repeatedly run your code when debugging, it is a good idea to enable Compile on Demand. This selection allows you to quickly access the areas of the system you want to test. If you plan to compile the code infrequently, you may want to deselect the Compile on Demand check box and allow all of your code to be compiled up front.

When you select the Compile on Demand check box, the Background Compile option becomes available. If you enable this option, Visual Basic uses idle time to continue compiling the project in the background. If you have Compile on Demand enabled, background compilation will help to improve run-time execution speed.

OLE DLL Settings

The OLE DLL group box contains a single setting: Use OLE DLL Restrictions. This setting allows you to instruct Visual Basic to run a DLL project in the development environment, using the same restrictions that apply to an OLE DLL when it is run in-process with another application.

A DLL cannot be run in-process when it is run in the development environment. Debugging must occur with a client application calling the DLL from another instance of Visual Basic. If you enable the Use OLE DLL Restrictions check box, Visual Basic will make the development environment more like an in-process environment. This will allow you to test your application in a real-world environment.

Command Line Arguments

The Command Line Arguments text box allows you to set sample command line arguments for testing your application. Command line arguments are used to provide data to your application at startup. For example, you might use a command line argument to allow a user to open an application and type in a user name. When running the application, a user could enter the following information:

```
MYAPP.EXE username
```

where *username* is the name of the user. This may cause a login screen that was displayed when the application opens to have the User ID field populated with *username*. If *username* was omitted, the login screen would be displayed without the user's ID populated.

Command line arguments are usually entered by a user by choosing the Run command from Windows 95's Start menu or from the Program Manager's File command. A user types the name and path of the application they want to run, followed by the command line arguments. Alternatively, command line arguments can be added when an icon or shortcut is created for a program.

Any arguments entered into the Command Line Arguments text box will be evaluated in the same way arguments entered through the Run command or through an application's icon or shortcut are evaluated. This feature gives you an opportunity to test the behavior of command line arguments on your application without requiring you to use the Run command to activate your application or create an icon on the Start menu or Program Manager.

Conditional Compilation Arguments

The Conditional Compilation Arguments text box allows you to specify constants that will be used for conditional compilation. Conditional compilation is a feature new to Visual Basic 4.0. It allows you to include statements in your Visual Basic application based on constants that Visual Basic makes available or that you create. You specify your compilation constants in the Conditional Compilation Arguments text box.

Conditional compilation makes it easy to create a run-time and debug version of your application. By specifying a RunMode constant as a compilation argument, you can instruct Visual Basic to compile additional debugging code. The additional code might display a message box, fully describing an error each time one occurs, or it might write information retrieved from a database to a log file, allowing you to verify that the information is correct.

In following sections of this chapter, we discuss using conditional compilation arguments to create a debugging version of an application. For more information on conditional compilation, see Chapter 8, "Architecting Tier 1: Client Applications."

A Summarization of Environment Recommendations

This section provides a brief review of all the development recommendations made in the previous sections. Rather than requiring you to reread the entire development environment sections, this section has been added to provide a quick reference.

The following list describes the recommendations, as well as the reasoning, behind each recommendation.

- **Save Before Run**   Selecting the Save Before Run option will ensure that your code is always secure and will help to prevent accidental data loss.

- **Option Explicit**   Choosing Option Explicit ensures that all variables in your application are properly declared. This also helps prevent bugs in your application that are caused by accidental mistyping of variable names.

- **Setting Compatible OLE Servers**   This setting ensures that changes you make to an OLE server will not be incompatible with versions already released.

- **No Compile on Demand or Background Compile**   Not requiring a complete compilation of your code each time you run it may let bugs in your code slide a long time.

- **Minimize the use of Variants**   Using specific data types, such as Integers and Strings, instead of the Variant data type will help your application to perform optimally.

Creating Coding Guidelines

The most important aspect of guidelines is not that one master set is constantly referred to by every project on which you ever work, but that all of the developers within a project adhere to the same guidelines. Guidelines also should ensure that clear, consistent code is created for every development project.

The following sections provide some suggestions for coding guidelines within your application.

Naming Conventions

When you open a new project, you should establish naming conventions that you will use when you create variables, controls, and modules in your application. Generally, these naming conventions are prefixes that indicate the type of variable, control, or module that you are creating.

The following sections discuss naming conventions for the following components of your project:

- Controls
- Form Modules
- Code Modules
- Class Modules
- Methods and Properties
- Variables

Controls

Controls in Visual Basic are uniquely identified by their Name property. Although Visual Basic provides you with the flexibility to use nearly any combination of numbers and characters to name controls, it's a good idea to lay out some guidelines for naming controls in your Visual Basic projects. Naming conventions for controls help to make your code more readable to both you and other developers.

Suppose that you placed a new text box control on a form. The form will be used to prompt a user for login information, such as a user ID and a password. If the new text box you created will be used to hold a user's password, you could name the text control **Password**.

Using the name, Password, doesn't provide much information about the new control. If a new developer looked at your code and saw the word, Password, he or she probably wouldn't have a good idea to what the word referred. They may think that Password is a variable, some type of control, or a function.

If, however, you had established naming guidelines for naming your controls, you may have named the password text box, **txtPassword**. The *txt* portion of the control name is often referred to as a *naming prefix*. The naming prefix provides information about the type of control being referred to. Now, when other developers look at your code and see the term, txtPassword, they would immediately know that the word refers to a text box control and not a variable or a function name.

In addition to providing clues to the type of control to which a name is referring, using naming prefixes causes Visual Basic to group together similar controls in the Controls drop-down list box at the top of the Properties window (see fig. 20.6).

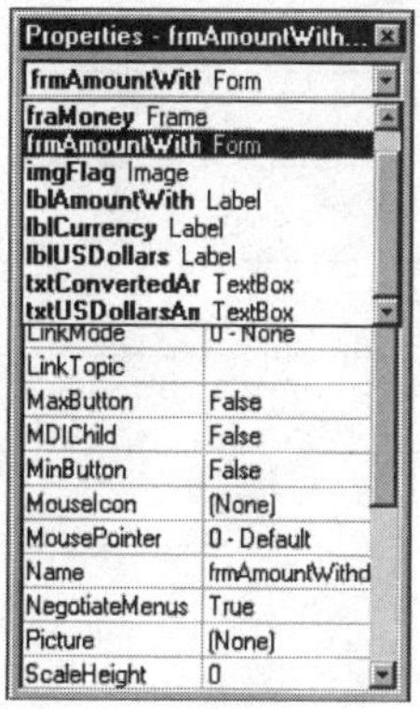

Fig. 20.6
The Controls drop-down list box of the Properties window displays the names of all controls on a Visual Basic form.

Controls are listed alphabetically in the Controls list box. If all of the text boxes on a form in your project are prefixed with the letters, "txt," all of the text boxes will be grouped together in the list box. If you are viewing a form and want to see the properties for a text box, you can scroll down the Control list and look for the controls, starting with the letters, "txt."

Table 20.1 shows a list of Visual Basic controls and the prefixes recommended by Microsoft Consulting Services.

Table 20.1 Recommended Control Name Prefixes

Control	Prefix
Check box	chk
Combo box	cbo
Data-bound combo box	dbc
Command button	cmd
Data	dat
Directory list box	dir
Drive list box	drv
File list box	fil
Frame	fra
Grid	grd
Data-bound grid	dbg
Horizontal scroll bar	hsb
Image	img
Label	lbl
Line	lin
List box	lst
Data-bound list box	dbl
Menu	mnu
OLE container	ole
Option button	opt
Picture box	pic
Shape (circle, square, oval, rectangle, rounded rectangle, and rounded square)	shp
Text box	txt
Timer	tmr
Vertical scroll bar	vsb

When creating naming guidelines for your projects, keep in mind that the prefixes you use for control names are less important than making sure that all developers on the project adhere to the same guidelines. If several developers use the "txt" prefix for text box controls and another group of developers use the prefix "tb," the naming convention loses a great deal of its value. If, however, all developers choose to use the tb prefix instead of the txt prefix, persons looking at your code will still understand that the *tbPassword* control name refers to a text box and all text box controls are still grouped alphabetically in the Controls drop-down list box.

Form Modules

Visual Basic provides three types of modules: form modules, code modules, and class modules. You can identify each type of module in the Project window by the icon that is displayed immediately to the left of the module's name. However, it is not so simple to identify a module's type in code.

If you create public property procedures or public functions for form modules in your Visual Basic project, they can be accessed from any other form or code module in your project. These procedures or functions are accessed by using either of the following two syntax examples:

```
form.function
```

or

```
form.propertyprocedure
```

Where `form` is the name of the form module that contains the function or property procedure, and `function` or `propertyprocedure` is the name of the public function or property procedure, respectively. This syntax, shown in the following two examples, is similar to the syntax that you use when you access a property or method of an OLE automation server:

```
object.method
```

or

```
object.property
```

When others view your code, they may not be able to easily determine if a statement, like the following example, is referring to the Login object or a form named Login:

```
Login.GetPassword
```

For this reason, it's important that you name forms properly. By including a naming prefix, such as "frm," at the beginning of the form's name, you help other developers understand that they are accessing a form module and not a class module. If a developer encounters the following code, he or she will immediately know that they are accessing a property procedure or function of a form module named `frmLogin`:

```
frmLogin.GetPassword
```

Code Modules

Code modules are generally used for declaring global variables or global functions. These functions and variables will be accessible only from within the Visual Basic project that stores them. When you access the global function or variable, you do not prefix them with a code module's name. For this reason, you do not need to provide any type of prefix for code modules.

You still should try to use descriptive names when naming code modules. For example, if you created a code module that contains all of the functions necessary to access a database, you might call it **DataAccess**. This naming convention will help another developer who is examining your code to quickly understand for what purpose the code module is used.

Class Modules

Because class modules may be exposed to other users in the form of OLE objects, you want to give them names that are as descriptive as possible. Try to use complete words rather than abbreviations whenever possible. Remember that end users who create their own applications may be accessing these objects. For example, naming a class module **Customer**, instead of Cstmr, makes the nature of the object much clearer to an end user.

Adding naming prefixes to a class module may confuse users. For example, adding the prefix **cls** to the Customer class module, which will make the name of the object **clsCustomer**, may make a user question whether or not he or she should select this object or continue to look for a Customer object. In addition, end users may not fully understand the concept of a class module, so the prefix, "cls," for an object will hold little, if any, meaning.

If you must use an abbreviation in place of a long name, use the first syllable of the word you are abbreviating. For example, if you wanted to abbreviate the name, "CustomerManager," you should use **CustManager** rather than CstmrManager. This helps make the class module more readable for other users.

Methods and Properties

Just as class modules are accessed by end users and other applications so are methods and properties of OLE automation servers. For this reason, it's important that you use proper conventions when naming methods and procedures.

It may seem logical to name methods and properties in the same way you name functions and variables, but methods and properties are exposed via an OLE automation server's interface. End users and other application developers may use them in other applications. Using the same prefixes that are recommended for functions and variables can cloud the meaning of methods and properties you create. In general, you should use the same guidelines used for naming class modules.

This means that methods and properties should not be prefixed. You should provide plain English words that adequately describe the functions. Abbreviations of words should be avoided as much as possible. If they are required, however, use the first syllable of the word or words that are being abbreviated. In addition, many OLE objects will provide a standard set of methods, such as Add and Delete.

For more information on creating OLE automation server methods and properties, see Chapter 6, "Creating OLE Objects."

Functions and Procedures

Unlike methods and properties of a class module, functions and procedures in modules are not exposed through an object interface. This means that end users will not call the functions and procedures that you create, and that you can provide function and procedure names that describe details about the sub-procedures, such as their scope, or in the case of a function, its return arguments.

When naming a function, for example, it's a good idea to provide a prefix that indicates the scope of the function. This prefix could be the letter g for global or the letter m for module-level. The following examples show a global function and a module-level function with prefixes:

```
gbOpenDatabase

fbAddOrder
```

From these names, other developers can quickly see that the OpenDatabase function has a global scope, while the AddOrder function has a module-level scope.

In addition to prefixing function names with a letter that indicates the function's scope, it is helpful to indicate the data type of the function's return value. This in turn helps other developers improve the performance of their code by using the proper data type to accept return values.

Suppose that you wrote a global function, `OpenWindow`, that is used to open a new instance of a window in your application. The function returns a Boolean value, indicating whether or not the new window was successfully opened. To help other developers prepare their code for the Boolean return value, you can add a letter that identifies the function's return value data type. The name of the `OpenWindow` function, when prefixed with its scope and return value data type, might look like the following:

    gbOpenWindow

With only a quick look, a developer knows that the `gbOpenWindow` function is global in scope and that it has returned a Boolean value.

As mentioned previously in this section, creating a guideline that uses scope and return value data type prefixes is less important than creating a guideline that will be used by all developers. As long as all of the developers who are working on your project can agree on a method for naming functions and procedures within the project, the details of the method are irrelevant.

Variables

Much like functions and procedures, it is often helpful to prefix variables used in your application with the variable's scope and data type. This helps other developers quickly determine the scope and data type of variables they want to employ.

In the following example, you can quickly see that the variable, `gbAppIsRunning` is a Boolean data type with a global scope:

    gbAppIsRunning

Had the variable been given the following name, there may be some doubt as to the scope and data type of the variable:

    AppIsRunning

This may require a developer to search for the declaration statement of the variable to identify its scope and data type, or a developer might be inclined to simply declare a new variable to perform the same function for which the `AppIsRunning` variable is currently used. In either case, time or application resources are wasted.

To restate this, the specific guideline that you choose to use in your project, such as using the letter **g** to indicate the global scope of a variable, is far less important than establishing a guideline on which all the developers can agree. If each developer is using a different method for declaring variables, the project as a whole will be disorganized.

Using Specific Variable Types

When you use variables in your code, it is important to always use a specific data type that can accommodate the information that you are storing. Suppose that you created an order processing application that allows a user to enter a PO number for each order generated. A business rule states that a PO number for the order processing application can contain only numbers. No alpha characters can be used. In addition, the PO number is always exactly six digits long.

To store the variable internally, you can use one of several data types. The variant data type, the long integer data type, or the string data type are all capable of holding a six-digit PO number. Which type is the best choice? You know that a variant can store any type of data. A string also can be used to store data that contains any combination of alpha and numeric characters.

To determine the best choice for storing data, you first need to look at which data type can contain the information you want to store. In the case of the PO number, you have already determined that the variant, long integer, and string data types are all capable of holding a six-digit number. The next step is determining which data type requires the least amount of overhead to store your value.

In the PO number example, you need to store a six-digit number. The string data type requires one byte of storage for each character—storing a six-digit number requires six bytes. The variant data type requires 16 bytes of storage plus an additional byte for each character to be stored. For a six-digit variant, 22 bytes are required. A long integer uses four bytes to store numbers between –2,147,483,648 and 2,147,483,648. From these numbers, you can see that using a long integer will save as much as 18 bytes of overhead.

If your application uses a larger number of variables, you can see how significant the overhead savings can be. If your application uses an array of variables to hold PO numbers, choosing the long integer data type over the variant data type may provide significant overhead reduction. All of the saved overhead results in improved performance in your application.

Using Indentation

You can make your code readable to other users by the indenting lines within functions and procedures. Using tab characters, you create logical groupings of If...Then...Else statements, For...Next loops, and With...End with constructs.

Indentation usually means indenting all code one tab character from the left margin of the screen. If you are creating a For...Next type construct, indent the code within the construct an additional tab character. When statements are nested, the nested code should be indented an additional character.

For example, if you look at the code fragment in Listing 20.1, taken from the OLE Document Manager's sample application's frmOLEDocList form, which you can find in the \CHAP20 directory on the companion disk, you can see how all code is indented one tab character from the left margin of the screen.

Listing 20.1   CODE01.TXT—The fiFillDirectories functions demonstrate the clarity that indentation adds to your code

```
Private Function fiFillDirectories(atvwTreeView As TreeView)

    ' Function fills the passed TreeView control
    ' with directories in the Directories collection
    Dim lsParentKey As String
    Dim lsKey As String
    Dim lsDescription As String
    Dim lnodNewNode As Node
    Dim ldirDirectory As Object
    Dim liCounter As Integer

    ' Clear the control
    atvwTreeView.Nodes.Clear

    ' Add the root directory
    Set lnodNewNode = atvwTreeView.Nodes.Add(, , "DirRoot",
    ➥"Documents", 1)

    For liCounter = 1 To gcolDirectories.Count
        ' Add each directory in the collection
        Set ldirDirectory = gcolDirectories.Item(liCounter)

        lsKey = "Dir" & ldirDirectory.Id
        lsDescription = ldirDirectory.Name

        If ldirDirectory.ParentID = 0 Then
            ' Dir is at parent level
            lsParentKey = "DirRoot"
        Else
            ' Dir is not at parent level
            lsParentKey = "Dir" & ldirDirectory.ParentID
        End If

        Set lnodNewNode = atvwTreeView.Nodes.Add(lsParentKey,
        ➥ tvwChild, lsKey, lsDescription, 1)
        lnodNewNode.ExpandedImage = 2
```

```
        Next

        atvwTreeView.Refresh

    End Function
```

The code within the For...Next loop is indented an additional tab character, and the code within the If...End If statement is indented still another tab character. You also can see how the indentation of code makes it easy to see where both the For...Next and If...End If constructs begin and end.

If you look at this same code with the indents removed, as shown in Listing 20.2, you can see how difficult it is to determine where the For...Next statement begins and ends, and also where the nested If...End If statement is located in this code.

Listing 20.2   CODE01.TXT—The fiFillDirectories functions with the indentations removed. Notice how much more difficult the code is to interpret

```
    Private Function fiFillDirectories(atvwTreeView As TreeView)

        ' Function fills the passed TreeView control
        ' with directories in the Directories collection
        Dim lsParentKey As String
        Dim lsKey As String
        Dim lsDescription As String
        Dim lnodNewNode As Node
        Dim ldirDirectory As Object
        Dim liCounter As Integer

        ' Clear the control
        atvwTreeView.Nodes.Clear

        ' Add the root directory
        Set lnodNewNode = atvwTreeView.Nodes.Add(, , "DirRoot",
        ➥"Documents", 1)

        For liCounter = 1 To gcolDirectories.Count
        ' Add each directory in the collection
        Set ldirDirectory = gcolDirectories.Item(liCounter)
        lsKey = "Dir" & ldirDirectory.Id
        lsDescription = ldirDirectory.Name

        If ldirDirectory.ParentID = 0 Then
        ' Dir is at parent level
        lsParentKey = "DirRoot"
        Else
        ' Dir is not at parent level
        lsParentKey = "Dir" & ldirDirectory.ParentID
        End If
```

(continues)

Listing 20.2   Continued

```
    Set lnodNewNode = atvwTreeView.Nodes.Add(lsParentKey,
➥ tvwChild, lsKey, lsDescription, 1)
    lnodNewNode.ExpandedImage = 2

    Next

    atvwTreeView.Refresh

End Function
```

The following is a list of the various constructs that should use indentation in your Visual Basic code:

- `For...Next, For Each...Next`

- `If...End If, If...Then...Else, If...ElseIf...End If`

- `#If...#Else...#End If`

- `Do...Loop`

- `While...Wend`

- `With...End With`

Debugging Code

Visual Basic provides several useful features and tools to aid in debugging your application. As part of any development effort, you should include two important components:

- A debugging version of your application

- An executable free of dead and unoptimized code

To implement each of these items, Visual Basic provides two useful features. To create a debugging version of your application, you can use Visual Basic's conditional compilation features. To create a version of your application that is free of dead code and highly optimized, you can use Visual Basic's Code Profiler.

The remainder of this section outlines both of these and describes how each can be used to debug and performance tune your Visual Basic project.

Creating a Debugging Version

In previous versions of Visual Basic, if you wanted to create a debugging version of an application, you had to use one of two methods.

In the first method, you could include all your debugging code in your application during development. You could activate and deactivate your debugging code by setting global constants. For example, you could declare a global variable, gbDebugMode, and set it to True. You then could create a series of If...Then statements that carried out your debugging steps, such as writing information to a log file. The code might look like the following example:

```
If gbDebugMode = True Then
    ..
    ..
    ' Debug code goes here
End If
```

When you deployed the application, you could set the gbDebugMode variable to False. This would ensure that your debug code was not run in the production version. However, the additional debug code added size to your compiled executable. When you had finished testing and debugging your code, you could go back through your project and remove all of your debugging code. This limited the size of the application but required additional work.

A second method that you could use in previous Visual Basic versions to create a debugging version of your application, one that required a large amount of extra work, was to create two separate versions of your code. One debug version and a second production version. Only the debug version contained debug code. This saved the step of removing debug code when you were ready to deploy your application but required you to keep two separate versions of the code in synch. If a developer added new code to the production version, it needed to be copied into the debug version.

Fortunately, Visual Basic 4.0 provides a much simpler means for creating a debugging version of your application. Conditional compilation allows you to add any amount of debugging code that you want. At compile time, you can instruct Visual Basic to ignore your debug code and include only the production code in the compiled executable.

Elements of a Debugging Version

Because the exact functionality of your application differs from project to project, it is impossible to outline a debugging version of an application that will fit all scenarios. However, this section provides some basic debugging features that will apply to most projects.

Your debugging version should include the following features:

- Detailed error logging
- Highly visible notification of errors

The first feature, detailed error logging, should write highly verbose information about the errors that occur in your application to a log file. Using this feature will help your debugging effort, especially in applications that run unattended for long periods. Suppose that you developed an application that ran a nightly batch job to distribute orders that were placed on the previous day. The application is responsible for processing several thousand orders each night. During the testing phase, you will use a similar number of orders as test data. You will not want to sit in front of the machine and watch thousands of orders being entered into the database, nor will you want to stop the entire process should one order present a problem.

A good solution is to add debugging code that writes to a log file all errors that occur during the order processing phase. The code simply writes a verbose message that describes the error, and then moves on to the next order. The error message might include information such as on which order the error occurred and the text that accompanied the error. In this way, your application could continue to process the remaining orders and still give you an accurate indication of all problems it encountered.

This code also would be conditionally compiled. When the application goes into production, you will still want to log your errors, but you may not want to include as much information about the error. Rather than edit your debugging code for the production, you can create a conditional compilation variable, named **DEBUG_VERSION**, and set it to True while you test. You might have a code fragment that looks like the following example:

```
' Sample Debug code
#If DEBUG_VERSION = True Then
    ..
    ..
    ' Detailed logging code goes here
#Else
    ..
    ..
    ' Production logging code goes here
#End If
```

To enable your debugging version, you set the DEBUG_VERSION compilation constant to True on the Advanced tab of the Options tabbed dialog (discussed previously in this chapter).

When an error occurs in a debugging environment, you want to be sure that a developer who is testing the application is made fully aware that an error has occurred. In addition to alerting the tester, you also want to provide detailed information about the error, such as the procedure name where the error occurred, the application that caused the error, the number of the error, the values of pertinent variables, and verbose text that describes the error. You also may want to give the tester the option of printing the error to a file or of ending the application immediately.

When your application is in production, however, you may not want to provide this level of detail about the error, nor will you want to give the end user the option of ending the application. Again, you can use conditional compilation to create a debugging version of your code and a production version. Both versions will be generated from the same set of source code and, because your code is conditionally compiled, the debugging code will be completely removed when you compile your production version.

Using the Code Profiler

Visual Basic 4.0 provides a powerful new tool, the *Code Profiler*. The Code Profiler is an Add-on extension that you can use to optimize your Visual Basic projects. The Code Profiler is capable of determining which portions of your Visual Basic code are used the most and which parts are not used. It also can determine how much time is required to run functions or parts of functions. This allows you to determine how efficiently portions of your code are running.

The Code Profiler also generates a report, detailing the activity it analyzed. The report tells you which portions of your code are using the most processor time, which functions are most commonly accessed, and which functions are not being used at all. This information will help you improve the performance of slow functions or removing dead code that is no longer being accessed by your application.

The rest of this section outlines the Code Profiler and explains how it can be used to help you optimize your Visual Basic application.

Installing the Code Profiler

The Code Profiler is a Visual Basic add-in, which means that it is an external tool that can interact with Visual Basic. Before an add-in can interact, however, it must be referenced within your Visual Basic project. This is done by referencing the add-in through the Add-In Manager.

The Add-In Manager is opened by choosing <u>A</u>dd-Ins, <u>A</u>dd-In Manager. When you select the options, the Add-In Manager dialog box appears (see fig. 20.7).

Fig. 20.7

The Add-in Manager dialog box displays the Code Profiler Add-In.

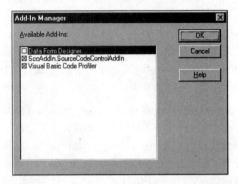

The Add-In Manager displays a list of all add-ins that are currently referenced by Visual Basic, as well as all add-ins that are available. Add-ins that were previously referenced have a marked check box to the right of their names. Add-ins that are not yet referenced have an unmarked check box to the left of the add-in name. To reference the Code Profiler Add-In, select the Visual Basic Code Profiler check box.

After you reference the Code Profiler add-in a new menu option, labeled <u>V</u>B Code Profiler, appears under the <u>A</u>dd-Ins menu. After you reference the Code Profiler, you can begin to use it.

Running the Code Profiler

After you reference the Code Profiler add-in, you can analyze a project by loading the Code Profiler, allowing the Code Profiler to add its analysis code, and running your project. When the analysis is complete, you can view the results.

The first step in the analysis process is loading your Visual Basic project. You should do this by opening the project as you would any other Visual Basic project. It's a good idea to make a back-up of your project before analyzing it. Although the Code Profiler makes copies of your project before adding its analysis code, always take the extra precaution of backing up your code. You also will want to make sure that all the files in your project are located on a local machine. The Code Profiler is not designed to analyze files located on a network drive. You also need to make sure all files that you plan to analyze are fully editable.

A fully editable file is a file whose read-only property is set to False. If you are using SourceSafe to store your code, you will want to retrieve an editable copy of each file in the project. Make sure that you retrieve only an editable copy from SourceSafe. Do not check out the files because they will be changed by the Code Profiler. If you are not using SourceSafe, you can make sure that the project files are fully editable by checking the file's properties in the Explorer or File Manager.

After you have loaded your project, the next step is to load the Code Profiler. To load the Code Profiler, select VB Code Profiler from the Add-Ins menu. When you do so, the Visual Basic Code Profiler dialog box, shown in figure 20.8, appears.

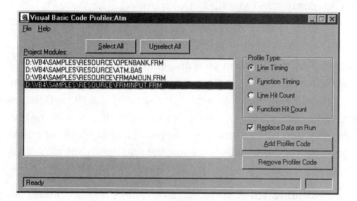

Fig. 20.8
The Visual Basic Code Profiler dialog box, displayed when the Visual Basic Code Profiler option is selected from the Add-ins menu.

The Visual Basic Code Profiler dialog box displays a list of all files included in your project and a list of analysis options on the right side of the dialog box. You first choose which files you want to analyze by selecting them from the Project Modules list box. You can quickly select all of your files for analysis by clicking the Select All button. Conversely, you can deselect all files by clicking the Unselect All button.

After selecting the files to analyze, you select the type of analysis you want to perform. You have four options, shown in the Code Profile dialog box's Profile Type group box:

- **Line Timing**   Allows you to determine how long it takes for individual lines of code to execute.

- **Function Timing**   Allows you to determine how long it takes for functions to execute.

- **Line Hit Count**   Allows you to determine how many times each line of code is executed.

- **Function Hit Count**   Allows you to determine how many times a function is executed.

You can choose only one type of analysis at a time. After you select your analysis, you click the Add Profiler Code button. This instructs the Code Profiler to add the lines of code necessary to complete your analysis. The Code Profiler will add information about your project to its internal database.

The Code Profiler will also make copies of all files in your project and store them in a separate directory, which helps ensure that the analysis procedure does not adversely affect any files in your project. The Code Profiler will create new copies of your files and place the code required to perform the analysis you selected within the new copies.

You are now ready to perform your analysis by switching back to your project in Visual Basic and running it. If you have certain functions that you want to analyze, you will want to make sure that they perform the actions necessary so that these functions are executed. For example, if you want to test the Form_Load function of a form in your project, you may want to repeatedly open and close the form. This gives you the maximum amount of analysis data.

When you have finished your testing, close your program, but do not exit Visual Basic. Now, you should switch back to the Code Profiler application.

Interpreting the Code Profiler's Analysis

After you have run your Visual Basic application, you can see the analysis that the Code Profiler performed. To do this, in Code Profiler choose View Results from the File menu. When you do this, the Analysis Grid appears (see fig. 20.9).

The Analysis Grid shows information that was gathered by the Code Profiler during its most recent analysis. The Analysis Grid displays the following columns shown in Table 20.2.

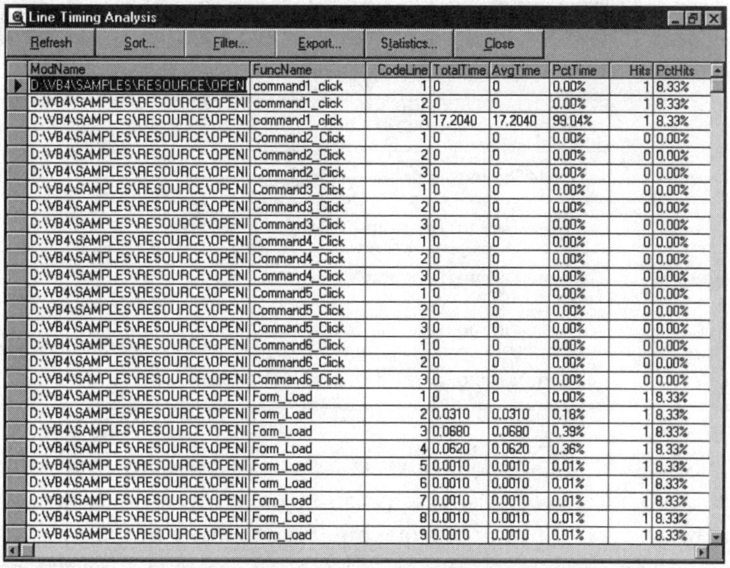

IV

Application Enhancements

Fig. 20.9
The Code Profiler's
Analysis Grid
displays the results
of a code analysis.

Table 20.2 The Columns Displayed in the Analysis Grid

Column	Description
ModName	The name of the code module or form
FuncName	The name of the function
CodeLine	The relative number of the inserted line of analysis code
TotalTime	The total time spent executing a line or function
AvgTime	The average time spent executing a line or function
PctTime	The percentage of time spent on a line or function compared to all the other lines or functions
Hits	The number of times a line or function ran
PctHits	The percentage of hits a particular line or function had compared to all the other lines or functions
LineText	The profiled line of executable code from the function

Several of these columns are displayed only when one of the four analysis types are selected. Table 20.3 shows these columns and indicates when they are displayed.

Table 20.3 Columns Displayed for Specific Analysis Types	
Column	**Included in Analysis Types**
CodeLine	Line Timing, Line Hit Count
TotalTime	Line Timing, Function Timing
AvgTime	Line Timing, Function Timing
PctTime	Line Timing, Function Timing
PctHits	Line Timing, Line Hit Count, Function Hit Count
LineText	Line Timing, Line Hit Count

If you are analyzing code in the hope of reducing its size or removing lines of code that are never used by your application, concentrate on the Hits column. This column indicates the total number of times a line of code is executed. If the number is zero, the code was never executed. However, before removing code that you suspect to be dead, you should thoroughly test it. This prevents you from accidentally removing lines of code that are infrequently used, but not dead.

If you are hoping to increase the performance of your code, concentrate on the Hits and PctHits columns. If either of the values in these two columns are high, you may want to reevaluate the particular line of code. You may have a recursive function. You should also pay attention to TotalTime, AvgTime, and PctTime columns. If a function or line of code is taking up a large amount of processor time, you may want to look at rewriting it or tuning its performance.

> **Note**
>
> Because the Code Profiler adds additional code to your project to perform its analysis, you may notice that your application slows down when you are analyzing. This decrease in speed because of the addition of Profiler code is accounted for when the Code Profiler performs its analysis.

The Analysis Grid provides several features to help interpret your code. These functions are accessed by choosing one of the six command buttons located at the top of the Analysis Grid. The functions carried out when each button is pushed are described in Table 20.4.

IV

Application Enhancements

Table 20.4   Additional Functions Available from the Analysis Grid

Function	Description
Refresh	Refreshes all data in the Analysis Grid to the state it was in before any sort or filter operations were executed.
Sort	Displays the Sort Column dialog box, allowing you to choose a column by which to sort the analysis data.
Filter	Displays the Filter dialog box, allowing you to define filter criteria to limit the amount and type of data displayed in the Analysis Grid.
Export	Displays the Export dialog box, allowing you to export data in the Analysis Grid to a tab delimited text file.
Statistics	Displays the statistics pertaining to the last analysis performed. Displays the number of modules, functions, and lines analyzed.
Close	Closes the Analysis Grid and displays the Visual Basic Code Profiler dialog box.

After you complete your analysis review, click the Close button to return to the Visual Basic Code Profiler dialog box.

Running a Subsequent Analysis

After you have completed an analysis of your code, you may want to run another analysis. You can choose a new type of analysis from the Profile Type group box. If you do this, the Code Profiler removes old code that it added to your Visual Basic project, and then adds the new code that is required to perform the analysis that you selected. After you select the new type of analysis you want to perform, you can switch to your Visual Basic program, run it, and return to the Code Profiler to display the Analysis Grid.

By selecting the Replace Data on Run check box from the Code Profiler dialog box, you can instruct the Code Profiler to remove data acquired during previous analysis and replace it with data gathered on the new run. It's a good idea to select the check box, especially if you are selecting a new type of analysis from the Profile Type group box, because old data in the analysis table may not be valid in the new Analysis grid.

Removing Analysis Code

When you complete your code analysis, click the Remove Profiler Code on the Visual Basic Code Profile dialog box. This action removes the Code Profiler files from your Visual Basic project and replaces the original files that the Code profiler copied out when you initially ran the Profiler.

Remember that the Code Profiler uses a copy of the files in your project. This means that all of the changes you made to files while the Code Profiler is running are lost when you stop the Profiler. For this reason, you need to make sure that all changes you make to the Code Profiler's copies of your files also need to be made in your original project files, after you have stopped the Profiler.

Performing Effective Analysis

When you are running the Code Profiler, generally, you are looking at two aspects of your code.

The first aspect, known as *Code Coverage*, is the process of learning which functions or lines of code in your application are not being run. You may find that your application contains many unused functions or lines of code that are never executed. The additional code increases the size of your executable file and therefore increases the overhead required by your application. This leads to decreased performance.

The Code Profiler provides two profile types that help in analyzing your project's Code Coverage—Line Hit Count and Function Hit Count. If you are only interested in how often functions are executed, select the Function Hit Count profile. If you are interested in how often individual lines of code are executed, select the Line Hit Count option.

The second aspect is known as *Code Optimization*. Code Optimization is the process of determining which lines of codes of functions in your project are run most often, as well as determining which functions or lines of code require the most time to execute. When you determine which processes take the most time, you can take steps to improve their speed, thereby improving the overall speed of your application.

The Code Profiler provides two profiles to help you determine your project's Code Optimization—Line Timing and Function Timing. If you want to look at your code from a high level, the Function Timing profile will allow you to quickly determine which functions are being accessed most often and requiring the largest amount of time to process. If you are interested in a low-level detail of the exact lines of code that are being executed most frequently or using the largest amount of processor time, use the Line Timing profile.

Regardless of whether you are testing your application's Code Coverage or Code Optimization, you should create a testing script to profile your application rather than randomly calling functions or executed lines of code. Using a testing strip enables you to consistently re-create testing situations and allows you to evaluate how changes you make to your code affect the profile.

From Here...

After reading this chapter, you should understand how to set up a development environment, a coding environment, and a debugging environment. You also should be familiar with the tools and features that Visual Basic 4.0 provides to make setting up each of these environments simpler.

For more information about the subjects covered in this chapter, read the following:

- Chapter 6, "Creating OLE Objects," details the creation of OLE Objects and the standard methods and properties that are included with them.

- Chapter 8, "Architecting Tier 1: Client Applications," describes guidelines for creating client applications including information on GUI design.

- Chapter 14, "Architecting Error Processing," for more information on creating error-trapping routines in your Visual Basic code.

- Chapter 19, "Version Control and Team Development," for more information on compatible OLE automation servers and using the Visual Basic SourceSafe Add-In.

IV

Application Enhancements

Chapter 21

Organizing the Development Approach

In the first 20 chapters, we discussed how to architect three-tier client/server applications. Construction of such applications takes time and involves people. This final chapter before the sample applications discusses how real people can organize themselves to approach three-tier client/server development.

This chapter doesn't provide a complete methodology, which is beyond the scope of this book. Instead, it provides you with a high-level overview of the characteristics of successful three-tier solutions development approaches. In doing so, we draw from Microsoft's own methodology, the Microsoft Solution's Framework (MSF), as well as from aspects from Clarity Consulting's refinement approach to application development, called Clarify.

Why talk about methodology at all in this book? Because traditional method-ologies do not adequately address the needs of three-tier client/server solu-tions. In particular, a project approach should incorporate the following characteristics:

- A milestone-based, risk-driven process model that incorporates proto-types, refinement steps, and user feedback

- Distribution of application services and developers to facilitate reusability

- Small teams with well-defined goals and relatively flat organizational hierarchies

- Flexibility to accommodate constantly changing technology and business requirements

These characteristics are common to both MSF and Clarify. Traditional development approaches don't necessarily prevent you from incorporating these characteristics' goals—they simply don't facilitate them. Traditional methodologies were designed for a more static environment, not today's component-based, technical, and evolving business environment. Changing the systems development process requires rethinking the development culture and infrastructure.

This chapter doesn't force-feed you a project approach. Rather, it gives you specific ideas that you should adapt to the way your organization currently develops applications. Because MSF is available publicly and Microsoft encourages people to become familiar with it, the bulk of this chapter will present these concepts within the context of MSF, and compare and contrast MSF with Clarify.

Microsoft Solutions Framework

The Microsoft Solutions Framework (MSF) was created by Microsoft Consulting Services (MCS) to provide a set of guidelines on how corporations should approach the creation of component-based, three-tier client/server solutions.

MCS provides a set of training seminars, CD-ROMs, white papers, case studies, and other materials to disseminate this information to the public. You can obtain these materials directly from Microsoft—see the end of the chapter for details.

The area of MSF on which this chapter will focus is the area most applicable to Visual Basic developers—the Solutions Development Discipline (SDD).

SDD acknowledges that the rapidly evolving development environment requires a framework for client/server development rather than specific methods, techniques, and tools. SDD provides such a framework for designing applications, structuring teams, and planning the delivery process.

SDD is divided into three primary models:

- **Application Model**—The MSF application model defines how applications should be architected and encourages service-based application architectures. The bulk of this book describes how to create these applications with Visual Basic 4 Enterprise Edition.

- **Team Model**—The MSF team model defines how groups of peers with differing roles make up the project teams.

■ **Process Model**—The MSF process model defines how projects are planned and executed with teams from the team model.

The SDD models incorporate all you need to know about building service-based applications. The application model shows how the application is designed, the team model shows who is involved, and the process model shows you how it all should be managed.

The Application Model

The application model describes how client/server systems should be designed. One of the fallacies of client/server development is that it is "easier" than traditional host-based development. Although GUIs have made users' lives easier, developing, maintaining, and enhancing two-tier client/server systems is challenging to the IT department.

An application model addresses this issue by defining a standard architecture that overcomes these development, maintenance, and enhancement challenges. The service-based application architecture detailed in this book and advocated by MSF addresses these issues.

For example, a single client/server solution can easily involve more than 10 rapidly changing technologies that address database design, stored procedure development, GUI design, business rule development, and other aspects. By isolating components, the services model enables developers to avoid acquiring expertise in many different technologies. Instead, the technical team can specialize in particular technologies.

Likewise, when a single piece of system functionality needs to change, or a key component has been enhanced by a third-party vendor, only the component that provides that functionality needs to be modified. Traditionally, the entire application would need to be modified, tested, and distributed to all users.

A clearly defined application model is critical: it defines how these distributed components interact. Without clearly defined guidelines and standards, it is unlikely that independent designers and developers will create components that interact well.

As discussed in this book, component services are defined in three layers: user services, business services, and data services. Because so much of this book was dedicated to describing such services, we will not discuss them here in the context of MSF.

The Team Model

The SDD team model advocates small teams of peers working in interdependent and cooperating roles. Each team member should have a well-defined role on the project and be working toward specific, well-defined goals and deliverables.

Team Roles

SDD has identified six team roles:

- Product Management
- Program Management
- Development
- Test and Quality Assurance
- User Education
- Logistics Planning

Depending on the project size, several people may play the same role. Likewise, multiple roles may be played by a single person. See figure 21.1 for the relationship of these roles.

Fig. 21.1
MSF's six project team roles.

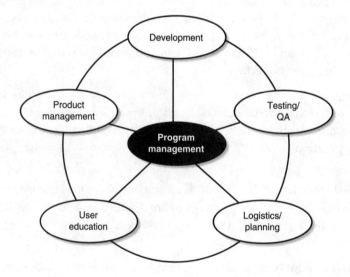

All of the responsibilities of these roles are critical to the success of *any* development project. You should think about the way you approach project development and think about how these roles fit into your organization's project structure. Consider formalizing these roles into your organization's project if they are not present. For example, many organizations fail to adequately address user education (for example, training) and logistics planning (for example, roll-out and conversions). Neglecting to address all of the missions of these roles is a primary contributor to initial client/server project failure.

Each team member role contributes to the team as a peer—no role is more important or has more authority than another. MSF defines each role in terms of a mission, responsibility, and skill-set.

The role's mission is a succinct statement that describes the ultimate goal of the role's responsibilities. No matter how your development team is organized, each role should have a mission. A mission enables you to constantly perform "reality-checks": Is this role's responsibility accomplishing its mission? The aggregation of all the missions of your project teams' roles should encompass everything that needs to occur for a successful project.

Product Management

Mission. Establish and maintain the project's business case. Communicate the project's vision and goals to the project development team as well as the user community.

Responsibilities. Product management is responsible for ensuring that the priorities of the project team address the priorities of the business. Product management is responsible for high-level interaction with the user community, such as budgeting, long-term strategic planning, major milestones, and staffing.

Skills. Product management should have a solid understanding of the business and the users' system requirements. They don't need development skills, but should have a strong understanding of the technology. Product management is most similar to the role of a typical IT organization's senior manager, who often manages multiple projects.

Program Management

Mission. Manage the day-to-day coordination of the project life cycle, and drive the application's specific features and functionality.

Responsibilities. Program management is responsible for the functional specification and scope of the system (what it will do). Program management is responsible for the following:

- Coordinating with external technical groups. This enables the developers to work without getting bogged down with external meetings, and enables program management to identify the opportunity to leverage others' work.

- Managing project scope and change.

- Managing and consolidating the overall project plan, although developers and other team members still maintain their own project schedules.

Skills. Program management needs strong communication skills to effectively coordinate and communicate across teams. Program management also needs management and discipline skills in order to keep people on track. Program management also should have solid technical skills so that they can understand cross-functional technical issues and specifications. Program management is most similar to a typical IT organization's middle project manager who maintains the project workplan and manages the day-to-day activities of the project.

Development

Mission. Construct a system that implements the original functional design.

Responsibilities. Development should actively participate in the design and sign-off of the functional specification. Many organizations don't proceed this way—development is not involved in deciding project functionality and timelines. Doing so, however, encourages accountability and actually leads to more accurate and more successful systems.

Skills. Client/server systems development requires familiarity with 3GLs, 4GLs, database design, database programming, and networking products all from multiple vendors. It's difficult to find people who have in-depth knowledge and experience in all areas. The services model enables developers to concentrate on a particular area of development expertise for a particular project. Typically, a development lead has the experience and skill to understand how all the technologies will integrate. The SDD development role is similar to the traditional IT developer role.

Testing and Quality Assurance (QA)

Mission. Verify and ensure compliance with all project deliverables, independently of other team members.

Responsibilities. Test/QA is responsible for ensuring that the system complies with the functional specification. Test/QA works closely with but independently of the development team. Test/QA implements test plans and tracks bugs.

Skills. The bulk of the testing team needs basic technical skills similar to the skills of developers. The test/QA team must be led, however, by someone who has solid architectural and development skills. Thorough testing of complex client/server systems encompasses many areas, including desktop configuration, performance, networks, and interoperability. Many IT organizations neglect to formalize and separate the testing team from the development team.

User Education

Mission. Ensure that the end-user community can use the system effectively.

Responsibilities. To ensure that the users can use the system effectively, user education is responsible for creating educational materials, such as online documentation, system documentation, and instructional materials. User education is responsible for coordinating all required training classes.

Skills. User education teams must have excellent communication skills and be capable of effectively communicating the technology to the end users. User educators should have excellent written and spoken communication skills. User education often isn't properly accounted for in the typical IT organization.

Logistics Planning

Mission. Ensure that the system rolls out smoothly.

Responsibilities. Rolling out complex distributed client/server systems requires careful planning. Logistics is responsible for managing a smooth transition from development to operations, including all conversions that must take place.

Skills. Logistics should be familiar with the corporate culture and infrastructure. They should have a solid understanding of the development and operations skills. A typical IT organization does not formalize logistics, instead leaving technically challenging roll-outs to already busy developers and operations.

Team Characteristics

Before discussing the characteristics of how these team roles are composed, take a step back to see the goals of the MSF team structure:

- To give all team members the opportunity to benefit from the success of the system

- To provide a project culture that encourages clarity, efficiency, and team member participation

- To improve accountability and task ownership

- To allow the developers to stay focused on their development tasks, instead of being pulled in many different unproductive directions

The most effective way to attain these goals with the team structure is to limit the size of each functional team to no more than three to seven people. If the project requires more work than can be accomplished by a such a team size, the work and the team should be partitioned into more manageable tasks.

Some characteristics of this team structure and goals follow:

- All team members participate and sign off on their schedule and deliverables.

- All team members focus on and understand the business problem, not just the technology solution.

- All team members understand how their role fits in and how they are critical to the success of the project.

In many situations, an entire project team consists of only a handful of people. In this case, project roles must be combined into the same individual or individuals.

Risky Combinations

Some roles have distinct skill sets and conflicting short-term goals. When combining multiple roles into the same individual, several combinations may have risk associated with them.

Product manager and program manager. A product manager is responsible for the big picture; his or her individual performance is often based upon meeting end-user expectations. A program manager, however, is responsible for the day-to-day activities of the project and the project team. A single person cannot impartially represent both parties.

Program management and development. Developers tend to focus on technology for technology's sake, even if it doesn't represent the business' best interest in terms of performance, business impact, release dates, and operational support. Program management, on the other hand, is responsible for managing the schedule and the functional specification. A single person may compromise project release dates or business functionality.

Development and test/QA. Developers cannot be expected to test their own code. Developers may show bias as to how well their code works or see the code from only a single perspective.

Complementary Combinations

Product management, user education, and logistics planning are all focused on end users and a smooth roll-out. These roles can be combined in a single person.

The Process Model

MSF's process model is designed to accommodate the characteristics of client/server platforms. The following Solutions Development Discipline (SDD) process model:

- Is driven by milestones

- Identifies team individual responsibility

- Prioritizes risk

- Is iterative

The traditional systems development life cycle (SDLC) used by many companies is task-driven. Generally, these traditional methodologies are composed of distinct steps, such as requirements, design, development, testing, and release.

These methodologies are often referred to as the "waterfall" process model. The name implies that a set of tasks must be completed before subsequent tasks can begin. This model has a number of bad characteristics, including: different people work on different phases of the project, each phase must be excruciatingly documented for a different team to continue the next phase, and early decisions are difficult to change later in the process. The waterfall model is task-driven, not milestone-driven.

Milestone-Based

The SDD process model is based on milestones (see fig. 21.2). The four high-level milestones are as follows:

- Vision- and Scope-Approved

- Functional Specification-Approved

- Code Complete

- Release

Fig. 21.2
The four Solutions
Development
Discipline
milestones.

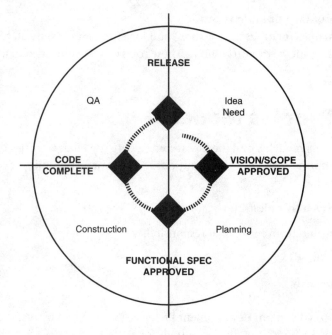

After a new project builds up momentum and interest within an organization, the project's vision and goals are defined. It's during this time that the user community and project teams come to agree on the scope and vision of the project, as well as to rough estimates of timelines and resources.

The next major milestone is the *functional specification*. The specification should provide the project team with enough detail about exact timelines and resource requirements. At the specification approval milestone, end users and the project team should be in agreement as to exactly what is going to be produced and in what time frame. This step incorporates prototypes and traditional requirements and design tasks.

When the functional specification is approved, heads-down development can begin. Development ends with an important milestone: Code Complete. At this milestone, the project and user teams approve the release, and the development of all new functionality is deferred to the next release.

Although testing and QA activities occur during development, they pick up after the Code Complete milestone. The Release milestone is where the application is formally turned over to the end users and operations groups.

Checkpoints within Milestones

For long projects, having only four milestones doesn't provide adequate visibility and control to the project's progression. In SDD, interim checkpoints are established by the teams to formally surface issues and status to program management and other teams.

These interim checkpoints are both external (inter-team) or internal (intra-team). You probably are familiar with these checkpoints and how they help manage lengthy projects. Examples of external checkpoints include the following:

- Regularly scheduled status meetings

- Making drafts of functional specifications publicly available

Examples of internal checkpoints include the following:

- Short-term deliverables managed in one- to two-week intervals

- Formal team synchronization to ensure that everyone's interpretation of the functional specification is consistent

Milestone Accountability and Tasks

Each team model's roles unambiguously owns each of the process model's milestones (see fig. 21.3).

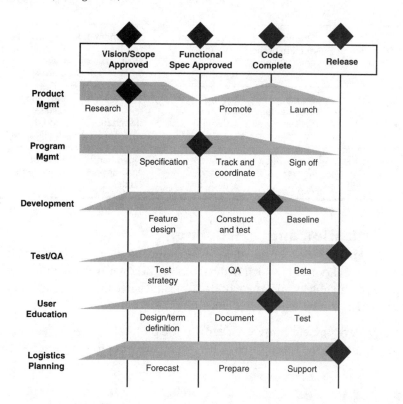

Fig. 21.3
Each process model milestone is owned by one or more of the team model's roles.

This ownership and clearly defined responsibility encourages team coordination. Table 21.1 shows the general tasks associated with each team role.

Table 21.1	General Tasks Associated with Each Team Role			
Team Role	Vision/ Scope Approved	Functional Specific. Approved	Code Complete	Release
	Requirements and needs definition	System Planning	Construction/ Development	Quality Assurance
Product Management	Product definition and research	Vision refinement and user expectations	Promotion, packaging, and pricing	Beta coordination and project launch
Program Management	Conceptual architecture	Feature analysis, specific., and schedule	Specification and project status management	Project status management
Development	Consulting	Evaluation, design, plan, and schedule	Development, internal releases	Bug fixing and performance tuning
User Education	Strategy: documentation and training	Documentation plan and help plan schedule	Documentation and help creation	Documentation help, and training delivery
Test/QA	Define acceptable delivery	Testing plan and schedule	Testing and stabilization	Beta and release candidate stabilization
Logistics Planning	Deployment impact	Roll-out plan and schedule	Operations and support guidelines	Roll-out management

Prioritization and Scheduling

The SDD process model is iterative, risk-driven, and milestone-based. Milestones are not points at which deliverables are necessarily frozen; they are points at which deliverables are understood and agreed upon, so subsequent scope changes can be properly handled.

Because development is involved early in the project lifecycle, development can take part in the specification with prototypes and proof-of-concepts to identify risk and increase project planning accuracy. This does not necessarily mean development can't begin developing before this milestone, nor does it mean that this early development work should be throw-away.

Important pieces of functionality and unproved technologies should be prioritized and addressed earlier in the lifecycle to enable the project team to more quickly identify and deal with risk. For example, if you are incorporating the first release of a vendor's product (such as a third-party OLE control) that is critical to the success of the system, it should probably be checked early in the process.

Phased and Versioned Releases

In a typical corporate IT department, a clear distinction exists between system development and system maintenance. Likewise, there is a tendency to pack as many features into an application as possible, sometimes at the expense of testing or delivery dates.

There are three finite project parameters that must be managed:

- *Schedule*. Refers to deliver date and project timeline.

- *Scope*. Refers to features.

- *Resources*. Refers to the number and type of project team members.

Because technology and business change so rapidly, SDD suggests that the schedule parameter be identified and fixed early. Typically, schedule is the parameter that fluctuates most. The thought is that it's better to release partial functionality and defer less-important features until a future release date.

For scope to be adjusted and accepted like this, however, organizations must change the traditional development versus maintenance mindset. Instead, SDD suggests a product mindset—that users *can* expect future releases and any organization's systems will continuously evolve, based on the changing organizational needs and priorities. Features not included in a given release will be methodically tracked and reevaluated for future releases.

Solution Design

The MSF solution design approach provides a model that accounts for distribution of both the processes and data. It ties together the application model, team model, and process model.

The enterprise architecture encompasses the following four perspectives:

- Business
- Application
- Data
- Technology

The sum of these four perspectives defines the corporate architectural direction. An organization should have a single enterprise architecture.

The Design Process

MSF defines a process for defining and managing the service-based components' functionality and interfaces. This helps manage the complexity of building distributed, component-based solutions with many team members.

Design evolves iteratively. However, design is viewed from the following three perspectives:

- A conceptual view, from the end-user community
- A logical view, from the project team
- A physical view, from the development team

MSF draws an analogy between this system architecture approach and building construction architecture.

First, the architect draws a conceptual view of the project incorporating basic concepts, metrics, prototypes, and scope. This stage corresponds to the conceptual view of the project.

Next, the architect draws up specific plans that contractors can use to determine specific resources, costs, and timelines. This stage corresponds to the logical view of a project.

Finally, plans are created for the builder. This step takes into account materials, equipment, and technology. Timelines are finalized. This stage corresponds to the physical view of the project.

As the design evolves through the conceptual, logical, and physical stages, all of the design views are captured in a single functional specification document to ensure that the original business requirements are constantly being addressed. The functional specification is an evolving document.

As defined in Chapter 9, "Architecting Tier 2: Business Servers," these design phases are driven by the following different attributes:

- User requirements drive the conceptual design.
- Business objects and services drive the logical design.
- Components drive the physical design.

Conceptual Design

The conceptual design audience is the end-user community. The conceptual design is user-centric and should reflect how the users view the solution. It should describe the different usage scenarios and their rationale. Although risk identification and planning should occur throughout the entire development lifecycle; the conceptual design phase should focus on risk assessment.

A *usage scenario* is more-or-less a flowchart of typical user actions with the application. Usage scenarios are used to answer questions about how the system will be used. They help maintain focus on the actual business problem to solve.

Usage scenarios can be used to describe both the existing system and the ideal new system. Examining the existing system ensures that dependencies, such as downstream effect, will surface.

Usage scenarios can be discovered several ways, such as the following:

- End-user interviews and observation
- Joint Application Development (JAD) sessions
- Prototyping
- Examination of the existing system and documentation

Usage scenarios can be documented in many ways. They can contain narrative text, work-flow diagrams, tables, and screen shots. It isn't important how usage scenarios are structured, provided they serve their purpose.

Logical Design

The logical design adds additional detail to the conceptual design to facilitate communication among the project team. Logical design defines business services and their objects so that the team has a clear view of how the system should operate. The functional specification should include this design as well as the rationale behind not choosing other alternatives.

The logical design should be technology independent. Realistically, however, the feasibility of the logical design may depend on existing technology.

MSF is an object-based approach. In MSF, objects are encapsulations of data and business logic; objects are not simply functions and procedures. Business objects are the key to reusing organizational code. An object-based approach such as MSF does not, however, require any specific object technology, such as C++.

A *business object* is a logical encapsulation of related business functionality derived from usage scenarios. Business objects should be designed so that they encapsulate related business functionality and have minimal dependency on other business objects.

Existing systems can be encapsulated by business objects so that the existing system appears as any other business object. This was described in Chapter 10, "Architecting Tier 3: Data Servers," where an example of encapsulating legacy host-based systems was presented.

You can break down the logical design process into three parallel tracks: the user interface track, the business service track, and the data service track.

Physical Design

The *physical design* maps the logical design to the tangible world. The physical design is primarily the concern of development. It provides a concrete definition of the system's components and interfaces. Like the conceptual and logical design, physical design is maintained in the functional specification.

The physical design maps the logical design to specific technologies. An application is a set of services that, working together, solves a business problem. When two applications require the same service, they share a common component that implements that service. The physical design process involves deciding on whether a service needs to be developed, or whether it can be accommodated by an existing component.

Component changes need to be applied consistently in all systems that utilize the component. The component can be maintained in several ways, such as a centralized file server, a CASE tool, a repository, or a source-code control system. Components can be distributed on floppy disks, over the network, or through automated tools. It's important to ensure that a clearly defined and workable method for managing components is in place.

Infrastructure

MSF defines *infrastructure* as the technologies and standards, operational processes, and people that are needed to support the enterprise. The infrastructure supports the overall business, technology, applications, and data architectures, with a focus on the technology architecture.

The technology architecture should identify both the organization's general technical need and the specific organizational-standard products that address the technical needs. Table 21.2 shows a Microsoft-centric view of possible standards.

Table 21.2   A Microsoft-Centric Technical Infrastructure

General Need	Specific Product Examples
Server hardware	Compaq, HP, Sequent, DEC
Server operating system	Windows NT, UNIX
Server relational database	SQL Server, Oracle
Server low-level language	Visual C++
Server high-level language	Visual Basic
Database language	SQL Server Transact-SQL
Client hardware	Compaq, Micron
Client operating system	Windows 95, Windows NT Workstation
Client relational database	Access
Client low-level language	Visual C++
Client high-level language	Visual Basic
Client meta language	OLE wrappers via VC or VB
Network hardware	Cisco, 3Com®
Network low-level protocol	TCP/IP
Network high-level protocol	Sockets -> RPC -> OLE
Gateway(s) and bridges	Micro Decisionware, SQL Solutions
Batch language and scheduler	MS Test, AT command
Other specific standards	WOSA

The technology infrastructure product list should be enforced as strongly as possible. Realistically, however, this list will grow and evolve as technology becomes obsolete or outdated. The infrastructure should be validated to ensure that all products will work together reliably. As new technologies are added, a formal impact analysis should occur and the technology should be validated. To remain competitive, organizations must be ready to respond relatively quickly to technology changes.

When new technologies are introduced in an organization, they generally affect existing operations and procedures. They typically affect corporate operations, disaster-recovery, and security.

The core project teams should already have most of the skills needed to implement the project. Some specialized skills, however, may be considered infrastructure and may need to be leveraged across projects. These skills include the following:

- Graphic design
- User training
- Database performance tuning
- Network and communications
- Database modeling and design
- Security
- Product-specific skills

Clarify

The authors' firm, Clarity Consulting, Inc., has its own refinement approach to application development, called Clarify. Clarify is similar to MSF, but it's geared more toward adapting to existing corporate IT culture and Clarity's specific project engagements.

This section highlights some of the key differences between Clarify and MSF. By reading this section, you will see how aspects of MSF differ from other service-based development approaches. In addition, you may find some aspects of Clarify applicable to your organization.

MSF is a reflection of Microsoft's roots in many-user, commercial software developed by exceptionally capable teams. Typical corporate applications, however, are characterized by few-user, custom database-centric applications that are developed by teams that don't necessarily have sophisticated skill sets.

Team Model

Clarity has found that, often, corporate projects have limited resources dedicated to the entire project lifecycle. It is common to find that an organization needs to build an entire application with approximately five to ten team members and one- to three-month releases. In addition, the development work often demands the bulk of the team's resources.

MSF's team model, which contains six different roles, must be adapted to accommodate such a small project team that may not have the luxury of devoting dedicated resources to all six roles' responsibilities, while still not deviating too sharply from existing corporate IT culture.

With Clarify, team roles might be organized as follows (with number of resources in parentheses):

- **Project Sponsor** (.25). Similar to MSF's product management and project management. Most likely, an IT senior manager who is devoted only part time to the project.

- **Project Manager** (1.0). Similar to MSF's program management. Responsible for overall team and milestone management.

- **Technical Manager** (1.0). Similar to MSF's development, test/QA, and logistics team leads, all rolled into a single individual. A jack-of-all technical trades.

- **Technical Architect** (2.0). Similar to MSF's development. Focuses on business and data service (DBA) development.

- **Analyst Developer** (1.0). Similar to MSF's development. Focuses on user and business service development.

Unfortunately, logistics, test/QA, and user-education responsibilities usually must be incorporated into these individual responsibilities. In this scenario, the risk of having developers perform test/QA tasks can be lessened by ensuring that the project manager takes a lead role in the process, as well as having developers not test their own code, only other developers' code.

These roles tend to require less of an organizational change for existing corporate IT structures, yet still provide the benefits of the MSF model.

Process Model

MSF draws analogies from Microsoft's commercial product-driven software approach which, although valid, is sometimes difficult to relate to in an existing corporate environment.

Most organizations need to identify project scope, risk, and business impact before significant resources can be dedicated to the project. MSF needs to address the need for up-front business impact and costs by creating such a business case without significant team resources.

Most organizations aren't ready to accept the product-driven approach to application development that views a system as constantly evolving and thereby completely abandons the traditional waterfall approach. This can be tempered by serializing the parallel aspect of versioned releases.

These trade-offs from the formal MSF approach generally lower the overall quality of the systems. But they also tend to lower the overall costs, timelines, and risks. Certainly the goal of corporate development should be zero-defect software. Most corporate development environments, however, have a greater tolerance for defects than commercial software.

Until organizations can fully appreciate the iterative client/server software development process, however, you'll need to adapt MSF and similar approaches to what your existing corporate culture will tolerate.

From Here...

For more information on MSF, contact your local Microsoft Consulting Services office or read the Microsoft Press book from Ken Spencer on MSF, due in early 1996.

For more information on three-tier client/server development with VB4, read *Building Client/Server Applications,* which is included with Visual Basic 4 Enterprise Edition.

For an excellent general overview of distributed applications, see *Client/Server Strategies: A Survival Guide for Corporate Reengineers*, by David Vaskevitch (IDG Press), who is the Director of Enterprise Computing for Microsoft.

In this chapter, you learned about techniques for changing a traditional development approach to better accommodate service-based application development. For more information about development approaches, go to the following chapters:

- Chapter 8, "Architecting Tier 1: Client Applications," provides more information on creating user services.

- Chapter 9, "Architecting Tier 2: Business Servers," provides more information on creating business services.

- Chapter 10, "Architecting Tier 3: Data Servers," provides more information on creating data services.

IV

Application Enhancemnets

Part V

Sample Applications

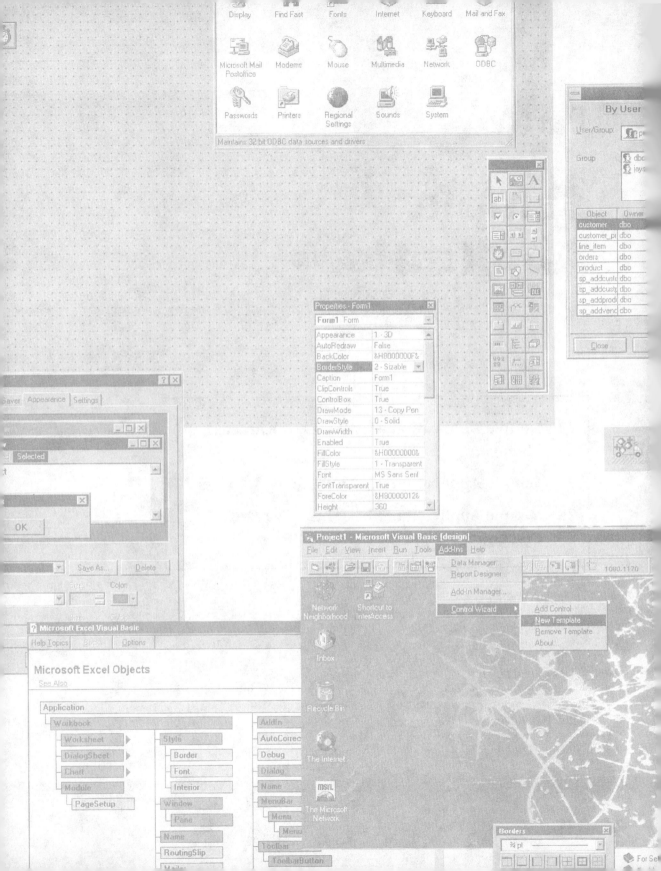

## Chapter 22

Sample Application #1: An OLE Document Manager

This chapter describes the overall architecture of the OLE Document Manager application included with this book. This chapter covers the following areas:

- Application description

- Summary of files included with application

- Steps to install the application

- A quick tour of the application's screens and functionality

- Design of the business, data, and user services

- Limitations of the OLE container control

OLE Documents in Applications

Many Windows applications use documents. Excel provides spreadsheet documents, Word provides word-processing documents, and Project provides project timeline documents. In each case, the document is the part of the application that can be edited by the user. The application provides tools and formatting features—such as fonts, colors, and spell checking—to aid the user in creating high-quality, professional-looking documents.

Usually, an application specializes in creating and editing one type of document. It includes a comprehensive list of features that make it the best solution for creating this type of document. You can use Excel, for example, to create a word-processing document because it allows you to type formatted text into cells. Word, however, provides a better interface for doing so, as well as several tools, such as table creation and bulleting, which makes it the choice for creating word-processing documents.

Business tasks often require that a user works with several kinds of documents. When creating a year-end marketing report, for example, you may need to create a word-processing document, a spreadsheet document, and a chart document. The user works with Word to create the word-processing document and Excel to create the spreadsheet and chart documents.

Trying to incorporate documents generated by different server applications can pose a few problems to the typical user in the enterprise. These problems are outlined in the following sections.

Launching Applications and Navigating Menus

As a user, you first need to know how to start each application from the Program Manager in Windows 3.1 or the Start menu in Windows 95. You also need to be familiar with the menu functions in each application. Does the Close menu option in Excel, for example, work in the same way as the Close menu option in Microsoft Word?

Many applications are part of application suites. These suites bundle four or five specialized products, such as Word and Excel, into one package. Although each application exists as a separate executable file, these suites usually provide a launching mechanism, such as the Microsoft Office Manager, which allows users to launch applications from a floating toolbar rather than from the Program Manager. Additionally, great effort was exerted to make the application's interfaces behave as similarly as possible. This similarity helps guarantee that the Close menu option in Word behaves in the same way as the Close menu option in Excel.

These models still require a user to navigate Windows and access different kinds of documents. After the applications are launched from the Microsoft Office Manager, Windows 3.1 users, for example, need to press Alt+Tab to move between applications. After an application becomes active, users must navigate the Window menu option to display the documents currently open within the application.

Lack of Central Storage

The suite model of applications doesn't provide a means for central storage of documents. You can create a folder called MyDocs, for example, in which you place all spreadsheets, word-processing documents, and charts. This folder requires a separate application, such as the Windows Explorer, to maintain. Additionally, the Explorer displays all types of files, such as application files, configuration files, and data files. You can lose documents easily in this mix. You also still need to launch the word-processing application to open any word-processing documents and the spreadsheet application to open any spreadsheet documents.

Addressing OLE Document Limitation Issues

Application suites begin to address the issue of windows navigation by providing a single interface that can display each type of document in the suite. Microsoft Office, for example, allows you to create a chart document, a spreadsheet, and a word-processing document, all from the same application. Each document is displayed in a separate window, but you don't need to use Alt+Tab to switch between applications.

These suites also allow you to store different kinds of documents in a single file, which makes them both portable and easy to manage. You can save and then e-mail to a colleague the file that contains the chart, word-processing document, and spreadsheet. Visual Basic also provides several features that allow developers to help simplify the task of generating OLE documents from different server applications.

Using Visual Basic's OLE Document Features

You learned in Chapter 5, "Controlling OLE Objects," that Visual Basic's OLE container control can be used to insert OLE documents exposed by applications, such as Word and Excel, into a Visual Basic application. Many server applications that expose the OLE documents are capable of visual editing. Visual editing enables the server application's menus and toolbars to merge with the container application's menus and toolbars. This merging provides many server application functions—formatting, spell-checking features, and so on—within the container application.

Merging the menus also means that a developer does not need to write code to duplicate the formatting features that are included with the server application, which saves development time and includes the functions needed to easily create professional-looking documents.

One exception does occur. When an OLE document is visually edited, the server application's File menu isn't merged with the container application's menu, which gives developers an opportunity to include custom Save, Open, and Close commands. You can develop a Visual Basic application, for example, that saves documents to a database when the Save menu option is selected. Additionally, after users understand the effects of selecting the Save option in the File menu of the container application, they know how to save any kind of document created in the application.

OLE Document Manager Sample App

The OLE Document Manager sample application included with this book is a demonstration of how to use Visual Basic to help a user perform the following two functions:

- Create different types of OLE document within a single application

- Store these OLE documents to a database

The OLE Document Manager is built upon a three-tier architecture, separating application components into user services, business services, and data services. Additionally, the application uses many of the new features that are included with Visual Basic, such as visual editing and the enhanced Windows 95 OLE Control set.

The Document Manager allows users to create Excel worksheets and Word documents, and then edit them in place. Toolbar and menu negotiation allows the OLE Document Manager to include many of the tools and formatting functions available in Word and Excel. After an OLE document is created, it can be stored in the OLE Document Manager's database, which provides a central, portable means of OLE document storage.

The OLE Document Manager Files

This section details all the files included in the document manager application. You can find these files on this book's companion disk, in the \DOCMGR\ directory.

Table 22.1 shows the sample application files found in the \DOCMGR\ directory.

Table 22.1	Document Manager Application Files	
Directory	**File**	**Description**
\DOCMGR\TIER1		**The client application**
	DOCMAN.EXE	Client application executable
	DOCHOLD.FRM	Document container form
	DOCHOLD.FRX	Dochold.frm's resource file
	DOCLIST.FRM	Document type list form
	DOCTREE.FRM	Document explorer form
	DOCTREE.FRX	Doctree.frm's resource file
	DOCMOD.BAS	Document manager's code module file
	DOCMAN.VBP	Document manager project file
\DOCMGR\TIER2		**The business services**
	DOCMGR.EXE	Object executable
	OLEAPP.CLS	The object's application class
	OLEDIR.CLS	The object's directory class
	OLEDIRS.CLS	The object's directories class
	OLEDOC.CLS	The object's document class
	OLEDOCS.CLS	The object's documents class
	OLETYPE.CLS	The object's doctype class
	OLETYPES.CLS	The object's doctypes class
	GENERAL.BAS	General module
	OLEMGR.VBP	Project file
\DOCMGR\TIER3		**The data services**
	DOCMGR.MDB	The document manager's Access database
	DOCMGR.LDB	The database's record locking file
	DOCMGR.SQL	SQL file for generating the SQL Server version of the database

V

Sample Applications

Installation Instructions

This section details installation of the Sample instance manager application.

> **Note**
>
> These are 32-bit applications, and must be installed under Windows 95 or Windows NT.

To install the Sample application locally, take the following steps:

1. Copy the entire \DOCMGR\ directory structure from the companion disk to your system's hard-drive.

2. From a DOS command prompt, type `\DocMgr\DocMgr.exe /regserver` to register the manager server.

To install the Sample application's database:

1. Click Start, and then Setting, and finally Control Panel.

2. Double-click the 32-bit ODBC manager.

3. On the Data Sources window, click the Add button.

4. You must create an ODBC data source, which allows the application to connect to the database using ODBC. The Document Manager application has been tested against a SQL Server 6.0 back-end and an Access 2.0 back-end.

> **Note**
>
> This application was not tested against Access 95.

When creating a data source, you must decide whether you will use the sample Access database supplied with the application, or create a SQL Server database and use the included SQL scripts to generate the appropriate tables and stored procedures. If you want to use SQL Server, move on to step 4a. If you would rather use Access 2.0, skip to step 5.

4a. If you plan to use a SQL Server database, enter the SQL Enterprise Manager and create a new database named **DOCMGR**. Then run the DOCMGR.SQL script (located in the DOCMGR\TIER3\ directory), using the SQL Enterprise Manager's Query Analzer tool, which can be found in the SQL Server group of the Program Manager. This script creates all the tables and stored procedures needed to run the Document Manager sample application.

4b. After the DOCMGR database is created, you will need to create a SQL Server data source. To do this, click the SQL Server driver from the list of 32-bit ODBC drivers on the 32-bit ODBC administrator application.

4c. Click the OK button.

4d. When the Database Setup window appears on-screen, enter the following information:

Data Source Name: **Document Manager Database**

Description: **Document Manager Sample App Database**

Server: Type the name of the SQL Server where your document manager database resides.

Network Address: Leave as default.

Network Language: Leave as default.

4e. Click the Options button and enter the following information:

> Database Name: **DOCMGR**.

4f. Click the OK button after you finish.

4g. You can now exit the 32-bit ODBC administrator application.

5. If you want to use the Access 2.0 database supplied with the application, you need a 32-bit ODBC driver for Access. This driver can be found in Microsoft's ODBC Desktop Driver Pack v2.0 or greater. After you have installed the 32-bit driver, you can click the Add button on the 32-bit ODBC administrator application. From the list of 32-bit ODBC drivers, Click the Microsoft Access Driver and then click the OK button.

5a. When the Database Setup window appears on-screen, enter the following information:

> Data Source Name: **Document Manager Database**
>
> Description: **Document Manager Sample App Database**

5b. Click the Select button on the Database frame.

5c. Click on the DOCMGR.MDB database (which is located in the \DOCMGR\TIER3\ directory), and click OK on the Select Database window.

The Setup Database window opens.

5d. Click the OK button on the Setup Database window, and then click on the Data Sources window.

After the sample application is installed, you are ready to take a quick tour of the OLE Document Manager.

A Quick Tour of the Application

When the OLE Document Manager application's .EXE file is run, the Document Explorer (see fig. 22.1), is the first window displayed. The left side of this window shows the hierarchical directory structure of folders used by the application to store OLE documents. When you click on a folder, the OLE document contained within it appears on the right side of the window.

Fig. 22.1

The Document Explorer, the initial window you see after running the OLE Document Manager.

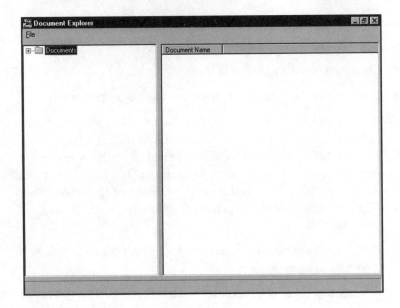

Using the Document Explorer

The Document Explorer uses a standard TreeView control to display the list of folders. If a folder contains one or more folders, a plus sign (+) appears to the left of the folder. This type of folder is known as a *parent* folder. Clicking on the plus sign displays all folders contained within the parent folder. The folders within the parent folder are collectively known as *child* folders.

In figure 22.1, the Main folder is shown in a collapsed state. Figure 22.2 shows the Main folder in an expanded state—after the plus sign was clicked—and all of the Main folder's child folders are visible.

When you click on a folder, the OLE documents contained within the folder appear in the right side of the Document Explorer, listed in alphabetical order. When you double-click on a document or select a document, and then select the Open command from the File menu, the document opens in its own OLE Document window.

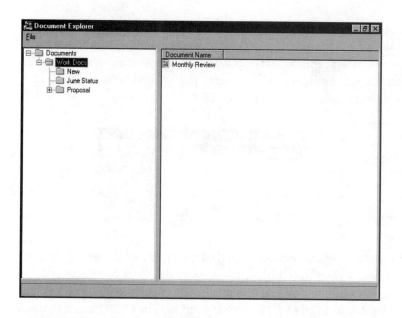

Fig. 22.2
The Main Folder in
an expanded state.

Adding Folders

The first time you run the OLE Document Manager, it contains no folder or documents. To add a new folder to the Document Manager, select the New command from the Document Explorer's File menu. This selection displays the sub-menu shown in figure 22.3 From the sub-menu, select Folder. A new folder is created in the currently selected folder.

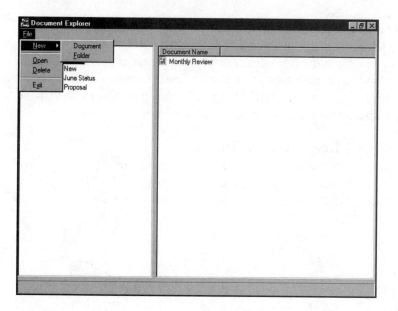

Fig. 22.3
The New menu
item's sub-menu.

Adding Documents

To add a new document, select the <u>N</u>ew command from the Document
Explorer's <u>F</u>ile menu, which displays the sub-menu shown in figure 22.3.
From the sub-menu, select Do<u>c</u>ument. This selection displays the Add
Document window shown in figure 22.4.

Fig. 22.4
The Add Docu-
ment window.

The Add Document window displays a list of OLE document types that can
be created within the OLE Document Manager. Click on the type of document you want to create, and then click OK, which creates a new document
and displays it in an OLE Document window. The OLE Document window is
explained in detail in following sections of this chapter.

Deleting Folders and Documents

To delete a folder or document from the database, highlight the folder
or document, and then select the <u>D</u>elete command from the Document
Explorer's <u>F</u>ile menu. If a folder contains child folders or documents, all
child folders and documents also are deleted.

Renaming Folders and Documents

To change the name of a folder or document, select by clicking on the folder
or document in the Document Explorer. After a short pause, click on the
folder or document again. The current name is highlighted and a cursor appears at the end of the name. After you are finished, type the new name and
click on another folder or outside of the edit area.

The OLE Document Window

Whenever you create a new OLE document or edit an existing document
stored in the database, the document is displayed in the OLE Document
Manager's OLE Document window. The OLE Document window is shown
in figure 22.5.

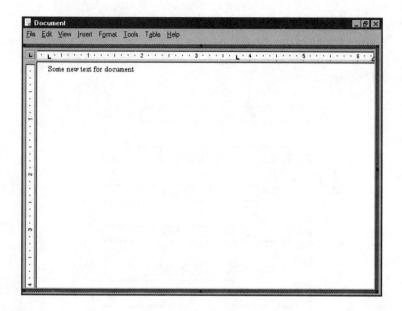

Fig. 22.5
The OLE Document window, showing a Word document.

Using the OLE Document Window

Each OLE document is displayed in a separate OLE Document window. When a new window is loaded, the window's menu and toolbar merge with the OLE document's server application's menu and toolbars. Figure 22.5 shows an OLE Document window, containing a Word document.

You can save the document to the database at any time by selecting the Save command from the File menu. If the document is new, you are asked to supply a file name. After you finish editing the document, select Close from the File menu.

Business Services

All business services of the sample application are contained in the DOCMGR.EXE OLE automation server. The following section details each class contained in the server. For each class, all properties of the class are listed with a brief description. For each method in the class, the code that comprises the method is listed and is followed with a brief description of the function of the method.

The business services contain one visual element—a form that is displayed whenever the DOCMGR.EXE server is running. This form is included for demonstration purposes only. In a production application, you normally would not include such a form, but it is very useful when demonstrating a business server.

The Application Class

The Application class sits at the top of the sample application's object hierarchy (see fig. 22.6). This class exposes two methods—the Directories method and the Documents method.

Fig. 22.6
The OLE Document Manager's object hierarchy.

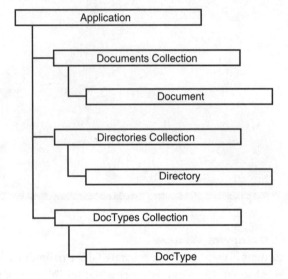

The remainder of this section explains the design of the Application class's methods.

Directories Method

The Directories method returns a collection of all current directories in the application by creating a new collection variable, ldDirCollection, and populating it by using the giFillDirectories function. The Directories method is shown in Listing 22.1. The giFillDirectories function is also used to populate the Directories class during initialization.

Listing 22.1   OLEAPP.CLS—The Directories method returns a collection of all Directory objects that have been stored in the database

```
Public Function Directories() As Collection

    ' Returns the current directories in the
    ' application
    Dim ldDirCollection As New Collection

    giFillDirectories ldDirCollection
    Set Directories = ldDirCollection

End Function
```

Both the Directories class and the `giFillDirectories` function are detailed in following sections of this chapter.

Documents Method

The `Documents` method is similar to the `Directories` method, except that it returns a collection of all documents currently existing in the application. It does so by calling the `giFillDocuments` function that populated the ldDocCollection collection variable. The `Documents` method's code is shown in Listing 22.2. The `giFillDocuments` function, described in a following section of this chapter, is also used by the Documents class.

Listing 22.2   OLEAPP.CLS—The Documents method returns a collection that contains all Documents objects stored in the database

```
Public Function Documents() As Collection

    ' Returns all Documents in Database
    Dim ldDocCollection As New Collection

    giFillDocuments ldDocCollection
    Set Documents = ldDocCollection

End Function
```

DocTypes Method

Finally, the `DocTypes` method returns all available DocTypes in the application. This method uses the `giFillDocTypes` function, described in a following section of this chapter, to populate the ldDocCollection collection variable. The code for the `DocTypes` method is shown in Listing 22.3.

Listing 22.3   OLEAPP.CLS—The DocTypes method returns a collection of all document types available for embedding

```
Public Function DocTypes() As Collection

    ' Returns all types of Documents in app
    Dim ldDocCollection As New Collection

    giFillDocTypes ldDocCollection
    Set DocTypes = ldDocCollection

End Function
```

The Directory Class

The Directory class represents a single directory available to the OLE Document Manager application. A directory can be the child of another directory or the parent of an OLE document. The following section describes the properties and methods of the Directory class.

Properties

A Directory object has the following properties:

- ID

- Name

- ParentID

The *ID* property uniquely identifies each Directory object. This property is set when a new Directory object is created by using the Add method of the Directories class.

The *Name* property is the displayed name of the Directory object as it appears in the client application. A user can change this property through the Update method.

The *ParentID* property identifies the Directory under which the current Directory object sits in the overall directory hierarchy. For example, figure 22.7 shows a sample directory hierarchy.

Fig. 22.7

A sample directory hierarchy.

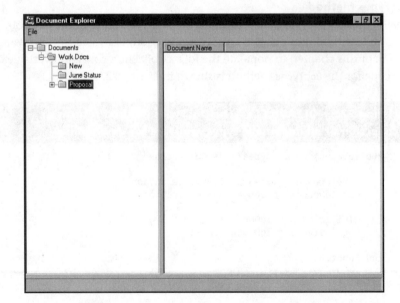

In figure 22.7, the *Work Docs* directory is the parent of the *New, June Status,* and *Proposal* directories.

Update Method

The Update method of the Directory class updates a directory object's Name property setting to the database by calling a stored procedure in the database, passing the Name and ID settings as parameters, and executing the procedure. Listing 22.4 shows the code that makes up the Update method.

Listing 22.4   OLEDIR.CLS—The Update function allows a user to change the name of a Directory object in the database

```
Public Function Update()

    ' Function updates the name of a directory
    ' in the tree view control

    ' Create prepared statement and execute it on database
    Dim lprepStatement As rdoPreparedStatement

    Set lprepStatement =
    gconConnection.CreatePreparedStatement
    ➡("sp_update_directory","{CALL sp_update_directory (?, ?)}")
    lprepStatement.rdoParameters(0).VALUE = Name
    lprepStatement.rdoParameters(1).VALUE = ID
    ' Execute the procedure
    lprepStatement.Execute

    lprepStatement.Close

End Function
```

Using Remote Data Objects, a stored procedure is declared, with an rdoPreparedStatement object. The object is set to a stored procedure in the database, using the CreatePreparedStatement method of a collection object. In the Update method, the following code associates the lprepStatement rdoPreparedStatement object with the sp_update_directory procedure:

```
Set lprepStatement = gconConnection.CreatePreparedStatement
➡("sp_update_directory","{CALL sp_update_directory (?, ?)}")
```

The question-marks (?) at the end of the statement indicate that parameters will be passed when this stored procedure is executed.

The following lines bind the two parameters passed to the stored procedure—the Name and ID properties of the Directory object—to the prepared statement:

V

Sample Applications

```
lprepStatement.rdoParameters(0).VALUE = Name
lprepStatement.rdoParameters(1).VALUE = ID
```

When the prepared statement is executed, the two parameters are passed to the stored procedure.

When associating stored procedures to prepared statement objects, it is important to use the {call *procedurename* (?, ?, ...)} syntax. In this construct, *procedurename* indicates the name of a stored procedure in the database, and a question-mark is used to indicate how many parameters will be passed to the procedure. This syntax is understood by all ODBC-complaint data sources. Using it when declaring prepared statements ensures that your code will run on all ODBC-complaint data sources.

All stored procedures used by the DOCMGR application are described in a following section of this chapter.

The Directories Class

The Directories class is a collection of all current directories in the application. Directories can be created or deleted by using the methods of the Directories class.

When a new instance of the Directories class is created, the Initialize event is fired. The code in the following event populates the class level collection object, prvDirectories, with all of the current directories in the application:

```
Private Sub Class_Initialize()

    giFillDirectories prvDirectories

End Sub
```

This process is done by calling the `giFillDirectories` function, which is explained in a following section of this chapter.

The methods and properties of the Directories class are detailed throughout the remainder of this section.

Count Property

The Count property returns the total number of directories existing in the application. It performs this process by executing the Count property of the prvDirectories class level collection.

```
Public Function Count() As Long

    Count = prvDirectories.Count

End Function
```

Add Method

The Add method of the Directories class creates a new Directory object and adds it to the Directories collection. The code that makes up the Add method is shown in Listing 22.5. This method also adds the new Directory to the database.

Listing 22.5   OLEDIRS.CLS—The Add method inserts a new Directory object into the Directories collection

```
Public Sub Add(aDirectory As Directory, DirKey As String)

    ' Add Item to the database
    Dim lsNewKey As String
    Dim llNewID As Long
    Dim lsNewBookmark As Variant

    ' Open the Directory table. Pull all directories back
    Dim lrsltDirectories As rdoResultset
    Dim ltbDirectories As rdoTable

    Set ltbDirectories = gconConnection.rdoTables("DOC_DIRECTORY")
    Set lrsltDirectories =
    ltbDirectories.OpenResultset
    ➥(rdOpenKeyset, rdConcurLock)

    lrsltDirectories.AddNew
    lrsltDirectories("DOC_PARENT_DIR_DESC").VALUE = aDirectory.Name
    lrsltDirectories("DIR_PARENT_DIR_ID").VALUE =aDirectory.ParentID
    lrsltDirectories.Update

    'Move to the most recently added record
    lsNewBookmark = lrsltDirectories.LastModified
    lrsltDirectories.Bookmark = lsNewBookmark

    llNewID = lrsltDirectories("DOC_PARENT_DIR_ID")

    ' Update the new Directory
    aDirectory.ID = llNewID
    lsNewKey = "Dir" & llNewID

    prvDirectories.Add aDirectory, lsNewKey

    lrsltDirectories.Close
    Set ltbDirectories = Nothing

End Sub
```

For a complete description of RDO methods and constants, see Chapter 11, "Remote Data Objects."

When the Add method is invoked by a client application, the method creates a rdoResultset object that is a representation of the DOC_DIRECTORY table in the database. This is done with the following code:

```
' Open the Directory table. Pull all directories back
  Dim lrsltDirectories As rdoResultset
  Dim ltbDirectories As rdoTable

  Set ltbDirectories = gconConnection.rdoTables("DOC_DIRECTORY")
  Set lrsltDirectories = ltbDirectories.OpenResultset
  ➡(rdOpenDynamic, rdConcurLock)
```

The preceding code creates an rdoTable object and associates it with the
DOC_DIRECTORY table in the database. Because rdoTable objects are read-
only, an updatable rdoResultset object must be created by invoking the
OpenResultset method of the rdoTable object.

After the result set is created, its AddNew method is called to create a new
record in the database. The new record is populated, using the following
code:

```
lrsltDirectories.AddNew
lrsltDirectories("DOC_PARENT_DIR_DESC").VALUE = aDirectory.Name
lrsltDirectories("DIR_PARENT_DIR_ID").VALUE =aDirectory.ParentID
lrsltDirectories.Update
```

The Update method of the result set saves the new record to the database.
After the Directory is saved to the database, its ID property—which uniquely
identifies it in the collection—is retrieved from the database by moving to
last record in the result set, as in the following example:

```
'Move to the most recently added record
  lrsltDirectories.Requery

  lrsltDirectories.MoveLast

  llNewID = lrsltDirectories("DOC_PARENT_DIR_ID")
```

After retrieving the ID, the local variable llNewID is set to the ID of the most-
recently added record. This new ID is assigned to the passed Directory object,
and a new key for the object is created:

```
' Update the new Directory
  aDirectory.ID = llNewID
  lsNewKey = "Dir" & llNewID
```

Finally, the newly created Directory is added to the Directories' collection
with the following code:

```
prvDirectories.Add aDirectory, lsNewKey
```

Item Method

The Item method of the Directories class returns a single Directory object. To
retrieve a Directory from the collection, a user passes the *Index* of the object
or the object's *Key* value.

```
Public Function Item(index As Variant) As Directory

    Set Item = prvDirectories.Item(index)

End Function
```

The *index* argument is passed to the method as a variant because the `item` method of a collection can accept either a number, indicating the order in which the directory appears in the collection—prvDirectories.Item(3) is the third item in the collection, for example, or the item's *Key*, which is a unique string that also identifies the item in the collection. Each item in a collection has a unique *Key* value that identifies it. For example, prvDirectories.Item("dirThree") returns the directory whose *Key* is "dirThree."

Remove Method

The `Remove` method removes an existing directory from the Directories collection and from the database. The code that makes up the `Remove` method is shown in Listing 22.6.

Listing 22.6   OLEDIRS.CLS—The Remove method deletes a Directory object from the Directories collection and removes it from the database

```
Public Sub Remove(asKey As Variant)

    'Function deletes the parent directory,
    ' all child directories, and all child
    ' documents

    'Look through collection to find matching dir
    Dim ldDirectory As Directory
    Set ldDirectory = prvDirectories(asKey)

    ' First delete child docs
    Dim lprepStatement As rdoPreparedStatement

    ' Delete Child Docs
    Set lprepStatement =
    gconConnection.CreatePreparedStatement
    ➥("sp_delete_child_docs", "{call sp_delete_child_docs (?)}")
    lprepStatement.rdoParameters(0).VALUE = ldDirectory.ID
    lprepStatement.Execute
    lprepStatement.Close

    ' Delete Child Directories
    Set lprepStatement =
    gconConnection.CreatePreparedStatement
    ➥("sp_delete_child_dirs", "{call sp_delete_child_dirs (?)}")
    lprepStatement.rdoParameters(0).VALUE = ldDirectory.ID
    lprepStatement.Execute
    lprepStatement.Close
```

```
' Delete Directory
Set lprepStatement =
gconConnection.CreatePreparedStatement
➥("sp_delete_child_dir", "{call sp_delete_dir (?)}")
lprepStatement.rdoParameters(0).VALUE = ldDirectory.ID
lprepStatement.Execute
lprepStatement.Close

' Remove the item from the collection
prvDirectories.Remove (asKey)


End Sub
```

In the directory hierarchy of the OLE Document Manager sample application, each Directory can contain other Directories or Documents. When a Directory is deleted, all Documents and Directories it contains also are deleted.

This is a good example of business rules encapsulated in the business services. From a client perspective, a user is interested in deleting a directory. Business rules dictate that when a directory that contains child documents and additional directories is deleted, the child documents and directories must also be deleted. The users may not be aware of which documents and directories are children of the directory they are deleting. The business server doesn't require the client to have any knowledge about a directory's children. It takes care of the deletions.

Programmatically, this process is accomplished by calling three stored procedures that delete the child documents, child directories, and finally the directory. Each procedure is associated with a prepared statement, assigned parameters, and executed. If your data services support cascading deletes, the parent and child Directories also could have been removed in this way. However, implementing cascading logic into your business services ensures that your code will run properly against any database, not just databases that support cascading deletes.

The following code shows the declaration and execution of the sp_delete_child_docs stored procedure:

```
' Delete Child Docs
  Set lprepStatement =
gconConnection.CreatePreparedStatement
➥("sp_delete_child_docs", "{call sp_delete_child_docs (?)}")
  lprepStatement.rdoParameters(0).VALUE = ldDirectory.ID
  lprepStatement.Execute
  lprepStatement.Close
```

Just as you saw in the Document class's Update method, the stored procedure that is used to delete the directories is associated with an rdoPreparedStatement object using the CreatePreparedStatement method of the gconConnection rdoConnection object. The CreatePreparedStatement method uses the {call *procedurename* (?, ?,...)} syntax to assure the portability of the code.

The sp_delete_child_docs procedure accepts one parameter—the ID of the Directory being deleted. This parameter is bound to the prepared statement, using the rdoParameters collection:

```
lprepStatement.rdoParameters(0).VALUE = ldDirectory.ID
```

After executing the prepared statement with the Execute method, the prepared statement object is closed. Closing the object removes it from the rdoPreparedStatements collection.

After deleting the child Documents, the child Directories are deleted. This is done in a manner nearly identical to the method used to delete the child Documents:

```
' Delete Child Directories
    Set lprepStatement =
    gconConnection.CreatePreparedStatement
➥("sp_delete_child_dirs", "{call sp_delete_child_dirs (?)}")
    lprepStatement.rdoParameters(0).VALUE = ldDirectory.ID
    lprepStatement.Execute
    lprepStatement.Close
```

Again, a prepared statement is associated with a stored procedure in the database—this time, the sp_delete_child_dirs procedure. This procedure also accepts a single input parameter, bound to the prepared statement by using the rdoParameters collection. After the prepared statement is executed, it is removed from the collection by using the Close method.

Finally, the Directory is removed by associating a prepared statement with the sp_delete_directory stored procedure, binding parameters, and executing the following statement:

```
' Delete Directory
    Set lprepStatement =
    gconConnection.CreatePreparedStatement
➥("sp_delete_child_dir", "{call sp_delete_dir (?)}")
    lprepStatement.rdoParameters(0).VALUE = ldDirectory.ID
    lprepStatement.Execute
    lprepStatement.Close
```

The final step of the method removes the Directory from the Directories collection:

V

Sample Applications

```
' Remove the item from the collection
    prvDirectories.Remove (asKey)
```

By calling one method from the client application, *directoriesobject*.Remove, we removed the Directory from the database *and* insured referential integrity by removing the Directory's child documents and directories from the database as well. All of this occurs without requiring the client application to pass any information other than the Directory's ID.

The Document Class

A *Document object* is used to represent a document existing in the database. A document is an OLE document, capable of visual editing in a Visual Basic application. The Document class's methods allow you to load a previously saved document from the database and update its properties. This section details both these methods and the Document object's properties.

Properties

The Document object has the following properties:

- ID
- Title
- ParentDirID
- FileName

The *ID* property is a unique identifier of a document in the database. This property is used by the Document object's Update and Load methods to identify the document.

The *Title* property indicates the display name of a document. You can update and save this property to the database, using the Document object's Update method.

The *ParentDirID* property is used to identify under which directory a document appears within the directory hierarchy. This property is used by the Remove method of the Directories class.

Because the OLE Container control is capable only of loading OLE documents to and from files, the *FileName* property is used to store and transfer the name of the file within which an OLE document is stored prior to reading or writing a document to the database.

Load Method

The Load method of the Document class is used to retrieve a document from the database. As you have seen in methods of other objects, the Load method uses a prepared statement to retrieve information from the database. The code for the Load method is shown in Listing 22.7. The sp_retrieve_doc stored procedure retrieves a document's ID, Title, ParentDirID, and OLE document values.

Listing 22.7   OLEDOC.CLS—The Load method retrieves information about a Document from the database

```
Public Sub Load()

    Dim liReturn As Integer
    ' Function retrieves a document record from the database

    ' Open the Document table
    Dim lrsltResults As rdoResultset
    Dim lcolResultColumn As rdoColumn
    Dim lprepStatement As rdoPreparedStatement

    Set lprepStatement =
    gconConnection.CreatePreparedStatement
    ➥("sp_retrieve_doc", "{call sp_retrieve_doc (?)}")
    lprepStatement.rdoParameters(0).VALUE = ID

  Set lrsltResults = lprepStatement.OpenResultset(rdOpenKeyset)

    Title = lrsltResults("DOC_TITLE")
    ParentDirID = lrsltResults("DOC_PARENT_DIR_ID")
    Set lcolResultColumn = lrsltResults.rdoColumns("DOC")
    liReturn = giOLEColumnToObject(lcolResultColumn, FileName)

    Set lcolResultColumn = Nothing
    lrsltResults.Close
    lprepStatement.Close

End Sub
```

The ID, Title, and ParentDirID properties can be written directly to the document object. No property exists, however, for the OLE document object because the OLE Container Control—which will display the document in the OLE Document Manager application—can only read an OLE document from a file. You cannot set the Object property of an OLE container control equal to an object. You must use the ReadFromFile method to load an existing OLE document or the CreateEmbed method to create a new OLE document, which means that the OLE document first must be written to a file, using the GetChunk method of an rdoColumn object.

V

Sample Applications

You accomplish this process by passing a reference to the column that contains the OLE document to the giOLEColumnToObject function. This function is explained in detail in a following section of this chapter. The giColumnToObject function also assigns the path of the OLE document file it creates to the FileName property of the document object.

The Load method retrieves the database columns, writes the values to the object for which properties exist, calls the function to write the OLE document to a file, and then passes back the FileName of the newly created file to the client application. The client application, as you will see, actually loads the files into the OLE container control.

Update Method

The Update method of the Document class is similar to the Update method of the Directory class described previously in this chapter. Both methods use the properties of a specified Document or Directory to update the database. The difference between the two is that, because an OLE document must be written to the database using the AppendChunk method of an rdoColumn object, the Update method of the Document class, whose code is shown in Listing 22.8, cannot use a stored procedure to pass all of a Document's information to the database as the directory class's Update method does. Rather, it uses the giOLEFiletoColumn function to write the OLE document to the database and an rdoResultset to update the other properties of a Document object.

Listing 22.8   OLEDOC.CLS—The Update method allows you to change Document information in the database

```
Public Sub Update()
     ' Function updates the name of a document
     ' in the tree view control
     ' and saves newer version of doc
     ' in database
     Dim liReturnResult As Integer
     Dim liCounter As Long
     Dim lbNotFound As Boolean
     Dim lvChunkHolder as Variant

     ' Open the Directory table. Pull first level nodes first
     Dim lrsltDocListing As rdoResultset
     Dim ltbDocuments As rdoTable
     Dim lcolColumn As rdoColumn

     Set ltbDocuments = gconConnection.rdoTables("OLE_DOCUMENT")
     Set lrsltDocListing = ltbDocuments.OpenResultset
     ➥(rdOpenKeyset, rdConcurLock)
```

```
            lrsltDocListing.MoveFirst
            lbNotFound = True
            ' Move to the row of the table that has the
            ' correct Document ID
            While lbNotFound = True

                If lrsltDocListing("DOC_ID") = ID Then
                'Update the document
                    lrsltDocListing.Edit
                        lrsltDocListing("DOC_TITLE").Value = Title
                        If Trim(FileName) <> "" Then
                            liReturnResult = giOLEFiletoColumn
                            ➥(FileName, lvChunkHolder)
                            lrsltDocListing("DOC").AppendChunk
                            ➥(lvChunkHolder)
                        End If
                    lrsltDocListing.Update
                    lbNotFound = False
                End If
                lrsltDocListing.MoveNext

        Wend
End Sub
```

The Update method creates a result set by using an rdoTable object similar to the Add method of the Directories class. Rather than using the AddNew method of the rdoResultset object, the Update method uses the rdoResultset's Edit method.

Because a stored procedure isn't used, the Update method must first locate the record being updated by cycling through the result set until it finds a match on the document's ID property, as in the following example:

```
' Move to the row of the table that has the
    ' correct Document ID
    While lbNotFound = True

        If lrsltDocListing("DOC_ID") = ID Then
        'Update the document
```

When updating an OLE document, the client application must first write the OLE document contained within the OLE container control to a file, using the WriteToFile method of the container control. The client application then assigns the name of the file to the FileName property of a Document object and calls the Document object's Update method. The Update method uses the giOLEFiletoColumn function to read the OLE file into the database.

```
lrsltDocListing.Edit
        lrsltDocListing("DOC_TITLE").VALUE = Title
        liReturnResult = giOLEFiletoColumn(FileName, lsChunkHolder)
    lrsltDocListing.Update
```

V

Sample Applications

The giOLEFiletoColumn function, described in a following section of this chapter, requires a variable of type variant. This variant will be populated with the data contained in the OLE file. The function also requires the FileName property of the document being updated, which indicates the path of the OLE file. When the file information has been retrieved, control returns to the Update method which updates the DOC column.

The Update method can write any changes to the document's title property directly to the database by assigning the value of the Title property to the value of the result set's DOC_TITLE column.

Ideally, the Document object should include an Object property. This property should be set to the OLE document contained in the OLE container control. The Update method can then read this value and write it to the database. This process is impossible because the database requires that OLE fields are added or updated by using the AppendChunk method and the AppendChunk method must read data from a file. Because an OLE Object can be written to a file only by using the OLE container control's WriteToFile method, including it as a property would be of little benefit.

The Documents Class

When an instance of the Documents class is created, the object calls the giFillDirectories function, which populates the prvDocuments collection variable. The giFillDirectories function is described later in this chapter.

The Documents class has a Count property that is identical to the Directories Count property. It returns the total number of documents in the database.

The methods of the Documents class are the same methods as the Directories class: Add, Item, and Remove. The results of each method are identical to the equivalent method of the Directories class. Although the code that executes the Item method is identical, except that it uses the prvDirectories collection variable, the Add and Remove methods are carried out in a slightly different manner.

Add Method

Just like the Add method of the Directories class, the Documents class's Add method creates a result set, uses the AddNew method to create a new record and submits the record to the database. It then moves to the end of the result set to retrieve the ID of the new record and assigns it to the Document's ID property. Listing 22.9 shows the code that makes up the Documents' Add method.

V

Sample Applications

Listing 22.9 OLEDOCS.CLS—The Add method of the Documents collection allows you to add a new Document to the collection as well as the database

```
Public Sub Add(aDocument As Document)

    ' Function adds a new document record to the database
    Dim liReturn As Integer
    Dim lsNewBookmark As Variant
    Dim llNewID As Long
    Dim lsKey As String

    ' Open the Document table
    Dim ltbDocTable As rdoResultset
    Dim lcolOLEField As rdoColumn
    Dim ltbTableObject As rdoTable
    Dim lvChunkHolder as Variant

    Set ltbTableObject = gconConnection.rdoTables("OLE_DOCUMENT")

    Set ltbDocTable = ltbTableObject.OpenResultset
    ➥(rdOpenKeyset, rdConcurLock)

    ' If the don has no name, it is new
    ' Create a new record
    If Len(Trim(aDocument.Title)) = 0 Then
        aDocument.Title = "Named"
    End If


    ltbDocTable.AddNew
        ltbDocTable("DOC_TITLE").VALUE = aDocument.Title
        ltbDocTable("DOC_PARENT_DIR_ID").Value =
        ➥aDocument.ParentDirID
        liReturn = giOLEFiletoColumn
        ➥(aDocument.FileName, lvChunkHolder)
        ltbDocTable("DOC").AppendChunk (lvChunkHolder)
    ltbDocTable.Update

    ltbDocTable.Requery
    ' Return the ID of the newly created doc
    ltbDocTable.MoveLast

    llNewID = ltbDocTable("DOC_ID")
    lsKey = "Doc" & llNewID
    aDocument.ID = llNewID

    prvDocuments.Add aDocument, lsKey

End Sub
```

Because the OLE container control must write the OLE document it contains to a file, the giOLEFiletoColumn function is called by the Add method. This function returns a string, *lvChunkHolder*, containing the binary data that makes up the new document. The Add method can then use the AppendChunk method of an rdoColumn object to write the binary data to the database. The giOLEFiletoColumn function is described in a following section of this chapter.

Remove Method

Like the Directories classes' Remove, the Document's Remove method also calls a stored procedure to delete records, and then removes the document from the collection. Because a Document has no child Documents or Directories, only one stored procedure needs to be called, which is shown in Listing 22.10.

> **Listing 22.10   OLEDOCS.CLS—The Remove method of the Documents collection allows you to remove a Document from the collection as well as the database**

```
Public Sub Remove(asKey As Variant)

    ' Function deletes a document from the database
    ' and the collection

    ' Find object in Collection
    Dim ldocObject As Document
    Set ldocObject = prvDocuments(asKey)

    ' Delete the document with a query
    Dim lprepDeleteChildDocs As rdoPreparedStatement

    ' Delete Doc
    Set lprepDeleteChildDocs =
    gconConnection.CreatePreparedStatement
    ➥("sp_delete_doc", "{call sp_delete_doc (?)}")
    lprepDeleteChildDocs.rdoParameters(0).VALUE = ldocObject.ID

    lprepDeleteChildDocs.Execute
    lprepDeleteChildDocs.Close

    ' Remove item from collection
    prvDocuments.Remove (asKey)

End Sub
```

The DocType Class

The DocType class is used to represent the different types of OLE documents that can be inserted into the OLE document container control. This section details the properties of the DocType class.

Properties

The DocType class has the following three properties:

- Name

- ID

- Class

The *Name* property contains the display name of the insertable object. This name is displayed in the Select Document Type list box of the client application. It is a more readable name than the object's class. The class of an Excel worksheet, for example, is "Excel.Sheet." The Name property contains the more lucid name, "Excel Worksheet."

The *ID* property is a unique identifier of each DocType.

The *Class* property contains the actual class name of the insertable object. The Class property, for example, of an Excel worksheet is "Excel.Sheet." This property is used by the OLE container control when creating a new embedded object.

The DocTypes Class

The DocTypes class is a collection of the available DocType objects. The DocTypes class has a Count property, which is identical to the Documents and Directories classes' Count properties. The DocTypes class also has an `Item` method that returns a single DocType from the collection. This method also is identical to the Directories and Documents classes' methods.

The Document Manager Module

Besides the classes contained in the DocMgr OLE server, several functions are included. The functions are not exposed to client applications or other OLE servers but are used internally by the servers classes. These functions, shown in the following list, are contained in the GENERAL.BAS file:

- `giOpenDatabase` function

- `giFillDirectories` function

- `giFillDocuments` function

- `giFillDocTypes` function

- OLE read/write functions

The remainder of this section details each of these functions and explains how the OLE Document Manager application makes use of them.

giOpenDatabase Function

The giOpenDatabase function creates a connection to the Document Managers database. It creates this connection by using the default rdoEnvironment object and a globally defined rdoConnection object.

```
Private Function giOpenDatabase()

    Set genvDataEnviron = rdoEnvironments(0)
    Set gconConnection = genvDataEnviron.OpenConnection
    ➥("Document Manager Database", True, _
    False, "UID=admin;")

    giOpenDatabase = True

End Function
```

The giOpenDatabase function requires that a data source was previously created with the name, Document Manager Database. It connects to the database by using the Admin or a user ID. Because this is an ODBC connection, the data source can be any type of database that supports ODBC.

giFillDirectories Function

The giFillDirectories function retrieves all directories from the database and adds them to the passed collection. The code that makes up the giFillDirectories function is shown in Listing 22.11. As you saw in other functions, the giFillDirectories function uses an rdoPreparedStatement object to reference a stored procedure in the database. This procedure is executed and its results are held in an rdoResultset object.

Listing 22.11   GENERAL.BAS—The giFillDirectories function is used to retrieve all directories stored in the database

```
Sub giFillDirectories(aDirectories As Collection)

    ' Fills the directories object
    ' Function fills the directory collection
    Dim lsKey As String

    ' Open the Directory table. Pull all directories back
    Dim lprepStatement As rdoPreparedStatement
    Dim lrsltResultSet As rdoResultset

    Set lprepStatement =
    gconConnection.CreatePreparedStatement
    ➥("sp_retrieve_directories", "{Call sp_retrieve_directories}")

    'Dim ltbDirListing As Recordset
    Set lrsltResultSet =
```

```
            lprepStatement.OpenResultset
            ➥(rdOpenForwardOnly, rdConcurReadOnly)

            ' Fill the collection
            While Not lrsltResultSet.EOF
                ' Create a new directory object
                Dim ldNewDirectory As New Directory

                ' Set the object's properties
                ldNewDirectory.ID = lrsltResultSet("DOC_PARENT_DIR_ID")
                ldNewDirectory.Name = lrsltResultSet("DOC_PARENT_DIR_DESC")
                ldNewDirectory.ParentID =
                ➥lrsltResultSet("DIR_PARENT_DIR_ID")
                ' Add the new item to the collection
                lsKey = "Dir" & ldNewDirectory.ID
                aDirectories.Add ldNewDirectory, lsKey

                Set ldNewDirectory = Nothing

                lrsltResultSet.MoveNext
            Wend

            lrsltResultSet.Close
            lprepStatement.Close

        End Sub
```

The function cycles through the result set, creating a new directory object
with each cycle, assigning the values stored in the database to the new directory object, and adding each directory to the passed collection. When the
end of the result set is reached, the result set and prepared statement objects
are closed.

giFillDocuments Function

The giFillDocuments function fills the passed collection with the documents contained in the database. It does so in the same manner as the
giFillDirectories function. The code that makes up the giFillDocuments
function is shown in Listing 22.12.

**Listing 22.12   GENERAL.BAS—The giFillDocuments function,
much like the giFillDirectories function in Listing 22.11, is used
to retrieve all documents stored in the database**

```
    Sub giFillDocuments(aDocuments As Collection)

        ' Function fills the Document collection
        Dim lsKey As String

        Dim lprepStatement As rdoPreparedStatement
        Dim lrsltResultSet As rdoResultset
```

```
        Set lprepStatement =
        gconConnection.CreatePreparedStatement
        ➥("sp_retrieve_docs", "{Call sp_retrieve_documents}")
        Set lrsltResultSet = lprepStatement.OpenResultset
        ➥(rdOpenForwardOnly, rdConcurReadOnly)

        ' Fill the collection
        While Not lrsltResultSet.EOF
            ' Create a new directory object
            Dim ldNewDocument As New Document

            ' Set the object's properties
            ldNewDocument.ID = lrsltResultSet("DOC_ID")
            ldNewDocument.Title = lrsltResultSet("DOC_TITLE")
            ldNewDocument.ParentDirID =
            ➥lrsltResultSet("DOC_PARENT_DIR_ID")
            ' Add the new item to the collection
            lsKey = "Doc" & ldNewDocument.ID
            aDocuments.Add ldNewDocument, lsKey

            Set ldNewDocument = Nothing

            lrsltResultSet.MoveNext
        Wend

        lrsltResultSet.Close
        lprepStatement.Close

    End Sub
```

giFillDocTypes Function

The giFillDocTypes function, shown in Listing 22.13, fills the passed collection with the available DocTypes objects. The sample app allows a user to create Excel worksheet objects and Word documents. The function creates two DocType objects, assigns the appropriate Name, ID, and Class values for the Excel worksheet and Word documents, and then adds the DocType object to the collection:

Listing 22.13   GENERAL.BAS—The giFillDocTypes function is used to determine the types of OLE documents the client application can insert into the database

```
Sub giFillDocTypes(asDocTypeCollection As Collection)

    ' Function fills the DocTypes collection
    Dim lsKey As String

    ' Create a new directory object
    Dim ldDocType As New DocType
```

```
' Add Excel Type
' Set the object's properties
ldDocType.Name = "Excel Worksheet"
ldDocType.ID = DOC_TYPE_EXCEL
ldDocType.Class = "Excel.Sheet"

' Add the new item to the collection
asDocTypeCollection.Add Item:=ldDocType

Set ldDocType = Nothing

' Add Word type
ldDocType.Name = "Word Document"
ldDocType.ID = DOC_TYPE_WORD
ldDocType.Class = "Word.Document"

' Add the new item to the collection
asDocTypeCollection.Add Item:=ldDocType

End Sub
```

OLE Read/Write Field Functions

Three functions exist in the DocManager OLE server that aid in writing and reading OLE documents to and from the database. These functions, detailed through the remainder of this section, are:

- giOLEColumnToObject function

- giObjectToFile function

- giOLEFiletoColumn function

giOLEColumnToObject Function

The giOLEColumnToObject function is called by the Load method of the document class. This function serves as the first step in retrieving and OLE document from the database and loading the file into an OLE container control. Its code is shown in Listing 22.14.

Listing 22.14   GENERAL.BAS—The giOLEColumnToObject function translates data stored in an OLE column in the database into an OLE document

```
Function giOLEColumnToObject
➥(acolObject As rdoColumn, asPathName As String) As Integer
' Function places data in an OLE database column
    ' into a binary file
    Dim liFileNumber As Integer
    Dim eError As Integer
    Dim b() As Byte
```

```
liFileNumber = FreeFile
asPathName = App.Path & "\OLE.TMP"
'Create temp
Open asPathName For Binary As liFileNumber

On Error Resume Next
'put getchunk into file until receive a Null back (which will
'generate a type mismatch error when trying to assign to b() )
Do
    b = acolObject.GetChunk(50)
    Put liFileNumber, , b
Loop While Err = 0

Close liFileNumber

End Function
```

The Load method calls the giOLEColumnToObject function and passes a reference to the column in the OLE_DOCUMENT table that contains the OLE
document. This reference is passed as acolObject. The Load method also
passes a reference to the FileName property of the Document object being
loaded as asPathName, which will be populated with the path name of the
recently created OLE file.

The giOLEColumnToObject function first generates a new file number. This
number is stored as liFileNumber. A file then is opened in binary mode and
the GetChunk method of the rdoColumn object is used to read the binary OLE
document from the database into a binary array. A byte array must be used in
this case. Writing the binary information to a string variable will result in
errors because the string data type automatically converts the binary data
to unicode data. After reading the data, the function places the data in the
binary array into the open file. Finally, the giOLEColumnToObject function
closes the binary file and writes the path of the file to the passed variable,
asPathName.

Because we are using ODBC to connect to the data source, we cannot determine the exact amount of information that is stored in the OLE column in
the database. Because of this, we have to cycle through the OLE column and
retrieve chunks of data by using the rdoColumn object's GetChunk method.
This data is incrementally added to the byte array *b*.

The Put statement writes the data stored in the byte array variable to the
binary file, aiFileNumber. This data is eventually read by the OLE container
control, allowing the OLE document stored in the database to be displayed to
the end user.

giOLEFiletoColumn Function

The `giOLEFiletoColumn` function performs the exact opposite action that the `giOLEColumnToObject` function performs. The `giOLEFiletoColumn` function writes the data stored in a binary file to an OLE Object column in the database. The `giOLEFiletoColumn` function is shown in Listing 22.15.

Listing 22.15 GENERAL.BAS—The giOLEFiletoColumn allows you to write information stored in a binary file to an OLE field in the database

```
Function giOLEFiletoColumn(asFilePath As String,
➥asChunk As Variant) As Integer
    ' Function extracts data from OLE file
    ' and writes it to a passed variant
    Dim liFileNumber As Integer
    Dim b() As Byte

    liFileNumber = FreeFile
    Open asFilePath For Binary As liFileNumber 'Create temp

    'get entire file into byte array
    ReDim b(LOF(liFileNumber))
    Get liFileNumber, 1, b

    'now we can assign to variant of VarType = vbByte + vbArra
    asChunk = b

    Close liFileNumber    'Close temp file
    Kill asFilePath       'Delete temp file
    giOLEFiletoColumn = 0
End Function
```

The `giOLEFiletoColumn` function is called by the Add and Update methods of the Document class. When a user creates a new OLE document in the Document Manager, or changes an existing document, the Add and Update methods are invoked, respectively. Both methods require that the data in the OLE container control was written to an OLE file, using the OLE container control's WriteToFile method. The path name of this file is stored in the FileName property of the document object being stored.

The Add and Update methods pass a reference to the document's FileName property as asFilePath, and a reference to a variant variable. As the `giOLEColumnToObject` function also does, the `giOLEFiletoColumn` function opens a binary file, asFilePath. The function then writes the data stored in the open binary file to the passed variant, asChunk. When control returns to the `giOLEFiletoColumn` function, the temporary OLE file closes and is deleted.

Data Services

The data services of the sample application consist of a stand-alone Access 2.0 database and a hard drive required to store the temporary files that are generated when reading and writing OLE documents to and from the OLE container control. The sample application also includes script files that allow you to set up a SQL Server 6.0 database.

Because the OLE Document Manager uses ODBC to communicate with data services, any ODBC-compliant database, such as SQL Server, can be used in place of the Access database without requiring modifications to the source code. The sample application does require that the DBMS permits stored procedures to return result sets, something that Oracle does not. However, when writing three-tier applications for the enterprise, you can overcome this limitation by using dynamic SQL in place of stored procedures to retrieve data from the database. Because all ODBC databases will support your ODBC compliant SQL statements, you can operate your client application and business services, regardless of your database back end.

To switch data sources, you only need to create an exact replica of the tables and stored procedures contained within the Access database. Exact means that all tables, columns, and stored procedures appearing in the Access database must appear in the new database with the same table names, column names, and stored procedure names. Any deviation from the template will prevent the application from operating properly. Additionally, the new database must be registered as an ODBC data source.

For more information on registering an ODBC data source, see the previous section in this chapter, "Installation Instructions."

Data Model

The OLE Document Manager application uses a single Access database to store documents and the information associated with them. The database consists of two tables. Figure 22.8 illustrates an entity-relationship (ER) diagram of the database.

This section details the components that make up the OLE Document Manager's data services.

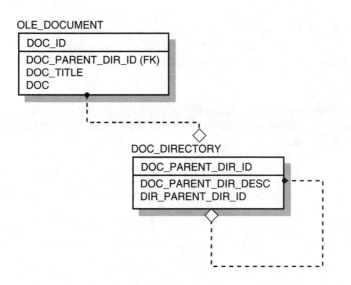

Fig. 22.8
The OLE Document Manager's database. The DOC_DIRECTORY table has a one-to-many relationship with the OLE_DOCUMENT table, indicating that each Directory can hold one or more Documents.

Table 22.2 shows the names of the columns in the OLE_DOCUMENT table and their descriptions. Table 22.3 shows the names of the columns in the DOC_DIRECTORY table.

Table 22.2 The OLE_DOCUMENT Table	
Column Name	**Description**
DOC_ID	A unique identifier for an OLE document
DOC_TITLE	The displayed title of an OLE document
DOC_PARENT_DIR_ID	The ID of a document's parent directory
DOC	The OLE document

Table 22.3 The DOC_DIRECTORY Table	
Column Name	**Description**
DOC_PARENT_DIR_ID	A unique identifier for a directory
DOC_PARENT_DIR_DESC	The displayed name of a Directory
DIR_PARENT_DIR_ID	The ID of a directory's parent directory

Stored Procedures

The OLE Document Manager uses several stored procedures to help complete routine tasks of the business servers. The stored procedures and their functions are listed in Table 22.4.

Table 22.4 The OLE Document Manager's Stored Procedures	
Procedure Name	**Description**
sp_delete_child_dirs	Deletes all child directories of a parent directory
sp_delete_child_docs	Deletes all child documents of a parent directory
sp_delete_dir	Deletes a directory from the database
sp_delete_doc	Deletes a document from the database
sp_retrieve_child_docs	Retrieves all child documents of parent directory
sp_retrieve_directories	Retrieves all directories from the database
sp_retrieve_doc	Retrieves a specific document from the database
sp_retrieve_documents	Retrieves all documents from the database
sp_update_directory	Updates the name of a directory in the database

Notice that every stored procedure performs one simple action on the database. As with the client application, no business logic should be present in the data services. You should use stored procedures to quickly perform simple queries, not to enforce business rules.

If a business rule existed, for example, that limited the number of documents that any parent directory can contain to four documents, this rule could be enforced in the data services. A trigger could be created for every insert that checks to see how many child documents the parent directory has, or a stored procedure could be created that first queried the database to determine how many child documents the parent directory has.

However, this type of logic should be maintained in the business servers, which ensures that changes to business rules need to be updated in only one place.

User Services

The application uses an Explorer-like main window to display a list of documents currently stored in the database, with a hierarchical view of the directories that contain these documents. From the main window (the Document Explorer), a user can open any document existing in the database or create a new OLE document. The user also has full control over creating and removing document directories.

New documents and existing documents are edited in the OLE Document window. The OLE Document Manager uses a Single Document Interface (SDI) similar to the Windows 95 InBox interface. Each copy of the OLE Document Window displays one OLE document. The toolbars and menus of the OLE Document Window merge with the OLE document's server application, allowing a user to use many of the OLE documents server's tools and functionality while editing.

The OLE Document Manager's business services house all the application's business logic. Through OLE Automation, the Document object exposes methods that allow a user to create and update OLE documents, add and remove document directories, and save and read OLE document to and from the application's database.

All access to the database is achieved through the business services. No code exists in the client application that directly accesses the Document Manager's database. At the same time, the business services allow users to create customized client application without redeveloping the functions needed to create and store OLE documents.

The following sections take a close look at the three windows—the Document Explorer, the Add Document window, and the OLE Document window—that comprise the user services tier, as well as the procedures and functions contained within these windows. Collectively, the elements make up the user services and are used to access the business services and display information to the user.

The Document Explorer

The Document Explorer window serves as square one for the OLE Document Manager application. This window appears on-screen when the program executes. From the window, a user can create and delete documents or open, view, and edit existing documents.

This section describes the events and procedures that the Document Manager window uses to carry out these functions.

Form Load Event

When the application starts, the Sub Main startup procedure loads the Document Explorer and triggers the Form_Load event of the Document Explorer window. The Form_Load event calls the giLoadCollection function. This function, detailed in a following section of this chapter, fills the globally declared Documents, Directories, and DocTypes objects with the available Directory, Document, and DocType objects in the database. The code that makes up the Form_Load event is shown in Listing 22.16.

> **Listing 22.16 DOCTREE.FRM—The Form_Load event of Document Explorer retrieves Directory and Document objects that represent OLE documents in the database**

```
Private Sub Form_Load()

    Screen.MousePointer = MP_HOURGLASS
    Me.Show
    lblStatus.Caption = "Retrieving directory list"

    ' Initialize global collection pointers
    giLoadCollections
    ' Call the function to fill directory list
    fiFillDirectories tvwDirectoryList

    ' Set Focus to TreeView
    tvwDirectoryList.SetFocus
    Screen.MousePointer = MP_DEFAULT

End Sub
```

After retrieving the collections, the event calls the fiFillDirectories function, which loads the available Directory objects into the passed TreeView control tvwDirectoryList.

File Menu—New Document

When the New Document command is selected from the File menu, the procedures required to create a new OLE document are enacted. The code that makes up the New Document option is shown in Listing 22.17.

Listing 22.17   DOCTREE.FRM—When user clicks New Document option on File menu, this code is used to call the method in the business services tier that creates a new Document object and stores it in the database

```
Private Sub mnuFileNewDocument_Click()

    Dim llDirID As Long

    ' Don't let user create documents under Root
    If tvwDirectoryList.SelectedItem.Index = 1 Then
        MsgBox "You cannot create documents
        ➥under the Document directory."
        Exit Sub
    End If

    ' Open the document select Window
    Set goObjectTypeSelected = Nothing
    gbFormReturnResult = False
    frmListForm.Show MODAL

    ' Determine if user made selection
    If gbFormReturnResult = False Then
        ' User Hit Cancel
        Exit Sub
    Else
        ' Retrieve ID of currently selected Directory
        llDirID = Val(Right(tvwDirectoryList.SelectedItem.KEY,
        ➥Len(tvwDirectoryList.SelectedItem.KEY) - 3))
        ' Show the MDI Child form
        Dim frmNewForm As New frmOLEDocContainer
        ' Create a new document object
        Set goNewDocObject = CreateObject("DocManager.Document")
        goNewDocObject.Id = 0
        goNewDocObject.ParentDirID = llDirID
        goNewDocObject.Title = ""
        goNewDocObject.filename = ""

        Load frmNewForm

        ' Call Method to create new OLE document
        ' Load the new type of Doc in the OLE control
        frmNewForm.oleOleForm.CreateEmbed "",
        ➥goObjectTypeSelected.Class
        frmNewForm.oleOleForm.DoVerb OPEN_OLE_OBJECT

        frmNewForm.Show

    End If

End Sub
```

The first block of code, shown in the following lines, ensures that a user-selected valid directory exists under which to create a new document:

```
' Don't let user create documents under Root
    If tvwDirectoryList.SelectedItem.Index = 1 Then
        MsgBox "You cannot create documents
        ➥under the Document directory."
        Exit Sub
    End If
```

New documents cannot be created under the root directory. If users attempt this, they are denied permission.

After it is determined that the directory is valid, the Add Document dialog window is displayed. The Add Document window, detailed in a following section of this chapter, prompts a user to select a type of document to create. The following code loads the form and waits for a return result:

```
' Open the document select Window
    Set goObjectTypeSelected = Nothing
    gbFormReturnResult = False
    frmListForm.Show MODAL
```

If the user clicks Cancel on the Add Document window, gbReturnResult is set to False. Otherwise, gbReturnResult is set to True. The following section of code checks for the users response:

```
If gbFormReturnResult = False Then
        ' User Hit Cancel
        Exit Sub
    Else
        ' Retrieve ID of currently selected Directory
        llDirID = Val(Right(tvwDirectoryList.SelectedItem.KEY,
        ➥Len(tvwDirectoryList.SelectedItem.KEY) - 3))
        ' Show the form
        Dim frmNewForm As New frmOLEDocContainer
        ' Create a new document object
        Set goNewDocObject = CreateObject("DocManager.Document")
        goNewDocObject.Id = 0
        goNewDocObject.ParentDirID = llDirID
        goNewDocObject.Title = ""
        goNewDocObject.filename = ""

        Load frmNewForm

        ' Call Method to create new OLE document
        ' Load the new type of Doc in the OLE control
        frmNewForm.oleOleForm.CreateEmbed "",
        ➥goObjectTypeSelected.Class
        frmNewForm.oleOleForm.DoVerb OPEN_OLE_OBJECT

        frmNewForm.Show

    End If
```

If the user clicks Cancel on the Add document screen, the code is ended. If the user selects a type of document to create, a new document object is created, a new instance of the form is displayed, and an embedded OLE document is inserted into the OLE container control on the new form.

At this point, only the ParentDirID property of the document object is known. All other values are set to cleared. When the document is added to the database from the OLE Document window, the other properties are assigned.

File Menu—New Directory

When the New Directory option is selected from the OLE Document Manager's File menu, a new Directory is created, added to the database, and displayed on the TreeView control. The code that allows this to happen is shown in Listing 22.18.

Listing 22.18   DOCTREE.FRM—When user clicks New Directory option on File menu, code calls the Add method of Directories collection, which adds a new Directory object to both the collection and the database

```
Private Sub mnuFileNewDirectory_Click()

    ' Create a New Directory Object
    Dim ldNewDirectory As Object
    Dim llParentID  As Long
    Dim lsKey As String
    Dim lsParentKey As String
    Dim lnodNewNod As Node

    ' Find the Parent ID
    lsParentKey = tvwDirectoryList.SelectedItem.KEY
    If tvwDirectory.SelectedItem.Index <> 1 Then
        llParentID = Val(Right(lsParentKey, Len(lsParentKey) - 3))
    Else
        llParentID = 0
    End If

    ' Create new Directory Object
    Set ldNewDirectory = CreateObject("DocManager.Directory")

    ldNewDirectory.Id = 0
    ldNewDirectory.Name = "TempName"
    ldNewDirectory.ParentID = llParentID

    ' Add it to the collection
    gcolDirectories.Add ldNewDirectory, ""
```

```
      ' Create the Key for TreeView control
      lsKey = "Dir" & ldNewDirectory.Id

      ' Add Document to TreeView
      Set lnodNewNod = tvwDirectoryList.Nodes.Add
      ➥(lsParentKey, tvwChild, lsKey, "", 1)
       ' Select the New Node
      lnodNewNod.Selected = True

      tvwDirectoryList.StartLabelEdit

      Set ldNewDirectory = Nothing

  End Sub
```

The first block of code, shown in the following example, determines the parent ID of the currently selected directory:

```
  ' Find the Parent ID
      lsParentKey = tvwDirectoryList.SelectedItem.KEY
      If tvwDirectory.SelectedItem.Index <> 1 Then
          llParentID = Val(Right(lsParentKey, Len(lsParentKey) - 3))
      Else
          llParentID = 0
      End If
```

This code will be used to determine where the new directory is displayed. When creating a new directory, the currently selected directory is always the parent of the new directory.

The next block of code, shown in the following lines, creates a new directory object, assigns it a temporary name and a parent ID, and invokes the Add method of the Directories class:

```
  ' Create new Directory Object
      Set ldNewDirectory = CreateObject("DocManager.Directory")

      ldNewDirectory.Id = 0
      ldNewDirectory.Name = "TempName"
      ldNewDirectory.ParentID = llParentID

      ' Add it to the collection
      gcolDirectories.Add ldNewDirectory, ""
```

The Add method adds the new directory to the database and adds the directory to the Directories collection. An optional Key value can be passed to the Add method. The method assigns a unique key, if one is not passed. If you do pass a key to the method, you risk passing a duplicate key. A directory with a duplicate key value will not be added to the collection.

After the new directory is added, the following function adds the directory to the TreeView control. Finally, it sets focus to the new directory and invokes the StartLabelEdit event:

```
        tvwDirectoryList.StartLabelEdit
```

Because the directory doesn't yet have a display name, setting focus to it requires the user to enter a valid directory name before continuing.

File Menu—Open

The Open command on the File menu opens an existing OLE document and displays a new instance of the OLE Document window. The code that makes up the Open options is shown in Listing 22.19.

Listing 22.19   DOCTREE.FRM—When Open option is selected from File menu, this code calls the Load event of the selected OLE document and displays the document to a user

```
    Private Sub mnuFileOpen_Click()

        ' Open an existing OLE File and place it in the
        ' OLE Doc Holder Form
        Dim lsKey As String
        Dim loDocObject As Object
        Dim liFileNumber

        ' Load new document from database. Can't create
        ' the form yet
        Set loDocObject = gcolDocuments.Item
    ➥(lvwDocList.SelectedItem.KEY)
        loDocObject.Load

        ' Now have document. Load the form
        ' Load the OLE Doc Form
        Dim frmNewForm As New frmOLEDocContainer

        Set goNewDocObject = loDocObject

        Load frmNewForm

        ' Load the OLE doc into the control and delete
        ' the temp file
        liFileNumber = FreeFile
        'Create temp file
        Open loDocObject.filename For Binary As liFileNumber
        frmNewForm.oleOleForm.ReadFromFile liFileNumber
        Close liFileNumber
        Kill loDocObject.filename

        ' Show the form
        frmNewForm.Show
        frmNewForm.oleOleForm.DoVerb OPEN_OLE_OBJECT

        Set loDocObject = Nothing

    End Sub
```

V

Sample Applications

The first block of code retrieves the document object from the Documents collection:

```
' Load new document from database. Can't create
' the form yet
Set loDocObject = gcolDocuments.Item
➥(lvwDocList.SelectedItem.KEY)
loDocObject.Load
```

The Load method of the existing document object is then invoked. As you saw previously, the Load method populates the Title and ParentDirID properties of the document object. Additionally, it writes the OLE document that is contained in the database to a temporary file. The path of this file is populated in the FileName property of the document object.

The next section of code, shown in the following lines, loads a new copy of the OLE Document window and inserts the OLE document saved to a temporary file into the OLE container control on the new form:

```
Set goNewDocObject = loDocObject

    Load frmNewForm

    ' Load the OLE doc into the control and delete
    ' the temp file
    liFileNumber = FreeFile
    'Create temp file
    Open loDocObject.filename For Binary As liFileNumber
    frmNewForm.oleOleForm.ReadFromFile liFileNumber
    Close liFileNumber
    Kill loDocObject.filename
```

This process is done by using the ReadFromFile method of the OLE container control.

After the OLE document is loaded, the temporary file is removed with the Kill command and the new OLE Document window is displayed.

File Menu—Delete
The Delete command from the File menu performs one of two functions. If the Directory TreeView control currently has focus, the selected directory is deleted. If the Document ListView control has focus, the selected document is deleted. When a directory is deleted, all child directories and documents also are deleted. Listing 22.20 shows the code that is required to perform this action.

Listing 22.20   DOCTREE.FRM—Delete option of File menu causes the selected Directory or Document object to be removed from the database

```
Private Sub mnuFileDelete_Click()

    ' Determine the currently selected Directory
    Dim lsDirKey As String
    Dim liReturn As Integer
    Dim lsDocKey As String

    lsDirKey = tvwDirectoryList.SelectedItem.KEY

    ' Determine which list has focus
    Select Case fiListWithFocus
        Case TREE_VIEW
            ' Tree View has focus
            liReturn = MsgBox("Are you sure you want
            ➥ to delete directory " &
            gcolDirectories.Item(lsDirKey).Name &
            " and all of its documents and directories?", vbYesNo)
            If liReturn = vbYes Then
                gcolDirectories.Remove lsDirKey
            Else
                Exit Sub
            End If

            ' Remove Node from TreeView
            tvwDirectoryList.Nodes.Remove lsDirKey
        Case Else
            ' List View has focus
            lsDocKey = lvwDocList.SelectedItem.KEY

            liReturn = MsgBox("Are you sure you want
            ➥to delete the document " & gcolDocuments.Item
            ➥(lsDocKey).Title & " ?", vbYesNo)
            If liReturn = vbYes Then
                gcolDocuments.Remove (lsDocKey)
            Else
                Exit Sub
            End If

            lvwDocList.ListItems.Remove (lsDocKey)

    End Select

End Sub
```

If the Directory TreeView control is selected, the following code is invoked:

```
Case TREE_VIEW
        ' Tree View has focus
        liReturn = MsgBox("Are you sure you want
    ➥ to delete directory " &
        gcolDirectories.Item(lsDirKey).Name &
        " and all of its documents and directories?", vbYesNo)
        If liReturn = vbYes Then
            gcolDirectories.Remove lsDirKey
        Else
            Exit Sub
        End If

        ' Remove Node from TreeView
        tvwDirectoryList.Nodes.Remove lsDirKey
```

This code asks users if they want to carry out the delete. If the user answers Yes, the Remove method of the Directories collection fires. This method deletes the directory selected and also all child directories and documents, from the database and the Directories collection. The directory then is removed from the TreeView control, using the Remove method of the TreeView's Nodes collection.

If the Document ListView control is selected, the same events occur, except the Remove method of the Documents collection is invoked. This method removes the document from the database and the Documents collection. The directory then is removed from the ListView control.

ListView—AfterLabelEdit Event

To change the name of an existing document, a user clicks on the doc-ument's title in the TreeView control and types the new title. After the user finishes editing and moves to a new document or directory, the AfterLabelEdit event of the TreeView control fires. The code to carry out this action is shown in Listing 22.21.

Listing 22.21 DOCTREE.FRM—After user edits the name of a Document, this code makes sure a valid name was entered and updates the database

```
Private Sub lvwDocList_AfterLabelEdit
➥(Cancel As Integer, NewString As String)

    Dim liDocObject As Object
    Dim llDocID As Long
    Dim lsNewDocName As String
```

```
    ' Make sure that a string was entered
    If Len(NewString) = 0 Then
        MsgBox "You must enter a name for this document."
        Cancel = True
        Exit Sub
    End If

    ' Find document in collection
    Set liDocObject = gcolDocuments(lvwDocList.SelectedItem.KEY)

    liDocObject.Title = Trim(NewString)

    ' Call Method to update directory name
    liDocObject.UPDATE

End Sub
```

The AfterLabelEdit event first ensures that a user has entered a title. If the title is left blank, the user is not permitted to leave the selected ListView item.

If the user enters a valid title, the code determines which document is being updated and retrieves it from the Documents collection:

```
    ' Find document in collection
        Set liDocObject = gcolDocuments(lvwDocList.SelectedItem.KEY)

        liDocObject.Title = Trim(NewString)

        ' Call Method to update directory name
        liDocObject.UPDATE
```

The code then resets the value of the document objects Title property and invokes the Update method of the document object. This saves the changes to the document's title in the database.

TreeView Control—AfterLabelEdit Event

The AfterLabelEdit event of the Directory control performs the same function as the AfterLabelEdit event of the TreeView control, but it also updates the name of a directory object by retrieving the directory being affected from the Directories collection, resetting the directory object's Name property, and calling the Update method. Listing 22.22 shows the code that makes up the AfterLabelEdit event.

V

Sample Applications

Listing 22.22   DOCTREE.FRM—After user changes the Directory name, this code makes sure that a valid name was entered, and then updates the database

```
Private Sub tvwDirectoryList_AfterLabelEdit
➡(Cancel As Integer, NewString As String)

    ' Change the name of the currently selected
    ' directory
    Dim llDirID As Long
    Dim lsKey As String

    ' Find the ID of the clicked directory
    lsKey = tvwDirectoryList.SelectedItem.KEY

    If lsKey = DIR_ROOT_KEY Then
        MsgBox "Cannot change name of Root."
        Cancel = True
        Exit Sub
    End If

    ' Make sure that a string was entered
    If Len(NewString) = 0 Then
        MsgBox "You must enter a name for this directory."
        Cancel = True
        Exit Sub
    End If

    Screen.MousePointer = MP_HOURGLASS

    ' Call the update method with the new file name
    gcolDirectories.Item(lsKey).Name = NewString
    gcolDirectories.Item(lsKey).UPDATE

    Screen.MousePointer = MP_DEFAULT

End Sub
```

TreeView Control—NodeClick Event

When a user clicks on a directory name in TreeView control, the NodeClick event fires, which causes the child documents of the directory to appear on-screen in the ListView control. The code that makes up the NodeClick event is shown in Listing 22.23.

Listing 22.23   DOCTREE.FRM— NodeClick event calls fiGetNodeKey function to retrieve the child Document objects of the selected Directory

```
Private Sub tvwDirectoryList_NodeClick(ByVal Node As Node)

    ' Determine the child documents for the Node
    ' and display them
    fiGetNodeKey lvwDocList, Node

End Sub
```

The code used to retrieve the child documents is held in the form-level function, `fiFillChildDocs`, detailed in the following section. The NodeClick event calls the `fiGetNodeKey` function, which determines the Key of the currently selected node.

fiFillChildDocs Function

The `fiFillChildDocs` function retrieves and displays all children of the passed directory in the Document ListView control. The code that makes up this function is shown in Listing 22.24.

Listing 22.24   DOCTREE.FRM—The fiFillChildDocs function cycles through the Documents collection and displays child Document objects to the end-user

```
Private Function fiFillChildDocs
➥(alvwListView As ListView, asDirectoryKey As String)

    Dim ldoDocObject As Object
    Dim ldDocObject As Object
    Dim llParentID As Long
    Dim lsKey As String
    Dim lsDescription As String
    Dim llstmListItem As ListItem
    Dim liCounter As Integer

    alvwListView.ListItems.Clear

    If asDirectoryKey = DIR_ROOT_KEY Then
        ' At root level. Return no Child docs
        Exit Function
    End If

    ' Find parent directory's ID
    llParentID = gcolDirectories.Item(asDirectoryKey).Id
```

```
    ' Find all occurrences of the Directory ID in each Document
    ' in the Documents collection
    For liCounter = 1 To gcolDocuments.Count
      Set ldDocObject = gcolDocuments.Item(liCounter)
      If ldDocObject.ParentDirID = llParentID Then
          ' The parent ID of the document equals the ID of the Node.
          ' Display the document
          lsKey = "Doc" & ldDocObject.Id
          lsDescription = ldDocObject.Title
          Set llstmListItem = alvwListView.ListItems.Add
          ➥(, lsKey, lsDescription, , 3)
      End If
    Next

    alvwListView.Refresh

End Function
```

The first portion of the fiFillChildDocs function, shown in the following
lines, determines the ID of the currently selected directory in the TreeView
control by searching for a match on the directory's key in the Directories
collection:

```
    ' Find parent directory's ID
        llParentID = gcolDirectories.Item(asDirectoryKey).Id
```

When a matching directory is found, the function cycles through the Documents collection and finds all documents with a ParentDirID property value
equal to the ID of the currently selected directory. If a match is found, the
document is displayed in the ListView control.

fiFillDirectories Function

When the Document Explorer form is loaded, the fiFillDirectories function
is called. This function cycles through the Directories collection and adds
each directory to the TreeView control. The code that makes up the
fiFillDirectories function is shown in Listing 22.25.

**Listing 22.25   DOCTREE.FRM—fiFillDirectories function cycles
through the Directories collection and adds each Directory object
in the TreeView control**

```
Private Function fiFillDirectories(atvwTreeView As TreeView)

    ' Function fills the passed TreeView control
    ' with directories in the Directories collection
    Dim lsParentKey As String
    Dim lsKey As String
    Dim lsDescription As String
    Dim lnodNewNode As Node
    Dim ldirDirectory As Object
    Dim liCounter As Integer
```

```
' Clear the control
atvwTreeView.Nodes.Clear

' Add the root directory
Set lnodNewNode = atvwTreeView.Nodes.Add
➥(, , "DirRoot", "Documents", 1)

For liCounter = 1 To gcolDirectories.Count
    ' Add each directory in the collection
    Set ldirDirectory = gcolDirectories.Item(liCounter)

    lsKey = "Dir" & ldirDirectory.Id
    lsDescription = ldirDirectory.Name

    If ldirDirectory.ParentID = 0 Then
       ' Dir is at parent level
       lsParentKey = "DirRoot"
    Else
       ' Dir is not at parent level
       lsParentKey = "Dir" & ldirDirectory.ParentID
    End If

    Set lnodNewNode = atvwTreeView.Nodes.Add
    ➥(lsParentKey, tvwChild, lsKey, lsDescription, 1)
    lnodNewNode.ExpandedImage = 2

Next

atvwTreeView.Refresh

End Function
```

The TreeView control permits a hierarchical display of Directories (a Directory can contain other Directories within it). In the Directory object, the ParentID property indicates if a directory has a parent. If a directory's ParentID property is set to 0, the directory sits at the highest level in the hierarchy.

The following code fragment looks at the value of a Directory's ParentID property:

```
For liCounter = 1 To gcolDirectories.Count
    ' Add each directory in the collection
    Set ldirDirectory = gcolDirectories.Item(liCounter)

    lsKey = "Dir" & ldirDirectory.Id
    lsDescription = ldirDirectory.Name

    If ldirDirectory.ParentID = 0 Then
       ' Dir is at parent level
       lsParentKey = "DirRoot"
    Else
       ' Dir is not at parent level
       lsParentKey = "Dir" & ldirDirectory.ParentID
    End If
```

V

Sample Applications

```
Set lnodNewNode = atvwTreeView.Nodes.Add
➥(lsParentKey, tvwChild, lsKey, lsDescription, 1)
lnodNewNode.ExpandedImage = 2

    Next
```

If the ParentID property equals 0, the directory is added to the TreeView at the highest possible level (one level below the root), by setting the parent argument of the Nodes collection's Add method to the key of the root directory. The loop also generates a unique key value for the new added directory.

If the value of a directory's ParentID is not 0, the parent argument of the Nodes collection's Add method is set to the Key of the directory's parent directory. For the demo application, directories can be added only at the first and second levels of the hierarchy (a directory that is a child of a directory other than the root cannot have children beneath it).

fiGetNodeKey Function

The fiGetNodeKey determines the Key of the currently selected Node in the TreeView control. The function then calls the fiFillChildDocs function to populate the Document ListView control. The code that makes up the fiGetNodeKey function is shown in Listing 22.26.

> **Listing 22.26 DOCTREE.FRM—The fiGetNodeKey function determines which Directory is currently selected in the TreeView function**

```
Private Function fiGetNodeKey
➥(alvwListView As ListView, anodNode As Node)

    ' Function retrieves child docs from the Documents collection
    Dim lsDirectoryKey As String

    ' Set local variable equal to the passed node's key
    lsDirectoryKey = anodNode.KEY

    ' Call the fill function
    fiFillChildDocs alvwListView, lsDirectoryKey

End Function
```

The Add Document Window

When you choose the New Document command from the Document Explorer's File menu, the Add Document dialog window is displayed. From this window, a user selects the type of document to create. This section details the functions used by the Add Document window.

The Form_Load Event

When the Add document form is loaded, the fiFillDocTypes function is called. This function, shown in the following code, populates a list box, passed as an argument to the function, with the names of document classes that are available for creation:

```
Private Sub Form_Load()

    'Fill Object Types
    fiFillDocTypes lstOLETypes

    gbFormReturnResult = False

End Sub
```

fiFillDocTypes Function

The fiFillDocTypes function populates the passed list box with all DocTypes available in the DocTypes collection. Additionally, the function sets the list box item's ItemData property equal to the DocType's ID. The fiFillDocTypes function is shown in Listing 22.27.

Listing 22.27   DOCLIST.FRM—The fiFillDocTypes function retrieves the types of OLE documents that are available to the end-user

```
Private Function fiFillDocTypes(alstListBox As ListBox)

    ' Function fills the past list box with available object types
    Dim loDocType As Object
    Dim liCounter As Long
    Dim llCounter As Long

    ' Clear list box
    alstListBox.Clear

    ' Add doc types to list box
    For llCounter = 1 To gcolDocTypes.Count
        alstListBox.AddItem gcolDocTypes.Item(llCounter).Name
        alstListBox.ItemData(alstListBox.NewIndex) =
        ➥ gcolDocTypes.Item(llCounter).Id
    Next

End Function
```

fiSelectObjectType

When the OK button on the Add Document window is clicked or an item in the Type list box is selected, the fiSelectObjectType function is called. This function determines which type of object was selected by the user and assigns its ID to the form level variable, foObjectType. After the selection is made, the form is unloaded. The code that makes up the fiSelectObjectType function is shown in Listing 22.28.

Listing 22.28 DOCLIST.FRM—The fiSelectObjectType function determines which type of OLE document a user wants to create

```
Private Function fiSelectObjectType() As Boolean

    ' Function determines which OLE object
    ' type was selected and assigns it to a global
    ' variable
    Dim liCounter As Integer

    For liCounter = 0 To lstOLETypes.ListCount - 1
        If lstOLETypes.Selected(liCounter) = True Then
            Set foObjectType =
            ➥gcolDocTypes.Item(lstOLETypes.ItemData(liCounter))
            fiSelectObjectType = True
            Exit Function
        End If
    Next liCounter

    MsgBox "Please select a type of object to create"
    fiSelectObjectType = False
End Function
```

The OLE Document Window

The OLE Document window displays both new documents and documents that were previously saved to the database. This section details the functions used by the OLE Document window.

Form_Load Event

When the OLE Document window is loaded, the Document Explorer window inserts the new or existing object into the OLE container control. The Load event places the title of the Document into the titlebar of the OLE Document window. Additionally, it assigns the value of the passed variable goNewDocObject to the local form variable, foDocObject. This object is used when a users saves or updates the OLE document. The code that makes up the Load event is shown in Listing 22.29.

Listing 22.29 DOCHOLD.FRM—The Form_Load event of the OLE Document window prepares the embedded OLE document for editing

```
Private Sub Form_Load()

    ' Set OLE control to only allow embedded objects
    oleOleForm.OLETypeAllowed = vbOLEEmbedded
```

```
' Set local variable from global
Set foDocObject = goNewDocObject

Set goNewDocObject = Nothing

If foDocObject.Id <> 0 Then
    ' Display Title of Doc in TitleBar
    Me.Caption = foDocObject.Title
End If

fbFormNeedsSaved = True

End Sub
```

fiSaveDocument

When a new OLE document is first saved, the fiSaveDocument function is called. The fiSaveDocument function prompts the user to enter a title for the new document. After a title is entered, the function writes the data in the OLE container control to a binary file, using the WriteToFile method of the container control because the only way to write the OLE object to the database is through the AppendChunk method. The fiSaveDocument function is shown in Listing 22.30.

Listing 22.30   DOCHOLD.FRM—The fiSaveDocument function saves a new OLE document to the database. It does this by calling the Add method of the Documents collection

```
Public Function fiSaveDocument() As Boolean

    ' Function saves the document currently in the
    ' OLE control
    Dim liFileNumber As Integer
    Dim lsFilePath As String
    Dim lsDocName As String
    Dim loDocObject As Object

    ' Make sure a document exists
    If oleOleForm.OLEType <> vbOLENone Then
        ' Retrieve Name for New file
        foDocObject.Title = InputBox
➥("Please select a Title for the new Document:",
➥ "Save Document", "New Document1")
        If Len(foDocObject.Title) = 0 Then
            ' User clicked cancel
            fiSaveDocument = False
            Exit Function
        End If

        ' Must first write data to file
        liFileNumber = FreeFile
```

```
                        'Open holder file for doc
                        Open App.Path & "\OLE.TMP" For Binary As liFileNumber
                        oleOleForm.SaveToFile liFileNumber
                        Close liFileNumber
                        foDocObject.filename = App.Path & "\OLE.TMP"
                        gcolDocuments.Add foDocObject
                        fbFormNeedsSaved = False
                        fiSaveDocument = True

                        ' Change title on form
                        Me.Caption = foDocObject.Title
                    End If

                End Function
```

After the data is written to a binary file, the Add method of the Documents collection is called. This method adds the new document both to the database and to the Documents collection.

fiUpdateDocument

The fiUpdateDocument function is similar to the fiSaveDocument, except that it uses the Update method of the Document class to save changes to a document. Because the document was already added to the Documents collection, calling the Add method of the collection isn't needed. After a new document is saved with the Add method, subsequent saves use the Update method exclusively. The fiUpdateDocument function is shown in Listing 22.31.

Listing 22.31 DOCLIST.FRM— fiUpdateDocument function updates changes made to a Document object to the database by calling the Document object's Update method

```
    Private Sub fiUpdateDocument()

        ' Function updates the document currently in the
        ' OLE control
        Dim liFileNumber As Integer
        Dim lsFilePath As String
        Dim lsDocName As String

        ' Make sure a document exists
        If oleOleForm.OLEType <> vbOLENone Then
            ' Must first write data to file
            liFileNumber = FreeFile
   'Open hold file for doc
            Open App.Path & "\OLE.TMP" For Binary As liFileNumber
            oleOleForm.SaveToFile liFileNumber
            Close liFileNumber
            foDocObject.filename = App.Path & "\OLE.TMP"
            foDocObject.UPDATE
            fbFormNeedsSaved = False
        End If
    End Sub
```

Limitations of the OLE Container Control

When developing applications that use the OLE container control to display and edit OLE documents, several limitations of the control should be kept in mind. This vigilance will help your development effort run smoothly.

The most-notable limit of the container control is that an existing OLE document can be loaded only from a binary file. You can, for example, create an Excel worksheet in an application by using the following code:

```
Dim loExcelSheet as Object
Set loExcelSheet = CreateObject("Excel.Sheet")
```

This code creates a reference to a new Excel worksheet. At this point, the sheet is invisible to the user. You then can use the methods and properties of the object to add a chart and populate some cells with data. If you then want to display this document to users with the OLE container control so they could look at and edit it, you need to write the data referenced in loExcelSheet to a binary file, and then use the ReadFromFile method of the OLE container control to display the worksheet. If you try to use the following statement, an error will occur:

```
Set oleContainerControl.Object = loExcelSheet
```

This limitation is the reason the giOLEFiletoColumn and giOLEColumntoObject functions are needed in the OLE Document Manager application—they automate the task of writing the contents of an OLE container control to and from binary files.

A second point to note is that toolbar negotiation can occur only between OLE document and MDIParent forms (unless your application is an MDI application, you will not have the added benefit of toolbar negotiation while you are visually editing an OLE document that has been inserted into the OLE container control). Menus still will merge. Some OLE document's toolbars, such as Word, will display as floating toolbars.

Finally, the size of an OLE container is difficult to manipulate programmatically. When you insert an OLE document into the OLE container control, the OLE document or the container control is resized, depending on the control's SizeMode property settings. Chapter 5, "Controlling OLE Objects," discusses the four SizeMode property options, which are shown in the following list:

- Clip
- Stretch

V

Sample Applications

- Autosize

- Zoom

For specific information on each property setting, see your Visual Basic documentation.

All of the SizeMode properties cause potential problems when resizing forms or the control. Some settings, such as Clip, may cause portions of the document, such as scroll bars, to be hidden. The AutoSize and Stretch settings may cause the OLE documents to re-dimension, which may cause edges of the displayed document to "hang" over the edge of the OLE container or "hang off" the edge of a form. The Zoom property can cause the text on a document to become too small to see.

Finally, some control and menu options are unavailable when visually editing an OLE document. When a Word document is displayed in an OLE container control, for example, only Page View viewing mode is available. Outline and Normal views are disabled.

From Here...

In this chapter, you examined the inner workings of a simple three-tier application. After reading this chapter, you should have an understanding of how the business logic of an application is divided between its tiers and how to create and use OLE automation server and documents.

For further information related to topics covered in this chapter, see the following:

- Chapter 5, "Controlling OLE Objects," provides details about controlling OLE documents and servers from client applications.

- Chapter 6, "Creating OLE Objects," provides more information about creating an OLE Automation server.

- Chapter 8, "Architecting Tier 1: Client Applications," provides more information about designing and creating a client application.

- Chapter 9, "Architecting Tier 2: Business Servers," provides more information about designing and creating a business server.

- Chapter 10, "Architecting Tier 3: Data Servers," provides more information about designing and creating data services.

Chapter 23

Sample Application #2: An Instance Manager

This chapter describes the instance manager sample application included on this book's companion disk. An instance manager is a program that maintains and makes available pools of already created objects on a server machine, accessible by remote automation.

Visual Basic includes sample code for another instance manager, called "Pool Manager." You can find this code in the SAMPLES\REMAUTO\POOLMNGR directory of your Visual Basic installation directory. The instance manager sample presented in this book takes a different approach than the sample included with VB so that you have a good feel for the flexibility in which instance managers can be architected.

This book uses the terms "instance manager" and "pool manager" interchangeably.

The instance manager sample code is divided into the following two main sections:

- A generic instance manager template that can form the basis of your own business object applications.

- A sample skeleton of the instance manager that is used by the GOLF system.

Read this chapter to become familiar with the concepts and features an instance manager can provide your remote OLE objects. In this chapter, you do the following:

- Review Visual Basic features that affect the design of an instance manager

- Learn feature ideas that you can implement in an instance manager

- Walk through the instance manager included with this book

- Learn the difference between the instance manager included with this book and Visual Basic's sample Pool Manager

Why Build an Instance Manager?

Many of the reasons we need an instance manager today will go away when remote automation is superseded by full-blown Distributed OLE (also known as the *Distributed Component Object Model*, or DCOM).

The instance manager is a tool for managing your custom server objects, usually business services. You probably will find most of the functionality of a particular instance manager useful for all objects. It may seem, therefore, like the kind of application you would buy or have included in the operating system rather than build yourself.

Because an instance manager is a powerful and necessary tool for managing server objects, the flexibility of a custom-developed instance manager probably outweighs the advantages of buying an off-the-shelf utility that may not do everything that you want.

Regardless, in the future DCOM and transaction processing monitors probably will incorporate all the features of today's instance manager. As you will see in the remainder of the chapter, for example, Microsoft's next generation operating system, code named "Cairo," will incorporate full-blown distributed OLE with integrated security.

Figure 23.1 shows the basic architecture of the sample *OrderMgrs* instance manager described in this chapter. This shell is the foundation upon which the full-blown GOLF system built its instance managers, which is presented in Chapter 24, "Sample Application #3: A Three-Tier Order Processing System."

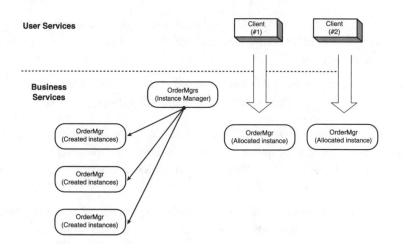

Fig. 23.1
The architecture
of the OrderMgrs
sample instance
manager.

Technology Review

Before you get into features and design of an instance manager, it's helpful to briefly review the Visual Basic technology and architecture that relates to remote automation and OLE automation servers.

Instance managers manage instances of object classes on a server being accessed by remote automation across a network.

Process Management

The object created by the Remote Automation Manager (RAM) for the client application must be an out-of-process object, because the Automation Manager cannot create in-process servers. This limitation is by design, because an errant in-process OLE server would be able to bring down the Automation Manager if it were to crash, and with it, all remotely automated servers.

OLE automation servers in Visual Basic are single-threaded (each process runs in one thread). An OLE automation server's *Instancing* property and the way in which it is compiled determines the process in which it runs. More specifically, an OLE automation server instancing property does the following things:

■ An out-of-process, creatable single-use server creates a new process on the server, and thus a new thread of execution, for every client create request.

- An out-of-process, creatable multi-use server creates a single process per server machine, and therefore a single thread of execution, for all client create requests.

- An in-process, creatable multi-use server uses the client process for all create requests. Therefore it shares the client's thread of execution.

If you want two or more object class instances to multi-task, then you need to create them so that they *live* in different processes. The operating system then will multi-task the instances. Each executing process uses about 500K of free memory.

In a services architecture, where multiple client applications must be served simultaneously by a business server object class, each client application needs its own process on the server. The instance manager's job is to allot these processes without unduly taxing the server's finite resources.

Remote Automation

The Automation Manager is a multi-threaded application. It maintains a thread of execution for each client connection (so the Automation Manager isn't going to be an execution bottleneck to your instance managers).

Because the Automation Manager runs all connections in the same process (but with multiple threads), it creates all processes in its security context (each OLE server on the server machine runs with the same user account in which the Automation Manager was started).

The Automation Manager, however, does implement security. Under Windows NT, it checks to see if a client was given specific access to a class's registry ACL (by temporarily impersonating the client) on the server before it allows the client access to the class, but it doesn't start the OLE server with the client's security context.

Designing an instance manager involves some trade-offs. You should thoroughly understand these often confusing server, process, and remote automation concepts before beginning the design of your instance manager.

Instance Manager Features

A number of features exist that you may want to implement in your instance manager. This section outlines some of these useful features.

The features you may want to implement in your instance manager include the following:

- Pre-load object instances
- Multi-tasking instances
- Exclusive instance manager creation
- Unobtrusive instance creation
- Integrated security
- Govern processes
- Minimize processes
- Load balance across machines
- Multiple classes
- Reuse object instances
- Management

Several of these features are implemented either in the sample instance manager provided with this book or in the sample Visual Basic Pool Manager. Possible implementation of features that aren't included in either application are discussed near the end of this chapter.

Pre-Load Object Instances

An important performance factor regarding remote automation is whether or not the client application must wait for the server to create a new object instance on demand. Instantiating an object in a new process often takes the server several seconds.

The instance manager can pre-create class instances and maintain a pool of free instances. When the client application asks for a particular instance, the instance manager need only pass a handle of the pre-created object to the client application from its free pool and mark it as allocated.

Pre-creating class instances is probably the most common task for which you use an instance manager because it's relatively easy to implement and yields a big performance gain on end-user wait time.

Because object variables can be passed by way of OLE automation and, thus, remote automation, the instance manager usually manages this pool of objects by storing references to them in a collection. After the client application assigns one of its own variables to the object, the instance manager then can release its reference, if desired, without destroying the object (because the client application still has a reference to it).

The instance manager needs to adjust the pool size asynchronously with respect to client requests, which means that the instance manager cannot adjust the pool size in immediate reaction to a client application requesting or releasing an instance. If it did, it would defeat the purpose of pre-loaded object instances: the client application still would have to wait while an object was created!

Because Visual Basic 4 is not multi-threaded, the instance manager cannot kick off an event asynchronously that adjusts the pool size. Rather, it can implement a timer in the instance manager that periodically wakes up and adjusts the pool size.

Multi-Tasking Instances

Several client applications need to use business objects simultaneously. When choosing and architecting a DBMS data service, one primary design consideration is concurrency—allowing multiple users simultaneous access to its services.

The same consideration applies to the business servers. The system's design should service multiple users simultaneously.

As you have learned, the only way you can multi-task objects of the same class is by running them in different processes. The instance manager needs to provide a mechanism of satisfactorily allocating objects by process.

The most straightforward way to accomplish this is by setting the Instancing property of the class to Creatable Single-Use, so that each instance created by the instance manager is automatically executed in its own process.

Another design consideration that relates to multi-tasking is the capability of the instance manager to serve multiple clients. Your instance manager, for example, probably will run in the same process for all client applications. It can, therefore, service only one client application create request at a time.

This limitation isn't a problem if the instance manager only creates objects asynchronously and allocates them to client applications. Although VB will serialize client requests, this shouldn't present a contention problem because it happens infrequently and quickly. When adding more features to your instance manager, however, you always must remember that the instance manager itself can service only one client application request at a time; any lengthy operations should be off-loaded to another process.

Exclusive Instance Manager Creation

OLE automation objects are fairly easy to access from desktop tools such as Microsoft Excel—just bring up the Object Browser and away you go.

You probably spent a lot of time designing how an instance manager can best manage server resources. You don't want an end user, or even an application developer, bypassing the instance manager and creating the business objects directly. Rather, the system should force the client application to use the instance manager to acquire an object.

You may have designed objects, for example, to load-balance across several machines. The instance manager should control the machine from which a client application gets its object. The client application should not be allowed to bypass the instance manager and choose a particular machine.

Enforcing object creation by the instance manager is accomplished in two different ways. The following two sections cover these two approaches.

Approach #1: Security by ACL

The simplest way to enforce object creation via the instance manager requires that the remote automation security policy on the server is set to allow remote creates by ACL. The client application can be given access to the instance manager but not to the managed object class. The instance manager is given rights to create the managed object. So, the client is allowed to create the instance manager but is not allowed to create the managed object.

Remember that security in remote automation is checked only during object creation, so the instance manager has no problem passing a reference to the created object back to the client application, even though the client application wasn't allowed to create the object directly.

Approach #2: Security by Key

A more complicated method of enforcing object creation via the instance manager, which works with just a security policy set to "allow remote creates by key," is to have the managed instances instantiate in a process other than the instance manager, and then have them actively pass a handle of themselves to the instance manager. The managed object is set to disallow remote creates.

In this scenario, neither the instance manager nor client applications create instances. Rather, another process running on the server creates the instances, and then gives them to the instance manager. Neither the client application nor the instance manager have permission to remotely create managed object instances.

Although this approach is more complicated than the first, it offers the same functionality as the first without requiring Windows NT-based user security.

Unobtrusive Instance Creation

In the services model, our goal is to allow different services to transparently interact. The design of your business objects should be intuitive, succinct, and easily used. Eventually, you want your end users to access the business services directly with desktop tools.

The instance manager adds a call-level between the client application and the business server object. The design of this extra step should be simple and consistent.

The managed object should not have to know about the instance manager. It should be designed so that it can be instantiated easily by means other than the instance manager.

The method in which an instance is retrieved should be consistent across all instance managers. After an instance manager interface is agreed upon, it shouldn't change and it also should be used for other business objects.

The instance manager should not count on client applications to perform a specific task. For example, the instance manager should not break or orphan instances if a special *terminate* method isn't called by the client application after it is done with the instance. Developers often forget to clean up properly. End-users who are accessing your business server will be even worse "housekeepers."

You design business servers so they can't break, cannot be placed in an invalid state, and cannot have their business rules bypassed. Likewise, you should design an instance manager so that it can't break or be placed in an invalid state.

The sample instance manager in this chapter requires only a single easy-to-use step to instantiate its managed objects.

Integrated Security

As you learned in Chapter 13, "Architecting Security," security should be an administrative task. The administrator should be able to change security settings without having to touch code.

Likewise, application developers should not have to build security systems. Operating systems such as Windows NT implement tighter security than most developers can implement. The goal of the system should be to universally leverage the operating-system security.

Besides allowing or disallowing all remote class creates, the Remote Automation Connection Manager allows you to specify two levels of security. The first level—allow remote creates by key—doesn't really provide discretionary security because it allows all users equal access to an OLE class. The second level—allow remote creates by ACL—enables you to provide selective access to creates.

Remote automation supports integrated security during remote-object instantiation (the client application's credentials are used to verify authority to create the object). Unfortunately, this impersonation concept doesn't extend into the object or into the data-services tier. With remote automation, the goal of integrated security cannot be achieved all the way down to the data services tier.

That remote automation checks security only during object creation creates another problem if you want to leverage operating-system security in an instance manager environment. In the instance manager environment, the objects were pre-created by the instance manager. So, when a client application asks for an instance, the client application is really instantiating the instance manager itself.

This means that client application credentials are checked against the instance manager, and not against the managed object.

One method of accomplishing the goal of leveraging OS security during object creation in an instance-manager environment is to create a separate instance manager application for each object class. You can then administer security on the instance manager the same way as its managed object class.

Govern Processes

Servers machines have finite resources. Each OLE automation process takes about 500K of free memory. An instance manager should govern the number of processes that are running on the server.

For example, you may want to enforce the rule that only 30 processes can run simultaneously on the server, or that a user can use only one of each type of process.

For an instance manager to govern processes, it needs to know how many are in use. Determining how many processes are allocated to client applications is fairly straightforward because the instance manager performed the allocations.

Determining when the client application is done with the instance, however, is more difficult because Visual Basic doesn't provide a means to determine the reference count on an object. This section outlines four approaches to determine when the client application is finished with an instance.

First Approach: Client Notification

The first approach to determine when the client application is finished with an instance is to require that the client application notify the instance manager when it is done with the object.

The client application, for example, may be expected to call a ReturnInstance method on the instance manager with a special ID to its instance. This approach probably is the easiest and most flexible option from a development vantage point but probably the most difficult approach from a deployment standpoint. The interface is cumbersome, objects cannot be terminated by the client application simply by setting them to *Nothing*, and client applications will forget to call the ReturnInstance method.

Second Approach: Business Object Notification

A second approach requires that the business server notify the instance manager when the client application is done with the object.

When the instance manager, for example, allocates an instance to a client application, the instance manager releases all its references to the instance. When the client application sets its references to the instance to Nothing, the instance is terminated. Before the instance terminates, however, the instance calls a method in the instance manager, telling the instance manager that it is shutting down.

The advantage of this approach is that the client application uses the instance like any other object—it doesn't have to do anything special to properly terminate the object. The downside is that the business server must know how to tell the instance manager that it is terminating.

Third Approach: Timeout

A third option to determine when the client application is finished with an instance is to simply set a timer in the instance manager that terminates instances after they are allocated for a specified period. This approach isn't very friendly from a client application standpoint but might be appropriate in an environment where business objects are supposed to have short or known life spans.

Fourth Approach: Process Monitoring

Finally, a fourth option to determine when the client application is finished with an instance is to have the instance manager monitor the operating system processes. The instance manager, for example, can periodically make Windows API calls that enumerate the loaded executables, tracking exactly how many executables are running. The downside of this option is that it doesn't work when an instance manager is managing instances across machines.

Minimize Processes

As mentioned in the preceding section, servers have limited resources. The instance manager should not only put an absolute ceiling on the number of instance processes running on the server, it also should intelligently manage instances so that a minimum number of processes are instantiated.

Idle processes, objects instantiated in their own processes but not actually executing code, still use server resources. A client application that sits idle with several business-server object instances still uses server resources. Each process takes about 500k, and each process is monitored and multitasked by the operating system.

If 60 users need access to a business object but only a maximum of 10 users ever use them simultaneously, then theoretically, 10 objects can serve all 60 users, if the process is intelligently managed.

The design challenge with this scenario is determining how to force client applications to release their objects when the objects are no longer needed and thus to free server resources. There are three approaches to determine how to handle this design challenge.

First Approach: Minimize Persistence

The first approach is to design business servers so that they won't live long. You can design a business object, for example, so that after any method is called, the business object terminates. Of course, this means the methods need to encapsulate a great deal of functionality to be of any use.

For example, an order manager business server may have two methods as its entire interface—GetOrders and CreateOrders. GetOrders may take some selection parameters, return an array of orders, and terminate. CreateOrders may take an array of order headers and line items, and then enter them in the database and terminate.

You can see that with this scenario we've abandoned a lot of the advantages a rich OLE interface provides, and our business server accomplishes nothing more than simple, non-persistent remote procedure calls. When the client application references the object a second time, the business server has no recollection of the first call.

Second Approach: Client-Side Management

The second approach is to require that client applications quickly release the object. Client applications, for example, may be required to be designed so that an object never remains instantiated while the client application is waiting for user input.

For example, rather than working directly with an *OrderMgr* during user input, the client application might gather a new order's information and store this information in private arrays and variables. Only when the user asks to update the data is the object created, populated, updated, and destroyed. The remote object never waits for user input from the client application.

The downside to this approach is that the business-server tier doesn't have complete control over its performance—it relies on properly designed client applications. Additionally, the client application doesn't get to work directly with the object during user input—it cannot store its information in the business object while the user is inputting.

This approach, however, mirrors its common data service counterpart: optimistic record locking. In this scenario, records don't stay locked nor do cursors stay open while user input occurs. Instead, the database record is accessed only after the user indicates.

Third Approach: In-Process Servers

The third approach probably is the most interesting. It uses in-process business servers exclusively on the server machine. This approach guarantees a client application uses no more than one process on the server at a time. So, if 20 users were active, only 20 processes would be running on the server, even if every user had a handle to 10 objects.

Figure 23.2 shows this architecture. In this case, the server runs only a single type of instance manager, the *ClientMgr*. The client application is allowed to create only one ClientMgr. After the *ClientMgr* process is created, the client application can ask the ClientMgr to instantiate any object and pass it a reference. All the business servers, however, are in-process. So when the ClientMgr instantiates an OrderMgr object, for example, the OrderMgr object runs in the ClientMgr's process. The client application can ask for 50 objects, and all will run in its ClientMgr process on the server.

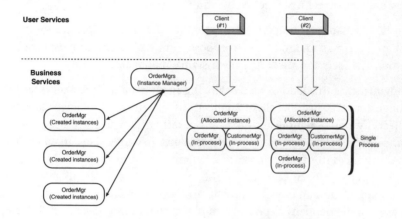

Fig. 23.2
An in-process instance manager.

There are a number of limitations to this architecture:

- All business servers must be in-process servers.

- Because all business objects are created with the ClientMgr's security context, you cannot individually secure objects with the operating system—anyone who has access to the instance manager has access to all of its object types.

- Although the server can serve multiple users at the same time, each user is limited to one server thread of execution. If the user is running a long process in the ClientMgr, for example, the user cannot run anything else on the server until the first request was finished.

If, however, an organization has a large number of business objects the advantages of this architecture are compelling—a system administrator knows that even if 50 users ask for 15 objects each, only 50 processes will run on the server.

The *LogonMgr* in the client application can help make interaction with the ClientMgr transparent. This architecture is probably best for a typical corporate environment with many users. It enables a typical NT machine to support over 50 concurrent users. In addition, when the business object is deployed on the client machine, this architecture runs very quickly because it runs in-process to the client application.

Load Balance across Machines

At some point, client applications' demand for object instances will exceed the server's capacity to service them. Ideally, the instance manager should load balance object instances across multiple server machines.

This load balancing should be transparent to the client application—the client application shouldn't have to choose from which machine its instance comes. This decision should be the instance manager's.

Implementing this kind of load balancing in an instance manager is fairly straightforward. Just like client applications, the instance manager can create objects by way of remote automation. So, rather than creating a pool of instances only off its own machine, the instance manager also can add to its pool instances from other machines. When a client machine asks for an instance from the instance manager, the instance manager simply passes the client application an object handle to an object in its pool. In this case, the object handle happens to point to an object that doesn't reside on the same machine as the instance manager.

Remember that because the object instantiation must be transparent to the client application, only one instance manager is running for all machines—not one instance manager per machine.

Multiple Classes

An instance manager shouldn't be tied to a specific object class. Ideally, the instance manager you build for one class should be universally employed by all classes. The same instance manager should manage multiple classes simultaneously.

A truly generic and flexible instance manager, for example, would be able to manage a pool of 15 OrderMgr instances, 15 CustomerMgr instances, and 12 ProdMgr instances.

The following list shows two roadblocks to this goal:

- If a single instance manager manages all objects, you can't apply security to objects selectively by user—anyone who has access to the instance manager also has access to all of its object types.

- Occasionally, you may want to manage different objects classes in very different ways. You may find it easier to build separate instance managers than to try and accommodate very different design goals into a consolidated instance manager.

Reuse Object Instances

When a client application is through with an instance, the instance manager can increase the size of its pool. The instance manager can either let the old instance terminate and create a new one, or it can try to reclaim the old instance.

New Instance

Creating a new instance is straightforward and was already discussed. For example, the instance manager releases its handle to the object when it is allocated to the client application. When the client application is done with the object, it releases its references and the object terminates. Before terminating, however, the business object notifies the instance manager that it is terminating.

Existing Instance

Reusing the instance is more difficult to implement. Visual Basic cannot monitor the reference count of an object instance, so as long as the instance manager maintains its handle to the object, it can't tell whether or not the client is done with the instance.

Instead, it must rely on the client application to proactively (through a method) tell the instance manager when it is done. As was mentioned previously, however, it isn't wise to require a client application to go through any special termination procedures.

Another problem is with objects that have persistent data. If an object only exposes a bunch of methods, reusing the object for another client application probably raises no persistent data issues. If, however, the object has properties and collections, the instance manager must clear the object before allocating it to another client application. This can be accomplished in the following two ways:

- The instance manager can know how to manually reset the object's properties and persistent data

- The object class can implement a special Clear method that resets the object

In the first scenario, special instance manager code must be written for each object. In the second scenario, the instance manager is capable only of managing instances that have the special Clear method.

Reusing pool objects is a noble effort, but usually is too difficult to implement cleanly.

Centralized Management

Because instance managers are a central router of all business object use, they make an ideal place to monitor business process usage. The instance manager, for example, can display a GUI interface on the server, indicating created and allocated pool sizes. It can keep a log of instance usage or write directly to the Windows NT event log.

An instance manager can allow the administrator to terminate instances, change pool size, and so on. In addition, it can expose a special management OLE automation interface so an administrator with a special monitoring client application can monitor the instance manager remotely.

The sample instance manager on the companion disk, for example, provides a GUI summary of all the instances it has managed.

Putting the Pieces Together

As you have seen, a number of ways are available in which you can implement an instance manager. Unfortunately, it's difficult to implement all features in the same instance manager. Because of the limitations of Visual Basic and Remote Automation, some features are mutually exclusive—if you implement one feature, you cannot implement another.

Rank the features that are most important to your organization and business service, and try to design an instance manager that meets these needs. Although you probably will need to run one instance manager per business object, try to keep them as consistent as possible.

The main goal when designing your own instance manager is to keep it simple. The best instance manager is unobtrusive, easy to administer, and easy to maintain.

Sample Instance Manager

This book includes a sample instance manager that incorporates some of the previously mentioned features.

This code includes a sample mini-application based on the GOLF system's *OrderMgr* business object, and also a template of the instance manager shell that you can adapt to your business objects.

Instance Manager Files

This section details all the files included in the instance manager application. You can find the files on the companion disk.

Table 23.1 describes the details of the files in the Sample application that you can find on the companion disk, in the \CHAP23\SAMPLE directory. Table 23.2 gives you the details of the files of the Template application in the \CHAP23\TEMPLATE directory.

Table 23.1 Instance Manager Sample Files		
Directory	**File**	**Description**
\TIER1\CLIENT	**The Client Application**	
	Client.exe	Client application executable
	Client.frm	Client form
	Client.vbp	Client project file
\TIER2\ORDMGR	**The OrderMgr Managed Object Class**	
	App.cls	The object's application class
	General.bas	General module
	OrdMgr.exe	Object executable
	OrdMgr.frm	Object form
	OrdMgr.tlb	Type library of OLE server
	OrdMgr.vbp	Project file
	OrdMgr.vbr	Remote automation file
\TIER2\ORDMGRS	**OrderMgr's Instance Manager**	
	App.cls	The object's application class
	General.bas	General module
	Inst.cls	Instance class
	InstMgr.frm	Status form
	InstMgr.frx	Status form resources

(continues)

Sample Applications

V

Table 23.1 Continued		
Directory	**File**	**Description**
\TIER2\ORDMGRS	**OrderMgr's Instance Manager**	
	OrdMgrs.exe	Instance manager executable
	OrdMgrs.tlb	Instance manager type library
	OrdMgrs.vbp	Instance manager project file
	OrdMgrs.vbr	Instance manager remote automation files

Table 23.2 Instance Manager Template Files		
Directory	**File**	**Description**
\TIER2\INSTMGR	**The Template Managed Object Class**	
	App.cls	The object's application class
	General.bas	General module
	InstMgr.exe	Object executable
	InstMgr.tlb	Type library of OLE server
	InstMgr.vbp	Project file
	InstMgr.vbr	Remote automation file
\TIER2\INSTMGRS	**Template Instance Manager**	
	App.cls	The object's application class
	General.bas	General module
	Inst.cls	Instance class
	InstMgr.exe	Instance manager executable
	InstMgr.frm	Status form
	InstMgr.frx	Status form resources
	InstMgr.tlb	Instance manager type library
	InstMgr.vbp	Instance manager project file
	InstMgr.vbr	Instance manager remote automation files

Installation Instructions

This section covers the details of installing the sample instance manager application. The sample application is based on a subset of the GOLF system's order entry business object functionality. It contains only the pieces relating to the instance manager.

You can perform installation locally or remotely. The *Client*, *OrderMgr* managed object class, and *OrderMgrs* instance manager all can reside on the same machine, or the *Client* can reside on a different machine, across the network from *OrderMgr* and *OrderMgrs*.

A local installation does not involve remote automation. A local installation can demonstrate all of the features of the instance manager, so you probably should play with the local installation before trying the added complexities of a remote installation.

Note that these are 32-bit applications that must be installed under Windows 95 or Windows NT 3.51 or greater.

To install the Sample application locally, take the following steps:

1. Copy the entire \SAMPLE\ directory structure from the companion disk to your hard-drive. If needed, create a new directory for the files (recommended).

2. From the MS-DOS command line, type `\OrderMgr\OrderMgr.exe /regserver` to register the manager server.

3. From the command line, type `\OrderMgrs\OrderMgrs.exe /regserver` to register the instance manager.

To install the sample application remotely, take the following steps:

1. From the client machine: Copy the entire \SAMPLE\ directory structure from the companion disk to your system's hard-drive.

2. From the client machine: From a DOS command line, execute `\OrderMgrs\OrderMgrs.exe /regserver` to register the instance manager.

3. From the client machine: Execute the Remote Automation Connection Manager, which is an icon in the Visual Basic 4 program group. Select the *Server Connections* tab, and select the *OrderMgrs.Application* instance manager class on the left list box (make sure you select *OrderMgrs.Application*, not *OrderMgr.Application*).

4. From the client machine: Enter the network address of your server machine (with no backslashes) in the Network Address combo box. Choose the network protocol that is running on your network in the Network Protocol combo box. Select the *Default* authentication level in the Authentication Level combo box. Click the left mouse button over the `OrderMgrs.Application` listbox entry, and choose *Remote*.

5. From the server machine: Copy the entire \SAMPLE\ directory structure on the companion disk to your server's hard-drive.

6. From the server machine: From the DOS command line, execute `\OrderMgr\OrderMgr.exe /regserver` to register the manager server.

7. From the server machine: From the DOS command prompt, execute `\OrderMgrs\OrderMgrs.exe /regserver` to register the instance manager.

8. From the server machine: Execute the Remote Automation Connection Manager, which is an icon in the Visual Basic 4 program group. Select the Client Access tab, and click the Allow All Remote Creates radio button. Finally, close the RACM.

Note

Allow All Remote Creates allows anyone to instantiate objects on the server. If you want, you can use the RACM to change the security policy back.

Now, whether or not you installed locally or remotely, you now are ready to run a quick tour of the sample instance manager.

A Quick Tour of Instance Manager

This chapter walks you through the sample instance manager, highlighting its features. You then will be ready to take a closer look at the design and code of the sample and template instance managers.

Step 1: Start the Instance Manager

Execute the `\SAMPLE\OrdMgrs.exe` application.

This step starts the instance manager. This application simulates what happens on your server machine—the instance manager will start automatically when the operating system boots.

Figure 23.3 shows what your screen should look like. The instance manager has a default pool size of 2 objects, so two instances of the *OrderMgr* were created. The *OrderMgr* object has a visible form for demonstration purposes only. Usually, a business object doesn't display a visible form.

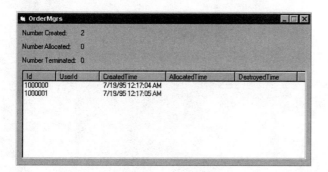

Fig. 23.3
The initialize Sample instance manager.

Each *OrderMgr* object and the *OrderMgrs* instance manager run in separate processes, so the 32-bit operating system is multitasking them.

The *OrderMgrs* windows shows the status of all the objects it managers. Initially, it has 2 created objects, 0 allocated objects, and 0 terminated objects. The instance manager is refreshed approximately every five seconds.

The instance manager assigns each object an ID that it tracks in the *ListView* control. It also tracks information relating to object allocation, such as to whom the object was allocated, when it was allocated, and when it was destroyed.

Step 2: Start the Client Application
Execute the \CLIENT\Client.exe application.

This step starts the Sample client application. Figure 23.4 shows what your screen should look like.

The *Client* application has three buttons: Get Instance, Use Instance, and Release Instance. The Get Instance button retrieves an instance from the OrderMgrs instance manager, Use Instance displays one of the instance's properties, and Release Instance releases the *Client's* reference to the instance.

Fig. 23.4
The Sample client
application.

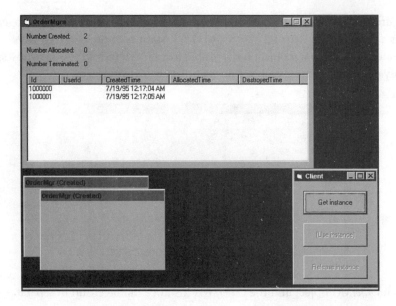

Step 3: Get an Instance

Press the Get Instance button on the Client. You should see several things
happen. Figure 23.5 shows what your screen should look like.

Fig. 23.5
The Sample client
application, with
an allocated
instance.

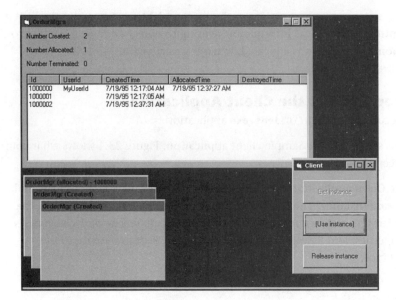

First, the first free instance from the instance manager was allocated to the Client. In the instance manager display, the first object now displays a *UserId* of "MyUserId," the *UserId* passed by the Client application. The allocated time was updated as well.

One *OrderMgr* instance now displays a caption, indicating that it was allocated.

After the object was allocated, *OrderMgrs* woke up on a timer event to check its pool size. It noticed its created pool size was only 1, and that its normal pool size should be 2. So it created a third instance and added it to the pool.

You can press the Use Instance button on the *Client* to prove that the *Client* is accessing the allocated *OrderMgr*.

Step 4: Release Instance

Press the Release Instance button on the *Client*. Again, you should notice several things happening. Figure 23.6 shows what the screen should look like.

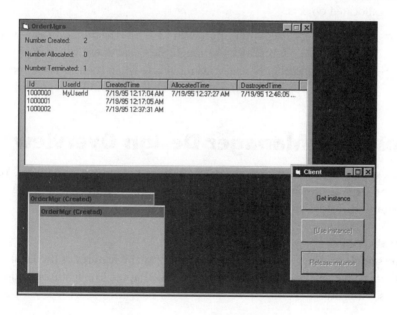

Fig. 23.6
Pressing the Release Instance button releases the instance and updates the instance manager's display.

When the *Client* released its reference to the allocated *OrderMgr* object, no other references existed so the object terminated and its form disappeared. Before it terminated, however, the *OrderMgr* notified *OrderMgrs* that is was terminating.

When *OrderMgrs* woke up to update its display (about every 5 seconds), it updated the *DestroyedTime* to indicate that the object no longer exists.

Note that *OrderMgrs* didn't adjust its pool size from two free instances because the pool is in place to maintain a minimum level of created instance for quick client application creation. The pool isn't in place to maintain a fixed number of created plus allocated instances.

Step 5

Try experimenting with the application. For example, try the following:

- Launch multiple *Clients* and allocate multiple instances. The maximum number of instances allowed by *OrderMgrs* is five, so after you allocate four instances you should notice that the pool is only 1. After you allocate five, *Client* no longer can retrieve an instance.

- Shut down *OrderMgrs*. Notice that only the unallocated objects are terminated because the *Clients*, not *OrderMgrs*, have references to the allocated objects.

- Terminate the *Client* application with Ctrl+Alt+Delete (End Task) while it has an *OrderMgr* instance. Although the *Client* doesn't shut down properly and explicitly release its reference, when it terminates, the reference is dropped and the allocated *OrderMgr* terminates properly.

Instance Manager Design Overview

This section presents a design overview of the sample instance manager. You see how the sample instance manager addresses the features listed in the beginning of this chapter. You also walk though the system's code.

Features

The sample instance manager addresses many of the features of the ideal instance manager presented previously in this chapter. The features it addresses well are:

- It pre-loads object instances so that *OrderMgrs* can quickly respond to client applications' requests for instances.

- It multitasks instances because each *OrderMgr* instance runs in its own process.

- If security is properly set up, client applications can be denied permission to instantiate an *OrderMgr* object directly. So, the client application cannot bypass the instance manager.

- The Sample instance manager also provides unobtrusive client application instance creation. As you will see, a client application that needs an *OrderMgr* instance through *OrderMgrs* only needs to make one extra OLE call, and the client application doesn't need to do anything special to release an object.

- Because each instance manager manages a specific object class, the ACL of the instance manager can be set the same as its managed class. Therefore, both the instance manager and the managed object receive the same level of security.

- The instance manager governs resources by setting an upper limit on the number of instances (processes) that can execute simultaneously.

- Although this version doesn't do it, the instance manager can easily be extended to create objects from multiple machines and add them to the pool.

- It provides basic management functionality, such as a display of the status of each individual instance. This functionality can easily be extended to provide more management capability.

The sample instance manager does not implement the following features well:

- The sample instance manager doesn't handle multiple classes. You must create a separate template instance manager for each object class. It cannot handle multiple classes without breaking the security model.

- The sample instance manager doesn't handle object reuse. The instance manager doesn't know when a client application is through with an object until after the object is terminating and it's too late to reuse. It cannot handle object reuse unless the client is forced to tell the instance manager when it is done.

Client

The sample *Client* application simulates how a client application would make use of the instance manager to instantiate an *OrderMgr* object. The *Client* application consists of a single form. It can reference a single sample *OrderMgr* object.

This section walks you through, in detail, the *Client* application's code. As mentioned previously, the *Client* code can be found on this book's companion disk, in the \CHAP24\SAMPLE\TIER1\CLIENT directory.

Declarations

The form contains two declarations:

```
'This is where we will store handle to the specific OrderMgr object
'given to us by the OrderMgrs Instance Manager.
Dim OrderMgr As Object

'This is the class name of the Instance Manager that manages
'OrderMgr objects.
Const ClassName = "OrderMgrs.Application"
```

The *OrderMgr* object stores a reference to the instance the instance manager creates. The *ClassName* constant is the class name of the instance manager object.

cmdGetInstance

The cmdGetInstance button retrieves an *OrderMgr* instance from the *OrderMgrs* instance manager and assigns it to the *OrderMgr* object variable. See Listing 23.1 for the code.

Listing 23.1   CLIENT.FRM—Code behind the cmdGetInstance button

```
Private Sub cmdGetInstance_Click()

'This is the handle to the Instance Manager. The Client Application
'can keep the handle around or release it; it doesn't matter.
'In this case, we get rid of it when it goes out of
'scope in this procedure.
Dim OrderMgrs As Object

Screen.MousePointer = 11

'When using the OrderMgrs Instance Manager (as opposed to
'instantiating the OrderMgr object directly), we just have
'to go through one extra, easily understood step:

'Get a handle to the OrderMgr Instance Manager
Set OrderMgrs = CreateObject(ClassName)

'Invoke the method on the Instance Manager that assigns us an
'object.
```

```
'We will remember this object in the form level OrderMgr variable even
'though we will forget the handle in the OrderMgrs variable to the
'Instance Manager itself when it goes out of scope in this procedure.
Set OrderMgr = OrderMgrs.GetInstance("MyUserId", "MyPassword")

'The OrderMgrs Instance Manager will return Nothing if now objects
'are available.
If OrderMgr Is Nothing Then
    Screen.MousePointer = 0
    MsgBox "No OrderMgr objects available."
    Exit Sub
End If

'Visual stuff
cmdGetInstance.Enabled = False
cmdUseInstance.Enabled = True
cmdReleaseInstance.Enabled = True
Screen.MousePointer = 0

End Sub
```

The routine first dimensions an *OrderMgrs* object variable. This object variable's scope is at the procedure level because once we have assigned an instance to *OrderMgr*, we no longer need to keep a reference to the *OrderMgrs* object.

The routine then uses the `CreateObject()` function to instantiate the *OrderMgrs* instance manager, which assigns a reference to the client application of the already executing instance manager on the server.

Then, the routine calls the instance manager's `GetInstance` method to retrieve an *OrderMgr* reference from the server:

```
Set OrderMgr = OrderMgrs.GetInstance((txtUserId), "MyPassword")
```

This is the only step needed to use an object managed by the sample instance manager beyond creating the object directly.

GetInstance may have returned *Nothing* if an instance wasn't available. The *If...Then* construct checks for this condition and notifies the user.

cmdUseInstance
The cmdUseInstance button shows how to access the properties of the *OrderMgr* object that is running on the server.

For example, the following code displays a message box with the value of the *OrderMgr.UserId* property:

```
Private Sub cmdUseInstance_Click()

'Demonstrate that we can access the OrderMgr object
MsgBox "The OrderMgr's UserId property is: " & OrderMgr.UserId

End Sub
```

cmdReleaseInstance

The cmdReleaseInstance button releases the *OrderMgr* object reference (see Listing 23.2), causing the object to terminate on the server.

Listing 23.2   CLIENT.FRM—Code behind the cmdReleaseInstance button

```
Private Sub cmdReleaseInstance_Click()

Screen.MousePointer = 11

'When done with the object, we just set its reference to Nothing,
'like any other object. Instance Manager handles it transparently.
Set OrderMgr = Nothing

'Visual stuff
cmdGetInstance.Enabled = True
cmdUseInstance.Enabled = False
cmdReleaseInstance.Enabled = False
Screen.MousePointer = 0

End Sub
```

The only thing that needs to occur to release the object is to set the *OrderMgr* object variable to Nothing.

OrderMgr

The *OrderMgr* application is a small OLE server that the *OrderMgrs* instance manager manages. It consists of a single class, form, and code module. The project name, *OrderMgr*, contains a single *Application* class. So, the full class name is *OrderMgr.Application*.

frmOrderMgr

The *frmOrderMgr* has no substantial code behind it. The *frmOrderMgr* is used just to provide a visual cue that an instance is running on the server.

General

The General module has no substantial code behind it. It contains the *Main( )* routine, which shows *frmOrderMgr* when instantiated.

Application

The *Application* class is the class instantiated by *OrderMgrs* and passed to *Client*.

Declarations. The *Application* class has several private variables that store properties of the object. The *UserId, Password, Id,* and *Parent* are properties that must be supported by all objects managed by the template instance manager (see Listing 23.3).

Listing 23.3   CLIENT.FRM—Code behind the Declarations section

```
'All business server's should have these objects.

'The UserId and Id property are read-only by the client application,
'the others are neither read nor write by the client application.

'Private copy of client application's user id
'This is read-only to the client application, because it might
'be helpful for debugging
Private prvUserId As String

'Private copy of client application's password
'It is neither read nor write by the client application because
'no one should ever be able to read a password
Private prvPassword As String

'Id and Parent are optional, and only make sense
'if the object is instantiated by an instance manager.

'Private copy of this instance's ID
'This is read-only to the client application, because it might
'be helpful for debugging
Private prvId As String

'Private copy of the parent object.
'It is neither read nor write by the client application because
'the client application has no reason to reference,
'the Instance Manager
 Private prvParent As Object
```

The *prvId* and *prvParent* variables point to the collection key and object in the instance manager's *Instances* collection. These properties are set when the object is allocated.

The *prvUserId* and *prvPassword* variables store the user ID and password of the user who was allocated this object.

AddInit

The AddInit method is used after the object is instantiated to set its write-once properties: *UserId, Password, Id,* and *Parent* (see Listing 23.4).

Listing 23.4 CLIENT.FRM—Code behind the AddInit button

```
Sub AddInit(UserId As String, Password As String, _
Optional Id As Variant, Optional Parent As Variant)

'This procedure is called once after the server is instantiated.

'If it is instantiated by an Instance Manager, the object Id and
'Parent will be passed by the Instance Manager.

'If it is instantiated by a client application, the client probably
'has no need to pass an Id or Parent.

'This shows how this generic object shell can be used in an
'Instance Manager environment or an environment where the client
'application is allowed to instantiate the object directly.

'------------------------------------------------------------
'make sure procedure is only called once
'------------------------------------------------------------

Static Initialized As Boolean
'only allow one initialization
If Initialized Then Exit Sub
Initialized = True


'------------------------------------------------------------
'Assign the initialized object values
'------------------------------------------------------------

prvUserId = UserId
prvPassword = Password
If IsMissing(Id) Then 'optional parm
    prvId = "<None>"
Else
    prvId = Id
End If
If IsMissing(Parent) Then 'optional parm
    Set prvParent = Nothing
Else
    Set prvParent = Parent
End If
```

```
'This pertains to OrderMgr specifically, not to a generic Instance
'Manager object.
'It just shows on the form that the object was initialized
frmOrderMgr.Caption = "OrderMgr (allocated) - " & Id

End Sub
```

The routine can be called only once. This limit is insured by setting the static *Initialized* variable.

Two parameters, *Id* and *Parent*, are optional because they apply only when an instance manager is managing the object and keeping track of it in its own collection.

Id & UserId. Two internal properties, *Id* and *UserId*, are readable, but not writable, by the controlling application, which is accomplished with two property procedures:

```
Property Get Id() As String

'The ID is read-only
Id = prvId

End Property

Property Get UserId() As String

'The UserId is read-only
UserId = prvUserId

End Property
```

Class_Terminate. The Class_Terminate event is fired when the instance is terminating. In the sample system, the instance terminates when the client application releases its reference.

```
Private Sub Class_Terminate()

'This pertains to OrderMgr specifically, not to a generic Instance
'Manager object. It unloads the visible form
Unload frmOrderMgr

'This checks to see if a parent object was assigned to this object
'instance. If a Parent was assigned, the Terminate method is
'called in the
'Parent Instance Manager to let the Instance Manager know the
'object is terminating.
```

V

Sample Applications

```
'This tells the Instance Manager it can readjust its pool size.

'By checking to see if a Parent exists, we insure,
'that this object can
'work either with or without an Instance Manager.

If prvParent Is Nothing Then
Else
    prvParent.Terminate
End If

End Sub
```

First, the event unloads the *frmOrderMgr* form. Then, if the instance was created by an instance manager, the instance notifies the instance manager that it is terminating—the instance checks to see if it has a *Parent* object. If so, the instance invokes the `Terminate` method on the parent object.

OrderMgrs

The *OrderMgrs* OLE object application is the instance manager. It consists of a single externally creatable class, *Application*. It also has a *frmInstMgr* form that displays the status of the managed instances. A private class, *Instance*, keeps track of the managed instances.

The object application is *Creatable Multi-Use* so that many client applications can use the same process to retrieve instances.

General

The general module contains some general purpose routines and declarations, including the *Main( )* program entry point.

Declarations. The *Declarations* section contains a number of global declarations. Several constants define this particular instance manager:

```
'The name of the class that the Instance Manager is managing
Global Const imgrClassName = "OrderMgr.Application"
'Maximum number of instances allowed to be instantiated at once.
Global Const MAX_INSTANCES = 5
'The size of pool of free objects the Instance Manager maintains
Global Const POOL_SIZE = 2
```

The constant, *imgrClassName*, contains the name of the managed class. *MAX_INSTANCES* and *POOL_SIZE* define the maximum number of instances allowed and the free instance pool size, respectively.

The *Application* variable points to a global copy of the *Application* object.

```
'A handle to shared application object. Each client application that
'requests an instance from the Instance Manager by calling the
'GetObject() method of this object
Global Application As New Application
```

The *Instances* collection stores information and a reference to each managed object. It will contain objects of the *Instance* class, defined as a class module in this project.

```
'This collection maintains a list of all instances either created,
'allocated, or terminated
Global Instances As New Collection
```

Several counters track the number of created, allocated, and terminated instances:

```
Global NumCreated As Long      'number of objects available and unallocated
Global NumAllocated As Long   'number of objects in use and allocated
Global NumTerminated As Long  'number of old objects used and destroyed
```

Each *Instance* object has a specific state, defined by these constants:

```
'constants apply to InstanceState
Global Const imgrInstanceStateCreated = 1      'available and unallocated
Global Const imgrInstanceStateAllocated = 2    'in use and allocated
Global Const imgrInstanceStateTerminated = 3   'old and destroyed
```

Main. The *Main* procedure is the entry point to the application. It displays the *frmInstanceMgr* status form and refreshes the pool size and display by using the RefreshInstance() function.

```
Sub Main()

'Show the status form
frmInstanceMgr.Show
'Change caption to the title of the Instance Manager Application
frmInstanceMgr.Caption = App.Title

'Update the pool size and status form
Call RefreshInstances

End Sub
```

RefreshInstances. *RefreshInstances* does two things—it adjusts the pool size, and it refreshes the display in the *frmInstanceMgr* status form.

```
Sub RefreshInstances()

'This procedure increases free instance pool size if appropriate
'and updates the status form.

Dim itmNext As Object
Dim itmNum As Long
Dim Instance As Instance

'Continue to add objects to the pool until we reach the maximum
'pool size or have reached the maximum number of instances allowed.
Do Until (NumCreated >= POOL_SIZE) Or _
         (NumCreated + NumAllocated >= MAX_INSTANCES)
    Call CreateInstance
Loop

'- - - - - - - - - - - - - - - - - - - - - - - - - - - - - - - - - - - -
'Update status form
'- - - - - - - - - - - - - - - - - - - - - - - - - - - - - - - - - - - -

'Labels
frmInstanceMgr.lblNumCreated(0) = NumCreated
frmInstanceMgr.lblNumAllocated(0) = NumAllocated
frmInstanceMgr.lblnumterminated(0) = NumTerminated

'ImageList
frmInstanceMgr.lstInstances.ListItems.Clear
For Each Instance In Instances
    With Instance
        Set itmNext = frmInstanceMgr.lstInstances.ListItems.Add()
        itmNext.TEXT = .Id
        itmNext.SubItems(1) = .UserId
        itmNext.SubItems(2) = .CreatedTime
        itmNext.SubItems(3) = .AllocatedTime
        itmNext.SubItems(4) = .TerminatedTime
    End With
Next

End Sub
```

This routine is called periodically by a timer on the status form (every five seconds, by default). It adds instances to the pool until either the maximum pool size is reached or until the maximum number of instances is created.

CreateInstance. The `CreateInstance` function creates a new instance of the managed object class and adds it to its collection of managed objects.

```
Sub CreateInstance()

'This routine creates new object instance and adds it to Instance
'Manager's Instance collection.

'Maintain a serialized ID number, beginning with INSTANCE_START
Static Id As String
Const INSTANCE_START = 1000000

'Create a new instance collection member
Dim NewInstance As New Instance

'Initialize Id to a large number, or add one to last used number
If Val(Id) < INSTANCE_START Then
    Id = INSTANCE_START
Else
    Id = CStr(CLng(Id) + 1)
End If
'Assign the next Id to the instance collection member
NewInstance.Id = Id

'Indicate that this instance is newly created
NewInstance.InstanceState = imgrInstanceStateCreated

'Create a new managed object
Set NewInstance.Object = CreateObject(imgrClassName)

'Indicate we have added a newly created object
NumCreated = NumCreated + 1
'Assign the created time of this object
NewInstance.CreatedTime = Now

'Add the Instance to our collection
Instances.Add Item:=NewInstance, KEY:=Id

End Sub
```

The preceding code assigns each object a unique ID, beginning at 100000. IDs are unique because the *CreateInstance* call is serialized.

The Instances collection of *Instance* objects keeps track of all managed instances. One property of the *Instance* object, *Object*, points to the actual instance.

After the new object is created and assigned to *NewInstance.Object* and the rest of the properties are set, the *NewInstance* is added to the Instances collection with the `Add` method.

V

Sample Applications

CloseAllInstances. *CloseAllInstances* is invoked when the application shuts down. It neatly closes all unallocated objects.

```
Sub CloseAllInstances()

'This routine shuts down reference to all objects in the Instance
'Manager collection. Note that only "Created" objects will have handles,
'because other collection members are already allocated.

Dim Instance As Object

For Each Instance In Instances
    Set Instance.Object = Nothing
Next

End Sub
```

Instance

The *Instance* class module is used by the *Instances* collection to keep track of the managed instances. It stores a number of attributes of the managed objects, such as *UserId*, *CreatedTime*, and the object.

Declarations. The *Declarations* section defines many public variable properties of the managed object. It stores the Id, the object, user ID, and password associated with the object:

```
'The ID of the managed object, set when the object is created
Public Id As Long
'The actual object, released to Nothing,
'when the object is destroyed
Public Object As Object

'The userid assigned to the object, set when object is allocated
Public UserId As String
'The password assigned to the object, set when object is allocated
Public Password As String
```

It also keeps track of the current state of the object as well as times in which the object changed state:

```
'The state of object, set to one of 3 global constants indicating
'created, allocated, or terminated
Public InstanceState As Integer

'The time in which the object changed states
Public CreatedTime As Variant
Public AllocatedTime As Variant
Public TerminatedTime As Variant
```

Terminate. The managed object calls the `Terminate` method of its corresponding *Instance* object when it is terminating.

```
Public Function Terminate()

'When the managed object was created, it remembered a reference to
'this particular class instance. When the object goes out of scope,
'it invokes this method in the Instance Manager so the Instance
'Manager is aware that the object is terminated and can adjust
'the pool size accordingly

'Decrease the number allocated, because an object was terminated
NumAllocated = NumAllocated - 1
'Decrease the number terminated, because an object was terminated
NumTerminated = NumTerminated + 1

'Set the terminated time in the collection
Me.TerminatedTime = Now
'Set the new instance state in the collection
Me.InstanceState = imgrInstanceStateTerminated

End Function
```

The `Terminate` method decrements the allocated pool size by one, updates the state of the managed object (terminated), and updates the terminated time.

Application

The *Application* class is instantiated by the client application. It contains a single method, `GetInstance`, that retrieves an instance for the client.

GetInstance. The `GetInstance` method returns an instance to the client application if one is available; otherwise this method returns nothing:

```
Public Function GetInstance(UserId As String, Password As String)
As Object

'When a client application wants an object from Instance Manager, it
'invokes this method on the Instance Manager.  This procedure allocates
'the instance and returns a handle to the client.

'The free instance we are handing to client
Dim Instance As Object
Dim Found As Boolean
Dim i As Long

'Find a free instance in the collection
For Each Instance In Instances
    If Instance.InstanceState = imgrInstanceStateCreated Then
        Found = True
        Exit For
    End If
```

```
    Next
    'If an instance isn't found, return Nothing to client application.
    'An instance won't be found if the number allocated equaled the
    'maximum number.
    If Not Found Then
        Set GetInstance = Nothing
        Exit Function
    End If

    'Since we are allocating, decrement the number created and increment
    'the number allocated
    NumAllocated = NumAllocated + 1
    NumCreated = NumCreated - 1

    'Allocate the instance
    With Instance
        'Remember the name and password we pass to the allocated object
        'in our collection.
        .UserId = UserId
        .Password = Password

        'Remember the allocated time and update the instance status
        .AllocatedTime = Now
        .InstanceState = imgrInstanceStateAllocated

        'Initialize allocated object by invoking its AddInit method.
        'Enables object to receive its UserId, Password, Id and Parent
        .Object.AddInit UserId:=.UserId, Password:=.Password, _Id:= _
        .Id, Parent:=Instance

        'Return the instance to the client application.  This increases
        'the reference count of the managed object to 2
        Set GetInstance = .Object

        'Unassign the Instance Manager's reference to object, so that
        'only the client application now has a reference. This
        'decreases the reference count of the managed object back to 1
        Set .Object = Nothing

        'The previous two lines of code are very important. They must
        'appear in the order shown, otherwise the reference count
        'would temporarily drop to 0 and the object would terminate!

        'Also, the Instance Manager _must_ release its reference to the
        'object, otherwise the object wouldn't terminate when the client
        'application was done with it.

    End With

    End Function
```

The `GetInstance` method searches the *Instances* collections and returns *Nothing* if an instance is not available.

If an instance is available, it initializes its write-once properties with the `AddInit` method. It sets the return value equal to the instance object, therefore increasing the object's reference count to 2. It then releases its reference to the instance object, therefore decreasing the object's reference count back to one.

This process must occur in the preceding order; otherwise the instance will terminate when its reference count hits 0.

frmInstanceManager

The *frmInstanceManager* form tracks the status of all instances. It also periodically updates the instance pool.

Form_Unload. The `Form_Unload` event cleans up all instances with the *CloseAllInstances* procedure and shuts down the application:

```
Private Sub Form_Unload(Cancel As Integer)

'When a user shuts down the Instance Manager on the server
'close down all the references objects.  Note that this doesn't
'close down objects that have been allocated to a client application,
'because the Instance Manager doesn't maintain a reference to the
'object after allocation.

Call CloseAllInstances

'Set the application object to nothing
Set Application = Nothing

End
```

tmrRefreshInstances_Timer. The `tmrRefreshInstances_Timer` event is invoked, by default, every five seconds. It calls the *RefreshAllInstances* routine, which updates the display and adjusts the pool size (if appropriate).

```
Private Sub tmrRefreshInstances_Timer()

'The pool size and form is adjusted on a regular basis by the timer.

'We could adjust it every time something changes, such as when
'an object is terminated, but that would mean the client application
'would have to wait while Instance Manager created a new object for
'the pool.
```

```
'With a timer, the Instance Manager wakes up every few seconds
'and checks to see if the pool needs adjusting and updates display
'to reflect created, allocated, and terminated objects.

Call RefreshInstances

End Sub
```

Using the Template

To use the template instance manager for your instance manager project, you need to follow a couple of rules.

The template is located in the \CHAP23\TEMPLATE\ directory. The template instance manager is almost identical to the sample instance manager just detailed. The sample was created from the template.

InstMgr

The *InstMgr* is the template business object. Your business object must follow a few specifications to work with the *InstMgrs* template.

InstMgr must do the following:

■ Expose a *Public, Creatable Single-Use* class (*Application* in the Template).

■ Be an out-of-process server.

■ Expose a public *AddInit* method with *UserId*, *Password*, *Id*, and *Parent* parameters.

To use the *InstMgr* as a template for your managed business object you must do the following:

1. Copy the \CHAP23\TEMPLATE\InstMgr from the companion disk to your own project directory on your system's hard drive.

2. Change the project name to the name of your project.

3. Add all changes to the template managed object that you want in your new project. That is, design the interface to your new managed object.

4. Make a new executable and give it the same name as your project name.

InstMgrs

To use *InstMgrs* as a template for your own instance manager, take these steps:

1. Copy the \CHAP23\TEMPLATE\INSTMGRS\ subdirectory into your project directory.

2. Change the `imgrClassName` global constant to the name of your managed class.

3. Change the `MAX_INSTANCES` and `POOL_SIZE` global constants to values appropriate for your instance manager.

4. Make a new executable, and give it the same name as your project name.

Instance Manager Versus Pool Manager

A few differences exist between the template instance manager and VB's sample Pool Manager.

- The Pool Manager manages multiple object types with the same manager; the template does not.

- The Pool Manager uses a linked list construct to track managed objects; the template uses a collection.

- The Pool Manager requires the client application to make a special function call to release an object; the template does not.

- The Pool Manager doesn't allow you to selectively secure managed objects; the template does.

From Here...

This chapter provided you with a detailed summary of the features of an instance manager, and detailed an instance manager scenario.

For more information about topics related to material covered in this chapter, see the following:

- Chapter 6, "Creating OLE Objects," shows how to create OLE servers.

- Chapter 7, "Managing OLE Objects," explains remote automation.

- Chapter 13, "Architecting Security," shows how to implement security in a three-tier architecture.

- Chapter 24, "Sample Application #3: A Three-Tier Order Processing System," describes the GOLF system in detail.

Chapter 24

Sample Application #3: A Three-Tier Order Processing System

The companion disk provided with this book contains a sample three-tier application, the GOLF System. In this chapter, we take a detailed look at the creation of the GOLF System, as well as a hands-on look at the concepts and techniques discussed throughout the book.

We first discuss the sample application, point you to where to find the executable and source code files on the companion CD-ROM, discuss how to install the application, and tour the application's user interface.

After looking at the finished product, we will discuss in detail the design and development of each of the service tiers. The tiers will be discussed in the order in which they were designed and developed when the application was created (and, therefore, in the order in which you might approach application development).

This chapter starts by determining what business objects the application needs to make available to the client services, and then covers the design and implementation of the data services tier. This chapter concludes by discussing the ways the client services can then use these objects to create an end-user application.

A consistent application architecture is important and desirable when developing real-world applications. To demonstrate the different implementation options available for aspects of the system, however, this sample application foregoes consistency.

Likewise, this application does not demonstrate some of the concepts that were also important in a two-tier environment, such as data service record locking and transaction management. This application is intended to place the concepts discussed in this book into a real-world scenario, while allowing you to become familiar with many of the available options. But do not consider this application as the final word on three-tier application architecture.

Purpose of the Application

The GOLF System is an example of a three-tier order processing and maintenance application developed with Visual Basic. The application uses Microsoft SQL Server 6.0 to provide the data services.

You will probably want to try to deploy the logical three-tier architecture in two different physical scenarios:

- All tiers on a single Windows NT machine

- The business and data services located on a Windows NT server machine, and the client application on a Windows 95/NT machine

When run in a distributed environment, the GOLF System uses Remote Automation to establish connections between the client services and the business services, and between the business services and the data services.

Summary of Files Distributed with the Book

This section details all of the files included with the GOLF System sample application. The files can be found on the companion disk, in the \CHAP24\GOLF directory.

SQL Server Scripts

SQL Server scripts are included for each stored procedure used by the GOLF Systems business services. You can find these scripts in the \CHAP24\GOLF\TIER3 directory on the companion disk. There also is one main script, SETUP.SQL, that is used to install all of the stored procedures required by the application.

Table 24.1 lists all the SQL script files included on the companion disk, and what each file contains.

Table 24.1 Stored Procedure Source Code Files	
File Name	**Description**
CUST01.SQL	Source for the sp_add_customer stored procedure
CUST02.SQL	Source for the sp_delete_customer stored procedure

File Name	Description
CUST03.SQL	Source for the sp_update_customer stored procedure
CUST04.SQL	Source for the sp_get_customers stored procedure
PRDT01.SQL	Source for the sp_add_product stored procedure
PRDT02.SQL	Source for the sp_delete_product stored procedure
PRDT03.SQL	Source for the sp_update_product stored procedure
PRDT04.SQL	Source for the sp_get_products stored procedure
ORDER01.SQL	Source for the sp_add_OrderHdr stored procedure
ORDER02.SQL	Source for the sp_delete_OrderHdr stored procedure
ORDER03.SQL	Source for the sp_get_orders stored procedure
ORDER04.SQL	Source for the sp_add_LineItem stored procedure

These stored procedures are automatically created by the installation script described later in this chapter.

Visual Basic Source Code

This section describes the Visual Basic source code files included in the GOLF System sample application. These files have been broken into two categories—Tier1, which contains the user services applications, and Tier2, which contains the business services used by the GOLF system. You can find these files on the companion disk, in the \CHAP24\GOLF\TIER1 and \CHAP24\GOLF\TIER2 directories, respectively.

Table 24.2 details the Visual Basic source code files that were used to develop the user services tier. You can find these files in the \CHAP24\GOLF\TIER1 directory.

Table 24.2   GOLF System User Services Source Code Files

Directory	File	Description
\TEST		**Test Client Applications**
	TCustMgr	Customer Manager test client
	TOrdMgr	Order Manager test client
	TprodMgr	Product Manager test client

(continues)

Table 24.2 Continued		
Directory	**File**	**Description**
\CLIENT		**Client Applications**
	Batch	The Batch client application files
	LogonMgr	The LogonMgr server files
	CustMntc	The Customer Maintenance application files
	OrdMntc	The Order Maintenance application files
	PrdtMntc	The Product Maintenance application files

Table 24.3 details the Visual Basic source code files used to develop the business services tier. These files can be found in the \CHAP24\GOLF\TIER2 directory on the companion disk.

Table 24.3 GOLF System Business Services Source Code Files		
Directory	**File**	**Description**
CUSTMGR		**The CustMgr Manager Object Class**
	App.cls	The objects application class
	Cust.cls	The objects Customer class
	CustMgr.exe	Object executable
	CustMgr.vbp	CustMgr Project file
	Custs.cls	The objects Customers class
	General.bas	General module
\CUSTMGRS		**CustMgrs Instance Manager**
	App.cls	Objects application class
	CustMgrs.exe	Object executable
	CustMgrs.tlb	Type library of OLE server
	CustMgrs.vbr	Remote Automation file
	General.bas	General module

Directory	File	Description
\CUSTMGRS		**CustMgrs Instance Manager**
	Instance.cls	Instance class
	InstMgr.frm	Status form
	InstMgr.frx	Status form resources
	CustMgrs.vbp	Instance manager project file
\ORDMGR		**The OrderMgr Managed Object Class**
	App.cls	The objects application class
	General.bas	General module
	Line.cls	The objects LineItem class
	Lines.cls	The objects LineItems class
	Order.cls	The objects Order class
	Orders.cls	The objects Orders class
	OrdMgr.exe	Object executable
	OrdMgr.tlb	Type library for OLE server
	OrdMgr.vbp	Project file
	OrdMgr.vbr	Remote Automation File
\ORDMGRS		**OrderMgrs Instance Manager**
	App.cls	The objects application class
	General.bas	General module
	Inst.cls	The objects instance class
	Instmgr.frm	Status form
	Instmgr.frx	Status form resources
	OrdMgrs.exe	Object executable
	OrdMgrs.tlb	Instance manager type library
	OrdMgrs.vbp	Project file
	OrdMgrs.vbr	Remote Automation file

V

Sample Applications

(continues)

Table 24.3   Continued

Directory	File	Description
\PRDTMGR		**The PrdtMgr Managed Object Class**
	App.cls	The objects application class
	General.bas	General module
	Prdt.cls	The objects product class
	PrdtMgr.exe	Object executable
	PrdtMgr.vbp	Project file
	Prdts.cls	The objects products class
\PRDTMGRS		**PrdtMgrs Instance Manager**
	App.cls	The objects application class
	General.bas	General module
	Inst.cls	The objects instance class
	Instmgr.frm	Status form
	Instmgr.frx	Status form resources
	PrdtMgrs.exe	Object executable
	PrdtMgrs.tlb	Instance manager type library
	PrdtMgrs.vbp	Project file
	PrdtMgrs.vbr	Remote Automation file
\BATCHMGR		**The Batch Object Class**
	App.cls	The objects application class
	Batch.frm	Batch managers form
	BatchMgr.exe	Executable file
	BatchMgr.vbp	Project file
	General.bas	General module

GOLF System Installation Instructions

This section details the procedures that you use to install the GOLF System sample application. You can deploy the installation on a single machine ("locally") or on distributed machines ("remotely").

In a local installation, the user service client applications, business server manager object classes (BatchMgr, OrderMgr, PrdtMgr, and CustMgr), business server instance managers (OrderMgrs, PrdtMgrs, and CustMgrs), and SQL Server data services all reside on a single machine. The local installation doesn't involve remote automation. A local installation demonstrates most features of the three-tier application architecture, except the communication layer.

In a remote installation, the user services reside on a different machine across the network from the business services and the data services. The remote installation uses Remote Automation to communicate between the client application and the business servers.

All of the GOLF System components are 32-bit and must, therefore, be installed under either the Windows 95 or the Windows NT 3.51 or later environments.

To install the GOLF System locally, take the following steps:

1. Copy the entire *GOLF* directory from the companion disk to your hard-drive. Doing this creates an image of the directory structure that exists on the companion disk.

2. From the command prompt (DOS or NT Command Prompt), type `\OrdMgr\OrdMgr.exe /regserver` to register the OrderMgr server.

3. From the command prompt, type `\OrdMgrs\Ordmgrs.exe /regserver` to register the OrderMgrs instance manager.

4. From the command prompt, type `\CustMgr\CustMgr.exe /regserver` to register the CustMgr server.

5. From the command prompt, type `\CustMgrs\CustMgrs.exe /regserver` to register the CustMgrs instance manager.

6. From the command prompt, type `\PrdtMgr\PrdtMgr.exe /regserver` to register the PrdtMgr server.

7. From the command prompt, type `\PrdtMgrs\PrdtMgrs.exe /regserver` to register the PrdtMgrs instance manager.

8. From the prompt, type **regsrvr32.exe\TIER1\CLIENT\LOGONMGR\ LogonMgr.dll** to register the Logon Manager. Regsrvr32 should be located in your \WINDOWS\SYSTEM32 directory (\WINDOWS\SYSTEM, under Windows 95).

9. Login to SQL Server by using the SQL Enterprise Manager and create a new database named **GOLF**. Then run the \TIER3\SETUP.SQL script, using the SQL Enterprise Managers Query Analyzer tool, which you can find in the SQL Server group of the Program Manager. This script creates a GolfUser login, creates the database tables and stored procedures, and populates some test data. Note that a different database name can be used by editing the script, TABLES.SQL, and by changing every reference to GOLF.

10. Using the 32-bit ODBC Administrator located in the Main group of the Program Manager, create an ODBC data source named **GOLF** to point to the freshly created SQLServer database. Refer to Chapter 10, "Architecting Tier 3: Data Servers," for step-by-step instructions on creating an ODBC data source.

To install the GOLF System remotely, take the following steps:

1. From the client, copy the entire \GOLF directory from the Companion disk to your client and server machine systems hard-drive. Again, this copy process will create an image of the directory and file structure that exists on the companion disk.

2. From the command prompt on the client machine, type **\ORDMGRS\ OrdMgrs.exe /regserver** to register the OrderMgrs instance manager.

3. From the command prompt on the client machine, type **\PRDTMGRS\ PrdtMgrs.exe /regserver** to register the PrdtMgrs instance manager.

4. From the command prompt on the client machine type **CUSTMGRS\ CustMgrs.exe /regserver** to register the CustMgrs instance manager.

5. From the command prompt, type **regsrvr32.exe\TIER1\CLIENT\ LOGONMGR\LogonMgr.dll** to register the Logon Manager. Regsrvr32 should be located in your \WINDOWS\SYSTEM32 directory (\WINDOWS\SYSTEM, under Windows 95).

6. From the client, execute the Remote Automation Connection Manager. Select the Server Connections tab and select the *OrderMgrs.Application* instance manager class from the left side of the window.

7. From the client, enter the address of your server machine (no backslashes). Choose the network protocol that runs on your network. Select the *Default* authentication level. Right-click on the *OrderMgrs.Application* list box entry, and choose *Remote*.

8. From the client, repeat steps 5 and 6 for the other instance managers (*PrdtMgrs.Application* and *CustMgrs.Application*).

9. From the server, copy the entire \GOLF directory onto your server's hard drive.

10. From the command prompt on the server, type **\ORDMGR\OrdMgr.exe /regserver** to register the OrderMgr server. Repeat this step for all the other servers (PrdtMgr.exe, CustMgr.exe).

11. From the command prompt on the server, type **\ORDMGRS\OrdMgrs.exe /regserver** to register the OrderMgrs instance manager. Repeat this step for all the other instance managers (\PRDTMGRS\PrdtMgrs.exe, \CUSTMGRS\CustMgrs.exe).

12. From the server, execute the Remote Automation Connection Manager. Select the Client Access tab, and select the Allow All Remote Create radio button. Close RACM. Note that this allows anyone to instantiate objects on the server, this can be changed later by going back into RACM.

13. From the server, login to SQL Server by using ISQL/w or the SQL Enterprise Manager and run the \SQL\Tables.sql script. This script creates the GOLF database, creates a GolfUser login, and populates some test data. Note that you can use a different database name by editing the Tables.sql script and by changing every reference to GOLF.

14. Using the 32-bit ODBC Administrator, create an ODBC data source named **GOLF** to point to the freshly created SQLServer database. For step-by-step instructions on creating an ODBC data source, refer to Chapter 10, "Architecting Tier 3: Data Servers."

The GOLF System's user services use the Logon Manager server described in Chapter 13, "Architecting Security." If the Logon Manager isn't installed on the client machine, refer to Chapter 13 for the installation instructions.

V

Sample Applications

Whether you installed locally or remotely, you now are ready to run a quick tour of the GOLF System sample application.

A Quick Tour of the GOLF System

Before going into details of the design and development of the application, you need to understand the functionality included in the application. Becoming familiar with the different pieces of the application helps you understand the interaction between the user services and business servers, and also the interaction that occurs between business servers.

The major focus of this book is to introduce the three-tier specific aspects available in the latest version of Visual Basic, not to rehash what was always available. So the sample application focuses on implementing an application in the three-tier environment, and doesn't spend a lot of time dealing with user-interface issues.

The GOLF Systems client applications were developed as Single Document Interface (SDI) applications. In this design, each major section of the application is its own stand-alone executable.

You can group the functionality of the GOLF client applications into three subsystems: the Customer Maintenance subsystem, the Product Maintenance subsystem, and the Order Processing subsystem.

Step 1: Run the Instance Manager

Execute the **\OrdMgrs\OrdMgrs.exe**, **\CustMgrs\CustMgrs.exe**, and **\PrdtMgrs\ PrdtMgrs.exe** applications, for example, by double-clicking on the files in the Windows NT File Manager.

This action starts the instance managers used by the GOLF System, which should be run on the server machine for remote installations. This step simulates what happens on your business server machine—the instance managers are started automatically when the operating system boots.

Figure 24.1 shows what the screen should look like now. The instance managers created their default pool sizes of 2 objects, which means that 2 instances of each manager server were created. You cannot see these server processes because they display no visible forms. The instance manager status forms show the creation time and status of each server instance.

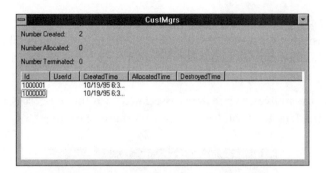

Fig. 24.1
The GOLF System,
with Customer
instance manager
initialized.

Each instance manager and its managed server runs as a separate process, which means that the operating system handles multitasking them. For more details on how the instance managers maintain the pools, refer to Chapter 23, "Sample Application #2: An Instance Manager."

Step 2: Run the Client Applications

Execute **\Client\OrdProc\OrdProc.exe** application.

This action starts the GOLF Systems Order Processor client application. Figure 24.2 shows the Order Processors main form, the order list.

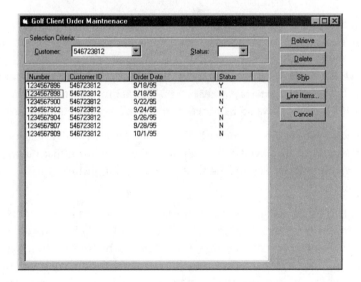

Fig. 24.2
The GOLF Order
Processor Client
Order List form.

V

Sample Applications

Step 3: Populate the Order List

Select a customer number and order status from the selection combo boxes. Click the Retrieve button to display the orders that match the selection criteria.

To display the individual line items associated with the order, select an order and click the Line Items button. Figure 24.3 shows the Order Line Items form.

Fig. 24.3

Order Processors Order Line Items form.

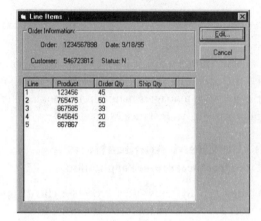

From this form, the user can change or add line items to the order. To change a line item, select the line item from the list, and click the Edit button.

Step 4: Run the Customer Maintenance Application

Execute `\Client\CustMntc\CustMntc.exe`, for example, by double-clicking the file with the Windows 95 Explorer, or the Windows NT File Manager.

This action starts the Customer Maintenance subsystem. The Customer List form should be displayed, which allows the user to begin maintaining customer information. Figure 24.4 shows the customer list form that now should be visible.

From this list of active customers, the user can perform maintenance on a specific customer by selecting that row in the list and choosing the Update option. You can add new customers by clicking the New button. Both of these options display the Customer Maintenance form shown in figure 24.5. As updates to an existing customer are being made, the form is populated with the current customer information.

From the list form, the user can delete customers from the system by selecting customers in the list and clicking the Delete button.

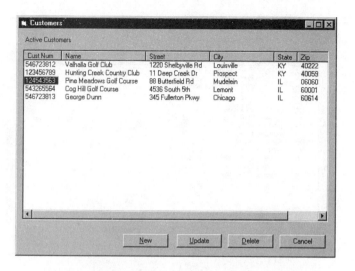

Fig. 24.4
Customer List
form.

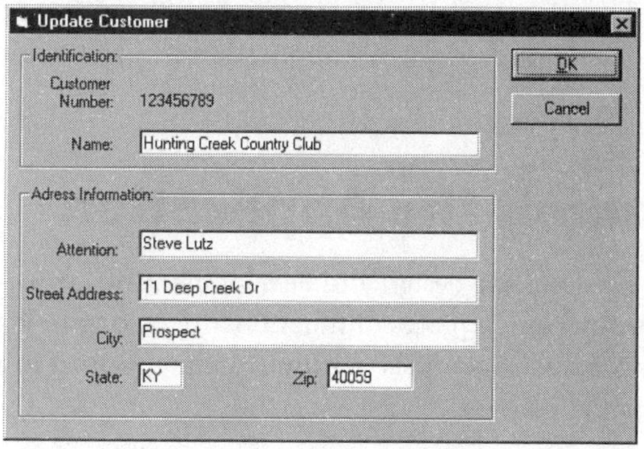

Fig. 24.5
Customer
Maintenance form.

Step 5: Run the Product Maintenance Application

Execute `\CLIENT\PRDTMNTC\PrdtMntc.exe`, for example, by double-clicking on the file in the Windows 95 Explorer or in the Windows NT File Manager.

This action starts the Product Maintenance subsystem. The Product List form shown in figure 24.6 now should be displayed. This form shows all the currently active products that were defined.

From this list, the user is allowed to update and delete existing products. This subsystem works in the same manner as the Customer maintenance subsystem.

Fig. 24.6
Product List form.

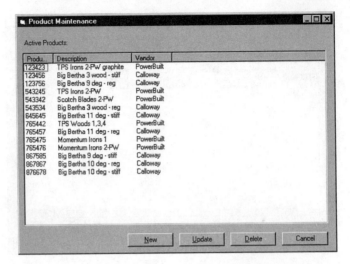

Now that you have the requirements for the application from the end-user perspective, you can look at how the application was partitioned across the three tiers.

Partitioning the Application

An important aspect of the design and development of a three-tier application is to determine which pieces of functionality belong in which tier. Throughout this book, some rules of thumb are mentioned to assist in the partitioning of applications.

The following list summarizes these general rules of thumb:

- Presentation logic should reside in the user services tier.

- Business rules and data service access should be handled in the business services tier.

- Basic data integrity, not directly related to business rules, should be handled by the data services tier.

These guidelines were used to partition the GOLF System between the three tiers. Figure 24.7 illustrates the basic application architecture that was developed.

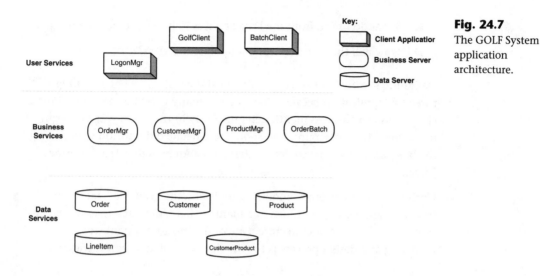

Fig. 24.7
The GOLF System application architecture.

The business services layer of this architecture provides all the access to the database objects that are used to store the order, product, and customer information. These objects also encapsulate the business rules applied to the data, which ensures that its integrity is maintained.

The application often isn't as cut-and-dry as the GOLF System. When complexities exist that make partitioning the application difficult, first try to check, and then adjust the rules of thumb.

The following section discusses the details of the business server objects created to support the GOLF System.

Designing the Business Servers/Objects

Now that you have an understanding of the requirements that the application needs to satisfy and how the application will be partitioned across the three tiers, you can begin designing the business services. In the two-tier environment, some developers prefer to create the data services first, and then work forward (back-end to front-end). The three-tier architecture, however, makes the business services layer the logic starting point.

Although the design efforts start with the business services, you should always have in mind the big picture of the application during all phases of design. A good way to ensure that you do so is to constantly ask yourself the following two questions:

- ■ "What do I need from the Data Services to be able to provide this data?"

- ■ "How will the User Services manipulate this data?"

Designing the business services is the most difficult aspect of designing a three-tier application because there are not many good Business object modeling tools available. As mentioned previously in the book, you will begin to see these tools emerging very soon. For a detailed discussion of designing the business services tier, refer to Chapter 9, "Architecting Tier 2: Business Servers."

Until good Business object modeling tools become available, you still need to be able to model your business in a manner that lends itself to easy adaptation into a three-tier architecture. One of the most important steps in the modeling and design process is the development of an object hierarchy.

Object Hierarchy

The *object hierarchy* is a physical representation of the business objects that are present within an organization. This hierarchy not only identifies each of these objects, but also illustrates the relationships between them.

Figure 24.8 illustrates the object hierarchy that exists in the GOLF System application. Chapter 9 details the standards and guidelines that can be applied to the task of creating an object hierarchy.

Fig. 24.8
The GOLF System
object hierarchy.

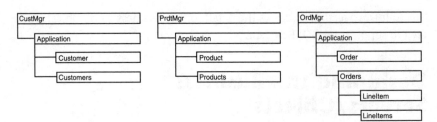

The objects defined in the applications object hierarchy contain properties and methods that client applications can use to manipulate the object. An object's properties and methods define what is referred to as the object interface. Figures 24.9, 24.10, and 24.11 illustrate the object interfaces of the OrderMgr, PrdtMgr, and CustMgr, respectively.

The following section discusses at a high level what properties and methods represent, and what features they provide. After getting an overview, this chapter discusses the specific properties and methods of the GOLF System objects in detail.

OrderMgr Object Interface

	Application	Orders	Order	LineItems	LineItem
Collections:	Orders		LineItems		
Member objects:		Item		Item	Parent
Properties	Id	Count	OrderID	Count	LineID
	UserId		CustomerID		ProductID
	Password		OrderDate		OrderQty
			ShippedFlag		ShipQty
			RemovedFlag		
Methods:	Initialize	LoadOrders		Add	
		UpdateOrders		Remove	
		Add			
		Remove			
(Performance tuning):		CollectionGet	PropertyGet	CollectionGet	PropertyGet
		CollectionSet	PropertySet	CollectionSet	PropertySet

Data Tier:		sp_Get_Orders	sp_Add_Order		sp_Add_LineItem
			sp_Delete_Order		

Fig. 24.9
The Order Manager's object interface.

V

Sample Applications

PrdtMgr Object Interface

	Application	Products	Product
Collections:	Products		
Member objects:		Item	
Properties	Id	Count	ProductID
	UserId		Description
	Password		Vendor
Methods:	Initialize	LoadProducts	
		UpdateProducts	
		Add	
		Remove	
(Performance tuning):		CollectionGet	PropertyGet
		CollectionSet	PropertySet

Data Tier:		sp_get_products	sp_add_products
			sp_update_products
			sp_delete_products

Fig. 24.10
The Product Manager's object interface.

Fig. 24.11

The Customer
Manager's object
interface.

CustMgr Object Interface

	Application	Customers	Customer
Collections:	Customers		
Member objects:		Item	
Properties	Id	Count	CustomerID
	UserId		Name
	Password		Street
			City
			State
			Zip
			Attention
Methods:	Initialize	LoadCustomers	
		UpdateCutomers	
		Add	
		Remove	
(Performance tuning):		CollectionGet	PropertyGet
		CollectionSet	PropertySet

Data Tier:		sp_get_customers	sp_add_customers
			sp_update_customers
			sp_delete_customers

Properties

Properties represent characteristics of the OLE server object that are meaningful to the user, the object itself, or both. Often, there are times when the OLE
server itself needs a property value, but the client application should not
be allowed to alter the value. These properties are known as *read-only*
properties.

Often, several properties are retrieved and set in sequence by the controlling
application. It's important for performance reasons, therefore, to minimize
the number of calls a client application must make to set the properties that
it needs.

To minimize the number of calls required to set the object's properties, you
should provide methods to update and retrieve all of an object's property
values at once. The main reason for providing these methods is to increase
the performance of the application.

Methods

Methods represent actions that the OLE server can take on behalf of the client
application. Methods most often perform an action of the business object
with which they are associated.

The OrderMgrs Orders collection, for example, has a `Remove` method that takes the order out of the system. In this case, the `Remove` method provides an interface for client applications to delete orders without being aware of business rules that apply to the process of deleting orders.

The GOLF System's Business Objects

After the business servers are defined, the object model established, and the data services in place, you can begin the development of the business services layer. This section goes into the details of the business servers that are part of the GOLF System.

The business services tier contains two types of objects, the managed instance classes ("Mgr" objects) and the instance managers ("Mgrs" objects). The Mgrs objects are the instance managers for the Mgr objects with the same name. The Mgr object is the actual business server that contains the business rules for the object.

The GOLF System contains the following four main business servers:

- **OrderMgr**—The Order Manager
- **CustMgr**—The Customer Manager
- **PrdtMgr**—The Product Manager
- **BatchMgr**—The Batch processing server

As previously mentioned, the business services tier of the GOLF System also contains three instance managers that maintain the pools of available and allocated business servers. These instance managers act as regulatory agents of the server machine to ensure that resources are not overused. Chapter 23, "Sample Application #2: An Instance Manager," details the design and workings of the instance manager, so they are not covered in detail in this chapter.

In later sections of this chapter, we discuss the details of each of the business servers that were developed for the GOLF System.

Designing the Data Services

After the Business objects are defined and the business services identified, it is time to design and develop the data services. This section discusses the details of the data services design that was implemented for the GOLF System.

Table Design

Because the GOLF System uses a relational database management system (Microsoft SQLServer 6.0), the business objects need to be mapped to relational database objects, tables, and views.

A number of tools on the market support the creation of database entity-relationship (ER) diagrams. Many of these tools also produce the schema script that can be used to actually create the database on the server. Figure 24.12 illustrates the ER diagram for the GOLF System's database.

Fig. 24.12

GOLF System's Entity-Relationship diagram.

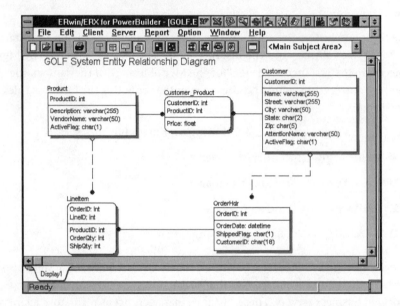

Use of Stored Procedures

When using RDBMS data services, you have a number of ways to increase performance by leveraging the advanced features of the data server.

The GOLF System uses SQL stored procedures to perform all of its forms of data access between the business services and the data services. Using stored procedures provides the following advantages over using embedded SQL statements:

- Increased performance

- Additional means of providing security for the data services

- Increased data integrity

Increased Performance

Stored procedures provide a performance increase over embedded SQL statements because the SQL engine has the capability to *pre-parse* the SQL statement and develop an execution plan.

When using stored procedures, SQL Server parses the SQL statement and develops a query-execution plan when the procedure is compiled. This is done by using the internal statistics that are maintained about the database objects. When embedded SQL statements are passed to the data service, they must be parsed and an execution plan developed when they are called.

Additional Security

As discussed in Chapter 13, all aspects of the three-tier applications should be secured. This is particularly true for the data services tier.

Stored procedures provide an additional layer of access to the data that can be leveraged when creating an application security architecture.

Access to the data service objects, for example, can be limited to just the stored procedures. In this way, clients are allowed to access the data through the pre-defined stored procedures, and cannot view the actual data.

Data Integrity

The primary responsibility of the data services is to ensure that the integrity of the applications data is maintained. Client applications should not be able to compromise the integrity of the applications data.

Allowing access to the database only through stored procedures insures that data is selected and updated in a pre-defined manner. Applications will not be able to manipulate the data in a manner that may potentially compromise the integrity of the data.

Listing 24.1 shows the stored procedure used to create a new order. The procedure expects parameters that represent the attributes of an Order Header, OrderId, CustomerID, OrderDate, and ShippedFlag. The OrderID parameter is an input/output parameter. When you first create an order, the business server will pass either a 0 or nothing for the OrderID. The stored procedure will assign a new OrderID and pass it back to the business server through this parameter. The source code for this stored procedure is located in the \CHAP24\GOLF\TIER3\ORDER01.SQL file of the companion disk.

Listing 24.1   ORDER01.SQL—Create Order stored procedure

```
create procedure sp_Add_OrderHdr
                    @OrderID int = 0 OUTPUT,
                    @CustomerID int,
                    @OrderDate varchar(25) ,
                    @ShippedFlag char(1) = "N"

as

begin

  /* Get the next order number if none passed */
  if @OrderID = 0
  begin
select @OrderID = max(OrderID) + 1 from OrderHdr
  end

  /* for the first order check for the null */
  if @OrderID = NULL
select @OrderID = 100000000

  insert into OrderHdr (OrderID, OrderDate, ShippedFlag, CustomerID)
  values(
        @OrderID,
        @OrderDate,
        @ShippedFlag,
        @CustomerID)

end
```

Chapter 10, "Architecting Tier 3: Data Servers," goes into more detail about the creation of the data services layer. Chapter 10 also offers additional information regarding the use of stored procedures.

Although stored procedures provide a number of advantages, they also have one major disadvantage—the loss of cross DBMS support. All database management systems on the market today do not provide the same functionality in their stored procedure implementations. This difference makes it difficult to create a DBMS independent application that uses stored procedures.

Use of RDO

As discussed in Chapter 11, "Remote Data Objects," RDO provides a set of objects, collections, properties, and methods that allows applications to remotely access data.

The RDO interface is built on top of ODBC, which means that it can be used to access any existing ODBC data source. Like ODBC, RDO provides the capability to change the back-end data services without affecting the code in the business services layer. Chapter 11 goes into greater detail about using RDO and its objects.

The GOLF System uses RDO as the means of communicating between the business services and the data services. The GOLF System uses the *rdoPreparedStatement* object to access stored procedures when updating and retrieving data. The rdoResultSet object is used to manage the result sets that are returned by select procedures.

Because RDO is the mechanism used to talk to the database, the GOLF system can be run against any database back-end that supports ODBC and provides the capability to retrieve results sets using stored procedures, including databases such as Microsoft SQL Server and Microsoft Access. Modifications are necessary to use Oracle as the database server because of the missing support for returning result sets from stored procedures.

Now that the data services are defined, stored procedures developed, and communications mechanism in place, we can begin the development of the business services.

Developing the Business Servers

In this section, we discuss the specific implementations of the business servers that exist in the GOLF System. First, we will examine one of the Test client applications that was used while developing the GOLF System's business servers.

The Test Clients

When developing the business servers, it is important to start at the most basic level. Although the GOLF System uses instance managers and the Logon Manager, none of these services is used during the development of the business objects. These layers should be included only after the business servers are tested by using a test application.

The GOLF System's business servers were developed by using simple test applications that provided nothing more than a hard-coded interface into the business servers themselves. The test application should be complete, attempting to manipulate all aspects of the object. The more complete the test application is, the easier it will be to develop the final client applications. Figure 24.13 illustrates the test client application that was used to develop the GOLF System's OrderMgr.

Fig. 24.13
OrderMgr Test
Client application.

Figure 24.14 illustrates the object layers that the client application goes
through when instantiating a business object in the test environment versus
the production environment.

Fig. 24.14
Client object
instantiation
requests.

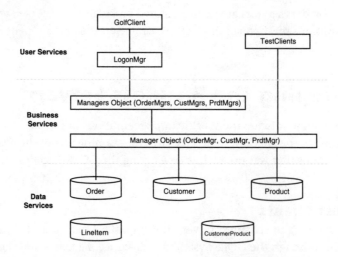

To gain a better understanding of the usefulness and design of a test client
application, we will discuss the details of the OrderMgr Test client. All Test
clients used while developing the GOLF System are included with the source
code. You can find these projects can be found in the \CHAP24\GOLF\TIER1
\TEST\ directory on the companion disk.

cmdGetObject

The cmdGetObject procedure tests the capability to instantiate the OrderMgr
object. The following code will instantiate the object in one of the three
methods available to the GOLF System: direct object creation, using the

instance manager, using the Logon Manager. This also shows how all the levels of access to the business objects can be testing in an incremental manner. This provides a simple interface for debugging object instantiation. Listing 24.2 is part of the test application, TordMgr.frm, found in the \CHAP24\GOLF\TIER1\TEST\ directory on the companion disk.

Listing 24.2   TORDMGR.FRM—Code to test business server instantiation

```
Private Sub cmdGetObject_Click()

Dim OrderMgrs As Object
Dim LogonMgr As Object


'basic logon
'Set OrderMgr = CreateObject("OrderMgr.Application")
'OrderMgr.Initialize UserId:="sa", Password:=""

'logon w/LogonMgr
'Set LogonMgr = CreateObject("LogonMgr.Application")
'Set OrderMgr = LogonMgr.GetInstance("OrderMgr.Application")

'instance manager logon (which uses instance mgr behind the scenes)
Set LogonMgr = CreateObject("LogonMgr.Application")
Set OrderMgr = LogonMgr.GetInstance("OrderMgr.Application", _
                                    "OrderMgrs.Application")

If OrderMgr Is Nothing Then
    Print "Did not get it"
Else
    Print "Got it"
End If


End Sub
```

The levels of object instantiation should be increased only after all of the other means of manipulating the objects have been tested.

cmdLoadOrders

The cmdLoadOrders procedure test the capability to populate the OrderMgrs Orders collection. Before the client application can manipulate the members of the Orders collection, it first must be populated.

This procedure simply populates the Orders collection with all the orders that currently exist. To further test the LoadOrders method, this procedure can be changed to pass the optional parameters it accepts. In Listing 24.3, which was taken from the TORDMGR.FRM form in the test client, you can see how the test application can be run multiple times to test different aspects of the business server.

Listing 24.3   TORDMGR.FRM—Populates the Orders collection

```
Private Sub cmdLoadOrders_Click()

 OrderMgr.Orders.LoadOrders
'OrderMgr.Orders.LoadOrders CustomerId:=123456789
'OrderMgr.Orders.LoadOrders ShippedFlag:="N"


Print "Loaded orders: " & OrderMgr.Orders.Count

End Sub
```

---

cmdModifyOrders

The cmdModifyOrders procedure tests the capability to access properties and methods of the Orders collection.

The procedure passes hard-coded values to the OrderMgrs Orders methods to test the capability to connect to and utilize them. There is no need for the test application to develop a fancy user interface and dynamically accept values. Remember that the goal of the test client is to validate that the business servers are working correctly, without requiring a great deal of time to set up. The output from the results is displayed directly on the client form.

In Listing 24.4, which was taken from the TORDMGR.FRM file of the test application, you can see how commenting and uncommenting sections of the procedure allow you to test all aspects of the OrderMgrs interface. The first section of this procedure uses the normal properties and methods exposed by the OrderMgr. The second section uses the `CollectionGet` and `CollectionSet` methods provide increased performance by accessing every member of the collection at once.

Listing 24.4   TORDMGR.FRM—Procedure to test Order Manager object interface

```
Private Sub cmdModifyOrders_Click()

'_ _ _ _ _ _ _ _ _ _ _ _ _ _
'Properties/methods
'_ _ _ _ _ _ _ _ _ _ _ _ _ _

'Dim NextOrder As Object
```

```
'remove second order
OrderMgr.Orders.Remove 2

'modify existing line items for 1st order
OrderMgr.Orders.Item(1).LineItems.Item(3).Productid = 867867
OrderMgr.Orders.Item(1).LineItems.Item(3).OrderQty = 111
OrderMgr.Orders.Item(1).LineItems.Item(3).ShipQty = 222

'add new order w/3 identical line items
'NextOrder = OrderMgr.Orders.Add(CustomerId:=543265564)
'NextOrder.LineItems.Add Productid:=867867, OrderQty:=333,
ShipQty:=444
'NextOrder.LineItems.Add Productid:=867867, OrderQty:=333,
ShipQty:=444
'NextOrder.LineItems.Add Productid:=867867, OrderQty:=333,
ShipQty:=444


'_____
'CollectionGet / CollectionSet
'_____

Dim LineItemArray As Variant
Dim OrderArray As Variant
Dim OrderIdx

'OrderArray = OrderMgr.Orders.CollectionGet

'remove second order
'OrderArray(ordRemovedFlag, 2) = "Y"

'modify existing line items for 1st order
'OrderArray(ordLineItems, 1)(linProductID, 3) = 867867
'OrderArray(ordLineItems, 1)(linOrderQty, 3) = 111
'OrderArray(ordLineItems, 1)(linShipQty, 3) = 222

'add new order w/3 identical line items
'OrderIdx = UBound(OrderArray, 2) + 1
'ReDim Preserve OrderArray(ordMaxAttribute, OrderIdx) 'add order
'OrderArray(ordCustomerID, OrderIdx) = 543265564
'    ReDim LineItemArray(linMaxAttribute, 3)
'    LineItemArray(linProductID, 1) = 867867
'    LineItemArray(linOrderQty, 1) = 333
'    LineItemArray(linShipQty, 1) = 444
'    LineItemArray(linProductID, 2) = 867867
'    LineItemArray(linOrderQty, 2) = 333
'    LineItemArray(linShipQty, 2) = 444
'    LineItemArray(linProductID, 3) = 867867
'    LineItemArray(linOrderQty, 3) = 333
'    LineItemArray(linShipQty, 3) = 444
'OrderArray(ordLineItems, OrderIdx) = LineItemArray

'OrderMgr.Orders.CollectionSet OrderArray

Print "Modified"

End Sub
```

cmdUpdateOrder

The cmdUpdateOrder procedure (see Listing 24.5) is used to test the capability to save the changes made to the collection back to the database. The UpdateOrders method will save all the changes that were made to the members of the Orders collection. This code was also taken from the OrderMgr test application's TORDMGR.FRM file.

Listing 24.5   TORDMGR.FRM—UpdateOrders test procedure

```
Private Sub cmdUpdateOrder_Click()

OrderMgr.Orders.UpdateOrders
Print "Updated"

End Sub
```

After the test application can successfully move through the various test procedures previously defined, the additional layers of object instantiation should be tested. The layers should be tested one at a time, starting with the instance managers, and then the Logon Manager. This technique makes it easier to debug any problems that occur.

At this point, the business servers are complete and the mechanism for accessing their interface has been tested. The creation of the final client application now is a matter of defining the presentation logic that is required to make the objects information meaningful.

In addition to using a simple test client application, it's also highly recommended that business objects be developed with local OLE automation. Remote Automation adds more complexities that can cause you endless nightmares during the development process. When the object works locally, it should be straightforward to test it remotely.

The OrderMgr

The OrderMgr allows users to manage orders in the application. It supports both the creation of new orders and the updating and canceling of existing orders.

The OrderMgr exposes three classes and two collections that client applications use to create and maintain orders. This section discusses each of these classes in detail.

Application Class

The *Application* class is instantiated by the *OrderMgrs* instance manager and passed to the client application. The application class represents an instance of the OrderMgr.

You can find all of the source code listings in this section in the \CHAP24\GOLF\TIER2\ORDMGR\App.cls file, on the companion disk.

Declarations. The Application class has several private variables that store properties of the object. The UserId, Password, Id, and Parent properties must be supported by all objects managed by the instance manager.

The Application class also contains public variables that store objects and collections that the client application can access. The Orders collection is used by the client to manipulate the order information. Listing 24.6 shows how the Application's object interface is created.

Listing 24.6 APP.CLS—Application class declaration

```
'All business server's should have these objects.

'The UserId and Id property are read-only by the client application,
'the others are neither read nor write by the client application.

'Private copy of client application's user id
'This is read-only to the client application, because it might
'be helpful for debugging
Private prvUserId As String

'Private copy of client application's password
'It is neither read nor write by the client application because
'no one should ever be able to read a password
Private prvPassword As String

'Id and Parent are optional, and only make sense
'if the object is instantiated by an instance manager.

'Private copy of this instance's ID
'This is read-only to the client application, because it might
'be helpful for debugging
Private prvId As String

'Private copy of the parent object.
'It is neither read nor write by the client application because
'the client application has no reason to reference the Instance
'Manager
Private prvParent As Object

'Declare the order objects
Public Orders As New Orders
```

V

Sample Applications

Initialize. The `Initialize` method, shown in Listing 24.7, is used after the object is instantiated to set the write-once properties: UserId, Password, Id, and Parent, as well as to establish a connection to the data server. Due to the way in which the OrderMgr uses its collections, it's necessary that the object maintain a connection to the data server to ensure data consistency.

Listing 24.7 APP.CLS—Application Initialize Method

```
Sub Initialize(UserId As String, _
               Password As String, _
               Optional Id As Variant, _
               Optional Parent As Variant)

'This procedure is called once when the server is instantiated.

'If it is instantiated by an Instance Manager, the object Id and
'Parent will be passed by the Instance Manager.

'If it is instantiated by a client application, the client probably
'has no need to pass an Id or Parent.

'This shows how this generic object shell can be used in an Instance
'Manager environment or in an environment where the client application
'is allowed to instantiate the object directly.

'_ _ _ _ _ _ _ _ _ _ _ _ _ _ _ _ _ _ _ _ _ _ _ _ _ _ _ _ _ _
'make sure procedure is only called once
'_ _ _ _ _ _ _ _ _ _ _ _ _ _ _ _ _ _ _ _ _ _ _ _ _ _ _ _ _ _

Static Initialized As Boolean
'only allow one initialization
If Initialized Then Exit Sub
Initialized = True

'_ _ _ _ _ _ _ _ _ _ _ _ _ _ _ _ _ _ _ _ _ _ _ _ _ _ _ _ _ _
'Assign the initialized object values
'_ _ _ _ _ _ _ _ _ _ _ _ _ _ _ _ _ _ _ _ _ _ _ _ _ _ _ _ _ _

prvUserId = UserId
prvPassword = Password
If IsMissing(Id) Then 'optional parm
    prvId = "<None>"
Else
    prvId = Id
End If
If IsMissing(Parent) Then 'optional parm
    Set prvParent = Nothing
Else
    Set prvParent = Parent
End If
```

```
'set up default environment
rdoEngine.rdoDefaultUser = UserId
rdoEngine.rdoDefaultPassword = Password
'open a connection to the database
Set db = rdoEngine.rdoEnvironments(0).OpenConnection( _
                DATA_SOURCE, _
                rdDriverNoPrompt, _
                False)

End Sub
```

The Initialize method is called only once, which is ensured by setting the
Initialized variable.

The Id and Parent parameters were made optional because they apply only
when the object is being managed by an instance manager.

Private Properties. The private object properties are used when instantiating the object, and are discussed in detail in Chapter 23, "Sample Application
#2: An Instance Manager." These properties provide the mechanism by which
the instance manager can maintain control of the business servers it has created and allocated to client applications in the user services tier.

Public Properties. The public property, Orders, is defined to allow the client
application the capability to access the Orders Collection.

Order Class

The Order class contains all of the properties that pertain to an order. This
class includes the order header and line item information.

You can find all of the source code for the Order class in the
\CHAP24\GOLF\TIER2\ORDMGR\Order.cls file, on the companion disk.

Declarations. The Declarations section, shown in Listing 24.8, contains the
properties of an order and also some read-only order properties that the object uses to maintain the object's integrity.

The order properties are exposed to client application through the use of
property procedures. Private variables are used to keep track of property values. This provides the most flexibility and control to the business server in
that it is aware every time a property value is changed, or accessed.

V

Sample Applications

Listing 24.8   ORDER.CLS—Order class declarations

```
'These values are read-only
Private prvOrderID As Long
Private prvCustomerID As Long
Private prvOrderDate As Date
Private prvShippedFlag As Variant
Private prvRemovedFlag As Variant 'Y if order marked for removal

Public LineItems As New LineItems
```

The Public LineItems object contains all of the individual line items associated with a particular order.

PropertyGet. The PropertyGet method, shown in Listing 24.9, allows the client application to retrieve the current values of all the properties that the OLE server makes available. The PropertyGet method contains an optional parameter list that accepts all the property values that the OLE server has chosen to make accessible to the client application.

The procedure uses the IsMissing function to determine which of the parameters the client application passed in, and populates them with the current value in the private property.

Listing 24.9   ORDER.CLS—PropertyGet procedure

```
Public Sub PropertyGet(Optional OrderID As Variant, _
                       Optional OrderDate As Variant, _
                       Optional CustomerID As Variant, _
                       Optional ShippedFlag As Variant, _
                       Optional RemovedFlag As Variant)

If IsMissing(OrderID) = False Then
    OrderID = prvOrderID
End If
If IsMissing(OrderDate) = False Then
    OrderDate = prvOrderDate
End If
If IsMissing(CustomerID) = False Then
    CustomerID = prvCustomerID
End If
If IsMissing(ShippedFlag) = False Then
    ShippedFlag = prvShippedFlag
End If
If IsMissing(RemovedFlag) = False Then
    RemovedFlag = prvRemovedFlag
End If


End Sub
```

Using this method, all five Order properties can be retrieved by using only one procedure call. Without this procedure, five individual calls would be required to obtain all of the information.

PropertySet. To update the property values, the Mgr objects expose a PropertySet method. This method works in the same manner as the PropertyGet, except that it updates the property values, as opposed to retrieving them.

The PropertySet method, shown in Listing 24.10, allows the OLE server object to control which properties the client application may update, as well as to implement integrity between any related properties.

Listing 24.10   ORDER.CLS—The PropertySet procedure

```
Public Sub PropertySet(Optional OrderDate As Variant, _
                       Optional CustomerID As Variant, _
                       Optional RemovedFlag As Variant)

If IsMissing(OrderDate) = False Then
    prvOrderDate = OrderDate
End If
If IsMissing(CustomerID) = False Then
    prvCustomerID = CustomerID
End If
If IsMissing(RemovedFlag) = False Then
    prvRemovedFlag = RemovedFlag
End If


End Sub
```

Orders Collection

The Orders collection provides the client with access to the OrderMgrs Orders collection, as well as individual Order objects through the use of its Item method.

All of the source code listings in this section are contained in the \CHAP24\GOLF\TIER2\ORDMGR\Orders.cls file, on the companion disk.

Declarations. To prevent the client application from directly using the default methods of a collection object, the Orders collection declares a private collection object, which it manipulates internally. The functionality of the default methods is exposed through Public methods of the Orders collection.

```
'Declare the private collection
Private prvOrders As New Collection
```

Add. The Add method, shown in Listing 24.11, allows the client application to create a new order and add it to the collection of existing orders being manipulated.

The Add method contains an optional parameters list which represents all the properties of an Order object. When the method is called by the client application, a new Order object is added to the collection, and a reference to this object is returned to the client application.

Listing 24.11   ORDERS.CLS—The Orders Add method

```
Public Function Add(Optional ByVal CustomerID As Variant, _
                    Optional ByVal OrderID As Variant, _
                    Optional ByVal OrderDate As Variant, _
                    Optional ByVal RemovedFlag As Variant, _
                    Optional ByVal ShippedFlag As Variant) As
Object

    Dim NewOrder As Order
    Set NewOrder = New Order

    With NewOrder
        .CustomerID = CustomerID
        If IsMissing(OrderID) Then
            .OrderID = 0
        Else
            .OrderID = OrderID
        End If
        If IsMissing(OrderDate) Then
            .OrderDate = Now
        Else
            .OrderDate = OrderDate
        End If
        If IsMissing(RemovedFlag) Then
            .RemovedFlag = "N"
        Else
            .RemovedFlag = RemovedFlag
        End If
        If IsMissing(ShippedFlag) Then
            .ShippedFlag = "N"
        Else
            .ShippedFlag = ShippedFlag
        End If
    End With
    prvOrders.Add NewOrder

    Set Add = NewOrder

End Function
```

The CustomerId property of the Add method is the only one that the client application needs to specify. The other order properties are handled within the object itself when it is saved to the database.

Orders created through the Add method are not saved to the database until the client calls the UpdateOrders method.

UpdateOrders. The UpdateOrders method, shown in Listing 24.12, updates the data server with all the changes that were made to the members of the Orders collection since they were retrieved.

This method takes a brute-force approach to updating the database, by first deleting the orders from the database, and then by inserting the orders again with their updated information. Using this method assures that new orders are inserted, and the existing orders are modified or deleted, based on the specification of the client application.

Listing 24.12   ORDERS.CLS—The UpdateOrders method

```
Public Sub UpdateOrders()

Dim qryDeleteOrder As rdoPreparedStatement
Dim qryAddOrder As rdoPreparedStatement
Dim qryAddLineItem As rdoPreparedStatement

Dim OrderIdx As Long
Dim LineItemIdx As Long
Dim NextLineItem As LineItem

'1) Delete all orders and line item keys in the original collection
'2) Insert all orders and line items in current collection,
'    ignoring those orders marked RemoveFlag="Y"


db.BeginTrans

'open a handle to the delete orders stored procedure
Set qryDeleteOrder = db.CreatePreparedStatement( _
                        "sp_Delete_OrderHdr", _
                        "{call sp_Delete_OrderHdr (?)}")
'delete orders
OrderIdx = 0
Do
    OrderIdx = OrderIdx + 1
    qryDeleteOrder.rdoParameters(0).Value =
Me.Item(OrderIdx).OrderID
    qryDeleteOrder.Execute
Loop Until OrderIdx >= Me.Count

'close the delete orders PreparedStatement handle
qryDeleteOrder.Close
```

(continues)

Listing 24.12 Continued

```
'open a handle to the add order stored procedure
Set qryAddOrder = db.CreatePreparedStatement( _
                        "sp_Add_OrderHdr", _
                        "{call sp_Add_OrderHdr (?, ?, ?, ?)}")
qryAddOrder.rdoParameters(0).Direction = rdParamInputOutput
qryAddOrder.rdoParameters(1).Direction = rdParamInput
qryAddOrder.rdoParameters(2).Direction = rdParamInput
qryAddOrder.rdoParameters(3).Direction = rdParamInput

'open a handle to the add line item stored procedure
Set qryAddLineItem = db.CreatePreparedStatement( _
                        "sp_Add_LineItem", _
                        "{call sp_Add_LineItem (?, ?, ?, ?, ?)}")

'reload all of the order currently in the orders collection
OrderIdx = 0
Do
    OrderIdx = OrderIdx + 1
    'only add if not marked for removal
    If Me.Item(OrderIdx).RemovedFlag = "N" Then
      With Me.Item(OrderIdx)
            qryAddOrder.rdoParameters(0).Value = .OrderID
            qryAddOrder.rdoParameters(1).Value = .CustomerID
            qryAddOrder.rdoParameters(2).Value = .OrderDate
            qryAddOrder.rdoParameters(3).Value = CStr(.ShippedFlag)
            qryAddOrder.Execute

            'update order id which was set by SP
            Me.Item(OrderIdx).OrderID = qryAddOrder.rdoParameters(0).Value
      End With

      'add the line items
      LineItemIdx = 0
      Do
        LineItemIdx = LineItemIdx + 1
          Set NextLineItem = Me.Item(OrderIdx).LineItems.Item(LineItemIdx)
          With NextLineItem
            qryAddLineItem.rdoParameters(0).Value = _
            Me.Item(OrderIdx).OrderID
            qryAddLineItem.rdoParameters(1).Value = LineItemIdx
            qryAddLineItem.rdoParameters(2).Value = .ProductId
            qryAddLineItem.rdoParameters(3).Value = .OrderQty
            qryAddLineItem.rdoParameters(4).Value = .ShipQty
            qryAddLineItem.Execute
          End With
      Loop Until LineItemIdx >= Me.Item(OrderIdx).LineItems.Count
    End If

Loop Until OrderIdx >= Me.Count
```

```
'close the PreparedStatement handles
qryAddOrder.Close
qryAddLineItem.Close

'commit the transaction
db.CommitTrans

Set prvOrders = Nothing


End Sub
```

LoadOrders. The LoadOrders method, shown in Listing 24.13, populates
the orders collection with order objects retrieved from the data service. The
LoadOrders method has two optional parameters that allow the client to limit
the number of orders that are retrieved.

Like the other methods that access the database, the LoadOrders method uses
a SQLServer stored procedure to retrieve the orders. These stored procedures
are accessed through the Remote Data Object (RDO) PreparedStatement
construct.

Listing 24.13   ORDERS.CLS—The LoadOrders method

```
Public Sub LoadOrders(Optional CustomerID As Variant, _
                      Optional ShippedFlag As Variant)


Dim qryGetOrders As rdoPreparedStatement
Dim rstGetOrders As rdoResultset
Dim NextOrder As Order
Dim NextLineItem As LineItem

Set prvOrders = Nothing

If IsMissing(CustomerID) Then
    CustomerID = "%"
End If
If IsMissing(ShippedFlag) Then
    ShippedFlag = "%"
End If


Set qryGetOrders = db.CreatePreparedStatement( _
                        "sp_Get_Orders", _
                        "{call sp_Get_Orders (?, ?)}")
'Set qryGetOrder = dbConnect.CreatePreparedStatement
➥("sp_getorders", "exec sp_getorders " & llCust & ",
➥'" & lsDate & "', '" & lsSts & "'")
qryGetOrders.rdoParameters(0).Value = CustomerID
qryGetOrders.rdoParameters(1).Value = ShippedFlag
```

(continues)

Listing 24.13 Continued

```
Set rstGetOrders = qryGetOrders.OpenResultset(rdOpenForwardOnly, _
                                              rdConcurReadOnly)

'populate the Orders collection with the new result set
Do Until rstGetOrders.EOF

    If rstGetOrders.rdoColumns("LineID") = 1 Then
        'new order
        Set NextOrder = New Order
        With NextOrder
            .OrderID = rstGetOrders.rdoColumns("OrderID")
            .CustomerID = rstGetOrders.rdoColumns("CustomerID")
            .OrderDate = rstGetOrders.rdoColumns("OrderDate")
            .ShippedFlag = rstGetOrders.rdoColumns("ShippedFlag")
            .RemovedFlag = "N"
        End With
        prvOrders.Add NextOrder, CStr(NextOrder.OrderID)
    End If

    'new line
    prvOrders(CStr(NextOrder.OrderID)).LineItems.Add _
            ProductId:=rstGetOrders.rdoColumns("ProductID"), _
            OrderQty:=rstGetOrders.rdoColumns("OrderQty"), _
            ShipQty:=rstGetOrders.rdoColumns("ShipQty")


    'get the next order
    rstGetOrders.MoveNext

Loop

rstGetOrders.Close
qryGetOrders.Close


End Sub
```

Count. As mentioned previously, to prevent the client application from calling the default methods of a collection, the OrderMgr manages the Orders
collection with a private collection variable. This allows the OrderMgr to
control the access to the collection through Public procedures.

The Count method, shown in Listing 24.14, is a public method that allows
the client to access the number of elements currently in the collection object.
This procedure provides the same functionality as the collection object's
default Count property.

Listing 24.14   ORDERS.CLS—The Count Property

```
Function Count() As Variant

    Count = prvOrders.Count

End Function
```

Item. The Item method, shown in Listing 24.15, also is a public function that allows the client to request a specific member of the Orders Collection. The method uses the collections Key value to identify the requested element.

Listing 24.15   ORDERS.CLS—The Item method

```
Function Item(Key As Variant) As Order

    Set Item = prvOrders.Item(Key)

End Function
```

Remove. The Remove method, shown in Listing 24.16, provides the capability to remove an order from the collection. The GOLF System's business rules actually require that the status of the order be set to canceled rather than deleting the order immediately. This rule is locked up in the OrderMgrs Remove method, therefore not requiring that users be aware of it.

Listing 24.16   ORDERS.CLS—The Remove method

```
Public Sub Remove(Key As Variant)

'Doesn't actually remove the order, just marks it to be removed.
'This allows the client-application to "undo", and enables
'the collection to remember which order to delete.

    prvOrders(Key).RemovedFlag = "Y"

End Sub
```

CollectionGet. As discussed in detail previously in this book, Remote Automation does present some performance issues that must be addressed. One of these issues is the manner in which information about objects and collections is retrieved by the client application. Because each time a client application references a property or method of a remote object an RPC call is required, accessing all of the elements of a large collection can be a performance bottleneck for your application.

To prevent this, the OrderMgr exposes a `CollectionGet` method, shown in Listing 24.17, which allows the client application to obtain all of the members of a collection by using a single method. This method passes back an array of variants, which contains all of the property settings for each object in the collection.

Listing 24.17 ORDERS.CLS—The CollectionGet method

```
Function CollectionGet() As Variant

Dim OrderIdx As Integer
Dim OrderArray As Variant
Dim NextLineItemArray As Variant

Dim OrderID As Variant
Dim CustomerID As Variant
Dim OrderDate As Variant
Dim RemovedFlag As Variant
Dim ShippedFlag As Variant

'redimension the OrderArray to contain make enough room
'for all the members of the collection
ReDim OrderArray(1 To ordMaxAttribute, 1 To Me.Count)

'loop through the collection elements
Do
    OrderIdx = OrderIdx + 1

    'get the order object properties
    Me.Item(OrderIdx).PropertyGet OrderID:=OrderID, _
                            CustomerID:=CustomerID, _
                            OrderDate:=OrderDate, _
                            RemovedFlag:=RemovedFlag, _
                            ShippedFlag:=ShippedFlag

    OrderArray(ordOrderID, OrderIdx) = OrderID
    OrderArray(ordCustomerID, OrderIdx) = CustomerID
    OrderArray(ordOrderDate, OrderIdx) = OrderDate
    OrderArray(ordRemovedFlag, OrderIdx) = RemovedFlag
    OrderArray(ordShippedFlag, OrderIdx) = ShippedFlag
    'get the line items of order
    NextLineItemArray = Me.Item(OrderIdx).LineItems.CollectionGet
    OrderArray(ordLineItems, OrderIdx) = NextLineItemArray

Loop Until OrderIdx >= Me.Count

'return the OrderArray
CollectionGet = OrderArray

End Function
```

CollectionSet. Like the `CollectionGet` method, `CollectionSet`, shown in Listing 24.18, allows the client application to update all of the objects within the Orders collection by using a single method. The `CollectionSet` method passes an array of variants to the OrderMgr, which contains all of the objects that are part of the collection.

Listing 24.18   ORDERS.CLS—The CollectionSet method

```
Public Sub CollectionSet(OrderArray As Variant)

Dim OrderIdx As Integer
Dim NextLineItemArray As Variant

'Delete private orders collection (note: this is different
'to what happens with the .Remove method)
Set prvOrders = Nothing

'update the orders collection with the information passed from the
'client application
OrderIdx = 0
Do
    'loop through the OrderArray
    OrderIdx = OrderIdx + 1

    'get the order information
    Me.Add OrderID:=(OrderArray(ordOrderID, OrderIdx)), _
           CustomerID:=(OrderArray(ordCustomerID, OrderIdx)), _
           OrderDate:=(OrderArray(ordOrderDate, OrderIdx)), _
           RemovedFlag:=(OrderArray(ordRemovedFlag, OrderIdx)), _
           ShippedFlag:=(OrderArray(ordShippedFlag, OrderIdx))

    'get the line items of order
    NextLineItemArray = OrderArray(ordLineItems, OrderIdx)
    Me.Item(OrderIdx).LineItems.CollectionSet NextLineItemArray

Loop Until OrderIdx >= UBound(OrderArray, 2)

End Sub
```

LineItem Class

The LineItem class contains all of the properties that apply to an order line item. These properties includes the product, quantity ordered, and quantity shipped.

You can find all of the source code for the LineItems class in the \GOLF\TIER2\ORDERMGR\Lines.cls file, on the companion disk.

Declarations. The Declaration section contains the available properties of an order line item. The LineItem class acts like a powerful user-defined structure.

```
Public pubLineNum As Long
Public pubPrdtId As Long
Public pubOrderQty As Long
Public pubShipQty As Long
```

PropertySet. The LineItem class exposes a `PropertySet` method. Like the `PropertySet` method of the Order class, this method allows the client application to update all the properties of a LineItem with only one procedure call.

PropertyGet. The LineItem class also exposes a `PropertyGet` method. Like the `PropertyGet` method of the Order class. Using the `PropertyGet` method, the client application can read all the properties of a LineItem with only one procedure call.

LineItems Collection

The LineItems collection provides the client application with a means of manipulating a group of LineItem objects.

Declarations. Like the Orders collection, the LineItems collection shouldn't expose all the default methods of a collection to the client application without the capability to intervene. To prevent this unwanted exposure, a private collection variable is declared internal to the class, which allows access to methods though Public procedures and functions.

```
'Declare the private collection
Private prvLineItems As New Collection
```

Add. The `Add` method allows the objects client to create a new LineItem and add it to the collection of LineItems for the current Order.

The implementation of the `Add` method is similar to the `Add` method of the Orders collection. Refer to the "Orders Collection" section for the details of the implementation.

Count. The `Count` method allows the client to determine how many line items exist for the current order. Like the `Orders.Count` method, the `LineItems.Count` method uses the default `Count` method of the private collection object.

Item. The `Item` method returns the LineItem object that corresponds to the collection Key value passed to the method.

Remove. The `Remove` method provides the client with the capability to use the default `Remove` method of the private collection. Again, no updates are made to the database until the `Orders.Modify` method is called.

The `LineItems.Remove` method removes the specified LineItem from the LineItems collection. Because the updates to orders were implemented by first deleting all the line items that existed in the database, and then inserting all the line items currently in the LineItems collection, the "Removed" line item is taken out.

CollectionGet/CollectionSet. Like the Orders collection, the LineItems collection's object interface contains methods that allow the client application to obtain and set all of the member objects by using only one method. This is done through the use of the `CollectionGet` and `CollectionSet` methods.

The CustMgr

The CustMgr allows users to manage customers in the application. It supports the creation of new customers, and also the updating and deactivating of existing customers.

The CustMgr exposes two classes and one collection that client applications use to create and maintain customer records. This section discusses these classes in detail.

Application Class

The Application class of the CustMgr contains the same methods and private properties as the OrderMgrs application class. Because these methods and properties are almost identical, they are not discussed again in this section. Refer to the "OrderMgr" section for more specifics on the Application Class and its properties and methods.

The CustMgr defines a public class (Customer), and a public collection (Customers) that client applications use to manipulate Customers

Customer Class

The Customer class defines all the attributes of a customer within the GOLF System.

Declarations. The Declarations section of the Customer class defines the available attributes or properties of a customer. The Customer class also contains a private read-only property that maintains the update status of the object. As in the OrderMgr, this value is used to determine when an object's properties have been changed.

```
'declare the object properties as read-only
Public CustomerId As Integer
Public Name As String
Public Street As String
```

```
Public City As String
Public State As String
Public Zip As String
Public Attn As String

Private prvModified As Boolean
```

Methods. The CustMgrs Customer class exposes many of the same methods present in the Order class of the OrderMgr. These include the `PropertySet`, `PropertyGet`, and `Remove` methods.

Customers class

The Customers collection is implemented in much the same way as the OrderMgrs Orders collection. In the CustMgr, it also is desirable to prevent the client from having access to the default methods of the collection.

The CustMgr also implements the desired standard methods as public functions.

Like the methods of the Orders collection, the database is not updated with changes until the `Customers.Modify` method is called.

The PrdtMgr

The PrdtMgr allows users to manage products in the application. It supports the creation of new products and also the updating and deactivating of existing products.

The PrdtMgr exposes two classes and one collection that client applications use to create and maintain product records. This section discusses these classes in detail.

Application Class

The Application class of the PrdtMgr contains the same methods and private properties as the OrderMgrs and CustMgrs application classes. Because these methods and properties are almost identical, they are not discussed again in this section. Refer to the "OrderMgr" section for more information on the Application Class and its properties and methods.

Product Class

The PrdtMgr defines a public class (Product) and a public collection (Products) that client applications use to manipulate Products that exist within the GOLF System. The Product class defines all of the attributes of a product within the GOLF System.

Declarations. The Declarations section of the Product class defines the available attributes or properties of a product. The product class also contains a private read-only property that maintains the update status of the object. As in the OrderMgr, this value is used to determine when an object's properties are changed.

```
'declare the object properties as read-only
Private prvPrdtNum As Integer
Private prvModified As Boolean

Public PrdtDesc As String
Public PrdtVendor As String
```

Methods. The PrdtMgrs Product class exposes many of the same methods that are present in the Order class of the OrderMgr and the Customer class of the CustMgr. These include the `PropertySet`, `PropertyGet`, and `Remove` methods.

Products Class

The Products collection is implemented much in the same way as the OrderMgrs Orders collection. In the PrdtMgr, it's also desirable to prevent the client from having access to the default methods of the collection.

The PrdtMgr also implements the desired standard methods as public functions.

Like the methods of the Orders collection, the database is not updated with changes until the `Products.Modify` method is called.

The Mgrs Objects

The GOLF System uses instance managers to handle pools of business servers that may be accessed by client applications. These instance managers are named by using the Mgrs suffix (for example, OrderMgrs) because they act like a collection of the business servers.

Using instance managers provides the following benefits to the entire application:

- Object instances pre-loaded
- Multitasking of instances by the operating system
- Exclusive point of object creation
- Integrated security
- Resource governing process

V

Sample Applications

- Minimized number of processes
- Capability to load balance business servers across multiple machines
- Reusability of object instances
- Object management

This list is not an exhaustive exposé of the benefits of implementing an instance manager for the business server objects; it merely mentions the major benefits.

For more details on the purpose, creation, and implementation of instance managers, refer to Chapter 23, which describes in detail the instance managers template used by the GOLF System.

Designing the Client

Now that the business and data services are in place, the construction of the client application is straightforward. The functionality of the business servers was already tested through the test client application, so all the object interfaces should be working.

By placing all of the complexity in the business servers and making the interface simple, the application developer now is given the capability to concentrate on the presentation logic that will make the application easy for the user to run.

Connecting to the Business Servers

As mentioned at the beginning of this chapter, the deployment of the three-tier application can be local (all components existing on a single machine) or remote (components distributed across multiple machines).

Remote Automation is used to communicate between the user services and the business services, and also to communicate between the business services and the data services.

The installation section earlier in this chapter briefly discussed the steps needed to make use of Remote Automation. For a more detailed description of Remote Automation and the steps that must be taken to implement it, refer to Chapter 7, "Managing OLE Objects."

Using Excel to Create Custom Apps

A practice that soon will become common with the introduction of three-tier applications is the distribution of template applications that end users can modify. Under this scenario, end users will have the ability to modify the manner in which they interact with the business servers, while not being allowed to alter the manner in which the business rules themselves are implemented.

One way this change will begin to occur is through the use of the macro languages provided with desktop applications. Microsoft Excel is an excellent example because its macro language is Visual Basic.

Application developers will develop templates that the user can modify or will even create application design wizards that step the end user through the creation of a custom application. These application wizards will handle the behind-the-scenes work of calling business servers, but allow the end user to dictate the presentation logic that is used.

Where to Go from Here...

This chapter provided a detailed look at the development of a three-tier application. Additional information related to the topics discussed in this chapter can be found in:

- Chapter 7, "Managing OLE Objects," which details the design of the user services.

- Chapter 8, "Architecting Tier 1: Client Applications," which covers in detail the design of business server applications.

- Chapters 10, "Architecting Tier 3: Data Servers," and 11, "Remote Data Objects," which detail the design of data services.

- Chapter 13, "Architecting Security," which details the process of architecting the application security model.

- Chapter 23, "Sample Application #2: An Instance Manager," which details the use of instance managers.

V

Sample Applications

Index

Symbols

. (dot) operator, 157
= (equal-sign character), 121
16-bit application DLL calls,
 597-600
32-bit
 applications
  DLL calls, 597-600
  Remote Automation
   performance, 242
 client applications
  advantages, 264-265
  recommendation, 265
  vs. 16-bit client
   applications, 261-264
 development environment,
  12
1NF (First Normal Form), 347
2NF (Second Normal Form),
 347
3NF (Third Normal Form), 347
4NF (Fourth Normal Form),
 347
5NF (Fifth Normal Form), 347

A

AbsolutePosition property
 (rdoResultset object), 405
Access Control Lists (ACLs),
 469-470
access rights (Visual
 SourceSafe), 697-703

accessing
 client application help files,
  530-540
 OLE automation object's
  interface, 134
 resource files from Visual
  Basic, 627-629
ACID (atomicity, consistency,
 isolation, durability)
 protocol, 348
ACLs (Access Control Lists),
 469-470
Action Technologies'
 ActionWorkflow, 377
Add Data Sources dialog
 box, 391
Add Directory dialog box
 (Visual SourceSafe), 657-658
Add Document window (OLE
 Document Manager sample
 application), 842-844
Add File command
 (File menu), 627
 Visual SourceSafe, 655-658
Add method, 125, 924
 collection objects, 182,
  186, 445
 ControlTemplates collection,
  608
 Directories class, 805-806
 Documents class, 814-816
Add SourceSafe Project dialog
 box, 720-722
Add to SourceSafe dialog box,
 720-722

Add user right (Visual
 SourceSafe), 698
Add Users command (Visual
 SourceSafe Users menu), 695
Add-In Manager command
 (Add-Ins menu), 717
add-ins, 600, 717-718
 Code Profiler, 755-762
 creating, 605-608
 deregistering, 604-605
 exposed objects, 601-603
 registering, 603-604
Add-Ins menu commands
 Add-In Manager, 717
 SourceSafe, 720-723
 Visual SourceSafe, 718-720
AddFormTemplate method
 (ProjectTemplate object),
 607-608
adding
 Component Catalogs (CC)
  to Component Manager
  (CM), 234-235
 components to Component
  Catalog, 232-234
 help to OLE automation
  servers, 538-539
 keys to Registry Editor
  (RE), 216
 named collections, 228
 properties to Component
  Catalogs (CC), 236
 resource files to projects, 627
 values to Registry Editor
  (RE), 216

Execute method
(rdoConnection object), 402
Execute method
(rdoPreparedStatement
object), 412
executing
WinHelp for client
application access, 534-537
executive information systems
(EISs), 370-374
explicit user rights (Visual
SourceSafe), 702-703
Explorer (SourceSafe), 686-688
Export Registry File command
(Registry menu), 218
exporting registry entries,
217-218
exposed objects for add-ins,
601-603
extending Visual Basic, 587
OCXes (OLE custom
controls), 588
VBXs, 588
Windows API, 588-597
calling by references, 593
declaring functions,
589-592
passing properties, 597
specifying parameter data
types, 593-596
user-defined types,
596-597
extensibility, 12-14

F

fat clients, 39
fatal errors, 512
fiFillChildDocs function,
839-840
fiFillDirectories function,
750-752, 840-842
fiFillDocTypes function, 843
Fifth Normal Form (5NF), 347
fiGetNodeKey function, 842
file dates, components, 226
File Input/Output
international applications,
637-639
Input # statement, 637

Print # statement,
637-638
Write # statement,
638-639
file list (SourceSafe Explorer),
652-653
File menu commands
Add File, 627
Make EXE File, 82, 575, 714
Make OLE DLL File, 82
Visual SourceSafe
Add File, 655-658
Create Project, 655
Delete, 668-669
Label, 707
Move Project, 659-660
Properties | Deleted Items
tab, 669-670
Rename, 660-661
Set Working Directory,
658-659
File To Include option (Find
database), 519
file-server application
architecture, 22
FileControl object, 602
files
configuration, 212
creating with Setup Wizard,
560-561
determining dependencies
for setup application
creation, 556-557
distribution files
copying/expanding, 567
creating, 575-576
executable versioning,
712-716
extensions
.OCX, 80
.TLB, 200
.VBR, 200
GOLF System application
source code, 893-896
SQL Server scripts,
892-893
help
client application access,
530-540
compiling, 529-530
content-sensitive,
528-529

creating, 516-520
design, 520-525
help topics, 525-528
OLE automation servers,
205-206
selecting for projects, 733
see also help files
INI, 609-611
log files, creting, 568
OLE Document Manager
sample application,
792-793
Project files, 552
REGCLEAN.EXE, 250
Remote Automation, 239
resource files
accessing from Visual
Basic, 627-629
adding to projects, 627
creating, 623-626
localizing, 626
runtime, 200-201
sample instance manager
application, 865-866
selecting to install, 557-559
SETUP.LST (Setup Toolkit),
562-563, 569-573
[FILES] section, 569-573
[SETUP] section, 572-573
modifying, 576-577
uninstalling copied files, 568
Visual SourceSafe, 649
adding to projects,
655-658
comparing versions,
691-693
filtering by extension,
environment settings,
690-691
history, displaying,
707-709
journal files, 705-706
keywords, 710-712
labels, 707
local, environment
settings, 684-686
naming, 650
reading from Visual
Basic, 724
removing/recovering,
668-670

L